Queue ADT–Linked List Implementation

Queue ADT–Array Implementation

AVL Tree ADT

(continued in the back of the book)

Data Structures
A Pseudocode Approach with C++

Richard F. Gilberg

De Anza College

Behrouz A. Forouzan

De Anza College

Brooks/Cole
Thomson Learning™

Australia • Canada • Mexico • Singapore • Spain
United Kingdom • United States

Sponsoring Editor: *Kallie Swanson*
Marketing Team: *Samantha Cabaluna and Christina De Veto*
Editorial Assistant: *Grace Fujimoto*
Production Coordinator: *Mary Vezilich*
Production Service: *Carlisle Publishers Services*
Print Buyer: *Vena Dyer*

Cover Designer: *Christine Garrigan*
Design Coordinator: *Roy Neuhaus*
Typesetting: *Carlisle Communications, Ltd.*
Printing and Binding: *R.R. Donnelley/Crawfordsville*

Printed in the United States of America

10 9 8 7 6 5 4 3 2

Library of Congress Cataloging-in-Publication Data

Gilberg, Richard F.
    Data structures: a pseudocode approach with C++/Richard F. Gilberg, Behrouz A. Forouzan.
  Richard F. Gilberg.
      p.   cm.
    Includes index.
    ISBN 0-534-95216-X
    1. C++ (Computer program language) 2. Data structures (Computer science). I.
Forouzan, Behrouz A. II. Title.

QA76.73.C153 G545 2001
005.13'3—dc21   00-025353
                                                                        CIP

In memory of my mother, Ann
R. F. Gilberg

To my nephew, Ryan Cameron Kioumehr
B. A. Forouzan

Contents

Preface

The study of data structures is both exciting and challenging. It is exciting because it presents a wide range of programming techniques that make it possible to solve larger and more complex problems. It is challenging because the complex nature of data structures brings with it many concepts that change the way we approach the design of programs.

Because the study of data structures encompasses an abundant amount of material, you will find that it is not possible to cover all of it in one term. In fact, data structures is such a pervasive subject that you will find it taught in lower-division, upper-division, and graduate programs.

Features of This Book

Our primary focus in this text is to present data structures as an introductory subject, taught in a lower-division course. With this focus in mind, we present the material in a simple, straightforward manner with many examples and figures. We also deemphasize the mathematical aspect of data structures, leaving the formal mathematical proofs of the algorithms for later courses.

Pseudocode

Pseudocode is an English-like presentation of the steps needed to solve a problem. It is written with a relaxed syntax that allows students to solve a problem at a level that hides the detail while they concentrate on the problem requirements. In other words, it allows students to concentrate on the big picture.

In addition to being an excellent design tool, pseudocode is also language independent. Consequently, students can use the same pseudocode design to implement an algorithm in several different languages. We developed our pseudocode syntax in our data structures classes over a 15-year period. During that time, our students have implemented the pseudocode algorithms in Pascal, C, and C++. In this text, we use C++ for all of our code implementations.

As we discuss the various data structures, we first present the general principles using diagrams to help the student visualize the concept. If the data structure is large and complex enough to require several algorithms, we use a structure chart to present a design solution. Once the design and structure are fully understood, we present a pseudocode algorithm, followed as appropriate by its C++ implementation.

Abstract Data Types

The second major feature of this text is its use of abstract data types (ADTs) implemented as C++ classes. To make ADTs data independent, we use template classes. All ADTs accept either one (data) or two (data and key) arguments. In this way any data type, including derived types and structures, can be used with all ADTs. Conversely, each ADT can be used with any data type as long as the required operators are predefined for that type. We introduce the concept immediately in Chapter 1 and use it extensively throughout the text.

Not every data structure should be implemented as an ADT class. However, where appropriate, we develop a complete C++ implementation for the student's study and use. Specifically, students will find ADT class implementations for Lists (Chapter 3), Stacks (Chapter 4), Queues (Chapter 5), AVL Trees (Chapter 8), B-Trees (Chapter 10), and Graphs (Chapter 12). The code for all of the ADTs is available on the Instructor's Materials page at the Brooks/Cole Web site www.brookscole.com

Structure and Style

One of our basic educational tenets is that good habits are formed early. The corollary is that bad habits are hard to break. Therefore, we consistently emphasize the principles of structured programming and software engineering. Every algorithm and program in the book uses a consistent style. As the algorithms and programs are analyzed, style and standards are further explained. While we acknowledge that there are many good styles, our experience has shown that if students are exposed to a good style and implement it, they will be better able to adapt to other good styles. On the other hand, unlearning sloppy short-cut habits is very difficult.

Visual Approach

A brief scan of the book will demonstrate that our approach is primarily visual. There are over 345 figures, 35 tables, 140 algorithms, 180 programs, and numerous code examples. Although this amount of material tends to create a large book, these materials make it much easier for students to follow the concepts.

Pedagogical End Materials

End of chapter materials reinforce what the student has learned. The important topics in the chapter are summarized in bulleted lists. Following the summary are three practice sets.

Exercises are multiple choice and short answer questions covering the material in the chapter. The answers to the odd numbered questions are included in the back of the book.

Problems are short assignments that ask the student to develop a pseudocode algorithm or write a short program to be run on a computer. These problems can usually be developed in 2 to 3 hours. The instructor's manual contains complete solutions for all exercises and problems.

Projects are longer, major assignments that may take an average student 6 to 9 hours or more to develop.

Organization And Order Of Topics

We have tried to build flexibility into the text so that the material may be covered in the order that best suits the needs of a particular class. Although we use the materials in the order presented in the text, there are other possible sequences (shown in the figure on this page). We recommend that you assign Chapter 1 as general reading. It contains basic information on pseudocode, abstract data types, and algorithmics students will need for the rest of the text.

The first two sections of Chapter 2 review sequential and binary search concepts. The third section, hashed list searches, may be new material. If you have covered search algorithms in your programming class, you may save this chapter for later. On the other hand, if your students have not studied searching algorithms, then you will need to cover at least the first section. Many of the algorithms in the following chapters require an understanding of sequential and ordered list searching. In many texts, sorting is covered with searching. Because our sorting chapter includes the recursive implementation of quick sort and heap sort (which requires an understanding of trees and heaps), we place it at the end of the text. With the exception of these two sorts, however, it could be covered before Chapter 3.

Chapter 3 introduces linear lists and the basic linked list data structures. It also introduces the first complete ADT class. For these reasons, Chapter 3 should be covered before the remaining chapters in the text.

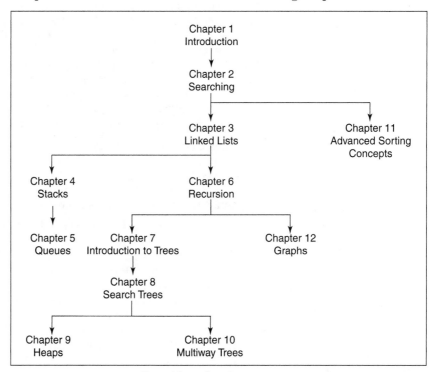

Possible subject sequences

The stack concept (Chapter 4) is basic to an understanding of recursion (Chapter 6), and recursion is in turn required to understand trees (Chapters 7, 8, and 10) and heaps (Chapter 9). Likewise, queues (Chapter 5) are used in breadth-first traversals in Chapters 7 and 12.

Chapter 9, Heaps, is a stand-alone chapter. Its only outside reference is the heap sort in Chapter 11.

We end the text with graphs in Chapter 12. Like many other data structure subjects, a complete course could be devoted to graphs. In this chapter, we review some basic graph concepts. Although this material could be covered anytime after Chapter 3, you will find that it contains some of the most difficult algorithms in the text. For this reason, we recommend that you present Chapter 12 at the end of the term, when your students will be much better prepared to handle the material.

Acknowledgments

No text of this scope can be developed without the support of many people. This is especially true for this text. The basic algorithms were field-tested by our students at De Anza College. Our first acknowledgment, therefore, has to be to the hundreds of students who by using and commenting on the text made a vital contribution. We especially thank our student, Scott Demouthe, who not only proofed the text, but verified every exercise and problem at the ends of the chapters.

We would also like to acknowledge the support of the De Anza staff. Their encouragement helped us launch the project, and their comments contributed to its success. To name them all is impossible, but we especially thank John Perry, Delia Garbacea, and George Rice.

To anyone who has not been through the process, the value of peer reviews cannot be fully appreciated. Writing a text rapidly becomes a myopic process. The important guidance of reviewers who can stand back and review the text as a whole cannot be measured. To twist an old cliche, "They are not valuable, they are priceless." We would especially like to acknowledge the contributions of the following reviewers:

James Clark, *University of Tennessee, Martin*
Roman Erenshteyn, *Goldey-Beacom College*
James Glenn, *University of Maryland*
Tracy Bradley Maples, *California State University—Long Beach*
Shensheng Zhao, *Governors State University*

Our thanks also go to our editors and staff at Brooks/Cole, Kallie Swanson, Grace Fujimoto, and Mary Vezilich. We would also like to acknowledge Kelli Jauron and Kathy Davis at Carlisle Publishers Services.

Last, and most obviously not the least, we thank our families and friends for their support. Many years ago an author described writing a text as a "locking yourself in a room" process. While the authors suffer through the writing process, families and friends suffer through their absence. We can only hope that as they view the final product, they feel that their sacrifices were worth it.

Richard F. Gilberg
Behrouz A. Forouzan

Introduction

1

This text assumes that the student has a solid foundation in structured programming principles and has written programs of moderate complexity. Although the text uses C++ for all of its implementation examples, the design and logic of the data structure algorithms are based on pseudocode. This approach creates a language-independent environment for the algorithms.

In this chapter we establish a background for the tools used in the rest of the text, most specifically pseudocode, the abstract data type, and algorithm efficiency analysis. We also introduce the measures we use throughout the text to discuss algorithm efficiency.

1-1   PSEUDOCODE

Although several tools are used to define algorithms, one of the most common is **pseudocode.** Pseudocode is an English-like representation of the code required for an algorithm. It is part English, part structured code. The English part provides a relaxed syntax that is easy to read. The code part consists of an extended version of the basic algorithmic constructs—sequence, selection, and iteration.

Note

> One of the most common tools for defining algorithms is pseudocode, which is part English, part structured code.

In this text we use pseudocode for both data structures and code. The basic format for data types consists of the name of the data and its type enclosed in pointed brackets as shown below

```
                         count <integer>
```

The structure of the data is indicated by indenting the data items as shown below.

```
node
       data      <dataType>
       link      <pointer to node>
end node
```

This data definition describes a node in a self-referential linked list that consists of a nested structure (`data`) and a pointer to the next node (`link`). It assumes that the data description for `dataType` has been previously defined.

As mentioned, the pseudocode is used to describe an algorithm. To facilitate a discussion of the algorithm statements, we number them using the hierarchical system shown in Algorithm 1-1 and fully described in the following sections.

Algorithm Header

Each algorithm begins with a header that names it, describes its parameters, and lists any pre- and postconditions. This information is important because the programmer using the algorithm often sees only the header information, not the complete algorithm. Therefore, the header information must be complete enough to communicate to the programmer everything he or she must know to use the algorithm.

In Algorithm 1-1 there is only one parameter, page number. Parameters are identified as pass by reference (`ref`) or pass by value (`val`). The type is included in pointed brackets after the identifier.

```
algorithm sample (ref pageNumber <integer>)
This algorithm reads a file and prints a report.
   Pre    pageNumber must be initialized
   Post   Report Printed. pageNumber contains number of pages
          in report.
   Return Number of lines printed.
 1 open file
 2 lines = 0
 3 loop (not end of file)
   1    read file
   2    if (full page)
        1    form feed
        2    pageNumber = pageNumber + 1
        3    write page heading
   3    end if
   4    write report line
   5    lines = lines + 1
 4 end loop
 5 close file
 6 return lines
end sample
```

Algorithm 1-1   Example of pseudocode

Purpose, Conditions, *and* Return

The purpose is a short statement about what the algorithm does. It needs to describe only the general algorithm processing. It should not attempt to describe all of the processing. For example, in Algorithm 1-1, the purpose does not need to state that the file will be opened or how the report will be printed. Similarly, in the search example, the purpose does not need to state which of the array searches will be used.

The precondition lists any precursor requirements for the parameters. For example, in Algorithm 1-1, the algorithm that calls `sample` must initialize the page number. Sometimes there are no preconditions, in which case we still list the precondition with the statement nothing, as shown below.

```
Pre    Nothing
```

If there are several input parameters, then the precondition should be shown for each. For example, a simple array search algorithm would have the following header:

```
algorithm search  (val list       <array>,
                    val argument    <integer>,
                    ref location    <index>)
Search array for specific item and return index location.
    Pre    list contains data array to be searched
           argument contains data to be located in list
    Post   location contains index of element matching argument
           -or- undetermined if not found
    Return <Boolean> true if found, false if not found
```

In search, two parameters are passed by value (val) and one by reference (ref). The precondition specifies that the two input parameters, list and argument, must be initialized. If a binary search were being used, the precondition would also state that the array data must be ordered.

The postcondition identifies any action taken and the status of any output parameters. In Algorithm 1-1, the postcondition contains two parts. First, it states that the report has been printed. Second, the reference parameter, pageNumber, contains the updated number of pages in the report. In the search algorithm shown above, there is only one postcondition, which may be one of two different values.

If a value is returned, it will be identified by a **return condition.** Often there is none, and no return condition is needed. In Algorithm 1-1, we return the number of lines printed. The search algorithm returns a **Boolean**—true if the argument was found, false if it was not found.

Statement Numbers

Statements are numbered using an abbreviated decimal notation in which only the last of the number sequence is shown on each statement. The expanded number of the statement in Algorithm 1-1 that reads the file is 3.1. The statement that writes the page heading is 3.2.3. This technique allows us to identify an individual statement while providing statements that are easily read.

Algorithm 1-1 also provides an example of all three structured programming constructs. Statement 2 is an example of a sequence, statement 3.2 is an example of a selection statement, and Statement 3 is an example of a loop. The end of the selection is indicated by the *end if* in Statement 3.3. Similarly, the end of the loop is indicated by end loop in Statement 4.

Variables

It is not necessary to define every variable used in the algorithm, especially when the context of the data is indicated by its name. To ensure that the meaning is understood, we use **intelligent data names**—that is, names that describe the meaning of the data. In Algorithm 1-1, pageNumber is an example of an intelligent data name.

The selection of the name for an algorithm or variable goes a long way toward making the algorithm and its coded implementation more readable. In general, you should follow these rules:

1. Do not use single character names. Even the traditional *for* loop variables of i and j should be avoided, although we sometimes use them in C++ *for* loops. There is always a better name. For example, if you are searching a two-dimensional array in which each row represents a different student and each column represents a quiz score, then student would be a better index for the rows than i. Likewise, quiz would be a better index for the columns than j.

2. Do not use generic names. Examples of generic names are count, sum, total, row, column, and file. In a program of any size there will be several counts, sums, and totals. Rather, add an intelligent qualifier to the generic name so that the reader knows exactly which piece of data is being referred to. For example, studentCount and numberOfStudents are both better than count.

3. Abbreviations are not excluded as intelligent data names. For example, stuCnt is a good abbreviation for studentCount and numOfStu is a good abbreviation for numberOfStudents. Note, however, that noStu would not be a good abbreviation for numberOfStudents because it is too easily read as *no students*.

Algorithm Analysis

For all but the simplest algorithms, we follow the algorithm with an analysis section that explains some of its salient points. Not every line of code is explained. Rather, the analysis examines only those points that either need to be emphasized or that may require some clarification. It also often introduces style or efficiency considerations.

Statement Constructs

When he first proposed the structured programming model, Niklaus Wirth stated that any algorithm could be written with only three programming **constructs:** sequence, selection, and loop. Our pseudocode contains only these three basic constructs. The implementation of these constructs relies on the richness of the implementation language. For example, the loop can be implemented as a *while, do . . . while,* or *for* statement in the C++ language.

Sequence

A **sequence** is a series of statements that do not alter the execution path within an algorithm. Although it is obvious that statements such as assign and add are sequence statements, it is not so obvious that a call to other algorithms is also considered a sequence statement. The reason it is lies in the structured programming concept that each algorithm has only one entry and one exit. Furthermore, when an algorithm completes, it returns to the statement immediately after the call that invoked it. Therefore, we can properly consider an algorithm call a sequence statement.

Selection

Selection statements evaluate one or more alternatives. If the alternatives are true, one path is taken. If the alternatives are false, a different path is taken. The typical selection statement is the two-way selection if (condition) action1 else action2. Whereas most languages provide for multiway selections, such as the *switch* in C++, we provide none in the pseudocode. The parts of the selection are identified by indentation, as shown in the short pseudocode statement below.

```
1  if (condition)
   1   action1
2  else
   1   action2
3  end if
```

Loop

Loop iterates a block of code. The loop that we use in our pseudocode most closely resembles the *while* loop. It is a pretest loop; that is, the condition is evaluated before the body of the loop is executed. If the condition is true, the body is executed. If the condition is false, the loop terminates.

Pseudocode Example

As an example of pseudocode, consider the logic required to calculate the deviation from a mean. In this problem, we must first read a series of numbers and calculate their average. Then, we subtract the mean from each number and print the number and its deviation. At the end of the calculation, we also print the totals and the average.

The obvious solution is to place the data in an array as they are read. Algorithm 1-2 contains the code for this simple problem as it would be implemented in a callable algorithm.

```
algorithm deviation
   Pre     nothing
   Post    average and numbers with their deviation printed
1  i = 0
2  loop (not end of file)
   1   read number into array[i]
   2   sum = sum + number
   3   i = i + 1
3  end loop
4  average =  sum / i
5  print (average)
6  j = 0
7  loop (j < i)
   1   devFromAve = array[j] – average
   2   print (array[j], devFromAve)
   3   j = j + 1
8  end loop
9  return
end deviation
```

Algorithm 1-2   Print deviation from mean for series of numbers

Algorithm 1-2 Analysis

Several points are worth mentioning in Algorithm 1-2. Note that there are no parameters. If there were, we would have indicated whether they were pass by reference (`ref`) or pass by value (`val`), their name, and their type. We do not define variables. Their type and purpose should be easily determined by their name.

We use a code-oriented pseudocode as opposed to a "tight English" pseudocode. Tight English uses a more natural language approach to the algorithm statements; it is more like spoken English than actual code. In Statement 2.3, we code the increment as it would appear in most computer languages. The tight English version of the same statement would be `Add one to i`.

Also note that our pseudocode arrays are indexed starting at 0, as is required by C++, not 1. Thus, we see in Statement 2.3 that we increment after we insert, making the first index 0.

We have broken the rule regarding intelligent data names in this algorithm for two reasons. First, it is an abstract example without an application reference so we do not have an intelligent name to use. Second, `i` and `j` are traditionally used in loops. When loops are short, and when they will be implemented using a *for* statement, we sometimes use the traditional names.

Finally, note that the algorithm ends with a return, even though no value is being returned. We find that use of a return eliminates an element of confusion in some students' minds.

1-2   THE ABSTRACT DATA TYPE

In the history of programming concepts, we started with nonstructured, linear programs, known as **spaghetti code,** in which the logic flow wound through the program like spaghetti on a plate. Next came the concept of **modular programming,** in which programs were organized in functions, each of which still used a linear coding technique. The structured programming concepts we still use today were formulated in the 1970s.

A **data type** consists of two parts, a set of data and the operations that can be performed on the data. Thus we see that the integer type consists of values (whole numbers in some defined range) and operations (add, subtract, multiply, divide, and any other operations appropriate for the application).

The latest development in the theory of program design is **object-oriented programming.** In an object-oriented approach, the functions are developed around an object, such as a linked list. One part of the object-oriented concept is **encapsulation,** in which all processing for an object is bundled together in a library and hidden from the user. All the programmer knows is the call formats that are required to communicate with the object and its functions. Encapsulation is one of the primary concepts behind the abstract data type. As we will see, the abstract data type is implemented as a C++ class.

Atomic and Composite Data

Atomic data are data that we choose to consider as a single, nondecomposable entity. For example, the integer 4562 may be considered as a single integer value. Of course, you can decompose it into digits, but the decomposed digits will not have the same characteristics of the original integer; they will be four single-digit integers in the range 0 to 9. In some languages, atomic data are known as scalar data because of their numeric properties.

An **atomic data type** is a set of atomic data with identical properties. These properties distinguish one atomic data type from another. Atomic data types are defined by a set of values and a set of operations that act on the values.

Note

> ### Atomic Data Type
>
> **1.** A set of values
> **2.** A set of operations on values

For example, we can define the three atomic data types shown below.

integer
values:	$-\infty, \ldots, -2, -1, 0, 1, 2, \ldots, \infty$
operations:	*, +, -, %, /, ++, --, ...

floating point
values:	$-\infty, \ldots, 0.0, \ldots, \infty$
operations:	*, +, -, /, ...

character
values:	\0, ... , 'A', 'B', ... , 'a', 'b', ... , ~
operations[1]:	<, >, ...

The opposite of atomic data is **composite data.** Composite data can be broken out into subfields that have meaning. As an example of a composite data item, consider your telephone number. A telephone number actually has three different parts. First, there is the area code. Then, what you consider to be your phone number is actually two different data items, a prefix consisting of a three-digit exchange and the number within the exchange, consisting of four digits. In the past, these prefixes were names such as DAvenport and CYpress. You will sometimes hear composite data referred to as structured data because they are implemented using structure statements such as *struct.* We do not use this term because it is easily confused with data structure.

Data Structure

A **data structure** is an aggregation of atomic and composite data types into a set with defined relationships. In this definition, *structure* means

---

1. C++ allows the addition and subtraction of characters, but + and – are not intrinsic character operators in pseudocode.

a set of rules that hold the data together. In other words, if we take a combination of data types and fit them into a structure such that we can define its relating rules, we have made a data structure. Data structures can be nested. We can have a data structure that consists of other data structures. For example, we can define the two structures array and record as shown in Table 1-1.

Note

Data Structure

1. A combination of elements each of which is either a data type or another data structure
2. A set of associations or relationships (structure) involving the combined elements

---

Array	Record
Homogeneous sequence of data or data types known as elements	Heterogeneous combination of data into a single structure with an identified key
Position association among the elements	No association

Table 1-1 Data structure examples

Most of the programming languages support several data structures. In addition, modern programming languages allow programmers to create new data structures for an application.

Abstract Data Type

Generally speaking, programmers' capabilities are determined by the tools in their tool kits. These tools are acquired by education and experience. Your knowledge of data structures is one of your tools.

When we first started programming there were no abstract data types. If we wanted to read a file, we wrote the code to read the physical file device. It did not take long to realize that we were writing the same code over and over again. So we created what is known today as an **abstract data type** (ADT). We wrote the code to read a file and placed it in a library for all programmers to use.

This concept is found in modern languages today. The code to read the keyboard is an ADT. It has a data structure, character, and a set of operations that can be used to read that data structure. The rules allow us to not only read the structure but also convert it into different data structures such as integers and strings.[2]

---

2. C++ programmers should recognize that *cin* is an object class, which fits our definition of an ADT.

With an ADT, users are not concerned with *how* the task is done but rather with *what* it can do. In other words, the ADT consists of a set of definitions that allow programmers to use the functions while hiding the implementation. This generalization of operations with unspecified implementations is known as **abstraction.** We abstract the essence of the process and leave the implementation details hidden.

Note

> ### The concept of abstraction means:
> **1.** We know *what* a data type can do.
> **2.** *How* it is done is hidden.

Consider the concept of a list. At least three data structures will support a list. We can use an array, a linked list, or a file. If we place our list in an ADT, users should not be aware of the structure we use. As long as they can insert and retrieve data, it should make no difference how we store the data. Figure 1-1 shows four logical structures that might be used to hold a list.

As another example, consider the system analyst who needs to simulate the waiting line of a bank to determine how many tellers are needed to serve customers efficiently. This analysis requires the simulation of a **queue.** However, queues are not generally available in programming languages. Even if a queue type were available, our analyst would still need some basic queue operations, such as enqueuing (insertion) and dequeuing (deleting), for the simulation.

There are two potential solutions to this problem: (1) we can write a program that simulates the queue our analyst needs (in this case, our solution is good only for the one application at hand) or (2) we can write

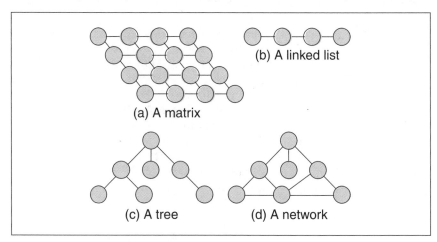

Figure 1-1   Some data structures

a queue ADT that can be used to solve any queue problem. If we choose the latter course, our analyst will still need to write a program to simulate the banking application, but doing so will·be much easier and faster because he or she will be able to concentrate on the application rather than the queue.

Let us now formally define an ADT. An **abstract data type** is a data declaration packaged together with the operations that are meaningful for the data type. In other words, we encapsulate the data and the operations on data and we hide them from the user.

Note

Abstract Data Type
1. Declaration of data
2. Declaration of operations
3. Encapsulation of data and operations

We cannot overstress the importance of hiding the implementation. The user should not have to know the data structure to use the ADT. Referring to our queue example, the application program should have no knowledge of the data structure. All references to and manipulation of the data in the queue must be handled through defined interfaces to the structure. Allowing the application program to directly reference the data structure is a common fault in many implementations that keep the ADT from being fully portable to other applications.

C++ programmers should recognize that hiding the implementation is exactly what happens in a class definition. Depending on the application requirements, a class defines structures and functions that are either completely hidden from the user application (private) or made available for use (public). C++ classes are therefore an ideal solution to the ADT software engineering concept.

1-3   A MODEL FOR AN ABSTRACT DATA TYPE

The ADT model is shown in Figure 1-2. The dark shaded area with an irregular outline represents the model. Inside the abstract area are two different aspects of the model: the data structure and the operational functions. Both are entirely contained in the model and are not within the user's scope. However, the data structure is available to all of the ADT's operations as needed, and an operation may call on other functions to accomplish its task. In other words, the data structure and the functions are within scope of each other.

ADT Operations

Data are entered, accessed, modified, and deleted through the operational interfaces drawn as rectangles partially in and partially out of

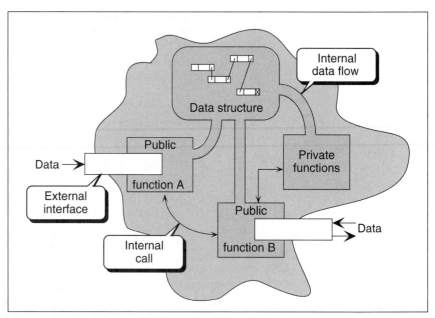

Figure 1-2   Abstract data type model

the structure. For each operation header there is an algorithm that performs its specific operation. Only the operation name and its parameters are visible to the user, and they provide the only interface to the ADT. Additional operations may be created to satisfy specific requirements. For example, in a file ADT, status calls for end-of-file or input/output error are generally provided.[3]

ADT Data Structure

When the list is controlled entirely by the program, it is often implemented using simple structures similar to those used in your programming class. Because the abstract data type must hide the implementation from the user, however, all data about the structure must be maintained inside the ADT. However, just encapsulating the structure in the ADT class is not sufficient. It is also necessary for multiple versions of the structure to be able to coexist. Consequently, we must hide the implementation from the user while being able to store different data. In C++, this task is easily accomplished with a class.

You have seen the ADT concept before. When you create a file, you use a predefined structure known as a file class. Defining a file in your program creates a stream object that becomes a part of your program.

---

3. Object-oriented design methods use different techniques for defining C++ classes. We have purposely kept the concept as simple and as language independent as possible.

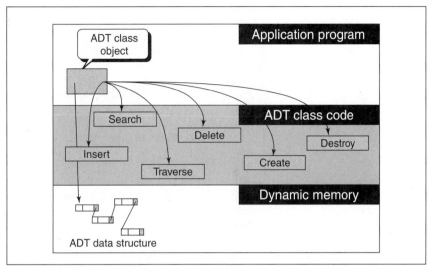

Figure 1-3   A pointer to a hidden structure

We will do the same thing with the ADT class. Each ADT class object will have a defined type that the users must use in their programs just as you must use the stream object names *cin* and *cout*. When the ADT class object is created, it contains any required structures. The exact format and type of the structures are not a concern of the application code. As a matter of practice, we will implement the structures used in this text in dynamic memory. This concept is shown in Figure 1-3.

In this text, we develop ADT classes for linked lists, stacks, queues, AVL trees, B-trees, and graphs. If you would like to preview them now, look at the list class in Chapter 3.

ADT Class Templates

The most difficult aspect of writing an ADT class is providing the flexibility to handle any type of data in a strongly typed language. Fortunately, C++ provides a solution in the form of templates. If you are not familiar with templates, see Appendix K.

All of the ADT classes in this text use the same template format. Two general components of a structure are the data and, optionally, a key identifier. The data structure is given a template identifier of TYPE, which the application programmer must use when the ADT class is defined. Also associated with the template is a key type identifier, KTYPE. The application programmer must use this type when creating the data structure in the program. Both of these ADT class keywords are seen in the class declarations in Program 1-1.

Now let's look at how an application programmer incorporates these elements into a program. First, the programmer must declare the structure that will hold the data. In Chapter 3, we create a list of

```
 1    // Node Declaration
 2      template <class   TYPE>
 3        struct NODE
 4          {
 5            . . .
 6          } ; //  End of Node Declaration
 7
 8    // List Class Declaration
 9      template <class   TYPE, class KTYPE>
10      class List
11        {
12          . . .
13          } ; // End of class List Declaration
```

Program 1-1   Typical ADT class template components

motion pictures that have received the Academy Award for Picture of the Year. The key is the year the picture won. The data are its title and the name of the director. In Program 1-2, we create a structure, PIC-TURE, and include in it the ADT class keyword key as one of the attributes. Then we define the list object (see Statement 11), designating that the structure type is PICTURE and the key type is *short*. The ADT class now has all of the information it needs to build the C++ class implementation for our list of award-winning pictures.

```
 1    struct PICTURE
 2      {
 3        short    key;
 4        char     picture [STR_MAX];
 5        char     director[STR_MAX];
 6      } ; // PICTURE
 7
 8    int main (void)
 9    {
10    // Local Definitions
11        List<PICTURE, short> list;
```

Program 1-2   ADT class template implementation

1-4   ALGORITHM EFFICIENCY

There is seldom a single algorithm for any problem. When comparing two different algorithms that solve the same problem, you will often find that one algorithm is an order of magnitude more efficient than the other. In this case, it only makes sense that you be able to recognize and choose the more efficient algorithm.

Although computer scientists have studied algorithms and algorithm efficiency extensively, the field has not been given an official name. Brassard and Bratley coined the term **algorithmics,** which they define as "the systematic study of the fundamental techniques used to design and analyze efficient algorithms."[4] We use the term in this book.

If a function is linear—that is, if it contains no loops—then its efficiency is a function of the number of instructions it contains. In this case, its efficiency depends on the speed of the computer and is generally not a factor in the overall efficiency of a program. On the other hand, functions that loop vary widely in their efficiency. The study of algorithm efficiency therefore focuses on loops.

As we study specific examples, we will generally discuss the algorithm's efficiency as a function of the number of elements to be processed. The general format is

$$f(n) = efficiency$$

The basic concepts are discussed in this section.

Linear Loops

Let us start with a simple loop. We want to know how many times the body of the loop is repeated in the following code:

```
1 i = 1
2 loop (i <= 1000)
   1  application code
   2  i = i + 1
3 end loop
```

Assuming i is an integer, the answer is 1000 times. The number of iterations is directly proportional to the loop factor, 1000. The higher the factor, the higher the number of loops. Because the efficiency is directly proportional to the number of iterations, it is

$$f(n) = n$$

However, the answer is not always as straightforward as it is in the above example. For instance, consider the following loop. How many times is the body repeated in this loop? Here the answer is 500 times. Why?

---

4. Gilles Brassard and Paul Bratley, *Algorithmics Theory and Practice* (Englewood Cliffs, N.J.: Prentice Hall, 1988), xiii.

```
1  i = 1
2  loop (i <= 1000)
   1  application code
   2  i = i + 2
3  end loop
```

In this example, the number of iterations is half the loop factor. Once again, however, the higher the factor, the higher the number of loops. The efficiency of this loop is proportional to half the factor, which makes it

$$f(n) = n / 2$$

If you were to plot either of these loop examples, you would get a straight line. For that reason, they are known as linear loops.

Logarithmic Loops

Now consider a loop in which the controlling variable is multiplied or divided in each loop. How many times will the body of the loops be repeated in the following program segments?

Multiply Loops	Divide Loops
``` 1 i = 1 2 loop (i < 1000) 1 application code 2 i = i × 2 3 end loop ```	``` 1 i = 1000 2 loop (i >= 1) 1 application code 2 i = i / 2 3 end loop ```

To help you understand this problem, Table 1-2 analyzes the values of i for each iteration. As you can see, the number of iterations is 10 in

Multiply		Divide	
Iteration	Value of i	Iteration	Value of i
1	1	1	1000
2	2	2	500
3	4	3	250
4	8	4	125
5	16	5	62
6	32	6	31
7	64	7	15
8	128	8	7
9	256	9	3
10	512	10	1
(exit)	1024	(exit)	0

Table 1-2   Analysis of multiply and divide loops

both cases. The reason is that in each iteration the value of i doubles for the multiply loop and is cut in half for the divide loop. Thus, the number of iterations is a function of the multiplier or divisor, in this case 2. That is, the loop continues while the condition shown below is true.

```
multiply   2^Iterations < 1000

divide     1000 / 2^Iterations >= 1
```

Generalizing the analysis, we can say that the iterations in loops that multiply or divide are determined by the following formula:

$$f(n) = \lceil \log_2 n \rceil$$

Nested Loops

When we analyze loops that contain loops, we must determine how many iterations each loop completes. The total is then the product of the number of iterations in the inner loop and the number of iterations in the outer loop.

```
Iterations = outer loop iterations × inner loop iterations
```

We now look at three nested loops: linear logarithmic, dependent quadratic, and quadratic.

Linear Logarithmic

The inner loop in the following code is a loop that multiplies. To see the multiply loop, look at the update expression in the inner loop (Statement 2.2.2).

```
1 i = 1
2 loop (i <= 10)
  1   j = 1
  2   loop (j <= 10)
    1     application code
    2   j = j * 2
  3   end loop
  4   i = i + 1
3 end loop
```

The number of iterations in the inner loop is therefore $\lceil \log_2 10 \rceil$. However, because the inner loop is controlled by an outer loop, the above formula must be multiplied by the number of times the outer loop executes, which is 10. This gives us

$$10 \times \lceil \log_2 10 \rceil$$

which is generalized as

$$f(n) = \lceil n \log_2 n \rceil$$

Dependent Quadratic

Now consider the nested loop shown below.

```
1 i = 1
2 loop (i <= 10)
   1   j = 1
   2   loop (j <= i)
       1   application code
       2   j = j + 1
   3   end loop
   4   i = i + 1
3 end loop
```

The outer loop is the same as the previous loop. However, the inner loop depends on the outer loop for one of its factors. It is executed only once the first iteration, twice the second iteration, three times the third iteration, and so forth. The number of iterations in the body of the inner loop is calculated as shown below.

$$1 + 2 + 3 + \ldots + 9 + 10 = 55$$

If we compute the average of this loop, it is 5.5 (55/10), which is the same as the number of iterations (10) plus 1 divided by 2. Mathematically, this calculation is generalized to

$$\frac{(n + 1)}{2}$$

Multiplying the inner loop by the number of times the outer loop is executed gives us the following formula for a dependent quadratic loop:

$$f(n) = n \left(\frac{n + 1}{2} \right)$$

Quadratic

In the final nested loop, each loop executes the same number of times as seen below.

The outer loop (Statement 2) is executed ten times. For each of its iterations, the inner loop (Statement 2.2) is also executed ten times.

```
1 i = 1
2 loop (i <= 10)
   1  j = 1
   2  loop (j <= 10)
      1   application code
      2   j = j + 1
   3  end loop
   4  i = i + 1
3 end loop
```

The answer, therefore, is 100, which is 10×10, the square of the loops. This formula generalizes to

$$f(n) = n^2$$

Big-O Notation

With the speed of computers today, we are not concerned with an exact measurement of an algorithm's efficiency as much as we are with its general order of magnitude. If the analysis of two algorithms shows that one executes 15 iterations while the other executes 25 iterations, they are both so fast that we can't see the difference. On the other hand, if one iterates 15 times and the other 1500 times, we should be concerned.

We have shown that the number of statements executed in the function for n elements of data is a function of the number of elements, expressed as $f(n)$. Although the equation derived for a function may be complex, a dominant factor in the equation usually determines the order of magnitude of the result. Therefore, we don't need to determine the complete measure of efficiency, only the factor that determines the magnitude. This factor is the **big-O,** as in "on the order of," and expressed as O(n)—that is, on the order of n.

This simplification of efficiency is known as **big-O analysis.** For example, if an algorithm is quadratic, we would say its efficiency is

$$O(n^2)$$

or on the order of n squared.

The big-O notation can be derived from $f(n)$ using the following steps:

1. In each term, set the coefficient of the term to 1.
2. Keep the largest term in the function and discard the others. Terms are ranked from lowest to highest as shown below.

$$\log_2 n \quad n \quad n\log_2 n \quad n^2 \quad n^3 \quad \dots \quad n^k \quad 2^n \quad n!$$

For example, to calculate the big-O notation for

$$f(n) = n\frac{(n+1)}{2} = \frac{1}{2}n^2 + \frac{1}{2}n$$

we first remove all coefficients. This gives us

$$n^2 + n$$

which after removing the smaller factors gives us

$$n^2$$

which in big-O notation is stated as

$$O(f(n)) = O(n^2)$$

To consider another example, let's look at the polynomial expression

$$f(n) = a_j n^k + a_{j-1} n^{k-1} + \ldots + a_2 n^2 + a_1 n + a_0$$

We first eliminate all of the coefficients as shown below.

$$f(n) = n^k + n^{k-1} + \ldots + n^2 + n + 1$$

The largest term in this expression is the first one, so we can say that the order of a polynomial expression is

$$O(f(n)) = O(n^k)$$

Standard Measures of Efficiency

Computer scientists have defined seven categories of algorithm efficiency. We list them in Table 1-3 in order of decreasing efficiency and show them graphically in Figure 1-4. Any measure of efficiency presumes that a sufficiently large sample is being considered. If you are dealing with only ten elements and the time required is a fraction of a second, there will be no meaningful difference between two algorithms. On the other hand, as the number of elements being processed grows, the difference between algorithms can be staggering. In Table 1-3, n is 10,000.

Returning for a moment to the question of why we should be concerned about efficiency, consider the situation in which you can solve a problem

Efficiency	Big-O	Iterations	Estimated Time[a]
Logarithmic	$O(\log_2 n)$	14	Microseconds
Linear	$O(n)$	10,000	0.1 seconds
Linear logarithmic	$O(n(\log_2 n))$	140,000	2 seconds
Quadratic	$O(n^2)$	$10,000^2$	15–20 minutes
Polynomial	$O(n^k)$	$10,000^k$	Hours
Exponential	$O(c^n)$	$2^{10,000}$	Intractable
Factorial	$O(n!)$	10,000!	Intractable

[a]Assumes instruction speed of 1 microsecond and 10 instructions in loop.

Table 1-3   Measures of efficiency

in three ways: one is linear, another is linear logarithmic, and a third is quadratic. The magnitude of their efficiency for a problem containing 10,000 elements shows that the linear solution requires a fraction of a second while the quadratic solution requires up to 20 minutes (see Table 1-3).

Looking at the problem from the other end, if we are using a computer that executes a million instructions per second and the loop contains ten instructions, then we would spend 0.00001 second for each iteration of the loop. Table 1-3 also contains an estimate of the time needed to solve the problem given different efficiencies.

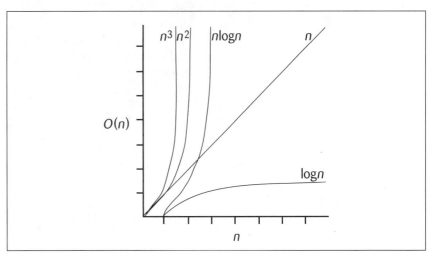

Figure 1-4   Big-O ranges

Big-O Analysis Examples

To demonstrate the concepts we have been discussing we examine two more algorithms: add and multiply two matrices.

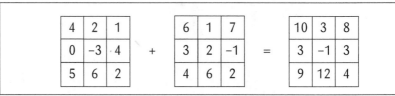

Figure 1-5 Add matrices

Add Matrices

To add two matrices, we add their corresponding elements; that is, we add the first element of the first matrix to the first element of the second matrix, the second element of the first matrix to the second element of the second matrix, and so forth. This concept is shown in Figure 1-5.

The pseudocode to add two matrices is seen in Algorithm 1-3.

```
algorithm addMatrix   (val matrix1   <matrix>,
                       val matrix2   <matrix>,
                       val size      <integer>
                       ref matrix3   <matrix>)
Add matrix1 to matrix2 and place results in matrix3
    Pre    matrix1 and matrix2 have data
           size is number of columns and rows in matrix
    Post   matrices added--result in matrix3
 1  r = 0
 2  loop (r < size)
    1   c = 0
    2   loop (c < size)
        1   matrix3[r, c] = matrix1[r, c] + matrix2[r, c]
        2   c = c + 1
    3   end loop
    4   r = r + 1
 3  end loop
 4  return
end addMatrix
```

Algorithm 1-3   Add two matrices

Algorithm 1-3 Analysis

In this algorithm, we see that the loop at Statement 2 loops "size" times. In each loop, it executes Statement 2.2, which also loops "size" times. This is the classic quadratic loop. The efficiency of Algorithm 1-3 is therefore $O(size^2)$ or $O(n^2)$.

Multiply Matrices

When two matrices are multiplied, we must *multiply* each element in a row of the first matrix by its corresponding element in a column of the second matrix. The value in the resulting matrix is then the *sum* of the products. For example, given the matrix in our addition example above, the first element in the resulting matrix—that is, the element at [0, 0]—

is the sum of the products obtained by multiplying each element in the first *row* (row 0) by its corresponding element in the first *column* (column 0). The value of the element at index location [0, 1] is the sum of the products of each element in the first row (again row 0) multiplied by its corresponding element in the second column (column 1). The value of the element at index location [1, 2] is the sum of the products of each element in the second *row* multiplied by the corresponding elements in the third *column*. Generalizing this concept, we see that

```
matrix3 [r, c] =
        matrix1[r, 0] x matrix2[0, c]
    +   matrix1[r, 1] x matrix2[1, c]
    +   matrix1[r, 2] x matrix2[2, c]
    ...
    +   matrix1[r, s-1] x matrix2[s-1, c]
where s = size of matrix
```

Figure 1-6 graphically shows how two matrices are multiplied. The pseudocode is provided in Algorithm 1-4.

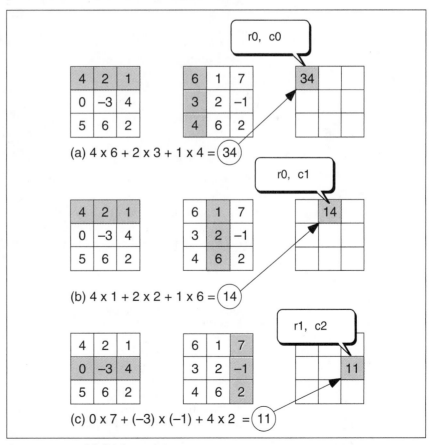

Figure 1-6 Multiply matrices

```
Algorithm addMatrix    (val matrix1   <matrix>,
                        val matrix2   <matrix>,
                        val size      <integer>
                        ref matrix3   <matrix>)
Multiply matrix1 by matrix2 and place product in matrix3
    Pre     matrix1 and matrix2 have data
            size is number of columns and rows in matrix
    Post    matrices multiplied--result in matrix3
  1 r = 0
  2 loop (r < size)
    1   c = 0
    2   loop (c < size)
        1   matrix3[r, c] = 0
        2   m = 0
        3   loop (m < size)
            1   matrix3[r, c] = matrix3[r, c]
                             + matrix1[r, m] × matrix2[m, c]
            2   m = m + 1
        4   end loop
        5   c = c + 1
    3   end loop
    4   r = r + 1
  3 end loop
  4 return
end addMatrix
```

Algorithm 1-4   Multiply two matrices

Algorithm 1-4 Analysis

In this algorithm we see three nested loops. Because each loop starts at the first element, we have a cubic loop. Loops with three nested loops have a big-O efficiency of $O(\text{size}^3)$ or $O(n^3)$.

1-5   SUMMARY

- One of the most common tools used to define algorithms is pseudocode.
- Pseudocode is an English-like representation of the code required for an algorithm. It is part English, part structured code.
- Atomic data are data that are single, nondecomposable entities.
- An atomic data type is a set of atomic data with identical properties.
- Atomic data types are defined by a set of values and a set of operations that act on the values.
- A data structure is an aggregate of atomic and composite data types into a set with defined relationship.

- An abstract data type (ADT) is a data declaration packaged together with the operations that are meaningful for the data type.
- Algorithm efficiency is generally defined as a function of the number of elements being processed and the type of loop being used.
- The efficiency of a logarithmic loop is $f(n) = \log_2 n$.
- The efficiency of a linear loop is $f(n) = n$.
- The efficiency of a linear logarithmic loop is $f(n) = n(\log_2 n)$.
- The efficiency of a dependent quadratic loop is $f(n) = n(n + 1)/2$.
- The efficiency of a quadratic loop is $f(n) = n^2$.
- The efficiency of a cubic loop is $f(n) = n^3$.
- The simplification of efficiency is known as big-O notation.
- The seven standard measures of efficiencies are $O(\log_2 n)$, $O(n)$, $O(n\log_2 n)$, $O(n^2)$, $O(n^k)$, $O(c^n)$, and $O(n!)$.

1-6   PRACTICE SETS

Exercises

1. Structure charts and pseudocode are two different design tools. How do they differ and how are they similar?
2. Using different syntactical constructs, write at least two pseudocode statements to add 1 to a number. For example, any of the following statements could be used to get data from a file:

```
read student file
read student file into student
read (studentFile into student)
```

3. Explain how an algorithm in an application program differs from an algorithm in an abstract data type.
4. Identify the atomic data types for your primary programming language.
5. Identify the composite data types for your primary programming language.
6. Reorder the following efficiencies from smallest to largest:
   a. 2^n
   b. $n!$
   c. n^5
   d. 10,000
   e. $n\log_2(n)$
7. Reorder the following efficiencies from smallest to largest:
   a. $n\log_2(n)$
   b. $n + n^2 + n^3$
   c. 2^4
   d. $n^{0.5}$
8. Determine the big-O notation for the following:
   a. $5n^{5/2} + n^{2/5}$
   b. $6\log_2(n) + 9n$
   c. $3n^4 + n\log_2(n)$
   d. $5n^2 + n^{3/2}$

9. Calculate the run-time efficiency of the following program segment:

```
1  i = 1
2  loop (i <= n)
   1  print (i)
   2  i = i + 1
3  end loop
```

10. Calculate the run-time efficiency of the following program segment:

```
1  i = 1
2  loop (i <= n)
   1  j = 1
   2  loop (j <= n)
      1  k = 1
      2  loop (k <= n)
         1  print (i, j, k)
         2  k = k + 1
      3  end loop
      4  j = j + 1
   3  end loop
   4  i = i + 1
3  end loop
```

11. If the algorithm doIt has an efficiency factor of $5n$, calculate the run-time efficiency of the following program segment:

```
1  i = 1
2  loop i <= n
   1  doIt (...)
   2  i = i + 1
3  end loop
```

12. If the efficiency of the algorithm doIt can be expressed as $O(n) = n^2$, calculate the efficiency of the following program segment:

```
1  i = 1
2  loop (i <= n)
   1  j = 1
   2  loop (j < n)
      1  doIt (...)
      2  j = j + 1
   3  end loop
   4  i = i + 1
3  end loop
```

13. If the efficiency of the algorithm doIt can be expressed as $O(n) = n^2$, calculate the efficiency of the following program segment:

```
1  i = 1
2  loop (i < n)
   1  doIt (...)
   2  i = i * 2
3  end loop
```

14. Given that the efficiency of an algorithm is $5n^2$, if a step in this algorithm takes 1 nanosecond (10^{-9}), how long does it take the algorithm to process an input of size 1000?

15. Given that the efficiency of an algorithm is n^3, if a step in this algorithm takes 1 nanosecond (10^{-9}), how long does it take the algorithm to process an input of size 1000?

16. Given that the efficiency of an algorithm is $5n\log_2(n)$, if a step in this algorithm takes 1 nanosecond (10^{-9}), how long does it take the algorithm to process an input of size 1000?

17. An algorithm runs a given input of size n. If n is 4096, the run time is 512 milliseconds. If n is 16,384, the run time is 2048 milliseconds. What is the efficiency? What is the big-O notation?

18. An algorithm runs a given input of size n. If n is 4096, the run time is 512 milliseconds. If n is 16,384, the run time is 8192 milliseconds. What is the efficiency? What is the big-O notation?

19. An algorithm runs a given input of size n. If n is 4096, the run time is 512 milliseconds. If n is 16,384, the run time is 1024 milliseconds. What is the efficiency? What is the big-O notation?

20. Three students wrote algorithms for the same problem. They tested the three algorithms with two sets of data as shown below:

a. Case 1: $n = 10$

    run time for student 1: 1
    run time for student 2: 1/100
    run time for student 3: 1/1000

b. Case 2: $n = 100$

    run time for student 1: 10
    run time for student 2: 1
    run time for student 3: 1

What is the efficiency for each algorithm? Which is the best? Which is the worst? What is the minimum number of test cases (n) in which the best algorithm has the best run time?

Problems

21. Write a pseudocode algorithm for dialing a phone number.

22. Write a pseudocode algorithm for giving all employees in a company a cost-of-living wage increase of 3.2%. Assume that the payroll file includes all current employees.

23. Write a language-specific implementation for the pseudocode algorithm in Problem 22.

24. Write a pseudocode definition for a textbook data structure.

25. Write a pseudocode definition for a student data structure.

Projects

26. Your college bookstore has hired you as a summer intern to design a new textbook inventory system. It is to include the following major processes:

a. Ordering textbooks
b. Receiving textbooks
c. Determining retail price
d. Pricing used textbooks
e. Determining quantity on hand
f. Recording textbook sales
g. Recording textbook returns

Write the abstract data type algorithm headers for the inventory system. Each header should include name, parameters, purpose, pre- and postconditions, and return value types. You may add additional algorithms as required by your analysis.

27. Write the pseudocode for an algorithm that converts a numeric score to a letter grade. The grading scale is the typical absolute scale in which 90% or more is an A, 80% to 90% is a B, 70% to 80% is a C, and 60% to 70% is a D. Anything below 60% is an F.

28. Write the pseudocode for an algorithm that receives an integer and then prints the number of digits in the integer and the sum of the digits. For example, given 12,345 it would print that there are 5 digits with a sum of 15.

29. Write the pseudocode for a program that builds a frequency array for data values in the range 1 to 20 and then prints their histogram. The data are to be read from a file. The design for the program is shown in Figure 1-7.

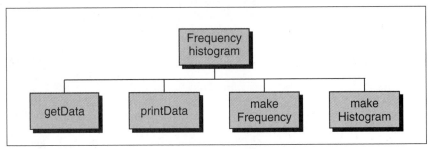

Figure 1-7   Design for frequency histogram program

Each of the subalgorithms is described below.

a. The getData algorithm reads the file and stores the data in an array.

b. The printData algorithm prints the data in the array.

c. The makeFrequency algorithm examines the data in the array, one element at a time, and adds 1 to the corresponding element in a frequency array based on the data value.

d. The makeHistogram algorithm prints out a vertical histogram using asterisks for each occurrence of an element. For example, if there were five value 1s and eight value 2s in the data, it would print

```
1: *****
2: ********
```

Searching

2

One of the most common and time-consuming operations in computer science is **searching,** the process used to find the location of a target among a list of objects. In this chapter we study several searching algorithms. We begin with list searching and a discussion of the two basic search algorithms, the sequential search—including three interesting variations—and the binary search.

After reviewing the concepts of list searches, we discuss hashed list searching, in which the data key is algorithmically manipulated to calculate the location of the data in the list. An integral part of virtually all hashed list algorithms is collision resolution, which we discuss in the last section.

Although we discuss the list search algorithms using an array structure, the same concepts can be found in linked list searches. The sequential search, along with the ordered list variation, is most commonly used to locate data in a linked list. The binary search tree is actually a structure built to provide the efficiency of the binary search of a tree structure. These searches are covered in their respective chapters.

2-1   LIST SEARCHES

The algorithm used to search a list depends to a large extent on the structure of the list. In this section, we study searches that work with arrays. The two basic searches for arrays are the sequential search and the binary search. The sequential search can be used to locate an item in any array. The binary search, on the other hand, requires an ordered list. The basic search concept is shown in Figure 2-1.

Sequential Search

The **sequential search** is used whenever the list is not ordered. Generally, you will use the technique only for small lists or lists that are not searched often. In other cases you should first sort the list and then search it using the binary search, discussed later.

In the sequential search, we start searching for the target at the beginning of the list and continue until we find the target or we are sure that it is not in the list. This approach gives us two possibilities: either we find it or we reach the end of the list. In Figure 2-2 we trace the steps to find the value 14. We first check the data at index 0, then 1, and then 2 before finding the 14 in the fourth element (index 3).

But what if the target were not in the list? In that case we would have to examine each element until we reach the end of the list. Figure 2-3 traces the search for a target of 72. At the end of the list, we discover that the target does not exist.

Sequential Search Algorithm

The **sequential search algorithm** needs to tell the calling algorithm two things: First, did it find the data it was looking for? And second, if it did, at what index are the target data found? To answer these questions, the search algorithm requires four parame-

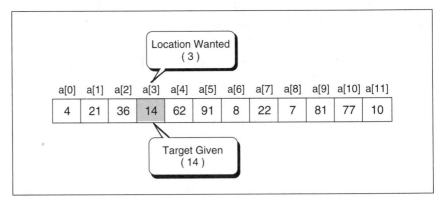

Figure 2-1   Locating data in unordered list

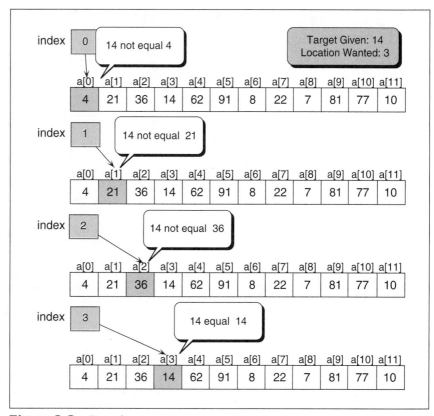

Figure 2-2 Search concept

ters: (1) the list we are searching, (2) an index to the last element in the list,[1] (3) the target, and (4) the address where the found element's index location is to be stored. To tell the calling algorithm whether the data were located, we return a Boolean—true for we found it or false for we didn't find it.

Although we could write a sequential search algorithm without passing the index to the last element, if we did so the search would have to know how many elements are in the list. To make the function as flexible as possible, we pass the index of the last data value in the array. Generalizing the algorithm by passing the index to the last item is also a good structured design technique. With this information, we are now ready to code Algorithm 2-1.

---

1. As an alternative to the index to the last element, the size of the list may be passed.

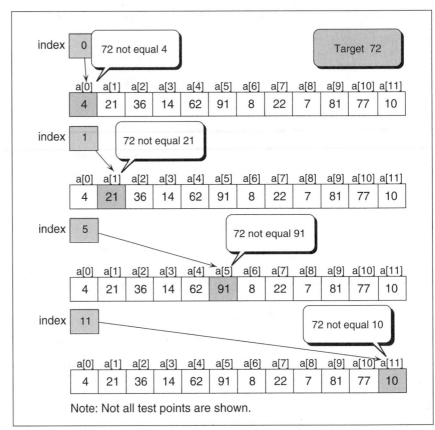

Note: Not all test points are shown.

Figure 2-3   Unsuccessful search in unordered list

```
algorithm SeqSearch (val list    <array>,
                      val last    <index>,
                      val target <keyType>,
                      ref locn    <index>)

Locate the target in an unordered list of elements.
   Pre    list must contain at least one element
          last is index to last element in the list
          target contains the data to be located
          locn is address of index in calling algorithm
   Post   if found--matching index stored in locn & found true
          if not found--last stored in locn & found false
   Return found <Boolean>
 1 looker = 0
 2 loop (looker < last AND target not equal list[looker])
```

Algorithm 2-1   Sequential search

```
   1   looker = looker + 1
 3 end loop
 4 locn = looker
 5 if (target equal list[looker])
   1   found = true
 6 else
   1   found = false
 7 end if
 8 return found
end SeqSearch
```

Algorithm 2-1   Sequential search *(continued)*

Algorithm 2-1 Analysis

Because this algorithm is rather straightforward, we have only one comment. We could have used the location parameter for the searching rather than create a looker index. However, it is generally not a good idea to use a parameter as a working variable because doing so destroys any initial value that may be needed later in the algorithm.

Variations on Sequential Searches

Three useful variations on the sequential search algorithm are (1) the sentinel search, (2) the probability search, and (3) the ordered list search. We look at each briefly in the following sections.

Sentinel Search

If you examine the search algorithm carefully, you will note that the loop tests two conditions, end of list and target not found. Knuth states that "When the inner loop of a program tests two or more conditions, an attempt should be made to reduce it to just one condition."[2] If we know that the target will be found in the list, we can eliminate the test for the end of the list. The only way to ensure that a target is actually in the list is to put it there yourself. A target is put in the list by adding an extra element (sentinel entry) at the end of the array and placing the target in the sentinel. We can then optimize the loop and determine after the loop completes whether we found actual data or the sentinel.[3] The obvious disadvantage is that the rest of the processing must be careful to never look at the sentinel element at the end of the list. The pseudocode for the sentinel search is shown in Algorithm 2-2.

---

2. Donald E. Knuth, *The Art of Computer Programming* Vol. 3, *Sorting and Searching* (Reading, MA: Addison-Wesley, 1973), 395.
3. It is not always possible to reduce a loop to only one test. We will see many loops that require two or more tests to satisfy the logic.

```
algorithm SentinelSearch (val list     <array>,
                          val last     <index>,
                          val target   <keyType>,
                          ref locn     <index>)
Locate the target in an unordered list of elements.
    Pre    list must contain element at the end for the sentinel
           last is index to last data element in the list
           target contains the data to be located
           locn is address of index in calling algorithm
    Post   if found--matching index stored in locn & found true
           if not found--last stored in locn & found false
    Return found <Boolean>
 1 list[last + 1] = target

 2 looker = 0

 3 loop (target not equal list[looker])
   1   looker = looker + 1

 4 end loop

 5 if (looker <= last)
   1   found  = true
   2   locn   = looker

 6 else
   1   found  = false
   2   locn   = last

 7 end if

 8 return found
end SentinelSearch
```

Algorithm 2-2   Sentinel search

Probability Search

One of the more useful variations is known as a **probability search.**
In the probability search, the array is ordered with the most probable search elements at the beginning of the array and the least probable at the end. It is especially useful when relatively few elements
are the targets for most of the searches. To ensure that the probability ordering is correct over time, in each search we exchange the
located element with the element immediately before it in the array.
A typical implementation of the probability search is shown in
Algorithm 2-3.

```
algorithm ProbabilitySearch  (val list      <array>,
                              val last      <index>,
                              val target    <keyType>,
                              ref locn      <index>)
```

Locate the target in a list ordered by the probability of each
element being the target--most probable first, least probable last.

    Pre   list must contain at least one element
               last is index to last element in the list
               target contains the data to be located
               locn is address of index in calling algorithm

    Post   if found--matching index stored in locn & found true
               and element moved up in priority.
               if not found--last stored in locn & found false

    Return found <Boolean>

```
1 looker = 0
2 loop (looker < last AND target not equal list[looker])
  1   looker = looker + 1
3 end loop
4 if (target equal list[looker])
  1   found = true
  2   if (looker > 0)
      1   temp             = list[looker - 1]
      2   list[looker - 1] = list[looker]
      3   list[looker]     = temp
      4   looker = looker - 1
  3   end if
5 else
  1   found = false
6 end if
7 locn = looker
8 return found
end ProbabilitySearch
```

Algorithm 2-3   Probability search

Ordered List Search

Although we generally recommend a binary search when searching a
list ordered on the key (target), if the list is small it may be more efficient to use a sequential search. When searching an ordered list sequentially, however, it is not necessary to search to the end of the list

to determine that the target is not in the list. We can stop when the target becomes less than or equal to the current element we are testing. In addition, we can incorporate the sentinel concept by bypassing the search loop when the target is greater than the last item. In other words, when the target is less than or equal to the last element, the last element becomes a sentinel, allowing us to eliminate the test for the end of the list.

Although it can be used with an array, the ordered list search is more commonly used when searching a linked list. The pseudocode for searching an ordered array is found in Algorithm 2-4.

```
algorithm OrderedListSearch (val list    <array>,
                             val last     <index>,
                             val target <keyType>,
                             ref locn    <index>)

Locate target in a list ordered on target.
    Pre     list must contain at least one element
            last is index to last element in the list
            target contains the data to be located
            locn is address of index in calling algorithm
    Post    if found--matching index stored in locn & found true
            if not found--locn is index of first element > target
                or locn equal last & found is false
    Return found <Boolean>
  1 if (target < list[last])
    1   looker = 0
    2   loop (target > list[looker])
        1   looker = looker + 1
    3   end loop
  2 else
    1   looker = last
  3 end if
  4 if (target equal list[looker])
    1   found = true
  5 else
    1   found = false
  6 end if
  7 locn = looker
  8 return found
end OrderedListSearch
```

Algorithm 2-4   Ordered list search

Binary Search

The sequential search algorithm is very slow. If we have an array of 1000 elements, we must do 1000 comparisons in the worst case. If the array is not sorted, the sequential search is the only solution. However, if the array is sorted, we can use a more efficient algorithm called the **binary search.** Generally speaking, we should use a binary search whenever the list starts to become large. Although the definition of large is vague, we suggest that you consider binary searches whenever the list contains more than 16 elements.

The binary search starts by testing the data in the element at the middle of the array to determine if the target is in the first or second half of the list. If it is in the first half, we do not need to check the second half. If it is in the second half, we do not need to test the first half. In other words, we eliminate half the list from further consideration. We repeat this process until we find the target or determine that it is not in the list.

To find the middle of the list, we need three variables, one to identify the beginning of the list, one to identify the middle of the list, and one to identify the end of the list. We analyze two cases here: the target is in the list and the target is not in the list.

Target Found

Figure 2-4 shows how we find 22 in a sorted array. We descriptively call our three indexes first, mid, and last. Given first as 0 and last as 11, we can calculate mid as follows:

$$mid = (first + last)/2$$

Because the index mid is an integer, the result will be the integral value of the quotient; that is, the result is truncated rather than rounded. Given the data in Figure 2-4, mid becomes 5 as a result of the first calculation.

$$mid = (0 + 11)/2 = 11/2 = 5$$

At index location 5, we discover that the target is greater than the list value (22 > 21). We can therefore eliminate the array locations 0 through 5. (Note that mid is automatically eliminated.) To narrow our search, we assign mid + 1 to first and repeat the search.

The next loop calculates mid with the new value for first and determines that the midpoint is now 8.

$$mid = (6 + 11)/2 = 17/2 = 8$$

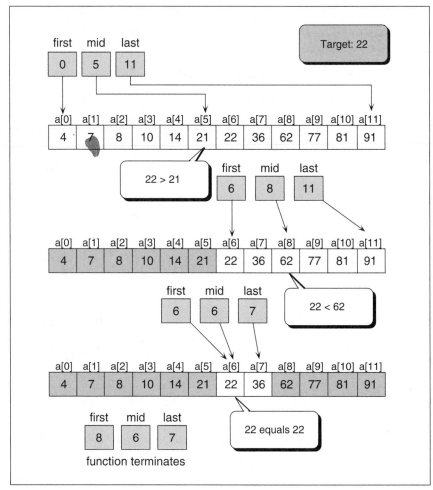

Figure 2-4 Binary search example

When we test the target to the value at mid a second time, we discover that the target is less than the list value (22 < 62). This time we adjust the end of the list by setting last to mid – 1 and recalculate mid. This step effectively eliminates elements 8 through 11 from consideration. We have now arrived at index location 6, whose value matches our target. This stops the search. (See Figure 2-4.)

Target Not Found

A more interesting case is when the target is not in the list. We must construct our search algorithm so that it stops when we have checked all possible locations. This is done in the binary search by testing for first and last crossing; that is, we are done when first becomes greater than last. We therefore see that two conditions terminate the binary search algorithm: The target is found or first becomes larger than last.

Let's demonstrate this situation with an example. Imagine we want to find 11 in our binary search array (see Figure 2-5). In this example,

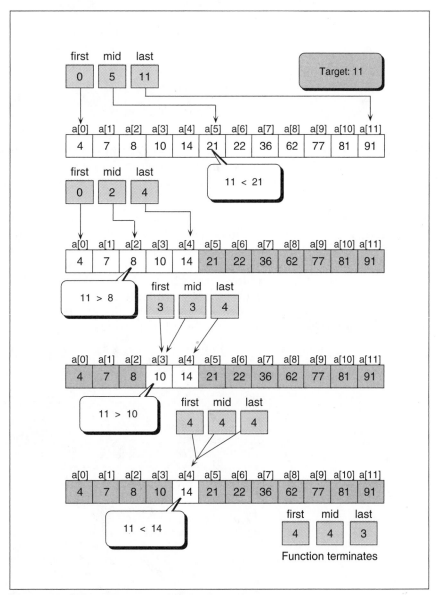

Figure 2-5   Unsuccessful binary search example

the loop continues to narrow the range as we saw in the successful search until we are examining the data at index locations 3 and 4. These settings of first and last set the mid index to 3.

$$mid = (3 + 4)/2 = 7/2 = 3$$

The test at index location 3 indicates that the target is greater than the list value, so we set first to mid + 1, or 4. We now test the data at location 4 and discover that 11 < 14.

$$mid = (4 + 4)/2 = 8/2 = 4$$

At this point, we have discovered that the target should be between two adjacent values; in other words, it is not in the list. We see this algorithmically because last is set to mid – 1, which makes first greater than last, the signal that the value we are looking for is not in the list.

Binary Search Algorithm

Algorithm 2-5 contains the implementation of the binary search algorithm we have been describing. It is constructed along the same design we saw for the sequential search. The first three parameters describe the list and the target we are looking for, and the last one contains the address into which we place the located index. One point is worth noting: When we terminate the loop with a not-found condition, the index returned is unpredictable—it may indicate the node greater than or less than the value in target.

```
algorithm binarySearch (val list     <array>,
                         val end      <index>,
                         val target   <keyType>,
                         ref locn     <index>)
Search an ordered list using Binary Search
    Pre    list is ordered; it must contain at least one element
           end is index to the largest element in the list
           target is the value of element being sought
           locn is address of index in calling algorithm
    Post   FOUND: locn assigned index to target element
                  found set true
           NOT FOUND: locn = element below or above target
                  found set false
    Return found <Boolean>
  1 first = 0
  2 last = end
```

Algorithm 2-5   Binary search

```
3  loop (first <= last)
   1   mid = (first + last) / 2
   2   if (target > list[mid])
       Look in upper half
       1   first = mid + 1
   3   else if (target < list[mid])
       Look in lower half
       1   last = mid - 1
   4   else
       Found equal: force exit
       1   first = last + 1
   5   end if
4  end loop
5  locn = mid
6  if (target equal list [mid])
   1   found = true
7  else
   1   found = false
8  end if
9  return found
end binarySearch
```

Algorithm 2-5   Binary search *(continued)*

Analyzing Search Algorithms

Of the five search algorithms discussed, which is the best? An application often determines which algorithm should be used, but we analyze the algorithms to determine which is most efficient.

Sequential Search

The basic loop for the sequential search is shown below.

```
while (looker < last && target != list[looker])
       looker++;
```

This is a classic example of a linear algorithm. In fact, in some of the literature, this search is known as a **linear search.** Because the algorithm is linear, its efficiency is $O(n)$.

```
The efficiency of the sequential search is O(n).
```

The search efficiency for the sentinel search is basically the same as for the sequential search. Although the sentinel search saves a few instructions in the loop, its design is identical. Therefore, it is also an $O(n)$ search. Likewise, the efficiency of the ordered list search is also $O(n)$. If we know the probability of a search being successful, we can construct a more accurate formula for searching an ordered list. This improved accuracy, however, turns out to be a coefficient in the formula, which as you will recall is dropped when using big-O analysis.

It is not possible to generalize the efficiency of the probability search without knowing the probability of each element in the list. On the other hand, if the probability of the first few elements of a list total more than 90%, it can be a very efficient search, even considering the additional overhead required to maintain the list. In general, however, we recommend the binary search, especially for large lists.

Binary Search

The binary search locates an item by repeatedly dividing the list in half. Its loop is

```
while (first <= last)
   {
   mid = (first + last) / 2;
   if (target > list[mid])
        first = mid + 1;
   else if (target < list[mid])
        last = mid - 1;
   else
        first = last + 1;
   } // while
```

This loop obviously divides, and it is therefore a logarithmic loop. The efficiency is thus $O(\log_2 n)$, which you should recognize as one of the most efficient of all the measures.

> The efficiency of the binary search is $O(\log_2 n)$.

Comparing the two searches, we see that, disregarding the time required to order the list, the binary search is obviously more efficient for searching a list of any significant size (see Table 2-1). For this reason, the binary search is recommended for all but the smallest of lists (i.e., lists with fewer than 16 elements).

The big-O concept is generally interested only in the largest factor. This focus tends to significantly distort the efficiency of the sequential sort in that it is always the worst case. If the search is always successful, it turns out that the efficiency of the sequential search is $(1/2)n$. We include the average in Table 2-1 for comparison. (The average for the binary search is only one less than the maximum, so it is less interesting.)

Size	Binary	Sequential (Average)	Sequential (Worst Case)
16	4	8	16
50	6	25	50
256	8	128	256
1000	10	500	1000
10,000	14	5000	10,000
100,000	17	50,000	100,000
1,000,000	20	500,000	1,000,000

Table 2-1 Comparison of binary and sequential searches

2-2 C++ SEARCH ALGORITHMS

In this section we develop the C++ code for the sequential and binary searches.

Sequential Search in C++

The sequential search in Program 2-1 parallels the pseudocode implementation in Algorithm 2-1 on page 32. In fact, it is virtually identical.

```
1   /* Locate the target in an unordered list of size elements.
2          Pre:    list must contain at least one item.
3                  last is index to last element in the list
4                  target contains the data to be located
5                  locn is address to index in calling function
6          Post:   FOUND:      matching index stored at locn
7                              return true (found)
8                  NOT FOUND: last stored in locn address.
9                              return false (not found)
10  */
11  bool seqSearch  (int   list[],
12                   int   last,
13                   int   target,
14                   int&  locn)
15  {
16  // Local Definitions
17     int looker;
18
19  // Statements
20     looker = 0;
```

Program 2-1 Sequential search

```
21    while (looker < last && target != list[looker])
22       looker++;
23
24    locn = looker;
25    return (target == list[looker]);
26 } // seqSearch
```

Program 2-1   Sequential search *(continued)*

Program 2-1 Analysis

Program 2-1 is simple but merits some discussion. First, why did we use a *while* statement rather than a *for* loop? Even though we know the limits of the array, it is still an event-controlled loop.[4] We search until we find what we are looking for or reach the end of the list. Finding something is an event, so we use an event loop.

Next, note that there are two tests in the limit expression of the loop. We have coded the test for the end of the array first. In this case, it doesn't make any difference which test is first from an execution standpoint, but in other search loops it might. Therefore, you should develop the habit of coding the limit test first because it doesn't use an indexed value and is therefore safer.

The call-by-reference use for locn also merits discussion. Because we need to pass the matching location back to the variable in the calling program, we need to pass it by reference.

Notice how succinct this function is. In fact, there are more lines of documentation than there are lines of code. The entire search is contained in one *while* statement. With this short code, you might be tempted to ask, "Why write the function at all? Why not just put the one line of code wherever it is needed?" The answer lies in the structured programming concepts that each function should do only one thing and in the concept of reusability. By isolating the search process in its own function, we separate it from the process that needs the search. This approach is better structured programming and also makes the code reusable in other parts of the program and portable to other programs that require searches.

Binary Search In C++

The C++ implementation of the binary search algorithm is shown in Program 2-2.

---

4. Event-controlled loops execute until an event, such as finding data or the end of the list, occurs. They are contrasted with count-controlled loops, which execute until a predetermined number of items have been processed. The *while* and *do . . . while* loops are event-controlled; the *for* loop is count controlled.

```
1   /* Search an ordered list using Binary Search
2        Pre:     list must contain at least one element
3                 end is index to the largest element in the list
4                 target is the value of element being sought
5                 locn is address to index in calling function
6        Post:    FOUND: locn = index to target element
7                        return true (found)
8                 NOT FOUND: locn = index below|above target
9                        return false (not found)
10  */
11  bool binarySearch  (int   list[],
12                      int   end,
13                      int   target,
14                      int&  locn)
15  {
16  // Local Definitions
17     int first;
18     int mid;
19     int last;
20
21  // Statements
22     first = 0;
23     last  = end;
24     while (first <= last)
25        {
26         mid = (first + last) / 2;
27         if (target > list[mid])
28            //  look in upper half
29            first = mid + 1;
30         else if (target < list[mid])
31            //  look in lower half
32            last = mid - 1;
33         else
34            //  found equal: force exit
35            break;
36        } //  end while
37     locn = mid;
38     return (target == list [mid]);
39  } //  binarySearch
```

Program 2-2 Binary search

Program 2-2 Analysis

To force the *while* loop to end when we find the target, we use a *break* statement (see Statement 35). One structured programming camp believes that *break* is not a good structured programming construct. However, we believe that it is more logical than the artificial end of loop we were forced to use in the pseudocode. If you work for a company that has rigorous standards against the *break* in loops, then you can force the loop to end with the following statement:

first = last + 1

Search Example

To demonstrate searches, let's create a program that looks up telephone numbers. Our input is a simple text file that contains names and phone numbers. When the program begins, it reads the file and loads the data into an array. A search function then loops and finds phone numbers. Program 2-3 contains the complete program.

```
 1   /* A small telephone lookup program.
 2       The input is a file of names and phone numbers.
 3          Written by:
 4          Date:
 5   */
 6   #include <fstream>
 7   #include <iomanip>
 8   #include <stdlib>
 9   #include <string>
10
11   // Global Declarations
12   typedef struct
13       {
14         char   name [31];
15         char   phone[16];
16       } LISTING;
17
18   const int MAX_SIZE = 53;
19
20   // Prototype Declarations
21   void buildList  (LISTING    phoneList[], int&  last);
22   void searchList (LISTING   *phoneList,   int   last);
23   bool seqSearch  (LISTING    list[],      int   last,
24                       char    *target,     int&  locn);
25
26   int main (void)
27   {
28   // Local Definitions
29      LISTING   phoneList[MAX_SIZE];
30      int       last;
31
32   // Statements
33      cout << "Begin Phone Listing\n";
34
```

Program 2-3   Sequential search example

```
35      last = MAX_SIZE - 1;
36      buildList (phoneList, last);
37      searchList(phoneList, last);
38
39      cout << "\nEnd Phone Listing\n";
40  } // main
41
42  /* ==================== buildList ====================
43     Read phone number file and load into array.
44         Pre    phoneList is array to be filled
45                last is index to last element loaded
46         Post   array filled
47  */
48  void buildList (LISTING phoneList[],
49                       int&    last)
50  {
51  // Local Definitions
52      ifstream fsPhoneNums;
53      int      i;
54
55  // Statements
56      fsPhoneNums.open ("P2-03.TXT");
57      if (!fsPhoneNums)
58         {
59          cout << "Can't open phone file\a\n";
60          exit (100);
61         } // if
62
63      i = 0;
64      while (i <= last && !fsPhoneNums.eof())
65         {
66          fsPhoneNums.getline(phoneList[i].name,
67                     sizeof(phoneList[0].name), ';');
68          fsPhoneNums.getline(phoneList[i].phone,
69                     sizeof(phoneList[0].phone));
70          i++;
71         } // while
72
73      if (!fsPhoneNums.eof())
74         cout << "File too large. Not all numbers read.\n";
75      last = i - 1;
76      return;
77  } // buildList
78
79  /* ==================== searchList ====================
80     Prompt user for name and look up in array.
```

Program 2-3 Sequential search example *(continued)*

```
 81            Pre    phoneList has been initialized
 82            Post   User requested quit
 83    */
 84    void searchList (LISTING  *phoneList,
 85                          int       last)
 86    {
 87    // Local Definitions
 88       char  srchName[31];
 89       char  more;
 90       bool  found;
 91       int   locn;
 92
 93    // Statements
 94       do
 95          {
 96            cout << "Enter name: ";
 97            cin  >> srchName;
 98
 99            found = seqSearch (phoneList, last, srchName, locn);
100            if (found)
101                cout << phoneList[locn].name
102                     << " (" << locn << ") "
103                     << phoneList[locn].phone << endl;
104            else
105              cout << srchName << " not found\n";
106
107            cout << "\nLook up another number <Y/N>? ";
108            cin  >> more;
109            } while (more == 'Y' || more == 'y');
110    } // searchList
111
112    /* ==================== seqSearch ====================
113       Locate the target in an unordered list.
114          Pre:    list must contain at least one item.
115                  last is index to last element in the list
116                  target contains the data to be located
117                  locn is address to index in calling function
118          Post:   FOUND:    matching index stored at locn
119                            return true (found)
120                  NOT FOUND: last stored in locn address.
121                            return false (not found)
122    */
123    bool seqSearch (LISTING  list[],
124                        int      last,
125                        char     *target,
126                        int&     locn)
```

Program 2-3   Sequential search example *(continued)*

```
127  {
128  // Local Definitions
129     int looker;
130
131  // Statements
132     looker = 0;
133     while (looker < last
134         && strcmp(target, list[looker].name) !=  0)
135        looker++;
136
137     locn = looker;
138     return (strcmp(target, list[looker].name) == 0);
139  } //  seqSearch
```

```
Results
   Begin Phone Listing
   Enter name: Behrouz
   Behrouz (0)   (555) 864-8888

   Look up another number <Y/N>? y
   Enter name: Wyan
   Wyan (10)   (555) 866-1234

   Look up another number <Y/N>? y
   Enter name: Wayn
   Wayn (11)   (555) 345-0987

   Look up another number <Y/N>? y
   Enter name: Richard
   Richard not found

   Look up another number <Y/N>? n

   End Phone Listing
```

Program 2-3 Sequential search example *(continued)*

Program 2-3 Analysis This program uses the same sequential search logic we saw in Program 2-1, on page 43. The only differences are in the code for the array type and the search argument. Because the array is an array of structures and the search argument is a string, we had to change the code. If you compare the logic, however, you will see that it is exactly the same.

2-3   HASHED LIST SEARCHES

The search techniques discussed in Section 2-1, "List Searches," on page 30 required several tests before we found the data. In an ideal search, we would know exactly where the data are and go directly there. This is the goal of a hashed search: to find the data with only one test. For our discussion, we use an array of data. The general concept is easily extended to other structures, such as files stored on a disk. These structures are beyond the scope of this text, however, and their discussion is left to other books.

Basic Concepts

A **hash search** is a search in which the key, through an algorithmic function, determines the location of the data. Because we are searching an array, we use a hashing algorithm to transform the key into the index that contains the data we need to locate. Another way to describe hashing is as a key-to-address transformation in which the keys map to addresses in a list. This mapping transformation is shown in Figure 2-6. At the top of Figure 2-6 is a general representation of the hashing concept. The rest of the figure shows how three keys might hash to three different addresses in the list.

Generally, the population of keys for a hashed list is greater than the storage area for the data. For example, if we have an array of 50 students for a class in which the students are identified by the last four digits of their Social Security numbers, then there are 200 possible

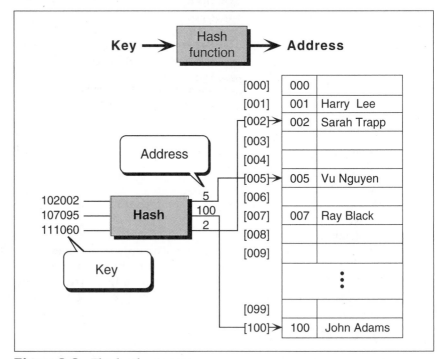

Figure 2-6   The hash concept

keys for each element in the array (10,000/50). Because there are many keys for each index location in the array, more than one student may hash to the same location in the array. We call the set of keys that hash to the same location in our list **synonyms.**

If the actual data that we insert into our list contain two or more synonyms, then we will have collisions. A **collision** occurs when a hashing algorithm produces an address for an insertion key and that address is already occupied. The address produced by the hashing algorithm is known as the **home address.** The memory that contains all of the home addresses is known as the **prime area.** When two keys collide at a home address, we must resolve the collision by placing one of the keys and its data in another location. The collision resolution concept is shown in Figure 2-7.

In Figure 2-7, we hash key A and place it at location 8 in the list. At some later time, we hash key B, which is a synonym of A. Because they are synonyms, they both hash to the same home address and a collision results. We resolve the collision by placing key B at location 16. When we hash key C, its home address is 16. Although B and C are not synonyms, they still collide at location 16 because we placed key B there when we resolved the earlier collision. We must therefore find another location for key C, which we place at location 4.

It should be obvious that when we need to locate an element in a hashed list, we must use the same algorithm that we used to insert it into the list. Consequently, we first hash the key and check the home address to determine whether it contains the desired element. If it does, the search is complete. If not, we must use the collision resolution algorithm to determine the next location and continue until we find the element or determine that it is not in the list. Each calculation of an address and test for success is known as a **probe.**

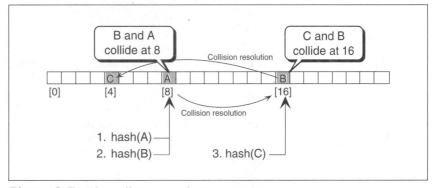

Figure 2-7   The collision resolution concept

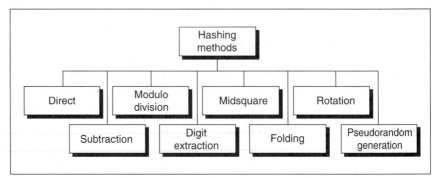

Figure 2-8   Basic hashing techniques

Hashing Methods

We are now ready to study several hashing methods. After we look at the different methods, we create a simple hashing algorithm that incorporates several of them. The hashing techniques that we study are shown in Figure 2-8.

Direct Method

In **direct hashing,** the key is the address without any algorithmic manipulation. The data structure must therefore contain an element for every possible key. The situations in which you can use direct hashing are limited, but it can be very powerful because it guarantees that there are no synonyms. Let's look at two applications.

First consider the problem in which we need to total monthly sales by the days of the month. For each sale, we have the date and the amount of the sale. In this case, we create an array of 31 accumulators. As we read the sales records for the month, we use the day of the month as the key for the array and add the sale amount to the corresponding accumulator. The accumulation code is shown below.[5]

```
dailySales[sale.day] = dailySales[sale.day]
                     + sale.amount;
```

Now let's consider a more complex example. Imagine that a small organization has fewer than 100 employees. Each employee is assigned an employee number between 1 and 100. In this case, if we create an array of 101 employee records (location 0 will not be used), the employee number can be directly used as the address of any individual record. This concept is shown in Figure 2-9.

As you study Figure 2-9, note that not every element in the array contains an employee's record. Although every element was used in

---

5. Because C++ arrays start at location 0, we will need to have 32 elements in our array. Element 0 will not be used.

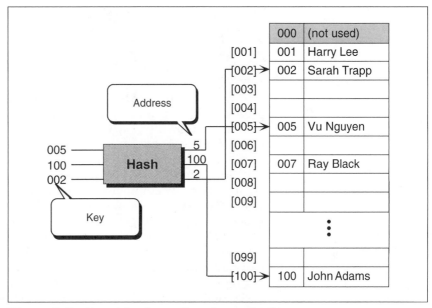

Figure 2-9   Direct hashing of employee numbers

our daily sales example, more often than not there are some empty elements in hashed lists. In fact, as we will see later, all hashing techniques other than direct hashing require that some of the elements be empty to reduce the number of collisions.

As you may have noticed, although this is the ideal method, its application is very limited. For example, we cannot have the Social Security number as the key using this method because Social Security numbers are nine digits. In other words, if we use the Social Security number as the key, we need an array as large as 1,000,000,000 records but we would use fewer than 100 of them. Let's turn our attention, then, to hashing techniques that map a large population of possible keys into a small address space.

Subtraction Method

Sometimes keys are consecutive but do not start from 1. For example, a company may have only 100 employees, but the employee numbers start from 1001 and go to 1100. In this case, we use a very simple hashing function that subtracts 1000 from the key to determine the address. The beauty of this example is that it is simple and guarantees that there will be no collisions. Its limitations are the same as direct hashing: It can only be used for small lists in which the keys map to a densely filled list.

Modulo-Division Method

Also known as **division remainder,** the **modulo-division** method divides the key by the array size and uses the remainder for the address.

This method gives us the simple hashing algorithm shown below when `listSize` is the number of elements in the array.

```
address = key MODULUS listSize
```

This algorithm works with any list size, but a list size that is a prime number produces fewer collisions than other list sizes. We should therefore try, whenever possible, to make the array size a prime number.

As our little company begins to grow, we realize that soon we will have more than 100 employees. Planning for the future, we create a new employee numbering system that will handle 1,000,000 employees. We also decide that we want to provide data space for up to 300 employees. The first prime number greater than 300 is 307. We therefore choose 307 as our list (array) size, which gives us a list with addresses that range from 0 through 306. Our new employee list and some of its hashed addresses are shown in Figure 2-10.

To demonstrate, let's hash Bryan Devaux's employee number, 121267.

```
121267/307 = 395 with remainder of 2
Therefore: hash(121267) = 2
```

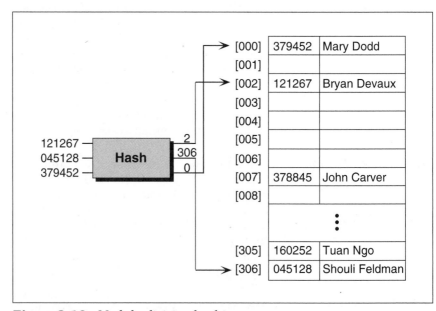

Figure 2-10   Modulo-division hashing

Digit-Extraction Method

Using **digit extraction,** selected digits are extracted from the key and used as the address. For example, using our six-digit employee number to hash to a three-digit address (000–999), we could select the first, third, and fourth digits (from the left) and use them as the address. Using the keys from Figure 2-10, we would hash them to the addresses shown below.

```
379452 ↝ 394
121267 ↝ 112
378845 ↝ 388
160252 ↝ 102
045128 ↝ 051
```

Midsquare Method

In **midsquare hashing,** the key is squared and the address selected from the middle of the squared number. The most obvious limitation of this method is the size of the key. Given a key of 6 digits, the product will be 12 digits, which is beyond the maximum integer size of many computers. Because most personal computers can handle a 9-digit integer, let's demonstrate the concept with keys of 4 digits. Given a key of 9452, the midsquare address calculation is shown below using a 4-digit address (0000–9999).

```
9452 * 9452 = 89340304: address is 3403
```

As a variation on the midsquare method, we can select a portion of the key, such as the middle three digits, and then use them rather than the whole key. Doing so allows the method to be used when the key is too large to square. For example, for the keys in Figure 2-10, we can select the first three digits and then use the midsquare method as shown below. (We select the third, fourth, and fifth digits as the address.)

```
379452: 379 * 379 = 143641 ↝ 364
121267: 121 * 121 = 014641 ↝ 464
378845: 378 * 378 = 142884 ↝ 288
160252: 160 * 160 = 025600 ↝ 560
045128: 045 * 045 = 002025 ↝ 202
```

Note that in the midsquare method, the same digits must be selected from the product. For that reason, we consider the product to have sufficient leading zeros to make it the full six digits.

Folding Methods

Two **folding methods** are used: fold shift and fold boundary.

In **fold shift,** the key value is divided into parts whose size matches the size of the required address. Then the left and right parts are shifted and added with the middle part. For example, imagine we want to

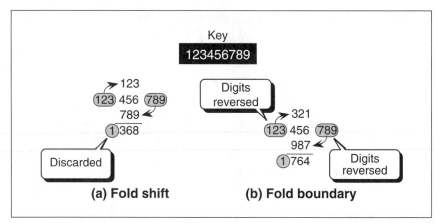

Figure 2-11   Hash fold examples

map Social Security numbers into three-digit addresses. We divide the nine-digit Social Security number into three three-digit numbers, which are then added. If the resulting sum is greater than 999, then we discard the leading digit. This method is shown in Figure 2-11(a).

In **fold boundary,** the left and right numbers are folded on a fixed boundary between them and the center number. The two outside values are thus reversed, as seen in Figure 2-11(b). It is interesting to note that the two folding methods give different hashed addresses.

Rotation Method

Rotation hashing is generally not used by itself but rather is incorporated in combination with other hashing methods. It is most useful when keys are assigned serially, such as we often see in employee numbers and part numbers. A simple hashing algorithm tends to create synonyms when hashing keys are identical except for the last character. Rotating the last character to the front of the key minimizes this effect. For example, consider the case of a six-digit employee number that might be used in a large company (see Figure 2-12).

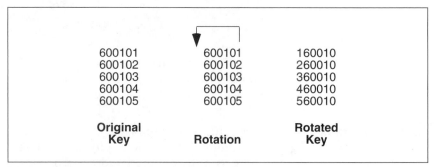

Figure 2-12   Rotation hashing

Examine the rotated key carefully. Because all keys now end in 60010, they would obviously not work well with modulo division. On the other hand, if we used a simple fold shift hash on the original key and a two-digit address, the addresses would be sequential starting with 62. Using a shift hash on the rotated key results in the series of addresses 26, 36, 46, 56, 66, which has the desired effect of spreading the data more evenly across the address space. Rotation is often used in combination with folding and pseudorandom hashing.

Pseudorandom Method

In the **pseudorandom method,** the key is used as the seed in a pseudorandom number generator and the resulting random number is then scaled into the possible address range using modulo division. A common random number generator is shown below.

$$y = ax + c$$

To use the pseudorandom number generator as a hashing method, we set x to the key, multiply it by the coefficient a, and then add the constant c. The result is then divided by the list size with the remainder plus 1 (see "Modulo-Division Method," on page 53) being the hashed address. For maximum efficiency, the factors a and c should be prime numbers. Let's demonstrate the concept with an example from Figure 2-10 on page 54. To keep the calculation reasonable, we use 17 and 7 for factors a and c, respectively. Also, the list size in the example is the prime number 307.

```
y = ((17 * 121267) + 7) modulo 307
y = (2061539 + 7) modulo 307
y = 2061546 modulo 307
y = 41
```

We will see this pseudorandom number generator again when we discuss collision resolution.

Hashing Algorithm

Before we conclude our discussion of hashing methods, we need to describe a complete hashing algorithm. Although the hashing methods may work well when we hash a key to an address in an array, hashing to large files is generally more complex. It often requires extensive analysis of the population of keys to be hashed to determine the number of synonyms and the length of the collision strings produced by the algorithm. The study of such analysis is beyond the scope of this text, but we present the algorithm described below as a simple example of a hashing algorithm for a large file.

Assume that we have an alphanumeric key consisting of up to 30 bytes that we need to hash into a 32-bit address. The first step is to convert the alphanumeric key into a number by adding the American Standard Code for Information Interchange (ASCII) value for each character to an accumulator that will be the address. As each character is added, we rotate the bits in the address to maximize the distribution of the values. After the characters in the key have been completely hashed, we take the absolute value of the address and then map it into the address range for the file. This logic is shown in Algorithm 2-6.

```
algorithm hash  (val key      <array of characters>,
                 val size      <integer>,
                 val maxAddr   <integer>,
                 ref addr      <integer>)
This algorithm converts an alphanumeric key of size characters
into an integral address.
    Pre    key is a key to be hashed
           size is the number of characters in the key
           maxAddr is the maximum possible address for the list
    Post   addr contains the hashed address
 1 looper = 0
 2 addr   = 0

Hash key
 3 loop (looper < size)
     1   if (key[looper] not space)
         1   addr = addr + key[looper]
         2   rotate addr 12 bits right
     2   end if
     3   looper = looper + 1
 4 end loop

Test for negative address
 5 if (addr < 0)
     1   addr = absolute(addr)
 6 end if
 7 addr = addr modulo maxAddr
 8 return
end hash
```

Algorithm 2-6   A hashing algorithm

Algorithm 2-6 Analysis

Two points merit discussion in this algorithm. First, the rotation in Statement 3.1.2 can often be accomplished by an assembly language instruction. If the algorithm is written in a high-level language, then the rotation is accomplished by a series of *bitwise and* instructions. For our purposes, it is sufficient that the 12 bits at the end of the address are shifted to be the 12 bits at the beginning of the address and the bits at the beginning are shifted to occupy the bit locations at the right.

Second, this algorithm actually uses three of the hashing methods discussed previously. We use fold shift when we add the individual characters to the address. We use rotation when we rotate the address after each addition. Finally, we use modulo division when we map the hashed address into the range of available addresses.

2-4 COLLISION RESOLUTION

With the exception of the direct and subtraction methods, none of the methods used for hashing are one-to-one mapping. Thus, when we hash a new key to an address, we may create a collision. There are several methods for handling collisions, each of them independent of the hashing algorithm. That is, each hashing method can be used with each of the collision resolution methods. In this section we discuss the collision resolution methods shown in Figure 2-13.

Before we discuss the collision resolution methods, however, we need to cover three more concepts. Because of the nature of hashing algorithms, there must be some empty elements in a list at all times. In fact, we define a full list as a list in which all elements except one contain data. As a rule of thumb, a hashed list should not be allowed to become more than 75% full. This guideline leads us to our first concept, load factor. The **load factor** of a hashed list is the number of elements in the list divided by the number of physical elements allocated for the list, expressed as a percentage. Traditionally, load factor is assigned the symbol alpha (α). The formula in which k represents the number of filled elements in the list and n represents the total number of elements allocated to the list is

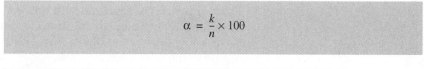

$$\alpha = \frac{k}{n} \times 100$$

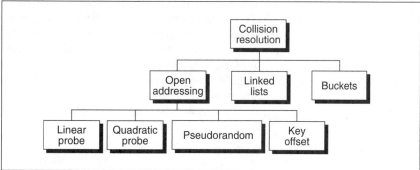

Figure 2-13 Collision resolution methods

Because there can never be more than n elements in a list, α will always be a percentage.

As data are added to a list and collisions are resolved, some hashing algorithms tend to cause data to group within the list. This tendency of data to build up unevenly across a hashed list is known as **clustering**, our second concept. Clustering is a concern because it is usually created by collisions. If the list contains a high degree of clustering, then the number of probes to locate an element grows and reduces the processing efficiency of the list.

Computer scientists have identified two distinct types of clusters. The first, **primary clustering,** occurs when data cluster around a home address. Primary clustering is easy to identify. Consider, for example, the population clusters found in the United States. If you have ever flown across the country on a clear night, you noticed that amid the darkness towns and cities were identified by their lights. If the whole country were a hashed list, and the lights each represented an element of data, then we would be looking at primary clustering, clustering around a home address in our list.

Secondary clustering, which occurs when data become grouped along a collision path throughout a list, is not as easy to identify. In secondary clustering, the data are widely distributed across the whole list so that the list appears to be well distributed. If the data all lie along a well-traveled collision path, however, the time to locate a requested element of data can increase. Consider an extreme example: Assume that we have a hashing algorithm that hashes each key to the same home address. Locating the first element inserted into the list takes only one probe. Locating the second element takes two probes. Carrying the analogy to its conclusion, locating the nth element added to the list takes n probes, even if the data are widely distributed across the addresses in the list.

From this discussion, it should be apparent that we need to design our hashing algorithms to minimize clustering. However, note that with the exception of the direct and subtraction methods, we cannot eliminate collisions. One of the surprises of hashing methods is how few elements need to be inserted into a list before a collision occurs. This concept is easier to understand if we recall a common party game used to encourage mingling. The host prepares a list of topics, and each guest is required to find one or more guests who satisfy each topic. One topic is often birthdays and requires that the guests find two people who have the same birthday (the year is not counted). If there are more than 23 party guests, chances are better than 50% that two of them have the same birthday.[6] Extrapolating this phenomenon to

---

6. This mathematical fact was first documented by von Mises in the 1930s and is known as the von Mises birthday paradox.

our hashing algorithms, if we have a list with 365 addresses, we can expect to get a collision within the first 23 inserts more than 50% of the time.

Our final concept is that the number of elements examined in the search for a place to store the data must be limited. The traditional limit of examining all elements of the list presents three difficulties. First, the search is not sequential, so finding the end of the list doesn't mean that every element has been tested. Second, examining every element would be excessively time-consuming for an algorithm that has as its goal a search effort of one. Third, some of the collision resolution techniques cannot physically examine all of the elements in a list. (For an example, see "Quadratic Probe," on page 62.)

Computer scientists therefore generally place a collision limit on hashing algorithms. What happens when the limit is reached depends on the application. One simple solution would be to abort the program. A more elegant solution would be to store the data in an area separate from the list (see "Linked List Resolution," on page 65). Whatever the solution, it is important to use the same algorithmic limit when searching for data in the list.

We are now ready to look at some collision resolution methods. Generally, there are two different approaches to resolving collisions: open addressing and linked lists. The third concept—buckets—defers collisions but does not prevent them.

Open Addressing

The first collision resolution method, **open addressing,** resolves collisions in the prime area—that is, the area that contains all of the home addresses. This technique is opposed to linked list resolution, in which the collisions are resolved by placing the data in a separate overflow area.

When a collision occurs, the prime area addresses are searched for an open or unoccupied element where the new data can be placed. We discuss four different methods: linear probe, quadratic probe, double hashing, and key offset.

Linear Probe

Our first collision resolution method is also the simplest. In a **linear probe,** when data cannot be stored in the home address, we resolve the collision by adding 1 to the current address. For example, let's add two more elements to the modulo-division method example in Figure 2-10, on page 54. The results are shown in Figure 2-14. When we insert key 070918, we find an empty element and insert it with no collision. When we try to insert key 166702, however, we have a collision at location 001. We try to resolve the collision by adding 1 to the address and inserting the new data at location 002. However, this address is also filled. We therefore add another 1 to the address and this time find an empty location, 003, where we can place the new data.

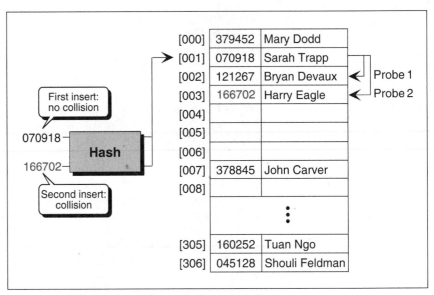

Figure 2-14 Linear probe collision resolution

As an alternative to a simple linear probe, we can add 1, subtract 2, add 3, subtract 4, and so forth until we locate an empty element. In either method, the code for the linear probe must ensure that the next collision resolution address lie within the boundaries of the list. Thus, if a key hashes to the last location in the list, adding 1 must produce the address of the first element in the list. Similarly, if the key hashes to the first element of the list, subtracting 1 must produce the address of the last element in the list.

Linear probes have two advantages. First, they are quite simple to implement. Second, data tend to remain near their home address. This tendency can be important in implementations for which being near the home address is important, such as when we hash to a disk address. On the other hand, linear probes tend to produce primary clustering. Additionally, they tend to make the search algorithm more complex, especially after data have been deleted.

Quadratic Probe

Primary clustering, although not necessarily secondary clustering, can be eliminated by adding a value other than 1 to the current address. One easily implemented method is to use the **quadratic probe.** In the quadratic probe, the increment is the collision probe number squared. Thus for the first probe we add 1^2, for the second collision probe we add 2^2, for the third collision probe we add 3^2, and so forth until we either find an empty element or we exhaust the possible elements. To ensure that we don't run off the end of the address list, we use the modulo of the quadratic sum for the new address. This sequence is shown in Table 2-2, which for simplicity assumes a collision at location 1 and a list size of 100.

A potential disadvantage of the quadratic probe is the time required to square the probe number. We can eliminate the multiply factor, however, by using an increment factor that increases by 2 each probe. Adding the increment factor to the previous increment gives us the next increment, which as you can see by the last column in Table 2-2 is the equivalent of the probe squared.

The quadratic probe has one limitation: It is not possible to generate a new address for every element in the list. For example, in Table 2-2, only 59 of the probes will generate unique addresses. The other 41 locations in the list will not be probed. The first duplicate address is found in probe 10. To see more examples of duplicate addresses, extend the table several probes. The solution to this problem is to use a list size that is a prime number. When the list size is a prime number, at least half of the list is reachable, which is a reasonable number.

Probe Number	Collision Location	Probe^2 and Increment	New Address
1	1	$1^2 = 1$	$1 + 1 \Rightarrow 02$
2	2	$2^2 = 4$	$2 + 4 \Rightarrow 06$
3	6	$3^2 = 9$	$6 + 9 \Rightarrow 15$
4	15	$4^2 = 16$	$15 + 16 \Rightarrow 31$
5	31	$5^2 = 25$	$31 + 25 \Rightarrow 56$
6	56	$6^2 = 36$	$56 + 36 \Rightarrow 92$
7	92	$7^2 = 49$	$92 + 49 \Rightarrow 41$
8	41	$8^2 = 64$	$41 + 64 \Rightarrow 5$
9	5	$9^2 = 81$	$5 + 81 \Rightarrow 86$
10	86	$10^2 = 100$	$86 + 100 \Rightarrow 86$

Table 2-2 Quadratic collision resolution increments

Pseudorandom Collision Resolution

The last two open addressing methods are collectively known as **double hashing.** In each method, rather than using an arithmetic probe function, the address is rehashed. As will be apparent from the discussion, both methods prevent primary clustering.

The first method uses a **pseudorandom** number to resolve the collision. We saw the pseudorandom number generator as a hashing method in "Pseudorandom Method," on page 57. We now use it as a collision resolution method. In this case, rather than using the key as a factor in the random number calculation, we use the collision address. Consider the collision we created in Figure 2-14, on page 62. We now resolve the collision using the following pseudorandom number generator, where a is 3 and c is 5:

```
y = (ax + c) modulo listSize
  = (3 × 1 + 5) Modulo 307
  = 8
```

In this example, we resolve the collision by placing the new data in element 008 (Figure 2-15). We have to keep the coefficients small to fit our example. A better set of factors would use a large prime number for a, such as 1663.

Pseudorandom numbers are a relatively simple solution, but they have one significant limitation: All keys follow only one collision resolution path through the list. (This deficiency also occurs in the linear and quadratic probes.) Because pseudorandom collision resolution can create significant secondary clustering, we should look for a method that produces different collision paths for different keys.

Key Offset

Key offset is a double hashing method that produces different collision paths for different keys. Whereas the pseudorandom number generator produces a new address as a function of the previous address, key offset calculates the new address as a function of the old address and the key. One of the simplest versions simply adds the quotient of

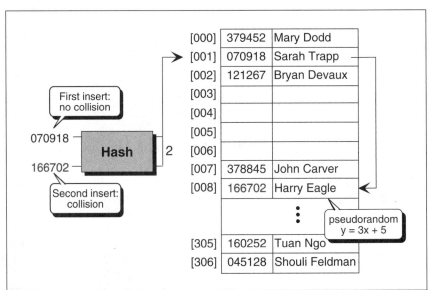

Figure 2-15   Pseudorandom collision resolution

the key divided by the list size to the address to determine the next collision resolution address, as shown in the formula below.

```
offSet     = ⌊key/listSize⌋
address    = ((offSet + old address) modulo listSize)
```

For example, when the key is 166702 and the list size is 307, using the modulo-division hashing method we generate an address of 1. As shown in Figure 2-15, this synonym of 070918 produces a collision at address 1. Using key offset to calculate the next address, we get 237, as shown below.

```
offSet     = ⌊166702/307⌋ = 543
address    = ((543 + 001) modulo 307) = 237
```

If 237 were also a collision, we would repeat the process to locate the next address, as shown below.

```
offSet     = ⌊166702/307⌋ = 543
address    = ((543 + 237) modulo 307) = 166
```

To really see the effect of key offset, we need to calculate several different keys, all hashing to the same home address. In Table 2-3 we calculate the next two collision probe addresses for three keys that collide at address 001.

Key	Home Address	Key Offset	Probe 1	Probe 2
166702	1	543	237	166
572556	1	1865	024	047
067234	1	219	220	132

Table 2-3 Key-offset examples

Note that each key resolves its collision at a different address for both the first and second probes.

Linked List Resolution

A major disadvantage to open addressing is that each collision resolution increases the probability of future collisions. This disadvantage is eliminated in the second approach to collision resolution, linked lists. A **linked list** is an ordered collection of data in which each element contains the location of the next element. For example, in Figure 2-16, array element 001, Sarah Trapp, contains a pointer to the next element, Harry Eagle, which in turn contains a pointer to the third element, Chris Walljasper. We study the maintenance of linked lists in the next chapter.

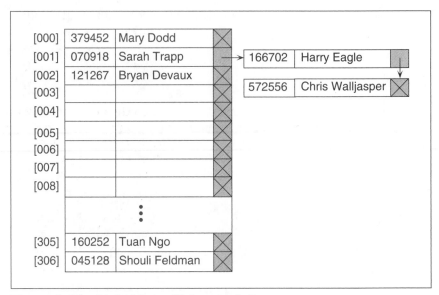

Figure 2-16   Linked list collision resolution

Linked list resolution uses a separate area to store collisions and chains all synonyms together in a linked list. It uses two storage areas, the prime area and the **overflow area.** Each element in the prime area contains an additional field, a link head pointer to a linked list of overflow data in the overflow area. When a collision occurs, one element is stored in the prime area and chained to its corresponding linked list in the overflow area. Although the overflow area can be any data structure, it is typically implemented as a linked list in dynamic memory. Figure 2-16 shows the linked list from Figure 2-15 with the three synonyms for address 001.

The linked list data can be stored in any order, but a last in–first out (LIFO) sequence or a key sequence is the most common. The LIFO sequence is the fastest for inserts because the linked list does not have to be scanned to insert the data. The element being inserted into overflow is simply placed at the beginning of the linked list and linked to the node in the prime area. Key sequenced lists, with the key in the prime area being the smallest, provide for faster search retrieval. Which sequence (LIFO or key-sequence) is used depends on the application.

Bucket Hashing

Another approach to handling the collision problem is to hash to **buckets,** nodes that accommodate multiple data occurrences. Because a bucket can hold multiple data, collisions are postponed until the bucket is full. Assume, for example, that in our Figure 2-16 list, each address is large enough to hold data about three employees. Under this

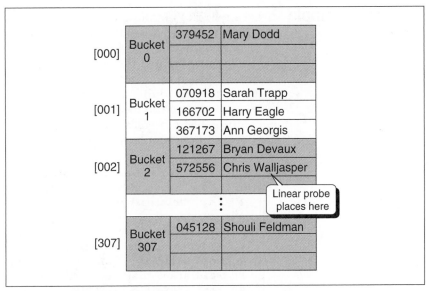

Figure 2-17 Bucket hashing

assumption, a collision would not occur until we tried to add a fourth employee to an address. There are two problems with this concept. First, it uses significantly more space because many of the buckets will be empty or partially empty at any given time. Second, it does not completely resolve the collision problem. At some point, a collision will occur and need to be resolved. When it does, a typical approach is to use a linear probe, assuming that the next element will have some empty space. Figure 2-17 demonstrates the bucket approach.

Study the second bucket in Figure 2-17. Note that it contains the data for three entries, all of which hashed to address 1. We will not get a collision until the fourth key, 572556 in our example, is inserted into the list. When a collision finally occurs—that is, when the bucket is full—any of the collision resolution methods may be used. For example, in Figure 2-17, a collision occurred when we inserted 572556 because bucket 1 was full. We then used a linear probe to insert it into location 2. Also note that for efficiency, we have placed the keys within a bucket in ascending key sequence.

Combination Approaches

There are several approaches to resolving collisions. As we saw with the hashing methods, a complex implementation often uses multiple steps. For example, one large database implementation hashes to a bucket. If the bucket is full, it uses a set number of linear probes, such as three, to resolve the collision and then uses a linked list overflow area.

Hash List Example

Let's rework Program 2-3, on page 46, as a hashed list search demonstration. We use a variation of Algorithm 2-6, on page 58 for the hashing and a linear probe for the collision resolution.

When we created the original program, we used a list size of 53 because it was a prime number. We also included two sets of names that are synonyms. Julie and Chris both hash to location 38; Wayn and Wyan both hash to location 52, the last location in our hash list. We can thus test our collision resolution at the end of the list. Our code is shown in Program 2-4.

```
 1   /* The telephone lookup program implemented using hashing.
 2      The input is a file of names and phone numbers.
 3         Written by:
 4         Date:
 5   */
 6   // Prototype Declarations
 7   void buildList  (LISTING   phoneList[], int&  last);
 8   void searchList (LISTING  *phoneList,   int   last);
 9   bool seqSearch  (LISTING   list[],      int   last,
10                    char     *target,      int&  locn);
11   int hashKey     (char     *key,         int   last);
12   int collision   (int       last,        int   locn);
13
14   int main (void)
15   {
16   // See Program 2-3 on page 46
17
18   } // main
19
20   /* ==================== buildList ====================
21      Read phone number file and load into array.
22         Pre    phoneList is array to be filled
23                last is index to last element loaded
24         Post   array filled
25   */
26   void buildList (LISTING phoneList[],
27                   int&    last)
28   {
29   // Local Definitions
30      ifstream fsPhoneNums;
31      LISTING  aListing;
32      int      locn;
33      int      cntCol;
34      int      end;
35      int      i;
36
```

Program 2-4   Hashed list search

```
37    // Statements
38       fsPhoneNums.open ("P2-03.TXT");
39       if (!fsPhoneNums)
40          {
41            cout << "Can't open phone file\a\n";
42            exit (100);
43          } // if
44
45       // Set keys to null
46       for (i = 0; i <= last; i++)
47            phoneList[i].name[0] = '\0';
48
49       while (!fsPhoneNums.eof())
50          {
51            fsPhoneNums.getline(aListing.name,
52                      sizeof(aListing.name), ';');
53            fsPhoneNums.getline(aListing.phone,
54                      sizeof(aListing.phone));
55            locn = hashKey(aListing.name, last);
56            if (phoneList[locn].name[0] != '\0')
57               {
58                 // Collision
59                 end     = last;
60                 cntCol  = 0;
61                 while (phoneList[locn].name[0] != '\0'
62                     && cntCol++ <= last)
63                     locn = collision(last, locn);
64
65                 if (phoneList[locn].name[0] != '\0')
66                    {
67                      cout << "List is full. Not all numbers read.\n";
68                      return;
69                    } // if full list
70               } // if collision
71            phoneList[locn] = aListing;
72          } // while
73       return;
74    } // buildList
75
76    /* ================== hashKey ==================
77       Given key, hash key to location in list.
78          Pre:    phoneList is hash array
79                  last is last index in list
80                  key is string to be hashed
81          Post:   returns hash location
82    */
```

Program 2-4 Hashed list search *(continued)*

```
 83   int hashKey (char *key,
 84                 int    last)
 85   {
 86   // Local Definitions
 87      int   addr;
 88      int   i;
 89      int   keyLen;
 90
 91   // Statements
 92      keyLen = strlen(key);
 93      addr   = 0;
 94
 95      for (i = 0; i < keyLen; i++)
 96          if (key[i] != ' ')
 97              addr += key[i];
 98
 99      return (addr % last + 1);
100   }  // hashKey
101
102   /* ==================== collision ====================
103      Have a collision. Resolve.
104          Pre:   phoneList is hashed list
105                 last is index of last element in list
106                 locn is address of collision
107          Post: returns next address in list
108   */
109   int collision (int   last,
110                  int   locn)
111   {
112   // Statements
113       return locn < last ? ++locn : 0;
114   }  // collision
115
116   /* ==================== searchList ====================
117      Prompt user for name and lookup in array.
118          Pre    phoneList has been initialized
119          Post   User requested quit
120   */
121   void searchList (LISTING  *phoneList,
122                    int          last)
123   {
124   // Local Definitions
125      char   srchName[31];
126      char   more;
127      int    locn;
128      int    maxSrch;
```

Program 2-4 Hashed list search *(continued)*

```
129        int    cntCol;
130
131    // Statements
132        do
133          {
134            cout << "Enter name: ";
135            cin  >> srchName;
136
137            locn = hashKey (srchName, last);
138            if (strcmp (srchName, phoneList[locn].name) != 0)
139               {
140                 // treat as collision
141                 maxSrch = last;
142               while (strcmp (srchName, phoneList[locn].name) != 0
143                    && cntCol++ <= maxSrch)
144                      locn = collision(last, locn);
145               } // if
146
147            // Test for success
148            if (strcmp (srchName, phoneList[locn].name) == 0)
149               cout << phoneList[locn].name
150                    << " (" << locn << ") "
151                    << phoneList[locn].phone << endl;
152            else
153               cout << srchName << " not found\n";
154
155            cout << "\nLook up another number <Y/N>? ";
156            cin  >> more;
157            } while (more == 'Y' || more == 'y');
158    } // searchList
```

```
    Results
      Begin Phone Listing
      Enter name: Julie
      Julie (38)   (555) 916-1212

      Look up another number <Y/N>? y
      Enter name: Chris
      Chris (39)   (555) 946-2859

      Look up another number <Y/N>? y
      Enter name: Wyan
      Wyan (52)   (555) 866-1234

      Look up another number <Y/N>? y
      Enter name: Wayn
      Wayn (0)   (555) 345-0987
```

Program 2-4 Hashed list search *(continued)*

```
Look up another number <Y/N>? y
Enter name: Bill
Bill not found

Look up another number <Y/N>? n
End Phone Listing
```

Program 2-4 Hashed list search *(continued)*

Program 2-4 Analysis

Many points in this program require discussion, although we tried to keep it as simple as possible. As we load the file, we use a function to hash the key. We use the same function to search the list. After hashing the key, we test for a collision. If the name in the hashed location is not a null string, we have a collision. To resolve the collision, we loop until we find an empty location. We used a separate collision function even though there is only one statement for two reasons. First, collision resolution is a separate process that should be placed in its own function because it will be used by multiple functions in the program. Second, if we later decide to change the collision resolution algorithm to key offset, for example, we can easily isolate and modify the code.

In the search function, we get the search argument from the user and then call the hash function to determine its location. If the search argument doesn't match the name in the location, we assume a collision. In this case, we loop until we find a matching key or until we have examined every location in the list.

The major problem with this simple search algorithm is that it must look in all locations to determine that a key is not in the list. In a productional program with a lot of data, we would have used a slightly different approach. If we used a flag to determine that a location had never been occupied, rather than one that was empty but had previously contained data, we could stop the search when we found an empty location.

2-5   SUMMARY

- Searching is the process of finding the location of a target among a list of objects.
- There are two basic searching methods for arrays: sequential and binary search.
- The sequential search is normally used when a list is not sorted. It starts at the beginning of the list and searches until it finds the data or hits the end of the list.
- One of the variations of the sequential search is the sentinel search. In this method, the condition ending the search is reduced to only one by artificially inserting the target at the end of the list.
- The second variation of the sequential search is called the probability search. In this method, the list is ordered with the most probable elements at the beginning of the list and the least probable at the end.

- The sequential search can also be used to search a sorted list. In this case, we can terminate the search when the target is less than the current element.
- If an array is sorted, we can use a more efficient algorithm called the binary search.
- The binary search algorithm searches the list by first checking the middle element. If the target is not in the middle element, the algorithm eliminates the upper half or the lower half of the list depending on the value of the middle element. The process continues until the target is found or the reduced list length becomes zero.
- The efficiency of a sequential list is $O(n)$.
- The efficiency of a binary search is $O(\log_2 n)$.
- In a hashed search the key, through an algorithmic transformation, determines the location of the data. It is a key-to-address transformation.
- There are several hashing functions: We discussed direct, subtraction, modulo division, digit extraction, midsquare, folding, rotation, and pseudorandom generation.
  - In direct hashing, the key is the address without any algorithmic manipulation.
  - In subtraction hashing, the key is transformed to an address by subtracting a fixed number from it.
  - In modulo-division hashing, the key is divided by the list size, recommended to be a prime number, and the remainder plus 1 is used as the address.
  - In digit-extraction hashing, selected digits are extracted from the key and used as an address.
  - In midsquare hashing, the key is squared and the address is selected from the middle of the result.
  - In fold shift hashing, the key is divided into parts whose sizes match the size of the required address. Then the parts are added to obtain the address.
  - In fold boundary hashing, the key is divided into parts whose sizes match the size of the required address. Then the left and right parts are reversed and added to the middle part to obtain the address.
  - In rotation hashing, the rightmost digit of the key is rotated to the left to determine an address. However, this method is usually used in combination with other methods.
  - In the pseudorandom generation hashing, the key is used as the seed to generate a pseudorandom number. The result is then scaled to obtain the address.
- Except in the direct and subtraction methods, collisions are unavoidable in hashing. Collisions occur when a new key is hashed to an address that is already occupied.
- Clustering is the tendency of data to build up unevenly across a hashed list.
  - Primary clustering occurs when data build up around a home address.
  - Secondary clustering occurs when data build up along a collision path in the list.
- To solve a collision, a collision resolution method is used.
- Three general methods are used to resolve collisions: open addressing, linked lists, and buckets.

- The open addressing method can be subdivided into linear probe, quadratic probe, pseudorandom rehashing, and key-offset rehashing.
  - **a.** In the linear probe method, when the collision occurs, the new data will be stored in the next available address.
  - **b.** In the quadratic method, the increment is the collision probe number squared.
  - **c.** In the pseudorandom rehashing method, we use a random number generator to rehash the address.
  - **d.** In the key-offset rehashing method, we use an offset to rehash the address.
- In the linked list technique, we use separate areas to store collisions and chain all synonyms together in a linked list.
- In bucket hashing, we use a bucket that can accommodate multiple data occurrences.

2-6　PRACTICE SETS

Exercises

1. An array contains the elements shown below. Using the binary search algorithm, trace the steps followed to find 88. At each loop iteration, including the last, show the contents of first, last, and mid.

    8　13　17　26　44　56　88　97

2. An array contains the elements shown below. Using the binary search algorithm, trace the steps followed to find 20. At each loop iteration, including the last, show the contents of first, last, and mid.

    8　13　17　26　44　56　88　97

3. Using the **modulo-division** method and **linear probing**, store the keys shown below in an array with 19 elements. How many collisions occurred? What is the density of the list after all keys have been inserted?

    224562, 137456, 214562

    140145, 214576, 162145

    144467, 199645, 234534

4. Repeat Exercise 3 using a linked list method for collisions. Compare the results in this exercise with the results you obtained in Exercise 3.

5. Repeat Exercise 3 using the **digit-extraction** method (first, third, and fifth digits) and **quadratic probing**.

6. Repeat Exercise 5 using a linked list method for collisions. Compare the results in this exercise with the results you obtained in Exercise 5.

7. Repeat Exercise 3 using the **midsquare** method, with the center two digits, for hashing. Use **pseudorandom number** generator for rehashing if a collision occurs. Use $a = 3$ and $c = -1$ as the factors.

8. Repeat Exercise 7 using a **key-offset** method for collisions. Compare the results in this exercise with the results you obtained in Exercise 7.

9. Repeat Exercise 3 using the **fold shift** method and folding two digits at a time and then **modulo division** of the folded sum.

10. Repeat Exercise 9 using the **fold boundary** method.

11. Repeat Exercise 3 using the **rotation method** for hashing. First rotate the rightmost digits two to the left and then use **digit extraction** (first, third, and fifth digits). Use the **linear probe** method to resolve collisions.

12. Repeat Exercise 11 using a **key-offset** method for collisions. Compare the results in this exercise with the results you obtained in Exercise 11.

Problems

13. Write a program that creates an array of 100 random integers in the range 1 to 200 and then, using the sequential search, searches the array 100 times using randomly generated targets in the same range. At the end of the program, display the following statistics:

a. The number of searches completed

b. The number of successful searches

c. The percentage of successful searches

d. The average number of tests per search

To determine the average number of tests per search, you will need to count the number of tests for each search.

After you run your program, write a paragraph on the similarities or differences between the expected efficiency (big-O) and your calculated results.

14. Repeat Problem 13 using an ordered list search. Rather than using a pseudorandom number generator, generate a sequenced array of numbers starting with 1 and alternately add 1 and then add 2 to create the next numbers in the series, as shown below.

1, 3, 4, 6, 7, 9, 10, 12, 13, 15, 16, . . . , 145, 147, 148, 150

For the search arguments, generate the 100 numbers in the range of 1 to 150.

15. Repeat Problem 14 using a binary search.

Projects

16. Modify Program 2-4, on page 68, to determine the efficiency of the hashed list search. Run your program with a list of at least 50 names and at least 10 searches. Include at least 3 search arguments that are not in the list.

17. Run your program from Problem 16 four times. The only differences between the runs should be the load factor. For the first program use a 60% load factor and then increase it by 10% for each of the following runs. Draw a graph that plots the search efficiency and write a short report about the differences.

18. Modify Program 2-4, on page 68, to use pseudorandom number generation to resolve collisions. Write a short report on the differences between the two methods.

19. Write a program that uses a hashing algorithm to create a list of inventory parts and their quantities sold in the past month. After creating the hashed list, write a simple menu-driven user interface that allows the user to select from the following options:

a. Search for an inventory item and report its quantity sold

b. Print the inventory parts and their quantity sold

c. Analyze the efficiency of the hashing algorithm

The parts data are contained in a text file, as shown in Table 2-4. The key is the three-digit part number. The quantity represents the units sold during the past month.

Part Number	Quantity
112	12
130	30
156	56
173	17
197	19
150	50
166	66
113	13
123	12
143	14
167	16
189	18
193	19
117	11
176	76

Table 2-4 Data for hashing problem

Three outputs are required from your program.

a. Test the following searches and return appropriate messages. You may test other part numbers if you desire, but the following tests must be completed first:
- Search for 112
- Search for 126
- Search for 173

b. When requested, analyze the efficiency of the hashing algorithm for this set of data. Your printout should follow the report format shown below.

```
Percentage of Prime Area Filled:    xx%
Average nodes in linked lists:      nn
Longest linked list                 nn
```

c. The printout of the entire contents of the list should use the following format:

```
Home Addr  Prime Area      Overflow List
    0      130/30
    1
    2      112/12
    3      123/12          143/14, 173/17, 193/19
    .
    .
    .
```

Linked Lists

3

A linear list is a list in which each element has a unique successor. In your programming classes you studied a linear list structure, the array. Arrays are easy to create and use, but they are inefficient when sequenced data need to be inserted or deleted. In our study of data structures, we extend the linear concept with the introduction of the linked list. Although the linked list efficiently handles insertions and deletions, it is inefficient for search and retrieval.

In this chapter we study the linked list implementation of linear lists. We start with some general concepts common to all linear lists and then develop the concept of the linked list. We conclude with some linked list applications and a basic implementation of a list abstract data type using a C++ class.

3-1   LINEAR LIST CONCEPTS

The sequential property of a linear list is basic to its definition and use. The simplest linear list structure, the array, is found in virtually all programming languages. The sequentiality of a linear list is diagrammed in Figure 3-1.

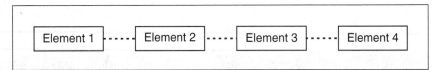

Figure 3-1   A linear list

Linear lists can be divided into two categories: general and restricted. In a **general list,** data can be inserted and deleted anywhere and there are no restrictions on the operations that can be used to process the list. General structures can be further described by their data as either random or ordered lists. In a **random list,** there is no ordering of the data. In an **ordered list,** the data are arranged according to a key. A **key** is one or more fields within a structure that are used to identify the data or otherwise control their use. In the simple array, the data are also the keys. In an array of records structure, the key is a field, such as employee number, that identifies the record.

In a **restricted list,** data can only be added or deleted at the ends of the structure and processing is restricted to operations on the data at the ends of the list. We describe two restricted list structures: the first in–first out **(FIFO)** list and the last in–first out **(LIFO)** list. The FIFO list is generally called a queue; the LIFO list is generally called a stack. We discuss stacks in Chapter 4 and queues in Chapter 5. Figure 3-2 shows the types of lists.

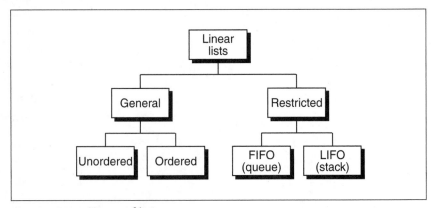

Figure 3-2   Types of lists

Four operations are generally associated with linear lists: insertion, deletion, retrieval, and traversal. The first three apply to all lists; list traversal is not applicable to restricted lists.

Insertion

Depending on the type of general list, an **insertion** can be made at the beginning of the list, in the middle of the list, or at the end of the list. Although there are no restrictions on inserting data into a random list, computer algorithms generally insert data at the end of the list. Thus, random lists are sometimes called **chronological lists.** The very nature of random lists, however, is counter to the computer concept in which algorithms are used to process data. The few computer applications in which random lists are used are found either in data-gathering applications, in which case the lists are chronological lists, or in situations in which the applications require randomness, such as simulation studies or games.

Data must be inserted into ordered lists so that the ordering of the list is maintained. Maintaining the order may require inserting the data at the beginning or at the end of the list, but most of the time data are inserted somewhere in the middle of the list. To determine where the data are to be placed, computer scientists use a search algorithm. Insertions are graphically shown in Figure 3-3.

In Figure 3-3, the inserted data are identified by the shaded element, in this case the third element of the revised list. If the data structure is an array, then all of the data following the inserted element must be shifted toward the rear of the array to make room for the new data. Other structures, such as the linked list, avoid this physical shifting of data by maintaining a logical sequencing of data that is separate from its physical sequence.

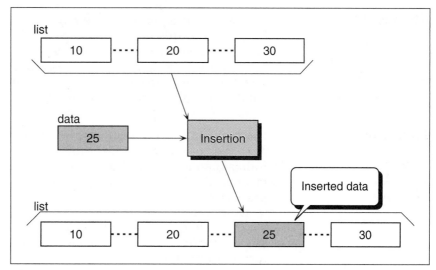

Figure 3-3   Ordered list insertion

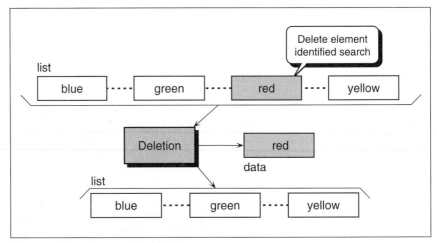

Figure 3-4   General list deletion

Deletion

Deletion from a general list requires that the list be searched to locate the data being deleted. Any sequential search algorithm can be used to locate the data. Once located, the data are removed from the list. Deletions from the restricted lists vary depending on which list is being used. We discuss restricted lists in their appropriate chapters. Figure 3-4 depicts a deletion from a general list.

When data are deleted from a random array, the data following the deleted item must be shifted to replace the empty element. As we will see with linked lists, other structures eliminate this shifting of data.

Retrieval

List **retrieval** requires that data be located in a list and presented to the calling module without changing the contents of the list. As with both insertion and deletion, any sequential search algorithm can be used to locate the data to be retrieved from a general list. Retrieval from a restricted list depends on the particular list being used. Retrieving data from a linear list is shown in Figure 3-5.

Traversal

List **traversal** is a special case of retrieval in which all elements are retrieved in sequence. List traversal requires a looping algorithm rather than a search. Each execution of the loop processes one element in the list. The loop terminates when all elements have been processed.

Other processes can be used with a linear list, such as sorting the list or totaling the value of all elements in the list. You have already studied these algorithms in your programming classes. We therefore turn our attention to linear lists that are stored in structures that do not require physical adjacency: linked lists.

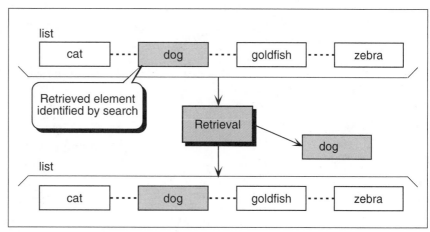

Figure 3-5   Linear list retrieval

3-2   LINKED LIST CONCEPTS

A **linked list** is an ordered collection of data in which each element contains the location of the next element; that is, each element contains two parts: **data** and **link.** The data part holds the useful information, the data to be processed. The link is used to chain the data together. It contains a pointer that identifies the next element in the list. In addition, a pointer variable identifies the first element in the list. The name of the list is the same as the name of this pointer variable. The simple linked list we describe here is commonly known as a **singly linked list** because it contains only one link to a single successor.

The major advantage of the linked list over other general list structures is that data are easily inserted and deleted. It is not necessary to shift elements of a linked list to make room for a new element or to delete an element. On the other hand, because the elements are no longer physically sequenced, we are limited to sequential searches: we cannot use a binary search.[1]

Figure 3-6 shows a linked list, pHead (for pointer to the head of the list), that contains four elements. The link in each element except the last points to its successor. The link in the last element contains a null pointer, indicating the end of the list. We define an **empty linked list** to be a null head pointer. Figure 3-6 also contains an example of an empty linked list.

Nodes

The elements in a linked list are traditionally called nodes. A **node** in a linked list is a structure that has at least two fields: one contains the

---

1. When we study trees, we will see several data structures that allow for easy updates and efficient searches.

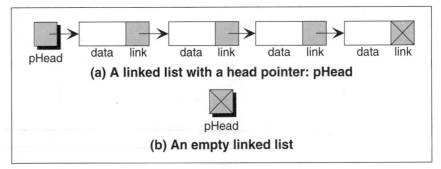

Figure 3-6   A linked list

data, the other the address of the next node in the sequence. Figure 3-7 shows three different node structures. The first node contains a single field, number, and a link. The second node is more typical. It contains three data fields, a name, id, and grade points (grdPts), and a link. The third example is the one we recommend. The fields are defined in their own structure, which is then put into the definition of a node structure. The one common element in all examples is the link field.

The nodes in a linked list are called **self-referential** structures. In a self-referential structure, each instance of the structure contains a pointer to another instance of the same structural type. In Figure 3-7, the shaded boxes with arrows are the links that make the linked list a self-referential structure.

Linked List Data Structure

One of the attributes of a linked list is that there is not a physical relationship between the nodes; that is, they are not stored contiguously. When a linear list is stored in an array, we know from the array structure where the list begins. The successor to each element is simply the next element in the array. But with a linked list, there is no physical relationship between the nodes.

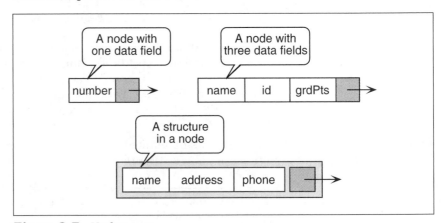

Figure 3-7   Nodes

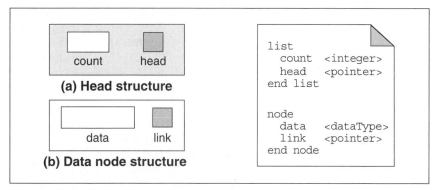

Figure 3-8 Linked list node structure

Without a physical relationship between the nodes, we need pointers to distinguish the beginning of the list—that is, to identify the first logical node in the list and the location of any given node's immediate successor. The pointer to the beginning of the list is known as a **head pointer** because it points to the node at the head of the list. In Figure 3-6, on page 82, we call the head pHead and the pointers that identified a node's immediate successor link.

Head Node Structure

Although only a single pointer is needed to identify the list, we often find it convenient to create a structure that stores the head pointer and other data about the list itself. When a node contains data about a list, the data are known as **metadata;** that is, they are data about data in the list. For example, the head structure in Figure 3-8 contains one piece of metadata: count, an integer that contains the number of nodes currently in the list. Other metadata, such as the maximum number of nodes during the processing of the list, are often included when they serve a useful purpose.

Data Node Structure

The data type for the list depends entirely on the application. A typical data type is shown below. The data types with ellipses must be tailored to the particular application being created.

```
dataType
    key      <keyType>
    field1   <...>
    field2   <...>
       ...
    fieldN   <...>
end dataType
```

We include a key field for applications that require searching by key. The key type defined above is a generic type that must be changed for each application.

We must study the node data structure, shown in Figure 3-8, in detail. First, note that it contains the data type. Now study the link structure carefully. Note that the link is a pointer to another data structure of its own type. We can thus create our linked list structure in which one instance of a node points to another instance of the node, making it a self-referential list.

Pointers to Linked Lists

A linked list must always have a head pointer. Depending on how you will use the list, you may have several other pointers as well. For example, if you are going to search a linked list, you will undoubtedly have a pointer to the location (pLoc) where you found the data for which you were looking. In many structures, programming is more efficient if there is a pointer to the last node in the list as well as a head pointer. This last pointer is often called either pLast for pointer to last or pRear for pointer to rear.

3-3   LINKED LIST ALGORITHMS

We define ten operations for a linked list, which should be sufficient to solve any sequential list problem. If an application requires additional list operations, they can be easily added. For each operation we define its name and provide a brief description and its calling parameters. We then develop algorithms for each operation.

Although implementating a linked list depends somewhat on the implementation language, it most commonly implemented with a pointer to a list head structure stored in dynamic memory. We use this design.

Create List

Create list receives the head structure and initializes the metadata for the list. At this time, there are only two metadata entries; later we will add more to expand the capabilities of the linked list. Figure 3-9 shows the header before and after it is initialized by create list.

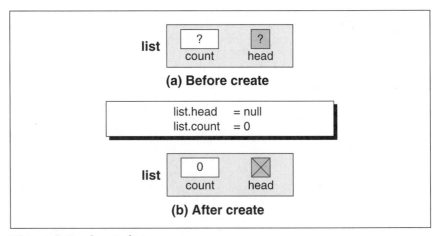

Figure 3-9   Create list

The pseudocode for create list is shown in Algorithm 3-1.

```
algorithm createList (ref list <metadata>)
Initializes metadata for a linked list.
    Pre     list is metadata structure passed by reference
    Post    metadata initialized
  1 list.head  = null
  2 list.count = 0
  3 return
end createList
```

Algorithm 3-1   Create linked list

Insert Node

Insert node adds data to a linked list. We need only its logical predecessor to insert a node into the list. Given the predecessor, there are three steps to the insertion:

1. Allocate memory for the new node and insert data.
2. Point the new node to its successor.
3. Point the new node's predecessor to the new node.

These steps appear to be simple, but a little analysis is needed to fully understand how to implement them. To insert a node into a list we need to know the location of the node that precedes the new node. This node is identified by a pointer that can be in one of two states: it can contain the address of a node or it can be null. When the predecessor is null, it means that there is no predecessor to the data being added. The logical conclusion is that we are either adding to an empty list or are at the beginning of the list. If the predecessor is not null, then we are adding somewhere after the first node—that is, in the middle of the list or at the end of the list. Let's discuss each of these situations in turn.

Insert into Empty List

When the head pointer of the list is null, then the list is empty. This situation is shown in Figure 3-10. All that is necessary to add a node to an empty list is to assign the list head pointer the address of the new node and make sure that its link field is a null pointer. Although we could use a constant to set the link field of the new node, we use the null pointer contained in the list head. Why we use the list head null pointer will become apparent in the next section.

The pseudocode statements to insert a node into an empty list are shown below.

```
pNew->link = list.head      Set link to null pointer
list.head  = pNew           Point list to first node
```

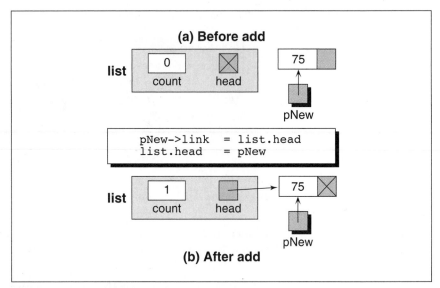

Figure 3-10   Add node to empty list

Note the order of these two statements. We must first point the new node to its successor; then we can change the head pointer. If we reverse these statements, we will end up with the new node pointing to itself, which would put our program into a never-ending loop when we process the list.

Insert at Beginning

We add at the beginning of the list anytime we need to insert a node before the first node of the list. We determine that we are adding at the beginning of the list by testing the predecessor pointer. If it is a null pointer, then there is no predecessor, so we are at the beginning of the list.

To insert a node at the beginning of the list we simply point the new node to the first node of the list and then set the head pointer to point to the new first node. We know the address of the new node. The question at this point is how we can find the address of the first node currently in the list so we can point the new node to it. The answer is simple: The first node's address is stored in the head pointer. The pseudocode statements to insert at the beginning of the list are shown below.

```
pNew->link    = list.head
list.head     = pNew
```

If you compare these two statements with the statements to insert into an empty list, you will see that they are the same. They are the same because, logically, inserting into an empty list is the same as inserting at the beginning of a list. We can therefore use the same logic

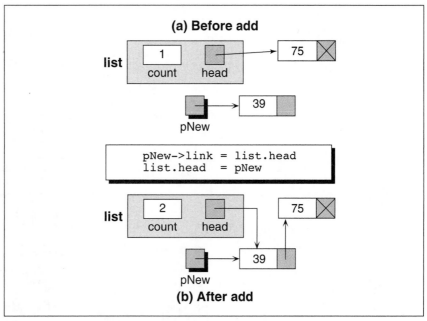

Figure 3-11   Add node at beginning

to cover both situations. Adding at the beginning of the list is shown in Figure 3-11.

Insert in Middle

When we add a node anywhere in the middle of the list, the predecessor contains an address. This case is shown in Figure 3-12.

To insert a node between two nodes, we point the new node to its successor and then point its predecessor to the new node. The address of the new node's successor can be found in the predecessor's link field.

The pseudocode statements to insert a node in the middle of the list are shown below.

```
pNew->link    = pPre->link
pPre->link    = pNew
```

Insert at End

When we are adding at the end of the list, we only need to point the predecessor to the new node. There is no successor to point to. It is necessary, however, to set the new node's link field to a null pointer. The statements to insert a node at the end of a list are shown below.

```
pNew->link    = null pointer
pPre->link    = pNew
```

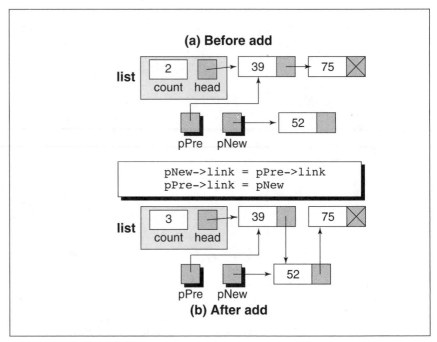

Figure 3-12   Add node in middle

Rather than have special logic in the algorithm for inserting at the end, however, we can take advantage of the existing linked list structure. We know that the last node in the list will have a null link pointer. If we use this pointer rather than a null pointer constant, then the code becomes exactly the same as the code for inserting in the middle of the list. The revised code is shown below. Compare it with the code for insert in the middle of the list.

```
pNew->link    = pPre->link
pPre->link    = pNew
```

Figure 3-13 shows the logic for inserting at the end of a linked list.

Insert Node Algorithm

Now let's write the algorithm that puts it all together and inserts a node into the list. We are given the head pointer, the predecessor, and the data to be inserted. We allocate memory for the new node and adjust the link pointers appropriately. When the algorithm is complete, it returns a Boolean—true if it was successful and false if there was no memory for the insert. The pseudocode is found in Algorithm 3-2.

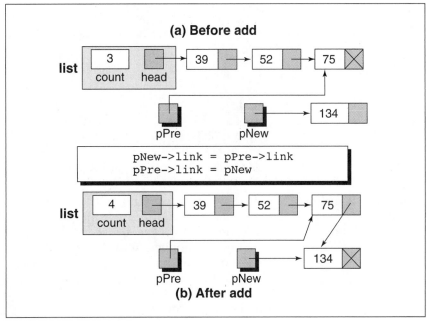

Figure 3-13   Add node at end

```
algorithm insertNode (ref list    <metadata>,
                      val pPre    <node pointer>,
                      val dataIn  <dataType>)
Inserts data into a new node in the linked list.
    Pre    list is metadata structure to a valid list
           pPre is pointer to data's logical predecessor
           dataIn contains data to be inserted
    Post   data have been inserted in sequence
    Return true if successful, false if memory overflow
1 allocate (pNew)
2 if (memory overflow)
    1   return false
3 end if
4 pNew->data = dataIn
5 if (pPre null)
    Adding before first node or to empty list.
    1   pNew->link = list.head
    2   list.head  = pNew
```

Algorithm 3-2   Insert linked list node

```
6 else
   Adding in middle or at end.
   1   pNew->link = pPre->link
   2   pPre->link = pNew
7 end if
8 list.count = list.count + 1
9 return true
end insertNode
```

Algorithm 3-2   Insert linked list node *(continued)*

Algorithm 3-2 Analysis

We have discussed all of the logic in this algorithm except for the memory allocation. When memory is exhausted, the insert is in an **overflow** state. The action taken depends on the application. Although the application will generally need to abort the program, that decision should not be made in the insert algorithm. We therefore return a Boolean indicating whether we were successful and let the calling module decide whether it needs to abort or whether some other action is appropriate.

Delete Node

The **delete node** algorithm logically removes a node from the linked list by changing various link pointers and then physically deleting the node from dynamic memory. To logically delete a node, we must first locate the node itself. A delete node is located by knowing its address and its predecessor's address. We will discuss location concepts shortly. Once we locate the node to be deleted, we can simply change its predecessor's link field to point to the deleted node's successor. We then recycle the node back to dynamic memory. We need to be concerned, however, about deleting the only node in a list. Deleting the only node results in an empty list, so we must be careful that in this case the head is set to a null pointer.

The delete situations parallel those for add. We can delete the only node, the first node, a node in the middle of the list, or the last node of a list. As we explain below, these four situations reduce to only two combinations: delete the first node and delete any other node. In all cases, the node to be deleted is identified by a pointer (pLoc).

Delete First Node

When we delete the first node, we must reset the head pointer to point to the first node's successor and then recycle the memory for the deleted note. We can tell we are deleting the first node by testing the predecessor. If the predecessor is a null pointer, we are deleting the first node. This situation is diagrammed in Figure 3-14.

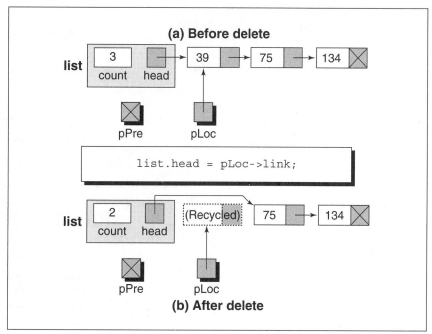

Figure 3-14   Delete first node

The statements to delete the first node are shown below. `Recycle` is the pseudocode command to return a node's space to dynamic memory.

```
list.head = pLoc->link
recycle (pLoc)
```

If you examine this logic carefully, you will note that it also applies when we are deleting the only node in the list. If the first node is the only node, then its link field is a null pointer. Because we move its link field (a null pointer) to the head pointer, the result is by definition an empty list.

General Delete Case

We call deleting any node other than the first node a general case because the same logic applies to deleting any node in either the middle or at the end of the list. For both of these cases, we simply point the predecessor node to the successor of the node being deleted. The logic is shown in Figure 3-15.

We delete the last node automatically. When the node being deleted is the last node of the list, its null pointer is moved to the predecessor's link field, making the predecessor the new logical end of the list. After the pointers have been adjusted, the current node is recycled.

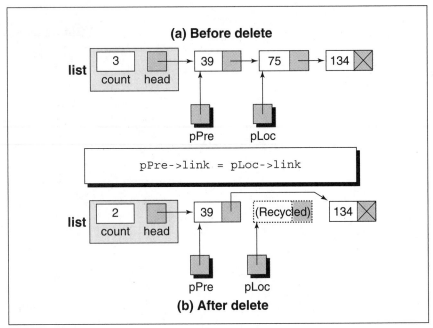

Figure 3-15   Linked list delete general case

The delete general case pseudocode is shown below.

```
pPre->link = pLoc->link
recycle (pLoc)
```

**Delete Node
Algorithm**

The logic to delete a node is shown in Algorithm 3-3. The algorithm is given a pointer to the head of the list, to the node to be deleted, and to the delete node's predecessor. It copies the deleted node's data to a data out area in the calling program and then adjusts the pointers before releasing the node's memory.

```
algorithm deleteNode (ref list      <metadata>,
                       val pPre      <node pointer>,
                       val pLoc      <node pointer>,
                       ref dataOut   <dataType>)
Deletes data from a linked list and returns it to calling module.
    Pre     list is metadata structure to a valid list
            pPre is a pointer to predecessor node
            pLoc is a pointer to node to be deleted
            dataOut is variable to received deleted data
    Post    data have been deleted and returned to caller
```

Algorithm 3-3   Linked list delete node

```
1  dataOut = pLoc->data
2  if (pPre null )
   Deleting first node
   1   list.head = pLoc->link
3  else
   Deleting other nodes
   1   pPre->link = pLoc->link
4  end if
5  list.count = list.count - 1
6  recycle (pLoc)
7  return
end deleteNode
```

Algorithm 3-3   Linked list delete node *(continued)*

Algorithm 3-3 Analysis

We need to discuss two points in this algorithm. The first, and most important, is that the node to be deleted must be identified before it is called. The algorithm assumes that the predecessor and current pointers are properly set. If they aren't, then the algorithm will most likely fail. Even if it doesn't fail, the data will be wrong. (It's better that the algorithm fail than that it report invalid results.)

Second, when we discussed the individual logic cases earlier, we placed the recycle statement after each delete statement. In the implementation, we moved it to the end of the algorithm. When the same statements appear in both the true and false blocks of a selection statement, they should be moved out of the selection logic. Moving common statements is similar to factoring common expressions in algebra. The result is a program that is smaller and easier to maintain.

Search List

A **Search list** is used by several algorithms to locate data in a list. To insert data, we need to know the logical predecessor to the new data. To delete data, we need to find the node to be deleted and identify its logical predecessor. To retrieve data from a list, we need to search the list and find the data. In addition, many user applications require that lists be searched to locate data.

When the data are stored in an array, we use a binary search for efficiency. When the data are stored in a linked list, however, we cannot use a binary search. We must use a sequential search because there is no physical relationship among the nodes. The classic sequential search returns the location of an element when it is found and the address of the last element when it is not found. Because our list is ordered, we need to return the location of the element when it is found and the location *where it should be placed* when it is not found. Knuth[2] calls this search "sequential search in ordered table." We simply call it an **ordered list search.**

To search a list on a key, we need a key field. For simple lists, the key and the data can be the same field. For more complex structures, we need a separate key field. We reproduce the data node structure from page 83 for your convenience.

```
dataType
    key      <keyType>
    field1   <...>
    field2   <...>
      ...
    fieldN   <...>
end dataType
```

Given a target key, the ordered list search attempts to locate the requested node in the linked list. If a node in the list matches the target value, the search returns true; if there are no key matches, it returns false. The predecessor and current pointers are set according to the rules in Table 3-1. Each of these conditions is also shown in Figure 3-16.

Condition	pPre	pLoc	Return
Target < first node	Null	First node	False
Target equal first node	Null	First node	True
First < target < last	Largest node < target	First node > target	False
Target equal middle node	Node's predecessor	Equal node	True
Target equal last node	Last's predecessor	Last node	True
Target > last node	Last node	Null	False

Table 3-1 List search results

We start at the beginning and search the list sequentially until the target value is no longer greater than the current node's key. At this point, the target value is either less than or equal to the current node's key while the predecessor is pointing to the node immediately before the current node. We then test the current node and set the return value true if the target value is equal to the list value or false if it is less (it cannot be greater) and terminate the search. The pseudocode for this search is shown in Algorithm 3-4.

2. Donald E. Knuth, *The Art of Computer Programming* Vol. 3, *Sorting and Searching* (Reading, MA: Addison-Wesley, 1973), 396.

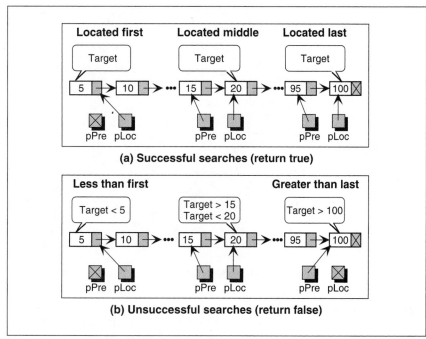

Figure 3-16 Ordered list search

```
algorithm searchList (val list      <metadata>,
                      ref pPre       <node pointer>,
                      ref pLoc       <node pointer>
                      val target     <key type>)
Searches list and passes back address of node containing target
and its logical predecessor.
   Pre     list is metadata structure to a valid list
           pPre is pointer variable for predecessor
           pLoc is pointer variable for current node
           target is the key being sought
   Post    pLoc points to first node with equal/greater key
           -or- null if target > key of last node
           pPre points to largest node smaller than key
           -or- null if target < key of first node
   Return  true if found, false if not found
1 pPre = null
2 pLoc = list.head
3 loop (pLoc not null AND target > pLoc->data.key)
   1   pPre = pLoc
```

Algorithm 3-4   Search linked list

```
   2   pLoc = pLoc->link
 4 end loop
   Set return value
 5 if (pLoc null)
   1   found = false
 6 else
   1   if (target equal pLoc->data.key)
     1   found = true
   2   else
     1   found = false
   3   end if
 7 end if
 8 return found
end searchList
```

Algorithm 3-4   Search linked list *(continued)*

Algorithm 3-4 Analysis

Examine the loop statement carefully. Note that there are two tests. The first test protects us from running off the end of the list; the second test stops the loop when we find the target or, if the target doesn't exist, when we find a node larger than the target. It is important that the null pointer test be done first. If the loop is at the end of the list, then the current pointer is no longer valid. Testing the key first would give unpredictable results.[3]

We could make the search slightly more efficient if we had a rear pointer. A rear pointer is a metadata field that contains the address of the last node in the list. With a rear pointer, we could test the last node to make sure that the target wasn't larger than its key value. If the target were larger, we would simply skip the loop, setting the predecessor pointer to the last node and the current pointer to a null pointer. Once we know that the target is not greater than the last node, we don't need to worry about running off the end of the list.

Unordered List Search

In the previous discussion we assumed that the list is ordered on a key. It is often necessary, however, to search the list on a list attribute rather than the key. For example, given a list of information about the employees in a company, we might want to find employees who have an engineering degree or employees who speak Japanese.

---

3. Note that some languages, such as Pascal, test both expressions in the condition before evaluating the results. In these situations, the loop limit test condition must be broken up into two separate expressions.

To search a list on any field other than the key we use a simple sequential search (see Chapter 2). The problem with nonkey searches, however, is that multiple elements often satisfy the search criteria. Although we might have only one employee who speaks Japanese, we might just as well have zero or many who do. One simple solution is to return a list of all elements that satisfy the criteria.

Retrieve Node

Now that we know how to locate a node in the list, we are ready to study **retrieve node.** Retrieve node uses search node to locate the data in the list. If the data are found, it moves the data to the output area in the calling module and returns true. If they are not found, it returns false. The pseudocode is shown in Algorithm 3-5.

```
algorithm retrieveNode (val list   <metadata>,
                        val key    <key type>,
                        ref dataOut <dataType>)
Retrieves data from a linked list.
    Pre    list is metadata structure to a valid list
           key is target of data to be retrieved
           dataOut is variable to receive retrieved data
    Post   data placed in dataOut
             -or- error returned if not found
    Return true if successful, false if data not found

1 found = searchList (list, pPre, pLoc, key)
2 if (found)
    1  dataOut = pLoc->data
3 end if
4 return found
end retrieveNode
```

Algorithm 3-5   Retrieve linked list node

Empty List

Processing logic often depends on whether there are data in a list. Thus, we provide **empty list,** a simple module that returns a Boolean indicating that there are data in the list or that it is empty (Algorithm 3-6).

```
algorithm emtpyList (val list <metadata>)
Returns Boolean indicating whether the list is empty.
    Pre    list is metadata structure to a valid list
    Return true if list empty, false if list contains data
1 return (list.count equal to zero)
end emptyList
```

Algorithm 3-6   Empty linked list

One of the questions often raised by students studying program design is "Why write a module when it contains only one statement—Isn't it more efficient to simply code the statement inline?" Although it is definitely more efficient to write the code inline, it is not a better design for a generalized module. Remember that we are implementing generalized code in which the user does not necessarily know the data structure. For example, virtually all systems have an algorithm that tests for end of file. This test is quite simple, most likely only one line of code. It is necessary, however, because the programmer doesn't know the file structure and therefore cannot check the end of file status without support.[4]

Full List

At first glance, **full list** appears to be as simple as empty list. It turns out to be a relatively complex algorithm to implement, however. Very few languages provide the programmer with the capability to test how much memory is left in dynamic memory. Given this limitation, the only way we can test for a full list is to try to allocate memory. If we are successful, we simply recycle the memory and return false—the list is not full. If we are unsuccessful, then we return true—dynamic memory is full. The pseudocode is shown in Algorithm 3-7.

```
algorithm fullList (val list  <metadata>)
Returns Boolean indicating whether or not the list is full.
    Pre      list is metadata structure to a valid list
    Return   false if room for new node; true if memory full
1  allocate (pNew)
2  if (allocation successful)
   1   recycle (pNew)
   2   return false
3  end if
4  return true
end fullList
```

Algorithm 3-7   Full linked list

List Count

List count is another simple, one-line module. It is necessary because the calling module has no direct access to the list structure. Its implementation is shown in Algorithm 3-8.

---

4. C++ programmers "can have their cake and eat it, too." Empty list could easily be implemented as a macro that supports the structured programming principle of data hiding while providing the efficiency of inline code, or as an inline function.

```
algorithm listCount (val list <metadata>)
Returns integer representing number of nodes in list.
   Pre      list is metadata structure to a valid list
   Return   count for number of nodes in list
1 return (list.count)
end listCount
```

Algorithm 3-8   Linked list count

Traverse List

Algorithms that **traverse** a list start at the first node and examine each node in succession until the last node has been processed. Traversal logic is used by several different types of algorithms, such as changing a value in each node, printing the list, summing a field in the list, or calculating the average of a field. Any application that requires that the entire list be processed uses a traversal.

To traverse the list we need a walking pointer, a pointer that moves from node to node as each element is processed. Assuming a linked list with a head structure, the following pseudocode uses a walking pointer to traverse the list. Each loop modifies the pointer to move to the next node in sequence as we traverse the list.

```
pWalker = list.head
loop (pWalker not null)
    process (pWalker->data)
    pWalker = pWalker->link
```

We begin by setting the walking pointer to the first node in the list. Then, using a loop, we continue until all of the data have been processed. Each loop calls a process module and passes it the data and then advances the walking pointer to the next node. When the last node has been processed, the walking pointer becomes null and the loop terminates.

We have two possible approaches in designing the traverse list implementation. In one approach the user controls the loop, calling traverse to get the next element in the list. In the other approach, the traverse module controls the loop, calling a user-supplied algorithm to process the data. We implement the first option because it provides the programmer with more flexibility. For example, if the application needs to process only half the list, the loop can simply terminate. The second design would loop through the second half of the data unnecessarily. Figure 3-17 is a graphic representation of a linked list traversal.

Because we need to remember where we are in the list from one call to the next, we need to add a current position pointer to the head structure. It keeps track of the node processed after the last call. The head structure is shown in Figure 3-17. The figure also shows how the position pointer is modified to move from one node to the next as the traversal algorithm is called.

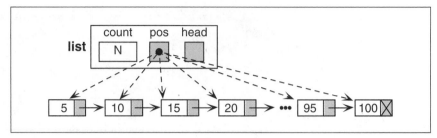

Figure 3-17   Linked list traversal

Each call also needs to know whether we are starting from the beginning of the list or continuing from the last node processed. This information is communicated through the parameter list. The basic logic
to traverse a list is shown in Algorithm 3-9. We name it `getNext` because it is called to get the next node in the traversal.

```
algorithm getNext  (ref list      <metadata>,
                     val fromWhere <Boolean>,
                     ref dataOut   <dataType>)
Traverses a linked list. Each call returns the location of an
element in the list.
    Pre     list is metadata structure to a valid list
            fromWhere is 0 to start at the first element
            dataOut is variable to receive data
    Post    dataOut contains data and true returned
            -or- if end of list, returns false
    Return  true if next element located, false if end of list
  1 if (fromWhere is 0)
    Start from first
    1   if (list.count is zero)
        1   success = false
    2   else
        1   list.pos  = list.head
        2   dataOut   = list.pos->data)
        3   success   = true
  2 else
    Continue from pos
    1   if (list.pos->link null)
        End of List
        1   success = false
    2   else
        1   list.pos = list.pos->link
        2   dataOut  = list.pos->data)
```

Algorithm 3-9   Traverse linked list

```
      3   success  = true
   3   end if
 3  end if
 4  return success
end getNext
```

Algorithm 3-9   Traverse linked list *(continued)*

Algorithm 3-9 Analysis

There are two major blocks of code in this algorithm. Statement 1 handles the processing when we start from the beginning of the list, and Statement 2 handles the processing when we continue from the current location. When we start from the beginning, we must guard against the traversal of a null list. We check the list count and if it is zero simply terminate with success set to false. Assuming that there are data in the list, we set the head structure's position pointer to the first node in the list and pass the first node's data back to the calling module.

If we are continuing the list traversal, we must ensure that there are more data by checking the current position's link field. If it is null, we set success to false and terminate. If there are more data, we set the current position to the next node and pass its data back to the calling module.

One final word of caution: This design supports only one traversal of any given list at a time. If an application needs more than one traversal at a time, then a different design is needed.

Destroy List

When a list is no longer needed but the application is not done, the list should be destroyed. **Destroy list** deletes any nodes still in the list and recycles their memory. It then sets the metadata to a null list condition. The code for destroy list is shown in Algorithm 3-10.

```
algorithm destroyList (ref pList <metadata>)
Deletes all data in list.
   Pre    list is metadata structure to a valid list
   Post   All data deleted
 1 loop (list.count not zero)
   1   dltPtr     = list.head
   2   list.head  = dltPtr->link
   3   list.count = list.count - 1
   4   recycle (dltPtr)
 2 end loop
   No data left in list. Reset metadata.
 3 list.pos = null
 4 return
end destroyList
```

Algorithm 3-10   Destroy linked list

3-4   PROCESSING A LINKED LIST

In the previous section, we wrote ten low-level algorithms for a linked list. In this section we add three high-level modules and a menu module that combines them all into one program. When you understand this program and can implement it, you will understand all of the basic linked list operations.

The design is shown in Figure 3-18. Study this design carefully and determine how many of the modules have already been developed.

Your analysis of Figure 3-18 should have indicated that there are six new algorithms required in this program: the main line, a menu module to interact with the user, a module to get data from the user, a module to add a node, a module to remove a node, and a module to print the list. The main line logic is shown in Algorithm 3-11. The pseudocode for the menu module is shown in Algorithm 3-12. The others are discussed in the sections that follow.

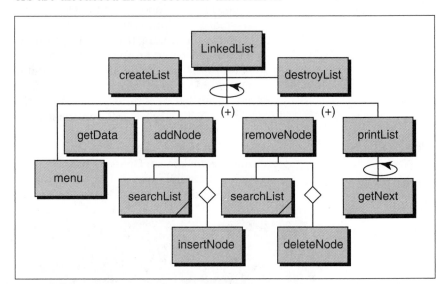

Figure 3-18   Design for build linked list

```
algorithm buildLinkedList
This program builds a linked list that can be modified or printed
by the user.
  1 print (Welcome to exploring linked lists.)
  2 createList (list)
  3 loop (option not quit)
    1   option = menu ()
    2   if (option add)
```

Algorithm 3-11   Build a linked list

```
      1   dataIn = getData()
      2   addNode (list, dataIn)
  3   elseif (option delete)
      1   print (Enter key of data to be deleted.)
      2   read (deleteKey)
      3   removeNode (list, deleteKey)
  4   elseif (option print)
      1   printList (list)
  5   end if
4 end loop
5 destroyList (list)
6 print (Exploration complete. Thank you.)
end buildLinkedList
```

Algorithm 3-11   Build a linked list *(continued)*

Algorithm 3-11 Analysis   There's not much to this program, as you can see. We start by printing a welcome message and then creating a null list. A call to the menu algorithm gets the user's first action. We then loop until the user quits. Each loop either adds a new node, removes a node, or prints the list.

```
algorithm menu
    Display a menu and read user option.
    Pre     Nothing
    Return Valid choice

1 print (......MENU......)
2 print (A: Add new data.)
3 print (D: Delete data.)
4 print (P: Print list.)
5 print (Q: Quit)
6 valid = false
7 loop (valid false)
  1   print (Enter your choice: ")
  2   read (choice)
  3   if (choice equal 'A' or 'D' or 'P' or 'Q')
      1   valid = true
  4   else
      1   print (Invalid choice. Choices are <A, D, P, Q>)
  5   end if
8 end loop
9 return choice
end menu
```

Algorithm 3-12   Menu for building a linked list

Algorithm 3-12 Analysis   If you are not already familiar with menus and data validation logic, you should study this algorithm carefully. It prompts the user to enter a choice from a menu and then makes sure that a valid choice was entered. If the choice is not valid, it prints an error message containing the valid options and asks the user to enter another choice. The loop continues until the user enters a valid choice, at which point it returns the choice to the calling algorithm.

Add Node

To add a node, we must get the data for the new node and then search the list to locate the insertion point. Once we know the insertion point, we can use insert node to physically place the data in the list. Search list and insert node are two of the basic algorithms developed earlier. The module to read the data depends on the application. We create a generic module, `getData` (see Statement 3.2.1 in Algorithm 3-11), for this purpose. It simply reads data from an appropriate source and places them in the reference parameter `dataIn`. The design for add node is seen in "Insert Node," which starts on page 85. The pseudocode for add node is found in Algorithm 3-13.

```
algorithm addNode (ref list    <metadata>,
                       val dataIn <dataType>)
Add data to a linked list.
    Pre    list is metadata structure to a valid list
           dataIn are data to be inserted into list
    Post   data have been inserted into list in key sequence

 1 found = searchList (list, pPre, pLoc, dataIn.key)
 2 if (found)
   Error: Key already exists
   1   print (Error: Data already in list. Not added.)
 3 else
   1   success = insertNode (list, pPre, dataIn)
   2   if (success false)
       1   print (Error: Out of memory. Program quitting.)
       2   abort algorithm
   3   end if
 4 return
end addNode
```

Algorithm 3-13   Add node to linked list

Algorithm 3-13 Analysis   The usefulness of structured programming becomes apparent when you can build programs by combining previously developed algorithms. We use two previously developed algorithms (`searchList` and `insertNode`) and a selection statement and we have a new algorithm. It's almost like magic.

When inserting data into a list, we need to decide whether duplicate data will be allowed. A node is generally considered a duplicate if its key matches an existing node's key. Some applications permit duplicates, and others do not. In this algorithm we have decided not to allow duplicates.

We also need to decide how to handle memory overflow. You will recall that in insert node, we pass a success flag back to the caller. If there is no memory for the new item, the flag is false. Now, in `addNode` we need to take appropriate action. If memory overflows we have decided to abort the program after printing a message to the user.

Remove Node

The design to remove a node is also simple. Given the key of the node to be removed, we call `searchList` to determine its location and its predecessor and then `deleteNode` to do the physical deletion. The design is shown in "Delete Node," which starts on page 90. The pseudocode is shown in Algorithm 3-14.

```
algorithm removeNode (ref list   <metadata>,
                      val key     <keyType>)
This algorithm deletes a node from the linked list.
   Pre    list is metadata structure to a valid list
          key is the key to be located and deleted
   Post   the node has been deleted
          -or- a warning message printed if not found

1  found = searchList (list, pPre, pLoc, key)
2  if (found)
   1   deleteNode (list, pPre, pLoc, deleteData)
3  else
   1   print (Error: Key not in list.)
4  end if
5  return
end removeNode
```

Algorithm 3-14   Remove data from linked list

Algorithm 3-14 Analysis   The most important logic in a delete algorithm is verifying that the data to be deleted actually exist. We do this in Statement 2. Search list returns a Boolean—true if the key was found and false if it doesn't exist. We test the Boolean to ensure that we found the data before calling the delete node algorithm.

Print List

One of the more common uses of link list traversals is to print the entire contents of a list. If the user selects the print list option from the menu, we traverse the list and print all of the key fields. In this program, we simply print a sequential number and the key from the data. To do this we need to call `traverse` (see page 99). The first call starts the traversal. Then, within a loop, we continue until all of the data have been printed. The code is shown in Algorithm 3-15.

```
algorithm printList (val list <metadata>)
This algorithm traverses a linked list and prints the key in each
node.
    Pre    list is metadata structure to a valid list
    Post   All keys have been printed

1  if (emptyList (list))
   1   print (No data in list.)
2  else
   1   print (**** Begin Data Print ****)
   2   count = 0
   3   moreData = getNext (list, 0, dataPtr)
   4   loop (moreData true)
       1   count = count + 1
       2   print (count, dataPtr->key)
       3   moreData = getNext (list, 1, dataPtr)
   5   end loop
   6   print (**** End Data Print ****)
3  end if
4  return
end printList
```

Algorithm 3-15   Print linked list

Algorithm 3-15 Analysis

There are several subtle points in this algorithm. First, note how we test for an empty list before starting the loop. We are thus able to print a unique error message if the user requests that an empty list be printed.

To assure the user that all of the data were printed, we print a start and end message. Then, the data from each node are numbered so that the user knows at a glance how many elements are in the list.

Because we know that there is at least one node in the list before we start the loop, we can simplify the printing. The first call to traverse must have a `whereFrom` flag of zero. It is therefore placed outside the loop. The loop then starts by incrementing the count and printing the data. The call at the end of the loop sets `moreData` so we know if we need to loop again.

Testing Insert and Delete Logic

Testing linked list algorithms requires careful planning. Because the list is ordered, you need at least four test cases to validate the insert logic.

1. Insert a node into a null list. This test is always done automatically because the list starts out in a null state.
2. Insert a node before the first data node. This test is not automatic, and you need to arrange the input so that this case is tested.
3. Insert between two data nodes. Again, this test is not automatic. Make sure that the test cases include the insertion of at least one node between two existing data nodes.
4. Insert after the last node. Because this case is the same as the insert into a null list, it is automatic. Nevertheless, we recommend a test case in which the new data are inserted after the last node in the list.

Testing the delete logic is similar.

1. Delete to a null list. To fully test the delete logic, one test case should delete all of the data from the list and then insert new data.
2. Delete the first data node in the list. When dealing with lists, the most common locations for errors are the first and last elements in the list. Make sure that one of the test cases deletes the first data node in the list.
3. Delete a node between two data nodes. Because this is the most common case, it is usually tested. Analyze the test data, however, to ensure that at least one of the delete cases deletes a node between two data nodes.
4. Delete the node at the end of the list. This test is not automatic. Make sure that one of the delete cases deletes the node at the end of the list.
5. Try to delete a node that doesn't exist. This test is not obvious. Some programs erroneously delete a node in the list even when the target node does not exist. It is thus very important that you also test the not-found conditions.
6. Try to delete a node whose key is less than the first data node's key. A subtle error in the program could result in the first node being deleted when the target does not exist. Make sure this case is tested.
7. Try to delete a node whose key is greater than the last data node's key.
8. Try to delete from an empty list. This is the opposite of the previous condition. It needs to be included in the test cases.

3-5   LIST APPLICATIONS

In this section we look at two list applications that use the linked list algorithms developed in the previous sections: append two lists and build an array of linked lists. As you study these algorithms, note how easy it is to develop new programs once you have built a library of basic algorithms.

Append Lists

In this application, we build two linked lists and then append the second one to the end of the first one. A pictorial representation of the data is shown in Figure 3-19.

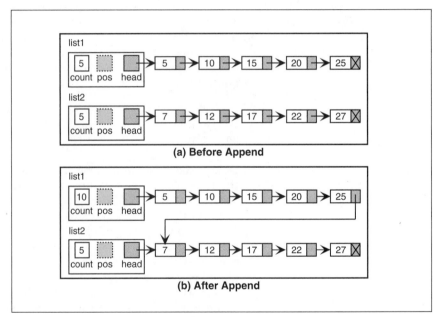

Figure 3-19   Append linked lists

When we began our discussion of the ten basic linked list algorithms on page 84, we said that they were sufficient to solve any basic problem. We have now found a problem that they will not solve. To append the second list to the end of the first list, we need to change the link pointer in the last node of the first list to point to the first node of the second list. None of the basic algorithms allow us to do so. We must therefore write a new algorithm to append two lists. The implementation is shown in Algorithms 3-16 through 3-18.

```
algorithm appendTwoLists
   Creates two linked lists and then appends the second to
   the first.
 1 print (This program creates two lists and then appends them)
 2 print (Enter first file name)
 3 read  (fileName)
 4 open  (fileName)
 5 build     (list1, fileName)
 6 printList (list1)
 7 print (Enter second file name)
 8 read  (fileName)
 9 open  (fileName)
10 build     (list2, fileName)
11 printList (list2)
12 append    (list1, list2)
   The lists are now appended. Print to prove success.
13 printList (list1)
14 return
end appendTwoLists
```

Algorithm 3-16   Append two linked lists

Algorithm 3-16 Analysis

This program's main line uses nothing but calls to algorithms. We will look at build and append in the algorithms that follow. We have already seen print list.

The algorithm to build the linked lists is shown in Algorithm 3-17.

```
algorithm build (ref list <metadata>,
                 val file <data file>)
This algorithm builds a linked list from data in a file.
   Pre  list is metadata structure for list to be built
        File must exist
   Post List has been built

 1 createList (list)
 2 loop (not end of file)
   1   read (file into dataIn)
   2   searchList (list, pPre, pLoc, dataIn.key)
   3   insertNode (list, pPre, dataIn)
 3 end loop
 4 return
end build
```

Algorithm 3-17   Build linked lists

Algorithm 3-17 Analysis

In Algorithm 3-11, "Build a linked list," on page 102 we used the add and remove algorithms. In this algorithm, we used the lower-level algorithms searchList and insertNode. Once again, this application points out the flexibility of good library algorithms.

We now need to write a new low-level algorithm to append two lists. Its pseudocode is shown in Algorithm 3-18.

```
algorithm append (ref list1 <metadata>,
                  val list2 <metadata>)
This algorithm appends the second list to the end of the first.
   Pre    both lists are metadata structures to valid list
   Post   Second list appended to the first list
1 if (list1.count zero)
   1    list1.head = list2.head
2 else
   1    pLoc = list1.head
   2    loop (pLoc->link not null)
      1    pLoc = pLoc->link
   3    end loop
   4    pLoc->link = list2.head
3 end if
4 list1.count = list1.count + list2.count
5 return
end append
```

Algorithm 3-18   Append linked lists

Algorithm 3-18 Analysis

The append algorithm is quite simple. We traverse the first list to find the last node. We then change the last node's link pointer to point to the beginning of the second list. Our only concern is that the first list might be null. If it is, then we simply set its head pointer to the head pointer of the second list. We are not concerned about the second list being null. The logic works when it is null and when it contains data. You should prove this to yourself. At the end of the algorithm, we add the counts for the two lists and place the sum in the count for the first list.

Array of Lists

In the next application we build an array of linked lists. The data for each linked list are read from a set of existing files and inserted into the list. After the program builds the lists, they are printed to verify that they are complete. The data structure is shown in Figure 3-20.

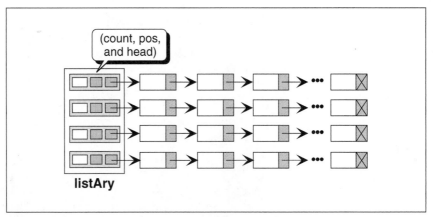

Figure 3-20   Structure for array of linked lists

Study the structure carefully. What we have is the linked list version of a two-dimensional array. Each linked list represents one row in the array. The nodes in the linked list represent the columns. This interesting and flexible structure can be used to solve many different problems.

The program to build the array of linked lists is shown in Algorithm 3-19.

```
algorithm arrayOfLists
Create an array of linked lists. Each list is read from
a file. After the lists have been created, they are
printed to verify that they were built properly.
  1  print (Begin array of linked lists)
  2  print (How many list do you want?)
  3  read   (numLists)
  4  buildArys (listArray, numLists)
  5  printArys (listArray, numLists)
  6  print (End of array of linked lists)
end arrayOfLists
```

Algorithm 3-19   Array of linked lists

Algorithm 3-19 Analysis   The main line is very simple. The first call creates the linked lists, the second one prints them. The logic to build the list is more interesting. It is shown in Algorithm 3-20.

```
algorithm buildArrays (ref listArray  <metadata>,
                       val numLists   <integer>)
Read files and insert contents into linked lists pointed to by
an array of head pointers.
   Pre   listArray and the number of elements in the array
   Post  Array of linked lists built
1 row = 0
2 loop (row < numLists)
   1   print (Enter file name)
   2   read  (fileName)
   3   open  (fileName)
   4   build (listArray[row], fileName)
   5   close (fileName)
   6   row = row + 1
3 end loop
4 return
end buildArrays
```

Algorithm 3-20   Build array of linked lists

Algorithm 3-20 Analysis

Statement 2.3 must be expanded in the implementation to open different files for each list. Other than that change, you should have no problems implementing the algorithm. Aside from the fact that each head node pointer is an element in an array, the code is identical to the linked list creation algorithms we have studied previously.

To prove that the array of linked lists was built successfully, we print it using Algorithm 3-21.

```
algorithm printArys (val listArray <metadata>,
                     val numLists  <integer>)
   This algorithm prints the contents of lists in listArray.
   Pre   lists in listArray has been filled
         numLists is the number of list pointers in array
   Post  The lists have been printed, one after the other
1 row = 0
2 loop (row < numLists)
   1   printList (listArray [row])
   2   row = row + 1
3 end loop
4 return
end printAry
```

Algorithm 3-21   Print array of linked lists

3-6   COMPLEX LINKED LIST STRUCTURES

In this section we introduce three useful linked list variations—the circularly linked list, the doubly linked list, and the multilinked list.

Circularly Linked Lists

In the **circularly linked list,** the last node's link points to the first node of the list, as shown in Figure 3-21. Cicrularly linked lists are primarily used in structures that allow access to nodes in the middle of the list without starting at the beginning. We will see one of these structures when we discuss the multilinked list.

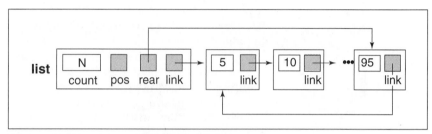

Figure 3-21   A circularly linked list

Insertion and deletion into a circularly linked list follow the same logic patterns used in a singly linked list except that the last node points to the first node. Therefore, when inserting or deleting the last node, in addition to updating the rear pointer in the header, we must also point the link field to the first node.

Given that we can directly access a node in the middle of the list through its data structure, we are then faced with a problem when searching the list. If the search target lies before the current node, how do we find it? In a singly linked list, when we arrive at the end of the list the search is complete. In a circular list, however, we automatically continue the search from the beginning of the list.

The ability to continue the search presents another problem. What if the target does not exist? In the singly linked list, if we didn't find the data we were looking for, we stopped when we hit the end of the list or when the target was less than the current node's data. With a circular list, we save the starting node's address and stop when we have circled around to it, as shown in the code below.

```
loop (target not equal to pLoc->data.key
   AND pLoc->link not equal to startAddress)
```

Doubly Linked Lists

One of the most powerful variations of linked lists is the doubly linked list. A **doubly linked list** is a linked list structure in which each node has a pointer to both its successor and its predecessor. Figure 3-22 is a representation of a doubly linked list.

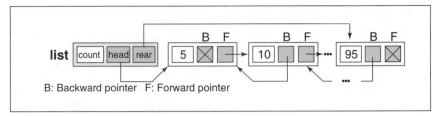

Figure 3-22   A doubly linked list

There are three pieces of metadata in the head structure: a count, a position pointer for traversals, and a rear pointer. Although a **rear pointer** is not required in all doubly linked lists, it makes some of the list algorithms, such as insert and search, more efficient.

Each node contains two pointers, a **backward pointer** to its predecessor and a **forward pointer** to its successor. In Figure 3-22 these pointers are designated B and F, respectively.

Another variation on the doubly linked list is the doubly linked circularly linked list. In this variation, the last forward pointer points to the first node of the list and the backward pointer of the first node points to the last node. If there is only one node in the list, both the forward and backward pointers point to the node itself.

Doubly Linked List Insertion

Inserting a node into a doubly linked list follows the basic pattern of inserting a node into a singly linked list, but we also need to connect both the forward and backward pointers.

A null doubly linked list's head and rear pointers are null. To insert a node into a null list, we simply set the head and rear pointers to point to the new node and set the forward and backward pointers of the new node to null. The results of inserting a node into a null list are shown in Figure 3-23(a).

Figure 3-23(b) shows the case for inserting between two nodes. The new node needs to be set to point to both its predecessor and its successor, and they need to be set to point to the new node. Because the insert is in the middle of the list, the head structure is unchanged except for adding to the count.

Inserting at the end of the list requires that the new node's back pointer be set to point to its predecessor. Because there is no successor, the forward pointer is set to null. The rear pointer in the head structure must also be set to point to the new rear node.

Algorithm 3-22 contains the code to insert a node into a doubly linked list.

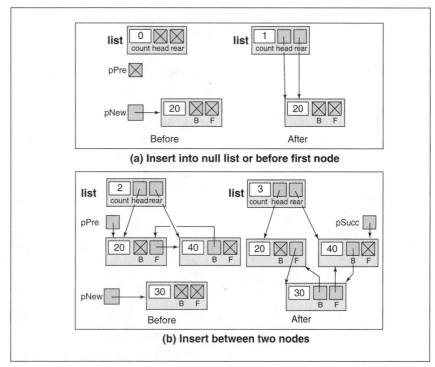

Figure 3-23   Doubly linked list insert

```
algorithm insertDbl (ref list    <metadata>,
                     val dataIn  <dataType>)
This algorithm inserts data into a doubly linked list.
   Pre    list is metadata structure to a valid list
          dataIn contains the data to be inserted
   Post   The data have been inserted in sequence
   Return <integer> 0: failed--dynamic memory overflow
                    1: successful
                    2: failed--duplicate key presented
1 if (full list)
   1   return 0
2 end if
Locate insertion point in list
3 found = searchList (list, pPre, pSucc, dataIn.key)
4 if (not found)
   1   allocate (pNew)
```

Algorithm 3-22   Doubly linked list insert

```
    2  pNew->data = dataIn
    3  if (pPre is null)
       Inserting before first node or into empty list
       1   pNew->back  = null
       2   pNew->fore  = list.head
       3   list.head   = pNew
    4  else
       Inserting into middle or end of list
       1   pNew->fore  = pPre->fore
       2   pNew->back  = pPre
    5  end if
       Test for insert into null list or at end of list
    6  if (pPre->fore null)
       Inserting at end of list--set rear pointer
       1   list.rear = pNew
    7  else
       Inserting in middle of list--point successor to new
       1   pSucc->back = pNew
    8  end if
    9  pPre->fore = pNew
   10  list.count = list.count + 1
   11  return (1)
  5  end if
     Duplicate data. Key already exists.
  6  return (2)
end insertDbl
```

Algorithm 3-22   Doubly linked list insert *(continued)*

Algorithm 3-22 Analysis   We must look at several points in this algorithm. First, rather than returning a simple success or failure, we have three different conditions and thus return three different values. If dynamic memory is full, we return a 0, indicating memory overflow (see Statement 1.1). If we are successful, then we return a 1 (see Statement 4.11). Finally, if the insert matches data already in the list, we return a 2 (see Statement 6).

The search algorithm provides the location of the target's logical predecessor and either (1) the location of the node with a key that matches the target, (2) the location of the first node with a key greater than the target, or (3) null if the target is greater than the last node. We named the last parameter in the search pSucc because that was what we expected. It could be confusing to the reader to use a pointer name that indicated we were looking for something other than the location of the successor.

Encapsulated Header Structures

Before the advent of abstract data types and classes, metadata were often embedded in the first node of a linked list. This concept, known as a header structure, is seen below.

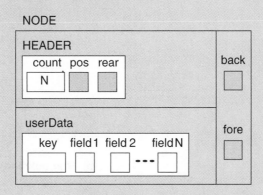

```
struct NODE;
struct HEADER
  {
  int      count;
  NODE     *pos;
  NODE     *rear;
  } ; // HEADER
union UN
  {
  DATA     userData;
  HEADER header;
  } ; // UN
struct NODE
  {
  NODE     *back;
  NODE     *fore;
  UN       un;
  } ; // NODE
```

Historically, there were two primary reasons for using the embedded header structure: First, it encapsulated the structure in the linked list. It thus created a self-contained structure in which one pointer referenced not only the linked list but also all of the metadata.

The second advantage of the header structure was that it slightly simplified insertions and deletions from the list. A null header list contains the header node, which is always the first node of the list. Therefore, all insertions take place either in the middle of the list or at the end of the list.

The primary disadvantage of the header structure is the complexity created by the union.

With abstract data types in general, and the class specifically, the concept of encapsulating the data in the linked list itself is no longer necessary. Rather, we now simply declare the metadata as member data in the class.

Finally, notice the comments. Although it is a short algorithm, the different conditions that can occur may be confusing. The comments should clarify the logic for the reader.

Doubly Linked List Deletion

Deleting from a doubly linked list requires that the deleted node's predecessor, if any, be pointed to the deleted node's successor and that the successor, if any, be set to point to the predecessor. This rather straight forward logic is shown in Figure 3-24. Once we locate the node

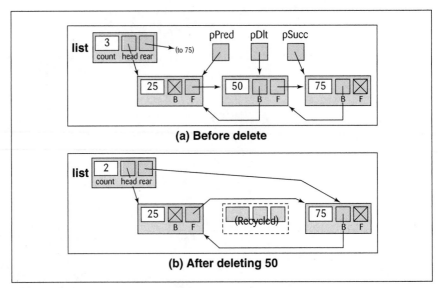

(a) Before delete

(b) After deleting 50

Figure 3-24   Doubly linked list delete

to be deleted, we simply change its predecessor's and successor's pointers and recycle the node.

The pseudocode is shown in Algorithm 3-23.

```
algorithm deleteDbl (ref list  <metadata>,
                     val pDlt  <node pointer>)
This algorithm deletes a node from a doubly linked list.
    Pre    list is metadata structure to a valid list
           pDlt is a pointer to the node to be deleted
    Post   node deleted
1 if (pDlt null)
    1   abort (Impossible condition in delete double)
2 end if
3 list.count  = list.count - 1
4 if (pDlt->back not null)
      Point predecessor to successor
    1   pPred       = pDlt->back
    2   pPred->fore = pDlt->fore
5 else
      Update head pointer
    1   list.head = pDlt->fore
6 end if
```

Algorithm 3-23   Doubly linked list delete

```
 7 if (pDlt->fore not null)
      Point successor to predecessor
   1   pSucc        = pDlt->fore
   2   pSucc->back = pDlt->back
 8 else
      Point rear to predecessor
   1   list.rear = pDlt->back
 9 end if
10 recycle (pDlt)
11 return
end deleteDbl
```

Algorithm 3-23   Doubly linked list delete *(continued)*

Algorithm 3-23 Analysis

Three points in this algorithm require further comment. First, the search was done in the calling algorithm. When we enter the doubly linked list delete algorithm, we already know the location of the node to be deleted.

Second, because it should never be called with a null delete pointer, we abort the program if we detect one. This is a logic error. Whenever a logic error is detected in a program, the program should be aborted and fixed.

The last point concerns style. Note that we created local variables to hold the predecessor pointer (Statement 4.1) and the successor pointer (Statement 7.1). We could have used the delete pointer (pDlt) but it is more difficult to read code when multiple pointers are chained together. To demonstrate the difference, compare the code in the algorithm with the alternative code shown below. Using descriptive pointers makes the logic easier to follow.

```
4.2 pDlt->back->fore = pDlt->fore
```

Multilinked Lists

A **multilinked list** is a list with two or more logical key sequences. For example, consider the list of the first ten presidents of the United States shown in Table 3-2.

The data in Table 3-2 are listed chronologically by the date the president first assumed office (year). Two additional sequences could be of interest. The data could be ordered by the president's name or by his first wife's name. Better yet, why not be able to traverse the list in any of these sequences? This is the power of the multilinked list: The same set of data can be processed in multiple sequences. It is important to understand that in a multilinked list, the data are not replicated. The data exist only once, but multiple paths connect the one set of data.

President	Year	First Wife
Washington, George	1789	Custis, Martha Dandridge
Adams, John	1797	Smith, Abigail
Jefferson, Thomas	1801	Skelton, Martha Wayles
Madison, James	1809	Todd, Dorothy Payne
Monroe, James	1817	Kortright, Elizabeth
Adams, John Quincy	1825	Johnson, Louisa Catherine
Jackson, Andrew	1829	Robards, Rachel Donelson
Van Buren, Martin	1837	Hoes, Hannah
Harrison, William H	1841	Symmes, Anna
Tyler, John	1841	Christian, Letitia

Table 3-2 First ten presidents of the United States

To process the data in multiple sequences, we create a separate set of links for each sequence. Each link structure can be singly linked, doubly linked, or circularly linked. To demonstrate the concept, let's create a singly linked multilinked list of the presidents and their wives. Figure 3-25 diagrams the data for the first three presidents.

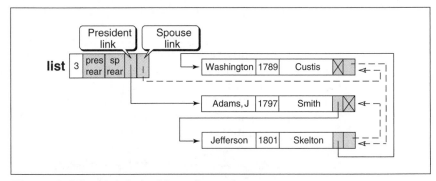

Figure 3-25 Multilinked list of presidents

Because there are two logical lists in the one physical list, we need two different link fields. Each node therefore contains two link fields, one for the president and one for the spouse. The president links are represented by solid lines. The spouse links are represented by dashed lines. If we follow the president links, we traverse the list through Adams, Jefferson, and Washington. If we follow the spouse links, we traverse the list through Custis (Mrs. Washington), Skelton (Mrs. Jefferson), and Smith (Mrs. Adams). Of course, in a real application, there would be many more data fields. We use just three to represent the structure.

With minor adjustments, the basic algorithms needed to maintain a multilinked list are the same as the algorithms for the singly linked or doubly linked lists.

Multilinked List Insert

Let's look first at the design to build a multilinked list. Using the president list as defined on page 120, we see that there are two logical lists. Therefore, when we add a node to the list, we need to insert it in each of the lists. We need to be careful, however, to make sure that we store the data only once. The design for the add node algorithm is shown in Figure 3-26.

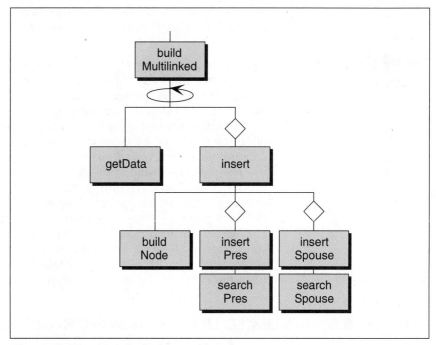

Figure 3-26   Multilinked list add node

This design assumes that the list will be built from a file. The build-multilinked module loops, reading the data for one president and inserting a node into the list. It then loops again, reading the data for the next president, and so on until the entire file has been read and the list built.

Each insert begins by allocating space for the data in `buildNode` and then building the president links in the insert president module and the spouse links in the insert spouse module. Because they are different logical lists with different keys, we use separate algorithms for each insertion and search.

There are three conditional calls in this design. We call insert as long as we successfully read data. If there is an error or when we get to the end of the file, we don't call it. Similarly, we call the inserts as long as the memory allocation in the build node module is successful. If it fails, then we cannot insert the data.

If you compare the insert logic for the singly linked and doubly linked lists with the logic for the multilinked list, you will see one major difference. In the multilinked list insert, the memory allocation is separate from the searching and pointer connections because the memory is allocated only once. Another minor variation is the count increment, which should also be coded in the build node module. We add to the count only once because we are inserting only one physical node, even though we inserted it into two logical lists.

Multilinked List Delete

The major algorithm variation for the multilinked list delete is that we need to reconnect the pointers for each logical list. Thus, if we delete a president's record, we need to adjust the spouse's successor pointer as well as the president's successor pointer.

Assuming that we follow the president's pointers to delete a president, the delete logic follows the same pattern that the other linked list deletions use. But how do we delete the spouse? One alternative is to use the spouse's name from the president search and then search the spouse list to find the pointers that need to be updated. When the lists are long, doing so can be very inefficient.

The standard solution uses a doubly linked list for the spouse links. Having arrived in the middle of the spouse list through our search of the president list, we can then easily set the spouse predecessor's pointers by following the backward pointer to the predecessor. This application is one of the more common uses of doubly linked lists.

3-7　BUILDING A LINKED LIST—C++ IMPLEMENTATION

To demonstrate how we can easily implement a linked list once we have an abstract data type (see next section), we implement a list of award-winning pictures and their directors as a linked list. The program has three major functions: print instructions, build the list, and process user inquiries. In addition, the process function calls three functions: get the user's choice, print the entire list, and search for a requested year. One other function is required. The complete design is shown in Figure 3-27.

Data Structure

The application data structure contains three fields: the year the movie was made, the name of the movie, and the name of the director. It is shown in Program 3-1.

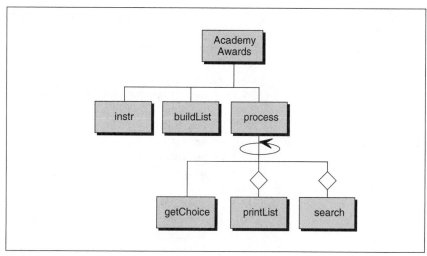

Figure 3-27   Build linked list design

```
1   const short STR_MAX = 41;
2
3   struct PICTURE
4      {
5       short    key;                           // year
6       char     picture [STR_MAX];
7       char     director[STR_MAX];
8      }; // PICTURE
```

Program 3-1   Build linked list data structure

Application Functions

In this section we describe the functions and their interface with the abstract data type.

Main

Main defines the list variable and then calls the three functions that do the job. It has no interface with the abstract data type. Its code is shown in Program 3-2.

```
1   // Prototype Declarations
2      void  instr       (void);
3      void  search      (List <PICTURE, short>& list);
4      void  printList   (List <PICTURE, short>& list);
5      void  process     (List <PICTURE, short>& list);
6      char  getChoice   (void);
```

Program 3-2   Main line for linked list

```
 7      void  buildList  (List <PICTURE, short>& list);
 8
 9  int main (void)
10  {
11    // Local Definitions
12      List<PICTURE, short> list;
13
14    // Statements
15      instr ();
16      buildList (list);
17      process   (list);
18
19      cout << "End Best Pictures\n"
20           << "Hope you found your favorite!\n";
21      return 0;
22  } // main
```

Program 3-2   Main line for linked list *(continued)*

Instructions

Instructions is a simple function that explains how the program works. Its code is shown in Program 3-3.

```
 1  /* ==================== instr ====================
 2      Print instructions to user.
 3         Pre     nothing
 4         Post    instructions printed
 5  */
 6  void instr (void)
 7  {
 8    // Statements
 9      cout << "This program will print the Academy Awards \n"
10           << "Best Picture of the Year and its director. \n"
11           << "Your job is to enter the year;  we will do \n"
12           << "the rest. Enjoy.\n\n";
13      return;
14  } // instr
```

Program 3-3   Print instructions for user

Build List

Build list is one of the two major processing modules in the program. The data for the linked list are contained in a text file. This module reads the text file and inserts the data into the list. Program 3-4 contains the code for build list.

```
 1   /* ===================== buildList =====================
 2      Reads a text data file and loads the linked list.
 3          Pre     file exists in format: yy;pic;dir\n
 4          Post    list contains data
 5                  -or- program aborted if problems
 6   */
 7   void buildList (List <PICTURE, short>& list)
 8   {
 9   // Local Definitions
10      ifstream fsData;
11      int      addResult;
12      PICTURE  pic;
13
14   // Statements
15      fsData.open("pictures.dat");
16      if (!fsData)
17         {
18          cerr << "\aError opening input file\n";
19          exit (110);
20         } // if
21
22      while (fsData >> pic.key)
23         {
24          fsData.getline (pic.picture,
25                          sizeof(pic.picture), ';');
26          fsData.getline (pic.director, sizeof(pic.director));
27
28          // Insert into list
29          addResult = list.addNode (pic);
30          if (addResult != 0)
31             if (addResult == -1)
32                {
33                 cout << "Memory overflow adding movie\a\n";
34                 exit (120);
35                } // Add overflow
36             else
37                cout << "Duplicate year: "
38                     << pic.key
39                     << " not added\n\a";
40         } // while
41      cout << endl;
42      return;
43   } //  buildList
```

Program 3-4   Build linked list

Program 3-4 Analysis

Program 3-4 contains the first module that interfaces with the abstract data type. It has some interesting design aspects.

Because the picture and director data both contain embedded spaces, we format the file with the year as a short integer and the picture title and director as delimited strings. The delimiter for the picture title is a semicolon; the delimiter for the director is a newline. This formatting allows us to use the C++ *getline* function.

The loop is controlled by reading a key from the file. If there is no key, then we are at the end of the file. If there is a key, we continue by reading the picture and director in turn. To read the picture, we use *getline* with a semicolon delimiter. To read the director, we use the default delimiter, newline.

After reading the data into the picture variable structure, we insert it into the list (see Statement 29). There are three possible results from add node. If the add is successful, add node returns zero. After calling add node, therefore, we check the results. If the return value is not 0, we check for memory overflow, in which case we abort the program; if there is a duplicate add, we just print an error message and continue.

Process User Requests

After the list has been built, we are ready to process the user requests. The user has three options, as shown in a menu displayed by get choice: print the entire list, search for a particular year, or quit the program. The code for process list is shown in Program 3-5.

```
1  /* ==================== process ====================
2      Process user choices.
3          Pre     list has been created
4          Post    all of user's choices executed
5  */
6  void process (List<PICTURE, short>& list)
7  {
8  // Local Definitions
9     char choice;
10
11 // Statements
12    do
13       {
14         choice = getChoice ();
15
16         switch (choice)
17            {
18              case 'P': printList (list);
19                        break;
20              case 'S': search (list);
21              case 'Q': break;
22            } // switch
23       } while (choice != 'Q');
24    return;
25 } // process
```

Program 3-5   Process user requests

Program 3-5 Analysis

There are no calls to the abstract data type in this function. The function simply calls a function to get the user's choice and then calls print list or search as appropriate.

Get User Choice

Get user choice is a simple function similar to many you have written. It reads the user's choice and ensures that it is valid. If the choice is not valid, the function loops until the user enters a correct choice. The code is shown in Program 3-6.

```
 1   /* ==================== getChoice ====================
 2      Prints the menu of choices.
 3           Pre     nothing
 4           Post    menu printed and choice returned
 5   */
 6   char getChoice (void)
 7   {
 8   // Local Definitions
 9      char choice;
10      bool valid;
11
12   // Statements
13      cout << "======= MENU ======= \n"
14           << "Here are your choices:\n"
15           << "  S: Search for a year\n"
16           << "  P: Print all years   \n"
17           << "  Q: Quit              \n\n"
18           << "Enter your choice: ";
19      do
20        {
21         cin >> choice;
22         choice = toupper(choice);
23         switch (choice)
24            {
25             case 'S':
26             case 'P':
27             case 'Q': valid = true;
28                       break;
29             default:  valid = false;
30                       cout << "\aInvalid choice\n"
31                            << "Please try again: ";
32                       break;
33            } // switch
34        } while (!valid);
35      return choice;
36   } // getChoice
```

Program 3-6 Get user's choice

Print List

Print list traverses the list, printing one movie with each call to the abstract data type traverse function. We begin by checking to make sure that there are data in the list and printing an appropriate message if the list is empty. Once we have verified that the list contains data, we call get next to read the first movie. We then use a *do . . . while* loop to process the rest of the data. The code is shown in Program 3-7.

```
 1  /*==================== printList ====================
 2      Prints the entire list.
 3          Pre     list has been created
 4          Post    list printed
 5  */
 6  void printList (List <PICTURE, short>& list)
 7  {
 8  // Local Definitions
 9      PICTURE pic;
10
11  // Statements
12
13      //Get first node
14      if (list.listCount () == 0)
15          cout <<"Sorry, nothing in the list\n\a";
16      else
17          {
18          cout << "\nBest Pictures List\n";
19          list.getNext (0, pic);
20          do
21              {
22              cout.setf (ios::left);
23              cout << pic.key << "   "
24                      << setw (sizeof(pic.picture))
25                      << pic.picture  << " "
26                      << setw (sizeof(pic.director))
27                      << pic.director << endl;
28              cout.unsetf (ios::left);
29              } while (list.getNext (1, pic));
30          cout << "End of Best Pictures List\n\n";
31          } // else
32      return;
33  } // printList
```

Program 3-7 Print list

Program 3-7 Analysis

The interesting logic in this function relates to the traversing of the linked list. The traverse function (`getNext`) in the abstract data type needs a "where from" flag to tell it to either start at the beginning of the list or to continue from its last location. Therefore, in Statement 19 we tell traverse that we want the first movie's data returned. Once we have a movie, we obtain the rest of the list using Statement 29. Because `getNext` returns a success flag, we can use it in the *do . . . while* expression. When all of the movies have been displayed, we display an end-of-list message and terminate.

Search List

The last function in our application allows the user to search for and display a movie for any year. The code is shown in Program 3-8.

```
1   /* ===================== search =====================
2      Searches for year and prints year, picture, and
3      director.
4      Pre     list has been created
5              user has selected search option
6      Post    year printed or error message
7   */
8   void search (List<PICTURE, short>& list)
9   {
10  // Local Definitions
11     short    year;
12     bool     found;
13
14     PICTURE pic;
15
16  // Statements
17
18     cout << "Enter a four digit year: ";
19     cin  >> year;
20
21     found = list.retrieveNode (year, pic);
22
23     if (found)
24        cout << pic.key       << " \""
25             << pic.picture  << "\"  Directed by: "
26             << pic.director << endl;
27     else
28        cout << "Sorry, but " << year
29             << " is not available.\n";
30     return;
31  } // search
```

Program 3-8   Search linked list

3-8   LIST ABSTRACT DATA TYPE—LINKED LIST IMPLEMENTATION

In this section we use the linked list implementation to create a list **abstract data type** (ADT). Recall that an ADT consists of a data type and the operations that manipulate the data. From the application program's perspective, it is also independent of the data structure used to implement it. Thus we could change the implementation from a linked list to an array and the application program would not need to be changed.

In C++, we implement the list ADT using class templates, which allows the application programmer to declare the data while allowing the class to control it. The class also encapsulates all of the list functions while hiding the linked list structure from the applications that use it.

Figure 3-28 shows the ADT structure. The linked list is implemented as a class (`List`) with its metadata encapsulated within the class. Although it is not apparent from the figure, the metadata are declared as private data.

We know the structure of metadata because we have analyzed the linked list operation. What we don't know, however, is what type of application data will be stored in the list. If our linked list class is to be able to store any type of data, we must have some way of letting the application programmer define them when the program is written. Fortunately, C++ provides this capability through class templates. A **class template** is a generic class declaration that allows the application programmer to provide the data structure through parameters that the compiler resolves. (For a short discussion of templates, see Appendix K.)

The structure template in Figure 3-28 declares two items, `data` and `link`. The link field is declared within the node structure to be a self-referential pointer to the next node. The data will be mapped to a programmer-declared type when the program is compiled.

Lists and many other data structures require that we be able to sequence the data. In the singly linked list, for example, the data in the

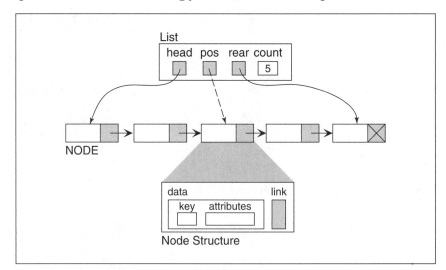

Figure 3-28   Linked list with template

list are generally stored in key sequence. Therefore—and this is a critical point that makes everything possible—the key type is identified within the user's declaration and can thus be used within the class to search through the data. Furthermore, the name of the key needs to be coordinated and agreed on by the class developer and the programmers who use the class. In our class, we named it key. As you study the example, note that the applications that use the class must use the same identifier—that is, key—in their data structures.

Finally, as long as the key's type is one of the standard C++ types, nothing else is needed. C++ knows how to compare all of the standard types automatically. However, if the key's type is not standard—for example, if it is a string or a structure—then the programmer must create a key structure that overloads the relational operators so that they can be compared.

With this understanding, we are now ready to create the structure template shown in Program 3-9.

```
1   // Node Declaration
2     template <class   TYPE>
3     struct NODE
4       {
5       TYPE      data;
6       NODE    *link;
7       }; //   End of Node Declaration
8
```

Program 3-9   Node template declaration

Program 3-9 Analysis

Before we continue, let's make sure we understand what this structure template does. First, it contains a structure named NODE that consists of two variables, data and link. The link is a self-referential pointer to NODE. The data type is symbolically specified as TYPE, and the actual type must be specified when the structure is defined in the program. In other words, the exact definition of TYPE is deferred until the template is used in a program.

List ADT Declaration

We now examine the declaration of the class template. Like the structure template, the class template begins with a template specification that describes the required type parameters that are needed to create it. In our linked list, two types must be specified, the data type (TYPE) and the key type (KTYPE). These are shown in the template at the beginning of the class declaration in Program 3-10. The template specification is immediately followed by the class declaration, which contains the class data members and list metadata and the member function declarations.

```
 1    // List Class Declaration
 2
 3    template <class  TYPE, class KTYPE>
 4    class List
 5      {
 6        private:
 7          NODE<TYPE> *head;
 8          NODE<TYPE> *pos;
 9          NODE<TYPE> *rear;
10          int        count;
11
12  //      Function Declarations
13          bool   _insert  (NODE<TYPE>   *pPre,
14                            TYPE          dataIn);
15          void   _delete  (NODE<TYPE>   *pPre,
16                            NODE<TYPE>   *pLoc,
17                            TYPE         *dataOutPtr);
18          bool   _search  (NODE<TYPE>  **pPre,
19                            NODE<TYPE>  **pLoc,
20                            KTYPE         key);
21
22        public:
23          List (void);
24          ~List (void);
25          int        addNode    (TYPE    dataIn);
26          bool       removeNode  (KTYPE   key,
27                                  TYPE    *dataOutPtr);
28          bool       retrieveNode (KTYPE   Argu,
29                                   TYPE&   dataOut);
30          bool       getNext    (int     fromWhere,
31                                  TYPE&   dataOut);
32          int        listCount  (void);
33          bool       emptyList  (void);
34          bool       fullList   (void);
35      }; // class List
```

Program 3-10   List ADT class declaration

The prototype declarations in Program 3-10 include all of the basic algorithms described in Section 3-3, "Linked List Algorithms," starting on page 84. Two of these algorithms, createList and destroyList, become the constructor and destructor, respectively. In addition, the insert, delete, and search functions require a high-level user interface, which is public, and a private function that completes the processing.

Each of these functions is discussed in turn in the following sections. Note that each function is written as a function template to allow the use of compilation-time types. Therefore, the template specification appears in the code at the beginning of each function.

List Constructor

The create list function is implemented as the class constructor. It instantiates the list in a null list state by setting all of the pointers to null and the count field to 0. The code is shown in Program 3-11.

```
1  /* =============== List Constructor  ===============
2     Initialize the list.
3        Pre     Class is being instantiated
4        Post    Class instantiated and initialized
5  */
6  template <class TYPE, class KTYPE>
7  List<TYPE, KTYPE> :: List (void)
8  {
9  // Statements
10     head     = NULL;
11     pos      = NULL;
12     rear     = NULL;
13     count    = 0;
14  } //  List Constructor
```

Program 3-11   Create linked list

Program 3-11 Analysis

The code in this function is very simple, but the template construction merits some discussion. Recall that the application program must provide both the data type and key type when it defines a class. The preprocessor then uses these types to declare a unique class with the program. The type of the class is symbolically declared as List<TYPE, KTYPE>, as seen in Statement 7.

Add Node

Add node is actually a higher-level function that receives the data to be inserted into the list and searches the list. Its logic follows the basic design shown in Algorithm 3-13, "Add note to linked list," on page 104, with the obvious changes required because of the ADT class.

In this program, we have chosen to prevent duplicate keys from being inserted into the list. Doing so leads to three possible return values: –1 indicates dynamic memory overflow, 0 indicates success, and +1 indicates a duplicate key. The using programmer is responsibile for correctly interpreting these return values. If an application required that duplicate keys could be inserted into the list, the programmer would need to rewrite insertion and several of the other algorithms to handle duplicate data. The code is shown in Program 3-12.

```
 1  /* ===================== addNode ====================
 2     Inserts data into linked list.
 3        Pre      dataIn contains data to be inserted
 4        Post     Data inserted or error
 5        Return -1 if overflow,
 6                    0 if successful,
 7                    1 if duplicate key
 8  */
 9  template <class TYPE, class KTYPE>
10  int List<TYPE, KTYPE> :: addNode (TYPE dataIn)
11  {
12  // Local Definitions
13     bool   found;
14     bool   success;
15
16     NODE<TYPE>  *pPre;
17     NODE<TYPE>  *pLoc;
18
19  //  Statements
20     found = _search (&pPre, &pLoc, dataIn.key);
21     if (found)
22        // Duplicate keys not allowed
23        return (+1);
24
25     success = _insert (pPre,  dataIn);
26     if (!success)
27        // Overflow
28        return (-1);
29     return (0);
30  } //  addNode
```

Program 3-12   Add node

Program 3-12 Analysis

Add node begins by searching the structure to find the insertion position, as identified by the predecessor (pPre) and current location (pLoc) pointers returned by the search. If the key of the new data matches a node in the list, the insert is rejected and +1 is returned. Assuming that the new data contain a unique key, the node is inserted by calling the private insertion function.

Insert Node

Insert node is a private function responsible for physically placing the new data into the linked list. Its code is shown in Program 3-13.

```
 1    /* ===================== _insert =====================
 2       Inserts data into a new node in the linked list.
 3          Pre      Insertion location identified by pPre
 4                   dataIn contains data to be inserted
 5          Post     data inserted in linked list or overflow
 6          Return   true  if successful, false if overflow
 7    */
 8    template <class TYPE, class KTYPE>
 9    bool List<TYPE, KTYPE> :: _insert (NODE<TYPE> *pPre,
10                                       TYPE        dataIn)
11    {
12    // Local Definitions
13       NODE <TYPE>  *pNew;
14
15    // Statements
16       if (! (pNew = new NODE<TYPE>))
17          return false;
18
19       pNew->data = dataIn;
20       pNew->link = NULL;
21
22       if (pPre == NULL)
23          {
24           //  Adding before first node or to empty list.
25           pNew->link = head;
26           head = pNew;
27          } // if pPre
28       else
29          {
30           // Adding in middle or at end
31           pNew->link  = pPre->link;
32           pPre->link  = pNew;
33          } // if else
34
35           // Now check for add at end of list
36           if (pNew->link == NULL)
37              // Adding to empty list. Set rear
38              rear = pNew;
39
40       count++;
41
42       return true;
43    } // _insert
```

Program 3-13   Insert node

Program 3-13 Analysis   This code closely follows the logic shown in Algorithm 3-2, "Insert linked list node," on page 89 with the addition of logic to maintain the rear pointer. The additional code is shown in Statements 35–38.

Remove Node

Remove node is also a high-level function that calls search list and delete node to complete the deletion. There are two possible completion states in remove node: either we were successful (true) or we were unsuccessful (false) because the data to be deleted could not be found. The code is shown in Program 3-14.

```
 1  /* ================= removeNode =================
 2     Removes data from linked list.
 3          Pre     dltkey is identifier of node to be deleted
 4                  pDataOut is pointer to data variable to
 5                  receive a copy of the deleted data
 6          Post    data copied to output variable and node
 7                  deleted or not found
 8          Return false if not found
 9                  true  if deleted
10  */
11  template <class TYPE, class KTYPE>
12  bool List<TYPE, KTYPE> ::
13          removeNode (KTYPE dltkey, TYPE *pDataOut)
14  {
15   // Local Definitions
16     bool          found;
17     NODE<TYPE>  *pPre;
18     NODE<TYPE>  *pLoc;
19
20   // Statements
21     found = _search (&pPre, &pLoc, dltkey);
22     if (found)
23         _delete (pPre, pLoc, pDataOut);
24     return found;
25  } // removeNode
```

Program 3-14   Remove node

Delete Node

The **delete node** function is called by remove node to physically delete the identified node from dynamic memory. As the data are deleted, they are copied to the calling function through the pointer (pDataOut) specified by the last parameter in the call. The code is shown in Program 3-15.

```
1   /* ================== _delete ==================
2      Deletes data from a linked list and returns
3      data to calling module.
4          Pre  pPre is a pointer to predecessor node
5               pLoc is a pointer to target node
6               pDataOut is pointer to output data area
7         Post Data have been deleted and returned
8              Data memory has been recycled
9   */
10  template <class TYPE, class KTYPE>
11  void List<TYPE, KTYPE> :: _delete (NODE<TYPE>    *pPre,
12                                     NODE<TYPE>    *pLoc,
13                                     TYPE          *pDataOut)
14  {
15  // Statements
16     *pDataOut = pLoc->data;
17     if (pPre == NULL)
18         // Deleting first node
19         head = pLoc->link;
20     else
21         // Deleting any other node
22         pPre->link = pLoc->link;
23
24     // Test for deleting last node
25     if (pLoc->link == NULL)
26         rear = pPre;
27
28     count--;
29     delete pLoc;
30
31     return;
32  } // _delete
```

Program 3-15   Delete node

Program 3-15 Analysis

Once again, the only difference between this function and its design algorithm (Algorithm 3-3, "Linked list delete node," on page 92) is the requirement to maintain the rear pointer. It is updated only if the last node in the list is being deleted. The code is shown in Statements 24–26.

Retrieve Node

Retrieve node locates a given node in the list and sends back its data to the calling function. Because retrieve node is an application interface, it needs only two parameters: the search argument (key) and the variable to receive the data (dataOut). To accomplish its function, it simply calls the internal class search function and returns the found Boolean from the search function. The code is shown in Program 3-16.

```
 1    /* =================== retrieveNode ===================
 2       Interface to search function.
 3            Pre      key is the search argument
 4                     dataOut is variable to receive data
 5            Post     dataOut contains located data if found
 6                     if not found, contents are unchanged
 7            Return true if successful, false if not found
 8    */
 9
10    template <class TYPE, class KTYPE>
11    bool List<TYPE, KTYPE>
12             :: retrieveNode (KTYPE  key, TYPE&  dataOut)
13    {
14    // Local Definitions
15       bool            found;
16       NODE <TYPE>    *pPre;
17       NODE <TYPE>    *pLoc;
18
19    // Statements
20       found = _search (&pPre, &pLoc, key);
21       if (found)
22          dataOut = pLoc->data;
23       return found;
24    } // retrieveNode
```

Program 3-16   Search interface function

Internal Search Function

The actual search work is done with an internal function available only within the ADT class. See Program 3-17.

```
 1    /* ==================== _search ====================
 2       Searches list and passes back address of node
 3       containing target and its logical predecessor.
 4            Pre      pPre is pointer variable for predecessor
 5                     pLoc is pointer variable for found node
 6                     key  is search argument
 7            Post     pLoc points to first node equal/greater key
 8                     -or- null if target > key of last node
 9                     pPre points to largest node smaller than key
10                     -or- null if target < key of first node
11            Return true if successful, false if not found
12    */
13    template <class TYPE, class KTYPE>
14    bool List<TYPE, KTYPE> :: _search (NODE<TYPE> **pPre,
15                                       NODE<TYPE> **pLoc,
16                                       KTYPE          key)
```

Program 3-17   Search list

```
17    {
18    // Statements
19        *pPre  = NULL;
20        *pLoc  = head;
21        if (count == 0)
22            return false;
23
24        // Test for argument > last node in list
25        if (key > rear->data.key)
26            {
27             *pPre = rear;
28             *pLoc = NULL;
29             return false;
30            } // if
31
32        while (key > (*pLoc)->data.key)
33            {
34             //  Have not found search argument location
35             *pPre = *pLoc;
36             *pLoc = (*pLoc)->link;
37            } // while
38
39        if (key == (*pLoc)->data.key)
40            //    argument found--success
41            return true;
42        else
43            return false;
44    } // _search
```

Program 3-17   Search list *(continued)*

Program 3-17 Analysis

The logic in this function is deceptively simple, although somewhat more complex than the design shown in Algorithm 3-4, "Search linked list," on page 95. We begin by testing for a null list and returning false if it is empty. If there are data in the list, we test the search argument (key) to see if it is greater than the last entry in the list. If it is, there is no need to search the list, so we return not found after setting the predecessor and location pointers. Because we now know that the search argument is less than or equal to the last entry, we can simplify the search loop itself by testing only for a search key greater than the list key (see Statement 32). You should recognize this logic as the ordered list search we studied in Chapter 2.

As long as the key type is one of the standard C++ types, the compare in Statement 32 is valid. However, if the key is a string or any other derived type, then it won't work unless the greater than operator has been overloaded for the key type. We leave the solution to this problem to the practice sets at the end of the chapter.

Empty List

Because the application programmer does not have access to the list structure, we provide three status functions that can be used to determine the list status. The first, **empty list**, is shown in Program 3-18.

```
 1  /* =============== emptyList ===============
 2     Returns Boolean indicating whether the
 3     list is empty.
 4        Pre    Nothing
 5        Return true if empty, false if list has data
 6  */
 7  template<class TYPE, class KTYPE>
 8  bool List<TYPE, KTYPE> :: emptyList (void)
 9  {
10  // Statements
11     return (count == 0);
12  } //   emptyList
```

Program 3-18   Empty list

Full List

The second status function, **full list,** determines whether there is enough room in dynamic memory for another node. It is available for applications that need to know before an insert if there is room available. The code is shown in Program 3-19.

```
 1  /* =================== fullList ===================
 2     Returns Boolean indicating whether the list is full
 3     or has room for more data.
 4        Pre    Nothing
 5        Return true if full, false if room for another node
 6  */
 7  template <class TYPE, class KTYPE>
 8  bool List<TYPE, KTYPE> :: fullList (void)
 9  {
10  // Local Definitions
11     NODE<TYPE>   *temp;
12
13  // Statements
14     if (temp = new NODE<TYPE>)
15        {
16         delete temp;
17         return false;
18        } // if
19
20     // Dynamic memory full
21     return true;
22  } // fullList
```

Program 3-19   Full list

Program 3-19 Analysis

This function is one of the more difficult to write. Because C++ does not provide a facility to determine free space in dynamic memory, we can only allocate a node; if it works we know there is room for at least one more node. However, because the allocation process may use the last available space, we must free the node before we return. Of course, if the allocation fails, then we know there is no more room in dynamic memory.

List Count

List count is the last of the status function. It returns an integer count for the number of nodes currently in the list. Its code is shown in Program 3-20.

```
1   /* ==================== listCount ====================
2       Returns integer representing number of nodes in list.
3           Pre     Nothing
4           Return  count for number of nodes in list
5   */
6   template <class TYPE, class KTYPE>
7   int List<TYPE, KTYPE> :: listCount(void)
8   {
9   // Statements
10      return count;
11  }  // listCount
```

Program 3-20   List count

Get Next Node

At one time or another, every list needs to be traversed. Because the programmer does not have access to the list structure, however, we need to provide a function to traverse the list. Because it is traversed one node at a time, we name the traversal function getNext. Depending on the fromWhere flag, each call returns either the data at the beginning of the list or the data in the next node. This algorithm is shown in Program 3-21.

```
1   /* ==================== getNext ====================
2       getNext traverses a linked list. Each call either starts
3       at the beginning of the list or returns the location of
4       the element in the list that was last returned.
5           Pre     fromWhere is 0 to start at the first element
6                   dataOut is reference to data variable
7           Post    if another element, address placed in output area
8           Return true if another element located,
9                   false if end of list
10  */
11  template <class TYPE, class KTYPE>
```

Program 3-21   Traverse list

```
12   bool List<TYPE, KTYPE> :: getNext (int    fromWhere,
13                                      TYPE&  dataOut)
14   {
15   // Local Definitions
16      bool success;
17
18   // Statements
19      if (fromWhere == 0)
20         {
21           // Start from first node
22           if (count == 0)
23               success = false;
24           else
25               {
26                pos      = head;
27                dataOut  = pos->data;
28                success  = true;
29               } // if else
30         } // if fromwhere is zero
31      else
32         {
33           // Continue from current position
34           if (pos->link == NULL)
35               success = false;
36           else
37               {
38                pos      = pos->link;
39                dataOut  = pos->data;
40                success  = true;
41               } // if else
42         } // if fromWhere else
43
44      return success;
45   } // getNext
```

Program 3-21   Traverse list *(continued)*

Program 3-21 Analysis   The traverse function needs to know if the traversal is just starting or if we are in the middle of the traversal. The stage is determined through the fromWhere flag, a technique similar to the position flag in the C++ seek function. Each time the function is called, it stores the address of the current node being returned in the position pointer in the head node. Then the next time, if we are not starting from the beginning of the list, we can use the position pointer to locate the next node. If a node is available, we return success (true); if we are at the end of the list, we return false.

Destroy List

The **destroy list** algorithm becomes the destructor in the ADT class. It is invoked any time an object is deleted. When invoked, the destructor deletes any nodes remaining in the list. The code is shown in Program 3-22.

```
1   /* =============== Destructor ===============
2      Deletes all data in list and recycles memory
3         Pre    List is being deleted
4         Post   Data and class structure have been deleted
5   */
6   template<class TYPE, class KTYPE>
7   List<TYPE, KTYPE > :: ~List (void)
8   {
9   // Local Definitions
10     NODE<TYPE>    *deletePtr;
11
12  // Statements
13     if (head)
14        {
15         while (count > 0)
16            {
17              deletePtr = head;
18              head      = head->link;
19              count--;
20              delete  deletePtr;
21            } // while
22        } //  if
23  }  // Destructor
```

Program 3-22   Destroy list

3-9   SUMMARY

- A linear list is a list in which each element has a unique successor.
- Linear lists can be divided into two categories: general and restricted.
  - In a general list, data can be inserted and deleted anywhere and there are no restrictions on the operations that can be used to process the list.
  - General lists can be further divided into random lists and ordered lists.
  - In a random list, there is no ordering of the data.
  - In an ordered list, the data are arranged according to a key, which is one or more fields used to identify the data or control their use.
  - In a restricted list, data can be added or deleted at the end of the structure and processing is restricted to the operations on the data at the ends of the list.
  - Two common restricted list structures are stacks, (last in–first out [LIFO] lists) and queues (first in–first out [FIFO] lists).

- Four common operations are associated with linear lists: insertion, deletion, retrieval, and traversal.
- A linked list is an ordered collection of data in which each element contains the location (address) of the next element; that is, each element contains two parts: data and link.
- A head node is a data structure that contains metadata about the list, such as a count, a head pointer to the first node, and a rear pointer to the last node. It may contain any other general list data required by the use of the structure.
- The node in a singly linked list contains only one link to a single successor unless it is the last, in which case it is not linked to any other node.
- When we want to insert into a linked list, we must consider four cases: adding to the empty list, adding at the beginning, adding to the middle, and adding at the end.
- When we want to delete a node from a list, we must consider two cases: delete the first node or delete any other node.
- To search a linked list for an item, we use the ordered list search.
- Traversing a linked list means going through the list, node by node, and processing each node. Three examples of list traversals are counting the number of nodes, printing the contents of nodes, and summing the values of one or more fields.
- A header node contains the same metadata found in the head structure and shares the pointer structure with the data node. It is physically positioned so that it is always the first node in the linked list.
- A circularly linked list is a list in which the last node's link points to the first node of the list.
- A doubly linked list is a linked list in which each node has a pointer to both its successor and its predecessor.
- A multilinked list is a linked list with two or more logical lists.

3-10   PRACTICE SETS

Exercises

1. Imagine we have the linked list shown in Figure 3-29.

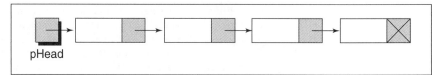

Figure 3-29   Linked list for Exercise 1

Show what happens if we use the following statement in a search of this linked list:

```
pHead = pHead->link
```

What is the problem with using this kind of statement? Does it justify the two walking pointers (pPre and pLoc) we introduced in the text?

2. Imagine we have the linked list shown in Figure 3-30. As discussed in "Search list," on page 93, search needs to be able to pass back both the location of the predecessor (pPre) and the location of the current (pLoc) node based on search criteria. A typical search design is shown in Figure 3-30.

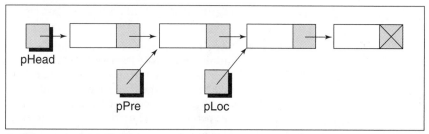

Figure 3-30 Linked list for Exercise 2

The following code to set pPre and pLoc contains a common error. What is it and how should it be corrected?

```
pLoc = pLoc->link
pPre = pPre->link
```

(Hint: What are the contents of these pointers at the beginning of the search?)

3. Imagine we have a dummy node at the beginning of a linked list. The dummy node does not carry any data. It is not the first data node, it is an empty node. Figure 3-31 shows a linked list with a dummy node.

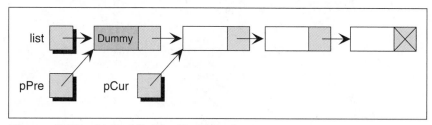

Figure 3-31 Linked list for Exercise 3

Write the code to delete the first node (the node after the dummy node) in the linked list.

4. Write the code to delete a node in the middle of a linked list with the dummy node (see Exercise 3). Compare your answer with the answer to Exercise 3. Are they the same? What do you conclude? Does the dummy node simplify the operation on a linked list? How?

5. Figure 3-32 shows an empty linked list with a dummy node. Write the code to add a node to this empty linked list.

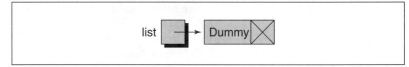

Figure 3-32   Linked list for Exercise 5

6. Write the statements to add a node in the middle of a linked list with the dummy node (see Exercise 3). Compare your answer with the answer to Exercise 5. Are they the same? What do you conclude? Does the dummy node simplify the operation on a linked list? How?

7. Imagine we have the two linked lists shown in Figure 3-33. What would happen if we applied the following statement to these two lists?

list1 = list2

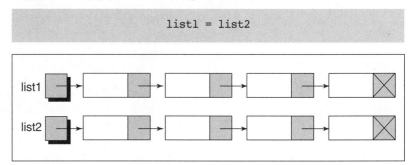

Figure 3-33   Linked lists for Exercise 7

8. What would happen if we applied the following statements to the two lists in Exercise 7?

```
1 temp = list1
2 loop (temp->link not null)
  1 temp = temp->link
3 end loop
4 temp->link = list2
```

9. Imagine we have the linked list shown in Figure 3-34.

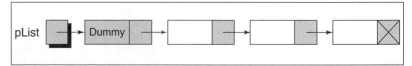

Figure 3-34   Linked list for Exercise 9

Show what would happen if we applied the following statements to this list.

```
1 temp = pList
2 loop (temp->link not null)
  1 temp = temp->link
3 end loop
4 temp->link = pList
```

Problems

10. Write an algorithm that reads a list of integers from the keyboard, creates a linked list out of them, and prints the result.

11. Write an algorithm that accepts a linked list, traverses it, and returns the data in the node with the minimum key value.

12. Write an algorithm that traverses a linked list and deletes all nodes whose keys are negative.

13. Write an algorithm that traverses a linked list and deletes the node following a node with a negative key.

14. Write an algorithm that traverses a linked list and deletes the node immediately preceding a node with a negative key.

15. Modify Algorithm 3-16, "Append two linked lists," on page 109 to count the number of nodes in the appended list. Display the count after printing the complete list.

16. Write a program to implement the modified append algorithm in Problem 15.

17. Write a program that creates a two-dimensional linked list. The nodes in the first column contain only two pointers, as shown in Figure 3-35. The left pointer points to the next row. The right pointer points to the data in the row.

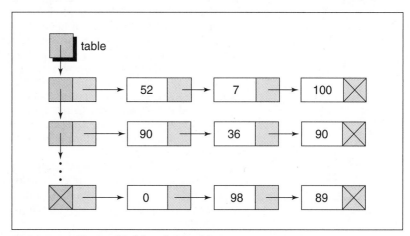

Figure 3-35 Linked list for Problem 17

18. We can simplify most of the algorithms in the text using a linked list with a dummy node at the beginning, as shown in Figure 3-36.

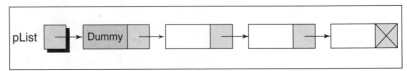

Figure 3-36   Linked list for Problem 18

   Write an algorithm `insertNode` (see "Insert Node," on page 134) using a linked list with a dummy node.

19. Write an algorithm `deleteNode` (Algorithm 3-3, "Linked list delete node," on page 92) using a linked list with a dummy node.

20. Write an algorithm `searchList` (Algorithm 3-4, "Search linked list," on page 95) using a linked list with a dummy node.

21. Write an algorithm that returns a pointer to the last node in a linked list.

22. Write an algorithm that appends two linked lists together.

23. Write an algorithm that appends a linked list to itself.

24. Write an algorithm that swaps (exchanges) two nodes in a linked list. The nodes are identified by number and are passed as parameters. For example, to exchange nodes 5 and 8, you would call `swap (5, 8)`. If the exchange is successful, the algorithm is to return 1. If it encounters an error, such as an invalid node number, it returns 0.

25. Write the C++ code for Algorithm 3-19, "Array of linked lists," on page 111 and Algorithm 3-20, "Build array of linked lists," on page 112.

26. Write a new ADT algorithm to merge two linked lists.

Projects

27. Write a program that reads a file and builds a linked list. After the list is built, display it on the monitor. You may use any appropriate data structure, but it should have a key field and data. Two possibilities are a list of your favorite CDs or your friends' telephone numbers.

28. Modify the program you wrote in Project 27. After you create the file, the program should present the user with a menu to insert new data, remove existing data, or print a list of all data.

29. Write a program to read a list of students from a file and create a linked list. Each entry in the link list should have the student's name, a pointer to the next student, and a pointer to a linked list of scores. There may be up to four scores for each student. The structure is shown in Figure 3-37.

   The program should initialize the student list by reading the students' names from the text file and creating null score lists. It should then loop through the list, prompting the user to enter the scores for each student. The scores' prompt should include the name of the student.

   After all scores have been entered, the program should print the scores for each student along with the score total and average score. The average should include only those scores present.

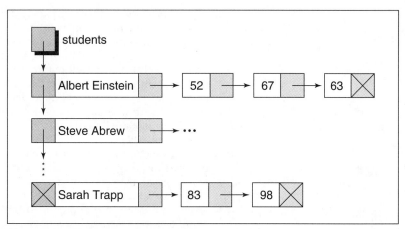

Figure 3-37   Data structure for Project 29

The data for each student are shown in Table 3-3.

Student Name	Score 1	Score 2	Score 3	Score 4
Albert Einstein	52	67	63	
Steve Abrew	90	86	90	93
David Nagasake	100	85	93	89
Mike Black	81	87	81	85
Andrew Dijkstra	90	82	95	87
Joanne Nguyen	84	80	95	91
Chris Walljasper	86	100	96	89
Fred Albert	70	68		
Dennis Dudley	74	79	77	81
Leo Rice	95			
Fred Flintstone	73	81	78	74
Frances Dupre	82	76	79	
Dave Light	89	76	91	83
Hua Tran	91	81	87	94
Sarah Trapp	83	98	94	93

Table 3-3   Data for Project 29

30. Modify Project 29 to insert the data into the student list in key (student name) sequence. Because the data are entered in a first name–last name format, you will need to write a special compare algorithm that reformats the name into last name–first name format and then does a string compare. All other algorithms should work as previously described.

31. Write a program to create an array of linked lists. The data are the same data and sequence as in Project 30. The first four students should be placed in the first linked list, the second four in the second linked list, and so forth until all lists have been built. Rather than have the last node in each list be a null pointer, it should point to the first node in the next list. Only the last linked list is to have a null pointer. This method effectively creates a singly linked list with an array structure that can be searched with a binary search to locate a student. For this application, provide a modified search algorithm that uses a binary search on the index to retrieve data.

32. Write a function that merges two ordered linked lists into one list. When two lists are merged,[5] the data in the resulting list are also ordered. The two original lists should be left unchanged; that is, the merged list should be a new list.

33. Write a program that adds and subtracts polynomials. Each polynomial should be represented as a linked list. The first node in the list represents the first term in the polynomial, the second node represents the second term, and so forth.

Each node contains three fields. The first field is the term's coefficient. The second field is the term's power, and the third field is a pointer to the next term. For example, consider the polynomials shown in Figure 3-38. The first term in the first polynomial has a coefficient of 5 and an exponent of 4, which then is interpreted as $5x^4$.

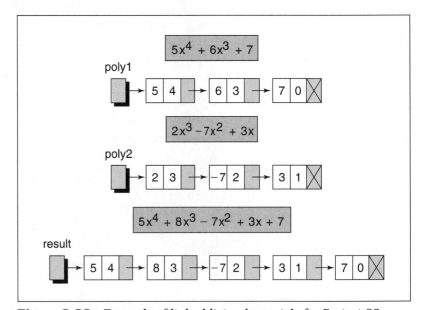

Figure 3-38 Example of linked list polynomials for Project 33

---

5. For more information about merge concepts, see Chapter 11.

The rules for the addition of polynomials are as follows:

a. If the powers are equal, the coefficients are algebraically added.

b. If the powers are unequal, the term with the higher power is inserted in the new polynomial.

c. If the exponent is 0, it represents x^0, which is 1. The value of the term is therefore the value of the coefficient.

d. If the result of adding the coefficients results in 0, the term is dropped (0 times anything is 0.)

A polynomial is represented by a series of lines, each of which has two integers. The first integer represents the coefficient; the second integer represents the exponent. Thus, the first polynomial in Figure 3-38 would be

```
5    4
6    3
7    0
```

To add two polynomials, the program reads the coefficients and exponents for each polynomial and places them into a linked list. The input can be read from separate files or entered from the keyboard with appropriate user prompts. After the polynomials have been stored, they are added and the results placed in a third linked list.

The polynomials are added using an operational merge process. An operational merge combines the two lists while performing one or more operations—in our case, addition. To add, we take one term from each of the polynomials and compare the exponents. If the two exponents are equal, then the coefficients are added to create a new coefficient. If the new coefficient is 0, then the term is dropped; if it is not 0, it is appended to the linked list for the resulting polynomial. If one of the exponents is larger than the other, the corresponding term is immediately placed into the new linked list, and the term with the smaller exponent is held to be compared with the next term from the other list. If one list ends before the other, the rest of the longer list is simply appended to the list for the new polynomial.

Print the two input polynomials and their sum by traversing the linked lists and displaying them as sets of numbers. Be sure to label each polynomial.

Test your program with the two polynomials shown in Table 3-4.

Polynomial 1		Polynomial 2	
Coefficient	Exponent	Coefficient	Exponent
7	9	−7	9
2	6	2	8
3	5	−5	7
4	4	2	4
2	3	2	3
6	2	9	2
6	0	−7	1

Table 3-4 Text data for Project 33

34. In most personal computers, the largest integer is 32,767 and the largest long integer is 2,147,483,647. Some applications, such as the national debt, may require an unbounded integer. One way to store and manipulate integers of unlimited size is by using a linked list. Each digit is stored in a node of the list. For example, Figure 3-39 shows how we could store a five-digit number in a linked list.

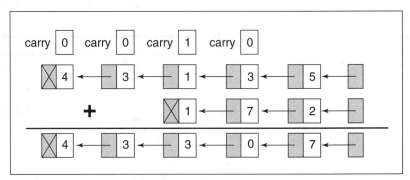

Figure 3-39   Integer stored in a linked list for Project 34

Although the linked list in Figure 3-39 is represented as moving from right to left, there is no physical direction in a linked list. We represent it in this way to clarify the problem.

To add two numbers, we simply add the corresponding digit in the same location in their respective linked lists with the carry from the previous addition. With each addition, if the sum is greater than 10, we need to subtract 10 and set the carry to 1. Otherwise, the carry is set to 0.

Write an algorithm to add two integer-linked lists. Design your solution so that the same logic adds the first numbers (units position) as well as the rest of the number. In other words, do not have special one-time logic for adding the units position.

35. Once you have written the function for adding two numbers, multiplication is relatively easy. You can use the basic definition of multiplication, repetitive addition. In other words, if we need to multiply two numbers, such as 45 × 6, we simply add 45 six times. Write an algorithm that multiplies two numbers using the algorithm developed in Project 34.

36. We have shown the linear list as being implemented as a linked list in dynamic memory, but it is possible to implement it in an array. In this case, the array structure has two basic fields, the data and the next index location. The next index field allows the array structure to take on the attributes of a linked list. A linked list array is shown in Figure 3-40.

Note that there are actually two lists in the array. The data list starts at element 2 and progresses through 6 and 0 and to the end of the data at element 9. The second list links all of the empty or available elements together. It starts at element 4, progresses through 1, 3, 7, and 8, and ends at 5.

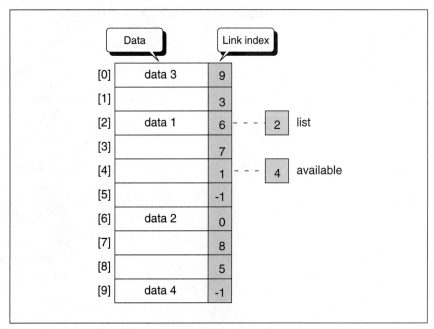

Figure 3-40   Linked list array for Project 36

Write a program that implements a linked list using an array. Your program should be menu driven and prompt the user to insert data, delete data, print the contents of the list, or search the list for a given piece of data.

To insert new data, you must delete an element from the available list and then insert it into the data list. Conversely, when you delete a node from the data list, you must insert it into the available list.

37. Rework the linked list ADT to be a doubly linked ADT list. Include a traverse backward as an additional algorithm.

38. Write a program to process stock data. The stock data should be read from a text file containing the following data: stock code, stock name, amount invested (xxx.xx), shares held, and current price. Use the Internet or your local paper to gather data on at least 20 stocks. (You may use mutual funds in place of stocks.)

As each stock is read, insert it into a doubly linked multilinked list. The first logical list should be ordered on the stock code. The second logical list should be ordered on the gain or loss for the stock. Gain or loss is calculated as the current value of the stock (shares held times current price) minus the amount invested. Include at least one loss in your test data.

After building the lists, display a menu that allows the user to display either logical list forward or backward (a total of four options). Each display should contain an appropriate heading and column captions.

Run your program and submit a list of your input data and a printout of each display option.

39. Modify Project 38 to include the following additional processes: search for a stock using the stock code and print the data for the stock, insert data for a new stock, modify data for an existing stock, and write the data back to a file when the program terminates.

40. You have been assigned to a programming team writing a system that will maintain a doubly linked multilinked list containing census data about cities in the United States. The first logical list maintains data in sequence by the 1990 population. The second logical list maintains the same data using the 1980 census data. Your assignment is to write the insert routine(s). To completely test your program, you will also need to write routines to print the contents of the lists.

The structure for the data is shown below.

```
Logical Definition:
City                     18 characters
State                    02 characters
Year Incorporated        04 characters
Population - 1990        long integer
Population - 1980        long integer
Civilian Workforce       long integer
Per Capita Income        integer
```

The input will be a file containing the census data in Table 3-5.

City	St.	Est	Pop90	Pop80	Wkfrce	Inc
Baltimore	MD	1797	736014	786741	346187	20267
Boston	MA	1822	574283	562994	297200	23746
Chicago	IL	1837	2783726	3005072	1434029	20349
Columbus	OH	1834	632910	565021	343288	17178
Dallas	TX	1856	1006877	904599	649527	19485
Detroit	MI	1815	1027974	1203368	441736	19660
Houston	TX	1837	1630553	1595138	1049300	17598
Indianapolis	IN	1832	744952	711539	405829	18080
Jacksonville	FL	1822	672971	571003	325187	16215
Los Angeles	CA	1850	3485398	2968528	1791011	19906
Memphis	TN	1826	610337	646174	337450	16484
Milwaukee	WI	1846	628088	636297	306256	18842
New York	NY	1898	7322564	7071639	3314000	22645
Philadelphia	PA	1701	1585577	1688210	736895	19750
Phoenix	AZ	1881	983403	789704	591142	17705

Table 3-5 Twenty largest cities in the United States

City	St.	Est	Pop90	Pop80	Wkfrce	Inc
San Antonio	TX	1837	935933	785940	446701	14144
San Diego	CA	1850	1110549	875538	553612	18651
San Francisco	CA	1850	723959	678974	390877	28170
San Jose	CA	1850	782248	629400	375309	24581
Washington	DC	1788	606900	638432	283702	24845

Table 3-5 Twenty largest cities in the United States *(continued)*

To verify your program, print the list in sequence, both forward and backward, for both census years. To conserve paper, print the data two-up, as shown in Table 3-6.

Census Data for 1980			Census Data for 1990		
City	St	Pop'l	City	St	Pop'l
01 Boston	MA	562994	01 Boston	MA	574283
02 Columbus	OH	565021	02 Washington	DC	606900
•			•		
•			•		
•			•		
19 Chicago	IL	3005072	19 Los Angeles	CA	3485398
20 New York	NY	7071639	20 New York	NY	7322564
20 New York	NY	7071639	20 New York	NY	7322564
19 Chicago	IL	3005072	19 Los Angeles	CA	3485398
•			•		
•			•		
•			•		
02 Columbus	OH	565021	02 Washington	DC	606900
01 Boston	MA	562994	01 Boston	MA	574283

Table 3-6 Sample output data for Project 40

41. Modify Project 40 to include the ability to delete an element from the list.

42. Using the data in Project 40, write a program that builds a singly linked list ordered on city. The program asks the user to enter a state and prints the statistics for all cities in the state. Use an unordered list search (see page 96) that returns a linked list of all cities for the state. Test your program by printing data for Maryland (MD), Oregon (OR), Washington, D.C. (DC), and California (CA).

4

Stacks

A **stack** is a linear list in which all additions and deletions are restricted to one end, called the **top.** If you inserted a data series into a stack and then removed it, the order of the data would be reversed. Data input as {5, 10, 15, 20} would be removed as {20, 15, 10, 5}. This reversing attribute is why stacks are known as the **last in–first out (LIFO)** data structure.

We use many different types of stacks in our daily lives. We often talk of a stack of coins or a stack of dishes. Any situation in which you can only add or remove an object at the top is a stack. If you want to remove any object other than the one at the top, you must first remove all objects above it. A graphic representation of a stack is shown in Figure 4-1.

Although nothing prevents you from designing a data structure that allows you to perform other operations, such as moving the item at the top of the stack to the bottom, the result would not be a stack.

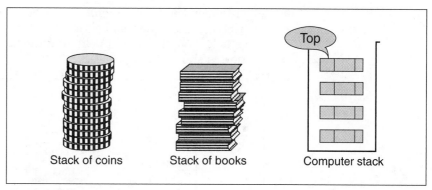

Figure 4-1 Stack

> **Note**
>
> A **stack** is a last in–first out (LIFO) data structure in which all insertions and deletions are restricted to one end, called the **top**.

4-1 BASIC STACK OPERATIONS

The three basic stack operations are push, pop, and stack top. Push is used to insert data into the stack. Pop removes data from a stack and returns the data to the calling module. Stack top returns the data at the top of the stack without deleting the data from the stack.

Push

Push adds an item at the top of the stack. After the push, the new item becomes the top. The only potential problem with this simple operation is that we must ensure that there is room for the new item. If there is not enough room, then the stack is in an **overflow** state and the item cannot be added. Figure 4-2 shows the push stack operation.

Pop

When we **pop** a stack, we remove the item at the top of the stack and return it to the user. Because we have removed the top item, the next

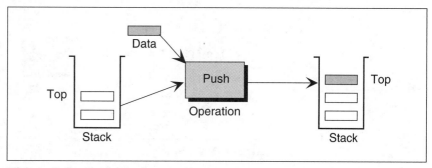

Figure 4-2 Push stack operation

older item in the stack becomes the top. When the last item in the stack is deleted, the stack must be set to its empty state. If pop is called when the stack is empty, then it is in an **underflow** state. The stack pop operation is shown in Figure 4-3.

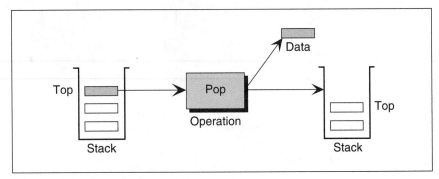

Figure 4-3   Pop stack operation

Stack Top

The third stack operation is **stack top.** Stack top copies the item at the top of the stack; that is, it returns the data in the top element to the user but does not delete it. You might think of this operation as reading the stack top. Stack top can also result in underflow if the stack is empty. The stack top operation is shown in Figure 4-4.

Figure 4-5 traces these three operations in an example. We start with an empty stack and push green and blue into the stack. At this point, the stack contains two entries. We then pop blue from the top of the stack, leaving green as the only entry. After pushing red, the stack again contains two entries. At this point, we retrieve the top entry, red, using stack top. Note that stack top does not remove red from the stack; it is still the top element. We then pop red, leaving green as the only entry. When green is popped, the stack is again empty. Note also how this example demonstrates the last

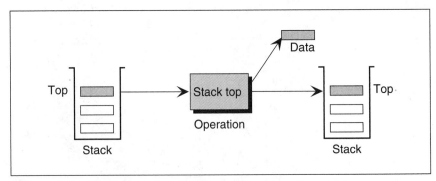

Figure 4-4   Stack top operation

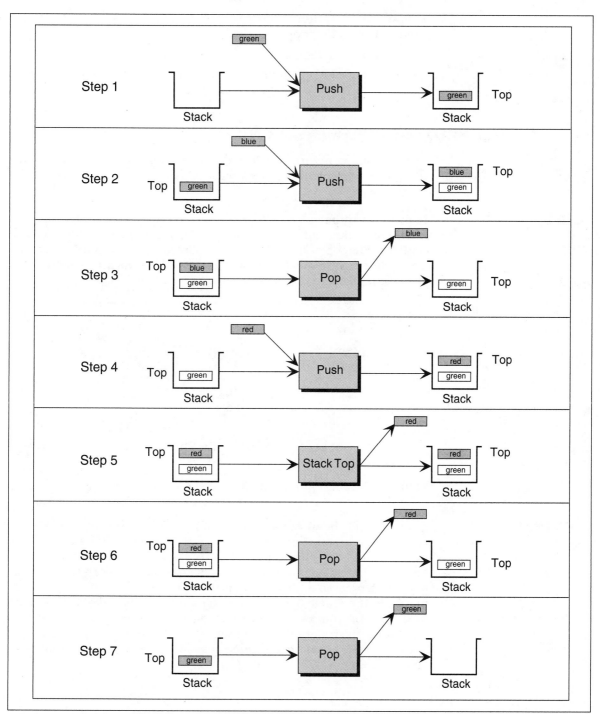

Figure 4-5 Stack example

in–first out operation of a stack. Although green was pushed first, it is the last to be popped.

Note

> The three basic stack operations are push, pop, and stack top.

4-2   STACK LINKED LIST IMPLEMENTATION

Several data structures could be used to implement a stack. In this section we implement the stack as a linked list.

Data Structure

To implement the linked list stack, we need two different structures, a head and a data node. The head structure contains metadata and a pointer to the top of the stack. The data structure contains data and a next pointer to the next node in the stack. The stack conceptual and physical implementations are shown in Figure 4-6.

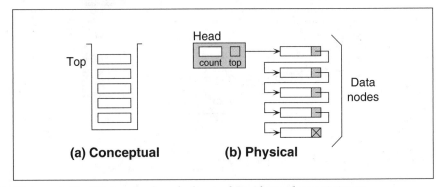

Figure 4-6 Conceptual and physical stack implementations

Stack Head

Generally the **head** for a stack requires only two attributes: a top pointer and a count of the number of elements in the stack. These two elements are placed in a structure. Other stack attributes can be placed here also. For example, it is possible to record the time the stack was created and the total number of items that have ever been placed in the stack. These two metadata items would allow the user to determine the average number of items processed through the stack in a given period. Of course, you would do this only if such a statistic were required for some reason. A basic head structure is shown in Figure 4-7.

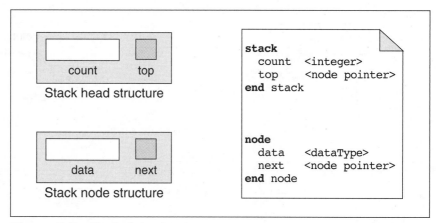

Figure 4-7   Stack data structure

Stack Data Node

The rest of the data structure is a typical linked list **data node.** Although the application determines the data that are stored in the stack, the stack data node looks like any linked list node. In addition to the data, it contains a next pointer to other data nodes, making it a self-referential data structure. The stack data node is also shown in Figure 4-7.

Stack Algorithms

The eight stack operations we define should be sufficient to solve any basic stack problem. If an application requires additional stack operations, they can be easily added. For each operation, we give its name, a brief description, and its calling sequence. We then develop algorithms for each one. The operations you need in a program depend on the application.

Although the implementation of a stack depends somewhat on the implementation language, it is usually implemented with a stack head structure or object. We use this design. It is reflected in Figure 4-8, along with the four most common stack operations: create stack, push stack, pop stack, and destroy stack.

Create Stack

Create stack initializes the metadata for the stack structure. The pseudocode for create stack is shown in Algorithm 4-1.

Push Stack

Push stack inserts an element into the stack. The first thing we need to do when we push data into a stack is find memory for the node. We must therefore allocate memory from dynamic memory. Once the memory is allocated, we simply assign the data to the

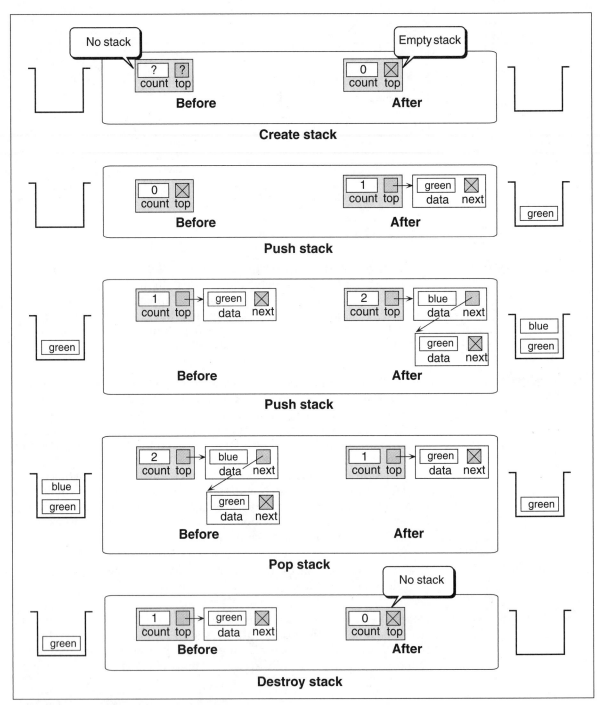

Figure 4-8 Linked list stack operations

```
algorithm createStack (ref stack <metadata>)
Initializes metadata for a stack.
    Pre     stack is structure for metadata
    Post    metadata initialized
  1 stack.count = 0
  2 stack.top   = null
  3 return
end createStack
```

Algorithm 4-1   Create stack

stack node and then set the next pointer to point to the node currently indicated as the stack top. We also need to update the stack top pointer and add 1 to the stack count field. Figure 4-9 traces a push stack operation in which a new pointer (pNew) is used to identify the data to be inserted into the stack.

To develop the insertion algorithm, we need to analyze three different stack conditions: (1) insertion into an empty stack, (2) insertion into a stack with data, and (3) insertion into a stack when the available memory is exhausted. The first two of these operations are shown in Figure 4-8. When we insert into a stack that contains data, the new node's next pointer is set to point to the node currently at the top, and the stack's top pointer is set to point to the new node. When we insert into an empty stack, the new node's next pointer is set to null and the stack's top pointer is set to point to the new node. However, because the stack's top pointer is null, we can use it to set the new node's next pointer to null. Thus the logic for inserting into a

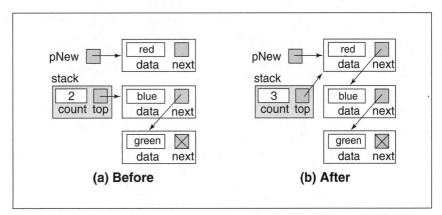

(a) Before   (b) After

Figure 4-9   Push stack example

stack with data and the logic for inserting into an empty stack are identical.

The logic for the third case, stack overflow, depends on the application. The action taken also depends on the application. When writing low-level algorithms, however, it is a good practice to defer potential errors to the calling algorithm. For a stack, this means passing back an overflow Boolean rather than handling the overflow in the stack push algorithm. Algorithm 4-2 contains the pseudocode for a stack push.

```
algorithm pushStack (ref stack   <metadata>,
                         val data    <dataType>)
Insert (push) one item into the stack.
    Pre     stack is metadata structure to a valid stack
            data contain data to be pushed into stack
    Post    data have been pushed in stack
    Return  true if successful; false if memory overflow
 1 if (stack full)
    1    success = false
 2 else
    1    allocate (newPtr)
    2    newPtr->data  = data
    3    newPtr->next  = stack.top
    4    stack.top     = newPtr
    5    stack.count   = stack.count + 1
    6    success       = true
 3 end if
 4 return success
end pushStack
```

Algorithm 4-2   Push stack design

Pop Stack

Pop stack sends the data in the node at the top of the stack back to the calling algorithm. It then deletes and recycles the node—that is, returns it to memory. After the count is adjusted by subtracting 1, the algorithm returns to the caller. If the pop was successful, it returns true; if the stack is empty when pop is called, it returns false. The operations for a stack pop are traced in Figure 4-10. The pop stack algorithm is shown in Algorithm 4-3.

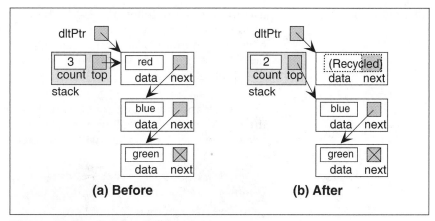

Figure 4-10   Pop stack

```
algorithm popStack (ref stack    <metadata>,
                    ref dataOut <dataType>)
This algorithm pops the item on the top of the stack and returns
it to the user.
    Pre    stack is metadata structure to a valid stack
           dataOut is a reference variable to receive the data
    Post   Data have been returned to calling algorithm
    Return true if successful; false if underflow
1 if (stack empty)
    1   success = false
2 else
    1   dltPtr      = stack.top
    2   dataOut     = stack.top->data
    3   stack.top   = stack.top->next
    4   stack.count = stack.count - 1
    5   recycle (dltPtr)
    6   success = true
3 end if
4 return success
end popStack
```

Algorithm 4-3   Pop stack

Algorithm 4-3 Analysis

It is interesting to follow the logic when the last node is being deleted. In this case, the result is an empty stack. No special logic is required, however: The empty stack is created automatically because the last node has a null next pointer that when assigned to top indicates that the stack is empty.

Stack Top

The **stack top** algorithm (Algorithm 4-4) sends the data at the top of the stack back to the calling module without deleting the top node. It allows the user to see what will be deleted when the stack is popped.

```
algorithm stackTop  (val stack     <metadata>,
                          ref dataOut <dataType>)
This algorithm retrieves the data from the top of the stack
without changing the stack.
    Pre     stack is metadata structure to a valid stack
            dataOut is a reference variable to receive the data
    Post    data have been returned to calling algorithm
    Return true if data returned, false if underflow
1 if (stack empty)
    1   success = false
2 else
    1   dataOut = stack.top->data
    2   success = true
3 end if
4 return success
end stackTop
```

Algorithm 4-4   Stack top pseudocode

Algorithm 4-4 Analysis

The logic for the stack top is virtually identical to that for the pop stack except for the delete and recycle. As with the pop, there is only one potential problem with the retrieve algorithm; the stack may be empty. If the retrieve is successful, it returns true; if the stack is empty, it returns false.

Empty Stack

Empty stack is provided to implement the structured programming concept of data hiding. If the entire program has access to the stack head structure, it is not needed. However, if the stack is implemented as a separately compiled program to be linked with other programs, the calling program may not have access to the stack head node. In these cases, it is necessary to provide a way to determine whether the stack is empty. The pseudocode for empty stack is shown in Algorithm 4-5.

```
algorithm emptyStack (val stack <metadata>)
Determines if stack is empty and returns a Boolean.
    Pre    stack is metadata structure to a valid stack
    Post   returns stack status
    Return Boolean, true: stack empty, false: stack contains data
  1 if (stack not empty)
    1   result = false
  2 else
    1   result = true
  3 end if
  4 return result
end emptyStack
```

Algorithm 4-5   Empty stack

Full Stack

Full stack is another structured programming implementation of data hiding. Depending on the language, it may also be one of the most difficult algorithms to implement. ANSI Pascal, for instance, provides no method to implement it. The pseudocode for full stack is shown in Algorithm 4-6.

```
algorithm fullStack (val stack <metadata>)
Determines if stack is full and returns a Boolean.
    Pre    stack is metadata structure to a valid stack
    Post   returns stack status
    Return Boolean, true: stack full, false: memory available
  1 if (memory available)
    1   result = false
  2 else
    1   result = true
  3 end if
  4 return result
end fullStack
```

Algorithm 4-6   Full stack

Stack Count

Stack count returns the number of elements currently in the stack. It is another implementation of the data-hiding principle of structured programming. The pseudocode is shown in Algorithm 4-7.

```
algorithm stackCount (val stack <metadata>)
Returns the number of elements currently in stack.
    Pre     stack is metadata structure to a valid stack
    Post    returns stack count
    Return integer count of number of elements in stack
  1 return (stack.count)
end stackCount
```

Algorithm 4-7   Stack count

Destroy Stack

Destroy stack deletes all data in a stack. Figure 4-8, on page 162 graphically shows the results of destroy stack, and Algorithm 4-8 contains the pseudocode. The function to return memory to the heap is language dependent. We use the pseudocode keyword **recycle**.

```
algorithm destroyStack (ref stack <metadata>)
This algorithm releases all nodes back to the dynamic memory.
    Pre     stack is metadata structure to a valid stack
    Post    stack empty and all nodes recycled
  1 loop (stack.top not null)
    1   temp      = stack.top
    2   stack.top = stack.top->next
    3   recycle (temp)
  2 end loop
  3 stack.count = 0
  4 return
end destroyStack
```

Algorithm 4-8   Destroy stack

Algorithm 4-8 Analysis

It is only necessary to destroy a stack when you no longer need it and the program is not complete. If the program is complete, the stack is automatically cleared from dynamic memory when the program terminates.

4-3   STACK APPLICATIONS

Stack applications can be classified into four broad categories: reversing data, parsing data, postponing data usage, and backtracking steps. For each of these applications we provide one or two examples. For reversing data we reverse a list. We also use reversing data to convert a decimal number to its binary equivalent. For parsing, we show how to match the parentheses in a source program. We use postponement to convert infix to postfix notation and also to evaluate a postfix expression. Finally, we use backtracking to choose between two or more paths. Each of these applications uses the stack algorithms described in the previous section. You should make sure that you fully understand these algorithms before studying the following applications.

Note

> Four common stack applications are: reversing data, parsing, postponing and backtracking.

Reversing Data

Reversing data requires that a given set of data be reordered so that the first and last elements are exchanged, with all of the positions between the first and last being relatively exchanged also. For example, {1 2 3 4} becomes {4 3 2 1}. We examine two different reversing applications: reverse a list and convert decimal to binary.

Reverse a List

One of the applications of a stack is to reverse a list of items. For example, the program in Algorithm 4-9 reads a list of integers and prints them in reverse.

```
algorithm reverseNumber
    This program reverses a list of integers read from
    the keyboard by pushing them into a stack and
    retrieving them one by one.
  1 createStack (stack)
  2 prompt (Enter a number)
  3 read (number)
    Fill stack
  4 loop (not end of data AND not fullStack(stack))
      1  pushStack (stack, number)
      2  prompt (Enter next number: <EOF> to stop)
      3  read (number)
  5 end loop
    Now print numbers in reverse
  6 loop (not emptyStack(stack))
      1  popStack (stack, dataOut)
      2  print (dataOut)
  7 end loop
  end reverseNumber
```

Algorithm 4-9   Reverse a number series

Algorithm 4-9 Analysis

This program is very simple. After creating a stack, it reads a series of numbers and pushes them into the stack. When the user keys end of file, the program then pops the stack and prints the numbers in reverse order.

The important point to note in this simple program is that we never referenced the stack structure directly. All stack references were through the stack ADT interface. This is an important concept in the structured programming principles of encapsulation and function reusability.

Convert Decimal to Binary

The idea of reversing a series can be used in solving classical problems such as transforming a decimal number to a binary number. The following simple code segment transforms a decimal number into a binary number:

```
1  read (number)
2  loop (number > 0)
    1    digit = number modulo 2
    2    print (digit)
    3    number = number/2
3  end loop
```

This code has a problem, however. It creates the binary number backward. Thus, 19 becomes 11001 rather than 10011.

We can solve this problem by using a stack. Instead of printing the binary digit as soon as it is produced, we push it into the stack. Then, after the number has been completely converted, we simply pop the stack and print the results one digit at a time in a line. This program is shown in Algorithm 4-10.

```
algorithm decimalToBinary
This algorithm reads an integer from the keyboard and
prints its binary equivalent. It uses a stack to reverse
the order of 0's and 1's produced.
1  createStack (stack)
2  prompt (Enter a decimal to convert to binary)
3  read (number)
```

Algorithm 4-10   Convert decimal to binary

```
4 loop (number > 0)
   1   digit   = number modulo 2
   2   pushOK  = push (stack, digit)
   3   if (pushOK false)
      1   print (Stack overflow creating digit)
      2   quit algorithm
   4   end if
   5   number = number / 2
5 end loop
   Binary number created in stack. Now print it.
6 loop (not emptyStack(stack))
   1   popStack (stack, digit)
   2   print (digit)
7 end loop
8 return
end decimalToBinary
```

Algorithm 4-10   Convert decimal to binary *(continued)*

Algorithm 4-10 Analysis

This program is similar to Algorithm 4-9, "Reverse a number series," on page 169. This time the data pushed into the stack are the binary digits. After the number has been completely converted, the stack is popped and the data printed on one line. The only potential problem is that there may not be enough room in memory. This problem is handled in Statement 4.3. If the push is not successful, a message is printed and the algorithm stops.

Parsing

Another application of stacks is **parsing.** Parsing is any logic that breaks data into independent pieces for further processing. For example, to translate a source program to machine language, a compiler must parse the program into individual parts such as keywords, names, and tokens.

One common programming problem is unmatched parentheses in an algebraic expression. When parentheses are unmatched, two types of errors can occur: The opening parenthesis can be missing or the closing parenthesis can be missing. These two errors are shown in Figure 4-11.

In Algorithm 4-11, we parse a source program to ensure that all of the parentheses are properly paired.

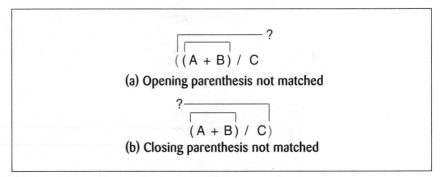

(a) Opening parenthesis not matched

(b) Closing parenthesis not matched

Figure 4-11   Unmatched parentheses examples

```
algorithm parseParens
This algorithm reads a source program and parses it to make
sure all opening-closing parentheses are paired.
  1 loop (more data)
     1   read (character)
     2   if (character is an opening parenthesis)
        1   pushStack (stack, character)
     3   else
        1   if (character is closing parenthesis)
           1   if (emptyStack (stack))
              1   print (Error: Closing parenthesis not matched)
           2   else
              1   popStack(stack, token)
           3   end if
        2   end if
     4   end if
  2 end loop
  3 if (not emptyStack (stack))
     1   print (Error: Opening parenthesis not matched)
end parseParens
```

Algorithm 4-11   Parse parentheses

Algorithm 4-11 Analysis

Whenever we find an opening parenthesis in a program, we push it into the stack. When we find a closing parenthesis, we pop its matching opening parenthesis from the stack. Note that there are two different pairing errors in the program: (1) a closing parenthesis without a matching parenthesis (see Statement 1.3.1.1.1) and (2) an opening parenthesis without a matching closing parenthesis (see Statement 3.1).

Postponement

When we used a stack to reverse a list, the entire list was read before we began outputting the results. Often the logic of an application requires that the usage of data be deferred until some later point. A stack can be useful when the application requires that the use of data be postponed for a while. We develop two stack postponement applications in this section: infix to postfix transformation and postfix expression evaluation.

Infix to Postfix Transformation

An arithmetic expression can be represented in three different formats: **infix, postfix,** and **prefix.** In an infix notation, the operator comes between the two operands, the basic format of the algebraic notation we learned in grammar school. In postfix notation,[1] the operator comes after its two operands, and in prefix notation it comes before the two operands. These formats are shown below.

```
Prefix:    + a b
Infix:     a + b
Postfix:   a b +
```

One of the disadvantages of the infix notation is that we need to use parentheses to control the evaluation of the operators. We thus have an evaluation method that includes parentheses and two operator priority classes. In the postfix and prefix notations, we do not need parentheses; each provides only one evaluation rule.

Although high-level languages use the infix notation, such expressions cannot be directly evaluated. Rather, they must be analyzed to determine the order in which the expressions are to be evaluated. A common evaluation technique is to convert the expressions to postfix notation before generating the code to evaluate them. We first examine a manual method for converting infix to postfix expressions and then develop an algorithm that can be implemented in a computer.

Note

In *prefix* notation, the operator comes *before* the operands.

In *infix* notation, the operator comes *between* the operands.

In *postfix* notation, the operator comes *after* the operands

Manual Transformation

The rules for manually converting infix to postfix expressions are as follows:

---

1. Postfix notation is also known as reverse Polish notation (RPN) in honor of its originator, the Polish logician Jan Lukasiewicz.

1. Fully parenthesize the expression using any explicit parentheses and the arithmetic precedence—multiply and divide before add and subtract.
2. Change all infix notations in each parenthesis to postfix notation, starting from the innermost expressions. Conversion to postfix notation is done by moving the operator to the location of the expression's closing parenthesis.
3. Remove all parentheses.

For example, for the following infix expression:

```
A + B * C
```

Step 1 results in

```
( A + ( B * C ) )
```

Step 2 moves the multiply operator after C

```
( A + ( B C * ) )
```

and then moves the addition operator to between the last two closing parentheses. This change is made because the closing parenthesis for the plus is the last parenthesis. We now have

```
( A (B C * ) +)
```

Finally, Step 3 removes the parentheses.

```
A B C * +
```

Let's look at a more complex example. This example is not only longer, but it already has one set of parentheses to override the default evaluation order.

```
( A + B ) * C + D + E * F - G
```

Step 1 adds parentheses.

```
( ( ( ( ( A + B ) * C ) + D ) + ( E * F ) ) - G )
```

Step 2 then moves the operators.

```
( ( ( ( ( A B + ) C * ) D + ) ( E F * ) + ) G - )
```

Step 3 removes the parentheses.

```
A B + C * D + E F * + G -
```

Algorithmic Transformation

This manual operation would be difficult to implement in a computer. Let's look at another technique that is easily implemented with a stack.

We start with a very simple example, transforming a multiply. The multiplication of two variables is shown below, first in infix notation and then in postfix notation.

```
A * B  ⮂  A B *
```

We can obviously read the operands and output them in order. The problem becomes how to handle the multiply operator; we need to postpone putting it in the output until we have read the right operand, B. In this simple case, we push the operator into a stack and, after the whole infix expression has been read, pop the stack and put the operator in the postfix expression.

Now let's look at a more complex expression. Again, the infix expression is given on the left and the equivalent postfix expression on the right.

```
A * B + C  ⮂  A B * C +
```

Here again we can read the infix operators and copy them to the postfix expression. If we were to simply put the operators into the stack as we did earlier and then pop them to the postfix expression after all of the operands had been read, we would get the wrong answer. Somehow we must pair the two operators with their correct operands. One possible rule might be to postpone an operator only until we get another operator. Then, before we push the second operator, we could pop the first one and place it in the output expression. This logic works in this case, but it won't for others. Consider the following example.

```
A + B * C  ⮂  A B C * +
```

As we discussed previously, infix expressions use a precedence rule to determine how to group the operands and operators in an expression. We can use the same rule when we convert infix to postfix. When we need to push an operator into the stack, if its priority is higher than the operator at the top of the stack, we go ahead and push it into the stack. Conversely, if the operator at the top of the stack has a higher priority than the current operator, it is popped and placed in the output expression. Using this rule with the above expression, we would take the following actions:

1. Copy operand A to output expression.
2. Push operator + into stack.
3. Copy operand B to output expression.
4. Push operator * into stack. (Priority of * is higher than +.)
5. Copy operand C to output expression.

6. Pop operator * and copy to output expression.

7. Pop operator + and copy to output expression.

We need to cover one more rule to complete the logic. When a current operator with a lower or equal priority forces the top operator to be popped from the stack, we must check the new top operator. If it is also greater than the current operator, it is popped to the output expression. Consequently, we may pop several operators to the output expression before pushing the new operator into the stack.

Let's work one more example before we formally develop the algorithm.

```
A + B * C - D/E   ➯   A B C * D E / - +
```

The transformation of this expression is shown in Figure 4-12. Because it uses all of the basic arithmetic operators, it is a complete test.

We begin by copying the first operand, A, to the postfix expression. See Figure 4-12(b). The add operator is then pushed into the stack and the second operand copied to the postfix expression. See Figure 4-12(d). At this point we are ready to insert the multiply operator into the stack. As we see in Figure 4-12(e), its priority is higher than that of the add operator at the top of the stack so we simply push it into the stack. After copying the next operand, C, to the postfix expression, we need to push the minus operator into the stack. Because its priority is lower than that of the multiply operator, however, we must first pop the multiply and copy it to the postfix expression. The plus sign is now popped and appended to the postfix expression because the minus and plus have the same priority. The minus is then pushed into the stack. The result is shown in Figure 4-12(g). After copying the operand D to the postfix expression, we push the divide operator into the stack because it is of higher priority than the minus at the top of the stack in Figure 4-12(i). After copying E to the postfix expression, we are left with an empty infix expression and three operators in the stack. See Figure 4-12(j). All that is left at this point is to pop the stack and copy each operator to the postfix expression. The final expression is shown in Figure 4-12(k).

We are now ready to develop the algorithm. We assume only the operators shown below. They have been adapted from the standard algebraic notation.

```
Priority 2:    *  /
Priority 1:    +  -
Priority 0:    (
```

The code is shown in Algorithm 4-12.

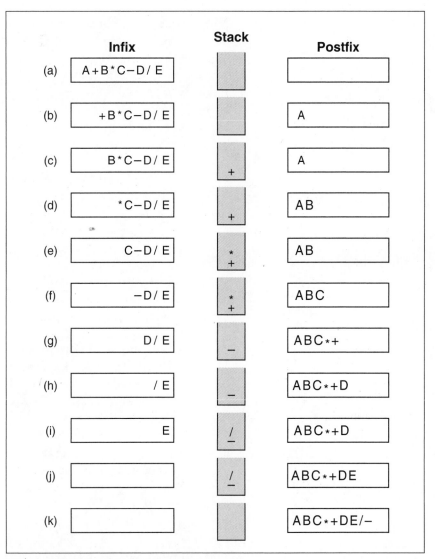

Figure 4-12 Infix transformations

```
algorithm inToPostFix (val formula <string>)
Convert infix formula to postfix.
    Pre    formula is infix notation that has been edited
           to ensure that there are no syntactical errors
```

Algorithm 4-12 Convert infix to postfix

```
        Post   postfix formula has been formatted as a string
        Return postfix formula
    1 createStack (stack)
    2 set postFix to null string
    3 looper = 0
    4 loop (looper < sizeof formula)
        1   token = formula[looper]
        2   if (token is open parenthesis)
            1   pushStack (stack, token)
        3   elseif (token is close parenthesis)
            1   popStack (stack, token)
            2   loop (token not open parenthesis)
                1   concatenate token to postFix
                2   popStack (stack, token)
            3   end loop
        4   elseif (token is operator)
                Test priority of token to token at top of stack
            1   stackTop (stack, topToken)
            2   loop (not emptyStack (stack)
                    AND priority(token) <= priority(topToken) )
                1   popStack (stack, tokenOut)
                2   concatenate tokenOut to postFix
                3   stackTop (stack, topToken)
            3   end loop
            4   pushStack (stack, token)
        5   else
                Character is operand
            1   Concatenate token to postFix.
        6   end if
        7   looper = looper + 1
    5 end loop
        Input formula empty. Pop stack to postFix
    6 loop (not emptyStack (stack))
        1   popStack (stack, token)
        2   concatenate token to postFix
    7 end loop
    8 return postFix
  end inToPostFix
```

Algorithm 4-12   Convert infix to postfix *(continued)*

Algorithm 4-12 Analysis

An infix expression can contain only three objects: a parenthetical set of operators, a variable identifier or a constant, and an operator. If we have an open parenthesis, we put it in the stack. It will then eventually be paired with a closing parenthesis that signals the end of an expression or subexpression. Variables and constants go immediately to the output string. Thus only operators require more analysis.

Given an operator to be processed, the question is, "Should it be pushed into the stack or placed in the output formula?" If the stack is empty, then the operator is pushed into the stack and we continue.

Infix operators have two priorities. The multiply and divide operators have a higher priority (2) than the add and subtract operators (1). Because the opening parenthesis is also pushed into the operator stack, we give it a priority of 0. We check the priority of the new current token against the priority of the token at the top of the stack at Statement 4.4.2 with an algorithm that is not included. This rather straightforward logic requires several compares. It is functionally described as priority for simplicity.

If the new operator's priority is lower than or equal to that of the operator at the top of the stack, then the token at the top of the stack is moved to the output string and we loop to recheck the operator at the top of the stack. If the new operator has a higher priority than the operator at the top of the stack, then it goes into the stack and we move to the next token in the input formula.

Several assumptions in this algorithm need to be understood. First, the input formula has been checked to ensure that it is a valid formula—that is, that its parentheses are matched and it contains only operators and valid operand characters. To keep the algorithm simple, we have also left the overflow testing out of the code. When implemented in a programming language, overflow would certainly need to be checked after Statements 4.2.1 and 4.4.4.

Now, let's use Algorithm 4-12 to convert the following expression.

A * B - (C + D) + E

Table 4-1 traces each step of the conversion.

Evaluating Postfix Expressions

Now let's see how we can use stack postponement to evaluate the postfix expressions we developed earlier. For example, given the expression shown below,

A B C + *

and assuming that A is 2, B is 4, and C is 6, what is the expression value?

The first thing you should notice is that the operands come before the operators. This means that we will have to postpone the use of the operands this time, not the operators. We therefore put them into the stack. When we find an operator, we pop the two operands at the top

Input Buffer	Operator Stack	Output String
A * B – (C + D) + E	Empty	Empty
* B – (C + D) + E	Empty	A
B – (C + D) + E	*	A
– (C + D) + E	*	A B
– (C + D) + E	Empty	A B *
(C + D) + E	–	A B *
C + D) + E	– (	A B *
+ D) + E	– (	A B * C
D) + E	– (+	A B * C
) + E	– (+	A B * C D
+ E	–	A B * C D +
+ E	Empty	A B * C D + –
E	+	A B * C D + –
	+	A B * C D + – E
	Empty	A B * C D + – E +

Table 4-1 Example: convert infix to postfix

of the stack and perform the operation. We then push the value back into the stack to be used later. Figure 4-13 traces the operation of our expression. (Note that we push the operand values into the stack, not the operand names. We therefore use the values in the figure.)

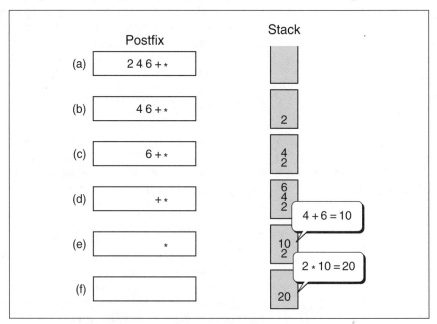

Figure 4-13 Evaluation of postfix expression

When the expression has been completely evaluated, its value is in the stack. See Algorithm 4-13.

```
algorithm postFixEvaluate (val expr <string>)
This algorithm evaluates a postfix expression and returns its
value.
    Pre    a valid expression
    Post   postfix value computed
    Return value of expression
1 exprSize = length of string
2 createStack (stack)
3 index = 0
4 loop (index < exprSize)
   1   if (expr[index] is operand)
      1   pushStack (stack, expr[index])
   2   else
      1   popStack (stack, operand2)
      2   popStack (stack, operand1)
      3   operator = expr[index]
      4   value    = calculate (operand1, operator, operand2)
      5   pushStack (stack, value)
   3   end if
   4   index = index + 1
5 end loop
6 popStack (stack, result)
7 return (result)
end postFixEvaluate
```

Algorithm 4-13   Evaluation of postfix expressions

Algorithm 4-13 Analysis

We have omitted all of the error handling in this algorithm. We assume that the expression is valid and that there is sufficient memory to evaluate it. An implementation would obviously need to guard against these problems.

Given these assumptions, the algorithm is relatively simple. We create a stack and then push operands into the stack until we find an operator. As we find each operator, we pop the two top operands and perform the operation. The result is then pushed into the stack and the next element of the expression examined. At the end, we pop the value from the stack and return it.

Backtracking

Backtracking is another stack use found in applications such as computer gaming, decision analysis, and expert systems. We examine two backtracking applications in this section: goal seeking and the eight queens problem.

Goal Seeking

Figure 4-14 is an example of a goal-seeking application. One way to portray the problem is to lay out the steps in the form of a graph that contains several alternate paths. Only one of the paths in the figure leads to a desired goal. Whereas we can immediately see the correct path when we look at the figure, the computer needs an algorithm to determine the correct path.

We start at node 1 and move right until we hit a branching node, 3. At this point we take the upper path. We continue until we get to node 5, at which time we again take the upper path. When we arrive at node 7 we can go no further. However, we have not yet reached our goal. We must therefore backtrack to node 5 and take the next path. At node 8 we again backtrack to node 5 and take the third path. Once again, at node 11, we must backtrack, this time way back to node 3. As we follow the path from node 12 we finally arrive at node 16, our goal. Note that we did not examine the path that contains nodes 17 and 18.

By now you should have begun to formulate an algorithm in your head. Every time we get to a decision point, we need to remember where it is so that we can get back to it if necessary. When we backtrack, we also want to backtrack to the nearest point before we continue. In this situation we use the LIFO data structure, the stack.

The question now is what to put into the stack. If we only needed to locate the node that contains the goal, we would just put the branch point nodes into the stack. However, when we are finished we want to print out the path that leads to our goal. Therefore, we must

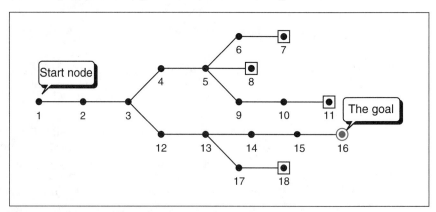

Figure 4-14   Backtracking example

also put the nodes in the valid path into the stack. Because we are putting two things into the stack, we need to be able to tell them apart. We do that with a flag. If the node is in the path, we push a path token. If we are storing a backtracking point, then we set the flag to a backtracking token.

Figure 4-15 contains our stack tracing of the path to our goal. We use B to indicate that we have stored a backtracking node. If there is no token, then the stack contains a path node.

We start by pushing 1, 2, and 3 into the stack. Because 3 is not our goal, we follow the upper path. However, we need to remember that we made a decision here. Therefore, we push the branch point, 12, into a stack with a backtracking token, as shown in Figure 4-15(a). At 5 we must make another decision. Again, we follow the upper path. This time we have two continue points, 8 and 9, that we need to remember. So, we push both into the stack with backtracking tokens. This point is shown in Figure 4-15(b). At 7 we have reached the end of the path without finding our goal. See Figure 4-15(c). To continue we pop the stack until we are at a backtracking point. We then push the backtracking point into the stack as a path node and move on. In our graph, we immediately hit another dead end, as shown in Figure 4-15(d). After backtracking to 9, we continue until we get to the dead end at node 11. See Figure 4-15(e). Once again we backtrack, this time to node 12. Following the path to 13 we push a decision node into the stack (B17) and continue on until we find our goal, at node 16.

We now know the path to our goal, we only need to print it out. The print loop simply pops the stack and prints the path. We ignore any backtracking points left in the stack, such as B17 in Figure 4-15(f). The pseudocode is found in Algorithm 4-14.

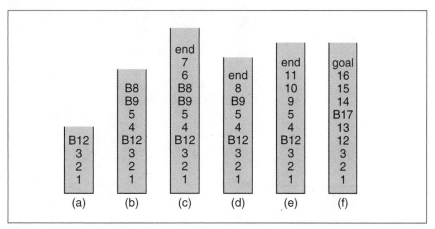

Figure 4-15 Backtracking stack operation

```
algorithm seekGoal (val map <map structure>)
This algorithm determines the path to a desired goal.
   Pre    a graph containing the path
   Post   path printed
1 createStack (stack)
2 pMap = map.start
3 loop (pMap not null AND goalNotFound)
   1  if (pMap is goal)
      1   set goalNotFound to false
   2  else
      1   pushStack (stack, pMap)
      2   if (pMap is a branch point)
         1   loop (more branch points)
            1   create branchPoint node
            2   pushStack (stack, branchPoint)
         2   end loop
      3   end if
      4   advance to next node
   3  end if
4 end loop
5 if (emptyStack (stack))
   1  print (There is no path to your goal)
6 else
   1  print (The path to your goal is:)
   2  loop (not emptyStack (stack))
      1   popStack (stack, pMap)
      2   if (pMap not branchPoint)
         1   print(pMap->nodeName)
      3   end if
   3  end loop
   4  print (End of Path)
7 end if
8 return
end seekGoal
```

Algorithm 4-14   Print path to goal (seekGoal)

Algorithm 4-14 Analysis   This algorithm demonstrates one of the values of pseudocode and why it is popular when discussing algorithms with users. You will not have enough data structure knowledge until Chapter 12 (graphs) to solve this problem on a computer. Yet even though we don't have

a data structure to solve it, we can still develop and understand the algorithm.

Eight Queens Problem

A classic chess problem requires that you place eight queens on the chessboard in such a way that no queen can capture another queen. There are actually several different solutions to this problem. The computer solution to the problem requires that we place a queen on the board and then analyze all of the attack positions to see if there is a queen that could capture the new queen. If there is, then we try another position.[2]

To demonstrate that the program would work, let's analyze how we would place four queens on a 4×4 chessboard. The queen's capture rules and one solution are shown in Figure 4-16.

We can solve this problem using a stack and backtracking logic. Because only one queen can be placed in any row, we begin by placing the first queen in row 1, column 1. This location is then pushed into a stack, giving the position shown in Figure 4-17, Step 1.

After placing a queen in the first row, we look for a position in the second row. Position 2,1 is not possible because the queen in the first row is guarding this location on the vertical. Likewise, position 2,2 is guarded on the diagonal. We therefore place a queen in the third column in row 2 and push this location into the stack. This position is shown in Figure 4-17, Step 2.

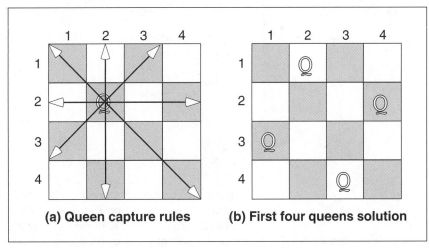

(a) Queen capture rules   **(b) First four queens solution**

Figure 4-16   Four queens solution

---

2. A queen can attack another queen if it is in the same row, in the same column, or on a diagonal.

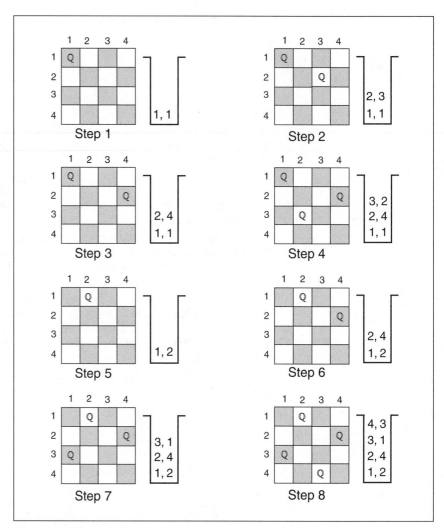

Figure 4-17   Four queens step-by-step solution

We now try to locate a position in row 3, but none are possible. The first column is guarded by the queen in row 1, and the other three positions are guarded by the queen in row 2. At this point we must backtrack to the second row by popping the stack and continue looking for a position for the second-row queen. Because column 4 is not guarded, we place a queen there and push its location into the stack (Step 3 in Figure 4-17).

Looking again at row 3, we see that the first column is still guarded by the queen in row 1 but that we can place a queen in the second column. We do so and push this location into the stack (Step 4 in Figure 4-17).

When we try to place a queen in row 4, however, we find that all positions are guarded. Column 1 is guarded by the queen in row 1 and the queen in row 3. Column 2 is guarded by the queen in row 2 and the queen in row 3. Column 3 is guarded by the queen in row 3, and column 4 is guarded by both the queen in row 1 and the queen in row 2. We therefore backtrack to the queen in row 3 and try to find another place for her. Because the queen in row 2 is guarding both column 3 and column 4, there is no position for a queen in row 3. Once again we backtrack by popping the stack and find that the queen in row 2 has nowhere else to go, so we backtrack to the queen in row 1 and move her to column 2. This position is shown in Figure 4-17, Step 5.

Analyzing row 2, we see that the only possible position for a queen is column 4 because the queen in row 1 is guarding the first three positions. We therefore place the queen in this location and push the location into the stack (Step 6 in Figure 4-17).

Column 1 in the third row is unguarded so we place a queen there (Step 7 in Figure 4-17). Moving to row 4, we find that the first two positions are guarded, the first by the queen in row 3 and the second by all three queens. The third column is unguarded, however, so we can place the fourth queen in this column for a solution to the problem.

Generalizing the solution, we see that we place a queen in a position in a row and then examine all positions in the next row to see if a queen can be placed there. If we can't place a queen in the next row, then we backtrack to the last positioned queen and try to position her in the next column. If there is no room in the next column, then we fall back again. Given that there is a solution[3] this trial and error method works well. A pseudocode solution using our stack abstract data type is shown in Algorithm 4-15.

```
Algorithm queens8 (val boardSize <integer>)
Position chess queens on a game board so that no queen can capture
any other queen.
    Pre    boardSize is number of rows & columns on board
    Post   queens' positions printed
  1 createStack (stack)
  2 set row to 1
```

Algorithm 4-15   Eight queens problem

_____

3. There are no solutions for boards less than 4×4 positions. All boards from 4×4 to 8×8 have at least one solution.

```
3  set col to 0
4  loop (row <= boardSize)
   1   loop (col <= boardSize AND row <= boardSize)
       1   add 1 to col
       2   if (not guarded (row, col))
           1   place queen at board [row][col]
           2   pushStack (stack, [row, col])
           3   add 1 to row
           4   set col to 0
       3   end if
           At end of row. Back up to previous position.
       4   loop (col >= boardSize)
           1   popStack (stack, [row, col])
           2   remove queen at board[row][col]
       5   end loop
   2   end loop
5  end loop
6  printBoard (stack)
7  return
end queens8
```

Algorithm 4-15   Eight queens problem *(continued)*

4-4   EIGHT QUEENS PROBLEM—C++ IMPLEMENTATION

To show how to use the stack abstract data type developed in the next section, we implement the eight queens problem found on page 185.

The program begins by requesting the board size from the user and then creating a stack to store the queens' positions. After creating the stack, the main line calls a function that fills the board with the maximum number of queens for the board size. It then prints the results. The design is shown in Figure 4-18.

As seen in the design, only one other function, guarded, is needed. It is called as each position surrounding the potential placement of a new queen is examined.

When designing a program, it is often necessary to resolve differences between the technical and user perspectives of the problem. In the eight queens program, this difference is seen in the terminology used to place the queens on the board. Users number the rows and columns starting at 1; C++ numbers them starting with 0. To resolve this difference, we added a dummy row and column to the board array, creating a 9 × 9 board. We then ignore row 0 and column 0 in the processing.

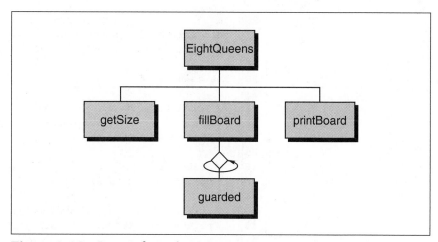

Figure 4-18   Design for eight queens

Main Line Logic

The global declarations and main line code are shown in Program 4-1.

```
 1    /* This program tests the eight queens algorithm. Eight
 2        queens is a classic chess problem in which eight queens
 3        are placed on a standard chessboard in positions such
 4        that no queen can capture another queen.
 5
 6        Written by:
 7        Date:
 8    */
 9    #include <iostream>
10    #include <stdlib>
11    #include "stackADT"
12
13    const int MAX_BOARD = 9;          // row 0 & col 0 not used
14
15    // Structure Declarations
16       struct POSITION
17          {
18           int  row;
19           int  col;
20          };
21
22    // Prototype Declarations
23    int  getSize     (void);
24    bool guarded     (int board[][MAX_BOARD],
25                       int chkRow, int chkCol,
```

Program 4-1   Eight queens main line

```
26                          int boardSize);
27   void fillBoard  (Stack <POSITION>& stack, int boardSize);
28   void printBoard (Stack <POSITION>& stack, int boardSize);
29
30   int main (void)
31   {
32   // Local Definitions
33      int            boardSize;
34      Stack<POSITION> stack;
35
36   // Statements
37      boardSize = getSize ();
38
39      fillBoard  (stack, boardSize);
40      printBoard (stack, boardSize);
41
42      cout << "\nWe hope you enjoyed Eight Queens.\n";
43      return 0;
44   } // main
```

Program 4-1   Eight queens main line *(continued)*

Get Board Size

The function to read the board size from the keyboard is shown in Program 4-2.

```
 1   /* ===================== getSize =====================
 2      Prompt user for a valid board size.
 3         Pre    nothing.
 4         Post   valid board size returned.
 5   */
 6   int getSize (void)
 7   {
 8   // Local Definition
 9      int boardSize;
10
11   // Statements
12      cout << "Welcome to the Eight Queens problem. You may\n"
13           << "select a board size from 4 x 4 up to 8 x 8.\n"
14           << "We will then position a queen in each row of\n"
15           << "the board so no queen may capture any other\n"
16           << "queen. Note: There are no solutions for  \n"
17           << "boards less than 4 x 4.\n";
18      cout << "\nPlease enter the board size: ";
19      cin  >> boardSize;
20
21      while (boardSize < 4 || boardSize > 8)
```

Program 4-2   Eight queens: get board size

```
22        {
23           cout << "The board size must be greater than 3 \n"
24                 << "and less than 9. You entered " << boardSize
25                 << "\nPlease re-enter. Thank you.\a\a\n\n"
26                 << "Your board size: ", boardSize;
27           cin  >> boardSize;
28         } // while
29      return boardSize;
30  } // getSize
```

Program 4-2 Eight queens: get board size *(continued)*

Fill Board

The longest function in the program is fill board. It loops using a trial and error concept to place the maximum number of queens on the board. Each possible position in a row is tested by calling guarded. If the position is good, its location is placed in the stack and the next row analyzed. If it is not good, then the stack is popped and we back up to try another position in the previous row. When all of the rows have a queen, then the problem is solved. The code is shown in Program 4-3.

```
 1  /* ==================== fillBoard =====================
 2     Position chess queens on a game board so that no queen
 3     can capture any other queen.
 4        Pre    boardSize is number of rows & columns on board
 5        Post   queens' positions filled
 6  */
 7  void fillBoard (Stack<POSITION>& stack,
 8                              int          boardSize)
 9  {
10  // Local Definition
11     int   row;
12     int   col;
13     //   on board--0 no queen: 1 queen
14     int   board[MAX_BOARD][MAX_BOARD] = {0};
15
16     POSITION boardPos;
17
18  // Statements
19     row = 1;
20     col = 0;
21
22     while (row <= boardSize)
23        {
24           while (col <= boardSize && row <= boardSize)
```

Program 4-3 Eight queens: fill board

```
25              {
26                col++;
27                if (!guarded(board, row, col, boardSize))
28                   {
29                    board[row][col] = 1;              // Place queen
30                    boardPos.row    = row;
31                    boardPos.col    = col;
32
33                    stack.pushStack(boardPos);
34
35                    row++;
36                    col = 0;
37                   } // if
38              // At end of row. Back up to previous position.
39              while (col >= boardSize)
40                 {
41                  stack.popStack(boardPos);
42                  row             = boardPos.row;
43                  col             = boardPos.col;
44                  board[row][col] = 0;
45                 } // while col
46             } // while col
47          } // while row
48     return;
49  } // fillBoard
```

Program 4-3   Eight queens: fill board *(continued)*

Program 4-3 Analysis

In this backtracking problem, we need to back up to the row and column that contains the last queen we placed on the board. In Statements 30 and 31 we save the row and column in a structure and then pass the position to pushStack in Statement 33.

Examine the *while* in Statement 39 carefully. It is used to backtrack when we could find no positions in a row. We must backtrack when the column becomes greater than or equal to the board size, indicating that we have examined all of the positions in the row and found none that satisfy the requirements. (If we had found an unguarded position, we would have advanced the row in Statement 35.)

Guarded

The logic for guarded is shown in Program 4-4. It uses a brute-force, trial and error method to determine whether the new queen is safe. Note that we only need to test for queens attacking from above. There can be no queens below the current row. If the queen is not safe, we return true—her current position is guarded. If she is safe, we return false.

```
 1    /* ====================== guarded ======================
 2       Checks rows, columns, and diagonals for guarding queens.
 3          Pre     board contains current positions for queens
 4                  chkRow & chkCol are position for new queen
 5                  boardSize is number of rows & cols in board
 6          Post    returns true if guarded; false if not guarded
 7    */
 8    bool guarded (int board[][MAX_BOARD],
 9                      int chkRow,
10                      int chkCol,
11                      int boardSize)
12    {
13    // Local Definitions
14       int row;
15       int col;
16
17    // Statements
18       //  Check current col for a queen
19       col = chkCol;
20       for (row = 1; row <= chkRow; row++)
21           if (board[row][col] == 1)
22              return true;
23
24       //  Check diagonal right-up
25       for (row = chkRow - 1, col = chkCol + 1;
26            row > 0 && col <= boardSize;
27            row--, col++)
28           if (board[row][col] == 1)
29              return true;
30
31       // Check diagonal left-up
32       for (row = chkRow - 1, col = chkCol - 1;
33            row > 0 && col > 0;
34            row--, col--)
35           if (board[row][col] == 1)
36              return true;
37
38       return false;
39    }  // guarded
```

Program 4-4   Eight queens: guarded

Print Board

The print board function simply prints out the positioning of the queens on the board. A sample output is shown at the end of Program 4-5.

```
1   /* ==================== printBoard ======================
2       Print positions of chess queens on a game board.
3          Pre    stack contains positions of queens
4                 boardSize is the number of rows and columns
5          Post   queens' positions printed
6   */
7   void printBoard (Stack<POSITION>& stack,
8                      int             boardSize)
9   {
10  // Local Definitions
11     int col;
12
13     POSITION         boardPos;
14     Stack<POSITION>  outStack;
15
16  // Statements
17     if (stack.emptyStack())
18        {
19         cout << "There are no positions on this board\n";
20         return;
21        } // if
22
23     //  Reverse stack for printing
24     while (!stack.emptyStack ())
25        {
26        stack.popStack (boardPos);
27        outStack.pushStack (boardPos);
28        } // while
29
30     //  Now print board
31     cout << "\nPlace queens in the following positions:\n";
32
33     while (!outStack.emptyStack ())
34        {
35        outStack.popStack (boardPos);
36        cout << "Row "
37             << boardPos.row
38             << "-Col "
39             << boardPos.col
40             << ": ";
41        for (col = 1; col <= boardSize;  col++)
42           {
43             if (boardPos.col == col)
44                cout << " Q |";
45             else
46                cout << "   |";
```

Program 4-5 Eight queens: print board

```
47        } // for
48      cout << "\n";
49    } // while
50  return;
51 } // printBoard
```

```
Results
    Welcome to the Eight Queens problem. You may
    select a board size from 4 x 4 up to 8 x 8.
    We will then position a queen in each row of
    the board so no queen may capture any other
    queen. Note: There are no solutions for
    boards less than 4 x 4.

    Please enter the board size: 4

    Place queens in the following positions:
    Row 1-Col 2:      | Q |   |   |
    Row 2-Col 4:      |   |   | Q |
    Row 3-Col 1:  Q |   |   |   |
    Row 4-Col 3:      |   | Q |   |

    We hope you enjoyed Eight Queens.
```

Program 4-5 Eight queens: print board *(continued)*

4-5   STACK ABSTRACT DATA TYPE IMPLEMENTATION

Each of the algorithms in the previous section used several stack operations. We could write them each time we need them, but this would certainly be an inefficient use of our time. What we need, therefore, is a stack abstract data type (ADT) that we can put in a library and call whenever we need it. In this section we develop a stack ADT that uses a linked list for its implementation structure.

Data Structure

The stack ADT implementation in C++ is straightforward. As we saw in Chapter 3, we use a template to declare the node structure; the major difference is that there is no key in a stack structure.

The stack metadata are declared within the private area of the ADT class. Also, unlike the linked list ADT, the class functions are all public.

One final design point: Because the stack inserts only at the top, we do not need a search algorithm for its ADT. This simplifies the calls to the ADT. The stack ADT structure is shown in Figure 4-19.

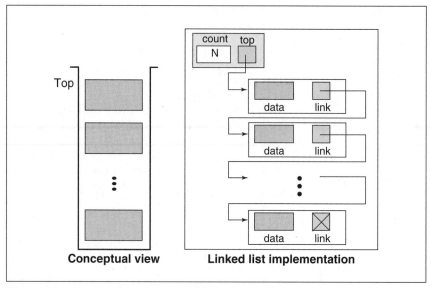

Figure 4-19   Stack ADT structural concepts

Stack ADT Implementation

As previously discussed, it takes more than a data structure to make an abstract data type: There must also be operations that support the stack. We develop the ADT class functions in the sections that follow.

Stack Structure

The stack ADT class is shown in Program 4-6. The node structure uses the structure template declared by the application programmer and a next node pointer.

The class template uses the structure template to declare the stack class. We need only two metadata fields, a top pointer and a count. Both are declared private. As previously noted, all stack functions are public. Their prototype statements are also shown in Program 4-6.

```
 1   /* Stack ADT Type Definitions
 2          Written by:
 3          Date:
 4   */
 5
 6   // Node Declaration
 7
 8      template<class TYPE>
 9      struct Node
10        {
11          TYPE   data;
12          Node<TYPE> *next;
```

Program 4-6   Stack ADT definitions

```
13        };
14
15    // Class Declaration
16       template<class TYPE>
17       class Stack
18       {
19        private:
20            int          count;
21            Node<TYPE> *top;
22
23        public:
24                Stack        (void);
25                ~Stack       (void);
26           bool  pushStack  (TYPE  dataIn);
27           bool  popStack   (TYPE& dataOut);
28           bool  stackTop   (TYPE& dataOut);
29           bool  emptyStack (void);
30           bool  fullStack  (void);
31           int   stackCount (void);
32       };  // class STACK
```

Program 4-6   Stack ADT definitions *(continued)*

Create Stack

Create stack is implemented as the class constructor. It simply initializes the metadata, top to null and count to zero.

Figure 4-8, on page 162, graphically demonstrates the results of creating a stack. The code for the constructor is shown in Program 4-7.

```
 1   /* =============== Constructor ===============
 2      This algorithm creates an empty stack.
 3           Pre   Nothing
 4           Post  Stack created and initialized
 5   */
 6
 7   template<class TYPE>
 8   Stack<TYPE> :: Stack (void)
 9   {
10   // Statements
11      top   = NULL;
12      count = 0;
13   } // Constructor
```

Program 4-7   Create stack

Push Stack

The first thing that we need to do when we **push** data into a stack is to find a node for the data. Finding a node requires that we allocate memory from the heap using *new*. Once the memory is allocated, we simply assign the data to the node and then set next to point to the node currently indicated as the stack top. We also need to add 1 to the stack count field. Figure 4-8, on page 162, shows several pushes into the stack. Program 4-8 contains the implementation code for the push stack algorithm.

```
1   /* =================== pushStack ===================
2      This function pushes an item onto the stack.
3          Pre     dataIn contains data to be inserted
4          Returns true if success; false if overflow
5   */
6
7   template<class TYPE>
8   bool Stack<TYPE> ::  pushStack (TYPE dataIn)
9   {
10  // Local Definitions
11     bool          success;
12     Node<TYPE>  *newPtr;
13
14  // Statements
15     if (!(newPtr =  new Node<TYPE>))
16         success  = false;
17     else
18         {
19         newPtr->data = dataIn;
20         newPtr->next = top;
21         top           = newPtr;
22         count ++;
23         success       = true;
24         } // else
25     return success;
26  } // pushStack
```

Program 4-8   Push stack

Program 4-8 Analysis

The ADT implementation of push differs from a traditional implementation only in its generality. Because it is an abstract data type, it needs to handle any type of data; therefore, we use a class template, as seen in Statement 7.

Because we are writing an ADT, we cannot assume that memory overflow is an error. That decision belongs to the application. All we can do is report status: Either the push was successful or it wasn't. If the memory allocation is successful, which is the normal case, we report that the push was successful by returning true. If dynamic memory is full, we report that the push failed by returning false. The calling function is then responsible for detecting and responding to an overflow.

Pop Stack

As shown in Program 4-9, pop stack returns the data in the node at the top of the stack. It then deletes and recycles the node. After the count is adjusted by subtracting 1, the function returns to the caller. Refer to Figure 4-8, on page 162, for a graphic example of a stack pop in a linked list environment.

```
 1   /* =============== popStack ==============
 2      This function pops the item on the top of the stack.
 3         Pre      dataOut is variable to receive data
 4         Post     popped data in dataOut
 5         Returns true if successful, false if underflow
 6   */
 7
 8   template<class TYPE>
 9   bool Stack<TYPE> :: popStack (TYPE& dataOut)
10   {
11   // Local Definitions
12      Node<TYPE>   *dltPtr;
13      bool          success;
14
15   // Statements
16      if (count == 0)
17           success = false;
18      else
19         {
20          dltPtr  = top;
21          dataOut = top->data;
22          top     = top->next;
23          count--;
24          delete dltPtr;
25          success = true;
26         } // else
27      return success;
28   }  // popStack
```

Program 4-9   Pop stack

Program 4-9 Analysis

The code for pop is rather straightforward. Despite its simplicity, it is interesting to follow the logic when the last node is being deleted. In this case, the result is an empty stack. No special logic is required: The empty stack is created automatically because the last node has a null next pointer, which when assigned to top indicates that the stack is empty.

Stack Top

The stack top function returns the data at the top of the stack without deleting the top node. It allows the user to see what will be deleted when the stack is popped. The logic is virtually identical to that of the pop stack except that the node is not deleted and recycled. The code is shown in Program 4-10.

```
1    /* ==================== stackTop ====================
2       This function retrieves the data from the top of the
3       stack without changing the stack.
4          Pre      dataOut is variable to receive data
5          Post     data in dataOut
6          Returns true if successful, false if underflow
7    */
8
9    template<class TYPE>
10   bool Stack<TYPE> :: stackTop (TYPE& dataOut)
11   {
12   // Local Definitions
13      bool success;
14
15   // Statements
16      if (count == 0)
17         success = false;
18      else
19         {
20          dataOut = top->data;
21          success = true;
22         } // else
23      return success;
24   }  // stackTop
```

Program 4-10   Retrieve stack top

Empty Stack

Because the metadata are private, the application program cannot determine whether there are data in the stack without actually trying to retrieve them. We therefore provide **empty stack,** a function (Program 4-11) that simply reports that the stack has data or that it is empty.

```
1    /* ================= emptyStack =================
2       This function determines if a stack is empty.
3          Pre      nothing
4          Returns true if empty, false if data in stack
5    */
6
7    template<class TYPE>
8    bool Stack<TYPE> :: emptyStack (void)
9    {
10   // Statements
11      return (count == 0);
12   }  // emptyStack
```

Program 4-11   Empty stack

Full Stack

Full stack is one of the most complex of the supporting functions. There is no straightforward way to tell whether the next memory allocation is going to succeed or fail. All we can do is try it. However, by trying to make an allocation, we use up part of the heap. Therefore, after allocating space for a node, we immediately delete it so that space will be available when the program requests memory. The code is shown in Program 4-12.

```
 1  /* =================== fullStack ===================
 2     This function determines if a stack is full.
 3     Full is defined as heap full.
 4          Pre     nothing
 5          Returns true if heap full, false if room
 6  */
 7
 8  template<class TYPE>
 9  bool Stack <TYPE> :: fullStack (void)
10  {
11  // Local Definitions
12     Node<TYPE>   *temp;
13
14  // Statements
15     temp = new Node<TYPE>;
16     if (temp != NULL)
17        {
18         delete  temp;
19         return false;
20        } // if
21
22     // allocation failed
23     return true;
24  } // fullStack
```

Program 4-12   Full stack

Stack Count

Stack count returns the number of items in the stack. Because this count is stored in the class ADT, we do not need to traverse the stack to determine how many items are currently in it. We simply return the count, as shown in Program 4-13.

```
 1  /* =================== stackCount ===================
 2     Returns the number of elements in the stack.
 3          Pre    nothing
 4          Post   count returned
 5  */
```

Program 4-13   Stack count

```
 6
 7    template<class TYPE>
 8    int Stack <TYPE> :: stackCount(void)
 9    {
10    // Statements
11       return count;
12    } //  stackCount
```

Program 4-13   Stack count *(continued)*

Destroy Stack

Destroy stack is implemented as the stack class destructor. To destroy the stack, we must first delete any data still in it so that its memory is available for reuse. This task is done with a *while* loop. The code is shown in Program 4-14.

```
 1    /* =============== Destructor  ==============
 2       This function releases all nodes to the heap.
 3          Pre    stack being destroyed
 4          Post   stack and data deleted
 5    */
 6
 7    template<class TYPE>
 8    Stack<TYPE> :: ~Stack (void)
 9    {
10    // Local Definitions
11       Node<TYPE>  *temp;
12
13    // Statements
14       //  Delete all nodes in stack
15       while (top != NULL)
16          {
17           temp = top;
18           top  = top->next;
19           delete temp;
20          } //  while
21    } // Destructor
```

Program 4-14   Destroy stack

4-6   STACK ADT—ARRAY IMPLEMENTATION

If a stack's maximum size can be calculated before the program is written, then an array implementation of a stack is more efficient than the dynamic implementation using a linked list. In addition, an array stack is a more easily understood and natural picture of a stack.

When implementing a stack in an array, the base is found at the first stack element, index 0 in C++. The top then moves up and down the array as data are inserted and deleted. To push an element into the stack, we add 1 to top and use it as the array index for the new data. To pop an element from the stack we copy the data at index location top and then subtract 1 from top. One additional metadata element is required, the maximum number of elements in the stack. The structure for the array implementation with a maximum size of 5 elements is shown in Figure 4-20.

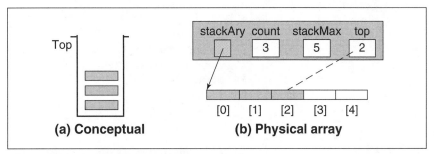

Figure 4-20   Stack array implementation

In this section we redesign the eight basic stack algorithms using an array rather than a linked list implementation.

Array Data Structure

There are three differences in the data structure for an array implementation: First, the stack top is an index rather than a pointer; second, we need to store the maximum number of elements allowed in the stack; and third, we don't need next fields. Because the stack is a LIFO structure, each element has a physical adjacency to its predecessor. The array class implementation declaration is shown in Algorithm 4-16.

```
Stack Definitions for Array Implementation

stack
    stackAry   <pointer to array of dataType>
    count      <integer>
    stackMax   <integer>
    top        <index>
end stack
```

Algorithm 4-16   Stack array definition

Although the data structure is significantly different, the array implementation of a stack requires the same basic algorithms used in the linked list implementation. The class ADT declaration is shown in Program 4-15. The algorithms are developed in the sections that follow.

```
 1  /* Stack ADT Type Definitions. This header file creates an
 2     array implementation of a stack. It can be substituted for
 3     the linked list implementation (stackADT.h) with no
 4     changes to the application program other than possibly
 5     assigning an array size other than the default (100).
 6
 7        Written by:
 8        Date:
 9  */
10
11  // NODE Declaration
12  template<class TYPE>
13  struct NODE
14  {
15    TYPE   data;
16  }; // NODE
17
18  // Class Declaration
19
20  template<class TYPE>
21  class Stack
22  {
23   private:
24
25     NODE<TYPE>   *stackAry;
26     int          count;
27     int           stackMax;
28     int            top;
29
30   public:
31         Stack      (int size = 100);
32        ~Stack      (void);
33    bool  pushStack  (TYPE  dataIn);
34    bool  popStack   (TYPE& dataOut);
35    bool  stackTop   (TYPE& dataOut);
36    bool  emptyStack (void);
37    bool  fullStack  (void);
38    int   stackCount (void);
39  } ; // class Stack
```

Program 4-15   Data structure for stack array

Create Stack Array

The class implementation of **create stack** is the class constructor. For flexibility, we create a default stack size of 100. The application program can override the default by specifying a new stack size when the class is defined as shown below. The following example defines the class stack first with the default of 100 elements and then as an array of 200 elements.

```
stack<TYPE> myStack;
stack<TYPE> myStack (200);
```

The code for create stack constructor is shown in Program 4-16.

```
1   /* =============== Constructor ===============
2      This algorithm creates an empty stack.
3          Pre    Array size passed or defaulted
4          Post   Array allocated in memory
5                 -or- NULL if overflow.
6   */
7
8   template<class TYPE>
9   Stack<TYPE> :: Stack (int size)
10  {
11  // Statements
12     // Verify memory available
13     stackMax =  size;
14     stackAry = new NODE<TYPE> [stackMax];
15     if (!stackAry)
16        {
17          cout << "\a\aMemory Overflow in Create Stack\n";
18          abort ();
19        } // Heap overflow
20     count    =  0;
21     top      = -1;
22  } // Constructor
```

Program 4-16   Create stack constructor

Program 4-16 Analysis

First, note that the default class size is actually coded in Program 4-15. The second major point to remember is that the metadata are stored as private data in the class.

There is only one possible error in the create stack constructor: If there is not enough room in dynamic memory for the stack array, we must abort the program. In Statement 14, we allocate memory for the stack. If this allocation fails, we display an error message and abort the program.

Because the newly created stack is by definition empty, we set the stack top index to -1. We must use -1 as the value for a null stack because a stack with only one item in it will have a stack top of 0.

Push Stack Array

The logic for the array implementation of push stack is very simple. We first test for overflow by comparing the count of the elements in the stack with the maximum stack size. If the stack is full, we return false indicating that the push failed. If there is room, we copy the data to the stack, increase the top index and stack count, and return 1 for success. The function code is shown in Program 4-17.

```
 1   /* ================= pushStack =================
 2      This function pushes an item onto the stack.
 3         Pre     dataIn contains data to be pushed
 4         Post    data pushed into array
 5         Returns true if success; false if overflow
 6   */
 7
 8   template<class TYPE>
 9   bool Stack<TYPE> ::  pushStack (TYPE dataIn)
10   {
11   // Statements
12      if (count >= stackMax)
13         return false;
14      count++;
15      top++;
16      stackAry[top].data = dataIn;
17      return true;
18   }  //  pushStack
```

Program 4-17   Push stack array

Pop Stack Array

The array implementation of pop stack is also quite simple and parallels the linked list implementation. The code is shown in Program 4-18.

```
 1   /* ==================== popStack ====================
 2      This function pops the item on the top of the stack.
 3         Pre     dataOut is variable to receive data
 4         Post    dataOut contains top data; top adjusted
 5         Returns true if successful; false if overflow
 6   */
 7
 8   template<class TYPE>
 9   bool Stack<TYPE> :: popStack (TYPE& dataOut)
10   {
11   // Local Definitions
12      bool success;
13
14   // Statements
15      if (count == 0)
16         success = false;
17      else
```

Program 4-18   Pop stack array

```
18      {
19        dataOut = stackAry[top].data;
20        top--;
21        count--;
22        success = true;
23        } // else
24    return success;
25  } // popStack
```

Program 4-18 Pop stack array *(continued)*

Program 4-18 Analysis

When working with data structures, you should always test what happens when you delete the only item in the structure. For our array stack, we need to ensure that when the only item in the stack is deleted, the stack is properly set to a null status. We have defined a null stack as a stack with a top index of –1. If there is only one element in the stack, then the top is 0. Subtracting 1 from 0 gives us –1, our designated flag for a null stack.

Stack Top Array

Stack top is a simple function. We test for data in the stack and return the data pointer in the top element if the stack is not empty or a null pointer if it is empty. The code is shown in Program 4-19.

```
1   /* ==================== stackTop ====================
2      This function retrieves the data from the top of the
3      stack without changing the stack.
4          Pre      dataOut is variable to receive data
5          Post     dataOut contains data at top of stack
6          Returns true if successful; false if stack empty
7   */
8
9   template<class TYPE>
10  bool Stack<TYPE> :: stackTop (TYPE& dataOut)
11  {
12  // Local Definitions
13     bool success;
14
15  // Statements
16     if (count == 0)
17        success = false;
18     else
19        {
20         dataOut = stackAry[top].data;
21         success = true;
22        } // else
23     return success;
24  } // stackTop
```

Program 4-19 Retrieve stack array top

Empty Stack Array

Empty stack logic is the same regardless of the implementation structure. It simply tests the stack count in the head structure and returns true if it is 0 or false if it is not. The code is shown in Program 4-20.

```
 1   /* ================== emptyStack ==================
 2       This function determines if a stack is empty.
 3          Pre      nothing
 4          Returns true if empty; 0 if data in stack
 5   */
 6
 7    template<class TYPE>
 8    bool Stack<TYPE> :: emptyStack (void)
 9    {
10   // Statements
11      return (count == 0);
12   } // emptyStack
```

Program 4-20   Empty stack

Full Stack Array

To determine whether the stack is full we simply compare the count with the maximum number of elements allocated for the array. If they are equal, the stack is full; if not, the stack has room for more data. The code is shown in Program 4-21.

```
 1   /* ================= fullStack =================
 2       This function determines if a stack is full.
 3       Full is defined as heap full.
 4          Pre      nothing
 5          Returns true if heap full; false if not
 6   */
 7
 8   template<class TYPE>
 9   bool Stack <TYPE> :: fullStack (void)
10   {
11   // Statements
12      return (count == stackMax);
13   } // fullStack
```

Program 4-21   Full stack

Stack Count Array

Like empty stack, the logic for stack count is identical in all implementations. We simply return the stack count found in the stack head structure. The code is shown in Program 4-22.

```
 1   /* ================= stackCount =================
 2      Returns the number of elements in the stack.
 3         Pre    nothing
 4         Post   count returned
 5   */
 6
 7   template<class TYPE>
 8   int Stack <TYPE> :: stackCount(void)
 9   {
10   // Statements
11      return count;
12   } //  stackCount
```

Program 4-22   Stack count

Destroy Stack Array

To destroy a stack implemented using an array, we must delete the array structure. The code is shown in Program 4-23.

```
 1   /* =============== Destructor  ==============
 2      This function deletes the array stack.
 3         Pre   stack being deleted
 4         Post  stack has been deleted
 5   */
 6
 7   template<class TYPE>
 8   Stack<TYPE> :: ~Stack (void)
 9   {
10   // Statements
11      delete [] stackAry;
12      stackAry = NULL;
13      count    = 0;
14      stackMax = 0;
15      top      = -1;
16   } // destroyStack
```

Program 4-23   Destroy stack

4-7   SUMMARY

- A stack is a linear list in which all additions are restricted to one end, called the top. A stack is also called a LIFO list.
- A stack is a list in descending chronological sequence.
- We have defined eight operations for a stack: create stack, push stack, pop stack, stack top, empty stack, full stack, stack count, and destroy stack.
- Create stack initializes the stack metadata.

- Push adds an item to the top of the stack. After the push, the new item becomes the top.
- Each push must ensure that there is room for the new item. If there is no room, the stack is in an overflow state.
- Pop removes the item at the top of the stack. After the pop, the next item, if any, becomes the top.
- Each pop must ensure that there is at least one item in the stack. If there is not at least one item, the stack is in an underflow state.
- The retrieve stack operation only copies the item at the top of the stack.
- Each retrieve must ensure that there is at least one item in the stack. If there is not at least one item, the stack is in an underflow state.
- Empty stack determines whether the stack is empty and returns a Boolean true if it is.
- Full stack determines whether there is room for at least one more item and returns a Boolean false if there is.
- Stack count returns the number of elements currently in the stack.
- Destroy stack releases all allocated data memory to dynamic memory.
- One of the applications of a stack is reversing data. The nature of a stack (last in, first out) allows us to push items into a stack and pop them in reverse order.
- Stacks are commonly used to parse data. We looked at an application to parse matching parentheses in a source program.
- Stacks can be used to postpone the use of data. Whenever an action must be postponed, we can use a stack. Two applications were covered: infix to postfix transformation and evaluation of postfix expressions.
- Stacks can be used to backtrack steps in a path. We looked at determining a path to a goal and the eight queens problem as examples of stack backtracking.

4-8   PRACTICE SETS

Exercises

1. Imagine we have two empty stacks of integers, s1 and s2. Draw a picture of each stack after the following operations:

```
pushStack  (s1, 3);
pushStack  (s1, 5);
pushStack  (s1, 7);
pushStack  (s1, 9);
pushStack  (s1, 11);
pushStack  (s1, 13);
while (!emptyStack (s1))
    {
      popStack  (s1, x);
      pushStack (s2, x);
    } // while
```

2. Imagine we have two empty stacks of integers, s1 and s2. Draw a picture of each stack after the following operations:

```
pushStack (s1, 3);
pushStack (s1, 5);
pushStack (s1, 7);
```

```
pushStack (s1, 9);
pushStack (s1, 11);
pushStack (s1, 13);
while (!emptyStack (s1))
    {
      popStack   (s1, x);
      popStack   (s1, x);
      pushStack  (s2, x);
    } // while
```

3. Using manual transformation, write the following infix expressions in their postfix and prefix forms:

   a. D − B + C

   b. A * B + C * D

   c. (A + B) * C − D * F + C

   d. (A − 2 * (B + C) − D * E) * F

4. Using manual transformation, change the following postfix or prefix expressions to infix:

   a. A B * C − D +

   b. A B C + * D −

   c. + − * A B C D

   d. − * A + B C D

5. If the values of A, B, C, and D are 2, 3, 4, and 5, respectively, manually calculate the value of the following postfix expressions:

   a. A B * C − D +

   b. A B C + * D −

6. If the values of A, B, C, and D are 2, 3, 4, and 5, respectively, manually calculate the value of the following prefix expressions:

   a. + − * A B C D

   b. − * A + B C D

7. Change the following infix expressions to postfix expressions using the algorithmic method (a stack):

   a. D − B + C

   b. A * B + C * D

   c. (A + B) * C − D * F + C

   d. (A − 2) * (B + C − D * E) * F

8. Determine the value of the following postfix expressions when the variables have the following values: A is 2, B is 3, C is 4, and D is 5.

   a. A B * C − D +

   b. A B C + * D −

Problems

9. Write a program to implement Algorithm 4-9, "Reverse a number series," on page 169. Test your program with the number series 1, 3, 5, 7, 9, 2, 4, 6, 8.

10. Write a program to implement Algorithm 4-10, "Convert decimal to binary," on page 170. Test it with the numbers 19, 127, and 255.

11. Write a function that changes a decimal number to an octal number.

12. Write a function that changes a decimal number to a hexadecimal number. Hint: If the remainder is 10, 11, 12, 13, 14, or 15, print A, B, C, D, E, or F, respectively.

13. Write a program to implement Algorithm 4-11, "Parse parentheses," on page 172, matching braces rather than parentheses. In your implementation, push the line number into the stack rather than the opening brace. When an error occurs, print the line number for the unmatched open brace or unmatched close brace. Test your program by running the source code through itself (there should be no errors) and then test it with the following small program:

```
Test brace errors.
} line 2 closing brace is not paired

No braces.
    {opening brace is paired on same line}

No braces.
    {opening brace paired later

  No braces.
  } Closing brace paired two lines up.

{{{ Line 9. Three braces--only two paired.
  } First closing brace

  } Second closing brace.
End of program. One opening brace left.
```

14. Write a program that implements the infix to postfix notation (see Algorithm 4-12, "Convert infix to postfix," on page 177). The program should read an infix string consisting of single alphabetic characters for variables, parentheses, and the +, −, *, and / operators; call the conversion algorithm; and then print the resulting postfix expression. After transforming an algorithm, it should loop and convert another infix string. To test your program, transform the expressions in Exercise 3, on page 211, with your program.

15. Change Problem 14 to allow multicharacter variable identifiers and numeric constants as shown in the following expression:

```
num + 18 * factor
```

16. Write a program to implement the postfix evaluation (see Algorithm 4-13, "Evaluation of postfix expressions," on page 181). The program should read a postfix string consisting of only multidigit numeric data and the +, −, *, and / operators, call the evaluation algorithm, and then print the result. After each evaluation, it should loop and process another evaluation. Evaluate the following expressions with your program:

```
25 7 * 14 − 6 +
1 24 3 + * 41 −
2 37 4 + * 15 −
```

17. One of the applications of a stack is to backtrack—that is, to retrace your steps. As an example, imagine we want to read a list of items and each time we read a negative number, we must backtrack and print the five numbers that come before the negative number and then discard the negative number.

We can use a stack to solve this problem. We read the numbers and push them into the stack (without printing them) until we read a negative number. At this time, we stop reading and pop five items from the stack and print them. If there are fewer than five items in the stack, we print an error message and stop the program.

After printing the five items, we resume reading data and placing them in the stack. When the end of the file is detected, we print a message and the items remaining in the stack.

Write a program that prints the five numbers preceding a negative number as described. If there are fewer than five numbers, print the numbers that exist. Test your program with the following data:

1 2 3 4 5 –1 1 2 3 4 5 6 7 8 9 10 –2 11 12 –3 1 2 3 4 5

18. Write a function called copyStack that copies the contents of one stack into another. The function must have two arguments of type stack, one for the source stack and one for the destination stack. The order of the stacks must be identical. Hint: Use a temporary stack to preserve the order.

19. Write a new ADT function, `catStack`, that concatenates the contents of one stack on top of another. Test your function by writing a program that uses the ADT to create two stacks and prints them. It should then concatenate the stacks and print the resulting stack.

20. A palindrome is a string that can be read backward and forward with the same result. For example, the following is a palindrome:

Able was I ere I saw Elba.

Write a function to test if a string is a palindrome using a stack. You can push characters in the stack one by one. When you reach the end of the string, you can pop the characters and form a new string. If the two strings are exactly the same, the string is a palindrome. Note: Palindromes ignore spacing, punctuation, and capitalization. Test your program with the following test cases:

Go dog
Madam, I'm Adam
Madam, I'm not a palindrome

21. Write a program that reads a text file, one line at a time, and prints the line as it was read and then prints the line with its text reversed. Print a blank line after each reversed line.

22. Write the pseudocode for an algorithm that reverses the contents of a stack (the top and bottom elements exchange positions, the second and the element just before the bottom exchange positions, and so forth until the entire stack is reversed). Hint: Use temporary stacks.

23. Write a function to check whether the contents of two stacks are identical. Neither stack should be changed. You will need to write a function that prints the contents of a stack to verify that your function works.

Projects

24. Given a square matrix, write a program that determines the number of white blocks and total number of squares in each of the white blocks. By definition, the outside boundaries of the matrix must be shaded. A block of white squares consists of all of the white squares whose side boundaries are next to another white square. White squares that touch only at a diagonal point are not adjacent.

In Figure 4-21, we have numbered the white blocks. Block 1 contains three squares, and block 4 contains nine squares. Note that block 3 contains only one square. It touches block 1 only on the diagonal.

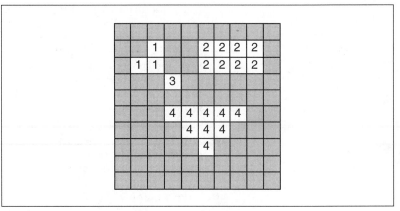

Figure 4-21   Project 24: find white blocks

Obtain the square definition from a text file. The file should contain a square matrix composed of zeros for shaded squares and nonzeros for white squares. The input for Figure 4-21 is shown below. The matrix should be allocated from dynamic memory.

```
0 0 0 0 0 0 0 0 0 0
0 0 1 0 0 2 2 2 2 0
0 1 1 0 0 2 2 2 2 0
0 0 0 3 0 0 0 0 0 0
0 0 0 0 0 0 0 0 0 0
0 0 0 4 4 4 4 4 0 0
0 0 0 0 4 4 4 0 0 0
0 0 0 0 0 4 0 0 0 0
0 0 0 0 0 0 0 0 0 0
0 0 0 0 0 0 0 0 0 0
```

At the end of the program, print a report showing the number of white blocks and the number of squares in each.

25. Write a program that simulates a mouse in a maze. The program must print the path taken by the mouse from the starting point to the final point, including all spots that have been visited and backtracked. Thus, if a spot is visited two times, it must be printed two times; if it is visited three times, it must be printed three times.

The maze is shown in Figure 4-22. The entrance spot, where the mouse starts its journey, will be chosen by the user who runs the program. It can be changed each time.

A two-dimensional array can be used as a supporting data structure to store the maze. Each element of the array can be black or white. A black element is a square that the mouse cannot enter. A white element is a square that can be used by the mouse. In the array, a black element can be represented by a 1 and a white element by a 0.

When the mouse is traversing the maze, it visits the elements one by one. In other words, the mouse does not consider the maze as an array of elements; at each moment of its journey, it is only in one element. Let's

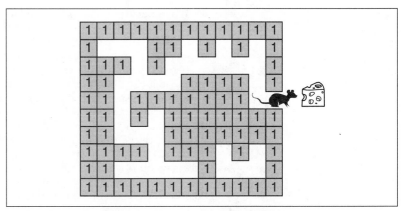

Figure 4-22 The mouse maze for Project 25.

call this element the `currentSpot`. It can be represented by a structure of two integer fields. The first field is the row and the second is the column coordinate of the spot in the maze. For example, the exit in Figure 4-22 is at (5, 12)—that is, row 5, column 12.

The program begins by creating the maze. It then initializes the exit spot and prompts the user for the coordinates of the entrance spot. The program must be robust. If the user enters coordinates of a black spot, the program must request new coordinates until a white spot is entered. The mouse starts from the entrance spot and tries to reach the exit spot and its reward. Note, however, that some start positions do not lead to the exit.

As the mouse progresses through its journey, print its path. As it enters a spot, the program determines the class of that spot. The class of a spot can be one of the following:

a. Continuing. A spot is a continuing spot if one and only one of the neighbors (excluding the last spot) is a white spot. In other words, the mouse has only one choice.

b. Intersection. A spot is an intersection spot if two or more of the neighbors (excluding the last spot) is a white spot. In other words, the mouse has two or more choices.

c. Dead end. A spot is a dead-end spot if none of the neighbors (excluding the last spot) is a white spot. In other words, the mouse has no spot to choose. It must backtrack.

d. Exit. A spot is an exit spot if the mouse can get out of the maze. When the mouse finds an exit, it is free and receives a piece of cheese for a reward.

To solve this problem, you need two stacks. The first stack, the visited stack, contains the path the mouse is following. Whenever the mouse arrives at a spot, it first checks to see whether it is an exit. If not, its location is placed in the stack. This stack is used if the mouse hits a dead end and must backtrack. Whenever the mouse backtracks to the last decision point, also print the backtrack path.

When the mouse enters an intersection, the alternatives are placed in a second stack. This decision point is also marked by a special decision token that is placed in the visited stack. The decision token has coordinates of (–1, –1). To select a path, an alternative is then popped from the alternatives stack and the mouse continues on its path.

While backtracking, if the mouse hits a decision token, the token is discarded and the next alternative is selected from the alternatives stack. At this point print an asterisk (*) next to the location to show that the next alternative path is being selected.

If the mouse arrives at a dead end and both stacks are empty, the mouse is locked in a portion of the maze with no exit. In this case, print a trapped message and terminate the search for an exit.

After each trial, regardless of the outcome, the user should be given the opportunity to stop or continue.

26. Write a program that implements the stack ADT described in Section 4-5, "Stack ADT Implementation," on page 195. To test your implementation, write a menu-driven user interface to test each of the operations in the ADT. For the test, use integer data as described below. Error conditions should be printed as a part of the test results. A suggested menu is shown below.

```
A. Push data into stack
B. Pop and print data
C. Print data at top of stack
D. Print entire stack (top to base)
E. Print stack status: Empty
F. Print stack status: Full
G. Print number of elements in stack
H. Destroy stack and quit
```

Test your program with the following test case. You may include additional test cases. The menu operation is shown at the end of the test.

a. Print stack status: Empty [E]
b. Pop and print data (should return error) [B]
c. Push data into stack: 1 [A]
d. Push data into stack: 2 [A]
e. Print stack status: Empty [E]
f. Print stack status: Full [F]
g. Print data at top of stack [C]
h. Print entire stack (top to base) [D]
i. Print number of elements in stack [G]
j. Pop and print data [B]
k. Pop and print data [B]
l. Pop and print data (should return empty) [B]
m. Push data into stack: 3 [A]
n. Print data at top of stack [C]
o. Destroy stack and quit [H]

27. Write a program to find all solutions to the eight queens problem. Your program will need to be able to handle a search for a configuration that has no solution.

28. Modify the user interface in Project 26 to manipulate two different stacks with two different types of data. The first stack should contain integer data. The second stack should contain alphabetic data. In addition to the test data in Project 26, create a set of alphabetic test data that tests the alphabetic stack with a similar set of operations.

Queues

5

A queue is a linear list in which data can only be inserted at one end, called the **rear,** and deleted from the other end, called the **front.** These restrictions ensure that the data are processed through the queue in the order in which they are received. In other words, a queue is a **first in–first out (FIFO)** structure.

A queue is the same as a line. In fact, if you were in England, you would not get into a line, you would get into a queue. A line of people waiting for the bus in a bus station is a queue, a list of calls put on hold to be answered by a telephone operator is a queue, and a list of waiting jobs to be processed by a computer is a queue.

Figure 5-1 shows two representations of a queue, one a queue of people and the other a computer queue. Both people and data enter the queue at the rear and progress through the queue until they arrive at the front. Once they are at the front of the queue, they leave the queue and are served.

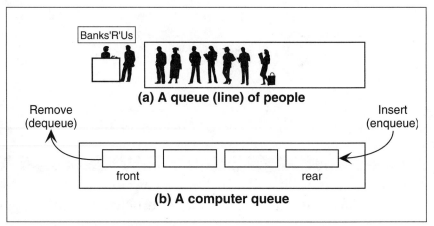

Figure 5-1   The queue concept

5-1   QUEUE OPERATIONS

There are four basic queue operations. Data can be inserted at the rear, deleted from the front, retrieved from the front, and retrieved from the rear. Although there are many similarities between stacks and queues, one significant structural difference is that the queue implementation needs to keep track of the front and the rear of the queue, whereas the stack only needs to worry about one end, the top.

Note

> A queue is a linear list in which data can be inserted at one end, called the rear, and deleted from the other end, called the front. It is a first in–first out (FIFO) data structure.

Enqueue

The queue insert is known as **enqueue.** After the data have been inserted into the queue, the new element becomes the rear. As we saw with stacks, the only potential problem with enqueue is running out of room for the data. If there is not enough room for another element in the queue, the queue is in an overflow state.

Note

> Enqueue inserts an element at the rear of the queue.

Figure 5-2 shows the enqueue operation.

Dequeue

The queue delete operation is known as **dequeue.** The data at the front of the queue are returned to the user and removed from the queue. If there are no data in the queue when a dequeue is attempted, the queue is in an underflow state.

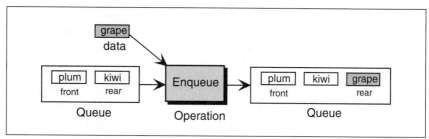

Figure 5-2   Enqueue

Note

> Dequeue deletes an element at the front of the queue.

The dequeue operation is shown in Figure 5-3.

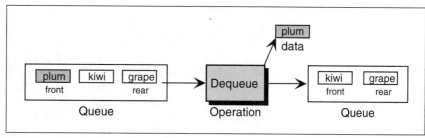

Figure 5-3   Dequeue

Queue Front

Data at the front of the queue can be examined with **queue front.** It returns the data at the front of the queue without changing the contents of the queue. If there are no data in the queue, then the queue is in an underflow state.

Note

> Queue front examines the element at the front of the queue.

The queue front operation is shown in Figure 5-4.

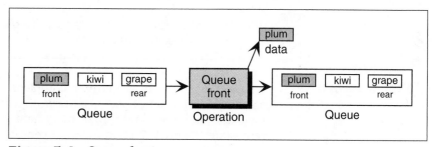

Figure 5-4   Queue front

Queue Rear

A parallel operation to queue front examines the data at the rear of the queue. It is known as **queue rear.** As with queue front, if there are no data in the queue, the queue is in an underflow state.

Note

> Queue rear examines the element at the rear of the queue.

The queue rear operation is shown in Figure 5-5.

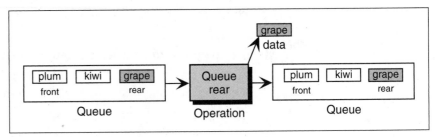

Figure 5-5 Queue rear

Queue Example

Figure 5-6 traces these four operations in an example. We start with an empty queue and enqueue green and blue. At this point, the queue contains two entries. We then dequeue, which removes the entry at the front of the queue, leaving blue as the only entry. After enqueuing red, a queue front operation returns blue to the caller but leaves it at the front of the queue. The next operation, queue rear, returns red but leaves it in the queue. A dequeue then removes blue, leaving red as the only entry in the queue. Finally, we dequeue red, which results in an empty queue.

5-2 QUEUE LINKED LIST DESIGN

As with a stack, we implement our queue as a linked list in dynamic memory. As we have stressed before, the actual implementation may be different. For example, at the end of the chapter we implement two different queue abstract data types, one for the linked list and one for an array structure.

Note

> For the linked list implementation of a queue, we use two types of structures: a head and a node.

Data Structure

We need two different structures to implement the queue, a queue head structure and a data node structure. After it is created, the queue will have one head node and zero or more data nodes, depending on its current state. Figure 5-7 shows the conceptual and physical implementations for our queue structure.

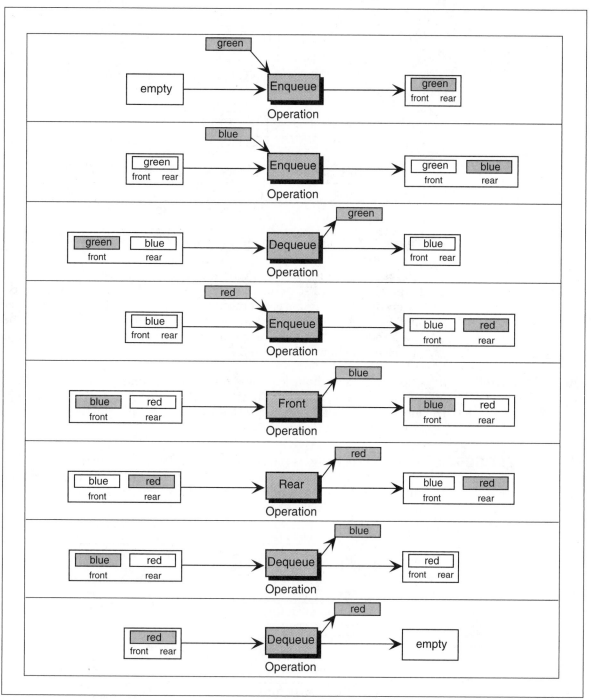

Figure 5-6 Queue example

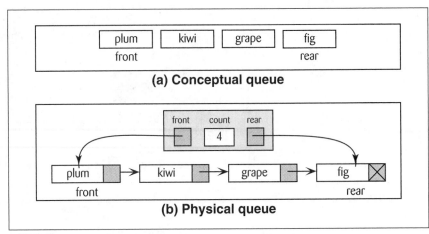

Figure 5-7   Conceptual and physical queue implementations

Queue Head

The queue requires two pointers and a count. These fields are stored in the **queue head** structure. Other queue attributes, such as the maximum number of items ever present in the queue and the total number that have been processed through the queue, could be stored in the head node if such data were relevant to an application. The queue head structure is shown in Figure 5-8.

Queue Data Node

The **queue data node** contains the user data and a link field pointing to the next node, if any. These nodes are stored in the heap and are inserted and deleted as requested by the using program. Its structure is also shown in Figure 5-8.

Queue Algorithms

The queue operations parallel those seen for a stack, with the addition of an algorithm to look at the data at the rear of the queue. We define these operations here and in the sections that follow. The four basic queue operations are shown in Figure 5-9.

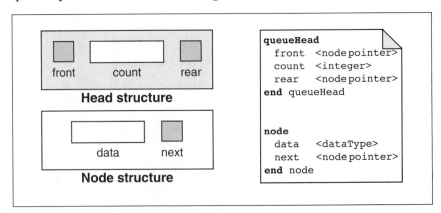

Figure 5-8   Queue data structure

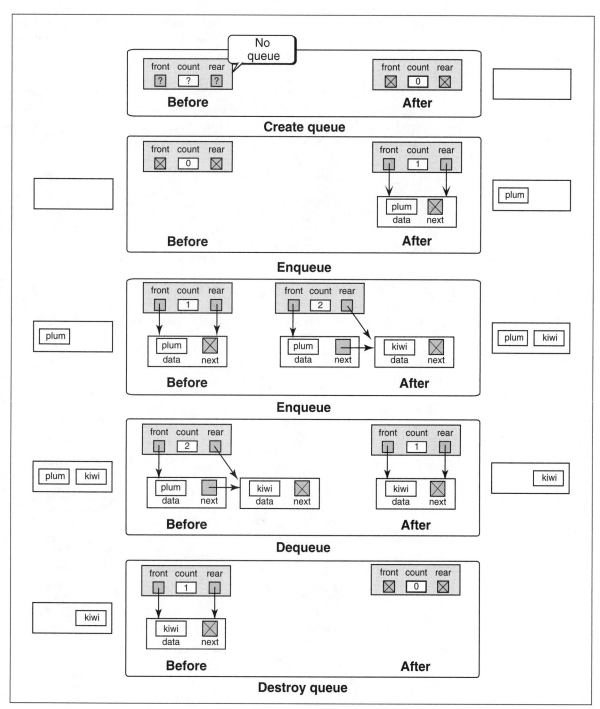

Figure 5-9 Basic queue functions

Create Queue

The **create queue** operation is rather simple. All we have to do is set the metadata pointers to null and the count to 0. The pseudocode for create queue is shown in Algorithm 5-1.

```
algorithm createQueue (ref queue <metadata>)
    Initializes the metadata elements of a queue structure.
    Pre    queue is a metadata structure
    Post   metadata elements have been initialized
  1 queue.front  = null
  2 queue.rear   = null
  3 queue.count  = 0
end createQueue
```

Algorithm 5-1   Create queue

Enqueue

The **enqueue** is a little more complex than inserting data into a stack. To develop the insertion algorithm, we need to analyze three different queue conditions: (1) insertion into an empty queue, (2) insertion into a queue with data, and (3) insertion into a queue when there is no memory left in the heap. The first two of these operations are shown in Figure 5-10.

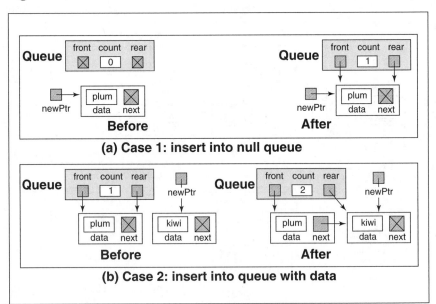

Figure 5-10   Enqueue example

When we insert data into an empty queue, the queue's front and rear pointers must both be set to point to the new node. When we insert data into a queue with data in it, we must point both the link field in the last node and the rear pointer to the new node. In either case, we must also check for overflow. If the insert was successful, we return a Boolean true; if there is no memory left for another node, we return a Boolean false. The pseudocode is shown in Algorithm 5-2.

```
algorithm enqueue  (ref queue    <metadata>,
                    val dataIn    <dataType>)
This algorithm inserts data into a queue.
     Pre    queue is a metadata structure
     Post   dataIn has been inserted
     Return true if successful, false if overflow
  1  if (queue full)
     1    return false
  2  end if
  3  allocate (newPtr)
  4  newPtr->data  = dataIn
  5  newPtr->next  = null pointer
  6  if (queue.count zero)
     Inserting into null queue
     1    queue.front = newPtr
  7  else
     Insert data and adjust metadata
     1    queue.rear->next = newPtr
  8  end if
  9  queue.rear   = newPtr
 10  queue.count  = queue.count + 1
 11  return true
end enqueue
```

Algorithm 5-2   Insert data into queue

Algorithm 5-2 Analysis There are three ways to test for an insertion into an empty queue: We can check either the front or the rear pointer for a null value or we can check the count for 0. We chose to check the count for 0 (see Statement 6). As an alternate method, we could have called the empty queue algorithm, but that involves extra overhead.

Dequeue

Although **dequeue** is also a little more complex than deleting data from a stack, it starts out much the same. We must first ensure that the

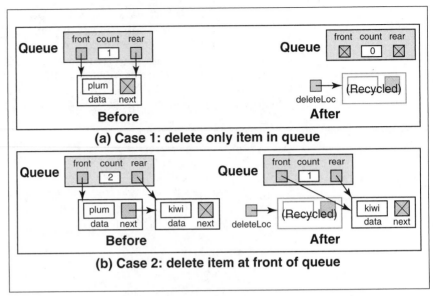

Figure 5-11   Dequeue examples

queue contains data. If the queue is empty, we have underflow and we return false, indicating that the delete was not successful.

Given that there are data to be deleted, we pass the data back through the parameter list and then set the front pointer to the next item in the queue. If we have just deleted the last item, then the queue front pointer automatically becomes a null pointer by assigning it the null pointer from the link field of the last node. However, if the queue is now empty, we must also set the rear pointer to null. There are several ways to determine whether the only element in the queue is being deleted. If the queue count is 1, indicating that we are deleting the only item in the queue, we assign a null pointer to the rear pointer. Finally, we recycle the node that we just deleted. The two successful cases are shown in Figure 5-11.

The pseudocode is shown in Algorithm 5-3.

```
algorithm dequeue (ref queue   <metadata>,
                   ref item    <dataType>)
This algorithm deletes a node from a queue.
    Pre     queue is a metadata structure
    Post    data at front of queue returned to user through item
            and front element deleted and recycled
    Return  true if successful, false if underflow
  1 if (queue.count is 0)
```

Algorithm 5-3   Delete data from queue

```
 1   return false
 2 end if
 3 item       = queue.front->data
 4 deleteLoc  = queue.front
 5 if (queue.count 1)
   Deleting only item in queue
   1   queue.rear  = null pointer
 6 end if
 7 queue.front    = queue.front->next
 8 queue.count    = queue.count - 1
 9 recycle (deleteLoc)
10 return true
end dequeue
```

Algorithm 5-3   Delete data from queue *(continued)*

Retrieving Queue Data

The only difference between the two retrieve queue operations is which pointer is used, front or rear. Let's look at **queue front.** Its logic is identical to that of dequeue except that the data are not deleted from the queue. It first checks for an empty queue and returns false if the queue is empty. If there are data in the queue, it passes the data back through dataOut and returns true. The pseudocode is shown in Algorithm 5-4.

```
algorithm queueFront (val queue    <metadata>,
                      ref dataOut  <dataType>)
This algorithm retrieves the data at the front of the queue
without changing the queue contents.
   Pre     queue is a metadata structure
   Post    data passed back to caller
   Return  true if successful, false if underflow
 1 if (queue.count is 0)
   1   return false
 2 end if
 3 dataOut = queue.front->data
 4 return true
end queueFront
```

Algorithm 5-4   Retrieve data at front of queue

To implement **queue rear**, copy Algorithm 5-4 but change the queue front to the queue rear.

Empty Queue

Empty queue returns true if the queue is empty and false if the queue contains data. As we discussed earlier, there are several ways to test for an empty queue. Checking the queue count is the easiest. The pseudocode is shown in Algorithm 5-5.

```
algorithm emptyQueue (val queue <metadata>)
This algorithm checks to see if a queue is empty.
    Pre      queue is a metadata structure
    Return   true if empty, false if queue has data
  1 return (queue.count equal 0)
end emptyQueue
```

Algorithm 5-5   Queue empty

Full Queue

Once again we must use the brute-force method of determining whether we have a **full queue** or whether there is room in the heap for another node. By allocating a node and then releasing the memory we can determine whether there is room for at least one more node, as shown in Algorithm 5-6.

```
algorithm fullQueue (val queue <metadata>)
This algorithm checks to see if a queue is full. The queue
is full if memory cannot be allocated for another node.
    Pre      queue is a metadata structure
    Return   true if full, false if room for another node
  1 allocate (tempPtr)
  2 if (allocation successful)
    1   recycle (tempPtr)
    2   return false
  3 else
    1   return true
  4 end if
end fullQueue
```

Algorithm 5-6   Full queue

Queue Count

Queue count returns the number of elements currently in the queue by simply returning the count found in the queue head node. The code is shown in Algorithm 5-7.

```
algorithm queueCount (val queue <metadata>)
This algorithm returns the number of elements in the queue.
    Pre    queue is a metadata structure
    Return queue count
 1 return queue.count
end queueCount
```

Algorithm 5-7   Queue count

Destroy Queue

Destroy queue deletes all data in the queue and recycles their memory. Algorithm 5-8 contains the code to destroy a queue.

```
algorithm destroyQueue (ref queue <metadata>)
This algorithm deletes all data from a queue.
    Pre    queue is a metadata structure
    Post   all data have been deleted and recycled
 1 pWalker = queue.front
 2 loop (pWalker not null)
    1   deletePtr = pWalker
    2   pWalker    = pWalker.next
    3   recycle (deletePtr)
 3 end loop
 4 queue.front = null
 5 queue.rear  = null
 6 queue.count = 0
 7 return
end destroyQueue
```

Algorithm 5-8   Destroy queue

5-3   QUEUING THEORY

Queuing theory is a field of applied mathematics that is used to predict the performance of queues. In this section we review a few basic queuing theory concepts. We leave the mathematics of queuing theory to advanced courses in the subject.

Note

> Queuing theory is a field of applied mathematics that is used to predict the performance of queues.

Queues can be divided into single-server and multiserver types. A **single-server queue** can provide service to only one customer at a time. An example of a single-server queue is the hot-food vendor found on street corners in most large cities. **Multiserver queues,** on the other hand, can provide service to many customers at a time. An example of a multiserver queue is a bank in which there is one line with many bank tellers providing service.

The two common elements to all queues are one or more customers who need a service and a server who provides the service. A **customer** is any person or thing needing service. Besides the examples cited, customers can be as diverse as jobs waiting to be run in a computer and packages being sent by express delivery. The **service** is any activity needed to accomplish the required result. The hot-food vendor provides food as a service; the package handler provides transportation and delivery of packages.

The two factors that most dramatically affect the queue are the arrival rate and service time. The rate at which customers arrive in the queue for service is known as the **arrival rate.** Depending on the service being provided, the arrival rate may be random or regular. The hot-food vendor's customers more than likely arrive randomly, although the rate may vary widely during the day. Jobs to be processed in the computer, however, may arrive at some regular rate created by a job-scheduling system.

Service time is the average time required to complete the processing of a customer request. If you have ever observed different bank customers while you stood in line, you noted the wide range in time required to process each customer. Obviously, the faster customers arrive and the higher the service time, the longer the queue will be.

In an ideal situation, customers would arrive at a rate that matches the service time. However, as we all know, things are seldom ideal. Sometimes the server will be idle because there are no customers to be served. At other times, there will be many customers waiting to be served. If we can predict the patterns, we may be able to minimize idle servers and waiting customers. Doing so is especially important when long-waiting customers are apt to switch to an alternative server, such as the hot-food vendor a block down the street.

Queuing theory attempts to predict such patterns. Specifically, it is able to predict queue time (which is defined as the average length of time customers wait in the queue), the average size of the queue, and the maximum queue size. To make these predictions, it needs two factors: the arrival rate and the average service time, which is defined as the average of the total service time between idle periods.

Given queue time and service time, we know response time, a measure of the average time from the point at which customers enter the queue until the moment they leave the server. Response time is an important statistic, especially in online computer systems. A queuing theory model is shown in Figure 5-12.

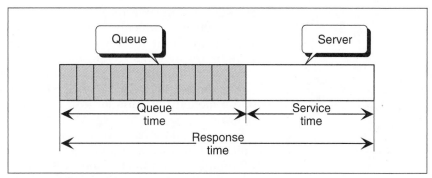

Figure 5-12 A queuing theory model

Once a model of a queue has been built, it can be used to study proposed changes to the system. For example, in the banking queue, if we were able to add automation improvements that would reduce the average service time by 15%, how many fewer tellers would we need? Or, given a model of a growing system that is currently under capacity, how long will it be before we need to add another server?

Note

> The two factors that most affect the performance of queues are the arrival rate and the service time.

5-4 QUEUE APPLICATIONS

Queues are one of the most common of all data-processing structures. They are found in virtually every operating system and network and in countless other areas. For example, queues are used in business online applications such as processing customer requests, jobs, and orders. In a computer system, a queue is needed to process jobs and for system services such as print spools.

Queues can become quite complex, but we demonstrate two simple queue implementations: The first is a queue simulation that can be used to study the performance of any queue application, and the second is an application that is useful in many problems, categorizing data.

Queue Simulation

An important application of queues is **queue simulation,** a modeling activity used to generate statistics about the performance of queues. Let's build a model of a single-server queue—for example, a saltwater taffy store on a beach boardwalk. The store has one window, and a clerk can service only one customer at a time. The store also ships boxes of taffy anywhere in the country. Because there are many flavors of saltwater taffy and because it takes longer to serve a customer who requests that the taffy be mailed, the time to serve customers varies between 1 and 10 minutes.

We want to study the store's activity over a theoretical day. The store is open 8 hours per day, 7 days a week. To simulate a day, we build a model that runs for 480 minutes (8 hours times 60 minutes per hour).

The simulation uses a digital clock that lets events start and stop in 1 minute intervals. In other words, customers arrive on the minute, wait an integral number of minutes in the queue, and require an integral number of minutes to be served. In each minute of operation, the simulation needs to check three events: the arrival of customers, start customer processing, and complete customer processing.

Events

The arrival of a new customer is determined in a module we name **new customer.** To determine the arrival rate, the store owner used a stopwatch and studied customer patterns over several days. The owner found that, on average, a customer arrives every 4 minutes. We simulate an arrival rate using a random number generator that returns a value between 1 and 4. If the number is 4, a customer has arrived. If the number is 1, 2, or 3, no customer has arrived.

We start processing a customer when the server is idle. In each minute of the simulation, therefore, the simulator needs to determine whether the clerk (the server) is busy or idle. In the simulation, this is done with a module called **server free.** If the clerk is idle, then the next waiting customer in line (the queue) can be served. If the clerk is busy, then the waiting customers remain in the queue.

Finally, at the end of each minute, the simulation determines whether it has **completed processing** for the current customer. The processing time for the current customer is determined by a random number generator when the processing is started. Then, for each customer, we loop the required number of minutes to complete the transaction. When the customer has been completely served, we gather statistics about the sale and set the server to an idle state.

Data Structures

Four data structures are required for the queue simulation: a queue head, a queue node, a current customer status, and a simulation statistics structure. All of these structures are shown in Algorithm 5-9, "Queue simulation: driver." These structures are described below and shown in Figure 5-13.

Queue Head

We use the standard head node structure for the queue. It contains two node pointers—front and rear—and a count of the number of elements currently in the queue.

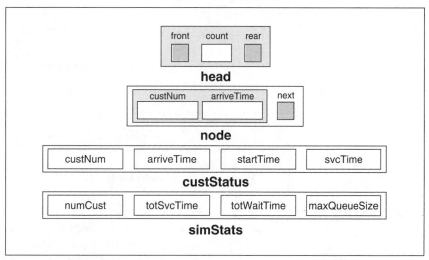

Figure 5-13 Queue data structures

Queue Node

The queue node contains only two elements, the customer data and a next node pointer. The customer data consist of a sequential customer number and the arrival time. The customer number is like the number you take when you go into a busy store with many customers waiting for service. The arrival time is the time the customer arrived at the store and got in line (was enqueued). The next node pointer is used to point to the next customer in line.

Customer Status

While we are processing the customer's order, we need to keep track of four pieces of data. First, we store the customer's number and arrival time. Because we need to know what time we started processing the order, we store the start time. Finally, as we start the processing, we use a random number generator to calculate the time it will take to fill the customer's order and store it in the customer status structure.

Simulation Statistics

At the conclusion of the simulation, we need to report the total number of customers processed in the simulation, the total and average service time, the total and average wait time, and the maximum number of customers in the queue at one time. We use a simulation statistics structure, simStats, to store these data.

Output

At the conclusion of the simulation, we print the statistics gathered during the simulation and the average queue wait time and average queue service time. To verify that the queue is working properly, we also print the basic statistics for each customer: arrival time, start time, wait time, service time, and the number of elements in the queue at the time the customer was completely served.

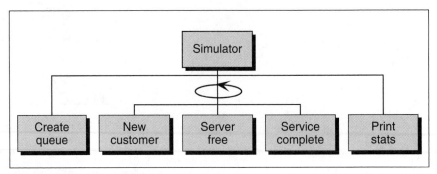

Figure 5-14   Design for queue simulation

Simulation Algorithm

We are now ready to write the simulation algorithm. The design consists of a driver module that calls three processing modules, as shown in Figure 5-14. It parallels the requirements discussed earlier. New customer determines whether a customer has arrived and needs to be enqueued. Server free determines whether the server is idle and if so starts serving the next customer, if any. Service complete determines whether the current customer has been completely served and if so collects the necessary statistical data and prints the data about the customer. We add an additional module, print stats, to print the end of simulation statistics.

Simulator

The pseudocode for the simulation driver is shown in Algorithm 5-9.

```
algorithm taffySimulation
This program simulates a queue for a saltwater taffy store.
Data Structures
   data
      number        <integer>
      arrivalTime   <integer>
   end data

   head
      front   <node pointer>
      count   <integer>
      rear    <node pointer>
   end head

   node
      custData   <data>
      next       <node pointer>
```

Algorithm 5-9   Queue simulation: driver

```
      end node

   custStatus
      custNum       <integer>
      arriveTime    <integer>
      startTime     <integer>
      svcTime       <integer>
   end custStatus

   simStats
      numCust       <integer>
      totSvcTime    <integer>
      totWaitTime   <integer>
      maxQueueSize  <integer>
   end simStats

Statements
 1 createQueue (queue)
 2 clock     = 1
 3 endTime   = 8 * 60
 4 custNum   = 0
 5 loop (clock <= endTime OR moreCusts)
    1   newCustomer  (queue, clock, custNum)
    2   serverFree   (queue, clock, custStatus, moreCusts)
    3   svcComplete  (queue, clock, custStatus,
                        runStats, moreCusts)
    4   if (not emptyQueue (queue))
        1   moreCusts = true
    5   end if
    6   clock = clock + 1
 6 end loop
 7 printStats  (runStats)
 8 return
end taffySimulation
```

Algorithm 5-9   Queue simulation: driver *(continued)*

Algorithm 5-9 Analysis   The driver creates the queue and then loops until the simulation is complete. Each loop tests to see whether a new customer needs to be enqueued, checks to see whether the server is idle so that a new customer can be started, and checks to see whether the current customer's service is complete.

To determine whether the simulation is complete, we need to test two conditions. We can only stop the simulation when we have run for the allocated time and there are no more customers. If there is more time left in the simulation, then we are not finished. Even when we reach the end of the processing time, however, we are not finished if a customer is being served or if customers are waiting in the queue. We use a more customers flag to determine whether either of these conditions is true. The server free logic sets the more customers flag to true when it starts a call (Statement 5.2). The service complete logic sets it to false when it completes a call (Statement 5.3). In the driver loop, we need to set it true if there are calls waiting in the queue (Statement 5.4). This test ensures that calls waiting in the queue are handled after the clock time has been exhausted.

At the end of the simulation, the driver calls a print algorithm that calculates the averages and prints all of the statistics.

New Customer

The pseudocode for new customer is shown in Algorithm 5-10.

```
algorithm newCustomer (ref queue     <metadata>,
                       val clock     <integer>,
                       ref custNum   <integer>)
This algorithm determines if a new customer has arrived.
    Pre    queue is a structure to a valid queue
           clock is the current clock minute
           custNum is the number of the last customer in line
    Post   if new customer has arrived, placed in queue
  1 arrival = (randum number modulo 4) + 1
  2 if (arrival equal 4)
    New customer has arrived
    1    custNum = custNum + 1
    2    custData.number    = custNum
    3    custData.arriveTime = clock
    4    enqueue (queue, custData)
  3 end if
  4 return
end newCustomer
```

Algorithm 5-10   Queue simulation: new customer

Algorithm 5-10 Analysis

The only complexity in this short algorithm is the calculation of new customer. As explained in the discussion above, customers arrive at a rate of one every 4 minutes. Taking a random number modulo 4 produces a random number in the range of 0 to 3. Adding 1 gives us a range of 1 to 4. Because we need to enqueue a new customer only once in four times (on the average), we add a customer when the calculated arrival flag is equal to 4.

It is important to note, however, that we could not simply add a customer every fourth call. For the simulation study to work, the customers must arrive in a random fashion, not exactly every 4 minutes. By using a random number as the basis for determining when a customer arrives, we may go several minutes without any customers and then have several customers arrive in succession. This random distribution is essential to queuing theory.

Server Free

The pseudocode to determine whether we can start serving a new customer is shown in Algorithm 5-11.

```
algorithm serverFree (ref queue      <metadata>,
                       val clock      <integer>,
                       ref status     <custStatus>,
                       ref moreCusts <Boolean>)
This algorithm determines if the server is idle and if so starts
serving a new customer.
    Pre    queue is a structure for a valid queue
           clock is the current clock minute
           status holds data about current/previous customer
    Post   moreCusts is set true if a call is started
  1 if (clock > status.startTime + status.svcTime - 1)
    Server is idle.
    1    if (not emptyQueue (queue))
       1    dequeue (queue, custData)
       2    status.custNum    = custData.number
       3    status.arriveTime = custData.arriveTime
       4    status.startTime  = clock
       5    status.svcTime    = random service time
       6    moreCusts         = true
    2    end if
  2 end if
  3 return
end serverFree status
```

Algorithm 5-11   Queue simulation: server free

Algorithm 5-11 Analysis

The question in this algorithm is, "How can we tell if the server is free?" The customer status record holds the answer. It represents either the current customer or, if there is no current customer, the previous customer. If there is a current customer, then we cannot start a new customer. We can tell if the record represents the new customer by comparing the clock time with the end time for the customer. The end time is the start time plus the required service time. If the clock time is greater than the calculated end time, then if the queue is not empty, we start a new customer.

One question remains to be answered: "How do we start the first call?" When we create the customer status structure, we initialize everything to 0. Now, using the formula in Statement 1, we see that a 0 start time plus a 0 service time minus 1 must be less than the clock time, so we can start the first customer.

Service Complete   The logic for service complete is shown in Algorithm 5-12.

```
algorithm svcComplete  (ref queue     <metadata>,
                        val clock      <integer>,
                        ref status     <custStatus>,
                        ref stats      <simStats>,
                        ref moreCusts <Boolean>)
This algorithm determines if the current customer's processing
is complete.
    Pre    queue is a structure for a valid queue
           clock is the current clock minute
           status holds data about current/previous customer
    Post   if service complete, data for current customer printed
           and simulation statistics updated
           moreCusts set to false if call completed
1 if (clock equal status.startTime + status.svcTime - 1)
   Current call complete
   1   waitTime          = status.startTime - status.arriveTime
   2   stats.numCust      = stats.numCust + 1
   3   stats.totSvcTime  = stats.totSvcTime + status.svcTime
   4   stats.totWaitTime = stats.totWaitTime + waitTime
   5   queueSize = queueCount (queue)
   6   if (stats.maxQueueSize < queueSize)
       1   stats.maxQueueSize = queueSize
   7   end if
   8   print  (status.custNum   status.arriveTime
                status.startTime status.svcTime
                waitTime          queueCount (queue))
   9   moreCusts = false
2 end if
3 return
end svcComplete
```

Algorithm 5-12   Queue simulation: service complete

Algorithm 5-12 Analysis

The question in this algorithm is similar to the server free question. To help analyze the logic, let's look at a few hypothetical services in the simulation. They are shown below.

start time	service time	complete time	
1	2	2	Minutes 1 and 2
3	1	3	Minute 3
4	3	6	Minutes 4, 5, and 6
7	2	8	Minutes 7 and 8

Because we test to start a new customer in server free before we test for the customer being complete, it is possible to start and finish serving a customer, who needs only 1 minute in the same loop. This is seen in minute 3 above. The correct calculation for the end of service time is therefore start time + service time − 1. This calculation is borne out in each of the examples above. We therefore test for the clock time equal to the end time, and, if they are equal, we print the necessary data for the current customer and accumulate the statistics needed for the end of the simulation.

Print Stats

The last algorithm in the simulation prints the statistics for the entire simulation. The code is shown in Algorithm 5-13.

```
algorithm printStats (stats <simStats>)
This algorithm prints the statistics for the simulation.
    Pre     stats contains the run statistics
    Post    statistics printed
 1 print (Simulation Statistics:)
 2 print (Total customers:     stats.numCust)
 3 print (Total service time:  stats.totSvcTime)
 4 avrgSvcTime  = stats.totSvcTime  / stats.numCust
 5 print (Average service time: avrgSvcTime)
 6 avrgWaitTime = stats.totWaitTime / stats.numCust
 7 print (Average wait time:  avrgWaitTime)
 8 print (Maximum queue size: stats.maxQueueSize)
 9 return
end printStats
```

Algorithm 5-13   Queue simulation: print statistics

Categorizing Data

It is often necessary to rearrange data without destroying their basic sequence. As a simple example, consider a list of numbers. We want to group the numbers while maintaining their original order in each group. This is an excellent multiple queue application.

To demonstrate, consider the following list of numbers:

> 3 22 12 6 10 34 65 29 9 30 81 4 5 19 20 57 44 99

We want to categorize them into four different groups:

- Group 1: less than 10
- Group 2: between 10 and 19
- Group 3: between 20 and 29
- Group 4: 30 and greater

In other words, we want the list rearranged as shown below.

> | 3 6 9 4 5 | 12 10 19 | 22 29 20| 34 65 30 81 57 44 99 |

This is not sorting. The result is not a sorted list but rather a list categorized according to the specified rules. The numbers in each group have kept their original order.

The solution is simple. We build a queue for each of the four categories. We then store the numbers in the appropriate queue as we read them. After all the data have been processed, we print each queue to demonstrate that we categorized the data correctly. This design is shown in Algorithm 5-14.

```
algorithm categorize
    Group a list of numbers into four groups using four queues.
    Written by:
    Date:
1   createQueue (q0to9)
2   createQueue (q10to19)
3   createQueue (q20to29)
4   createQueue (qOver29)
5   fillQueues  (q0to9, q10to19, q20to29, qOver29)
6   printQueues (q0to9, q10to19, q20to29, qOver29)
7   return
end categorize
```

Algorithm 5-14   Category queues

Algorithm 5-14 Analysis   The main line for the category queue simply creates the queues and then calls algorithms to fill and print them. Note that when we complete, we do not destroy the queues. We leave this process for the operating system. If we had more work to do, however, we would have to delete them to release their memory.

The algorithm to fill the queue is shown in Algorithm 5-15. We demonstrate the logic for printing the queues when we write the C++ implementation in the next section.

```
algorithm fillQueues  (ref q0to9    <metadata>,
                       ref q10to19  <metadata>,
                       ref q20to29  <metadata>,
                       ref qOver29  <metadata>)
This algorithm reads data from the keyboard and places them in
one of four queues.
   Pre    all four queues have been created
   Post   queues filled with data
 1 loop (not EOF)
     1   read (number)
     2   if (number < 10)
         1   enqueue (q0to9, number)
     3   elseif (number < 20)
         1   enqueue (q10to19, number)
     4   elseif (number < 30)
         1   enqueue (q20to29, number)
     5   else
         1   enqueue (qOver29, number)
     6   end if
 2 end loop
 3 return
end fillQueues
```

Algorithm 5-15   Fill category queues

Algorithm 5-15 Analysis

What sounded like a long and difficult program is really a short and simple algorithm, thanks to code reusability. The most difficult decision in this algorithm is determining how to write the categorizing code. We simply used a multiway selection implemented with an *elseif* construct. Once we made that decision, the algorithm practically wrote itself.

5-5   CATEGORIZING DATA—C++ IMPLEMENTATION

We demonstrate one use of queues with a program that categorizes data. Rather than read the data from a file, however, we simply generate 25 random numbers in the range 0 to 50. The C++ functions use the abstract data type created in the next section.

Main Line Logic

The main line logic for the categorizing program begins by creating the queues. Once the queues have been created, it calls a function to create and enqueue the data and another function to print them. The code is shown in Program 5-1.

```
1   /* Groups list of numbers into four groups using four queues.
2          Written by:
3          Date:
4   */
5   #include <iostream>
6   #include <stdlib.h>
7   #include "queueADT.h"
8   #include <iomanip>
9
10  // Prototype Statements
11  void fillQueues       (Queue<int>&  q0to9,
12                         Queue<int>&  q10to19,
13                         Queue<int>&  q20to29,
14                         Queue<int>&  qOver29);
15
16  void printQueues      (Queue<int>&  q0to9,
17                         Queue<int>&  q10to19,
18                         Queue<int>&  q20to29,
19                         Queue<int>&  qOver29);
20
21  void printOneQueue   (Queue<int>&  anyQueue);
22
23  int main (void)
24  {
25  // Local Definitions
26     Queue<int>  q0to9;
27     Queue<int>  q10to19;
28     Queue<int>  q20to29;
29     Queue<int>  qOver29;
30
31  // Statements
32     cout << "Welcome to a demonstration of categorizing \n"
33          << "data. We generate 25 random numbers and then\n"
34          << "group them into categories using queues.\n\n";
35     fillQueues  (q0to9, q10to19, q20to29, qOver29);
36     printQueues (q0to9, q10to19, q20to29, qOver29);
37
38     return 0;
39  } //  main
```

Program 5-1   Categorizing data main line

Fill Queues

Fill queues uses a random number generator to create 25 random numbers between 0 and 50. As each number is generated, it is displayed so that we can verify the accuracy of the program and then inserted into the appropriate queue. The code is shown in Program 5-2.

```
 1    /* ================= fillQueues =================
 2       This function generates data using rand() and
 3       places them in one of four queues.
 4          Pre    nothing
 5          Post   queues filled with data
 6    */
 7    void fillQueues (Queue<int>&  q0to9,
 8                     Queue<int>&  q10to19,
 9                     Queue<int>&  q20to29,
10                     Queue<int>&  qOver29)
11    {
12    // Local Definitions
13       int   category;
14       int   i;
15       int   item;
16
17    // Statements
18       cout << "Categorizing data:\n";
19       srand(79);
20
21       for (i = 1; i <= 25; i++)
22           {
23            item = rand() % 51;
24            category = item / 10;
25            cout << setw(3) << item;
26            if (!(i % 11))
27               cout << endl;
28
29            switch (category)
30               {
31                case 0  : q0to9.enqueue (item);
32                          break;
33                case 1  : q10to19.enqueue (item);
34                          break;
35                case 2  : q20to29.enqueue (item);
36                          break;
37                default : qOver29.enqueue (item);
38                          break;
39               } // switch
40           } // for
41
42       cout << "\nEnd of data categorization\n\n";
43       return;
44    } // fillQueues
```

Program 5-2 Categorizing data: fill queues

Program 5-2 Analysis   The code is very simple: as each random number is generated, we use a switch statement to insert it into its proper queue. Perhaps more interesting is the pagination logic to write a maximum of 11 numbers on each line. Although there are more efficient methods, using the *for* counter modulo 11 is the simplest.

Print Queues

Print queues is a simple driver that calls a function to print one queue at a time. Its code is shown in Program 5-3.

```
 1   /* ==================== printQueues ====================
 2      This function prints the data in each of the queues.
 3          Pre    queues have been filled
 4          Post   data printed and dequeued
 5   */
 6   void printQueues (Queue<int>&  q0to9,
 7                     Queue<int>&  q10to19,
 8                     Queue<int>&  q20to29,
 9                     Queue<int>&  qOver29)
10   {
11   // Statements
12      cout << "Data    0.. 9:";
13      printOneQueue (q0to9);
14
15      cout << "Data   10..19:";
16      printOneQueue (q10to19);
17
18      cout <<  "Data   20..29:";
19      printOneQueue (q20to29);
20
21      cout <<  "Data over 29:";
22      printOneQueue (qOver29);
23
24      return;
25   } //  printQueues
```

Program 5-3   Categorizing data: print queues

Print One Queue

Print one queue uses a straightforward approach. Each call prints a queue by dequeuing a node and printing it. The loop continues as long as there are data in the queue. Because we do not have access to the data structure, however, we use emptyQueue to test for more data to be printed. We could also have used queueCount and tested for greater than zero. The code is shown in Program 5-4. It also contains the results from a sample run.

```
1    /* ================ printOneQueue ================
2       This function prints the data in one queue,
3       ten entries to a line.
4          Pre    queue has been filled
5          Post   data deleted and printed; queue is empty
6    */
7    void printOneQueue (Queue<int>& anyQueue)
8    {
9    // Local Definitions
10      int lineCount;
11      int data;
12
13   // Statements
14      lineCount = 0;
15      while (anyQueue.dequeue (data))
16          {
17           if (lineCount++ >= 10)
18              {
19               lineCount = 1;
20               cout << endl;
21              } //  if
22           cout <<  setw(3) << data;
23          } // while !emptyQueue
24      cout << endl;
25
26      return;
27   }  // printOneQueue
```

```
Results
    Welcome to a demonstration of categorizing
    data. We generate 25 random numbers and then
    group them into categories using queues.

    Categorizing data:
     24   7 31 23 26 14 19  8  9  6 43
     16 22   0 39 46 22 38 41 23 19 18
     14   3 41
    End of data categorization

    Data   0.. 9:  7  8  9  6  0  3
    Data  10..19: 14 19 16 19 18 14
    Data  20..29: 24 23 26 22 22 23
    Data over 29: 31 43 39 46 38 41 41
```

Program 5-4   Categorizing data: print queues

Program 5-4 Analysis   Note how we control the loop in this simple algorithm. The dequeue function returns true if data were deleted from the queue and false if the queue is empty. We use its return value in Statement 15: As long as data were deleted from the queue, we print; when the queue becomes empty, we terminate the loop.

5-6   QUEUE ADT—LINKED LIST IMPLEMENTATION

The queue abstract data type (ADT) follows the basic design of the stack ADT. We begin by examining the queue data structure, and then we develop each of the queue algorithms that are discussed starting on page 222.

Queue Structure   The **queue data structure** is shown in Program 5-5. The class ADT structure is similar to the structure we used for a stack. Each node contains a data declaration and a link pointer to the next element in the queue. The data are declared using a structure created by the application programmer. The major difference between the two classes is the addition of the rear pointer and the functions that use it. Program 5-5 also contains the prototype declarations for the queue functions. In a productional environment, it would be the queue header file (queue.h).

```
 1   /* Queue ADT Definitions
 2          Written by:
 3          Date:
 4   */
 5   // Node Declaration
 6      template <class TYPE>
 7      struct NODE
 8      {
 9       TYPE         data;
10       NODE<TYPE> *next;
11      };
12
13   // Class Declaration
14      template <class TYPE>
15      class Queue
16      {
17        private:
18           NODE<TYPE>   *front;
19           int          count;
```

Program 5-5 Queue ADT data structures

```
20      NODE<TYPE>   *rear;
21
22   public:
23          Queue       (void);
24          ~Queue      (void);
25   bool   dequeue     (TYPE& dataOut);
26   bool   enqueue     (TYPE  dataIn);
27   bool   queueFront  (TYPE& dataOut);
28   bool   queueRear   (TYPE& dataOut);
29   int    queueCount  (void);
30   bool   emptyQueue  (void);
31   bool   fullQueue   (void);
32   }; // class Queue
```

Program 5-5   Queue ADT data structures *(continued)*

Queue ADT Implementation

This section contains the C++ code for each of the queue algorithms. As you study them, trace them through the queue example on page 221.

Create Queue

Create queue is implemented as the queue class constructor. It initializes the front and rear pointers to null and sets the count to 0. The code for create queue is shown in Program 5-6.

```
 1   /* ================= Constructor  =================
 2      Instantiates a queue and initializes private data.
 3          Pre      queue being defined
 4          Post     queue created and initialized
 5   */
 6
 7   template <class TYPE>
 8   Queue<TYPE> :: Queue (void)
 9   {
10   // Statements
11      front  = NULL;
12      rear   = NULL;
13      count  = 0;
14   } // Constructor
```

Program 5-6   Create queue

Enqueue

The logic for enqueue is straightforward. If memory is available, it creates a new node, inserts it at the rear of the queue, and returns a Boolean true. If memory is not available, it returns a Boolean false. The code is shown in Program 5-7.

```
 1 | /* ================== enqueue ==================
   |    This algorithm inserts data into a queue.
   |       Pre    dataIn contains data to be enqueued
   |       Post   data have been inserted
   |       Return true if successful, false if overflow
   | */
 2 |
 3 | template <class TYPE>
 4 | bool Queue<TYPE> :: enqueue (TYPE dataIn)
 5 | {
 6 | // Local Definitions
 7 |    NODE<TYPE>   *newPtr;
 8 |
 9 | // Statements
10 |    if (!(newPtr = new NODE<TYPE>))
11 |        return false;
12 |
13 |    newPtr->data = dataIn;
14 |    newPtr->next = NULL;
15 |
16 |    if (count == 0)
17 |        // Inserting into empty queue
18 |        front  = newPtr;
19 |    else
20 |            rear->next = newPtr;
21 |
22 |    count++;
23 |    rear = newPtr;
24 |    return true;
25 | } //enqueue
```

Program 5-7 Enqueue

Program 5-7 Analysis

Because we must maintain both a front and a rear pointer, we need to determine whether we are inserting into an empty queue. If we are, we must set both pointers to the data just inserted. If there are already data in the queue, then we need to set the next field of the node at the rear of the queue and the rear pointer to the new node. In this case, the front pointer is unchanged. Because the rear pointer is updated in either case, we changed it after the *if* statement (see Statement 23).

Dequeue

Dequeue begins by checking to make sure there are data in the queue. If there are, dequeue copies the data being deleted back to the calling function through a reference parameter, adjusts the pointers, and subtracts one from the queue count. If the delete is successful, it returns a Boolean true; if it is empty, it returns a Boolean false. The code is shown in Program 5-8.

```
 1   /* ================= dequeue =================
 2      This algorithm deletes a node from the queue.
 3         Pre    dataOut variable to receive data
 4         Post   front data placed in dataOut and front deleted
 5         Return true if successful, false if underflow
 6   */
 7   template<class TYPE>
 8   bool Queue<TYPE> :: dequeue (TYPE& dataOut)
 9   {
10   // Local Definitions
11      NODE<TYPE>   *deleteLoc;
12
13   // Statements
14      if (count == 0)
15         return false;
16
17      dataOut   = front->data;
18      deleteLoc = front;
19      if (count == 1)
20         // Deleting the only item in queue
21         rear = front = NULL;
22      else
23         front = front->next;
24      count--;
25      delete deleteLoc;
26
27      return true;
28   } // dequeue
```

Program 5-8 Dequeue

Program 5-8 Analysis

The logic for dequeue is rather basic. The major concern is that we may have deleted the last element in the queue, in which case we must set it to a null state. Setting the queue to a null state requires that the queue front and rear be set to a null pointer. Note that we always set the queue front to the next pointer in the node being deleted. If the last node is being deleted, then the deleted node's next pointer is guaranteed to be null (because it is the last node in the queue). In this case, queue front is automatically set to null. If it is not the last node in the queue, then after the update, queue front will point to the new node at the front of the queue.

Queue Front

Queue front also passes the data at the front of the queue back to the calling function through a reference parameter. It differs from dequeue only in that the queue is not changed. The code is shown in Program 5-9.

```
1    /* ================= queueFront =================
2       Retrieves data at the front of the queue
3       without changing the queue contents.
4            Pre    dataOut is variable for data
5            Post   data in dataOut
6            Return true if successful, false if underflow
7    */
8
9    template <class TYPE>
10   bool Queue<TYPE> :: queueFront (TYPE& dataOut)
11   {
12   // Statements
13      if (count == 0)
14          return false;
15      else
16         {
17            dataOut = front->data;
18            return true;
19         } //else
20   }  // queueFront
```

Program 5-9   Queue front

Queue Rear

The code for **queue rear,** shown in Program 5-10, is identical to that of queue front except that the data at the rear of the queue are sent back to the calling function.

```
1    /* =============== queueRear ==============
2       Retrieves   data at the rear of the queue
3       without changing the queue contents.
4            Pre    dataOut is variable to receive data
5            Post   dataOut contains data at rear of queue
6            Return true if successful, false if underflow
7    */
8
9    template <class TYPE>
10   bool Queue<TYPE> :: queueRear (TYPE& dataOut)
11   {
12   // Statements
13      if (count == 0)
14          return false;
15      else
16         {
17            dataOut = rear->data;
18            return true;
19         } // else
20   }  // queueRear
```

Program 5-10   Queue rear

Queue Empty

Queue empty is one of the simplest functions in the ADT. It simply uses the count in the queue object to determine whether the queue is empty or contains data (see Program 5-11).

```
 1    /* =================== emptyQueue ==================
 2        This algorithm checks to see if a queue is empty.
 3            Pre     nothing
 4            Return true if empty, false if queue has data
 5    */
 6
 7    template <class TYPE>
 8    bool Queue<TYPE> ::  emptyQueue (void)
 9    {
10    // Statements
11        return (count == 0);
12    }  // emptyQueue
```

Program 5-11 Empty queue

Full Queue

Like the full stack algorithm, **full queue** is one of the most difficult algorithms to implement because C++ provides no way to test the amount of space left in the heap. We use the same implementation we used for the stack. For a complete discussion, see "Full Stack," on page 201. The code for full queue is shown in Program 5-12.

```
 1    /* =================== fullQueue ===================
 2        This algorithm checks to see if a queue is full.
 3        The queue is full if memory cannot be allocated
 4        for another node.
 5            Pre     nothing
 6            Return true if full, false if room for a node
 7    */
 8
 9    template <class TYPE>
10    bool Queue<TYPE> :: fullQueue (void)
11    {
12    // Local Definitions
13        NODE<TYPE>   *temp;
14
15    // Statements
16        temp = new NODE<TYPE>;
17        if (temp != NULL)
18            {
19             delete temp;
20             return false;
21            } // if
```

Program 5-12 Full queue

```
22
23        // Heap full
24        return true;
25    } //  fullQueue
```

Program 5-12   Full queue *(continued)*

Queue Count

Queue count simply returns the count found in the queue head node. Its code is shown in Program 5-13.

```
1    /* =============== queueCount ===============
2        Returns the number of elements in the queue.
3            Pre     nothing
4            Return queue count
5    */
6
7    template <class TYPE>
8    int Queue<TYPE> :: queueCount(void)
9    {
10   // Statements
11       return count;
12   } // queueCount
```

Program 5-13   Queue count

Destroy Queue

The implementation of the **destroy queue** is the class destructor. It simply cycles through the queue, deleting all of the elements, and then terminates. The code is shown in Program 5-14.

```
1    /* ================== Destructor ==================
2        Deletes all data from a queue and recycles
3        its memory.
4            Pre    queue is being destroyed
5            Post   all data have been deleted and recycled
6    */
7
8    template <class TYPE>
9    Queue<TYPE> :: ~Queue (void)
10   {
11   // Local Definitions
12       NODE<TYPE>    *deletePtr;
13
14   // Statements
15       while (front != NULL)
```

Program 5-14   Destroy queue

```
16        {
17          deletePtr = front;
18          front = front->next;
19          delete deletePtr;
20        } // while
21    } // Destructor
```

Program 5-14   Destroy queue *(continued)*

Program 5-14 Analysis   In the normal course of events, the queue being destroyed will be empty. If it is, the queue front will be null and we are finished. If there are data in the queue, however, then we delete the queue nodes. Eventually we will get to the end of the queue, at which time we are finished.

5-7   QUEUE ADT—ARRAY IMPLEMENTATION

The linked list implementation is very popular, but it is not the only way to implement a queue. Queues can also be implemented in arrays and for very large queues, in files. Because a file can be thought of as an array stored on a disk, the array and file implementations have similar solutions. In this section, we rewrite the queue ADT using an array.

An enqueue to an empty queue is placed in the first element of the array, which becomes both the front and the rear. Subsequent enqueues are placed at the array location following rear; that is, each enqueue stores the queue data in the next element after the current queue rear. Thus, if the last element in the queue is stored at array location 11, then the data for the next enqueue are placed in element 12.

Dequeues take place at the front of the queue. As an element is deleted from the queue, the queue front is advanced to the next location; that is, queue front becomes queue front plus 1. Figure 5-15 shows a queue after it has been in operation for a period. At the point shown, the data have migrated from the front of the array to its center.

When we implement a queue in an array, we use indexes rather than pointers. Thus, the front of the queue in Figure 5-15 is 5 and the rear is 11.

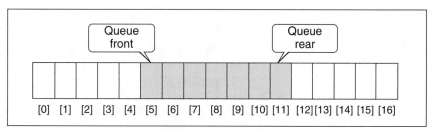

Figure 5-15   A queue stored in an array.

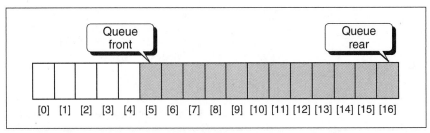

Figure 5-16   Array queue with last element filled

The definition of a full queue changes when we implement a queue in an array. A full queue is defined as every element filled. Because arrays have a finite number of elements, we can determine that the queue is full by testing the queue count against the maximum number of elements.

When data arrive faster than the queue service time, the queue will tend to advance to the end of the array. Consequently, the last element in the array is occupied, but the queue is not full because there are empty elements at the beginning of the array. This situation is shown in Figure 5-16.

When the data are grouped at the end of the array, we need to find a place for the new element when we enqueue data. One solution is to shift all of the elements from the end to the beginning of the array. For example, in Figure 5-16 element 5 is shifted to element 0, element 6 to 1, 7 to 2, and so forth until element 16 is shifted to 11.

A more efficient alternative is to use a circular array. In a circular array, the last element is logically followed by the first element. This is done by testing for the last element and rather than adding 1, setting the index to 0. Given our array queue above, the next element after 16 is 0. A circular queue is shown in Figure 5-17.

With this understanding of a circular queue, we are ready to rewrite the abstract data type. The only difference in the calling sequence between the two implementations is the addition of an optional maximum queue size when the queue is instantiated.

Array Queues Implementation

The data structure requires two changes for the queue object. We need to store the address of the queue array, which we allocate from dynamic memory. We also need to store the maximum number of elements in the array. These changes are shown in Figure 5-18.

The revised ADT class is shown in Program 5-15. We also include the declarations for the queue class functions. As you study the data structure, compare it with the linked list structure shown in Program 5-5, on page 246.

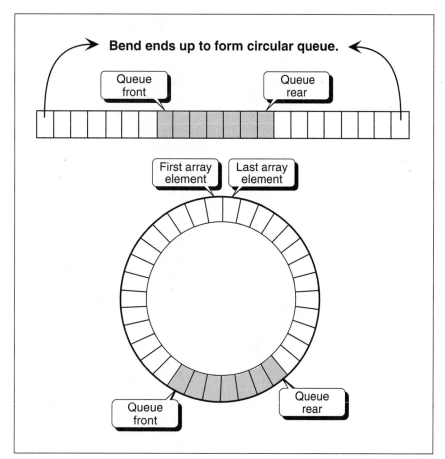

Figure 5-17 A circular queue

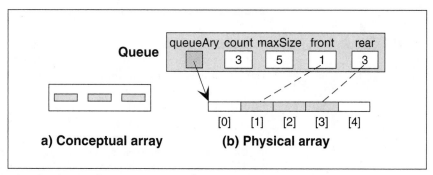

Figure 5-18 Queue array implementation

```
 1    /* Queue ADT Definitions
 2          Written by:
 3          Date:
 4    */
 5       template <class TYPE>
 6       struct NODE
 7          {
 8            TYPE  data;
 9          }; // NODE
10
11       template <class TYPE>
12       class Queue
13          {
14            private:
15
16              NODE<TYPE> *queueAry;
17              int        count;
18              int        maxSize;
19              int        front;
20              int        rear;
21
22            public:
23                   Queue      (int size = 100);
24                   ~Queue     (void);
25              bool  dequeue    (TYPE& dataOut);
26              bool  enqueue    (TYPE  dataIn);
27              bool  queueFront (TYPE& dataOut);
28              bool  queueRear  (TYPE& dataOut);
29              int   queueCount (void);
30              bool  emptyQueue (void);
31              bool  fullQueue  (void);
32          }; // class Queue
```

Program 5-15   Data structure for queue array

Create Queue Array

The **create queue** function is the class constructor. It allocates memory for a queue array from dynamic memory and initializes the class data members and metadata. If there is not enough memory for the queue structure, the program is aborted. The code for create queue is shown in Program 5-16.

```
 1    /* =============== Constructor   ===============
 2        Allocates memory for a queue array from dynamic
 3        memory and initializes data members and metadata.
 4           Pre     class being instantiated; if no queue size
```

Program 5-16   Create queue: array implementation

```
 5                        specified, default of 100 will be used
 6           Post        queue has been allocated and initialized
 7     */
 8     template <class TYPE>
 9     Queue<TYPE> :: Queue (int size)
10     {
11     // Statements
12        maxSize  = size;
13        front    = -1;
14        rear     = -1;
15        count    = 0;
16        queueAry = new NODE<TYPE> [maxSize];
17        if (!queueAry)
18           {
19            cout << "\a\aNot enough memory to allocate queue\n";
20            exit (100);
21           } // if
22     }  // Constructor
```

Program 5-16   Create queue: array implementation *(continued)*

Program 5-16 Analysis

To create an empty queue, we set the front and rear indexes to –1. We have chosen –1 as the index for an empty queue to make the enqueue logic as simple as possible. Whenever we insert an element into the queue, we add 1 to the rear index. When the queue is null, this automatically sets rear to 0 for the first element.

Note that we have set the queue up with a default array size of 100 elements. If the application program needs a larger queue, it can override the default with an initializer for the queue definition. An example of each definition is shown below.

```
Queue<int>   queue;
Queue<int>   bigQueue (200);
```

Enqueue: Array Implementation

The parameter list for the array implementation of **enqueue** is identical to the linked list implementation. The logic, however, differs considerably. First, there is no memory to be allocated. We simply need to determine in which array element to store the data.

The test for a full queue has also been changed. To determine whether the queue is full, we compare the queue count with the maximum queue size. If they are equal, we have a full queue.

To complete the insert, we add 1 to the rear index. If rear is at the last element, we need to wrap around to the first element of the queue. The code is shown in Program 5-17.

```
 1  /* ================= enqueue =================
 2     This algorithm inserts data into a queue.
 3         Pre     dataIn contains data to be inserted
 4         Post    data have been inserted
 5         Return  true if successful, false if overflow
 6  */
 7  template <class TYPE>
 8  bool Queue<TYPE> :: enqueue (TYPE dataIn)
 9  {
10  // Statements
11     if (count == maxSize)
12        // Queue is full
13        return false;
14     rear++;
15     if (rear == maxSize)
16        // Queue wraps to element 0
17        rear = 0;
18
19     queueAry[rear].data = dataIn;
20
21     if (count == 0)
22        // Inserting into empty queue
23        front  = 0;
24     count++;
25     return true;
26  } // enqueue
```

Program 5-17   Enqueue: array implementation

Program 5-17 Analysis

Two points in this function require careful study. First, note how the wraparound logic in Statements 15 to 17 is handled. At this point in the function, we know that the queue is not full. If the rear index is equal to the maximum queue size, however, we need to wrap around to the first element. (Remember, C++ uses 0 indexing so when the new rear is equal to the count, the last element has been filled.)

Second, if we are inserting into an empty queue, identified by a count of 0, then we must set the front index to 0. The rear index is set to 0 automatically when we add 1 to the rear index, which is set to −1 whenever the queue is empty.

Dequeue: Array Implementation

Dequeue deletes data at the front of the queue and stores them in a calling function variable. Its code is shown in Program 5-18.

```
1    /* =============== dequeue ===============
2        This algorithm deletes a node from the queue.
3            Pre     dataOut is variable to receive data
4            Post    data returned and front element deleted
5            Return true if successful, false if underflow
6    */
7    template<class TYPE>
8    bool Queue<TYPE> :: dequeue (TYPE& dataOut)
9    {
10   // Statements
11      if (count == 0)
12          return false;
13
14      dataOut = queueAry[front].data;
15      front++;
16      if (front == maxSize)
17          // queue front has wrapped to element 0
18          front = 0;
19      if (count == 1)
20          // Deleting the only item; -1 for empty queue
21          rear = front = -1;
22      count--;
23      return true;
24   } // dequeue
```

Program 5-18   Dequeue: array implementation

Program 5-18 Analysis

Take note of two pieces of code in this function. First, once again we must wrap around from the end of the queue. For dequeue, we test for a wrap after we have deleted the data from the queue. If front was in the last element of the array, then we must set the new front to the first element, 0.

The second point is that we need to reset both front and rear to –1 when we delete the last item in the queue (see Statements 19 to 21).

Queue Front: Array Implementation

The queue front logic parallels dequeue logic except that the status of the queue is not changed. Its logic is shown in Program 5-19.

```
1    /* ================== queueFront ==================
2        This algorithm retrieves the data at the front of
3        the queue without changing the queue contents.
4            Pre     dataOut is variable to receive data
5            Post    data at front in dataOut
```

Program 5-19   Queue front: array implementation

```
 6              Return   true if successful, false if underflow
,7     */
 8     template <class TYPE>
 9     bool Queue<TYPE> :: queueFront (TYPE& dataOut)
10     {
11     // Statements
12        if (count == 0)
13           return false;
14        else
15           {
16             dataOut = queueAry [front].data;
17             return true;
18           } // else
19     } // queueFront
```

Program 5-19   Queue front: array implementation *(continued)*

Queue Rear: Array Implementation

Queue rear returns the data at the rear of the queue without changing the contents of the queue. Its logic is shown in Program 5-20.

```
 1     /* =============== queueRear ==============
 2        This algorithm retrieves the data at the rear of
 3        the queue without changing the queue contents.
 4           Pre     dataOut is variable to receive data
 5           Post    data passed back to caller
 6           Return true if successful, false if underflow
 7     */
 8
 9     template <class TYPE>
10     bool Queue<TYPE> :: queueRear (TYPE& dataOut)
11     {
12     // Statements
13        if (count == 0)
14           return false;
15        else
16           {
17             dataOut = queueAry[rear].data;
18             return true;
19           } // else
20     } // queueRear
```

Program 5-20   Queue rear: array implementation

Full Queue: Array Implementation

The **full queue** logic is much simpler in the array implementation than in the linked list. We simply test the count against the maximum queue size. If they are equal, the queue is full. The code is shown in Program 5-21.

```
1    /* =================== fullQueue ===================
2       This algorithm checks to see if a queue is full.
3       The queue is full if the array is full.
4          Pre    nothing
5          Return true if full, false if room for a node
6    */
7
8    template <class TYPE>
9    bool Queue<TYPE> :: fullQueue (void)
10   {
11   // Statements
12      return  (count == maxSize);
13   } //  fullQueue
```

Program 5-21   Queue full: array implementation

Destroy Queue: Array Implementation

The last function for the array implementation is **destroy queue**. It is implemented as the ADT class destructor. The **queue count** and **empty queue** functions are identical for the linked list implementation and the array implementation, so we won't repeat them.

To destroy the queue, we simply delete the array. The code is shown in Program 5-22.

```
1    /* =================== Destructor ===================
2       Deletes queue array.
3          Pre    queue is being destroyed
4          Post   queue array deleted
5    */
6    template <class TYPE>
7    Queue<TYPE> :: ~Queue (void)
8    {
9    // Statements
10      delete [] queueAry;
11   } // Destructor
```

Program 5-22   Destroy queue: array implementation

5-8   SUMMARY

- A queue is a linear list in which data can only be inserted at one end, called the rear, and deleted from the other end, called the front.
- A queue is a first in–first out (FIFO) structure.
- There are four basic queue operations: enqueue, dequeue, queue front, and queue rear.
  - The enqueue operation inserts an element at the rear of the queue.
  - The dequeue operation deletes the element at the front of the queue.

- The queue front operation examines the element at the front of the queue without deleting it.
- The queue rear operation examines the element at the rear of the queue without deleting it.
- To implement the queue using a linked list, we use two types of structures: a head and a node.
- Queuing theory is a field of applied mathematics that is used to predict the performance of queues.
- Queue applications can be divided into single servers and multiservers.
  - A single-server queue application provides services to only one customer at a time.
  - A multiserver queue application provides service to several customers at a time.
- The two features that most affect the performance of queues are the arrival rate and the service time.
  - The rate at which the customers arrive in the queue for service is known as the arrival rate.
  - Service time is the average time required to complete the processing of a customer request.
- The queue time is the average length of time customers wait in the queue.
- The response time is a measure of average time from the point at which customers enter the queue until the moment they leave the server. It is queue time plus service time.
- One application of queues is queue simulation, which is a modeling activity used to generate statistics about the performance of a queue.
- Another application of queues is categorization. Queues are used to categorize data into different groups without losing the original ordering of the data.
- Queues can be implemented using linked lists or arrays.

5-9   PRACTICE SETS

Exercises

1. Imagine you have a stack of integers, S, and a queue of integers, Q. Draw a picture of S and Q after the following operations:

```
 1  pushStack  (S, 3)
 2  pushStack  (S, 12)
 3  enqueue    (Q, 5)
 4  enqueue    (Q, 8)
 5  popStack   (S, x)
 6  pushStack  (S, 2)
 7  enqueue    (Q, x)
 8  dequeue    (Q, y)
 9  pushStack  (S, x)
10  pushStack  (S, y)
```

2. What would be the value of queues Q1, Q2, and stack S, after the following algorithm segment:

```
 1 S  = createStack
 2 Q1 = createQueue
 3 Q2 = createQueue
 4 enqueue (Q1, 5)
 5 enqueue (Q1, 6)
 6 enqueue (Q1, 9)
 7 enqueue (Q1, 0)
 8 enqueue (Q1, 7)
 9 enqueue (Q1, 5)
10 enqueue (Q1, 0)
11 enqueue (Q1, 2)
12 enqueue (Q1, 6)
13 loop (not emptyQueue (Q1))
    1   dequeue (Q1, x)
    2   if (x == 0)
        1   z = 0
        2   loop (not emptyStack (S))
            1   popStack (S, &y)
            2   z = z + y
        3   end loop
        4   enqueue (Q2, z)
    3   else
        1   pushStack (S, x)
    4   end if
14 end loop
```

3. What would be the contents of queue Q after the following code is executed and the following data are entered?

```
1 Q = createQueue
2 loop (not end of file)
    1   read number
    2   if (number not 0)
        1   enqueue (Q, number)
    3   else
        1   queuerear (Q, x)
        2   enqueue (Q, x)
    4   end if
3 end loop
```

The data are: 5, 7, 12, 4, 0, 4, 6, 8, 67, 34, 23, 5, 0, 44, 33, 22, 6, 0.

4. What would be the contents of queue Q1 and queue Q2 after the following code is executed and the following data are entered?

```
1  Q1 = createQueue
2  Q2 = createQueue
3  loop (not end of file)
   1    read number
   2    enqueue (Q1, number)
   3    enqueue (Q2, number)
   4    loop (not empty Q1)
        1    dequeue (Q1, x)
        2    enqueue (Q2, x)
   5    end loop
4  end loop
```

The data are 5, 7, 12, 4, 0, 4, 6.

5. What would be the contents of queue Q1 after the following code is executed and the following data are entered?

```
1  Q1 = createQueue
2  S1 = createStack
3  loop (not end of file)
   1    read number
   2    if (number not 0)
        1    pushStack (S1, number)
   3    else
        1    popStack (S1, x)
        2    popStack (S1, x)
        3    loop (not empty S1)
             1    popStack (S1, x)
             2    enqueue (Q1, x)
        4    end loop
   4    end if
4  end loop
```

The data are 5, 7, 12, 4, 0, 4, 6, 8, 67, 34, 23, 5, 0, 44, 33, 22, 6, 0.

6. Imagine that the contents of queue Q1 and queue Q2 are as shown. What would be the content of Q3 after the following code is executed? The queue contents are shown front (left) to rear (right).

Q1: 42 30 41 31 19 20 25 14 10 11 12 15
Q2: 4 5 4 10 13

```
1  Q3 = createQueue
2  count = 0
3  loop (not empty Q1 and not empty Q2)
   1    count = count + 1
   2    dequeue (Q1, x)
   3    dequeue (Q2, y)
   4    if (y equal count)
      1    enqueue (Q3, x)
   5    end if
4  end loop
```

Problems

7. Using only the algorithms in the queue ADT, write an application algorithm called copyQueue that copies the contents of one queue to another.

8. It doesn't take much analysis to determine that the solution for Problem 7 is not very efficient. It would be much more efficient to write a new ADT method that would copy a queue using its knowledge of the ADT. Rewrite Problem 7 as a new ADT algorithm.

9. Rewrite the ADT queue copy in Problem 8 by overriding the assignment operator (=).

10. Rewrite the ADT queue copy in Problem 9 by overriding the plus/assignment operator (+=).

11. Using only the algorithms in the queue ADT, write an algorithm called catQueue that concatenates two queues together. The second queue should be put at the end of the first queue.

12. Rewrite Problem 11 as a new method to be included in the queue ADT.

13. Write an algorithm called stackToQueue that creates a queue from a stack. After the queue has been created, the top of the stack should be the front of the queue and the base of the stack should be the rear of the queue. At the end of the algorithm, the stack should be empty.

14. Write an algorithm called queueToStack that creates a stack from a queue. At the end of the algorithm, the queue should be unchanged; the front of the queue should be the top of the stack, and the rear of the queue should be the base of the stack.

15. Write an algorithm that compresses a string by deleting all space characters in the string. One way to do so is to use a queue of characters. Insert nonspace characters from the string into the queue. When you reach the end of the string, dequeue the characters from the queue and place them back into the string.

16. Given a queue of integers, write an algorithm that, using only the queue ADT, calculates and prints the sum and the average of the integers in the queue without changing the contents of the queue.

17. Given a queue of integers, write an algorithm that deletes all negative integers without changing the order of the remaining elements in the queue.

18. Rewrite Problem 17 as a new method to be included in the queue ADT.
19. Write an algorithm that reverses the contents of a queue.
20. Using only the algorithms in the queue ADT, write an algorithm that checks the contents of two queues and returns true if they are identical and false if they are not.
21. Rewrite Problem 20 as a new method to be included in the queue ADT.
22. Rewrite Problem 20 by overloading the equal operator (==).

Projects

23. Using the linked list abstract data type described in Section 5-6 "Queue Abstract Data Type—Linked List Implementation," on page 246, write a menu-driven user interface to test each of the operations in the ADT. Error condition should be printed as a part of the test result. A suggested menu is shown below.

```
A.  Enqueue data into queue
B.  Dequeue and print data
C.  Print data at the front
D.  Print data at the rear
E.  Print entire queue
F.  Print queue status: Empty
G.  Print queue status: Full
H.  Print number of elements and quit
```

Test your program with the following test cases. You may include additional test cases after you have executed the tests shown below.
a. Print queue status, Empty (F).
b. Dequeue and print data (B). Should return error.
c. Enqueue data into queue: 5 (A).
d. Enqueue data into queue: 8 (A).
e. Print queue status, Empty (F).
f. Print queue status, Full (G).
g. Print data at the front (C).
h. Print data at the rear (D).
i. Print entire queue (E).
j. Print number of elements in queue (H).
k. Dequeue and print data (B).
l. Dequeue and print data (B).
m. Dequeue and print data (B). Should return error.
n. Enqueue data into stack: 14 (A).
o. Print data at the front (C).
p. Print data at the front (C).
q. Enqueue data into queue: 32 (A).
r. Print data at the front (C).
s. Print data at the rear (D).
t. Destroy queue and quit (I).
24. One way to evaluate a prefix expression is to use a queue. To evaluate the expression, scan it repeatedly until you know the final expression value. In each scan, read the tokens and store them in a queue. In each

scan, replace an operator followed by two operands by the calculated values. For example, the following expression is a prefix expression that is evaluated to 159:

$$- + * \ 9 + 2 \ 8 * + 4 \ 8 \ 6 \ 3$$

We scan the expression and store it in a queue. During the scan, when an operator is followed by two operands, such as + 2 8, we put the result, 10, in the queue.

After the first scan, we have

− + * 9 10 * 12 6 3

After the second scan, we have

− + 90 72 3

After the third scan, we have

− 162 3

After the fourth scan, we have

159

Write a C++ program to evaluate a prefix expression.

25. Write the C++ implementations for the saltwater taffy store described in "Queue Simulation," on page 231.

26. Using the C++ ADT class, write a program that simulates the operation of a telephone system that might be found in a small business, such as your local pizza parlor. Only one person can answer the phone (a single-server queue), but there can be an unlimited number of calls waiting to be answered.

Queue analysis considers two primary elements, the length of time a requester waits for service (the queue wait time—in this case, the customer calling for pizza) and the service time (the time it takes the customer to place the order). Your program should simulate the operation of the telephone and gather statistics during the process.

The program will require two inputs to run the simulation: (1) the length of time in hours that the service will be provided and (2) the maximum time it takes for the operator to take an order (the maximum service time).

Four elements are required to run the simulation: a timing loop, a call simulator, a call processor, and a start call function.

a. Timing loop: This is simply the simulation loop. Every iteration of the loop will be considered 1 minute in real time. The loop will continue until the service has been in operation the requested amount of time (see input above). When the operating period is complete, however, any waiting calls must be answered before ending the simulation. The timing loop has the following subfunctions:

- Determine whether a call was received (call simulator)
- Process active call
- Start new call

This sequence allows a call to be completed and another call to be started in the same minute.

b. **Call simulator:** The call simulator will use a random number generator to determine whether a call has been received. Scale the random number to an appropriate range, such as 1 to 10.

The random number should be compared with a defined constant. If the value is less than the constant, a call was received; if it is not, then no call was received. For the simulation, set the call level to 50%; that is, on the average, a call will be received every 2 minutes. If a call is received, place it in a queue.

c. **Process active call:** If a call is active, test whether it has been completed. If completed, print the statistics for the current call and gather the necessary statistics for the end-of-job report.

d. **Start new call:** If there are no active calls, start a new call if there is one waiting in the queue. Note that starting a call must calculate the time the call has been waiting.

During the processing, print the data shown in Table 5-1 after each call is completed. (Note: You will not get the same results.)

Clock Time	Call Number	Arrival Time	Wait Time	Start Time	Service Time	Queue Size
4	1	2	0	2	3	2
6	2	3	2	5	2	4

Table 5-1   Sample queue output

At the end of the simulation, print out the following statistics gathered during the processing. Be sure to use an appropriate format for each statistic, such as a float for averages.

a. Total calls: calls received during operating period
b. Total idle time: total time during which no calls were being serviced
c. Total wait time: sum of wait times for all calls
d. Total service time: sum of service time for all calls
e. Maximum queue size: maximum number of calls waiting during simulation
f. Average wait time: total wait time/number of calls
g. Average service time: total service time/number of calls

Run the simulator twice. Both runs should simulate 2 hours. In the first simulation, use a maximum service time of 2 minutes. In the second run, use a maximum service time of 5 minutes.

27. Repeat the queue simulation in Project 26, using multiple queue servers such as you might find in a bank. There should be only one queue. The number of servers, to be read from the keyboard, may range from two to five.

To simulate multiple servers, you will need to provide a separate customer status structure for each server. In the processing loop, each server should be tested for completion. Similarly, in start new call, a call should be started for each idle server.

You will also need to modify the call simulator to handle up to three customers arriving at the same time. To determine the number of customers, generate a random number in the range of 0 to 3. If the number is 0, no customer arrived. If the number is not 0, enqueue the number of customers indicated by the random number.

28. Write a stack and queue test driver. A test driver is a program created to test functions that are to be placed in a library. Its primary purpose is to completely test functions; therefore, it has no application use.

The functions to be tested are create stack, create queue, push stack, pop stack, enqueue, and dequeue. You may include other stack and queue functions as required. All data should be integers. You will need two stacks and two queues in the program, as described below.

a. Input stack: used to store all user input
b. Input queue: used to store all user input
c. Output stack: used to store data deleted from input queue
d. Output queue: used to store data deleted from input stack

Use a menu-driven user interface that prompts the user to select either insert or delete. If an insert is requested, the system should prompt the user for the integer to be inserted. The data are then inserted into the input stack and input queue. If a delete is requested, the data are deleted from both structures: The data popped from the input stack are enqueued in the output queue, and the data dequeued from the input queue are pushed into the output stack.

Processing continues until the input structures are empty. At this point, print the contents of the output stack while deleting all of its data. Label this output "Output Stack." Then, print all of the data in the output queue while deleting all of its data. Label this output "Output Queue." Your output should be formatted as shown below.

```
Output Stack: 18  9 13  7  5  1
Output Queue:  7 13  9 18  5  1
```

Test your program with the following operations:

```
1 input 1    5 delete     9 input 6   13 input 8
2 input 2    6 input 0   10 delete    14 delete
3 delete     7 input 5   11 input 7   15 delete
4 input 3    8 delete    12 delete    16 delete
```

In addition to the computer output from your test, write a short report (less than one page) describing what structural concepts were demonstrated by your output.

29. Queues are commonly used in network systems. For example, e-mail is placed in queues while it is waiting to be sent and after it arrives at the recipient's mailbox. A problem occurs, however, if the outgoing mail processor cannot send one or more of the messages in the queue. For example, a message might not be sent because the recipient's system is not available.

Write an e-mail simulator that processes mail at an average of 40 messages per minute. As messages are received, they are placed in a queue. For the simulation, assume that the messages arrive at an average rate of 30 messages per minute. Remember, the messages must arrive randomly, so you will need to use a random number generator to determine when messages are received (see "Queue Simulation," on page 231).

Each minute, you can dequeue up to 40 messages and send them. Assume that 25% of the messages in the queue cannot be sent in any processing cycle. Again, you will need to use a random number to determine whether a given message can be sent. If it can't be sent, put it back at the end of the queue (enqueue it).

Run the simulation for 24 hours, tracking the number of times each message had to be requeued. At the end of the simulation, print the statistics that show

a. The total messages processed
b. The average arrival rate
c. The average number of messages sent per minute
d. The average number of messages in the queue in a minute
e. The number of messages sent on the first attempt, the number sent on the second attempt, and so forth
f. The average number of times messages had to be requeued (do not include the messages sent the first time in this average)

Recursion

6

In general, there are two approaches to writing repetitive algorithms. One uses iteration; the other uses recursion. **Recursion** is a repetitive process in which an algorithm calls itself. Note, however, that some older languages, including COBOL, do not support recursion.

In this chapter we study recursion. We begin by studying a classical recursive case, factorial. Once we understand how recursion works, we develop some principles for developing recursive algorithms and then use them to develop another recursive case study, Fibonacci numbers. We conclude the theory of recursion with a discussion of a classic recursive algorithm, the Towers of Hanoi. In the last section, we develop C++ implementations for Fibonacci numbers, prefix to postfix conversion, and the Towers of Hanoi.

6-1   FACTORIAL—A CASE STUDY

To begin with a simple example, let's consider the calculation of **facto-rial.** The factorial of a number is the product of the integral values from 1 to the number. This definition is shown in Figure 6-1.

$$\text{Factorial}(n) = \begin{bmatrix} 1 & \text{if } n = 0 \\ n \times (n-1) \times (n-2) \times \ldots \times 3 \times 2 \times 1 & \text{if } n > 0 \end{bmatrix}$$

Figure 6-1   Iterative algorithm definition

Note that this definition is iterative. A repetitive algorithm is defined iteratively whenever the definition involves only the algorithm param-eter(s) and not the algorithm itself. We can calculate the value of fac-torial(4) using Figure 6-1, as follows:

$$\text{factorial}(4) = 4 \times 3 \times 2 \times 1 = 24$$

Recursion Defined

A repetitive algorithm uses **recursion** whenever the algorithm appears within the definition itself. For example, the factorial algorithm can be defined recursively as shown in Figure 6-2.

The decomposition of factorial(3) using Figure 6-2 is shown in Figure 6-3. If you study Figure 6-3 carefully, you will note that the re-cursive solution for a problem involves a two-way journey: first we de-compose the problem from the top to the bottom, and then we solve it from the bottom to the top.

Note

Recursion is a repetitive process in which an algorithm calls itself.

Judging by this example, the recursive calculation appears to be much longer and more difficult. So why would we want to use the re-cursive method? Although the recursive calculation looks more diffi-cult when using paper and pencil, it is often a much easier and more elegant solution when we use computers. Also, it offers a conceptual simplicity to the creator and the reader.

$$\text{Factorial}(n) = \begin{bmatrix} 1 & \text{if } n = 0 \\ n \times (\text{Factorial}(n-1)) & \text{if } n > 0 \end{bmatrix}$$

Figure 6-2   Recursive algorithm definition

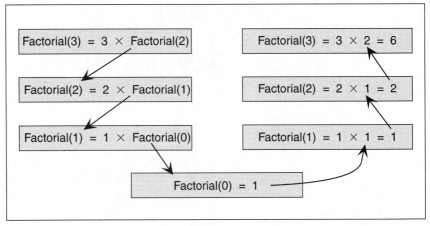

Figure 6-3   Factorial(3) recursively

Iterative Solution

Let's write an algorithm to solve the factorial problem iteratively. This solution usually involves using a loop such as that shown in Algorithm 6-1.

```
algorithm iterativeFactorial (val n <integer>)
Calculates the factorial of a number using a loop.
    Pre    n is the number to be raised factorially
    Return n! is returned
1  i = 1
2  factN = 1
3  loop (i <= n)
   1   factN = factN * i
   2   i = i + 1
4  end loop
5  return factN
end iterativeFactorial
```

Algorithm 6-1   Iterative factorial algorithm

Recursive Solution

Now let's write the same algorithm recursively. The recursive solution does not need a loop; recursion is itself repetition. In the recursive version, we let the algorithm `factorial` call itself, each time with a different set of parameters. Figure 6-4 shows this mechanism and the parameters for each individual call. The algorithm for recursive factorial is shown in Algorithm 6-2.

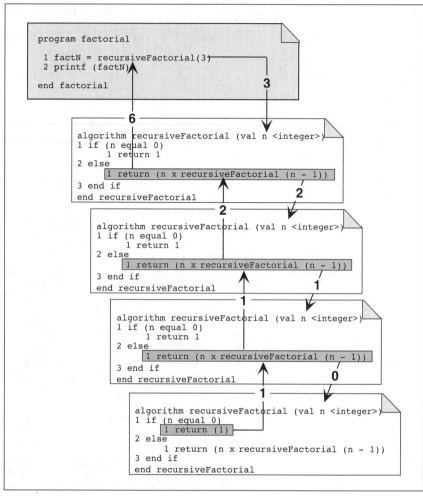

Figure 6-4   Calling a recursive algorithm

```
algorithm recursiveFactorial (val n <integer>)
Calculates factorial of a number using recursion.
    Pre    n is the number being raised factorially
    Post   n! is returned
 1 if (n equal 0)
    1   return 1
 2 else
    1   return (n * recursiveFactorial (n - 1))
 3 end if
end factorial
```

Algorithm 6-2   Recursive factorial

Algorithm 6-2 Analysis   If you compare the iterative and recursive versions of factorial, you should be immediately struck with how much simpler the code in the recursive version is. First, there is no loop. The recursive version consists of a simple selection statement that either returns the value 1 or the product of two values, one of which is a call to factorial itself.

6-2 HOW RECURSION WORKS

To understand how recursion works, we need to first explore how any call works. When a program calls a subroutine—for example, a function in C++ or a procedure in Pascal—the current module suspends processing and the called subroutine takes over control of the program. When the subroutine completes its processing and returns to the module that called it, the module wakes up and continues its processing. One important point in this interaction is that, unless changed through call by reference, all local data in the calling module are unchanged. Every local variable must be in the same state when processing resumes as it was in when processing suspended. Similarly, the parameter list must not be changed. The value of the parameters must be the same before and after a call, unless they are reference parameters.

Let's look at an example of a simple call and see how it works. Figure 6-5 contains an algorithm called `testPower` that prints the value of a number x raised to a power y. To illustrate the function call, we use a separate algorithm, `power`, to determine the actual value of x^y.

Our little program contains three local variables: the base number, `base`; the exponent, `exp`; and the answer, `result`. The base and exponent values must not be changed by the call to power.[1] When

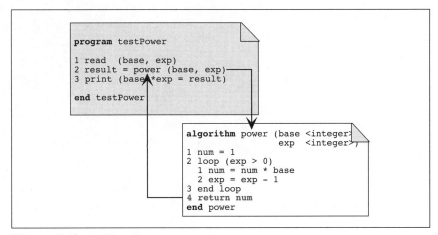

Figure 6-5   Call and return

---

1. In this discussion, we assume a recursive compiler. Languages such as COBOL and FORTRAN operate under a different, nonrecursive design in which there are no local variables.

power terminates, it returns the value of x^y, which is stored in the local variable, `result`.

When `power` begins to execute, it must know the values of the parameters so that it can process them. It must also know where it needs to return when its processing is done. Finally, because `power` returns a value, it must know where the value is to be placed when it terminates. The physical implementation is determined by the compiler writer, but these data are conceptually placed in a **stackframe.** When `power` is called, the stackframe is created and pushed into a system stack. When it concludes, the stackframe is popped, the local variables are replaced, the return value is stored, and processing resumes in the calling algorithm.

Note

A stackframe contains four different elements:

1. The parameters to be processed by the called algorithm
2. The local variables in the calling algorithm
3. The return statement in the calling algorithm
4. The expression that is to receive the return value (if any)

Now that you understand how a call works, you are ready to see how recursion works. Algorithm 6-3 contains a recursive version of the power algorithm discussed earlier.

```
algorithm power (val base <integer>,
                 val exp  <integer>)
This algorithm computes the value of a number, base, raised to
the power of an exponent, exp.
    Pre    base is the number to be raised
           exp is the exponent
    Post   value of base raised to power exp computed
    Return value of base raised to power exp returned
  1 if (exp equal 0)
    1   return (1)
  2 else
    1   return (base * power (base, exp - 1))
  3 end if
end power
```

Algorithm 6-3   Recursive power algorithm

In Figure 6-4, on page 274, we traced the calls for a recursive factorial algorithm. This example is logically correct, but it oversimplifies the calls. Figure 6-6 traces the execution of Algorithm 6-3 in its recursive version and shows the contents of the system stack for each call.

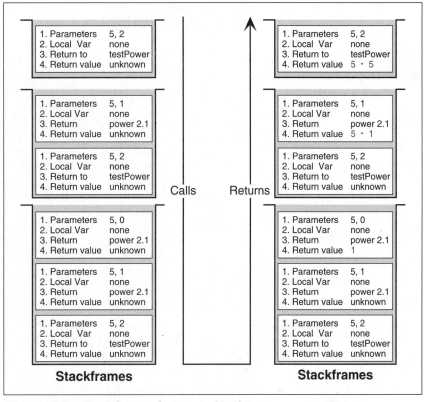

Figure 6-6 Stackframes for power (5, 2)

Referring to Figure 6-6, power is called initially by `testPower` with base and exponent set to 5 and 2, respectively. The first stackframe was created by the original call and contains a return location in the calling algorithm, `testPower`. In the second call, the base is unchanged but the exponent becomes 1. This call creates the second stackframe in Figure 6-6. Note that the parameters are changed and the return address is now `power 2.1`. In the third iteration, the exponent becomes 0. This call is shown in the third stackframe.

At this point, we have reached the base case and begin backing out of the recursion. As each return statement is executed, we return to Statement 2.1 in `power`, first with the value of 1 (the base case), then with a value of 5 (5×1), and finally with a value of 25 (5×5). When we return the third time, we return to the original calling algorithm, `testPower`.

6-3   DESIGNING RECURSIVE ALGORITHMS

Now that we have seen how recursion works, let's turn our attention to the steps for designing a recursive algorithm. We first look at the basic design methodology, then we discuss the limitations of recursion, and finally we design and implement another recursive algorithm.

The Design Methodology

If you examined all hypothetically possible recursive algorithms, you would see that they all have two elements: Each call either *solves* one part of the problem or it reduces *the size* of the problem. In Algorithm 6-2, on page 274, Statement 1.1 solves a small piece of the problem—factorial(0) is 1. Statement 2.1, on the other hand, reduces the size of the problem by recursively calling factorial with n – 1. Once the solution to factorial (n – 1) is known, Statement 2.1 provides a part of the solution to the general problem by returning a value to the calling algorithm.

As we see in Statement 2.1, the general part of the solution is the recursive call: Statement 2.1 calls itself to solve the problem. We also see this in Figure 6-4, on page 274. At each recursive call, the size of the problem is reduced, from the factorial of 3, to 2, to 1, and finally to factorial 0.

The statement that "solves" the problem is known as the **base case.** *Every recursive algorithm must have a base case.* The rest of the algorithm is known as the **general case.** In our factorial example, the base case is factorial (0); the general case is n × factorial (n – 1). The general case contains the logic needed to reduce the size of the problem.

Note

> Every recursive call must either solve a part of the problem or reduce the size of the problem.

In the factorial problem, once the base case has been reached, the solution begins. We now know one part of the answer and can return that part to the next more general statement. Thus, in Algorithm 6-2, on page 274, we know that factorial(0) is 1, and we return that value. This allows us to solve the next general case,

$$\text{factorial(1)} \rightsquigarrow 1 \times \text{factorial(0)} \rightsquigarrow 1 \times 1 \rightsquigarrow 1$$

We can now return the value of factorial(1) to the more general case, factorial(2), which we know to be

$$\text{factorial(2)} \rightsquigarrow 2 \times \text{factorial(1)} \rightsquigarrow 2 \times 1 \rightsquigarrow 2$$

As we solve each general case in turn, we are able to solve the next higher general case until we finally solve the most general case, the original problem.

Returning to the purpose of this section, we are now ready to state the rules for designing a recursive algorithm.

1. First, determine the base case.
2. Then determine the general case.
3. Combine the base case and general case into an algorithm.

In combining the base and general case into an algorithm, you must pay careful attention to the logic. Each call must reduce the size of the problem and move it toward the base case. The base case, when reached, must terminate without a call to the recursive algorithm; that is, it must execute a return.

Limitations of Recursion

We have introduced only a brief explanation of recursion in this section. Recursion works best when the algorithm uses a data structure that naturally supports recursion. For example, in the next chapter we will study trees. Trees are a naturally recursive structure and recursion works well with them. In other cases, the algorithm is naturally suited to recursion. For example, the binary search algorithm lends itself to a natural recursive algorithm, as does the Towers of Hanoi, which we discuss later in this chapter. On the other hand, not all looping algorithms can or should be implemented with recursion, as we discuss below.

Recursive solutions may involve extensive overhead because they use calls. When a call is made, it takes time to build a stackframe and push it into the stack. Conversely, when a return is executed, the stackframe must be popped from the stack and the local variables reset to their previous values. Again, this takes time. A recursive algorithm therefore generally runs slower than its nonrecursive implementation.[2]

Each time we make a call we use up some of our memory allocation. If the recursion is deep—that is, if there are many recursive calls—then we may run out of memory. Therefore, the algorithms we have discussed so far (factorial and powers) are better developed iteratively if large numbers are involved. As a general rule, recursive algorithms should be used only when their efficiency is logarithmic.

Note

You should not use recursion if the answer to any of the following questions is no:

1. Is the algorithm or data structure naturally suited to recursion?
2. Is the recursive solution shorter and more understandable?
3. Does the recursive solution run in acceptable time and space limits?

Design Implementation— Reverse a Linked List

Having studied the design methodology for recursive algorithms and their limitations, we are now ready to put the concepts into practice. Assume that we have a linked list, such as the one shown in Figure 6-7. We need to print the list in reverse but do not have reverse pointers. The easiest way to print the list in reverse is to write a recursive algorithm.

---

2. Most of today's compilers optimize code when possible. When the recursion occurs at the end of a function (known as tail recursion), an optimized compiler will turn the recursive code into a simple loop, thus eliminating the function call inefficiency.

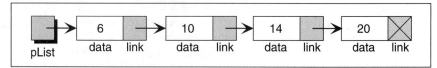

Figure 6-7 A linked list

It should be obvious that to print the list in reverse, we must traverse it to find the last node (20). The **base case,** therefore, is that we have found the end of the list. Similarly, the **general case** is to find the next node. The question is, when do we print? If we print before we find the last node, we print the list in sequence. If we print the list after we find the last node—that is, if we print it as we back out of the recursion—we print it in reverse sequence. Printing in reverse is shown in Figure 6-8. The code is shown in Algorithm 6-4.

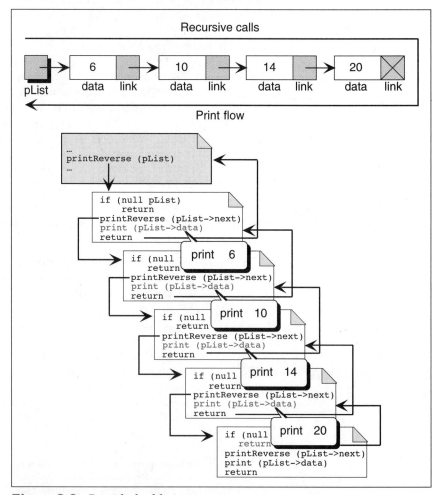

Figure 6-8 Print linked list in reverse

```
algorithm printReverse (val list <pointer to node>)
Print singly linked list in reverse.
    Pre    list has been built
    Post   list printed in reverse
  1 if (null list)
    1   return
  2 end if
  3 printReverse (list->next)
Have reached end of list: print nodes
  4 print (list->data)
  5 return
end printReverse
```

Algorithm 6-4 Print linked list reverse

Algorithm 6-4 Analysis

As you study Algorithm 6-4, remember that Statement 4 cannot be executed until we reach the end of the list. It is not executed immediately after Statement 3, because Statement 3 is a recursive call. We get to Statement 4 only after we return in Statement 1.1 or after we return from the end statement at the end of the algorithm.

Now that we've designed the algorithm, we need to analyze it to determine whether it is really a good solution; that is, is the recursive algorithm a good candidate for recursion? To analyze this algorithm, we turn to the three questions we developed in the note to "Limitations of Recursion," on page 279.

1. Is the algorithm or data structure naturally suited to recursion? A linear list, such as a linked list, is not a naturally recursive structure. Furthermore, the algorithm is not naturally suited to recursion; that is, it is not one of the logarithmic algorithms.

2. Is the recursive solution shorter and more understandable? The answer to this question is yes.

3. Does the recursive solution run in acceptable time and space limits? The number of iterations in the traversal of a linear list can become quite large. Also, because the algorithm has a linear efficiency—that is, it is $O(n)$—it is not a good candidate for recursion.

We thus see that the answer to two of the three questions is no. Therefore, although we can successfully write the algorithm recursively, we should not. It is not a good candidate for recursion.

6-4 ANOTHER CASE STUDY—FIBONACCI NUMBERS

Now let's look at another example of recursion, an algorithm that generates Fibonacci numbers. Named after an Italian mathematician who lived in the early thirteenth century, Leonardo Fibonacci, Fibonacci numbers are a series in which each number is the sum of the previous two numbers. The first few numbers in the Fibonacci series are

```
0, 1, 1, 2, 3, 5, 8, 13, 21, 34, ...
```

The pseudocode for a program that prints Fibonacci numbers is shown in Algorithm 6-5. It begins by asking the user how many Fibonacci numbers are needed. This algorithm is not recursive, but it calls a recursive algorithm that calculates the next number in the series.

```
program Fibonacci
This program prints out a Fibonacci series.
  1 print (This program prints a Fibonacci series.)
  2 print (How many numbers do you want?)
  3 read  (seriesSize)
  4 if (seriesSize < 2)
     1   seriesSize = 2
  5 end if
  6 print (First seriesSize Fibonacci numbers are:)
  7 looper = 0
  8 loop (looper < seriesSize)
     Get next Fibonacci number
     1   nextFib = fib(looper)
     2   print (nextFib)
     3   looper = looper + 1
  9 end loop
end Fibonacci
```

Algorithm 6-5   Fibonacci numbers

To start the series, however, we need to know the first two numbers. As you can see from the above series, they are 0 and 1. Because we are discussing recursion, you should recognize these two numbers as the base cases.

We can generalize the Fibonacci series as follows:

```
Given:
  Fibonacci(0) = 0
  Fibonacci(1) = 1
Then
  Fibonacci(n) = Fibonacci(n - 1) + Fibonacci(n - 2)
```

The generalization of Fibonacci(4) is shown in Figure 6-9. The top half of the figure shows the components of Fibonacci(4) using a

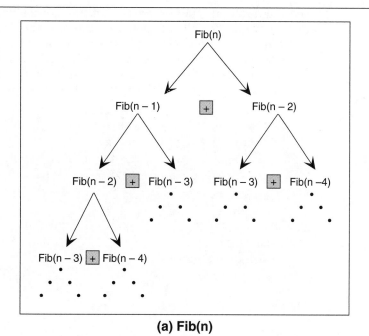

(a) Fib(n)

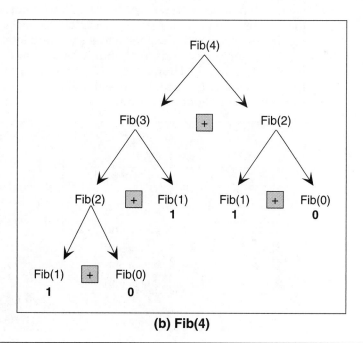

(b) Fib(4)

Figure 6-9   Fibonacci numbers

general notation. The bottom half of the figure shows the components as they would be called to generate the numbers in the series.

To determine the `Fibonacci(4)`, we can start at 0 and move up until we have the number, or we can start at `Fibonacci(4)` and move down to 0. The first technique is used in the iterative solution; the second is used in the recursive solution, which is shown in Algorithm 6-6.

```
algorithm fib (val num <integer>)
Calculates the nth Fibonacci number.
    Pre   num identified the ordinal of the Fibonacci number
    Post  returns the nth Fibonacci number
  1 if (num is 0 OR num is 1)
    Base Case
    1   return num
  2 end if
  3 return (fib (num - 1) + fib (num - 2))
end fib
```

Algorithm 6-6   Recursive Fibonacci

Algorithm 6-6 Analysis

Compare fib in Algorithm 6-5 with the solution in Figure 6-9. To determine the fourth number in the series, we call fib with num set to 4. Determining the answer requires that fib be called recursively eight times, as shown in Figure 6-9, which with the original call gives us a total of nine calls.

This number sounds reasonable. Now, how many calls does it take to determine `Fibonacci(5)`? The answer is 15. As you can see from Table 6-1, the number of calls goes up quickly as we increase the size of the Fibonacci number we are calculating.

No.	Calls	Time[a]	No.	Calls	Time[a]
1	1	< 1 second	11	287	< 1 second
2	3	< 1 second	12	465	< 1 second
3	5	< 1 second	13	753	< 1 second
4	9	< 1 second	14	1219	< 1 second
5	15	< 1 second	15	1973	< 1 second
6	25	< 1 second	20	21,891	< 1 second
7	41	< 1 second	25	242,785	1 second
8	67	< 1 second	30	2,692,573	7 seconds
9	109	< 1 second	35	29,860,703	1 minute
10	177	< 1 second	40	331,160,281	13 minutes

[a] Run on a Power Macintosh 7100/66 with 32 megabytes of memory.

Table 6-1 Fibonacci run time

Table 6-1 leads us to the obvious conclusion that a recursive solution to calculate Fibonacci numbers is not efficient for more than 20 numbers.

6-5 THE TOWERS OF HANOI

The Towers of Hanoi is a classic recursion problem that is relatively easy to follow, is efficient, and uses no complex data structures. Let's look at it.

According to the legend, the monks in a remote mountain monastery knew how to predict when the world would end. They had a set of three diamond needles. Stacked on the first diamond needle were 64 gold disks of decreasing size. The monks moved one disk to another needle each hour, subject to the following rules:

1. Only one disk could be moved at a time.
2. A larger disk must never be stacked above a smaller one.
3. One and only one auxiliary needle could be used for the intermediate storage of disks.

The legend said that when all 64 disks had been transferred to the destination needle, the stars would be extinguished and the world would end. Today we know that we need to have $2^{64} - 1$ moves to do this task. Figure 6-10 shows the Towers of Hanoi with only three disks.

This problem is interesting for two reasons. First, the recursive solution is much easier to code than the iterative solution would be, as is often the case with good recursive solutions. Second, its solution pattern is different from the simple examples we have been discussing. As you study the towers solution, note that after each base case, we return to a decomposition of the general case for several steps. In other words, the problem is divided into several subproblems, each of which has a base case, moving one disk.

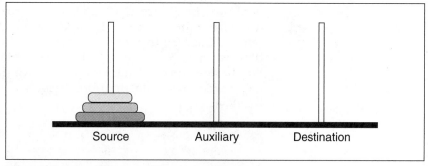

Figure 6-10   Towers of Hanoi—start position

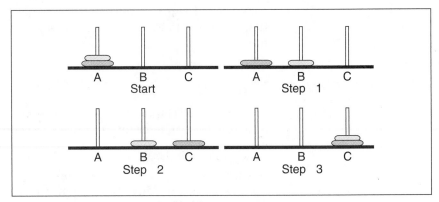

Figure 6-11   Towers solution for two disks

Recursive Towers of Hanoi

To solve this problem, we must study the moves to see if we can find a pattern. We will use only three disks because we do not want the world to end. First, imagine that we have only one disk to move. This is a very simple case, as shown below.

```
Case 1: Move one disk from source to destination needle.
```

Now imagine that we have to move two disks. Figure 6-11 traces the steps for two disks. First, we move the top disk to the auxiliary needle. Then we move the second disk to the destination. Finally, we move the first disk to the top of the second disk on the destination. This gives us the second case, as shown below.

```
Case 2:   Move one disk to auxiliary needle.
          Move one disk to destination needle.
          Move one disk from auxiliary to destination needle.
```

We are now ready to study the case for three disks. Its solution is shown in Figure 6-12. The first three steps move the top two disks from the source to the auxiliary needle. (To see how to do this, refer to Case 2.) In Step 4, we move the bottom disk to the destination. We now have one disk in place. This is an example of Case 1. We then need three more steps to move the two disks on the auxiliary needle to the destination. These steps are summarized in Case 3 below.

```
Case 3:   Move two disks from source to auxiliary needle.
          Move one disk from source to destination needle.
          Move two disks from auxiliary to destination needle.
```

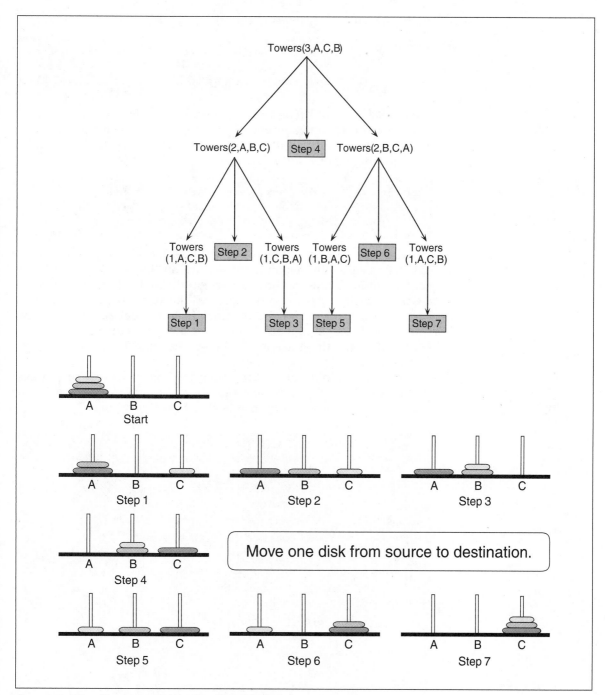

Figure 6-12 Towers solution for three disks

We are now ready to generalize the problem.

```
1 Move n - 1 disks from source to auxiliary      General Case
2 Move one disk from source to destination       Base Case
3 Move n - 1 disks from auxiliary to destination General Case
```

Our solution will require an algorithm with four parameters: the number of disks to be moved, the source needle, the destination needle, and the auxiliary needle. Using pseudocode, the three moves in the generalization shown above are then

```
Call Towers (n - 1, source, auxiliary, destination)
Move one disk from source to destination
Call Towers (n - 1, auxiliary, destination, source)
```

Study the second call above carefully. After we complete the move of the first disk, the remaining disks are on the auxiliary needle. We need to move them from the auxiliary needle to the destination. In this case, the original source needle becomes the auxiliary needle. (Remember that the positions of the parameters in the **called** algorithm are source, destination, and auxiliary. The calling algorithm must remember which of the three needles is the source and which is the destination for each call.)

We can now put these three calls together. In place of physical moves, we use print statements to show the moves that need to be made. The complete pseudocode is shown in Algorithm 6-7.

```
algorithm towers (val disks     <integer>,
                  val source    <character>,
                  val dest      <character>,
                  val auxiliary <character>,
                  ref step      <integer>)
Recursively move disks from source to destination.
    Pre   the tower consists of integer disks
          source, destination, and auxiliary towers given
    Post  steps for moves printed
1 print("Towers: ", disks, source, dest, auxiliary)
2 if (disks 1)
    1   print ("Step ", step,
                "Move from ", source, " to ", dest)
    2   step = step + 1
3 else
    1   towers (disks - 1, source, auxiliary, dest, step)
```

Algorithm 6-7 Towers of Hanoi

```
   2   print ("Step ", step,
                "Move from ", source, " to ", dest)
   3   step = step + 1
   4   towers (disks - 1, auxiliary, dest, source, step)
 4 end if
 5 return
end towers
```

Algorithm 6-7   Towers of Hanoi *(continued)*

Algorithm 6-7 Analysis

Each time we enter the algorithm, we print the current parameters, with the exception of the step. We can thus keep track of which tower is currently the source, which is the destination, and which is the auxiliary. Because the towers are constantly changing their role among the three, printing the call parameters helps us keep them straight.

Two statements print the move instructions. The first is at Statement 2.1. It prints the instructions when there is only one disk left on a tower. The second move instruction is printed at Statement 3.2. It is printed whenever we return from the recursion and provides the instructions to move a disk when there are more than one on a tower.

It is important to study the parameters in the two calls. Note how they are moving the towers' roles from destination to auxiliary in Statement 3.1 and from auxiliary to source in Statement 3.4.

The output from the algorithm is shown in Figure 6-13. You will undoubtedly need to trace the program with the output to follow the recursion.

Calls:	Output:
Towers (3, A, C, B)	
Towers (2, A, B, C)	
Towers (1, A, C, B)	
	Step 1: Move from A to C
	Step 2: Move from A to B
Towers (1, C, B, A)	
	Step 3: Move from C to B
	Step 4: Move from A to C
Towers (2, B, C, A)	
Towers (1, B, A, C)	
	Step 5: Move from B to A
	Step 6: Move from B to C
Towers (1, A, C, B)	
	Step 7: Move from A to C

Figure 6-13   Tracing of Algorithm 6-7, Towers of Hanoi

6-6   C++ IMPLEMENTATIONS OF RECURSION

In this section we implement three recursive algorithms in C++. The first, Fibonacci numbers, is limited because of the memory it requires to determine a large Fibonacci number. The second uses recursion to convert a prefix expression to a postfix format, and the third, the Towers of Hanoi, demonstrates a good application of recursion. But be careful that you don't solve it for 64 disks or the world might end.

Fibonacci Numbers

In our Fibonacci program, we begin by asking the user how many numbers are needed. We then use a *for* loop that calls the Fibonacci function the prescribed number of times, printing the next number in the series in each loop.

The C++ implementation of Fibonacci follows the pseudocode statement for statement. It is interesting to note that the bulk of the code in the algorithm is the main line code to read the number of numbers to be generated and to print the results. There are actually only three statements in the recursive algorithm. (See Program 6-1.)

```
 1   /* This program prints out a Fibonacci series.
 2          Written by:
 3          Date:
 4   */
 5   #include <iostream>
 6   #include <iomanip.h>
 7
 8   // Prototype Statements
 9      long fib (long num);
10
11   int main (void)
12   {
13   // Local Definitions
14      int looper;
15      int seriesSize;
16
17   // Statements
18      cout << "This program prints a Fibonacci series.\n";
19      cout << "How many numbers do you want? ";
20      cin  >> seriesSize;
21      if (seriesSize < 2)
22          seriesSize = 2;
23
24      cout << "\nFirst " << seriesSize
25          << " Fibonacci numbers: \n";
26      for (looper = 0; looper < seriesSize; looper++)
```
Program 6-1   Recursive Fibonacci

```
27            {
28               if (looper % 5)
29                    cout << setw (8) << fib(looper);
30               else
31                    cout << endl << setw (8) << fib(looper);
32            } // for
33      cout << endl;
34      return 0;
35   } //  main
36
37   /* ==================== fib ====================
38      Calculates the nth Fibonacci number.
39           Pre     num identifies Fibonacci number
40           Post    returns nth Fibonacci number
41   */
42   long fib (long num)
43   {
44   // Statements
45      if (num == 0 || num == 1)
46           // Base Case
47           return num;
48      return (fib (num - 1) + fib (num - 2));
49   } // fib
```

Results
```
    This program prints a Fibonacci series.
    How many numbers do you want? 30

    First 30 Fibonacci numbers:

            0        1        1        2        3
            5        8       13       21       34
           55       89      144      233      377
          610      987     1597     2584     4181
         6765    10946    17711    28657    46368
        75025   121393   196418   317811   514229
```

Program 6-1 Recursive Fibonacci *(continued)*

Program 6-1 Analysis

If you have difficulty following the code, refer to Figure 6-9, on page 283, and trace the first four Fibonacci numbers. The first 30 numbers are shown at the end of the algorithm. Unless you have a very fast computer, we recommend that you not try to calculate more than 30 to 35 numbers.

Prefix to Postfix Conversion

In Chapter 4 we used a stack to convert infix expressions to the postfix format. In this section, we use recursion to convert prefix expressions to the postfix format.

Before looking at the algorithms, let's make sure that we understand the basic concept. Given the following prefix expression

*AB

we convert it by moving the operator (*) after the operands (A and B). The postfix format of the expression is shown below. To keep the algorithm as simple as possible, we assume that each operand is only one character and that there are only four operators: add (+), subtract (−), multiply (*), and divide (/).

AB*

As stated, to convert a prefix expression, we must find its operator and move it after the two operands. By definition, the operator will always be the first character in the prefix string. Following the operator are its two operands. As the expression grows in complexity, however, we can have multiple operators and operands in an expression. Consider the following prefix expression, which we will use for our discussions.

−+*ABC/EF

This expression consists of several binary expressions combined into one complex expression. To parse it, we begin at the left and work right until we isolate one binary expression, in this case *AB. Once we have a simple prefix expression, we can convert it to postfix and put it in the output.

The first step in designing a recursive algorithm is determining the base case. The question, therefore, is "What is the base case?" Obviously, it is not finding an operator. Not so obviously, the base case turns out to be finding an operand—in our example, any of the alphabetic characters.

Because the operand can contain another expression, the general case is to find the operator and the left and right operands in the binary expression. We then concatenate them into one postfix expression.

To find the left and right operands in the prefix expression, we need a second algorithm that determines the length of a prefix expression. The length of an expression is the length of the first subexpression plus the length of the second expression plus 1 for the operator. We also use recursion for this algorithm. Because each operand is one character long, our base case is finding one operand.

Prefix to Postfix

We are now ready to design the algorithms. Algorithm 6-8 contains the pseudocode to build the postfix expression.

```
algorithm preToPostFix (val preFixIn  <string>,
                            ref postFix   <string>)
Convert a preFix string to a postFix string.
    Pre    preFix is a valid preFixIn expression
    Post   postFix contains converted expression
  1 if (length of preFixIn is 1)
    Base case: one character string is an operand
    1    postFix = preFixIn
    2    return
  2 end if
If not an operand, must be an operator
  3 operator = first character of preFixIn
Find first expression
  4 lengthOfExpr = findExprLen (preFixIn less first char)
  5 temp = substring(preFixIn[2, lengthOfExpr])
  6 preToPostFix (temp, postFix1)
Find second postFix expression
  7 temp = prefixIn[lengthOfExpr + 1, end of string]
  8 preToPostFix (temp, postFix2)
Concatenate postfix expressions and operator
  9 postFix = postFix1 + postFix2 + operator
 10 return
end preToPostFix
```

Algorithm 6-8   Convert prefix expression to postfix

Algorithm 6-8 Analysis

The algorithm is rather straightforward. The most difficult part is finding the prefix expression. We find it by determining its length and then storing it in a temporary string. The notation in Statement 5 indicates that the substring starting at the first location and through the second location is to be assigned to `temp`. Once we have identified a prefix expression, we recursively call Algorithm 6-8 to convert it to postfix.

Find Length of Prefix Expression

Now let's look at the algorithm that determines the length of the prefix expression. As stated earlier, this algorithm needs to return the length of the expression. Once again, the base case is finding an operand. From the definition of the problem, we know that each operand is one character long. The minimum length of a prefix expression is therefore three: one for the operator and one for each operand. As we recursively decompose the expression, we continue to add the size of its combined expressions until we have the total length. The code is shown in Algorithm 6-9.

```
algorithm findExprLen (val exprIn <string>)
Recursively determine the length of a prefix expression.
  Pre    exprIn is a valid prefix expression
  Post   length of expression returned
 1 if (first character is operator)
   Find length of first prefix expression
   1   lenExpr1 = findExprLen (exprIn + 1)
   Find length of second prefix expression
   2   lenExpr2 = findExprLen (exprIn + 1 + lenExpr1)
   3   return 1 + lenExpr1 + lenExpr2
 2 else
   1   return 1
 3 end if
end findExprLen
```

Algorithm 6-9   Find length of prefix expression

Algorithm 6-9 Analysis

We examine the first character of a string containing a prefix expression or a substring. If it is an operator, we recursively add the length of its two operands. The algorithm returns either 1 (the base case) or the length of the prefix expression (the solution).

Prefix to Postfix Implementation

With the design complete, we are ready to write Program 6-2. The main line is simply a test driver that calls preToPostFix and prints the results. The two functions parallel the pseudocode developed in the previous section. The results are shown at the end.

```
 1  /* Convert prefix to postfix expression.
 2        Written by:
 3        Date:
 4  */
 5  #include <fstream>
 6  #include <string.h>
 7
 8  // Prototype Declarations
 9  void preToPostFix  (char *preFixIn, char *exprOut);
10  int  findExprLen   (char *exprIn);
11
12  int main (void)
13  {
14  // Local Definitions
15     char  preFixExpr[256]  = "-+*ABC/EF";
```

Program 6-2   Prefix to postfix

```
16    char  postFixExpr[256] = "";
17
18  // Statements
19    cout << "Begin prefix to postfix conversion\n\n";
20
21    preToPostFix (preFixExpr, postFixExpr);
22    cout << "Prefix expr:  " << preFixExpr  << endl;
23    cout << "Postfix expr: " << postFixExpr << endl;
24
25    cout << "\nEnd prefix to postfix conversion\n";
26    return 0;
27  } // main
28
29  /* ==================== preToPostFix ====================
30    Convert prefix expression to postfix format.
31       Pre   preFixIn is string containing prefix expression
32               expression can contain no errors/spaces
33             postFix is string variable to receive postfix
34       Post  expression has been converted
35  */
36  void preToPostFix (char *preFixIn,
37                     char *postFix)
38  {
39  // Local Definitions
40    char  operatr [2];
41    char  postFix1[256];
42    char  postFix2[256];
43    char  temp    [256];
44    int   lenPreFix;
45
46  // Statements
47    if (strlen(preFixIn) == 1)
48       {
49        *postFix        = *preFixIn;
50        *(postFix + 1) = '\0';
51        return;
52       } // if only operand
53
54    *operatr        = *preFixIn;
55    *(operatr + 1) = '\0';
56
57    // Find first expression
58    lenPreFix = findExprLen (preFixIn + 1);
59    strncpy (temp, preFixIn + 1, lenPreFix);
60    *(temp + lenPreFix) = '\0';
61    preToPostFix (temp, postFix1);
```

Program 6-2 Prefix to postfix *(continued)*

```
62
63      // Find second expression
64      strcpy (temp, preFixIn + 1 + lenPreFix);
65      preToPostFix (temp, postFix2);
66
67      // Concatenate to postFix
68      strcpy (postFix, postFix1);
69      strcat (postFix, postFix2);
70      strcat (postFix, operatr);
71
72      return;
73   } // preToPostFix
74
75   /* ==================== findExprLen ====================
76      Determine size of first prefix substring in an expression.
77         Pre    exprIn contains prefix expression
78         Post   size of expression is returned
79   */
80   int findExprLen (char *exprIn)
81   {
82   // Local Definitions
83      int  lenExpr1;
84      int  lenExpr2;
85
86   // Statements
87      switch (*exprIn)
88         {
89          case '*':
90          case '/':
91          case '+':
92          case '-':
93              // Find length of first prefix expression
94              lenExpr1  =  findExprLen (exprIn + 1);
95
96              // Find length of second prefix expression
97              lenExpr2  =  findExprLen (exprIn + 1 + lenExpr1);
98              break;
99          default:
100             // base case--first char is operand
101             lenExpr1 = lenExpr2 = 0;
102             break;
103         } // switch
104     return lenExpr1 + lenExpr2 + 1;
105   } // findExprLen
```

Results:
Begin prefix to postfix conversion

Program 6-2 Prefix to postfix *(continued)*

```
Prefix expr:  -+*ABC/EF
Postfix expr: AB*C+EF/-

End prefix to postfix conversion
```

Program 6-2   Prefix to postfix *(continued)*

Towers of Hanoi

Once again we see the elegance of recursion. With only 69 lines of code we solve a relatively difficult problem. Furthermore, the recursive portion of the algorithm that does all of the work is only eight statements long, including three print statements. As is often the case with recursive algorithms, the analysis and design of the algorithm take longer than the time to write it. The code is shown in Program 6-3.

```
 1   /* Test Towers of Hanoi
 2         Written by:
 3         Date:
 4   */
 5   #include <iostream.h>
 6
 7   // Prototype Statements
 8      void towers (int  n,    char source,
 9                      char dest, char auxiliary);
10
11   int main (void)
12   {
13   // Local Definitions
14      int numDisks;
15
16   // Statements
17      cout << "Please enter number of disks: ";
18      cin  >> numDisks;
19
20      cout << "Start Towers of Hanoi\n\n";
21
22      towers (numDisks, 'A', 'C', 'B');
23
24      cout  << "\nI hope you didn't select 64 "
25            << "and end the world!\n";
26
27      return 0;
28   } // main
29
30   /* ==================== towers ====================
31      Move one disk from source to destination through the
```

Program 6-3   Towers of Hanoi

```
32      use of recursion.
33          Pre    the tower consists of n disks
34                 source, destination, and auxiliary towers given
35          Post   steps for moves printed
36  */
37  void towers (int    n,
38                char  source,
39                char  dest,
40                char  auxiliary)
41  {
42  // Local Definitions
43      static int step = 0;
44
45  // Statements
46      cout << "Towers ("
47          << n           << ", "
48          << source      << ", "
49          << dest        << ", "
50          << auxiliary << ")"  << endl;
51
52      if (n == 1)
53          cout << "\t\t\t\t\t\tStep " << setw(3) << ++step
54               << ": Move from "
55               << source <<   " to "
56               << dest    << endl;
57      else
58          {
59            towers (n - 1, source, auxiliary, dest);
60
61            cout << "\t\t\t\t\t\tStep " << setw(3) << ++step
62                 << ": Move from "
63                 << source <<   " to "
64                 << dest    << endl;
65
66            towers (n - 1, auxiliary, dest, source);
67          } // if  else
68      return;
69  } // towers
```

Results:
    Please enter number of disks: 3
    Start Towers of Hanoi

    Towers (3, A, C, B)
    Towers (2, A, B, C)
    Towers (1, A, C, B)
                              Step   1: Move from A to C

Program 6-3 Towers of Hanoi *(continued)*

```
                                          Step    2: Move from A to B
        Towers (1, C, B, A)
                                          Step    3: Move from C to B
                                          Step    4: Move from A to C

        Towers (2, B, C, A)
        Towers (1, B, A, C)
                                          Step    5: Move from B to A
                                          Step    6: Move from B to C

        Towers (1, A, C, B)
                                          Step    7: Move from A to C


        I hope you didn't select 64 and end the world!
```

Program 6-3 Towers of Hanoi *(continued)*

6-7   SUMMARY

- There are two approaches to writing repetitive algorithms: iteration and recursion.
  - Recursion is a repetitive process in which an algorithm calls itself.
  - A repetitive algorithm uses recursion whenever the algorithm appears within the definition itself.
- When a program calls a subroutine, the current module suspends processing and the called subroutine takes over the control of the program. When the subroutine completes its processing and returns to the module that called it, the module wakes up and continues its processing.
- When control is returned to a calling module, it must know four pieces of information, which are stored in a stackframe:
  a. The values of parameters
  b. The values of local variables
  c. Where it should return when its processing is done
  d. The return value
- When a module calls a subroutine recursively, in each call, all of the information needed by the subroutine is pushed in the stackframe. The information is popped in the reverse order when subroutines are terminated one after another, and finally the control is returned to the calling module.
- A recursive algorithm has two elements: Each call either solves only part of the problem or reduces the size of the problem.
- The statement that solves the problem is known as the base case; every recursive algorithm must have a base case.
- The rest of the recursive algorithm is known as the general case.
- The general rule for designing a recursive algorithm is as follows:
  a. First, determine the base case.
  b. Then, determine the general case.
  c. Combine the base case and the general case into an algorithm.
- You should not use recursion if the answer to any of the following questions is no:
  a. Is the algorithm or data structure naturally suited to recursion?
  b. Is the recursive solution shorter and more understandable?
  c. Does the recursive solution run in acceptable time and space limits?

6-8   PRACTICE SETS

Exercises

1. Consider the following algorithm:

```
algorithm fun1 (x <integer>)
1 if (x < 5)
   1   return (3 * x)
2 else
   1   return (2 * fun1 (x - 5) + 7)
3 end if
end fun1
```

What would be returned if fun1 is called as
a. fun1 (4)?
b. fun1 (10)?
c. fun1 (12)?

2. Consider the following algorithm:

```
algorithm fun2 (x <integer>
                y <integer>)
1 if (x < y)
   1   return -3
2 else
   1   return (fun2 (x - y, y + 3) + y)
3 end if
end fun2
```

What would be returned if fun2 is called as
a. fun2 (2, 7)?
b. fun2 (5, 3)?
c. fun2 (15, 3)?

3. Consider the following algorithm:

```
algorithm fun3 (x <integer>
                y <integer>)
1 if (x > y)
   1   return -1
2 elseif (x equal y)
   1   return 1
3 else
   1   return (x * fun3 (x + 1, y))
4 end if
end fun3
```

What would be returned if `fun3` is called as
a. `fun3 (10,4)`?
b. `fun3 (4,3)`?
c. `fun3 (4,7)`?
d. `fun3 (0,0)`?

4. One of the methods to calculate the square root of a number is Newton's method. The formula for Newton's method is shown in Figure 6-14. Write the pseudocode for a recursive algorithm to compute a square root using Newton's method. Verify your algorithm by using it to manually calculate the following test cases: `squareRoot (5, 2, 0.01)` and `squareRoot (4, 2, 0.01)`.

$$
\text{squareRoot (num, ans, tol)} =
\begin{bmatrix}
\text{ans} & \text{if } | \text{ans}^2 - \text{num} | \leq \text{tol} \\
\text{squareRoot(num, (ans}^2 + \text{num)/(2} \times \text{ans), tol)} & \text{otherwise}
\end{bmatrix}
$$

Figure 6-14   Newton's method for Exercise 4

5. The greatest common divisor (gcd) of two integers can be found using Euclid's algorithm. Euclid's algorithm is shown in Figure 6-15.

$$
\text{gcd (x, y)} =
\begin{bmatrix}
\text{gcd (y, x)} & \text{if } x < y \\
\text{x} & \text{if } y = 0 \\
\text{gcd (y, x mod y)} & \text{otherwise}
\end{bmatrix}
$$

Figure 6-15   Euclid's algorithm for Exercise 5

   Write a recursive algorithm that calculates the gcd of two integers. Verify your algorithm by using it to manually calculate the following test cases: `gcd(4, 28)`, `gcd(22, 4)`, and `gcd(22, 5)`.

6. The combination of n objects, such as balls in a basket, taken k at a time can be calculated recursively using the formula shown in Figure 6-16. This is a useful formula. For example, several state lotteries require players to choose six numbers out of a series of possible numbers. This formula can be used to calculate the number of possible combinations, k, of n objects. For example, for 49 numbers, there are `C(49, 6)`, or 13,983,816, different combinations of six numbers. Write a recursive algorithm to calculate the combination of n objects taken k at a time.

7. Ackerman's number, used in mathematical logic, can be calculated using the formula shown in Figure 6-17. Write a recursive algorithm that calculates Ackerman's number. Verify your algorithm by using it to manually calculate the following test cases: `Ackerman(2, 3)`, `Ackerman(2, 5)`, `Ackerman(0, 3)`, and `Ackerman(3, 0)`.

$$C(n, k) = \begin{bmatrix} 1 & \text{if } k = 0 \text{ or } n = k \\ C(n, k) = C(n - 1, k) + C(n - 1, k - 1) & \text{if } n > k > 0 \end{bmatrix}$$

Figure 6-16   Selection algorithm for Exercise 6

$$\text{Ackerman } (M, \ N) = \begin{bmatrix} N + 1 & \text{if } M = 0 \\ \text{Ackerman } (M - 1, 1) & \text{if } N = 0 \\ \text{Ackerman } (M - 1, \text{Ackerman } (M, N - 1)) & \text{otherwise} \end{bmatrix}$$

Figure 6-17   Ackerman formula for Problem 7

Problems

8. Write a recursive algorithm that calculates and returns the length of a linked list.

9. Write a recursive algorithm that converts a string of numerals to an integer. For example, "43567" will be converted to 43567.

10. Write a recursive algorithm to add the first n elements of the series

$$1 + 1/2 + 1/3 + 1/4 + 1/5 + \ldots + 1/n$$

11. Write a recursive algorithm to determine whether a string is a palindrome. A string is a **palindrome** if it can be read forward and backward with the same meaning. Capitalization and spacing are ignored. For example, *anna* and *go dog* are palindromes. Test your algorithm with the following two palindromes and at least one case that is not a palindrome.

    Madam, I'm Adam
    Able was I ere I saw Elba

12. Write a recursive algorithm to check whether a specified character is in a string.

13. Write a recursive algorithm to count all occurrences of a specified character in a string.

14. Write a recursive algorithm that removes all occurrences of a specified character from a string.

15. Write a recursive algorithm that finds all occurrences of a substring in a string.

16. Write a recursive algorithm that changes an integer to a binary number.

17. A perfect number is a number that is the sum of its factors. For example, 6 is a perfect number because 6 = 1 + 2 + 3. Write a recursive algorithm to calculate all perfect numbers smaller than a given number.

18. Write the recursive version of the binary search algorithm.

19. Write a recursive C++ function to calculate the square root of a number using Newton's method. (See Exercise 4.) Test your function by printing the square root of 125, 763, and 997.

20. Write a recursive algorithm that reads a string of characters from the keyboard and prints them reversed.

21. The greatest common divisor (gcd) of two integers can be found using Euclid's algorithm. (See Exercise 5.) Write a recursive C++ function that calculates the gcd of two integers. Test your function by printing the greatest common divisor of the following factors: 4, 28; 22, 4; 22, 5; 128, 16; 802, 800; and 997, 19.

22. The combination of n objects, such as balls in a basket, taken k at a time can be calculated recursively using the combination formula. (See Exercise 6.) Write a C++ function to calculate the number of combinations present in a number. Test your function by computing and printing C(10, 3).

23. Ackerman's number, used in mathematical logic, can be calculated using the formula shown in Exercise 7. Write a recursive C++ function that calculates Ackerman's number. Verify your algorithm by using it to calculate the following test cases: Ackerman(5,2), Ackerman(2,5), Ackerman(0,3), and Ackerman(3,0).

24. Write the C++ function for the recursive algorithm that prints the elements of a linked list in reverse order. (See Algorithm 6-4, "Print linked list reverse," on page 281.)

Projects

25. In Chapter 4 we used a stack to solve the eight queens problem. Any problem that can be solved with a stack can be solved with recursion. Rewrite Algorithm 4-15, "Eight queens problem," on page 187, to solve it using recursion.

26. Rewrite Algorithm 4-13, "Evaluation of postfitx expressions," on page 181, using recursion.

27. If a recursion call is the last executable statement in the algorithm, **tail recursion,** it can easily be removed using iteration. Tail recursion is so named because the return point of each call is at the end of the algorithm. Thus, there are no executable statements to be executed after each call. To change a tail recursion to an iteration, we can use the following steps:

  a. Use a variable to replace the procedure call.
  b. Use a loop with the limit condition as the base case (or its complement).
  c. Enclose all executable statements inside the loop.
  d. Change the recursive call to an appropriate assignment statement.
  e. Use appropriate statements to reassign values to parameters.
  f. Return the value of the variable defined in Step a.

  Write the iterative version of the recursion factorial algorithm (Algorithm 6-2, on page 274) and test it by printing the value of factorial(5) and factorial(20).

28. Write the iterative version of Fibonacci, algorithm (Algorithm 6-6, on page 284), using the hints given in Project 27. Note that Step c in Project 27 will be different because factorial uses two recursive calls in the last statement.

29. Even if a recursion call is not the last executable statement in the algorithm, it can still be removed using a stack. However, it is easier to remove the recursion from an algorithm that returns no value (returns void). We can create a stack of records in which each record holds the local variables, parameters, and return address. In this case, the recursive calls and the return statements in the algorithm can be removed using the following steps:

a. Each recursive call can be simulated by
- Pushing a record containing the local variables, parameters, and return address of the line into the stack
- Resetting all of the parameters to their new values
- Going to the beginning of the algorithm

b. Each return statement can be simulated by
- Popping the stack and restoring the value of parameters and local variables
- Going to the address defined by the returning address popped from the stack

Write the iteration version of recursion Tower of Hanoi (Algorithm 6-7, on page 289) and test it using eight disks.

Introduction to Trees

7

The study of trees in mathematics can be traced to Gustav Kirchhoff in the middle nineteenth century and several years later to Arthur Cayley, who used trees to study the structure of algebraic formulas. Cayley's work undoubtedly laid the framework for Grace Hopper's use of trees in 1951 to represent arithmetic expressions. Hopper's work bears a strong resemblance to today's binary tree formats. [1]

Trees are used extensively in computer science to represent algebraic formulas, as an efficient method for searching large, dynamic lists, and for such diverse applications as artificial intelligence systems and encoding algorithms. In this chapter we discuss the basic concepts behind the computer science application of trees. Then, in the following two chapters, we develop the application of trees for specific problems.

---

1. Donald E. Knuth, *The Art of Computer Programming* Vol. 1, *Fundamental Algorithms*, 2nd ed. (Reading, MA: Addison-Wesley, 1972), 405, 458.

7-1   BASIC TREE CONCEPTS

A **tree** consists of a finite set of elements, called **nodes,** and a finite set of directed lines, called **branches,** that connect the nodes. The number of branches associated with a node is the **degree** of the node. When the branch is directed toward the node, it is an **indegree** branch; when the branch is directed away from the node, it is an **outdegree** branch. The sum of the indegree and outdegree branches is the degree of the node.

Note

> A tree consists of a finite set of elements, called nodes, and a finite set of directed lines, called branches, that connect the nodes.

If the tree is not empty, then the first node is called the **root.** The indegree of the root is, by definition, zero. With the exception of the root, all of the nodes in a tree must have an indegree of exactly one. All nodes in the tree can have zero, one, or more branches leaving them; that is, they may have an outdegree of zero, one, or more. Figure 7-1 is a representation of a tree.

Terminology

In addition to *root*, many different terms are used to describe the attributes of a tree. A **leaf** is any node with an outdegree of zero. A node that is not a root or a leaf is known as an **internal node** because it is found in the middle portion of a tree.

A node is a **parent** if it has successor nodes—that is, if it has an outdegree greater than zero. Conversely, a node with a predecessor is a **child.** A child node has an indegree of one. Two or more nodes with the same parent are **siblings.** Fortunately, we don't have to worry about aunts, uncles, nieces, nephews, and cousins. Although some literature uses the term *grandparent*, we do not. We prefer the more general term *ancestor*. An **ancestor** is any node in the path from the root to the node. A **descendent** is any node in the path below the parent node; that is, all nodes in the paths from a given node to a leaf are descendents of the node. Figure 7-2 shows the usage of these terms.

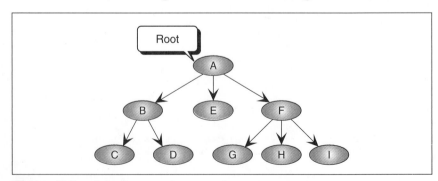

Figure 7-1   A tree

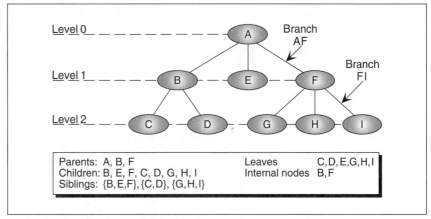

Figure 7-2   Tree nomenclature

Several terms drawn from mathematics or created by computer scientists are used to describe attributes of trees and their nodes. A **path** is a sequence of nodes in which each node is adjacent to the next one. Every node in the tree can be reached by following a unique path starting from the root. In Figure 7-2, the path from the root to the leaf I is designated as AFI. It includes two distinct branches, AF and FI.

The **level** of a node is its distance from the root. Because the root has a zero distance from itself, the root is at level 0. The children of the root are at level 1, their children are level 2, and so forth. Note the relationship between levels and siblings in Figure 7-2. Siblings are always at the same level, but all nodes in a level are not necessarily siblings. For example, at level 2, C and D are siblings, as are G, H, and I. However, D and G are not siblings because they have different parents.

The **height** of the tree is the level of the leaf in the longest path from the root plus 1. By definition, the height of an empty tree is –1. Figure 7-2 contains nodes at three levels: 0, 1, and 2. Its height is 3. Because the tree is drawn upside down, some texts refer to the **depth** of a tree rather than its height.

Note

> The level of a node is its distance from the root. The height of a tree is the level of the leaf in the longest path from the root plus 1.

A tree may be divided into subtrees. A **subtree** is any connected structure below the root. The first node in a subtree is known as the root of the subtree and is used to name the subtree. Furthermore, subtrees can be subdivided into subtrees. In Figure 7-3, BCD is a subtree, as are E and FGHI. Note that by this definition, a single node is a subtree. Thus, the subtree B can be divided into two subtrees, C and D, and the subtree F contains the subtrees G, H, and I.

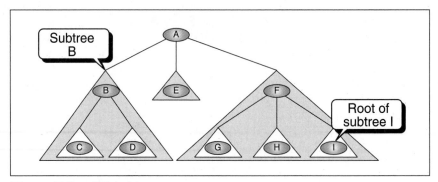

Figure 7-3   Subtrees

The concept of subtrees leads us to a recursive definition of a tree: A tree is a set of nodes that either (1) is empty, or (2) has a designated node, called the root, from which hierarchically descend zero or more subtrees, which are also trees.

Tree Representation

Whereas a tree is generally implemented in the computer using pointers, outside the computer there are three different representations for trees. The first is the organization chart format, which is basically the notation we use to represent trees in our figures. The term we use for this notation is **general tree.** The general tree representation of a computer's components is shown in Figure 7-4; it is discussed in Section 7-5.

The second representational notation is the indented list. You will find it most often used in bill-of-materials systems in which a parts list represents the assembly structure of an item. The graphical representation of a computer system's components in Figure 7-4 clearly shows the relationship among the various components of a computer, but graphical representations are not easily generated from a database

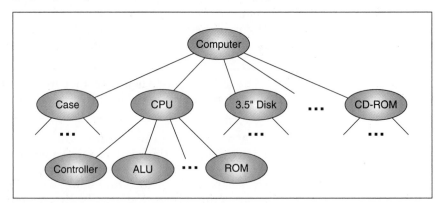

Figure 7-4   Computer parts list as a general tree

system. The bill-of-materials format was therefore created to show the same information using a textual parts list format. In a bill of materials, each assembly component is shown indented below its assembly. Some bills of materials even show the level number of each component. Because a bill of materials shows which components are assembled into each assembly, it is sometimes called a **goezinta** (goes into) list. Table 7-1 shows the computer bill of materials in an indented parts list format.

Part Number	Description
301	Computer
301-1	Case
. . .	. . .
301-2	CPU
301-2-1	Controller
301-2-2	ALU
. . .	. . .
301-2-9	ROM
301-3	3.5" Disk
301-3-1	. . .
...	. . .
301-9	CD-ROM
. . .	. . .

Table 7-1 Computer bill of materials

There is another common bill of materials with which you should be familiar. When you write a structured program, the entire program can be considered an assembly of related functions. Your structure chart is a general tree representing the relationship among the functions.

The third user format is the parenthetical listing. This format is used with algebraic expressions. When a tree is represented in parenthetical notation, each open parenthesis indicates the start of a new level; each closing parenthesis completes the current level and moves up one level in the tree. Consider the tree shown in Figure 7-1, on page 306. Its parenthetical notation is

A (B (C D) E F (G H I))

To convert a general tree to its parenthetical notation, we use the code in Algorithm 7-1.

Using this algorithm with Figure 7-1, we start by placing the root (A) in the output. Because A is a parent, we insert an opening parenthesis

```
algorithm ConvertToParen (val root    <node pointer>,
                              ref output <string>)
Convert a general tree to parenthetical notation.
    Pre   root is a pointer to a tree node
    Post  output contains parenthetical notation
  1 Place root in output
  2 If (root is a parent)
     1   Place an open parenthesis in the output
     2   ConvertToParen (root's first child)
     3   loop (more siblings)
        1   ConvertToParen (root's next child)
     4   end loop
     5   Place close parenthesis in the output
  3 end if
  4 return
end ConvertToParen
```

Algorithm 7-1   Convert general tree to parenthetical notation

in the output and then process the subtree B by first placing its root (B) in the output. Again, because B is a parent, we place an open parenthesis in the output and recursively call ConvertToParen to insert C. This time, however, the root has no children. The algorithm therefore terminates with a return to Statement 2.3. After placing D in the output, we return to the loop statement to discover that there are no more siblings. We now place a close parenthesis in the output and return to Statement 2.3 to continue placing B's siblings in the output.

After I's children have been completely processed, we add a closing parenthesis (2.5), which takes us up one level to complete the processing of B's siblings and the addition of a closing parenthesis. Note that when the processing is correctly done, the parentheses are balanced. If they are not balanced, you have made a mistake in the conversion.

7-2   BINARY TREES

A **binary tree** is a tree in which no node can have more than two subtrees. In other words, a node can have zero, one, or two subtrees. These subtrees are designated as the **left subtree** and **right subtree**. Figure 7-5 shows a binary tree with its two subtrees. Note that each subtree is itself a binary tree.

To better understand the structure of binary trees, study Figure 7-6. It contains eight trees, the first of which is a null tree. A **null tree** is

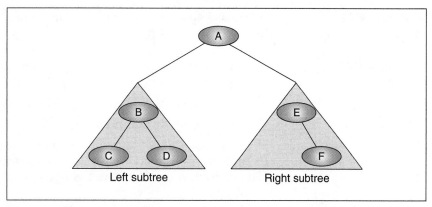

Figure 7-5   Binary tree

a tree with no nodes (see Figure 7-6[a]). As you study this figure, note that symmetry is not a tree requirement.

Note

A binary tree node cannot have more than two subtrees.

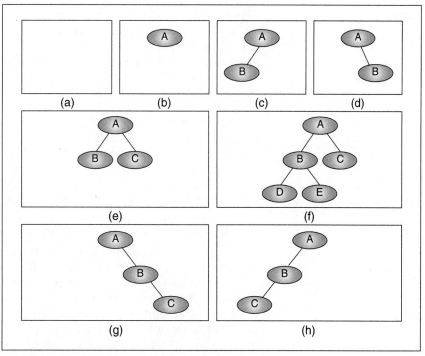

Figure 7-6   A collection of binary trees

Properties

We now define several properties for binary trees that distinguish them from general trees.

Height of Binary Trees

The height of binary trees can be mathematically predicted. Given that we need to store N nodes in a binary tree, the maximum height, H_{max}, is

$$H_{max} = N$$

A tree with a maximum height is rare. It occurs when the entire tree is built in one direction, as shown in Figure 7-6(g) and Figure 7-6(h). The minimum height of the tree, H_{min}, is determined by the following formula:

$$H_{min} = \lfloor \log_2 N \rfloor + 1$$

Given a height of the binary tree, H, the minimum and maximum number of nodes in the tree are given as

$$N_{min} = H \quad \text{and} \quad N_{max} = 2^H - 1$$

Balance

The distance of a node from the root determines how efficiently it can be located. For example, the children of any node in a tree can be accessed by following only one branch path, the one that leads to the desired node. Similarly, the nodes at level 2 of a tree can all be accessed by following only two branches from the root. It stands to reason, therefore, that the shorter the tree, the easier it is to locate any desired node in the tree.

This concept leads us to a very important characteristic of a binary tree, its **balance.** To determine whether a tree is balanced, we calculate its balance factor. The **balance factor** of a binary tree is the difference in height between its left and right subtrees. If we define the height of the left subtree as HL and the height of the right subtree as HR, then the balance factor of the tree, B, is determined by the following formula:

$$B = H_L - H_R$$

Using this formula, the balances of the eight trees in Figure 7-6 are (a) 0 by definition, (b) 0, (c) 1, (d) –1, (e) 0, (f) 1, (g) –2, and (h) 2.

A tree is **balanced** if its balance factor is 0 and its subtrees are also balanced. Because this definition occurs so seldomly, an alternate definition is more generally applied: A binary tree is balanced if the height of its subtrees differs by no more than one (its balance factor is –1, 0, or +1) and its subtrees are also balanced. As we shall see, this definition was created by Adelson-Veskii and Landis in their definition of an AVL tree.

Complete Binary Trees

A **complete tree** has the maximum number of entries for its height (see formula N_{max}, on page 312). The maximum number is reached when the last level is full (see Figure 7-7). A tree is considered **nearly complete** if it has the minimum height for its nodes (see formula H_{min}, on page 312) and all nodes in the last level are found on the left. Complete and nearly complete trees are shown in Figure 7-7.

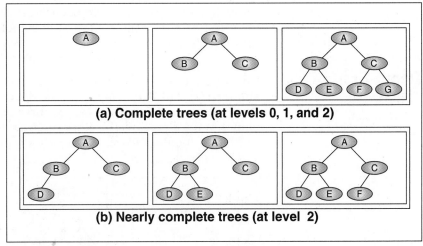

Figure 7-7   Complete and nearly complete trees

Binary Tree Structure

The representation of a binary tree structure is relatively straightforward. Each node in the structure must contain the data to be stored and two pointers, one to the left subtree and one to the right subtree. For example, in a typical binary tree, the node would contain data and two pointers, as shown below.

```
Node
    leftSubTree    <pointer to Node>
    data           <dataType>
    rightSubTree   <pointer to Node>
End Node
```

Traditionally, the subtree pointers are simply called left and right. In specific applications, as we will see later, they are sometimes given names that better describe their application.

7-3   BINARY TREE TRAVERSALS

A **binary tree traversal** requires that each node of the tree be processed once and only once in a predetermined sequence. The two general approaches to the traversal sequence are depth first and breadth first. In the **depth-first traversal,** the processing proceeds along a path from the root through one child to the most distant descendent of that first child before processing a second child. In other words, in the depth-first traversal, you process all of the descendents of a child before going on to the next child.

In a **breadth-first traversal,** the processing proceeds horizontally from the root to all of its children, then to its children's children, and so forth until all nodes have been processed. In other words, in the breadth-first traversal, each level is completely processed before the next level is started.

Depth-First Traversals

Given that a binary tree consists of a root, a left subtree, and a right subtree, we can define six different depth-first traversal sequences. Computer scientists have assigned three of these sequences standard names in the literature; the other three are unnamed but are easily derived. The standard traversals are shown in Figure 7-8.

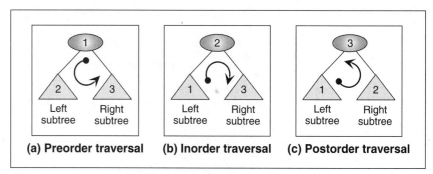

(a) Preorder traversal   (b) Inorder traversal   (c) Postorder traversal

Figure 7-8   Binary tree traversals

The traditional designation of the traversals uses a designation of node (N) for the root, `left` (L) for the left subtree, and `right` (R) for the right subtree. To demonstrate the different traversal sequences for a binary tree, we will use Figure 7-9.

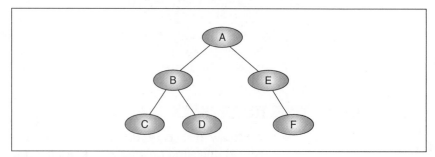

Figure 7-9   A binary tree for traversals

Preorder Traversal (NLR)

In the **preorder traversal,** the root node is processed first, followed by the left subtree, and then the right subtree. It draws its name from the Latin prefix *pre*, which means to go before. Thus, the root goes before the subtrees.

Note

> In the preorder traversal, the root is processed first, before the left and right subtrees.

Given the recursive characteristics of trees, it is only natural to implement tree traversals recursively. First we process the root, then the left subtree, and then the right subtree. The left subtree is in turn processed recursively, as is the right subtree. The code for the preorder traversal is shown in Algorithm 7-2.

```
algorithm preOrder (val root <node pointer>)
Traverse a binary tree in node-left-right sequence.
    Pre   root is the entry node of a tree or subtree
    Post  each node has been processed in order
  1 if (root is not null)
    1   process (root)
    2   preOrder (root->leftSubtree)
    3   preOrder (root->rightSubtree)
  2 end if
  3 return
end preOrder
```

Algorithm 7-2   Preorder traversal of a binary tree

Figure 7-9 contains a binary tree with each node named. The processing sequence for a preorder traversal processes this tree as follows: First we process the root A. After the root, we process the left subtree. To process the left subtree, we first process its root, B, then its left subtree and right subtree in order. When B's left and right subtrees have been processed in order, we are then ready to process A's right subtree, E. To process the subtree E, we first process the root and then the left subtree and right subtree. Because there is no left subtree, we continue immediately with the right subtree, which completes the tree.

Figure 7-10 shows another way to visualize the traversal of the tree. Imagine that you are walking around the tree, starting on the left of the root and keeping as close to the nodes as possible. In the preorder traversal you process the node when you are on its left. This is shown as

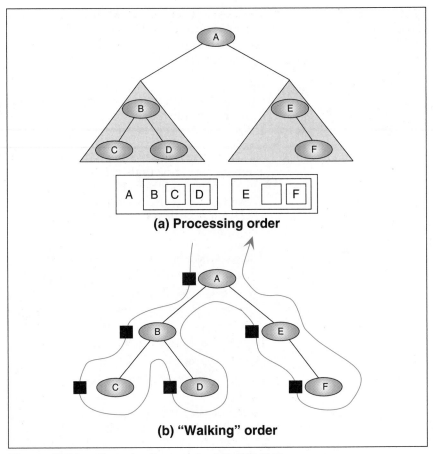

Figure 7-10   Preorder traversal—A B C D E F

a black box on the left of the node. The path is shown as a line following a route completely around the tree and back to the root.

Figure 7-11 shows the recursive algorithmic traversal of the tree. The first call processes the root of the tree, A. It then recursively calls itself to process the root of the subtree B (Figure 7-11[b]). The third call, shown in Figure 7-11(c), processes node C, which is also subtree C. At this point, we call preorder with a null pointer, which results in an immediate return to subtree C to process its right subtree. Because C's right subtree is also null, we return to node B so that we can process its right tree, D, in Figure 7-11(d). After processing node D, we make two more calls, one with D's null left pointer and one with its null right pointer. Because subtree B has now been completely processed, we return to the tree root and process its right subtree, E, in Figure 7-11(e). After a call to E's null left subtree, we call E's right

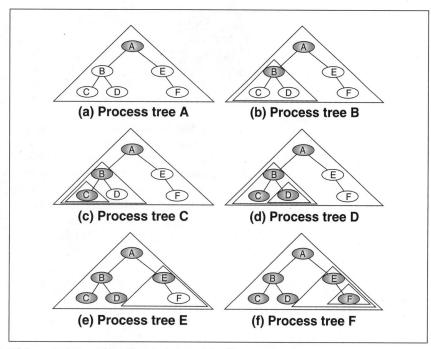

(a) Process tree A

(b) Process tree B

(c) Process tree C

(d) Process tree D

(e) Process tree E

(f) Process tree F

Figure 7-11 Algorithmic traversal of binary tree

subtree, F, in Figure 7-11(f). Although the tree is completely processed at this point, we still have two more calls to make, one to F's
null left subtree and one to its null right subtree. We can now back
out of the tree, returning first to E and then to A, which concludes the
traversal of the tree.

Inorder Traversal (LNR)

The **inorder traversal** processes the left subtree first, then the root,
and finally the right subtree. The meaning of the prefix *in* is that the
root is processed *in between* the subtrees. Once again we implement
the algorithm recursively, as shown in Algorithm 7-3.

```
algorithm inOrder (val root <node pointer>)
Traverse a binary tree in left-node-right sequence.
    Pre    root is the entry node of a tree or subtree
    Post   each node has been processed in order
  1 if (root is not null)
    1    inOrder (root->leftSubTree)
    2    process (root)
```

Algorithm 7-3   Inorder traversal of a binary tree

```
    3   inOrder (root->rightSubTree)
  2 end if
  3 return
end inOrder
```

Algorithm 7-3   Inorder traversal of a binary tree *(continued)*

Because the left subtree must be processed first, we trace from the root to the leftmost leaf node before processing any nodes. After processing the leftmost subtree, C, we process its parent node, B. We are now ready to process the right subtree, D. Processing D completes the processing of the root's left subtree, and we are now ready to process the root, A, followed by its right subtree. Because the right subtree, E, has no left child, we can process its root immediately followed by its right subtree, F. The complete sequence for inorder processing is shown in Figure 7-12.

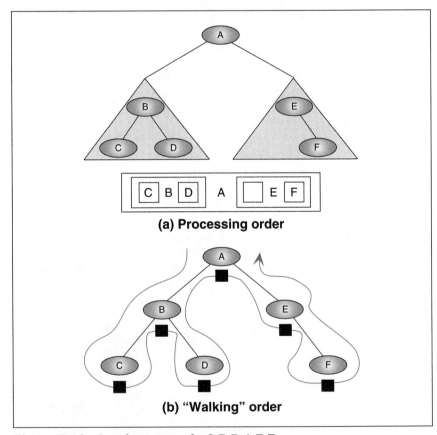

(a) Processing order

(b) "Walking" order

Figure 7-12   Inorder traversal—C B D A E F

To walk around the tree in inorder sequence, we follow the same path but move the processing to the bottom on the node. This processing route is also shown in Figure 7-12.

Note

> In the inorder traversal, the node is processed between its subtrees.

Postorder Traversal (LRN)

The last of the standard traversals is the **postorder traversal.** It processes the root node after (*post*) the left and right subtrees have been processed. It starts by locating the leftmost leaf and processing it. It then processes its right sibling, including its subtrees (if any). Finally, it processes the root node.

Note

> In the postorder traversal, the root is processed after the subtrees.

The recursive postorder traversal logic is shown in Algorithm 7-4.

```
algorithm postOrder (val root <node pointer>)
Traverse a binary tree in left-right-node sequence.
    Pre    root is the entry node of a tree or subtree
    Post   each node has been processed in order
  1 if (root is not null)
    1   postOrder (root->leftSubtree)
    2   postOrder (root->rightSubtree)
    3   process (root)
  2 end if
  3 return
end postOrder
```

Algorithm 7-4   Postorder traversal of a binary tree

In the tree walk for a postorder traversal, we move the processing block to the right of the node so that we process it as we are leaving the node. The postorder traversal is shown in Figure 7-13. Note that we took the same path in all three walks; only the time of the processing changed.

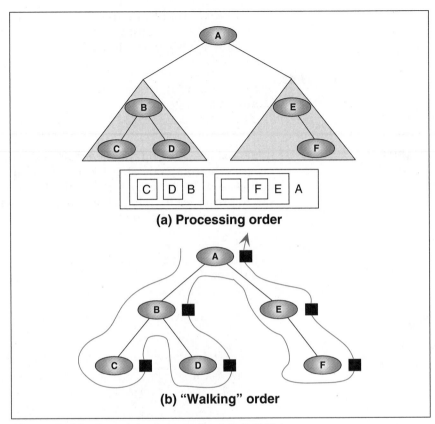

Figure 7-13   Postorder traversal—C D B F E A

Breadth-First Traversals

In the breadth-first traversal of a binary tree, we process all of the children of a node before proceeding with the next level. In other words, given a root at level *n*, we process all nodes at level *n* before proceeding with the nodes at level *n* + 1. To traverse a tree in depth-first order, we used a stack. (Remember that recursion uses a stack.) On the other hand, to traverse a tree in breadth-first order, we use a queue. The code for a breadth-first traversal of our binary tree is shown in Algorithm 7-5.

```
algorithm breadthFirst (val root <node pointer>)
Process tree using breadth-first traversal.
    Pre    root is a pointer to a tree node
    Post   tree has been processed
  1 pointer = root
  2 loop (pointer not null)
    1   process (pointer)
    2   if (pointer->left not null)
```

Algorithm 7-5   Breadth-first tree traversal

```
      1    enqueue (pointer->left)
   3  end if
   4  if (pointer->right not null)
      1    enqueue (right pointer)
   5  end if
   6  if (not emptyQueue)
      1    dequeue (pointer)
   7  else
      1    pointer = null
   8  end if
 3 end loop
 4 return
end breadthFirst
```

Algorithm 7-5   Breadth-first tree traversal *(continued)*

Like the depth-first traversals, we can trace the traversal with a walk. This time, however, the walk proceeds in a stairlike fashion, first across the root level, then across level 1, then at level 2, and so forth until the entire tree is traversed. The breadth-first traversal is shown in Figure 7-14.

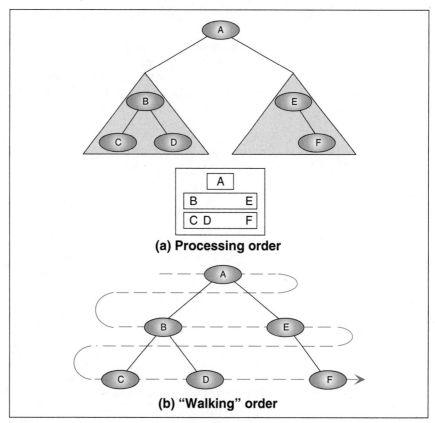

(a) Processing order

(b) "Walking" order

Figure 7-14   Breadth-first traversal

7-4   EXPRESSION TREES

One interesting series of binary tree applications are expression trees. An **expression** is a sequence of tokens that follow prescribed rules. A **token** may be either an operand or an operator. In this discussion, we consider only binary arithmetic operators in the form operand–operator–operand. The standard arithmetic operators are

+, −, *, /

An **expression tree** is a binary tree with the following properties:

1. Each leaf is an operand.
2. The root and internal nodes are operators.
3. Subtrees are subexpressions, with the root being an operator.

Figure 7-15 is an infix expression and its expression tree.

For an expression tree, the three standard traversals represent the three different expression formats: infix, postfix, and prefix. The inorder traversal produces the infix expression, the postorder traversal produces the postfix expression, and the preorder traversal produces the prefix expression.

Infix Traversal

To demonstrate the **infix traversal** of an expression tree, let's write an algorithm that traverses the tree and prints the expression. When we print the infix expression tree, we must add an opening parenthesis at the beginning of each expression and a closing parenthesis at the end of each expression. Because the root of the tree and each of its subtrees represent a subexpression, we print the opening parenthesis when we start a tree or subtree and the closing parenthesis when we have processed all of its children. Figure 7-16 shows the placement of the pa-

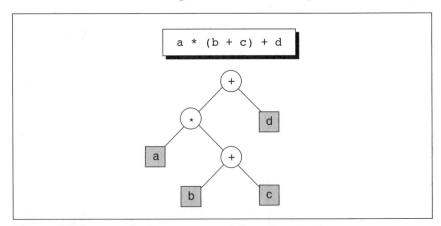

Figure 7-15   An infix expression and its expression tree

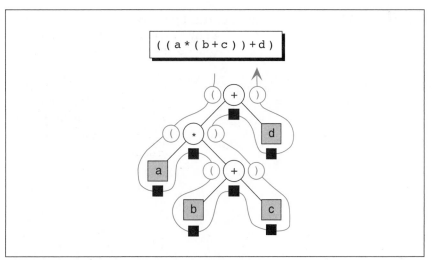

Figure 7-16 Infix traversal of an expression tree

rentheses as we walk through the tree using an inorder traversal. The pseudocode for the infix expression tree traversal is shown in Algorithm 7-6.

```
algorithm infix (val tree <tree pointer>)
Print the infix expression for an expression tree.
    Pre    tree is a pointer to an expression tree
    Post   the infix expression has been printed
 1 if (tree not empty)
    1   if (tree->token is an operand)
        1   print (tree-token)
    2   else
        1   print (open parenthesis)
        2   infix (tree->left)
        3   print (tree->token)
        4   infix (tree->right)
        5   print (close parenthesis)
    3   end if
 2 end if
 3 return
end infix
```

Algorithm 7-6 Infix expression tree traversal

Postfix Traversal

The **postfix traversal** of an expression uses the basic postorder traversal of any binary tree. Note that it does not require parentheses. The pseudocode is shown in Algorithm 7-7.

```
algorithm postfix (val tree <tree pointer>)
Print the postfix expression for an expression tree.
    Pre    tree is a pointer to an expression tree
    Post   the postfix expression has been printed
1 if (tree not empty)
    1   postfix (tree->left)
    2   postfix (tree->right)
    3   print (tree->token)
2 end if
3 return
end postfix
```

Algorithm 7-7   Postfix traversal of an expression tree

Prefix Traversal

The final expression tree traversal is the **prefix traversal.** It uses the standard preorder tree traversal. Again, no parentheses are necessary. The pseudocode is shown in Algorithm 7-8.

```
algorithm prefix (val tree <tree pointer>)
Print the prefix expression for an expression tree.
    Pre    tree is a pointer to an expression tree
    Post   the prefix expression has been printed
1 if (tree not empty)
    1   print  (tree->token)
    2   prefix (tree->left)
    3   prefix (tree->right)
2 end if
3 return
end prefix
```

Algorithm 7-8   Prefix traversal of an expression tree

7-5   GENERAL TREES

A **general tree** is a tree in which each node can have an unlimited outdegree. Each node may have as many children as is necessary to satisfy its requirements. Although general trees have little use in computer science, they are commonly found in user applications. For example, the bill of materials discussed on page 308 is an example of a general tree. We therefore need to be able to process general trees.

Changing General Tree to Binary Tree

It is considerably easier to represent binary trees in programs than it is to represent general trees. We would therefore like to be able to represent general trees with a binary tree format. The binary tree format can be adopted by changing the meaning of the left and right pointers. In a general tree, we can use two relationships: parent to child and sibling to sibling. Using these two relationships, we can represent any general tree as a binary tree.

Consider the tree shown in Figure 7-17. To change it to a binary tree, we first identify the branch from the parent to its first or leftmost child. These branches from each parent become left pointers in the binary tree. They are shown in Figure 7-17(b). Then, we connect siblings, starting with the leftmost child, using a branch for each sibling to its right sibling. These branches, shown in Figure 7-17(c), are the right pointers in the binary tree. The third and last step in the conversion process is to remove all unneeded branches from the parent to its children. The resulting binary tree is shown in Figure 7-17(d). Although this is a valid tree structure, it does not have a traditional binary tree format. We therefore redraw it as shown in Figure 7-17(e).

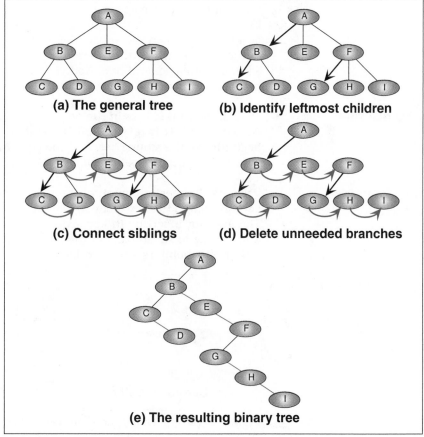

(a) The general tree

(b) Identify leftmost children

(c) Connect siblings

(d) Delete unneeded branches

(e) The resulting binary tree

Figure 7-17 Converting general trees to binary trees

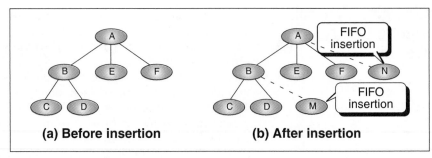

Figure 7-18   FIFO insertion into general trees

Insertions into General Trees

To insert a node into a general tree, the user must supply the parent of the node. Given the parent, three different rules may be used: (1) first in–first out (FIFO) insertion, (2) last in–first out (LIFO) insertion, and (3) key-sequenced insertion.

FIFO Insertion

When using **FIFO insertion,** we insert the nodes at the end of the sibling list, much as we insert a new node at the rear of a queue. When the list is then processed, the siblings will be processed in FIFO order. FIFO order is used when the application requires that the data be processed in the order in which they were input. Figure 7-18 shows two FIFO insertions into a general tree. Node N has been inserted into level 1 after node F, and node M has been inserted at level 2 after node D.

LIFO Insertion

To process sibling lists in the opposite order in which they were created, we use **LIFO insertion.** LIFO insertion places the new node at the beginning of the sibling list. It is the equivalent of a stack. Figure 7-19 shows the insertion points for a LIFO tree.

Key-Sequenced Insertion

Perhaps the most common of the insertion rules, **key-sequenced insertion** places the new node in key sequence among the sibling nodes. The logic for inserting in key sequence is similar to that for insertion into a linked list. Starting at the parent's first child, we follow the sibling (right) pointers until we locate the correct insertion point and

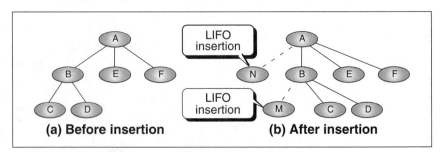

Figure 7-19   LIFO insertion into general trees

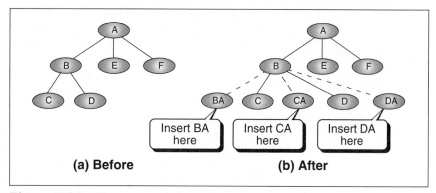

Figure 7-20 Key-sequenced insertion into general tree

then build the links with the predecessors and successors (if any). Figure 7-20 shows the correct key-sequenced insertion locations for several different values in a general tree.

General Tree Deletions

Although we cannot develop standard rules for general tree insertions, we can develop standard deletion rules. The first rule is similar to all other binary tree delete rules (see Chapter 8): a node may be deleted only if it is a leaf. In the general tree, this means a node cannot be deleted if it has any children; that is, it cannot have a left subtree (it is okay if it has right subtrees). If the user tries to delete a node that has children, the program provides an error message that the node cannot be deleted until its children are deleted. It is then the user's responsibility to first delete any children. As an alternative, the application could be programmed to delete the children first and then delete the requested node. If this alternative is used, it should be with a different user option, such as purge node and children, and not the simple delete node option.

When a node is deleted, we must also check for siblings; that is, does the node have a right subtree pointer? If there are siblings, then the logic follows the basic rules for linked lists. If the first node is deleted, then the parent's left pointer must be updated. If any other node is deleted, then its predecessor's right pointer must be updated to point to the deleted node's successor.

7-6   HUFFMAN CODE

ASCII and EBCDIC are fixed-length codes. Each ASCII character consists of 7 bits.[2] Each EBCDIC character consists of 8 bits. Character

_____

2. When ASCII code is stored in an 8-bit byte, only the first 128 values are considered ASCII. The second 128 characters are used for special characters or graphics and are considered "extended ASCII."

length does not vary. Although the character E occurs more frequently than the character Z, both are assigned the same number of bits in a given code. This consistency means that every character uses the maximum number of bits.

Huffman code, however, makes character storage more efficient. In Huffman code, we assign shorter codes to characters that occur more frequently and longer codes to those that occur less frequently. For example, E and T, two characters that occur frequently in the English language, could be assigned 1 bit each. A, O, R, and N, which also occur frequently but less frequently than E and T, could be assigned 2 bits each. S, U, I, D, M, C, and G are the next most frequent and could be assigned 3 bits each, and so forth. In a given piece of text, only some of the characters will require the maximum bit length. When used in a network transmission, the overall length of the transmission is shorter if Huffman-encoded characters are transmitted rather than fixed-length encoding; Huffman code is thus a popular **data compression** algorithm.

Before we can assign bit patterns to each character, we assign each character a weight based on its frequency of use. In our example, we assume that the frequency of the character E in a text is 15% and the frequency of the character T is 12%. (See Table 7-2.)

E = 15	T = 12	A = 10	O = 08	R = 07	N = 06	S = 05
U = 05	I = 04	D = 04	M = 03	C = 03	G = 02	K = 02

Table 7-2 Character weights for a sample of Huffman code

Once we have established the weight of each character, we build a tree based on those values. The process for building this tree is shown in Figures 7-21 through 7-24. It follows three basic steps:

1. First we organize the entire character set into a row, ordered according to frequency from highest to lowest (or vice versa). Each character is now a node at the leaf level of a tree.
2. Next, we find the two nodes with the smallest combined frequency weights and join them to form a third node, resulting in a simple two-level tree. The weight of the new node is the combined weights of the original two nodes. This node, one level up from the leaves, is eligible to be combined with other nodes. Remember, the sum of the weights of the two nodes chosen must be smaller than the combination of any other possible choices.
3. We repeat Step 2 until all of the nodes, on every level, are combined into a single tree.

Figure 7-21 shows the first part of this process. The first row of the figure shows Step 1, with the leaf-level nodes representing the original

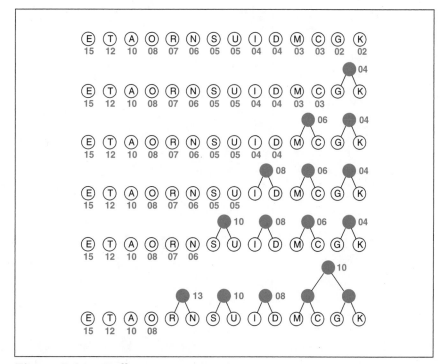

Figure 7-21 Huffman tree, part 1

characters arranged in descending order of value; then, as explained in Step 2, we locate the two nodes with the smallest values and combine them. This step is shown in the second row. As you can see, this process results in the creation of a new node (represented by a solid circle). The frequency value (weight) of this new node is the sum of the weights of the two nodes. In the third row, we combine two more nodes, and so on.

In the sixth row, the nodes with the lowest values are found one level up from the characters rather than among the characters themselves. We combine them into a node two levels up from the leaves.

Also in the sixth row, the lowest-value node is 08 (O) and the second lowest value is 10 (A). But there are three 10s—one at the leaf level (A), one a level up from the leaves (S-U), and one two levels up from the leaves (M-C-G-K). Which should we choose? We choose whichever of the 10s is adjacent to the 8. This decision keeps the branch lines from crossing and allows us to preserve the legibility of the tree.

If none of the higher values are adjacent to the lower value, we can rearrange the nodes for clarity (see Figure 7-22). In the figure (third row), we have moved the character T from the left side of the tree to the

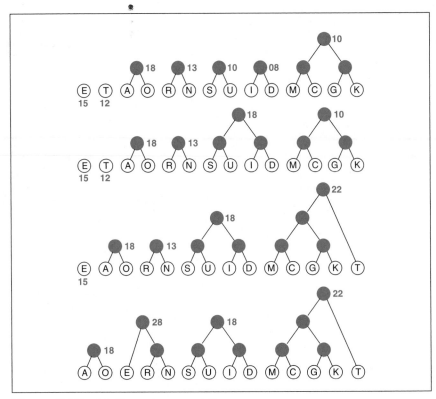

Figure 7-22   Huffman tree, part 2

right to combine it with a node on that side. We move the character E for the same reason.

Figure 7-23 shows the rest of the process. As you can see, the completed tree results in a single node at the root level (with a value of 86).

Once the tree is complete, we use it to assign codes to each character. First, we assign a bit value to each branch (see Figure 7-24). Starting from the root (top node), we assign 0 to the left branch and 1 to the right branch and repeat this pattern at each node. Which branch becomes 0 and which becomes 1 is left to the designer—as long as the assignments are consistent throughout the tree.

A character's code is found by starting at the root and following the branches that lead to that character. The code itself is the bit value of each branch on the path taken in sequence. In our example, for instance, A = 000, G = 11010, and so on. The code for each character and the frequency of the character are shown in Figure 7-24. If you examine the codes carefully, you will note that the leading bits of each code are unique; that is, no code is the prefix of any other code because each has been obtained by following a different path from the root.

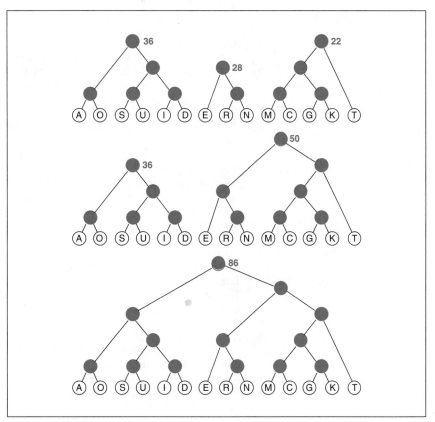

Figure 7-23   Huffman tree, part 3

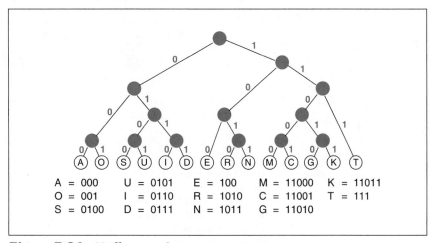

A = 000	U = 0101	E = 100	M = 11000	K = 11011
O = 001	I = 0110	R = 1010	C = 11001	T = 111
S = 0100	D = 0111	N = 1011	G = 11010	

Figure 7-24   Huffman code assignment

7-7   SUMMARY

- A tree consists of a finite set of elements called nodes and a finite set of directed lines called branches that connect the nodes.
- The number of branches associated with a node is the degree of the node.
- When the branch is directed toward the node, it is an indegree branch; when the branch is directed away from the node, it is an outdegree branch. The sum of indegree and outdegree branches is the degree of the node.
- If the tree is not empty, the first node is called the root, which has the indegree of zero.
- All nodes in the tree, except the root, must have an indegree of one.
- A leaf is a node with an outdegree of zero.
- An internal node is a node that is neither the root nor a leaf.
- A node can be a parent, a child, or both. Two or more nodes with the same parent are called siblings.
- A path is a sequence of nodes in which each node is adjacent to the next one.
- An ancestor is any node in the path from the root of a given node. A descendent is any node in all of the paths from a given node to a leaf.
- The level of a node is its distance from the root.
- The height of a tree is the level of the leaf in the longest path from the root plus 1; the height of an empty tree is -1.
- A subtree is any connected structure below the root.
- A tree can be defined recursively as a set of nodes that either (1) is empty or (2) has a designated node called the root from which hierarchically descend zero or more subtrees, which are also trees.
- A binary tree is a tree in which no node can have more than two children.
- The minimum and maximum height of a binary tree can be related to the number of nodes:

$$H_{min} = \lfloor \log_2 N \rfloor + 1 \qquad\qquad H_{max} = N$$

- Given the height of a binary tree, the minimum and maximum number of nodes in the tree can be calculated as

$$N_{min} = H \quad \text{and} \quad N_{max} = 2^H - 1$$

- The balance factor of a binary tree is the difference in height between its left and right subtrees.

$$B = H_L - H_R$$

- A tree is balanced if its balance factor is 0 and its subtrees are also balanced; a binary tree is balanced if the heights of its subtrees differ by no more than 1 and its subtrees are also balanced.
- A complete tree has the maximum number of entries for its height; a tree is complete when the last level is full.
- A nearly complete tree is a tree that has the minimum height for its nodes and all nodes in the last level are found on the left.

- A binary tree traversal visits each node of the tree once and only once in a predetermined sequence.
- The two approaches to binary tree traversal are depth first and breadth first.
- Using the depth-first approach, we traverse a binary tree in six different sequences; however, only three of these sequences are given standard names: preorder, inorder, and postorder.
- In the preorder traversal, we process the root first, followed by the left subtree, and then the right subtree.
- In the inorder traversal, we process the left subtree first, followed by the root, and then the right subtree.
- In the postorder traversal, we process the left subtree first, followed by the right subtree, and then the root.
- In the breadth-first approach, we process all nodes in a level before proceeding to the next level.
- A general tree is a tree in which each node can have an unlimited outdegree.
- To change a general tree to a binary tree, we first identify the leftmost children, connect the siblings from left to right, and delete the connection between each parent and all children except the leftmost.
- The three approaches for inserting data into general trees are FIFO, LIFO, and key sequenced.
- To delete a node in a general tree, we must ensure that it does not have a child.
- Huffman code is an encoding method that uses a variable-length code to represent characters.
- In Huffman code, we assign shorter codes to characters that occur more frequently and longer codes to those that occur less frequently.
- To create Huffman codes for a set of characters, use the following steps:
  1. Determine the number of occurrences for each character in the set.
  2. Put the entire character set into a row (leaves of a tree).
  3. Find the two nodes with the smallest combined frequency weights and link them to a new node to form a tree whose parent's weight is the sum of the two nodes.
  4. Repeat Step 3. until all nodes on all levels are combined into a single tree.

7-8 PRACTICE SETS

Exercises

1. Show the tree representation of the following parenthetical notation:

a (b (c d) e f (g h))

2. In Figure 7-25 find the
   a. Root
   b. Leaves
   c. Internal nodes
   d. Ancestors of H
   e. Descendents of F

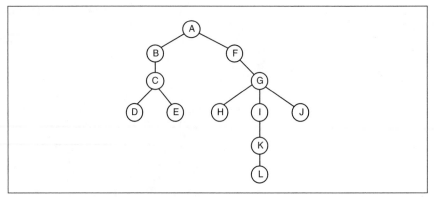

Figure 7-25   Tree for Exercises 2, 3, 4, 5, 6, and 7

3. In Figure 7-25 find the
   a. Indegree of node F
   b. Outdegree of node B
   c. Siblings of H
   d. Parent of K
   e. Children of C

4. In Figure 7-25 find the
   a. Height of the tree
   b. Height of node G
   c. Level of node G
   d. Level of node A
   e. Height of node E

5. In Figure 7-25 show the subtrees of node F.

6. In Figure 7-25 show the indented list representation of the tree.

7. In Figure 7-25 show the parenthetical representation of the tree.

8. Find a binary tree whose preorder and inorder traversal create the same result.

9. What are the maximum and minimum heights of a tree with 28 nodes?

10. In a binary tree, what is the maximum number of nodes that can be found in level 3? In level 4? In level 12?

11. What is the balance factor of the tree in Figure 7-26?

12. Draw a complete tree to level 4.

13. How many different nearly complete trees can exist at level 4?

14. Show the depth-first traversals (preorder, inorder, and postorder) of the binary tree in Figure 7-26.

15. Show the breadth-first traversal of the tree in Figure 7-26.

16. Find the root of each of the following binary trees:
   a. Tree with postorder traversal: FCBDG
   b. Tree with preorder traversal: IBCDFEN
   c. Tree with inorder traversal: CBIDFGE

17. A binary tree has ten nodes. The inorder and preorder traversal of the tree are shown below. Draw the tree.
   Preorder: JCBADEFIGH
   Inorder: ABCEDFJGIH

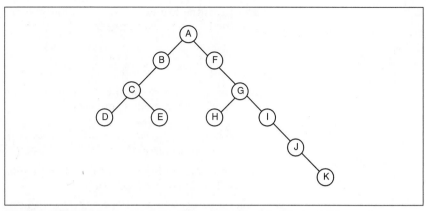

Figure 7-26   Binary tree for Exercises 11, 14, 15, and 30

18. A binary tree has eight nodes. The inorder and postorder traversal of the tree are given below. Draw the tree.
   Postorder: FECHGDBA
   Inorder: FCEABHDG

19. A binary tree has seven nodes. The preorder and postorder traversal of the tree are given below. Can you draw the tree? If not, explain.
   Preorder: GFDABEC
   Postorder: ABDCEFG

20. A nearly complete binary tree has nine nodes. The breadth traversal of the tree is given below. Draw the tree.
   Breadth: JCBADEFIG

21. Draw all possible nonsimilar binary trees with three nodes (A, B, C).

22. Draw the corresponding binary tree of Figure 7-18(b), on page 326.

23. What is the smallest number of levels a binary tree with 42 nodes can have?

24. What is the largest number of levels a ternary tree with 42 nodes can have?

25. What is the maximum number of nodes at level five of a binary tree?

26. Find the infix, prefix, and postfix expressions in the expression tree of Figure 7-27.

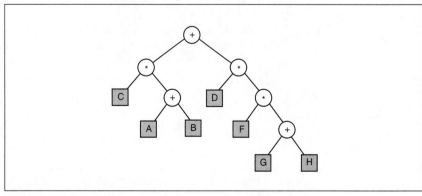

Figure 7-27   Expression tree for Exercise 26

27. Draw the expression tree and find the prefix and postfix expressions for the following infix expression:

$$(C + D + A * B) * (E + F)$$

28. Draw the expression tree and find the infix and postfix expressions for the following prefix expression:

$$* - A B + * C D / E F$$

29. Draw the expression tree and find the infix and prefix expressions for the following postfix expression:

$$A B * C D / + E F - *$$

30. Show the result of the recursive function in Algorithm 7-9 using the tree in Figure 7-26.

```
algorithm treeTraversal (val tree <tree pointer>)
1 if tree is null
   1  print "Null"
2 else
   1  treeTraversal (tree->right)
   2  print "right is done"
   3  treeTraversal (tree->left)
   4  print (tree->data)
3 end if
4 return
end treeTraversal
```

Algorithm 7-9   Tree traversal for Exercise 30

31. Supply the missing factor (the question mark) in the following recursive definition (Figure 7-28) of the maximum number of nodes based on the height of a binary tree.

$$N(H) = \begin{bmatrix} 1 & \text{if } H = 1 \\ N(H-1) + ? & \text{if } H \geq 2 \end{bmatrix}$$

Figure 7-28   Recursive definition for Exercise 31

Problems

32. Write an algorithm that counts the number of nodes in a binary tree.

33. Write an algorithm that counts the number of leaves in a binary tree.

34. Write an algorithm to delete all the leaves from a binary tree, leaving the root and intermediate nodes in place. Hint: Use a preorder traversal.

35. Write an algorithm that, given the number of nodes in a complete or nearly complete binary tree, finds the height of the tree.

36. Write an algorithm that determines whether a binary tree is complete.

37. Write an algorithm that determines whether a binary tree is nearly complete.

38. Rewrite the binary tree preorder traversal algorithm using a stack instead of recursion.

39. Rewrite the binary tree inorder traversal algorithm using a stack instead of recursion.

40. Rewrite the binary tree postorder traversal algorithm using a stack instead of recursion.

41. Write the FIFO insertion algorithm for general trees.

42. Write the LIFO insertion algorithm for general trees.

43. Write the key-sequenced insertion algorithm for general trees.

44. Write the deletion algorithm for a general tree.

45. Write an algorithm that creates a mirror image of a binary tree. All left children become right children and vice versa.

Projects

46. Write a C++ function to compute the balance factor of a binary tree. If it is called initially with the root pointer, it determines the balance factor of the entire tree. If it is called with a pointer to a subtree, it determines the balance factor for the subtree.

47. Write a pseudocode algorithm to build a Huffman tree. Use the alphabet as shown in Table 7-3.

A = 7	B = 2	C = 2	D = 3	E = 11	F = 2	G = 2
H = 6	I = 6	J = 1	K = 1	L = 4	M = 3	N = 7
O = 9	P = 2	Q = 1	R = 6	S = 6	T = 8	U = 4
V = 1	W = 2	X = 1	Y = 2	Z = 1		

Table 7-3 Huffman character weights for Project 47

48. Write the C++ implementation for the Huffman algorithm developed in Project 47. After it has been built, print the code. Then write a C++ program to read characters from the keyboard and convert them to your Huffman code. Include a function in your program that converts Huffman code back to text. Use it to verify that the code entered from the keyboard was converted correctly.

8

Search Trees

We now turn our attention to search trees, with an in-depth discussion of two standard tree structures: binary search trees and AVL trees. Both are used when data need to be ordered. They differ only in that AVL trees are balanced whereas binary search trees are not. We examine each of these structures in turn and give examples of their use. Then, at the end of the chapter, we discuss the AVL tree as an abstract data type and write a program that uses it.

8-1   BINARY SEARCH TREES

When we store ordered data in an array structure, we have a very efficient search algorithm, the binary search, but very inefficient insertion and deletion algorithms that require shifting data in the array. To provide for efficient insertion and deletion algorithms, we created a linked list. The problem with linked lists, however, is that their search algorithms are sequential searches, which are very inefficient. What we really need is a data structure that has an efficient search algorithm and at the same time efficient insert and delete algorithms. The binary search tree provides that structure.

Definition

A **binary search tree** is a binary tree with the following properties:

1. All items in the left subtree are less than the root.
2. All items in the right subtree are greater than or equal to the root.
3. Each subtree is itself a binary search tree.

Note

> A binary search tree is a binary tree in which the left subtree contains key values less than the root and the right subtree contains key values greater than or equal to the root.

Generally, the information represented by each node is a record rather than a single data element. When the binary search tree definition is applied to a record, the sequencing properties refer to the key of the record. Figure 8-1 reflects the properties of a binary tree in which K is the key.

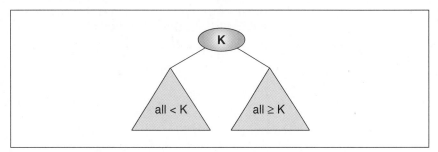

Figure 8-1   A binary search tree

Figure 8-2 contains five binary search trees. As you study them, note that the trees in Figure 8-2(a) and (b) are complete, the tree in Figure 8-2(d) is nearly complete, and the trees in Figure 8-2(c) and (e) are neither complete nor balanced.

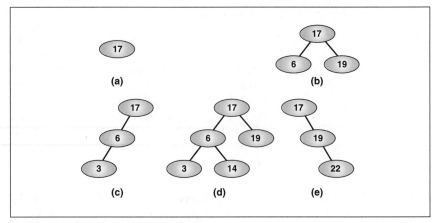

Figure 8-2   Binary search trees

Now let's look at some binary trees that do not have the properties of a binary search tree. Examine the binary trees in Figure 8-3. The first tree, Figure 8-3(a), breaks Rule 1: All items in the left subtree must be less than the root. The key in the left subtree (22) is greater than the key in the root (17). The second tree, Figure 8-3(b), breaks Rule 2: All items in the right subtree must be greater than or equal to the root. The key in the right subtree (11) is less than the key in the root (17). Figure 8-3(c) breaks Rule 3: Each subtree must be a binary search tree. In this tree, the left subtree key (6) is less than the root (17), and the right subtree key (19) is greater than the root. However, the left subtree is not a valid binary search tree because it breaks Rule 1: Its left subtree (11) is greater than the root (6). Figure 8-3(d) also breaks one of the three rules. Do you see which one? (Hint: What is the largest key in the left subtree?)

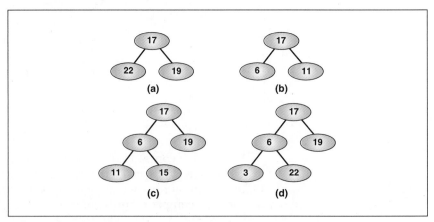

Figure 8-3   Invalid binary search trees

Operations on Binary Search Trees

We now examine several operations used on binary search trees. We start with the traversal algorithms you studied in Chapter 7. We then look at some simple search algorithms and conclude with the algorithms that build a binary search tree.

Binary Search Tree Traversals

The binary search tree traversal algorithms are identical to the ones in Chapter 7. Our interest here is not in the algorithm itself but rather in the results it produces. Let's begin by traversing the tree in Figure 8-4.

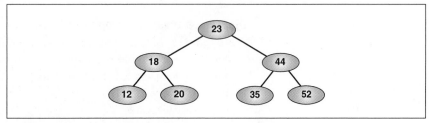

Figure 8-4   A binary search tree

If we traverse the tree using a preorder traversal, we get the results shown below.

```
23 18 12 20 44 35 52
```

Although this traversal is valid, it is not very useful. Let's try a postorder traversal and see if it is more useful.

```
12 20 18 35 52 44 23
```

Again, this sequence holds little promise of being useful. Let's try an inorder traversal.

```
12 18 20 23 35 44 52
```

This traversal has some very practical use: The inorder traversal of a binary search tree produces an ordered list. What happens if you traverse the tree using a right-node-left sequence? Try it and see.[1]

Note

> The inorder traversal of a binary search tree produces an ordered list.

---

1. As you can see, the right-node-left traversal produces a descending sort order of the data in the tree. This is not a standard traversal, but it can be very useful.

Binary Search Tree Search Algorithms

In this section we study three binary search tree search algorithms: find the smallest node, find the largest node, and find a requested node.

Find Smallest Node

If you examine the binary search tree in Figure 8-4, you will note that the node with the smallest value (12) is the leftmost leaf node in the tree. To find the smallest node, therefore, we simply follow the left branches until we get to a leaf. Algorithm 8-1 contains the pseudocode to find the smallest node in a binary search tree (BST).

```
algorithm findSmallestBST (val root <pointer>)
This algorithm finds the smallest node in a BST.
    Pre      root is a pointer to a nonempty BST or subtree
    Return   address of smallest node
 1  if (root->left null)
    1    return (root)
 2  end if
 3  return findSmallestBST (root->left)
end findSmallestBST
```

Algorithm 8-1   Find smallest node in a BST

Algorithm 8-1 Analysis

As is typical with trees, this algorithm is recursive. The first call starts with the root of the tree, as shown in Figure 8-5. We then follow a path down the left pointers. If the left pointer is not null, then we must keep looking further to the left. We do so with a recursive call to findSmallestBST with a new root pointing to the left subtree. The base case in this algorithm occurs when we find a null left pointer. At this point we return

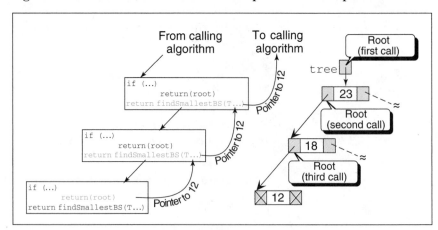

Figure 8-5   findSmallestBST

the address of the current node, which returns the root pointer containing 12 as the base case. Because the recursive call is part of a return statement, as we move back up the tree we continue to return the pointer to the smallest node until we finally return it to the initiating module.

Find Largest Node

The logic to find the largest node in a binary search tree is the reverse of findSmallestBST. This time we start at the tree root and follow the right branches to the last node in the tree, which by definition must be the largest. The pseudocode is shown in Algorithm 8-2.

```
algorithm findLargestBST (val root <pointer>)
This algorithm finds the largest node in a BST.
    Pre      root is a pointer to a nonempty BST or subtree
    Return   address of largest node returned
  1 if (root->right null)
    1    return (root)
  2 end if
  3 return findLargestBST (root->right)
end findLargestBST
```

Algorithm 8-2   Find largest node in a BST

Binary Search Tree Search

We now examine the most important feature of binary search trees, finding a specific node in the tree. Before we begin, however, let's revisit the binary search algorithm, as shown in Figure 8-6. This figure traces each of the possible search paths from the middle element in the array. Starting with 23, the binary search examines either 18 or 44, depending on the search key. From 18 it examines either 12 or 20; from 44 it examines

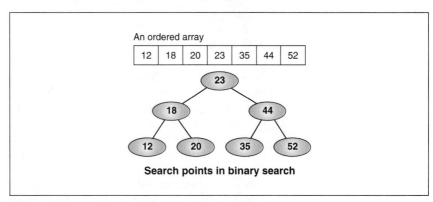

Figure 8-6   BSTs and the binary search

either 35 or 52. As is clear in the figure, tracing all possible search paths results in a binary search tree.

Now let's reverse the process. Find a given node in a binary search tree. Assume we are looking for node 20. We begin by comparing the search argument, 20, with the value in the tree root. Because 20 is less than the root value, 23, and because we know that all values less than the root lie in its left subtree, we go left. We now compare the search argument with the value in the subtree, 18. This time the search argument is greater than the tree value, 18. Because we know that values greater than the tree root must lie in its right subtree, we go right and find our desired value. This logic is shown in Algorithm 8-3.

```
algorithm searchBST   (val root      <pointer>,
                       val argument <key>)
Search a binary search tree for a given value.
    Pre    root is the root to a binary tree or subtree
           argument is the key value requested
    Return the node address if the value is found
           null if the node is not in the tree
  1 if (root is null)
    1    return null
  2 end if
  3 if (argument < root->key)
    1    return searchBST (root->left, argument)
  4 elseif (argument > root->key)
    1    return searchBST (root->right, argument)
  5 else
    1    return root
  6 end if
end searchBST
```

Algorithm 8-3   BST search

Algorithm 8-3 Analysis   We implement the BST search using recursion. In this algorithm, there are two base cases: either we find the search argument in the tree, in which case we return the address of its node (Statement 5.1), or the search argument doesn't exist, in which case we return null (Statement 1.1).

Study the returns at Statements 3.1 and 4.1 carefully. Note that they are returning the value given by the recursive call, which as we saw earlier is either null or the address of the node we are trying to locate. These statements are necessary to pass the located address back through the recursion to the original requester. Figure 8-7 traces the path through the binary search tree from Figure 8-4, on page 341, as we search for node 20 using Algorithm 8-3.

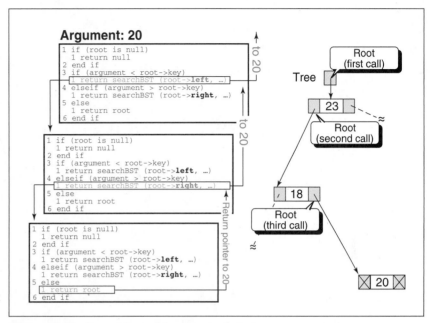

Figure 8-7 Searching a binary search tree

Insert Node

When we insert data into an ordered array, we must first locate the insertion point and then shift all elements from that point to the end of the array. Inserting data into a binary search tree is much simpler. All we need to do is follow the branches to an empty subtree and then insert the new node. In other words, all inserts take place at a leaf or a leaflike node, a node that has only one null branch.

Note

> All BST inserts take place at a leaf or a leaflike node.

Figure 8-8 shows our binary search tree after we have inserted two nodes. We first added node 19. To locate its insertion point, we searched the tree through the path 23, 18, and 20 to a null left branch. After locating the insertion point, we inserted the new node as the left subtree of 20. We then added 38. This time we searched the tree through 23, 44, and 35 to a null right subtree and inserted the new node.

Insertions of both 19 and 38 were made at a leaf node. If we inserted a duplicate of the root, 23, it would become the left subtree of 35. Remember that in a binary search tree, nodes with equal values are found in the right subtree. The path for its insertion would therefore be 23, 44, and 35. In this case, the insertion takes place at a leaflike node. Although 35 has a right subtree, its left subtree is null. We would therefore place the new node, 23, as the left subtree of 35.

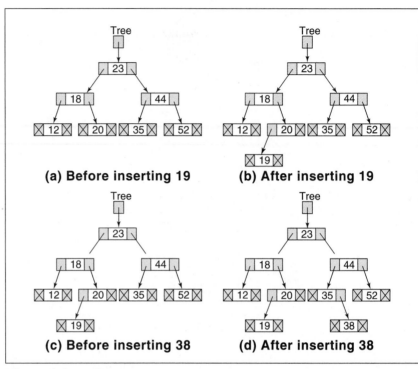

Figure 8-8   BST insert

We are now ready to develop the insert algorithm. We first write it using an iterative search for the insertion point, and then we write it using recursion.

Iterative Insert

The iterative insert requires that we search the tree and insert the new data at a leaf node. Given data to insert, we must first search the tree and then insert the data as a new subtree of its logical parent. The pseudocode is seen in Algorithm 8-4.

```
algorithm insertBST (ref root  <pointer>,
                     val new   <pointer>)
Insert node containing new node into BST using iteration.
    Pre   root is address of first node in a BST
          new is address of node containing data to be inserted
    Post  new node inserted into the tree
1 if (root is null)
1    root = new
2 else
```

Algorithm 8-4   Iterative binary search tree insert

```
    1   pWalk = root
    2   loop (pWalk not null)
        1   parent = pWalk
        2   if (new->key < pWalk->key)
            1   pWalk = pWalk->left
        3   else
            1   pWalk = pWalk->right
        4   end if
    3   end loop
        Location for new node found
    4   if (new->key < parent->key)
        1   parent->left = new
    5   else
        1   parent->right = new
    6   end if
  3 end if
  4 return
end insertBST
```

Algorithm 8-4   Iterative binary search tree insert *(continued)*

Algorithm 8-4 Analysis   This algorithm is quite simple. Given a new node containing the data to be inserted, we simply follow the left or right branch down the tree until we find a null subtree. To search down the tree structure, we use a *while* loop with a trailing address pointer, `parent`, that will eventually become the parent of the new node. When a null subtree is found, we then need only determine whether the data are to be inserted on the left branch or the right branch. Figure 8-9 shows the steps to insert 19 iteratively.

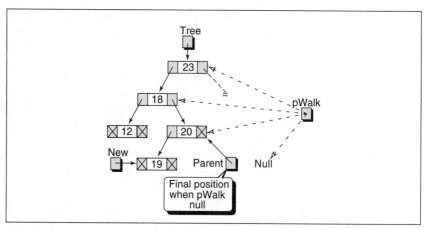

Figure 8-9   Iterative insert of node 19

Recursive Insert Node

We can write an elegant algorithm that will insert the data into the tree using recursion. The design is even simpler than Algorithm 8-4. If we are at a null tree or subtree, we simply assign the new node's address to replace the null tree. If we are not at a null tree, then we determine which branch we need to follow and call recursively to determine whether we are at a leaf yet. The code is shown in Algorithm 8-5.

```
algorithm addBST  (ref root <pointer>,
                        val new  <pointer>)
Insert node containing new data into BST using recursion.
    Pre     root is address of current node in a BST
            new is address of node containing data to be inserted
    Post    new node inserted into the tree
  1 if (root is null)
    1   root = new
  2 else
    Locate null subtree for insertion
    1   if (new->key < root->key)
        1   addBST (root->left, new)
    2   else
        1   addBST (root->right, new)
    3   end if
  3 end if
  4 return
end addBST
```

Algorithm 8-5   Add node to BST recursively

Algorithm 8-5 Analysis

The algorithm is quite elegant, but it is not easy to see how the address of the new node is inserted at the correct location. To help, let's insert four nodes into a null tree, as shown in Figure 8-10.

We start with a null tree, which is identified by a variable named tree. When the tree is null, the variable tree contains a null value. When we call addBST to insert node 23, root receives the address of the variable tree. At Statement 1.1, therefore, tree receives the address of the new tree root, 23. When we add node 18, the algorithm starts at node 23 and recursively calls itself with the root's left child (because 18 is less than 23). At the time of the insert, therefore, root is pointing to 23's left pointer, which is null. At this point, Statement 1.1 assigns the address of node 18 to root, 23's left child. Similarly, when we insert 44, we again start at the root and this time follow the right child's branch, which is null. When Statement 1.1 then assigns the address of node 44 to root, it is actually placing it in node 23's right child. The last insert, which adds the node with a value of 9, requires two recursive calls. The

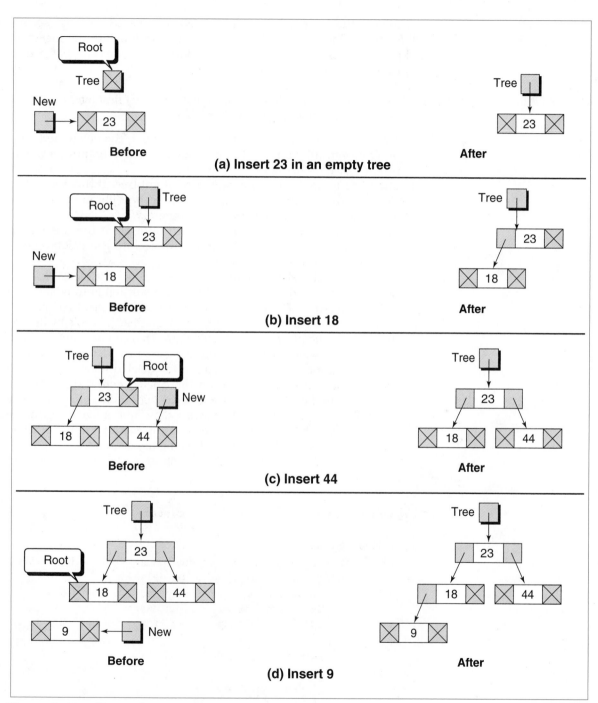

Figure 8-10 Trace of recursive BST insert

first follows the left pointer from node 23 to node 18, and the second call follows the left pointer from 18, which is null before the insert. At this point, Statement 1.1 assigns the address of node 9 to root, which is pointing at node 18's left child.

Delete Node

To delete a node from a binary search tree, we must first locate it. There are four possible cases when we delete a node:

1. The node to be deleted has no children. When the delete node has no children, all we need to do is set the delete node's parent to null, recycle its memory, and return.

2. The node to be deleted has only a right subtree. If there is only a right subtree, then we can simply attach the right subtree to the delete node's parent and recycle its memory.

3. The node to be deleted has only a left subtree. If there is only a left subtree, then we attach the left subtree to the delete node's parent and recycle its memory.

4. The node to be deleted has two subtrees. It is possible to delete a node from the middle of a tree, but the result tends to create very unbalanced trees. Rather than simply delete the node, therefore, we try to maintain the existing structure as much as possible by finding data to take the place of the deleted data. This can be done in one of two ways: (1) we can find the largest node in the deleted node's left subtree and move its data to replace the deleted node's data or (2) we can find the smallest node on the deleted node's right subtree and move its data to replace the deleted node's data. Regardless of which logic we use, we will be moving data from a leaf or a leaflike node that can then be deleted. Prove to yourself that either of these moves will preserve the integrity of the binary search tree.

The pseudocode for the binary search tree delete is shown in Algorithm 8-6.

```
algorithm deleteBST (ref root      <pointer>,
                     val dltKey  <key>)
This algorithm deletes a node from a BST.
    Pre    root is pointer to tree containing data to be deleted
           dltKey is key of node to be deleted
    Post   node deleted and memory recycled
           if dltKey not found, root unchanged
    Return true if node deleted, false if not found
1 if (root null)
    1    return false
2 end if
3 if (dltKey < root->data.key)
```

Algorithm 8-6   Binary search tree delete

```
   1    return deleteBST (root->left, dltKey)
 4 elseif (dltKey > root->data.key)
   1    return deleteBST (root->right, dltKey)
 5 else
        Delete node found--test for leaf node
   1    If (root->left null)
      1    dltPtr = root
      2    root = root->right
      3    recycle (dltPtr)
      4    return true
   2    elseif (root->right null)
      1    dltPtr = root
      2    root    = root->left
      3    recycle (dltPtr)
      4    return true
   3    else
           Node to be deleted not a leaf. Find largest node on
           left subtree.
      1    dltPtr = root->left
      2    loop (dltPtr->right not null)
         1    dltPtr = dltPtr->right
           Node found. Move data and delete leaf node.
      3    root->data = dltPtr->data
      4    return deleteBST (root->left, dltPtr->data.key)
   4    end if
 6 end if
end deleteBST
```

Algorithm 8-6   Binary search tree delete *(continued)*

Algorithm 8-6 Analysis

You will need to study this algorithm carefully to fully understand it. First, note that it is a recursive algorithm. There are two base cases: First, we do not find the node. In that case, the root pointer is null. This case is handled in Statement 1.1. The second base occurs after we have deleted the node, at either Statement 5.1.4 or Statement 5.2.4.

The first two delete cases on page 350 have been combined in one case in the actual implementation of the algorithm. If the left subtree is null, then we can simply connect the right subtree to the parent (root). If the right subtree is null, then we will be connecting a null subtree, which would be correct. If the right subtree is not null, then its data are connected to the deleted node's parent, which is Case 2. Figure 8-11(a) shows the results of deleting a node with no children, and Figure 8-11(b) shows the results of deleting a node with only a right subtree.

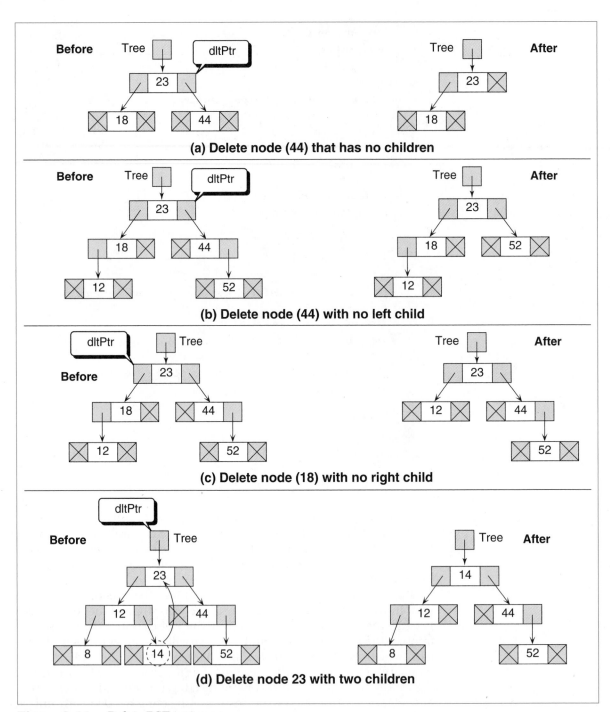

Figure 8-11   Delete BST test cases

On the other hand, if the left subtree is not null, then we test to see whether the right subtree is null. If the right subtree is null, then we can move the left subtree pointer to its parent. Deleting a node with a left subtree but with no right subtree is shown in Figure 8-11(c).

The most difficult logic in this algorithm occurs when the node is not a leaf. You will need to study this situation carefully to fully understand it; see Figure 8-11(d). We begin by searching for the largest node on the left subtree and move its data to replace the data to be deleted. We then call the algorithm recursively, giving it a new delete target, the key of the leaf node that contains the data we moved to the internal or root node. This guarantees that when we find the target key this time, at least one of its subtrees will be null.

8-2 AVL TREES

In 1962, the two Russian mathematicians G. M. Adelson-Velskii and E. M. Landis created the balanced binary tree structure that is named after them—the AVL tree. An **AVL tree** is a search tree in which the heights of the subtrees differ by no more than 1. It is thus a balanced binary tree. To understand the significance of the tree being balanced, let's look at two different trees containing the same data. The first is a search tree in which each node is larger than its predecessor. The second is an AVL tree. These trees are shown in Figure 8-12.

If you study the tree in Figure 8-12(a), you should quickly note that it is the equivalent of a linear list in a binary tree's clothing. It takes two tests to locate 12. It takes three tests to locate 14. It takes eight tests to locate 52. In other words, the search effort for this particular binary search tree is $O(n)$.

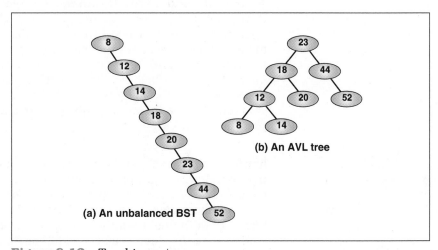

(b) An AVL tree

(a) An unbalanced BST

Figure 8-12 Two binary trees

Now consider the tree in Figure 8-12(b). Although we have labeled it an AVL tree, it looks like a binary search tree because both trees are built on the same structure. Locating nodes 8 and 14 requires four tests. Locating nodes 20 and 52 requires three tests. In other words, the maximum search effort for this tree is either three or four. Its search effort is $O(\log_2 n)$. In this sample of two small trees, we see that the worst search effort was reduced from eight to four by simply balancing the tree. For a tree with 1000 nodes, the worst case for a completely unbalanced tree is 1000, whereas the worst case for a nearly complete tree is 10. We thus see that balancing a tree can lead to significant performance improvements.

We are now ready to define an AVL tree. An AVL tree is a binary tree that is either empty or that consists of two AVL subtrees, T_L, and T_R, whose heights differ by no more than 1, as shown below.

$$|H_L - H_R| \leq 1$$

where H_L is the height of the left subtree and H_R is the height of the right subtree (the bar symbols indicate absolute value). Because AVL trees are balanced by working with their height, they are also known as **height-balanced trees**.

Note

> An AVL tree is a height-balanced binary search tree.

Referring back to Figure 8-12(b), we see that the tree appears to be balanced when we look at the root. The height of the left subtree (root 18) is 3; the height of the right subtree (root 44) is 2. Therefore, if the subtrees 18 and 44 are balanced, the tree is balanced, as shown in Figure 8-13(a).

Now examine the left subtree, 18, in Figure 8-13(b). It also appears to be balanced because the heights of its subtrees differ by only 1. If its subtrees 12 and 20 are balanced, then it is a balanced tree. Looking at Figure 8-13(c), we see that the right subtree (root 44) is balanced because the heights of its subtrees differ by only 1. Prove to yourself that the remaining subtrees are also balanced, which makes the tree balanced.

AVL Balance Factor

In Chapter 7 we defined the balance factor as the height of the left subtree minus the height of the right subtree. Because the balance factor for any node in an AVL tree must be +1, 0, or –1, we will use the descriptive identifiers LH for left high (+1) to indicate that the left subtree is higher than the right subtree, EH for even high (0) to indicate that the subtrees are the same height, and RH for right high (–1) to indicate that the left subtree is shorter than the right subtree. We find that this sys-

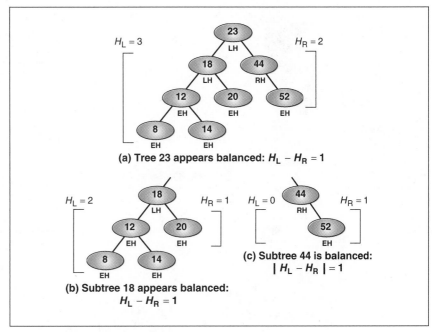

(a) Tree 23 appears balanced: $H_L - H_R = 1$

(b) Subtree 18 appears balanced: $H_L - H_R = 1$

(c) Subtree 44 is balanced: $|H_L - H_R| = 1$

Figure 8-13   An AVL tree

tem allows us to more easily concentrate on the structure, and because most programming languages provide methods for implementing identifiers for constant values, it should prove no problem when implementing the algorithms. These balance factors are shown in Figure 8-13.

Balancing Trees

Whenever we insert a node into a tree or delete a node from a tree, the resulting tree may be unbalanced. When we detect that a tree has become unbalanced, we must rebalance it. AVL trees are balanced by rotating nodes either to the left or to the right. In this section, we discuss the basic balancing algorithms.

We consider four cases that require rebalancing. All unbalanced trees fall into one of these four cases: (1) **left of left,** a subtree of a tree that is left high has also become left high; (2) **right of right,** a subtree of a tree that is right high has also become right high; (3) **right of left,** a subtree of a tree that is left high has become right high. (4) **left of right,** a subtree of a tree that is right high has become left high. These four cases are shown in Figure 8-14.

Case 1: Left of Left

When the out of balance condition has been created by a left high subtree of a left high tree, we must balance the tree by rotating the out of balance node to the right. Let's begin with a simple case. In Figure 8-15(a), node 20 (the tree) is out of balance because the left

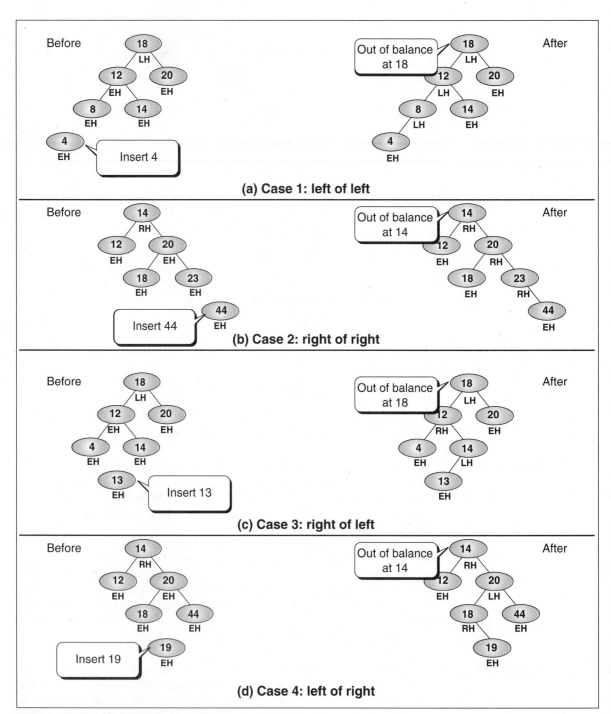

Figure 8-14   Out of balance AVL trees

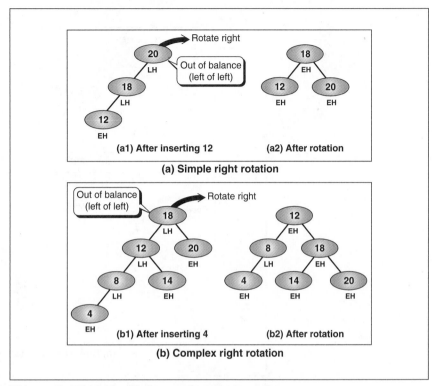

Figure 8-15 Left of left—single rotation right

subtree 18 is left high and it is on the left branch of node 20, which is also left high. In this case, we balance the tree by rotating the root, 20, to the right so that it becomes the right subtree of 18.

The tree in Figure 8-15(b) presents a more complex problem. The subtree 12 is balanced, but the whole tree (18) is not. Therefore, we must rotate 18 to the right, making it the right subtree of the new root, 12. This creates a problem, however. What can we do with node 14, the current right subtree of 12? If you study the tree carefully, you will note that the old root, 18, loses its left subtree in the rotation (it becomes the root). We can therefore use 18's empty left subtree to attach 14, which also preserves the search tree relationship that all nodes on the right of the root must be greater than or equal to the root.

In both cases in Figure 8-15, after the rotation the rotated node is even high. Other balance factors may also have changed along the way, depending on the complexity of the tree and how the out of balance condition was created. We will see how the balance factors are changed when we study the insert and delete algorithms.

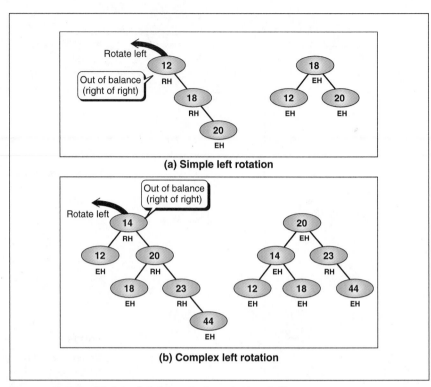

Figure 8-16   Right of right—single rotation left

Case 2: Right of Right

Case 2 is the mirror of Case 1. Figure 8-16(a) contains a simple left rotation. The subtree 18 is balanced, but the root is not. We therefore rotate the root to the left, making it the left subtree of the new root, 18.

Now let's look at the more complex case shown in Figure 8-16(b). In this case, we have a right high root with a right high subtree and thus a right of right, out of balance condition. To correct the imbalance, we rotate the root to the left, making the right subtree, 20, the new root. In the process, 20's left subtree is connected as the old root's right subtree, preserving the order of the search tree.

Case 3: Right of Left

The first two cases required single rotations to balance the trees. We now study two out of balance conditions in which we need to rotate two nodes, one to the left and one to the right, to balance the tree.

Again, let's start with a relatively simple case. In Figure 8-17(a) we see an out of balance tree in which the root is left high and the left subtree is right high—a right of left tree. To balance this tree, we first rotate the left subtree to the left, then we rotate the root to the right, making the left node the new root.

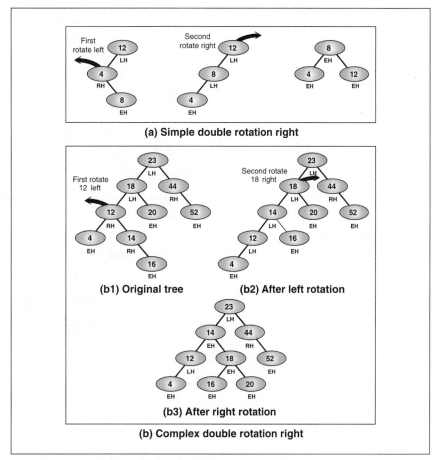

Figure 8-17   Right of left—double rotation right

Now let's examine the complex case. In Figure 8-17(b) we see an out of balance tree in which a node (18) is left high and its left subtree (12) is right high. To balance this tree, we first rotate the left subtree (12) of the node that is out of balance (18) to the left, which aligns the subtree nodes in search tree sequence. This rotation is shown in Figure 8-17(b2). We now rotate the left subtree (18) to the right, which results in the new left subtree (14) being balanced.

In this example, the resulting tree is still left high, and the newly balanced subtree, 14, is even high.

Case 4: Left Of Right

Case 4 is also complicated. Figure 8-18(a) shows a simple case. To balance the tree, we first rotate the right subtree (44) right and then rotate the root (12) left.

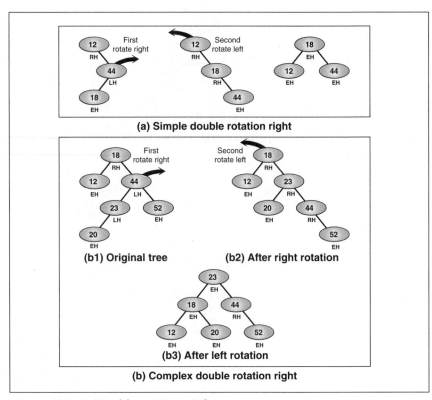

Figure 8-18   Double rotation right

Figure 8-18(b) shows the complex case. In this example, the subtree 44 is balanced but the tree is not. Because the out of balance condition is created by a left high subtree on a right high branch, we must double rotate. We begin by rotating the right subtree (44) to the right, which creates the tree in Figure 8-18(b2). We then rotate the root left, which gives us the balanced tree in Figure 8-18(b3). Note that the root of the balanced tree has an even high balance factor.

AVL Node Structure

The **AVL node structure** follows the same design as the binary search tree, with the addition of the balance factor. Each node must contain the key and data to be stored, a left subtree pointer and a right subtree pointer, and the balance factor. The node structure is shown below.

```
Node
    key          <keyType>
    data         <dataType>
    left         <pointer to Node>
    right        <pointer to Node>
    bal          <LH, EH, RH>
End Node
```

AVL Insert

Now that we have seen how to balance a tree, we are ready to look at the algorithms. The search and retrieval algorithms are the same as for any binary tree. Naturally, you will want to use an inorder traversal because AVL trees are search trees.

As with the binary search tree, all inserts take place at a leaf node. To find the appropriate leaf node, we follow the path from the root, going left when the new data's key is less than a node's key and right otherwise. Once we have found a leaf, we connect it to its parent node and begin to back out of the tree. Here is where the AVL tree differs from the binary search tree. *As we back out of the tree,* we constantly check the balance of each node. When we find that a node is out of balance, we balance it and then continue up the tree.

Not all inserts create an out of balance condition. When we add a node on the right branch of a left high node, automatic balancing occurs and the node is now even high, as shown in Figure 8-19. Conversely, when we add a node on the left branch of a right high node, the node is automatically balanced.

When the leaf is evenly balanced before the add, however, the subtree that the leaf is on grows one level. Whether this addition creates an out of balance condition depends on the balance of its ancestor's nodes. In the insert algorithm we set a flag whenever a tree has potentially grown higher. Then, as we back out of the insertion, we test this taller flag. We can thus determine whether we need to rotate a node.

The design of the AVL insert algorithm is shown in Figure 8-20. It clearly shows that inserting on the right branch of a tree is a mirror of inserting on the left. On the left in the structure chart is the design for inserting on a left branch. On the right is the design for inserting on a right branch. Both start with a recursive call to locate a leaf. Once we locate the leaf and begin to back out of the recursion, we call either left balance or right balance if the insert has set the taller flag true. When the taller flag is no longer true, no more balancing is needed.

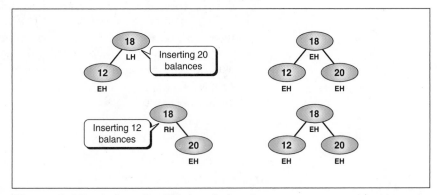

Figure 8-19 Automatic AVL tree balancing

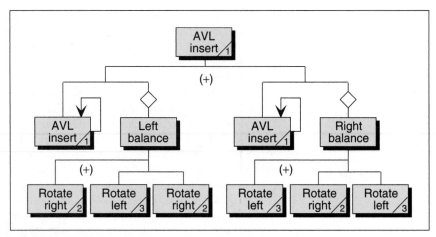

Figure 8-20   AVL tree insert design

To balance a left subtree node, we rotate either singly to the right or doubly, first to the left and then to the right. To balance a right subtree node, we rotate either singly to the left or doubly, first to the right and then to the left. Before you move on to the algorithms, compare this design with the balancing figures in "Balancing Trees," on pages 356–360 (Figures 8-14 through 8-18).

AVL Insert Algorithm   The AVL insert pseudocode is shown in Algorithm 8-7. This algorithm requires that the space be allocated for the new node before it is called. The calling algorithm therefore manages memory.

```
algorithm AVLInsert  (ref root    <tree pointer>,
                       val newPtr  <tree pointer>,
                       ref taller  <Boolean>)
Using recursion, insert a node into an AVL tree.
    Pre    root is a pointer to first node in AVL tree/subtree
           newPtr is a pointer to new node to be inserted
    Post   taller is a Boolean: true indicating the subtree
           height has increased, false indicating same height
    Return root returned recursively up the tree
 1 if (root null)
    Insert at root
    1   root  = newPtr
    2   taller = true
    3   return root
```

Algorithm 8-7   AVL tree insert

```
2  end if
3  if (newPtr->key < root->key)
   1   root->left = AVLInsert (root->left, newPtr, taller)
   2   if (taller)
       Left subtree is taller
       1   if (root left-high)
           1   root = leftBalance (root, taller)
       2   elseif (root even-high)
           1   root->bal = left-high
       3   else
           Was right high--now even high
           1   root->bal = even-high
           2   taller = false
       4   end if
   3   end if
4  else
   New data >= root data
   1   root->right = AVLInsert (root->right, newPtr, taller)
   2   if(taller)
       Right subtree is taller
       1   if (root left-high)
           1   root->bal = even-high
           2   taller = false
       2   elseif (root even-high)
           Was balanced--now right high
           1   root->bal = right-high
       3   else
           1   root = rightBalance (root, taller)
       4   end if
   3   end if
5  end if
6  return root
end AVLInsert
```

Algorithm 8-7   AVL tree insert *(continued)*

Algorithm 8-7 Analysis   As we discussed earlier, the algorithm begins much the same as the binary search tree add node on page 348. If we are at a leaf, we set the root to point to the new node. At this point, we don't know if the root has grown taller or has become balanced. We therefore set the taller flag to true and let the previous module determine the situation as we back out of the recursion.

When we return from the recursive call, there are two possibilities: Either the tree has grown taller or it hasn't. If it is not taller, no balancing is required.

If the tree is taller, there are again two possibilities. We need to balance if the tree is left high and we inserted on the left (Statement 3.2.1.1) or if the tree is right high and we inserted on the right (Statement 4.2.3.1). Automatic balancing has occurred if the insertion was on the right branch of a left high node or on the left branch of a right high node. In these cases, we simply set the node to even height and turn off the taller flag because the tree will be balanced the rest of the way up to the root.

One final note: This algorithm does not check for duplicate insertions. If an application does not allow duplicates, then the algorithm must search before it inserts to ensure that the insert is not a duplicate.

AVL Left Balance Algorithm

Because the logic for balancing a left subtree and the logic for balancing a right subtree are mirrors of each other, we show only the logic to balance a left subtree. If you understand it, you should be able to construct the algorithm for balancing a right subtree. The pseudocode for balancing a left high node is shown in Algorithm 8-8.

```
algorithm leftBalance (ref root    <tree pointer>,
                       ref taller  <Boolean>)
This algorithm is entered when the root is left heavy (the left
subtree is higher than the right subtree).
    Pre    root is a pointer to the root of the [sub]tree
           taller is true
    Post   root has been updated (if necessary)
           taller has been updated
  1 leftTree = root->left
  2 if (leftTree left-high)
    Case 1: Left of left. Single rotation right.
    1    rotateRight (root)
    2    root->bal     = even-high
    3    leftTree->bal = even-high
    4    taller = false
```

Algorithm 8-8   AVL left balance

```
3 else
  Note: even balance factor is impossible!
  Case 2: Right of left. Double rotation required.
  1   rightTree = leftTree->right
  adjust balance factors
  2   if (rightTree->bal left-high)
    1   root->bal      = right-high
    2   leftTree->bal = even-high
  3   elseif (rightTree->bal even-high)
    1   leftTree->bal = even-high
  4   else
    rightTree->bal is right-high)
    1   root->bal      = even-high
    2   leftTree->bal = left-high
  5   end if
  6   rightTree->bal = even-high
  7   root->left = rotateLeft (leftTree)
  8   root        = rotateRight  (root)
  9   taller = false
4 end if
5 return root
end leftBalance
```

Algorithm 8-8   AVL left balance *(continued)*

Algorithm 8-8 Analysis

When the left balance algorithm is called, we know that the tree has grown taller, the parent is left high, and we are on a left branch. Now we need to know whether we have Case 1, left of left, or Case 3, right of left. We can determine the case by examining the balance factor of the left subtree. If it is left high, we have Case 1, left of left; if it is right high, we have Case 2, right of left. Once we determine which case we have, the rest of the logic is straightforward.

Rotate Algorithms

To rotate a node we simply exchange the root and the appropriate subtree pointers. This process takes four steps, three for the exchange and one to reset the root pointer. The steps to rotate a left high tree are shown in Figure 8-21. Note that in this figure we are dealing with just a portion of a tree. Therefore, we cannot determine the final balance factors. The pseudocode for rotate right and for rotate left are shown in Algorithm 8-9 and Algorithm 8-10, respectively.

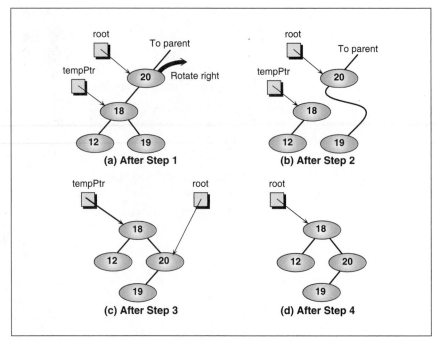

Figure 8-21   AVL tree rotate right

```
algorithm rotateRight (ref root <tree pointer>)
This algorithm exchanges pointers to rotate the tree right.
    Pre    root points to tree to be rotated
    Post   node rotated and root updated

 1 tempPtr        = root->left
 2 root->left     = tempPtr->right
 3 tempPtr->right = root
 4 return tempPtr
end rotateRight
```

Algorithm 8-9   Rotate AVL tree right

```
algorithm rotateLeft (ref root <tree pointer>)
This algorithm exchanges pointers to rotate the tree left.
    Pre    root points to tree to be rotated
    Post   node rotated and root updated
```

Algorithm 8-10   Rotate AVL tree left

```
1 tempPtr        = root->right
2 root->right    = tempPtr->left
3 tempPtr->left  = root
4 return tempPtr
end rotateLeft
```

Algorithm 8-10   Rotate AVL tree left *(continued)*

AVL Delete Algorithm

As we saw with the binary search tree, all deletions must take place at a leaf node. The AVL delete (Algorithm 8-11) follows the basic logic of the binary search tree delete with the addition of the logic to balance the tree. As with the insert logic, the balancing occurs as we back out of the tree.

```
algorithm AVLDelete  (ref root       <tree pointer>,
                      val deleteKey   <key>,
                      ref shorter     <Boolean>,
                      ref success     <Boolean>)
This algorithm deletes a node from an AVL tree and rebalances if
necessary.
   Pre    root is a pointer to a [sub]tree
          deleteKey is the key of node to be deleted
   Post   node deleted if found, tree unchanged if not found
          shorter is true if subtree is shorter
          success is true if deleted, false if not found
   Return pointer to root of [potential] new subtree

1 if (tree null)
   1   shorter = false
   2   success = false
   3   return null
2 end if
3 if (deleteKey < root->key)
   1   root->left = AVLDelete
               (root->left, deleteKey, shorter, success)
   2   if (shorter)
      1   root = deleteRightBalance (root, shorter)
   3   end if
4 elseif (deleteKey > root->key)
   1   root->right = AVLDelete
               (root->right, deleteKey, shorter, success)
   2   if (shorter)
```

Algorithm 8-11   AVL tree delete

```
          1    root = deleteLeftBalance (root, shorter)
      3   end if
    5 else
      Delete node found--test for leaf node
      1   deleteNode = root
      2   if (no right subtree)
          1    newRoot    = root->left
          2    success = true
          3    shorter = true
          4    recycle (deleteNode)
          5    return newRoot
      3   elseif (no left subtree)
          1    nwRoot     = root->right
          2    success = true
          3    shorter = true
          4    recycle (deleteNode)
          5    return newRoot
      4   else
          Deleted node has two subtrees
          Find substitute--largest node on left subtree
          1    exchPtr = root->left
          2    loop (exchPtr->right not null)
               1   exchPtr = exchPtr->right
          3    end loop
          4    root->key   = exchPtr->key
          5    root->data  = exchPtr->data
          6    root->left = AVLDelete
                   (root->left, exchPtr->key, shorter, success)
          7    if (shorter)
               1   root = dltRightBalance (root, shorter)
          8    end if
      5   end if
    6 end if
    7 return root
  end AVLDelete
```

Algorithm 8-11　　AVL tree delete *(continued)*

Algorithm 8-11 Analysis　　　Although the basic logic parallels that of the binary search tree delete, there are significant differences. It begins much the same: If we find a null tree, then the node we are trying to delete does not exist. In this case we set both success and shorter to false. We then return a null root. Returning a null root is necessary because the tree's or subtree's root may have changed during rotation. The original calling algorithm must therefore save the new root and then test for success before automatically changing the tree's root, just in case the delete key was not found. This logic is shown below.

```
1 newTree = AVLDelete (root, deleteKey, shorter, success)
2 if (success is true)
   1   root = newTree
3 else
   1   error (deleteKey "not found")
4 end if
```

Once we find the node to be deleted (Statement 5), we need to determine whether the delete node is a leaf. If there is no right subtree, then we connect the left subtree (which, as we saw in the binary search tree delete, may be null also) to the parent, set the shorter and success flags to true, and return the new root. If there is a right subtree but not a left subtree, then we connect the right subtree to the parent and again set the flags and return the new root.

If there is a left subtree and a right subtree, then we need to find a node to take the delete node's place. We therefore loop to find the largest node on the left subtree. When we find it, we copy its data to the delete node. We then continue the delete at the deleted node's left subtree, this time looking for the substitute data we copied to replace the deleted data. If after deleting the copied data from its leaf the tree is shorter, we balance it. Because data were deleted, we conclude by returning the new root.

Delete Right Balance

Again, we show only one side of the balancing algorithm, delete right balance. The logic for delete left balance mirrors that for Algorithm 8-12.

```
algorithm deleteRightBalance (ref root    <pointer>,
                              ref shorter <Boolean>)
The [sub]tree is shorter after a deletion on the left branch.
Adjust the balance factors and if necessary balance the tree by
rotating left.
   Pre    tree is shorter
   Post   balance factors updated and balance restored
          root updated
          shorter updated
1 if (root left-high)
   1   root->bal = even-high
2 elseif (root even high)
```

Algorithm 8-12   AVL delete right balance

```
    1   root->bal = right-high
    2   shorter   = false
3 else
  Tree was right high already--rotate left
    1   rightTree = root->right
    2   if (rightTree left-high)
        Double rotation required
        1   leftTree       = rightTree->left
            Adjust balance factors
        2   if (leftTree left-high)
            1   rightTree->bal = right-high
            2   root->bal       = even-high
        3   elseif (leftTree even-high)
            1   root->bal       = left-high
            2   rightTree->bal = even-high
        4   else
            leftTree right-high
            1   root->bal       = left-high
            2   rightTree->bal = even-high
        5   end if
        6   leftTree->bal = even-high
        7   root->right   = rotateRight (rightTree)
        8   root          = rotateLeft  (root)
    3   else
        Single rotation required
        1   if (rightTree not even-high)
            1   root->bal       = even-high
            2   rightTree->bal = even-high
        2   else
            1   root->bal       = right-high
            2   rightTree->bal = left-high
            3   shorter         = false
        3   end if
        4   root = rotateLeft (root)
    4   end if
4 end if
5 return root
end deleteRightBalance
```

Algorithm 8-12   AVL delete right balance *(continued)*

Algorithm 8-12 Analysis

We begin by determining whether we need to balance the tree. Remember, we do not necessarily need to rebalance the tree just because we deleted a node. For example, we first check to see whether the root is left high. If it is, because we deleted a node on the left, it is now even high and we can exit after setting the balance factor. Note that we leave shorter unchanged in this case.

On the other hand, if the root is even high and we have deleted on the left, it becomes right high. In this case, we know that the tree cannot be shorter because the height of the subtree remains the same even though we deleted the left subtree. We therefore set shorter false and return.

The final case requires that we rebalance the tree: We have deleted on the left and the tree was already right high. It is now doubly right high (the delete is right of right). We therefore need to rotate the right subtree to the left.

If the right subtree is left high, we need to rotate twice, first to the right and then to the left. This case is shown in Figure 8-18, on page 360. After the rotation, we adjust the balance factor of the right subtree's left subtree, which was rotated up and is now even high. Shorter is left unchanged because the tree may need more rotations as we move up toward the root.

If the right subtree is not left high, we need to rotate only once. This situation is shown in Figure 8-16, on page 358. Because we deleted on the left, we need to rotate the root to the left. Before the rotation, however, we adjust the balance factors. If the right subtree is even high, then after the rotation the root will be right high and the right subtree will be even high. These rotations are shown in Figure 8-22.

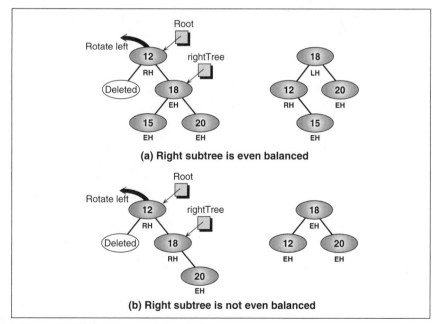

(a) Right subtree is even balanced

(b) Right subtree is not even balanced

Figure 8-22   AVL tree delete balancing

Adjusting the Balance Factors

After an insert or delete, as we balance the tree we must adjust the balance factors. Although the adjustments to the balance factors must be analyzed individually for each case, there is a general pattern:

1. If the root was even balanced before an insert, it is now high on the side in which the insert was made.
2. If an insert was in the shorter subtree of a tree that was not even balanced, the root is now even balanced.
3. If an insert was in the higher subtree of a tree that was not even balanced, the root must be rotated.

We develop the code for adjusting the balance factors fully in the implementation of the AVL tree abstract data type.

8-3   AVL TREE IMPLEMENTATION

In this section we create an AVL tree application that uses a tree structure containing all of the words in a document, with a count of the number of times each word is used. This program uses the AVL abstract data type found in Section 8-4. Because the key is a word, we also need to create a string class that allows comparison of two strings. The string class is found in Appendix G.

Data Structure

The application data structure is shown in Figure 8-23. Each entry in the AVL tree contains a word from the document and a pointer to an integer that contains a count of the number of times the word appears in the document. Had the AVT tree contained a function to write a node back to the tree—that is, to update it—we could have simply stored the node in the tree.

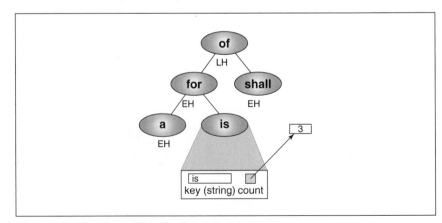

Figure 8-23   Count words data structure

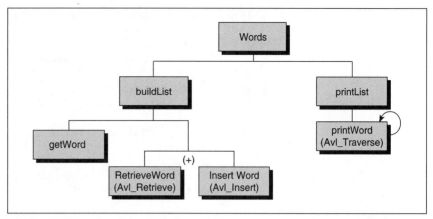

Figure 8-24 Count words design

Program Design

As we process the file, we parse a word and then search the tree to see if we can find it. If it's already in the tree, we simply add to its counter. If it's not in the tree, we insert a new entry into the tree. Figure 8-24 contains the program design. We have indicated the AVL tree class functions where they are used. The code for each of the functions is shown in the following sections.

Words Main Line

The program's data structure and its main line are found in Program 8-1. As you study it, note that DATA is the name of the template that the AVL tree will use to store the words in the document.

```
 1   struct DATA
 2     {
 3      String  key;                  // One word
 4      int     *count;
 5     } ;
 6
 7   //  Prototype Functions
 8   void insertWord    (AvlTree<DATA, String>& words);
 9   void deleteWord    (AvlTree<DATA, String>& words);
10   void buildList     (AvlTree<DATA, String>& wordList);
11   void printList     (AvlTree<DATA, String>& wordList);
12   void printWord     (DATA    wordList);
13   bool getWord       (DATA&   aWord, ifstream& fsWords);
14
15   int main ( void )
16   {
17   //  Local Definitions
```

Program 8-1 Count words main line

```
18    AvlTree<DATA, String> wordList;
19
20 //   Statements
21    cout << "Start count words in document\n";
22
23    buildList (wordList);
24    printList (wordList);
25
26    cout << "End count words\n";
27    return 0;
28 } // main
```

Program 8-1   Count words main line *(continued)*

Program 8-1 Analysis

A good design keeps the code in the main line function to a minimum. In this program, we start with a hello message, call buildList and printList, and then conclude with a good-bye message. Like a good manager, main delegates all of the processing to subordinate functions.

Build List

Build list (Program 8-2) reads one word from the file, looks it up in the tree, and if found simply adds 1 to its counter. If the word is not yet in the tree, it creates a counter, sets it to 1, and adds the word to the tree.

```
 1 /* ==================== buildList ==================
 2    Reads file and creates AVL tree containing list
 3    of all words used in the file with count of the
 4    number of times each word is found in the file.
 5       Pre    nothing
 6       Post  AVL tree (list) built or error returned
 7 */
 8 void buildList (AvlTree<DATA, String>& wordList)
 9 {
10 // Local Definitions
11    bool       found;
12    char       fileName[25];
13    DATA       aWord;
14    DATA       newWord;
15    ifstream   fsWords;
16
17 // Statements
18    cout << "Please enter name of file to be processed: ";
19    cin  >> fileName;
20
21    fsWords.open (fileName);
```

Program 8-2   Count words: build list

```
22      if (!fsWords)
23          {
24            cout << fileName << "\a\a could not be opened\n";
25            cout << "Please verify name and try again.\n";
26            exit (100);
27          } // !fsWords
28
29      while (getWord (newWord, fsWords))
30          {
31            found = wordList.AVL_Retrieve (newWord.key, aWord);
32            if (found)
33                (*aWord.count)++;
34            else
35                {
36                  newWord.count = new int;
37                  if (!newWord.count)
38                      {
39                        cout << "Memory failure in build list\a\a\n";
40                        exit (120);
41                      } // if
42                  // Add word to list
43                  *(newWord.count) = 1;
44                  if (!wordList.AVL_Insert (newWord))
45                      {
46                        cout << "\a\aMemory full. Can't continue\n";
47                        exit (121);
48                      } // if overflow test
49                } // else
50          } // while
51
52      cout << "End AVL Tree\n";
53      return;
54  } // buildList
```

Program 8-2   Count words: build list *(continued)*

Program 8-2 Analysis

As you study this function, pay close attention to four important points. First, we allow the user to enter the name of the file. This program is designed to support any text file and by reading the filename from the keyboard, we make it as flexible as possible.

One of the most difficult loops to write in any program is a read file loop. We use a simple technique in this program: We call a read function that returns true if it was able to parse a word and false if there was no word to parse. This makes the control of the processing loop very simple.

Note the "intelligent" data names we use for words. The first, aWord, is used to retrieve a word from the list. The second, newWord, is used to create a new entry in the tree. Good names make a program more readable.

Finally, note that we check for memory failures. When we allocate memory for the new word's counter, we test for an overflow. Again, when we insert the new word into the tree, we test the return from the insert function. If either function fails, we print an error message and exit the program.

Get Word

The get word function parses the file input and extracts one word from the file. Its code is shown in Program 8-3.

```
 1   /* =================== getWord ==================
 2      Reads one word from file.
 3         Pre    nothing
 4         Post   word read into reference parameter
 5   */
 6   bool getWord        (DATA&      aWord,
 7                           ifstream& fsWords)
 8   {
 9   // Local Definitions
10      int wordEnd;
11      char strIn[25];
12
13   // Statements
14      fsWords >> strIn;
15      if ( !(fsWords.good()) )
16         return false;
17
18      wordEnd = strlen(strIn) - 1;
19      if ( !isalpha(strIn[wordEnd]) )
20         strIn[wordEnd] = '\0';
21      aWord.key = strIn;
22
23      return true;
24   } // getWord
```

Program 8-3 Count words: get one word

Program 8-3 Analysis

Parsing words simply means copying all of the characters between two or more spaces to a string. Because we are processing a text document, however, we had to remove any punctuation from the end of the word. We did this by simply testing the last character to make sure it was alphabetic. If it wasn't, we deleted it from the word by moving a null character over it.

Depending on the application, it might be necessary to use a different set of editing criteria. For example, to parse the words in a program, we would need to keep numbers and the underscore character as a part of the word. We might also want to eliminate the reserved words. To keep the rest of the program as simple as possible, these changes would be programmed in getWord.

Print Words

Because the implementation of the tree is hidden in the class ADT, we cannot directly traverse the tree to print the list. Rather, we must call on the tree traversal function, AVL_Traverse. On the other hand, the traverse function doesn't know how to process the data as it traverses the tree. For this reason, we pass the process function to the traversal function when we call it. Program 8-4 contains both the call to the traversal function and the function that prints one word.

```
1   /* ================= printList =================
2      Prints the list with the count for each word.
3         Pre    list has been built
4         Post   list printed
5   */
6   void printList      (AvlTree<DATA, String>  wordList)
7   {
8   // Statements
9      cout << "\n\nWords found in list\n";
10     wordList.AVL_Traverse (printWord);
11     cout << "\nEnd of word list\n";
12     return;
13  } // printList
14
15  /* ================= printWord =================
16     Prints one word from the list with its count.
17        Pre    ADT calls function to print data
18        Post   data printed
19  */
20  void printWord      (DATA  aWord)
21  {
22  // Statements
23     cout.setf (ios::left);
24     cout << setw (25) << aWord.key;
25     cout.unsetf (ios::left);
26     cout << setw ( 4) << *(aWord.count) << endl;
27     return;
28  } // printWord
```

Program 8-4 printList

Count Words Summary

After studying this application, it should be apparent that it is very easy to build an application once we have built abstract data types such as an AVL tree and string. Writing reusable code is one of the strengths of C++. In the next section we create the AVL abstract data type class.

8-4   AVL ABSTRACT DATA TYPE

No programming language has intrinsic operations for an AVL tree. Its operations must be simulated using C++ functions. The model for the AVL tree abstract data type (ADT) is the ADT we developed for linked lists in Chapter 2. Both structures use dynamic memory to store nodes containing a pointer to the application data. Both structures require pointers to identify each node's successor. Whereas the linked list contains only one pointer to each successor, the AVL tree uses two, one for the left subtree and one for the right subtree. Because there is order in the AVL tree, just as there was in the linked list, we need to know the key for the application. If it is a standard type, we simply identify it in a structure template. If it is not a standard type, such as the word string in Section 8-3, then we must create a class for the key type and write the necessary compare functions.

A major difference between the two structures lies in the traversal of the structure. In the linked list, we provided a function to retrieve the next node in the list. We use recursion in the AVL traversal, so this design is not possible. Because the ADT must process the data in a traversal, the design requires that the application programmer develop the traversal-processing algorithm and pass its address to the ADT. Given that there may be more than one process required for any application, the function must be passed when the traversal is initiated.

With the basic design understood, we are ready to describe the ADT class. In addition to the constructor and destructor, we define the nine functions that make up the basic set needed to build and maintain AVL trees. Other functions may be added as required by specific applications. The basic functions are shown in Figure 8-25 and described below.

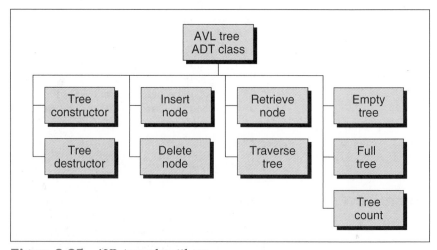

Figure 8-25   AVL tree algorithms

AVL Tree Data Structures

The AVL tree class requires one internal data structure and two pieces of metadata, the tree root and a count of the number of nodes in the tree.

To implement the nine application functions described in Figure 8-25, the ADT class requires 11 private functions. The class declaration is shown in Program 8-5.

```
 1  // ==================== MACROS ====================
 2  #define LH +1      // Left High
 3  #define EH  0      // Even High
 4  #define RH -1      // Right High
 5
 6  // NODE Definitions
 7  template <class TYPE>
 8  struct NODE
 9    {
10     TYPE     data;
11     NODE    *left;
12     int     bal;
13     NODE    *right;
14    } ; // NODE
15
16  // Class Declaration
17  template <class TYPE, class KTYPE>
18  class AvlTree
19    {
20     private:
21       int            count;
22       NODE<TYPE>    *tree;
23
24       NODE<TYPE> *_insert       (NODE<TYPE> *root,
25                                      NODE<TYPE>  *newPtr,
26                                  bool&       taller);
27
28       NODE<TYPE> *leftBalance   (NODE<TYPE> *root,
29                                  bool&       taller);
30
31       NODE<TYPE> *rotateLeft    (NODE<TYPE> *root);
32       NODE<TYPE> *rightBalance  (NODE<TYPE> *root,
33                                  bool&       taller);
34       NODE<TYPE> *rotateRight   (NODE<TYPE> *root);
35       NODE<TYPE> *_delete       (NODE<TYPE> *root,
36                                  KTYPE       dltKey,
37                                  bool&       shorter,
38                                  bool&       success);
```

Program 8-5 AVL class definition

```
39
40         NODE<TYPE>  *dltLeftBalance  (NODE<TYPE>   *root,
41                                       bool&         smaller);
42         NODE<TYPE>  *dltRightBalance (NODE<TYPE>   *root,
43                                       bool&         shorter);
44         NODE<TYPE> *_retrieve        (KTYPE         key,
45                                       NODE<TYPE>   *root);
46
47         void _traversal  (void (*process)(TYPE dataProc),
48                                  NODE<TYPE>    *root);
49
50         void _destroyAVL (NODE<TYPE>  *root);
51
52     public:
53          AvlTree (void);
54          ~AvlTree  (void);
55     bool  AVL_Insert   (TYPE    dataIn);
56     bool  AVL_Delete   (KTYPE   dltKey);
57     bool  AVL_Retrieve (KTYPE   key,     TYPE& dataOut);
58     void  AVL_Traverse (void (*process)(TYPE  dataProc));
59
60     bool  AVL_Empty    (void);
61     bool  AVL_Full     (void);
62     int   AVL_Count    (void);
63     } ; // class AvlTree
```

Program 8-5   AVL class definition *(continued)*

Now that we understand the class structure, we are ready to develop the algorithms.

AVL Tree Functions

We describe a basic set of AVL tree functions in this section. Depending on the application, other algorithms could be required. For example, some applications may need to include descending-key traversals.

AVL Tree Constructor

The class constructor is very simple. It sets the tree pointer to null and the tree count to 0. The code is shown in Program 8-6.

```
1   /* =================== Constructor ===================
2      Initializes private data.
3          Pre     class is being defined
4          Post    private data initialized
5   */
6
7   template <class TYPE, class KTYPE>
```

Program 8-6   AVL tree constructor

```
 8   AvlTree<TYPE, KTYPE> ::  AvlTree (void)
 9   {
10   // Statements
11      tree    = NULL;
12      count   = 0;
13   }  //  Constructor
```

Program 8-6 AVL tree constructor *(continued)*

AVL Tree Insert

AVL tree insert is the function called by the application program. It receives a pointer to the tree structure and a pointer to the data to be inserted into the tree. After allocating a node, it calls a recursive insert function to make the physical insertion. The application called insert function is shown in Program 8-7.

```
 1   /* ================== AVL_Insert ===================
 2      This function inserts new data into the tree.
 3         Pre    dataIn contains data to be inserted
 4         Post   data have been inserted or memory overflow
 5         Return success (true) or overflow (false)
 6   */
 7
 8   template <class TYPE, class KTYPE>
 9   bool    AvlTree<TYPE, KTYPE> :: AVL_Insert (TYPE dataIn)
10   {
11   // Local Definitions
12      NODE<TYPE>    *newPtr;
13      bool          taller;
14
15   // Statements
16      if (!(newPtr = new NODE<TYPE>))
17         return false;
18      newPtr->bal     = EH;
19      newPtr->right   = NULL;
20      newPtr->left    = NULL;
21      newPtr->data    = dataIn;
22
23      tree = _insert(tree, newPtr, taller);
24      count++;
25      return true;
26   }  //  Avl_Insert
```

Program 8-7 Application AVL insert function

Program 8-7 Analysis

Because all additions take place at a leaf node, we initialize the balance factor to even height (EH) and the subtree pointers to null. We then call the recursive insert function. When it returns, we update the tree count and return success.

Note the name of the recursive insert module. Following the guide for system software, we call it _insert so that the name will not be duplicated by application programmers.

Recursive Insert

The recursive function, initially called by AVL_Insert, requires three parameters: a pointer to the root of the tree or the subtree, a pointer to the node being inserted, and a Boolean to tell whether the tree has grown taller. The taller flag is used for rotation processing as we back out of the tree after the insert. If the tree is taller, the function calls one of two subfunctions, one to balance a left subtree or another to balance a right subtree. Also handled as we back out of the tree are the changes to the balance factors. The function is shown in Program 8-8.

```
 1   /* ======================= _insert =======================
 2      This function uses recursion to insert the new data into
 3      a leaf node in the AVL tree.
 4         Pre    application has called AVL_Insert, which passes
 5                   root and data pointers
 6         Post   data have been inserted
 7         Return pointer to [potentially] new root
 8   */
 9
10   template <class TYPE, class KTYPE>
11   NODE<TYPE>*  AvlTree<TYPE,  KTYPE>
12            ::  _insert (NODE<TYPE>  *root,
13                         NODE<TYPE>  *newPtr,
14                         bool&        taller)
15   {
16   // Statements
17      if (!root)
18         {
19         root     = newPtr;
20         taller   = true;
21         return  root;
22         } //  if NULL tree
23
24      if (newPtr->data.key < root->data.key)
25         {
26         root->left = _insert(root->left,
27                              newPtr,
28                              taller);
29         if (taller)
30            //  Left subtree is taller
31            switch (root->bal)
32               {
33               case LH: // Was left high--rotate
34                        root = leftBalance (root, taller);
```

Program 8-8   Recursive insert function

```
35                              break;
36
37                      case EH: // Was balanced--now LH
38                              root->bal = LH;
39                              break;
40
41                      case RH: // Was right high--now EH
42                              root->bal = EH;
43                              taller    = false;
44                              break;
45                  } // switch
46           } //  new < node
47      else
48           //  new data >= root data
49           {
50            root->right = _insert (root->right,
51                                        newPtr,
52                                        taller);
53          if (taller)
54              // Right subtree is taller
55              switch (root->bal)
56                  {
57                      case LH: // Was left high--now EH
58                              root->bal = EH;
59                              taller    = false;
60                              break;
61
62                      case EH: // Was balanced--now RH
63                              root->bal = RH;
64                              break;
65
66                      case RH: // Was right high--rotate
67                              root = rightBalance (root, taller);
68                              break;
69                  } //  switch
70           } //  else new data >= root data
71      return root;
72  } //  _insert
```

Program 8-8 Recursive insert function *(continued)*

Program 8-8 Analysis

You must carefully study this rather difficult algorithm to fully understand its logic. It begins with a recursive search to locate the correct insertion point in a leaf node. After completing the insert (Statement 19) and setting the taller flag, we begin to back out of the tree, examining its balance as we go. If we are out of balance after a left insert, we call left balance (see Statement 34). If we are out of balance after a right insert, we call right balance (see Statement 67).

The balance factors are adjusted in three functions. The current root's balance factor is adjusted in the insert function. The subtree balance factors are adjusted in left and right balance as the tree is rotated. All follow the general rules discussed in "Adjusting the Balance Factors," on page 372.

After we have adjusted each node, if necessary, we return the root. We must return the root because the root of a tree may change as we add data. This is one of the major differences between the binary search tree and the AVL tree. In the binary search tree, the first node inserted is always the root unless it is deleted.

Because this is a recursive function, it must have a base case. Can you see it? The base case occurs when we locate a leaf (null root) and return the new root in Statement 21.

Insert Left Balance

If the tree is taller after an insert on the left subtree, we need to determine whether a rotation is necessary. As we saw earlier, rotation is necessary only if the tree was already left high. In this case we call the left balance function to restore the balance by rotating the left subtree. This algorithm is shown in Program 8-9.

```
 1  /* ==================== leftBalance ====================
 2      The tree is out of balance to the left. This function
 3      rotates the tree to the right.
 4          Pre      the tree is left high
 5          Post     balance restored
 6          Returns potentially new root
 7  */
 8
 9  template <class TYPE, class KTYPE>
10  NODE<TYPE>  *AvlTree<TYPE,  KTYPE>
11          :: leftBalance (NODE<TYPE>   *root,
12                              bool&        taller)
13  {
14  // Local Definitions
15      NODE<TYPE>   *rightTree;
16      NODE<TYPE>   *leftTree;
17
18  // Statements
19      leftTree = root->left;
20      switch (leftTree->bal)
21          {
22          case LH:  // Left High--Rotate Right
23                      root->bal     = EH;
24                      leftTree->bal = EH;
25
```

Program 8-9 AVL tree insert left balance

```
26              // Rotate Right
27                  root     = rotateRight (root);
28                  taller   = false;
29              break;
30      case EH: // This is an error
31                  cout <<"\n\a\aError in leftBalance\n";
32                  exit (100);
33      case RH: // Right High - Requires double rotation:
34               // first left, then right
35                  rightTree = leftTree->right;
36                  switch (rightTree->bal)
37                     {
38                      case LH: root->bal    = RH;
39                               leftTree->bal = EH;
40                               break;
41                      case EH: root->bal    = EH;
42                               leftTree->bal = EH;
43                               break;
44                      case RH: root->bal    = EH;
45                               leftTree->bal = LH;
46                               break;
47                     } //  switch rightTree
48
49                  rightTree->bal = EH;
50                  //  Rotate Left
51                  root->left = rotateLeft (leftTree);
52
53                  // Rotate Right
54                  root     = rotateRight (root);
55                  taller   = false;
56          } // switch leftTree
57      return root;
58  } // leftBalance
```

Program 8-9   AVL tree insert left balance *(continued)*

Program 8-9 Analysis

The function examines the left subtree's balance factor to determine what action must be taken. If the subtree is left high—that is, if it is left of left—then a simple right rotation is all that is required. If it is right high, then it is right of left and a double rotation is required. The third possible balance factor, even high, is not possible. If we find an even high balance factor, we abort the program because it must contain a logic error to arrive at this impossible situation.

Rotation Functions

The rotation of a subtree requires an exchange of pointers among four subtree pointers. The logic is a relatively simple extension of the logic to exchange two values. The code to rotate left and right is shown in Program 8-10. As you study the logic, you may find it helpful to refer to Figure 8-21, on page 366.

```
1   /* ==================== rotateLeft ====================
2      This function exchanges pointers so as to rotate the
3      tree to the left.
4         Pre   root points to tree to be rotated
5         Post NODE rotated and new root returned
6   */
7
8   template <class TYPE, class KTYPE>
9   NODE<TYPE>*  AvlTree<TYPE,  KTYPE>
10            :: rotateLeft (NODE<TYPE>  *root)
11  {
12  // Local Definitions
13     NODE<TYPE>  *tempPtr;
14
15  // Statements
16     tempPtr        = root->right;
17     root->right    = tempPtr->left;
18     tempPtr->left  = root;
19
20     return tempPtr;
21  } //  rotateLeft
22
23  /* ==================== rotateRight ====================
24     This function exchanges pointers to rotate the tree
25     to the right.
26        Pre   root points to tree to be rotated
27        Post  NODE rotated and new root returned
28  */
29
30  template <class TYPE, class KTYPE>
31  NODE<TYPE>*  AvlTree<TYPE,  KTYPE>
32            :: rotateRight (NODE<TYPE> *root)
33  {
34  // Local Definitions
35     NODE<TYPE>  *tempPtr;
36
37  // Statements
38     tempPtr        = root->left;
39     root->left     = tempPtr->right;
40     tempPtr->right = root;
41
42     return tempPtr;
43  } //  rotateRight
```

Program 8-10 AVL tree rotate left and right

AVL Tree Delete

Deleting from an AVL tree produces many of the same problems we saw when we inserted data. Interestingly, however, only the rotation algorithms can be reused; the balancing algorithms must be rewritten for deletion.

We use the same design for deletion as we used for insertion. The application program interface receives the key of the node to be deleted and calls a private function to locate and delete its node. If the deletion is successful, delete returns true; if the node cannot be found, it returns false. The code for the application interface is shown in Program 8-11.

```
 1  /* ===================== AVL_Delete =====================
 2     This function deletes a node from the tree and rebalances
 3     it if necessary.
 4         Pre     dltKey contains key to be deleted
 5         Post    the node is deleted and its space recycled
 6                 -or- an error code is returned
 7         Return success (true) or not found (false)
 8  */

10  template <class TYPE, class KTYPE>
11  bool  AvlTree <TYPE, KTYPE> :: AVL_Delete (KTYPE  dltKey)
12  {
13  // Local Definitions
14     bool shorter;
15     bool success;
16
17     NODE<TYPE>   *newRoot;
18
19  // Statements
20     newRoot = _delete (tree, dltKey, shorter, success);
21     if (success)
22        {
23          tree = newRoot;
24          count--;
25        } // if
26     return success;
27  } // AVL_Delete
```

Program 8-11 AVL tree delete application interface

Program 8-11 Analysis

The application interface delete function simply accepts the key from the user and calls the recursive delete function. When the delete has been completed, it updates the tree count and passes success back to the calling function.

Recursive AVL Delete

The real work is done by the recursive AVL delete function shown in Program 8-12.

```
 1   /* ======================== _delete ========================
 2      This function deletes a node from the tree and rebalances
 3      it if necessary.
 4         Pre    dltKey contains key of node to be deleted
 5                shorter is Boolean indicating tree is shorter
 6         Post   the node is deleted and its space recycled
 7                -or- if key not found, tree is unchanged
 8         Return true if deleted, false if not found
 9                pointer to root
10   */
11
12   template <class TYPE, class KTYPE>
13   NODE<TYPE>*  AvlTree<TYPE,  KTYPE>
14              :: _delete (NODE<TYPE> *root,
15                          KTYPE        dltKey,
16                          bool&        shorter,
17                          bool&        success)
18   {
19   //  Local Definitions
20      NODE<TYPE> *dltPtr;
21      NODE<TYPE> *exchPtr;
22      NODE<TYPE> *newRoot;
23
24   // Statements
25      if (!root)
26         {
27          shorter = false;
28          success = false;
29          return NULL;
30         } //  if -- base case
31
32      if (dltKey < root->data.key)
33         {
34          root->left = _delete (root->left, dltKey,
35                                shorter,    success);
36          if (shorter)
37              root    = dltRightBalance (root, shorter);
38         } // if less
39      elseif (dltKey > root->data.key)
40         {
41          root->right = _delete (root->right, dltKey,
42                                 shorter,      success);
43          if (shorter)
```

Program 8-12 AVL tree recursive delete

```
44              root = dltLeftBalance (root, shorter);
45          } //  if greater
46      else
47          // Found equal node
48          {
49           dltPtr  = root;
50           if (!root->right)
51              // Only left subtree
52              {
53                newRoot  = root->left;
54                success  = true;
55                shorter  = true;
56                delete (dltPtr);
57                return newRoot;              // base case
58              } //  if true
59          else
60              if (!root->left)
61                  // Only right subtree
62                  {
63                    newRoot  = root->right;
64                    success  = true;
65                    shorter  = true;
66                    delete (dltPtr);
67                    return newRoot;         // base case
68                  } // if
69              else
70                  // Delete NODE has two subtrees
71                  {
72                    exchPtr = root->left;
73                    while (exchPtr->right)
74                        exchPtr = exchPtr->right;
75
76                    root->data = exchPtr->data;
77                    root->left = _delete (root->left,
78                                          exchPtr->data.key,
79                                          shorter,
80                                          success);
81                    if (shorter)
82                        root = dltRightBalance (root, shorter);
83                  } // else
84
85          } // equal node
86      return root;
87  } // _delete
```

Program 8-12 AVL tree recursive delete *(continued)*

Program 8-12 Analysis   Again we see a long, relatively complex implementation. This function is definitely longer than the structured programming guideline of one page, but it does not readily lend itself to decomposition.

As we saw with the recursive insert, the first part of the function searches for the node to be deleted. If it reaches a leaf before finding the delete node, it sets the success flag false and returns a null pointer. This is the first of three base cases.

Once we find the delete node, we determine if it is at a leaf or leaf-like node. Remember that deletes can take place only at a leaf. If a node has two subtrees, we must search for a leaf node to take its place. We first determine whether there is a right subtree. If there is none, then we simply save the left subtree pointer as the pointer to take the root's place. If there is a right subtree, we check the left subtree pointer. If there is none, then we save the right subtree pointer as the pointer to take the root's place. Assuming for the moment that there are zero or one subtree, we set success and shorter true, recycle the deleted node's memory, and return the new root pointer. These are the second (Statement 57) and third (Statement 67) base cases.

If the node to be deleted has two subtrees, then we must find a node to take its place. Our design searches the left subtree for its largest node. When we find it, we move its data to replace the deleted data and then recursively call the delete function to delete what we know to be a valid leaf node. This logic is shown in Statements 72 through 83.

As we back out of the tree, we must ensure that it is still balanced. If we have deleted a node on the left and the tree is shorter, we call delete right balance (Statement 37). We also call delete right balance when we return from deleting the largest node on the left subtree (Statement 82). If we have deleted a node on the right and the tree is shorter, we call delete left balance (Statement 44). Of course, if the tree is not shorter, then we don't need to balance it.

AVL Tree Delete Right Balance   Delete right balance is used when we delete a node on a left subtree and the tree needs to be rebalanced. We need to rebalance only if the root is right high. In this case, we have deleted a node on the left side of a right high tree, making it out of balance on the right subtree by two levels. Conversely, if the root is left or even high, then no rotation is needed. The code is shown in Program 8-13.

```
1   /* =================== dltRightBalance ===================
2      The tree is shorter after a delete on the left.
3      Adjust the balance factors and rotate the tree
4      to the left if necessary.
5         Pre      the tree is shorter
6         Post     balance factors adjusted and balance restored
```

Program 8-13   AVL tree delete right balance

```
 7            Returns potentially new root
 8     */
 9
10     template <class TYPE, class KTYPE>
11     NODE<TYPE>*  AvlTree<TYPE,  KTYPE>
12              ::  dltRightBalance (NODE<TYPE>  *root,
13                                    bool&          shorter)
14     {
15     //  Local Definitions
16        NODE<TYPE>  *rightTree;
17        NODE<TYPE>  *leftTree;
18
19     // Statements
20        switch (root->bal)
21           {
22           case LH: //  Deleted Left--Now balanced
23                    root->bal  = EH;
24                    break;
25           case EH: //  Now Right high
26                    root->bal  = RH;
27                    shorter    = false;
28                    break;
29           case RH: //  Right High - Rotate Left
30                    rightTree = root->right;
31                    if (rightTree->bal == LH)
32                        // Double rotation required
33                        {
34                         leftTree  = rightTree->left;
35
36                         switch (leftTree->bal)
37                             {
38                              case LH: rightTree->bal = RH;
39                                       root->bal       = EH;
40                                       break;
41                              case EH: root->bal       = EH;
42                                       rightTree->bal = EH;
43                                       break;
44                              case RH: root->bal       = LH;
45                                       rightTree->bal = EH;
46                                       break;
47                             } // switch
48
49                         leftTree->bal = EH;
50
51                         // Rotate Right then Left
52                         root->right = rotateRight (rightTree);
```

Program 8-13 AVL tree delete right balance (*continued*)

```
53              root          = rotateLeft  (root);
54          } //  if rightTree->bal == LH
55      else
56      {
57          //  Single Rotation Only
58          switch (rightTree->bal)
59          {
60            case LH:
61            case RH: root->bal      = EH;
62                     rightTree->bal = EH;
63                     break;
64            case EH: root->bal      = RH;
65                     rightTree->bal = LH;
66                     shorter        = false;
67                     break;
68          } // switch rightTree->bal
69          root = rotateLeft (root);
70      } // else
71  } //  switch root bal
72  return root;
73 } //  dltRightBalance
```

Program 8-13 AVL tree delete right balance *(continued)*

Program 8-13 Analysis

As we mentioned earlier, we need to rotate only if the right tree's height is two larger than the left tree's height. Therefore, if the tree was left high or even high before the deletion, no rotation is necessary. If it was right high, then it needs to be rotated. If its right subtree is left high (Statement 31), then a double rotation is necessary; otherwise, only a single rotation is necessary (Statement 57). In either case, we first adjust the balance factors and then rotate. As you study the logic, you will find it helpful to refer back to Figure 8-22, on page 371.

AVL Tree Data Processing

Now that we know how to build a tree, let's study the functions that retrieve data from the tree. We include two basic functions: retrieve one node and process the whole tree. These functions use the basic binary search tree algorithms.

Retrieve AVL Tree Node

The retrieve follows the left-right structure of the tree until the desired node is found. When it is located, the data are passed back to the calling function through a reference parameter. The retrieve function returns a Boolean—true if found and false if not found.

The design is similar to those of the insert and delete algorithms previously described. An application interface function provides the key to be located and the variable to receive the data. We then call a private function to locate the data. The code for the retrieve function is shown in Program 8-14. The code for the internal function is shown in Program 8-15.

```
 1   /* =================== AVL_Retrieve ===================
 2      Retrieve node searches the tree for the node containing
 3      the requested key and returns pointer to its data.
 4         Pre      dataOut is variable to receive data
 5         Post     tree searched and data returned
 6         Return   true if found, false if not found
 7   */
 8
 9   template <class TYPE, class KTYPE>
10   bool    AvlTree<TYPE, KTYPE>
11      ::  AVL_Retrieve  (KTYPE    key, TYPE& dataOut)
12   {
13   // Local Definitions
14      NODE<TYPE> *node;
15
16   // Statements
17      if (!tree)
18         return false;
19
20      node    = _retrieve (key, tree);
21      if (node)
22         {
23           dataOut = node->data;
24           return true;
25         } // if found
26      else
27         return false;
28   } //   AVL_Retrieve
```

Program 8-14   AVL retrieve data

Program 8-14 Analysis   The retrieve data function is quite simple. It is needed only because the recursive function requires a parameter for the root, which is private data that the using application can't reference.

```
 1   /* =================== _retrieve ===================
 2      Retrieve searches tree for node containing requested
 3      key and returns its data to the calling function.
 4         Pre      AVL_Retrieve called: passes key to be located
 5         Post     tree searched and data pointer returned
 6         Return   address of matching node returned
 7                  if not found, NULL returned
 8   */
```

Program 8-15   AVL tree recursive retrieve function

```
 9
10    template <class TYPE, class KTYPE>
11    NODE<TYPE>*  AvlTree<TYPE, KTYPE>
12              ::  _retrieve (KTYPE          key,
13                             NODE<TYPE> *root)
14    {
15    // Statements
16      if (root)
17          {
18           if (key < root->data.key)
19               return _retrieve (key, root->left);
20           elseif (key > root->data.key)
21               return _retrieve (key, root->right);
22           else
23               // Found equal key
24               return (root);
25          } // if root
26      else
27          //Data not in tree
28          return root;
29    } //  _retrieve
```

Program 8-15   AVL tree recursive retrieve function *(continued)*

Program 8-15 Analysis

The retrieve function searches the tree. If the search argument, key, is less than the root data's key, it calls itself with the left subtree as the root. If the search argument is greater than the root data's key, it calls itself with the right subtree as the root. If the argument is not greater or less than the root, then it must be equal so it returns the root's data pointer.

Study the recursive call's functions in Statements 19 and 21 carefully. Note that they return the address returned by the recursive call. In this fashion, the address returned by the base cases is passed back up the tree structure until it is finally returned to the original application call by the interface function.

Traverse AVL Tree

The traverse uses an inorder traversal of the tree, calling the application-dependent process function when the node is to be processed. Although the traversal is standard, the application-processing function is not. Therefore, whenever the using application calls the traversal, it must also pass the address of the function that processes the data. The processing function uses only one parameter, the data to be processed. It in turn calls the ADT internal function that actually traverses the tree. As seen in the insert and delete functions, we use a user interface function and call a private recursive function to do the actual traversal. The code for both functions is shown in Program 8-16.

```
 1  /* ==================== AVL_Traverse ====================
 2     Process tree using inorder traversal.
 3        Pre    process used to "visit" nodes during traversal
 4        Post   all nodes processed in LNR (inorder) sequence
 5  */
 6
 7  template <class TYPE, class KTYPE>
 8  void  AvlTree<TYPE, KTYPE>
 9    ::  AVL_Traverse (void (*process)(TYPE dataProc))
10  {
11  // Statements
12    _traversal (process, tree);
13    return;
14  } // end AVL_Traverse
15
16  /* ==================== _traversal ====================
17     Traverse tree using inorder traversal. To process a
18     node, we use the function passed when traversal is called.
19        Pre    tree has been created (may be null)
20        Post   all nodes processed
21  */
22
23  template <class TYPE, class KTYPE>
24  void  AvlTree<TYPE, KTYPE>
25    ::  _traversal (void(*process)(TYPE dataproc),
26                    NODE<TYPE> *root)
27  {
28  // Statements
29    if (root)
30       {
31        _traversal  (process, root->left);
32        process     (root->data);
33        _traversal  (process, root->right);
34       } //  if
35    return;
36  } //  _traversal
```

Program 8-16 Traverse AVL tree

AVL Tree Utility Functions

In this section we cover the four remaining functions for the AVL tree abstract data type class: empty tree, full tree, tree count, and destroy tree.

AVL Empty Tree

Empty tree simply checks the tree count. If it is 0, it returns true; otherwise, it returns false. The code is shown in Program 8-17.

```
 1   /* ================== AVL_Empty ==================
 2      Returns true if tree is empty, false if any data.
 3          Pre      tree has been created; may be null
 4          Returns  true if tree empty, false if any data
 5   */
 6
 7   template <class TYPE, class KTYPE>
 8   bool   AvlTree<TYPE, KTYPE> ::  AVL_Empty (void)
 9   {
10   // Statements
11      return (count == 0);
12   } //  AVL_Empty
```

Program 8-17   AVL empty tree

AVL Full Tree

Because there is no way to test for available memory in C++, we must actually try to allocate a node. If we are successful, we delete it and return false. If the allocation fails, then we return true, there is not enough memory for another node. The code is shown in Program 8-18.

```
 1   /* ================== AVL_Full ==================
 2      If there is no room for another node, returns true.
 3          Pre      tree has been created
 4          Returns  true if no room, false if room
 5   */
 6
 7   template <class TYPE, class KTYPE>
 8   bool   AvlTree<TYPE, KTYPE> ::  AVL_Full (void)
 9   {
10   // Local Definitions
11      NODE<TYPE>  *newPtr;
12
13   // Statements
14      newPtr = new NODE<TYPE>;
15      if (newPtr)
16          {
17           delete  newPtr;
18           return false;
19          } // if
20      else
21          return true;
22   } //  AVL_Full
```

Program 8-18   AVL full tree

AVL Count

The count function simply returns the number of nodes currently in the tree (Program 8-19).

```
 1    /* =================== AVL_Count ===================
 2       Returns number of nodes in tree.
 3          Pre      tree has been created
 4          Returns tree count
 5    */
 6
 7    template <class TYPE, class KTYPE>
 8    int  AvlTree<TYPE, KTYPE> ::  AVL_Count (void)
 9    {
10    // Statements
11       return (count);
12    } //  AVL_Count
```

Program 8-19   AVL tree count

Destroy AVL Tree

The last function in the AVL tree abstract data type is the AVL tree class destructor. It physically deletes all the data nodes when the tree is no longer needed. Because we need to traverse the tree to find all of the data and nodes that need to be deleted, we call a recursion to do the physical deletions.

The logic for destroy list parallels that for the destructor functions we have seen previously. The code for the destructor interface is shown in Program 8-20.

```
 1    /* =================== Destructor ===================
 2       Deletes all data in tree and recycles memory.
 3       The nodes are deleted by calling a recursive
 4       function to traverse the tree in inorder sequence.
 5          Pre      tree is a pointer to a valid tree
 6          Post     all data have been deleted
 7    */
 8
 9    template <class TYPE, class KTYPE>
10    AvlTree<TYPE, KTYPE> :: ~AvlTree  (void)
11    {
12    // Statements
13       if (tree)
14          _destroyAVL (tree);
15    } // Destructor
```

Program 8-20   Destroy tree

Program 8-20 Analysis

The logic is simple. We first make sure that we have a valid tree by testing the tree pointer. If it is valid—that is, if the tree pointer is not null—we call the recursive subfunction that does the physical deletions. The code for the recursive deletion function is shown in Program 8-21.

```
 1  /* ==================== _destroyAVL ====================
 2     Deletes all data in tree and recycles memory.
 3     The nodes are deleted by calling a recursive
 4     function to traverse the tree in postorder sequence.
 5        Pre    tree is being destroyed
 6        Post   all data have been deleted
 7  */
 8
 9  template <class TYPE, class KTYPE>
10  void  AvlTree<TYPE, KTYPE>
11     :: _destroyAVL (NODE<TYPE>  *root)
12  {
13  // Statements
14     if (root)
15        {
16         _destroyAVL (root->left);
17         _destroyAVL (root->right);
18         delete root;
19        } // if
20     return;
21  } // _destroyAVL
```

Program 8-21   Recursive destroy tree

Program 8-21 Analysis   The logic in the recursive deletion function is a little more complex. The big question is when to delete the root. Because we can't delete a root until both of its subtrees have been deleted, we must use a postorder traversal. Once we understand that concept, the rest of the algorithm is simple.

8-5   SUMMARY

- A binary search tree is a binary tree with the following properties:
  a. All items in the left subtree are less than the root.
  b. All items in the right subtree are greater than or equal to the root.
  c. Each subtree is itself a binary search tree.
- The inorder traversal of a binary search tree produces an ordered list.
- In a binary search tree, the node with the smallest value is the leftmost node in the tree. To find the smallest node, we simply follow the left branches until we get to a null left pointer.
- In a binary search tree, the node with the largest value is the rightmost node. To find the largest node, we follow the right branches until we get to a null right pointer.
- To search for a value in a binary search tree, we first compare the target value with the root. If the target value is smaller than the root, we repeat the procedure for the left subtree. If the target is greater than the root, we

repeat the procedure for the right subtree. If the target value is equal to the root, the search is complete.

■ To insert a node in a binary search tree, we follow the left or right branch down the tree, depending on the value of the new node, until we find a null subtree.

■ To delete a node from a subtree, we must consider four cases:

    a. The node to be deleted has no children.

    b. The node to be deleted has only a left subtree.

    c. The node to be deleted has only a right subtree.

    d. The node to be deleted has two subtrees.

■ An AVL tree is a search tree in which the heights of the subtrees differ by no more than 1, which means that the tree is balanced.

■ We consider four different cases when we want to rebalance a tree after deletion or insertion: left of left, right of right, right of left, and left of right.

■ We must balance a left of left, unbalanced AVL tree by rotating the out of balance node to the right.

■ We must balance a right of right, unbalanced tree by rotating the out of balance node to the left.

■ We must balance a right of left, unbalanced tree by double rotation: first the left subtree to the left and then the out of balance node to the right.

■ We must balance a left of right, unbalanced tree by double rotation: first the right subtree to the right and then the out of balance node to the left.

■ Inserting a new node into an AVL tree is the same as inserting into a binary search tree except that when we back out of the tree, we must constantly check the balance of each node and rebalance if necessary.

■ Deleting a node from an AVL tree is the same as deleting from a binary search tree except that when we back out of the tree, we must constantly check the balance of each node and rebalance if necessary.

8-6   PRACTICE SETS

Exercises

1. Draw all possible binary search trees for the data elements 5, 9, and 12.

2. Create a binary search tree using the following data entered as a sequential set:

        14, 23, 7, 10, 33, 56, 80, 66, 70

3. Create a binary search tree using the following data entered as a sequential set:

        7, 10, 14, 23, 33, 56, 66, 70, 80

4. Create a binary search tree using the following data entered as a sequential set:

        80, 70, 66, 56, 33, 23, 14, 10, 7

5. Insert 44 and 50 into the tree created in Exercise 2.

6. Insert 44 and 50 into the tree created in Exercise 3.

7. Insert 44 and 50 into the tree created in Exercise 4.

8. Give the balance factor for the trees created in Exercises 2, 3, and 4.

9. Which one of the trees in Figure 8-26 is a valid binary search tree and which one is not? Explain your answer.

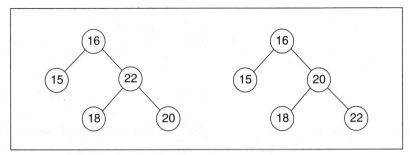

Figure 8-26   Figure for Exercise 9

10. Traverse the binary search tree in Figure 8-27 using an inorder traversal.

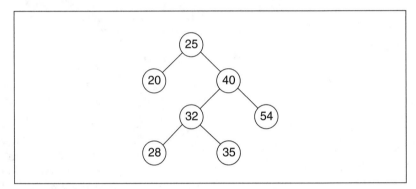

Figure 8-27   Figure for Exercise 10

11. The binary search tree in Figure 8-28 was created by starting with a null tree and entering data from the keyboard. In what sequence were the data entered? If there is more than one possible sequence, identify the alternatives.

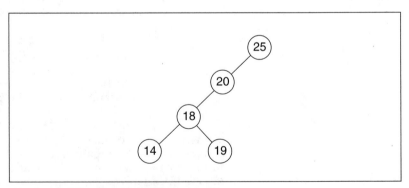

Figure 8-28   Figure for Exercise 11

12. The binary search tree in Figure 8-29 was created by starting with a null tree and entering data from the keyboard. In what sequence were the data entered? If there is more than one possible sequence, identify the alternatives.

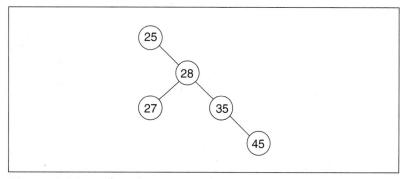

Figure 8-29   Figure for Exercise 12

13. Insert 44, 66, and 77 into the binary search tree in Figure 8-30.

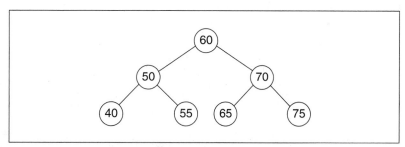

Figure 8-30   Figure for Exercise 13

14. Delete the node containing 60 from the binary search tree in Figure 8-31.

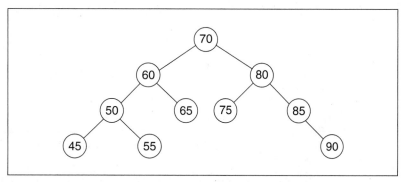

Figure 8-31   Figure for Exercises 14 and 15

15. Delete the node containing 85 from the binary search tree in Figure 8-31.

16. Balance the tree in Figure 8-32.

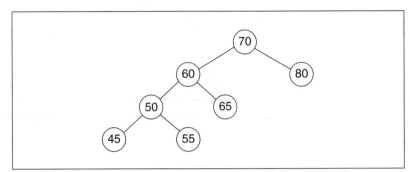

Figure 8-32   Figure for Exercise 16

17. Balance the tree in Figure 8-33.

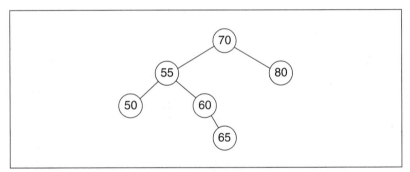

Figure 8-33   Figure for Exercise 17

18. Add 49 to the AVL tree in Figure 8-34. The result must be an AVL tree. Show the balance factors in the resulting tree.

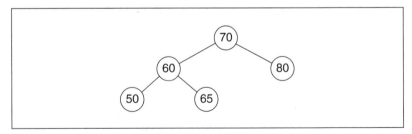

Figure 8-34   Figure for Exercises 18 and 19

19. Add 68 to the AVL tree in Figure 8-34. The result must be an AVL tree. Show the balance factors in the resulting tree.

Problems

20. Develop a nonrecursive algorithm for Algorithm 8-1, "Find smallest node in a BST," on page 342.
21. Develop a nonrecursive algorithm for Algorithm 8-3, "BST search," on page 344.
22. Write the C++ code for Algorithm 8-1, "Find smallest node in a BST," on page 342.
23. Write the C++ code for Algorithm 8-4, "Iterative binary search tree insert," on page 346.
24. Write the C++ code for Algorithm 8-5, "Add node to BST recursively," on page 348.
25. Write the C++ code for Algorithm 8-6, "Binary search tree delete," on page 350.

Projects

26. When writing BST algorithms, you need to be able to print the tree in a hierarchical order to verify that the algorithms are processing the data correctly. Write a special print function that can be called to print the tree. The printed output should contain the node level number and its data. Present the tree using a bill-of-materials format, as shown in Figure 8-35, for several popular breeds of dogs recognized by the American Kennel Club (AKC).

```
      1.  Labrador
          2.  German Shepherd
              3. Cocker Spaniel
                 4. Beagle
                 4. Dachshund
                    5. Dalmatian
              3. Golden Retriever
          2. Rottweiler
              3. Poodle
              3. Shetland Sheepdog
```

Figure 8-35   Top popular breeds of dogs recognized by the AKC

27. Rewrite the print algorithm in Project 26 to print the data hierarchically. A vertical presentation of the data in Figure 8-35 is shown in Figure 8-36. If you tilt the page sideways, the data are presented in the binary tree format.
28. Write a program that reads a list of names and telephone numbers from a text file and inserts them into an AVL tree. Once the tree has been built, present the user with a menu that allows him or her to search the list for a specified name, insert a new name, delete an existing name, or print the entire phone list. At the end of the job, write the data in the list back to the file. Test your program with at least ten names.
29. Write an algorithm that prints an AVL tree. See Projects 26 and 27.
30. Work Project 28 using a binary search tree.

```
                3. Shetland Sheepdog
            2. Rottweiler
                3. Poodle
        1.  Labrador
                3. Golden Retriever
            2.  German Shepherd
                        5. Dalmatian
                    4. Dachshund
                3. Cocker Spaniel
                    4. Beagle
```

Figure 8-36   AKC data presented hierarchically

31. Create the ADT for a binary search tree using the array implementation. In an array implementation, the pointers become indexes to the subtree elements. When you create the tree, you will need to know the maximum number of nodes to be stored in the tree. To test the ADT, use it to run the program in Project 28.

32. Build an index for the words in a document containing pages identified by a form-feed character at the end of each page. Hint: See count words example starting on page 372. Print the index at the end of the program.

33. An index generally contains only keywords. Write a program that uses a file of keywords to index a document. It begins by reading the keyword file and inserting the words into an AVL tree. It then reads the document and builds an AVL tree index of the keywords in the document. Print the keyword index at the end of the document.

34. Binary tree traversal algorithms are written using either recursion or programmer-written stacks. If the tree must be traversed frequently, using stacks rather than recursion may be more efficient. A third alternative is a **threaded tree.** In a threaded tree, null pointers are replaced with pointers to their successor nodes.

Using a stack for each call makes the binary tree traversal inefficient, particularly if the tree must be traversed frequently. The reason we use recursion or a stack is that, at each step, we cannot access the next node in the sequence directly and we must use backtracking. The traversal is more efficient if the tree is a threaded tree.

For example, in the inorder traversal of a binary tree, we must traverse the left subtree, the node, and the right subtree. Because an inorder traversal is a depth-first traversal, we follow left pointers to the leftmost leaf.

When we find the leftmost leaf, we must begin backtracking to process the right subtrees we passed by on our way down. This is especially inefficient when the parent node has no right subtree. Consider the tree shown in Figure 8-37(a).

The inorder traversal of this tree is BCDAE. When we traverse the tree in inorder sequence, we follow the left pointers to get the first node, B. However, after locating the leftmost node, we must go back to C,

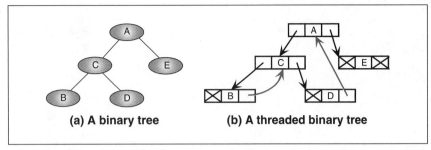

(a) A binary tree   **(b) A threaded binary tree**

Figure 8-37   A threaded binary tree for Project 34

which is why we need recursion or a stack. Note that when we are processing B, we do not need recursion or a stack because B's right subtree is empty.

Similarly, when we finish processing node D using recursion or stacks we must return to node C before we go to A. But again, we do not need to pass through C. The next node to be processed is the root, A.

From this small example, it should be clear that the nodes whose right subtrees are empty create more work when we use recursion or stacks. This leads to the threaded concept: When the right subtree pointer is empty, we can use the pointer to point to the successor of the node. In other words, we can use the right null pointer as a thread. The threaded tree is shown in Figure 8-37(b).

To build a threaded tree, first build a standard binary search tree. Then traverse the tree, changing null right pointers to point to their successors.

The traversal for a threaded tree is straightforward. Once you locate the leftmost node, you loop, following the thread (the right pointer) to the next node. No recursion or stack is needed. When you find a null thread (right pointer), the traversal is complete.

Write an algorithm to create a threaded binary tree for inorder traversal. Then write the algorithm to traverse the subtree inorder.

35. Rework Project 34 using a preorder traversal.

36. Rework Project 34 using a postorder traversal.

37. One of the problems with hashed lists (Chapter 2) is that the data cannot be processed sequentially. Rewrite Project 19 in Chapter 2 on page 75, to include a search tree for the part numbers. Add a user option to print the list in part number sequence.

9

Heaps

As a fourth use of trees, let's look at heaps. Like the binary trees, which we have studied so far, heaps have a meaning for the left and right subtrees—smaller. The root of a heap is guaranteed to hold the largest node in the tree; its subtrees contain data that have lesser values. Unlike the binary search tree, however, the smaller nodes of a heap can be placed on either the right or left subtree. Therefore, both the left and right branches of the tree have the same meaning.

Heaps have another interesting facet: They are often implemented in an array rather than a linked list. When we implement a binary tree in an array, we are able to calculate the location of the right and left subtrees. Conversely, given the address of a node, we can calculate the address of its parent. This makes for very efficient processing.

9-1   HEAP DEFINITION

A **heap** is a binary tree structure with the following properties:

1. The tree is complete or nearly complete.
2. The key value of each node is greater than or equal to the key value in each of its descendents.

Figure 9-1 shows a heap.

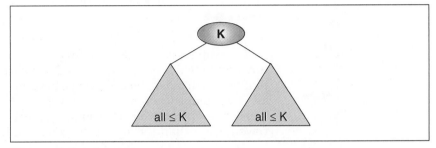

Figure 9-1   A heap

Sometimes this structure is called a **max-heap.** The second property of a heap, the key value is greater than the keys of the subtrees, can be reversed to create a **min-heap.** That is, we can create a minimum heap in which the key value in a node is *less than* the key values in all of its subtrees. Generally speaking, whenever the term *heap* is used by itself, it refers to a max-heap.

Note

> A heap is a complete or nearly complete binary tree in which the key value in a node is greater than the key values in all of its subtrees and the subtrees are in turn heaps.

9-2   HEAP STRUCTURE

To better understand the structure of a heap, let's examine the heaps in Figure 9-2. Study the two- and three-level heaps. Note that the left node of two siblings can be either larger or smaller than the right node. Compare this ordering with the binary search tree that we studied earlier. It is obviously different.[1] Finally, in the three-level heap, note that the third level is being filled from the left. This is the definition of a nearly complete tree and is a requirement for a heap.

---

1. It is interesting to note that in a complete binary search tree with no equal nodes, the root always contains the median value of the keys, whereas in the heap it contains the largest value.

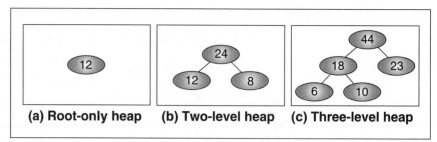

Figure 9-2   Heap trees

To complete our understanding of a heap, let's look at some structures that are not heaps. Figure 9-3 shows four examples of structures that are not heaps. The first two structures are not heaps because they are not complete or nearly complete trees. Although the third and fourth examples are nearly complete, the keys of the nodes are not always greater than the keys of their descendents.

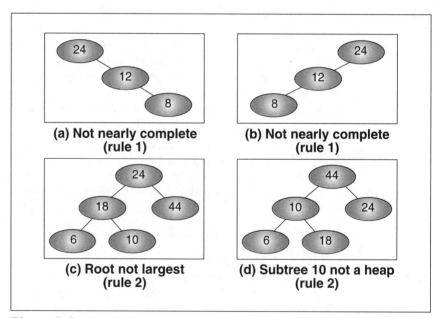

Figure 9-3   Invalid heaps

9-3   BASIC HEAP ALGORITHMS

Two basic maintenance operations are performed on a heap: insert a node and delete a node. Although the heap structure is a tree, it is meaningless to traverse it, search it, or print it out. In these respects, it is much like a restricted data structure. To implement the insert and delete operations, we need two basic algorithms: reheap up and reheap down. All of the other heap algorithms build on these two. We therefore study them first.

ReheapUp

Imagine that we have a nearly complete binary tree with N elements whose first $N-1$ elements satisfy the order property of heaps, but the last element does not. In other words, the structure would be a heap if the last element were not there. The **reheapUp** operation repairs the structure so that it is a heap by floating the last element up the tree until that element is in its correct location in the tree. We show this restructuring graphically in Figure 9-4. Before reheapUp, the last node in the heap was out of order. After the reheap, it is in its correct location and the heap has been extended one node.

Like the binary search tree, inserts into heaps take place at a leaf. Furthermore, because the heap is a complete or nearly complete tree, the node must be placed in the last leaf level at the first (leftmost) empty position. This creates the situation we see in Figure 9-4. If the new node's key is larger than that of its parent, it is floated up the tree by exchanging the child and parent keys and data. The data eventually rise to the correct place in the heap by repeatedly exchanging child-parent keys and data.

Note

> The reheapUp operation repairs a "broken" heap by floating the last element up the tree until it is in its correct location in the heap.

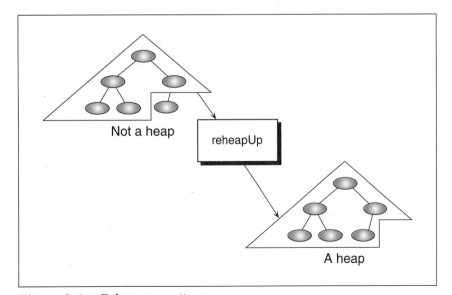

Figure 9-4   Reheap operation

Figure 9-5 traces the `reheapUp` operation in a heap. At the beginning, we observe that 25 is greater than its parent's key, 12. Because 25 is greater than 12, we also know from the definition of a heap that it is greater than the parent's left subtree keys. We therefore exchange 25 and 12 and call `reheapUp` to test its current position in the heap. Once again, 25 is greater than its parent's key, 21. Therefore, we again exchange the nodes' data. This time, when `reheapUp` is called, the value of the current node's key is less than the value of its parent key, indicating we have located the correct position and the operation stops.

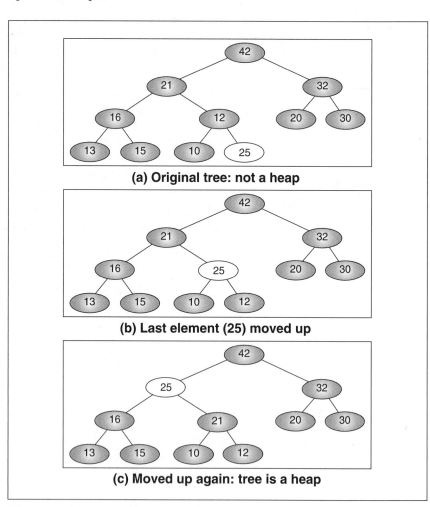

(a) Original tree: not a heap

(b) Last element (25) moved up

(c) Moved up again: tree is a heap

Figure 9-5   `reheapUp` example

ReheapDown

Now let's examine the reverse situation. Imagine we have a nearly complete binary tree that satisfies the heap order property except in the root position. This situation occurs when the root is deleted from the tree, leaving two disjointed heaps. To correct the situation, we move the data in the last tree node to the root. Obviously this action destroys the tree's heap properties.

Note

> ReheapDown repairs a "broken" heap by pushing the root down the tree until it is in its correct position in the heap.

To restore the heap property we need an operation that will sink the root down until it is in a position where the heap-ordering property is satisfied. We call this operation **reheapDown.** The reheapDown operation is shown in Figure 9-6.

Figure 9-7 demonstrates the reheapDown operation. When we start, the root (10) is smaller than its subtrees. We examine them and select the larger of the two to exchange with the root, in this case 32. Having made the exchange in Figure 9-7(b), we check the subtrees to see if we are finished and see that 10 is smaller than their keys. Once again we exchange 10 with the larger of the subtrees, 30. At this point we have reached a leaf and are finished.

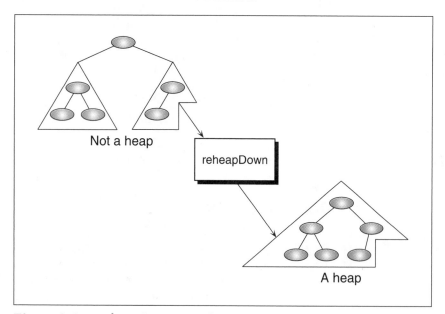

Not a heap

reheapDown

A heap

Figure 9-6   reheapDown operation

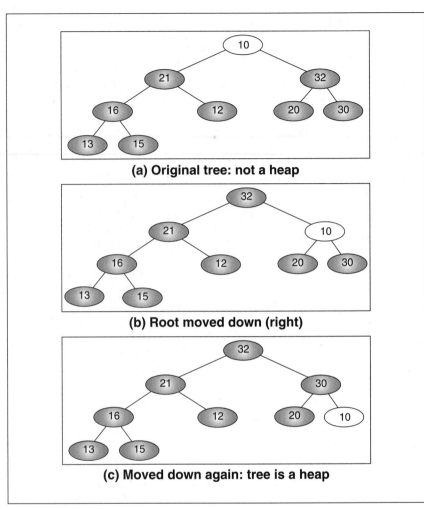

(a) Original tree: not a heap

(b) Root moved down (right)

(c) Moved down again: tree is a heap

Figure 9-7   reheapDown

9-4   HEAP DATA STRUCTURE

Although a heap can be built in a dynamic tree structure, it is most often implemented in an array. This implementation is possible because the heap is, by definition, complete or nearly complete. Therefore, the relationship between a node and its children is fixed and can be calculated as shown below.

1. For a node located at index i, its children are found at
   a. Left child: $2i + 1$
   b. Right child: $2i + 2$
2. The parent of a node located at index i is located at $\lfloor (i - 1)/2 \rfloor$.

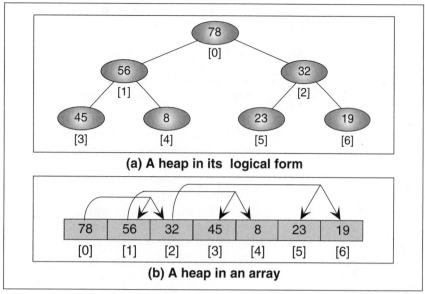

Figure 9-8   Heaps in arrays

3. Given the index for a left child, *j*, its right sibling, if any, is found at *j* + 1. Conversely, given the index for a right child, *k*, its left sibling, which must exist, is found at *k* − 1.

4. Given the size, *n*, of a complete heap, the location of the first leaf is $\lfloor (n/2) \rfloor$. Given the location of the first leaf element, the location of the last nonleaf element is 1 less.

To demonstrate these relationships, let's examine Figure 9-8. We have the following relationships:

1. The index of 32 is 2, so the index of its left child, 23, is 2 * 2 + 1, or 5. The index of its right child, 19, is 2 * 2 + 2, or 6 (Relationship 1).

2. The index of 8 is 4, so the index of its parent, 56, is $\lfloor (4 - 1)/2 \rfloor$, or 1 (Relationship 2).

3. In Relationship 1 we found the address of the left and right child. To find the right child, we could also have used the location of the left child (5) and added 1 (Relationship 3).

4. The total number of elements is 7, so the index of the first leaf element, 45, is $\lfloor (7/2) \rfloor$, or 3 (Relationship 4).

5. The location of the last nonleaf element, 32, is 3 − 1, or 2 (Relationship 4).

Finally, these heap relationships are unique to C++ and other languages that use base-zero index addressing for their arrays.[2] They

---

2. In Pascal, the programmer can create a zero-based array by declaring the array starting at 0.

would need to be modified slightly for other languages that use base-one index addressing.

Note

> A heap can be implemented in an array because it must be a complete or nearly complete binary tree, which allows a fixed relationship between each node and its children.

Figure 9-8 shows a heap in its tree form and in its array form. Study both of these representations carefully. In the logical form, note that each node's data are greater than the data in its descendents. In the array format, follow the arrows to both successors for a node and confirm that the array properly represents the logical (tree) format. In Figure 9-8, the tree is complete and the array is full. Therefore, to add another node to the tree we would have to add a new level to the tree and double the size of the array, because the physical array should always represent the complete tree structure.

9-5   HEAP ALGORITHMS

There are two ways to build a heap. We can start with an empty array and insert elements into the array one at a time, or, given an array of data that are not a heap, we can rearrange the elements in the array to form a heap. After looking at the two basic algorithms, reheapUp and reheapDown, we examine both approaches. Then we look at the logic for deleting data from a heap.

ReheapUp

ReheapUp uses recursion to move the new node up the tree. It begins by determining the parent's address using the relationships we discussed on page 409. If the key of the new data is greater than the key of its parent, it exchanges the nodes and recursively calls itself (Figure 9-5, on page 410). The base case is determined when either there is no parent, meaning we are at the heap's root, or the nodes are in the proper heap sequence. The logic is shown in Algorithm 9-1.

```
algorithm reheapUp (ref heap      <array>,
                    val newNode  <index>)
Reestablishes heap by moving data in child up to its correct
location in the heap array.
    Pre   heap is array containing an invalid heap
          newNode is index location to new data in heap
    Post  heap has been reordered
```

Algorithm 9-1   reheapUp

```
1 if (newNode not zero)
   1   parent = (newNode - 1) / 2
   2   if (heap[newNode].key > heap[parent].key)
      1   swap (heap, newNode, parent)
      2   reheapUp (heap, parent)
   3   end if
2 end if
3 return
end reheapUp
```

Algorithm 9-1   reheapUp *(continued)*

ReheapDown

The logic for reheapDown is a little more complex. As we push nodes down the heap, we need to determine whether the current entry is less than either of its children (one or both). If it is, we need to exchange it with the larger entry (see Figure 9-7, on page 412).

To determine whether the current entry is less than either of its children, we first determine which of the two subtree keys is larger. Once we know which one is larger, we need only test the current node with it. If the current node is smaller than the larger node, we exchange them and recursively call reheapDown. As you study Algorithm 9-2, you will see that most of the code is used to determine which of the subtree keys is larger.

```
algorithm reheapDown (ref heap  <array>,
                      val root  <index>,
                      val last  <index>)
Reestablishes heap by moving data in root down to its correct
location in the heap.
   Pre    heap is an array of data
          root is root of heap or subheap
          last is an index to the last element in heap
   Post   heap has been restored
Determine which child has larger key
1 if (root * 2 + 1 <= last)
   There is at least one child
   1   leftKey = heap[root * 2 + 1].data.key
   2   if (root * 2 + 2 <= last)
      1   rightKey = heap[root * 2 + 2].data.key
   3   else
      1   rightKey = lowKey
```

Algorithm 9-2   reheapDown

```
    4    end if
    5    if (leftKey > rightKey)
         1    largeChildKey    = leftKey
         2    largeChildIndex  = root * 2 + 1
    6    else
         1    largeChildKey    = rightKey
         2    largeChildIndex  = root * 2 + 2
    7    end if
    Test if root > larger subtree
    8    if (heap[root].data.key < largeChildKey)
         1    swap (heap, root, largeChildIndex)
         2    reheapDown (heap, largeChildIndex, last)
    9    end if
  2 end if
  3 return
end reheapDown
```

Algorithm 9-2   reheapDown *(continued)*

Algorithm 9-2 Analysis

We need to test only one subtree because we know from logic that if the root is greater than the left subtree and the left subtree is greater than the right subtree, then the root is also greater than the right subtree. This argument is logically stated as "If A > B and if B > C, then A > C."

There are two base cases in this algorithm. First, if there are no leaves, then we are finished. This case is shown in Statement 1. The second base case is shown in Statement 1.8. If the root is greater than the larger subtree, we have a valid heap.

BuildHeap

Given a filled array of elements in random order, to build the heap we need to rearrange the data so that each node in the heap is greater than its children. We begin by dividing the array into two parts, the left being a heap and the right being data to be inserted into the heap. At the beginning, the root (the first node) is the only node in the heap and the rest of the array are data to be inserted. This structure is shown in Figure 9-9. Note the "wall" between the first and second nodes. The lines at the top of figures point to the nodes' children. Each iteration of the insertion algorithm uses reheap up to insert the next element into the heap and moves the wall separating the elements one position to the right.

To insert a node into the heap, we follow the parent path up the heap, swapping nodes that are out of order. If the nodes are in order, then the insertion terminates and the next node is selected and inserted into the heap. This process is sometimes referred to as **heapify.**

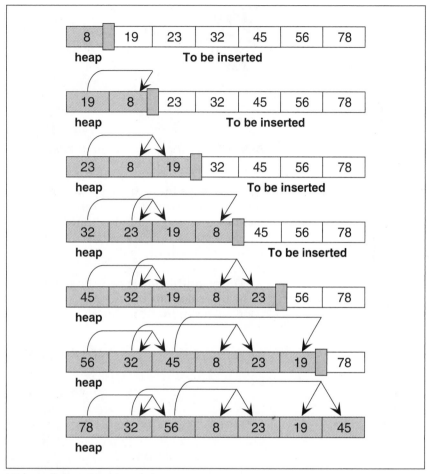

Figure 9-9   Building a heap

The buildHeap algorithm is very simple. We walk through the array that we need to convert to a heap, starting at the second element, calling reheapUp for each array element to be inserted into the heap. The code is shown in Algorithm 9-3.

```
algorithm buildHeap (ref heap  <array>,
                     val size  <integer>)
Given an array, rearrange data so that they form a heap.
    Pre    heap is an array containing data in nonheap order
           size is number of elements in array
    Post   array is now a heap
```

Algorithm 9-3   buildHeap

```
1 walker = 1
2 loop (walker < size)
    1   reheapUp(heap, walker)
    2   walker = walker + 1
3 end loop
4 return
end buildHeap
```

Algorithm 9-3   `buildHeap` (continued)

InsertHeap

Once we have built the heap, we can insert a node as long as there is room in the array. To insert a node we need to locate the first empty leaf in the array. We find it immediately after the last node in the tree, which is given as a parameter. To insert a node, we move the new data to the first empty leaf and reheap up. The concept is shown in Figure 9-10.

The algorithm for `insertHeap` is straightforward. It moves the data to be inserted into the heap to the first leaf and calls `reheapUp`. The code is shown in Algorithm 9-4.

```
algorithm insertHeap (ref heap <array of dataType>,
                      ref last <index>,
                      val data <dataType>)
Inserts data into heap.
    Pre     heap is a valid heap structure
            last is index to last node in heap
    Post    data have been inserted into heap
    Return  true if successful; false if array full
1 if (heap full)
    1   return false
2 end if
3 last = last + 1
4 heap[last] = data
5 reheapUp (heap, last)
6 return true
end insertHeap
```

Algorithm 9-4   `insertHeap`

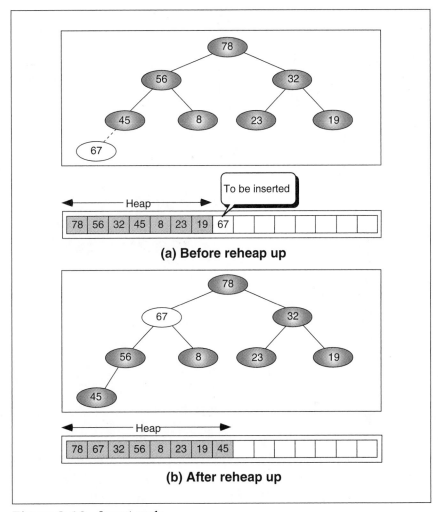

Figure 9-10 Insert node

DeleteHeap

When deleting a node from a heap, the most common and meaningful logic is to delete the root. The heap is thus left without a root. To reestablish the heap, we move the data in the last heap node to the root and reheapDown. The concept is shown in Figure 9-11.

The logic to delete the root from a heap is shown in Algorithm 9-5. Note that we return the data at the top of the heap to the calling algorithm for processing.

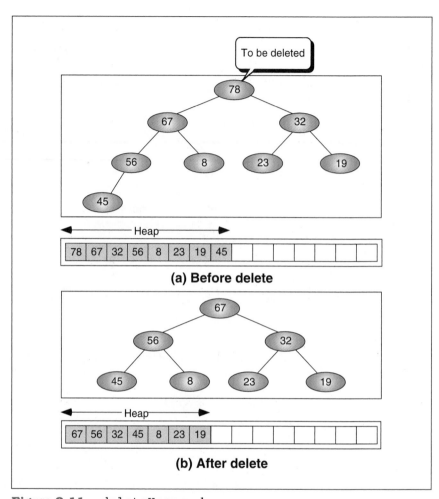

Figure 9-11   deleteHeap node

```
algorithm deleteHeap (ref heap      <array of dataType>,
                      ref last      <index>,
                      ref dataOut   <dataType>)
Deletes root of heap and passes data back to caller.
    Pre    heap is a valid heap structure
           last is index to last node in heap
```

Algorithm 9-5   deleteHeap node

```
            dataOut is reference parameter for output data
     Post   root has been deleted from heap
            root data placed in dataOut
     Return true if successful; false if array empty
   1 if (heap empty)
     1   return false
   2 end if
   3 dataOut = heap[0]
   4 heap[0] = heap[last]
   5 last    = last - 1
   6 reheapDown (heap, 0, last)
   7 return true
   end deleteHeap
```

Algorithm 9-5   `deleteHeap` node *(continued)*

9-6   HEAP APPLICATIONS

Three common applications of heaps are selection algorithms, priority queues, and sorting. We discuss heap sorting in Chapter 11 and selection algorithms and priority queues here.

Selection Algorithms

There are two solutions to the problem of determining the kth element in an unsorted list. We could first sort the list and select the element at location k, or we could create a heap and delete $k - 1$ elements from it, leaving the desired element at the top. Because we are studying heaps, let's look at the second solution, using a heap.

Creating the heap is simple enough. We have already discussed the heap algorithms. Once we have a heap, however, how do we select the desired element? Rather than simply discarding the elements at the top of the heap, a better solution would be to place the deleted element at the end of the heap and reduce the heap size by 1. After the kth element has been processed, the temporarily removed elements can then be reinserted into the heap.

For example, if we want to know the fourth largest element in a list, we can create the heap shown in Figure 9-12. After deleting three times, we have the fourth largest element, 21, at the top of the heap. After selecting 21, we reheap, to restore the heap so that it's complete and we are ready for another selection. The heap selection logic is shown in Algorithm 9-6.

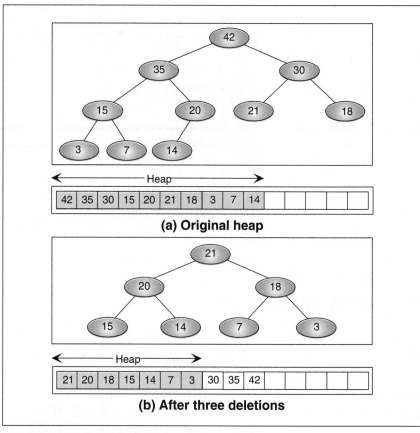

Figure 9-12   Heap selection

```
algorithm selectK  (ref heap      <array>,
                    val k         <integer>,
                    ref heapLast  <index>)
Select the k-th largest element from a list
    Pre    heap is an array implementation of a heap
           k is the ordinal of the element desired
           heapLast is index to last element in heap
    Post   k-th largest value returned
1 if (k > heapLast + 1)
  1    return 0
2 end if
3 i = 1
4 origHeapSize = heapLast + 1
```

Algorithm 9-6   selectK—heap selection

```
5 loop (i < k)
  1   temp = heap[0]
  2   deleteHeap (heap, heapLast,dataOut)
  3   heap[heapLast + 1] = temp
  4   i = i + 1
6 end loop
Desired element is now at top of heap
7 holdOut = heap[0]
Reconstruct heap
8 loop (heapLast < origHeapSize)
  1   heapLast = heapLast + 1
  2   reheapUp (heap, heapLast)
9 end loop
10 return holdOut
end SelectK
```

Algorithm 9-6   selectK—heap selection *(continued)*

Priority Queues

The queue structure that we studied in Chapter 4 uses a linear list in which each node travels serially through the queue. It is not possible for any element to advance faster than the others. Although this system may be very equitable, it is often not very realistic. Oftentimes, for various reasons, we want to prioritize one element over the others. As a rather trivial example, consider the line waiting for show seats in one of the large Las Vegas casinos. Most people wait in one long line, but there is usually a celebrity line that is very short if not empty. This line is reserved for special customers of the casino.

The heap is an excellent structure to use for a **priority queue**. As an event enters the queue, it is assigned a priority number that determines its position relative to the other events already in the queue. It is assigned a priority number even though the new event can enter the heap in only one place at any given time, the first empty leaf. However, once in line, the new event quickly rises to its correct position relative to all other events in the heap. If it has the highest priority, it rises to the top of the heap and becomes the next event to be processed. If it has a low priority, it remains relatively low in the heap, waiting its turn.

The key in a priority queue must be carefully constructed to ensure that the queue works properly. One common technique is to use an encoded priority number that consists of the priority plus a sequential number representing the event's place within the queue. For example, given a queue with five priority classes, we could construct a key in which the first digit of the priority number represented the queue priority, 1 through 5, and the rest of the number represented

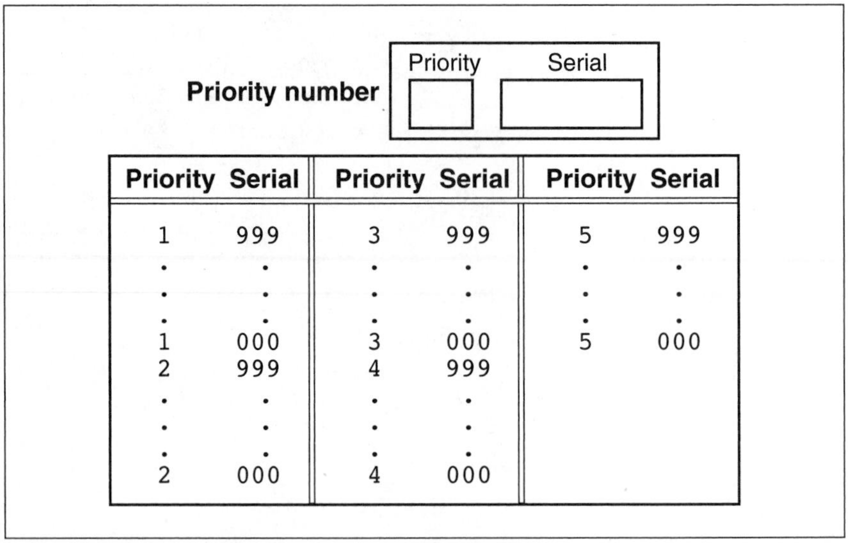

Figure 9-13 Priority queue priority numbers

the serial placement within the priority. Because we are using a priority heap, however, the serial number must be in descending order—that is, 999 down to 0 within each priority.

If we assume that there will be a maximum of 1000 events for any priority at any one time, then we could assign the lowest-priority sequential numbers in the range 1999 down to 1000, the second-lowest-priority sequential numbers in the range 2999 to 2000, the third-lowest-priority numbers in the range 3999 to 3000, and so forth. This concept is shown in Figure 9-13.

9-7   A HEAP PROGRAM

No programming language has intrinsic heap operators: To work with a heap, we must write the heap operations. Before writing the algorithms, we need to determine the data structure we will use. As mentioned earlier, we will use an array (see Figure 9-8, on page 413). Therefore, we need only the array itself and two other pieces of data, the index location of the last element in the heap and the maximum size of the heap. We use a variable, `heapLast`, for the first and a defined constant, `HEAP–SIZE`, for the second.[3]

---

3. With C, It would be possible to use *calloc* and implement the array in dynamic memory. In this environment, if the heap needed to be extended, we could use *realloc*.

Heap Program Design

To test the heap algorithms, we will write a simple program. It creates an array of random numbers in heap order and allows the user to interact with the heap by inserting and deleting data. The design of the program is shown in Figure 9-14.

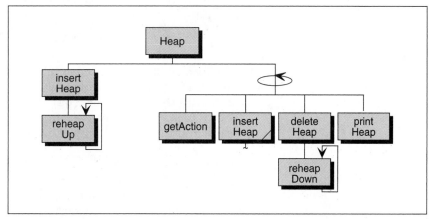

Figure 9-14   Heap program design

We begin by writing the prototype statements for the new functions that we need:

1. Insert heap. This function inserts new data. It needs three parameters: the heap array, an index to the new element in the array, and the data to be inserted.

```
bool insertHeap (int heap[], int& last, int data);
```

2. Delete heap. This function deletes the largest node from the heap. Because the largest node is always found at the top of the heap, we know its location. To complete its job, the function needs the heap, the index location to the last node in the heap, and a place to put the deleted data in the calling function.

```
bool deleteHeap (int  heap[],
                 int& heapLast,
                 int& dataOut);
```

3. To verify that the heap has been properly built, we need a print heap function. As we pointed out earlier, the operations on a heap are actually limited to just inserting and deleting data. While we are debugging these functions, however, we need to verify that the heap is correct. Like the insert and delete functions, the print function needs a pointer to the heap and the location of the last data in it. Because the heap is a form of binary tree, we use a recursive traversal to print it. Recursion adds one additional parameter, the root of the current subtree that is being processed. For formatting, we added one last parameter, a level number for the root. The complete prototype statement is shown below.

```
void printHeap (int   heap[],    int root,
                int   heapLast, int level);
```

4. Once we build the heap, we allow the user to interact with the heap through a menu-driven interaction. The function that interfaces with the user is called getAction. Its prototype statement is shown below. As you can see from the prototype, it reads the keyboard and returns a character, which is a valid user action code.

```
char getAction (void);
```

Program 9-1 contains main and the nonheap functions. The heap functions are developed in the next section.

```
 1  /* This program tests the heap functions used in the text.
 2     It uses a random number from rand() to build a heap. It
 3     then presents a menu that allows the user to insert to,
 4     delete from, and print the heap.
 5        Written by:
 6        Date:
 7  */
 8  #include <iostream>
 9  #include <iomanip>
10  #include <stdlib.h>
11  #include <ctype.h>
12
13  #define HEAP_SIZE 15
14  #include "P9-heap.h"          // Must be placed AFTER HEAP_SIZE
15
16  // Prototype Declarations
17  char getAction   (void);
18
19  // ===================== main =====================
20  int main (void)
21  {
22  // Local Definitions
23     int heap[HEAP_SIZE];
24
25     int data;
26     int heapLast;
```
Program 9-1   Heaps

```
27     int bldLooper;
28     int bldIndex;
29     int result;
30
31     char action;
32
33  // Statements
34     cout <<  "Begin Heap Test\n";
35
36     //  Fill half the heap with random numbers
37     heapLast = HEAP_SIZE / 2 - 1;
38     bldIndex = -1;
39     for (bldLooper = 0;
40          bldLooper <= heapLast;
41          bldLooper++)
42         {
43          data = rand() % 999 + 1;
44          insertHeap (heap, bldIndex, data);
45         } // for
46     cout << "\nEnd of heap creation\n\n";
47
48     // List built. Now test by inserting and deleting data
49     do
50         {
51         action = getAction ();
52         switch (action)
53             {
54             case 'I':
55                 cout << "Enter an integer: ";
56                 cin >>  data;
57                 result = insertHeap (heap, heapLast, data);
58                 if (result)
59                     cout << data << " inserted\n";
60                 else
61                     cout << "Heap full\a\n";
62                 break; // case I
63             case 'D':
64                 result = deleteHeap (heap, heapLast, data);
65                 if (result)
66                     cout << data << " deleted.\n";
67                 else
68                     cout << "Heap empty. Can't delete\a\n";
69                 break;  //  case D
70             case 'P':
71                 printHeap (heap, 0, heapLast, 0);
72                 break;
```

Program 9-1   Heaps *(continued)*

```
 73              case 'Q':
 74                  break;
 75              default :
 76                  cout << "Impossible error in main.\a\a\n";
 77                  exit    (100);
 78                  break;
 79              } // switch
 80      } while (action != 'Q');
 81
 82      cout <<   "End of Heap Test\n";
 83      return 0;
 84  } // main
 85
 86  /* ================== getAction ==================
 87     Get and return a valid action from keyboard.
 88         Pre    nothing
 89         Post   valid action read and returned
 90  */
 91  char getAction (void)
 92  {
 93  // Local Definitions
 94     char action;
 95     bool OK;
 96
 97  // Statements
 98     do
 99        {
100         cout << "\nPlease enter action <P, I, D, Q>: ";
101         cin >>  action;
102         action = toupper(action);
103         switch (action)
104            {
105            case 'P':
106            case 'I':
107            case 'D':
108            case 'Q': OK = true;
109                    break;
110
111            default:
112                    OK = false;
113                cout <<"<" << action << ">" << "invalid:";
114                cout << "Please re-enter\a\a\n" << action;
115                    break;
116            } // switch
117        } while (!OK);
118     return action;
```

Program 9-1   Heaps *(continued)*

```
119  } // getAction
120
121  /* ================== printHeap ==================
122     Print the heap. It is used only to verify that
123     the heap is valid.
124
125        Pre   heap is a pointer to a valid heap structure
126              root is the top of a tree or subtree
127              heapLast is the index to last node in the tree
128              level is the level number of the current root
129        Post  contents of heap array have been printed
130  */
131  void printHeap (int  heap[],
132                  int  root,
133                  int  heapLast,
134                  int  level)
135  {
136  // Local Definitions
137     int child;
138     int i;
139
140  // Statements
141     if (root <= heapLast)
142         {
143          child = (root * 2 + 1);
144          printHeap (heap, child + 1, heapLast, level + 1);
145
146          for (i = 0; i < level; i ++)
147             cout << "    ";
148          cout << setw(4) << heap[root] << endl;
149
150          printHeap (heap, child, heapLast, level + 1);
151         } // if  root
152     return;
153  } // printHeap
```

```
Results: (After heap built)

Please enter action <P, I, D, Q>: p
             34            (Rightmost node)
       633
             124
   855
             83
       764
             533          (Leftmost node)
```

Program 9-1   Heaps *(continued)*

Program 9-1 Analysis

This program contains a lot of code, but most of it is relatively simple. Nevertheless, some code is worth discussing. First, note how we build the heap in Statements 39 through 45. Using only half the array so that the user can add more data, we loop, assigning a random number to the next element to be inserted into the array and then calling `insertHeap`, which uses `reheapUp` to insert the new number into the heap.

The `getAction` function prompts the user and reads an action from the keyboard. If the action is not valid, it prints an error message and asks the user to reenter. When we return to the main line, therefore, we know that we have a valid action code. Now study the default (Statement 75) for the switch that drives the processing. If the action does not match any of our case options, we exit the program. Because we know that `getAction` checks for a valid action and the switch says the action is not valid, we also know our program has a bug and we need to fix it. Therefore, we exit the program after displaying an appropriate message.

Finally, study `printHeap` carefully. Note how it prints the heap as a sideways tree using a reverse-order (RNL) traversal. The reverse-order traversal prints the right subtrees first, which puts them on the right when the tree is viewed sideways. `PrintHeap` also uses a level number to determine how many spaces to print so that the result is a tree. By adding one with each call, it keeps track of how far down the tree it has traversed.

Heap Functions

This section contains the C++ code for the heap functions discussed earlier.

ReheapUp

`ReheapUp` parallels the pseudocode algorithm developed earlier. Its code is shown in Program 9-2.

```
 1  /* ==================== reheapUp ====================
 2     Reestablishes heap by moving data in child up to
 3     correct location in the heap array.
 4        Pre  heap is array containing an invalid heap
 5             newNode is index location to new data in heap
 6        Post newNode has been inserted into heap
 7  */
 8  void reheapUp (int   heap[],
 9                 int   newNode)
10  {
11  // Local Definitions
12     int parent;
13     int hold;
14
15  // Statements
16     // if not at root of heap
17     if (newNode)
```

Program 9-2 `reheapUp`

```
18          {
19            parent = (newNode - 1) / 2;
20            if (heap[newNode] > heap[parent])
21               {
22                // child is greater than parent
23                hold          = heap[parent];
24                heap[parent]  = heap[newNode];
25                heap[newNode] = hold;
26                reheapUp (heap, parent);
27               } // if
28          } //if newNode
29      return;
30  } // reheapUp
```

Program 9-2 reheapUp *(continued)*

ReheapDown

Although reheapDown is a rather long algorithm, it follows the pseudocode closely. The major difference is that we chose to code the swap inline rather than calling a swap function. The logic is shown in Program 9-3.

```
 1   /* ==================== reheapDown ====================
 2      Reestablishes heap by moving data in root down to its
 3      correct location in the heap.
 4         Pre   heap is an array of data
 5               root is root of heap or subheap
 6               last is an index to the last element in heap
 7         Post heap has been restored
 8   */
 9   void reheapDown    (int  heap[],
10                       int  root,
11                       int  last)
12   {
13   // Local Definitions
14      int hold;
15      int leftKey;
16      int rightKey;
17      int largeChildKey;
18      int largeChildIndex;
19
20   // Statements
21      if ((root * 2 + 1) <= last)
22         // There is at least one child
23         {
24            leftKey   = heap[root * 2 + 1];
25            if ((root * 2 + 2) <= last)
```

Program 9-3 reheapDown

```
26              rightKey   = heap[root * 2 + 2];
27          else
28              rightKey   = -1;
29
30          // Determine which child is larger
31          if (leftKey > rightKey)
32              {
33                largeChildKey    = leftKey;
34                largeChildIndex = root * 2 + 1;
35              } //  if
36          else
37              {
38                largeChildKey    = rightKey;
39                largeChildIndex = root * 2 + 2;
40              } // else
41          //   Test if root > larger subtree
42          if (heap[root] < largeChildKey)
43              {
44                // parent < children
45                hold                      = heap[root];
46                heap[root]                = heap[largeChildIndex];
47                heap[largeChildIndex] = hold;
48                reheapDown (heap, largeChildIndex, last);
49              } // if
50      } // if
51      return;
52  } // reheapDown
```

Program 9-3   reheapDown *(continued)*

InsertHeap

InsertHeap inserts one entry into the heap and reheaps up to reestablish the heap. Its code is shown in Program 9-4.

```
1  /* ================== insertHeap ==================
2     Inserts data into heap.
3        Pre     heap is a valid heap structure
4                last is pointer to index for last element
5                data is data to be inserted
6        Post    data have been inserted into heap
7        Return true if successful; false if array full
8  */
9  bool insertHeap (int& heap[],
10                  int& last,
11                  int  data)
12  {
13  // Statements
14     if (last == HEAP_SIZE - 1)
```

Program 9-4   insertHeap

```
15        return false;
16      ++last;
17      heap[last] = data;
18      reheapUp (heap, last);
19      return true;
20   } // insertHeap
```

Program 9-4 `insertHeap` *(continued)*

DeleteHeap Node

`DeleteHeap` deletes the element at the top of the heap and returns it to the caller. It then calls `reheapDown` to reestablish the heap. The code is shown in Program 9-5.

```
 1   /* ================= deleteHeap ==================
 2      Deletes root of heap and passes data back to caller.
 3          Pre    heap is a valid heap structure
 4                 last is index to last node in heap
 5          Post   element removed and heap rebuilt
 6                 deleted data passed back to user
 7          Return true if successful; false if array empty
 8   */
 9   bool deleteHeap (int  heap[],
10                    int& last,
11                    int& dataOut)
12   {
13   // Statements
14      if (last < 0)
15          return false;
16      dataOut = heap[0];
17      heap[0]  = heap[last];
18      last--;
19      reheapDown (heap, 0, last);
20      return true;
21   } // deleteHeap
```

Program 9-5 `deleteHeap`

9-8 SUMMARY

- A heap is a complete or nearly complete binary tree structure in which the key value of each node is greater than or equal to the key value in each of its descendents.
- A heap can be recursively defined as a complete or nearly complete binary tree in which the key value in a node is greater than or equal to the key values in all of its subtrees and each subtree is itself a heap.
- The only operations that generally apply to a heap are insert and delete.
- To be able to insert or delete from a heap, we need two algorithms: `reheapUp` and `reheapDown`.

- The `reheapUp` algorithm repairs a nonheap structure, which is a heap except for the last element. It floats the last element up the tree until that element is in its correct location. The `reheapUp` algorithm is needed when we insert an element into the heap and when we build a heap from an array.

- The `reheapDown` algorithm repairs a nonheap structure, which is made of two heaps and a root. The algorithm floats the root element down the tree until that element is in its correct location. We need a `reheapDown` algorithm when we delete an element from a heap.

- A heap can be implemented in an array because a heap is a complete or nearly complete binary tree in which there is a fixed relationship between each node and its children.

- Three common applications of heaps are selection, priority queue, and sorting.

- A heap can be used to select the *k*th largest (or smallest) element in an unsorted list.

- A heap can be used to implement a priority queue, in which every element has a priority number that determines its relationship to other elements.

- A heap can also be used to implement a sorting algorithm called the heap sort.

9-9   PRACTICE SETS

Exercises

1. Show which of the structures in Figure 9-15 is a heap and which is not.

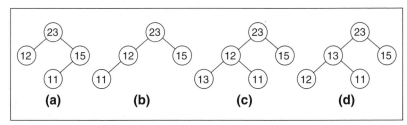

Figure 9-15   Heaps for Exercise 1

2. Make a heap out of the following data read from the keyboard:

       23 7 92 6 12 14 40 44 20 21

3. Apply the `reheapUp` algorithm to the nonheap structure shown in Figure 9-16.

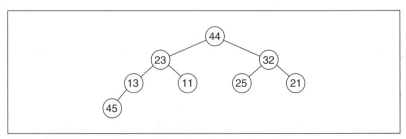

Figure 9-16   Nonheap structure for Exercise 3

4. Apply the `reheapDown` algorithm to the partial heap structure shown in Figure 9-17.

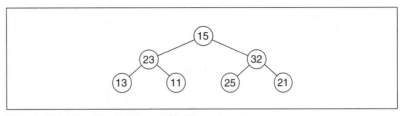

Figure 9-17   Partial heap for Exercise 4

5. Show the array implementation of the heap in Figure 9-18.

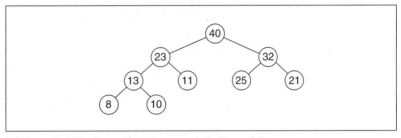

Figure 9-18   Heap for Exercises 5, 6, and 7

6. Apply the delete operation to the heap in Figure 9-18. Repair the heap after the deletion.

7. Insert 38 into the heap in Figure 9-18. Repair the heap after the insertion.

8. Show the left and right children of 32 and 27 in the heap in Figure 9-19. Also show the left children of 14 and 40.

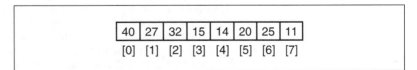

Figure 9-19   Heap array for Exercises 8 and 9

9. In the heap in Figure 9-19, show the parent of 11, parent of 20, and parent of 25.

10. If a node is at index 25, what is the index of its right child? What is the index of its left child? Assume the indexes start from 0.

11. If a node is at index 37, what is the index of its parent?

12. Which of the following sequences are heaps?
   a. 42 35 37 20 14 18 7 10
   b. 42 35 18 20 14 30 10
   c. 20 20 20 20 20 20

13. Show which item would be deleted from the following heap after calling the delete algorithm three times:

    50 30 40 20 10 25 35 10 5

14. Show the resulting heap after 33, 22, and 8 are added to the following heap:

    50 30 40 20 10 25 35 10 5

15. Draw a tree that is both a heap and a binary search tree.

16. Create a priority queue using the following data. The first number is the priority and the letter is the data.

    3-A, 5-B, 3-C, 2-D, 1-E, 2-F, 3-G, 2-H, 2-I, 2-J

17. Show the contents of the priority queue in Exercise 16 after deleting three items from the queue.

18. Show the contents of the original priority queue in Exercise 16 after the following operations:

    Insert 4-K, Insert 3-L, Delete, Insert 2-M, Delete

Problems

19. Rewrite the `reheapUp` (page 414) algorithm to build a minimum heap.
20. Rewrite the `reheapDown` (page 415) algorithm to recreate a minimum heap.
21. Rewrite the `insertHeap` (page 418) algorithm to build a minimum heap.
22. Rewrite the `deleteHeap` (page 420) algorithm to recreate a minimum heap.
23. Write an algorithm to combine two heaps and produce a third heap.
24. Write the C++ code for Problem 19.
25. Write the C++ code for Problem 20.
26. Write the C++ code for Problem 21.
27. Write the C++ code for Problem 22.
28. Write the C++ code for Problem 23.

Projects

29. Our study of tree algorithmics has shown that most tree structures are quite efficient. Let's examine the efficiency of heaps. Modify the `buildHeap` program (see Program 9-1, "Heaps," on page 426) to determine the complexity of building a heap. For this program, measure efficiency as the number of data moves necessary to build the heap.

    To determine a pattern, run your program with arrays filled with random numbers. Use five different array sizes: 100, 200, 500, 1000, and 2000. Then analyze the heuristics developed in these runs and determine which big-O notation would best apply. Prepare a short report of your findings with appropriate tables and graphs.

30. Modify Project 29 to determine the efficiency of the `reheapUp` and `reheapDown` algorithms only. Again, analyze the data and prepare a short report of your conclusions regarding their efficiency.

31. The `buildHeap` algorithm (Algorithm 9-3, on page 417) uses the `reheapUp` algorithm to build a heap from an array. Another slightly faster way to build a heap from an array is to use `reheapDown` in a loop starting from the middle of the array $\lfloor N/2 \rfloor - 1$, which is the root of the last nonempty subtree, and working up the tree to the root. This concept is shown in Figure 9-20.

    Rewrite the `buildHeap` algorithm and then write a C++ code to implement it using the above approach.

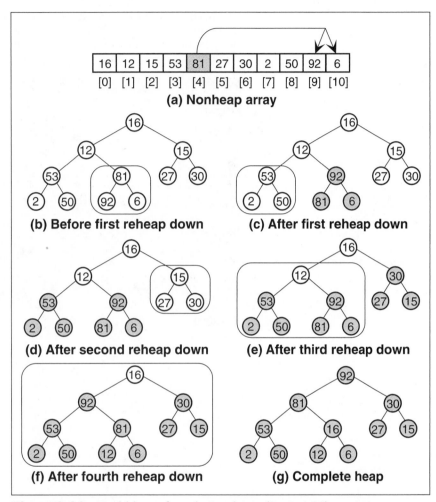

Figure 9-20 Build heap from last subtree (Project 31)

32. Add heuristic code to Project 31 to determine the efficiency of building the heap from the middle up.

33. An airline company uses the formula shown below to determine the priority of passengers on the waiting list for overbooked flights.

$$\text{priority number} = A/1000 + B - C$$

where
   A is the customer's total mileage in the past year
   B is the number of years in his or her frequent flier program
   C is a sequence number representing the customer's arrival position when he or she booked the flight

Given a file of overbooked customers as shown in Table 9-1, write a program that reads the file and determines the customer's priority number. The program then builds a priority queue using the priority number and prints a list of waiting customers in priority sequence.

Name	Mileage	Years	Sequence
Bryan Devaux	53,000	5	1
Amanda Trapp	89,000	3	2
Baclan Nguyen	93,000	3	3
Sarah Gilley	17,000	1	4
Warren Rexroad	72,000	7	5
Jorge Gonzales	65,000	2	6
Paula Hung	34,000	3	7
Lou Mason	21,000	6	8
Steve Chu	42,000	4	9
Dave Lightfoot	63,000	3	10
Joanne Brown	33,000	2	11

Table 9-1 Data for Project 33

Multiway Trees **10**

We have studied four different binary trees: binary search trees (Chapter 8), AVL trees (Chapter 8), internal structures for general trees (Chapter 7), and heaps (Chapter 9). Because they are all binary trees, their outdegree is restricted to 2. As the trees grow in size, their heights can become significant. For example, a tree with 1000 entries has a height of at least 10, and a tree with 100,000 entries has a height of at least 17. If the trees are unbalanced, their heights can be significantly larger.

In this chapter we explore trees whose outdegree is not restricted to 2 but that retain the general properties of binary search trees. Whereas each node in a binary tree has only one entry, multiway trees have multiple entries in each node and thus may have multiple subtrees. You will find these structures in applications such as internal search trees, spelling checkers, and external file indexes.

10-1　　*m*-WAY SEARCH TREES

An **m-way tree** is a search tree in which each node can have from 0 to *m* subtrees, where *m* is defined as the **order** of the tree. Given a nonempty multiway tree, we can identify the following properties:

1. Each node has 0 to *m* subtrees.
2. A node with $k < m$ subtrees contains *k* subtree pointers, some of which may be null, and $k - 1$ data entries.
3. The key values in the first subtree are all less than the key value in the first entry; the key values in the other subtrees are all greater than or equal to the key value in their parent entry.
4. The keys of the data entries are ordered $key_1 \leq key_2 \leq \ldots \leq key_k$.
5. All subtrees are themselves multiway trees.

Figure 10-1 is a diagrammatic representation of an *m*-way tree of order 4.

Study Figure 10-1 carefully. The first thing to note is that it has the same structure as the binary search tree: Subtrees to the left of an entry contain data with keys that are less than the key of the entry, and subtrees to the right of an entry contain data with keys that are greater than or equal to the entry's key. This ordering is best seen in the first and last subtrees.

Now study the second subtree. Note that its keys are greater than or equal to K_1 and less than K_2. It serves as the right subtree for K_1 and at the same time the left subtree for K_2. In other words, whether a subtree is a left or a right subtree depends on which node entry you are viewing.

Also note that there is one more pointer than there are entries in the node; there is a separate pointer at the beginning of each node. This first pointer identifies all of the subtrees that contain keys less than the first entry in the node. In addition, because each node has a variable number of entries, we need some way to keep track of how many entries are currently in the node. This is done with an entry count, which is not shown in Figure 10-1. Figure 10-2 is a four-way tree.

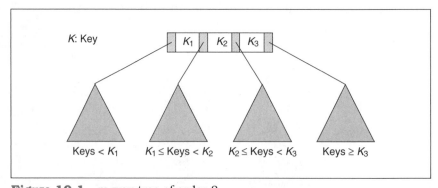

Figure 10-1　*m*-way tree of order 3

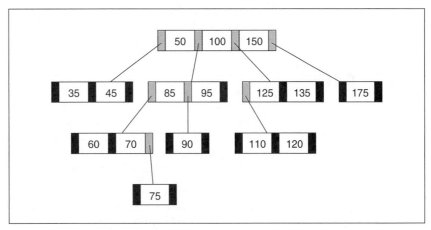

Figure 10-2   A four-way tree

We are now ready to code the description of an *m*-way tree node. Let's first build a structure for the entries. Because the number of entries varies up to a specified maximum, the best structure in which to store them is an array. Each entry needs to hold the key of the data, the data (or a pointer to the data if stored elsewhere), and a pointer to its right subtree; Figure 10-3(a) depicts the structure.

The node structure contains the first pointer to the subtree with entries less than the key of the first entry, a count of the number of entries currently in the node, and the array of entries. It is shown in Figure 10-3(b).

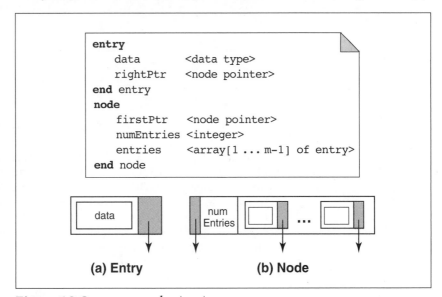

Figure 10-3   *m*-way node structure

Before leaving the discussion of *m*-way trees, there is one more thought we would like to leave with you. The binary search tree is an *m*-way tree of order 2.

10-2   B-TREES

The *m*-way tree has the potential to greatly reduce the height of a tree. However, it still has one major deficiency: It is not balanced. In 1970, two computer scientists working for the Boeing Company in Seattle created a new tree structure they called the B-tree.[1]A **B-tree** is an *m*-way search tree with the following additional properties:

1. The root is either a leaf or it has 2 . . . *m* subtrees.
2. All internal nodes have at least $\lceil m/2 \rceil$ nonnull subtrees and at most *m* nonnull subtrees.
3. All leaf nodes are at the same level; that is, the tree is perfectly balanced.
4. A leaf node has at least $\lceil m/2 \rceil - 1$ and at most $m - 1$ entries.

From the definition of a B-tree, it should be apparent that a B-tree is a perfectly balanced *m*-way tree in which each node, with the possible exception of the root, is at least half full. Table 10-1 defines the minimum and maximum numbers of subtrees in a nonroot node for B-trees of different orders.

Order	Number of Subtrees	
	Minimum	Maximum
3	2	3
4	2	4
5	3	5
6	3	6
...	...	...
m	$\lceil m/2 \rceil$	*m*

Table 10-1 Entries in B-trees of various orders

Figure 10-4 contains a B-tree of order 5. Let's examine its design. First, by the *m*-way rules on page 440, the tree is a valid *m*-way tree. Now let's look at the B-tree rules. The root is not a leaf—it has two subtrees (Rule 1). The left internal node has the minimum number of subtrees (three), and the right internal node has the maximum number of subtrees (five) (Rule 2). All leaf nodes are at level 2 (Rule 3). The leaves all have between the minimum (two) and the maximum (four) entries (Rule 4). Therefore, the tree is a valid B-tree.

1. R. Bayer and E. McCreight, "Organization and Maintenance of Large Ordered Indexes," *Acta Informatica 1,* no. 3 (1972): 173–189.

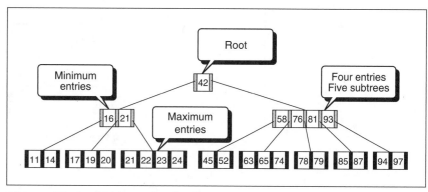

Figure 10-4   A B-tree of order 5

The four basic operations for B-trees are: insert, delete, traverse, and search. In this section we discuss these four algorithms and any algorithms they call.

B-Tree Insertion

Like the binary search tree, B-tree insertion takes place at a leaf node. The first step, therefore, is to locate the leaf node for the data being inserted. If the node is not full—that is, if it has fewer than $m - 1$ entries, then the new data are simply inserted in sequence in the node.

Note

> **A B-tree grows from the bottom up.**

When the leaf node is full, we have a condition known as **overflow.** Overflow requires that the leaf node be split into two nodes, each containing half of the data. To split the node, we allocate a new node from the available memory and then copy the data from the end of the full node to the new node. After the data have been split, the new entry is inserted into either the original or the new node, depending on its key value. Then the median data entry is inserted into the parent node.

To help us understand how to build a B-tree, let's run through a simple example. Given a B-tree structure with an order of 5, we begin by inserting 11, 21, 14, and 78. The first insert creates a node that becomes the root. The next three inserts simply place the data in the node in ascending key sequence. At this point, we have a tree that looks like the tree in Figure 10-5(a).

When we try to insert 97, we discover that the node is full. We therefore create a new right subtree and move the upper half of the data to it, leaving the rest of the data in the original node. This situation is shown in Figure 10-5(b). Note that the new value (97) has been placed in the new node because it logically belongs to the upper half of the data.

After creating the new node, we insert the median valued data (21) into the parent of the original node. Because the original node was a

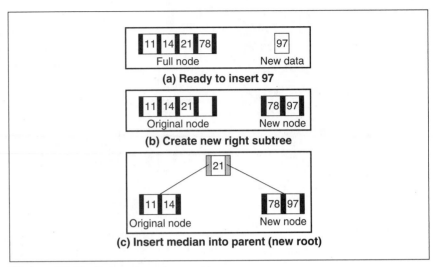

Figure 10-5   B-tree insert overview

root, we create a new root and insert 21 into it. This step completes the insertion of 97 into the B-tree, which has now grown by one level. The resulting B-tree is shown in Figure 10-5(c).

B-Tree Insert Design

The B-tree insert design is shown in Figure 10-6. The process of inserting an entry into the parent provides an interesting contrast to the binary search tree. Recall that the binary search tree grew in an unbalanced fashion from the top down. B-trees grow in a balanced fashion from the bottom up. When the root node of a B-tree overflows and the median entry is pushed up, a new root node is created and the tree grows one level. The B-tree insert code is shown in Algorithm 10-1.

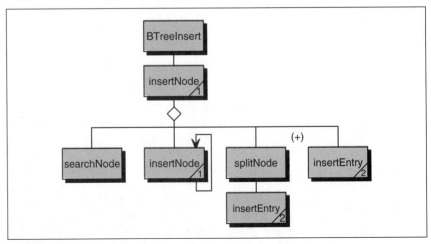

Figure 10-6   B-tree insert design

```
algorithm BTreeInsert (ref tree  <pointer>,
                       val data  <record>)
Inserts data into B-tree. Equal keys placed on right branch.
    Pre    tree is a pointer to the B-tree; may be null
    Post   data inserted

1 if (tree null)
  Empty tree. Insert first node.
  1    allocate (newPtr)
  2    if (allocate successful)
    1    newPtr->firstPtr          = null
    2    newPtr->numEntries        = 1
    3    newPtr->entries[0].data   = dataIn
    4    newPtr->entries[0].rightPtr = null
    5    tree = newPtr
    6    return true
  3    else
    1    abort program (Out of Memory)
  4    end if
2 end if
3 taller = insertNode (tree, data, upEntry)
4 if (taller true)
  Tree has grown. Create new root.
  1    allocate (newPtr)
  2    if (allocate successful)
    1    newPtr->entries[0]    = upEntry
    2    newPtr->firstPtr      = tree
    3    newPtr->numEntries    = 1
    4    tree = newPtr
  3    else
    1    abort program (Out of Memory)
  4    end if
5 end if
6 return
end BTreeInsert
```

Algorithm 10-1   B-tree insert

Algorithm 10-1 Analysis

The B-tree insert algorithm has just two processes. First it calls the insert node algorithm. As we will see, insert node is a recursive algorithm that not only inserts data into a leaf but also inserts the median entries into their parent nodes. If the root overflows, however, there is no parent in which to insert the median entry. The second process of B-tree insert node is creating a new root when the tree overflows. Whenever there is an overflow, insert node passes the median entry back to B-tree insert, through the parameter upEntry. The median entry contains the data and a pointer to its right subtree. The original root, which was split in insert node, then becomes the new root's left subtree (firstPtr). After the insertion is complete, the root is returned to the calling algorithm.

B-Tree Insert Node

As we mentioned earlier, the insert node algorithm is the heart of the B-tree insert. Because it is complex, you will need to walk through an example to understand it. Let's trace the building of a B-tree of order 5. We have already shown an overview of the first part of the process. Let's pick it up where we are ready to insert the data, 57, into the tree. We begin by calling B-tree insert (Algorithm 10-1), passing it the root and the new data to be inserted (57) (see Figure 10-7). We trace Figure 10-7 through insertNode, as shown in Algorithm 10-2.

```
algorithm insertNode (ref root      <pointer>,
                      val dataIn    <data type>,
                      ref upEntry   <entry>)
Recursively searches tree to locate leaf for data. If node
overflows, inserts median key's data into parent.
    Pre     root is pointer to tree or subtree; may be null
    Post    data inserted
            upEntry is overflow entry to be inserted into parent
    Return  tree taller <Boolean>
  1 if (root null)
    1   upEntry.data      = dataIn
    2   upEntry.rightPtr  = null
    3   taller = true
    4   return taller
  2 end if
  3 entryNdx = searchNode (root, data.key)
  4 newEntryLow = dataIn.key < root->entries[entryNdx].data.key
  5 if (entryNdx equal 0 AND newEntryLow)
    1   subTree = root->firstPtr
  6 else
    1   subTree = root->entries[entryNdx].rightPtr
  7 end if
  8 taller = insertNode (subTree, data, upEntry)
```

Algorithm 10-2   B-tree insert node

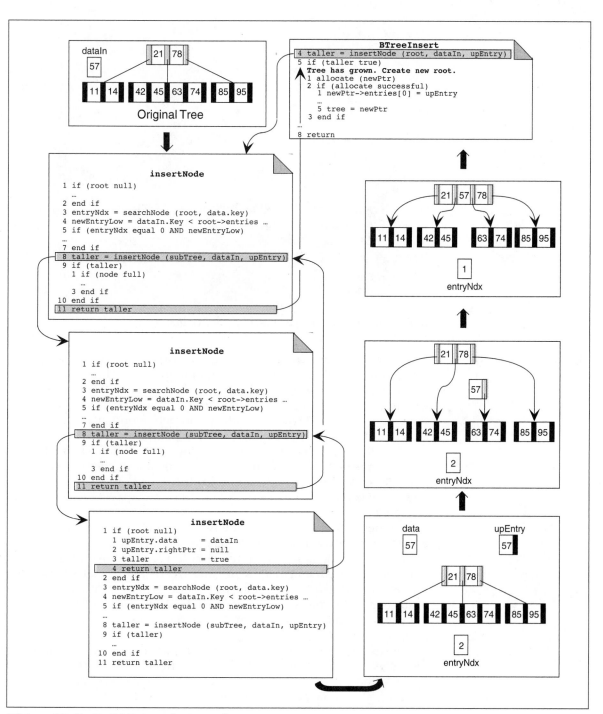

Figure 10-7 Build B-tree, first overflow

```
 9  if (taller)
    1    if (node full)
         1    splitNode (root, entryNdx, newEntryLow, upEntry)
         2    taller = true
    2    else
         1    if (newEntryLow)
              1    insertEntry (root, entryNdx, upEntry)
         2    else
              1    insertEntry (root, entryNdx + 1, upEntry)
         3    end if
         4    root->numEntries = root->numEntries + 1
         5    taller = false
    3    end if
10  end if
11  return taller
end insertNode
```

Algorithm 10-2 B-tree insert node *(continued)*

Algorithm 10-2 Analysis

B-tree insert node (`insertNode`) is a recursive algorithm (see Statement 8). Let's follow the code through Figure 10-7. The base case is a null subtree, indicating that the leaf node was located in the previous call. In the first call, the root is not null, so `insertNode` calls `searchNode` to determine the correct subtree branch, found at 21, and recursively calls itself using 21's right subtree pointer.

The third call reaches the base case for this insert. Because the root is null, `insertNode` moves the new data and a null pointer to the new entry (Statements 1.1 and 1.2) and returns true, indicating that the new entry is ready to be inserted. Note that the new entry is passed by reference.

We then return to `insertNode` in Statement 8 and are ready to insert the new entry into the leaf node as we back out of the recursion. Because the node is full, we must split it and then insert the median entry into the current node's parent. We therefore call `splitNode` (Statement 9.1.1). The logic for `splitNode` is shown in Algorithm 10-4, on page 450, and will be discussed in detail shortly. For now it is sufficient to understand that `splitNode` creates a new right subtree node and moves data to it.

Because 57 is the median valued entry, we insert it upward into the parent node containing 21 and 78. This step completes the insertion, because there is room for 57 in the parent node. We must still complete the recursion, however, by backing all of the way out.

Search Node

Search node first checks to see if the target is less than the first entry's key. If it is, it returns entry 0. If the target is not less than the first node, it locates the target's node by starting at the end and working toward the beginning of the entries. This design is more efficient than starting at the beginning (see "Algorithm 10-3 Analysis" below). The detail code is found in Algorithm 10-3.

```
algorithm searchNode (val nodePtr  <pointer>,
                      val target    <key>)
Search B-tree node for data entry containing key <= target.
    Pre    nodePtr is pointer to non-null node
           target is key to be located
    Return index to entry with key <= target
           -or- zero if key < first entry in node
    (Note: for B-trees with large order, use binary search.)
 1 if (target < nodePtr->entry[0].data.key)
    1   walker = 0
 2 else
    1   walker = nodePtr->numEntries - 1
    2   loop (target < nodePtr->entries[walker].data.key)
        1   walker = walker - 1
    3   end loop
 3 end if
 4 return walker
end searchNode
```

Algorithm 10-3   B-tree search node

Algorithm 10-3 Analysis

This algorithm is simple, but you need to pay close attention to the search technique used. Note that it starts at the end of the entry array and works toward the beginning. We use this search technique because each entry points to a subtree with data whose keys are greater than or equal to the current entry's key and less than the next entry's key. If we searched from the beginning, we would overshoot our target and have to back up. By searching from the end, when we find an entry less than or equal to the target, we have also found the subtree pointer to the subtree that contains the desired target.

Split Node

Split node takes a full node, an entry that needs to be inserted into the node, and the index location for the new entry and splits the data between the existing node, a median entry, and a new node. The code is shown in Algorithm 10-4.

```
algorithm splitNode (val node        <pointer>,
                     val entryNdx     <index>,
                     val newEntryLow  <Boolean>
                     ref upEntry      <entry>)
Node has overflowed. Split node.
   Pre    node is pointer to node that overflowed
          entryNdx contains index location of parent
          newEntryLow true if new data < entryNdx data
          upEntry contains entry being inserted in split node
   Post   upEntry contains entry to be inserted into parent
 1 minEntries = minimum number of entries
 2 allocate (rightPtr)
   Build right subtree node
 3 if (entryNdx < minEntries)
   1   fromNdx = minEntries
 4 else
   1   fromNdx = minEntries + 1
 5 end if
 6 toNdx = 0
 7 rightPtr->numEntries = node->numEntries - fromNdx
 8 loop (fromNdx < node->numEntries)
   1   rightPtr->entries[toNdx] = node->entries[fromNdx]
   2   toNdx                    = toNdx   + 1
   3   fromNdx                  = fromNdx + 1
 9 end loop
10 node->numEntries = node->numEntries - rightPtr->numEntries

11 if (entryNdx < minEntries)
   Insert in original (lower) node
   1   if (newEntryLow)
       1   insertEntry (node, entryNdx, upEntry)
   2   else
       1   insertEntry (node, entryNdx + 1, upEntry)
   3   end if
12 else
```

Algorithm 10-4   B-tree split node

```
    Insert in new (right) node
    1   insertEntry(rightPtr, entryNdx - minEntries + 1, upEntry)
    2   rightPtr->numEntries = rightPtr->numEntries + 1
    3   node->numEntries     = node->numEntries     - 1
    Build entry for parent
13  end if
14  upEntry.data         = node->entries[medianNdx].data
15  upEntry.rightPtr     = rightPtr
16  rightPtr->firstPtr   = node->entries[minEntries].rightPtr
17  return
end splitNode
```

Algorithm 10-4   B-tree split node *(continued)*

Algorithm 10-4 Analysis

We need to analyze three different insert positions: The new key is less than the median key, the new key is the median key, and the new key is greater than the median key. The first two reduce to the same case. Figure 10-8(a) shows the step-by-step logic for splitting a node when the new entry is less than or equal to the median, and Figure 10-8(b) shows the steps when the new entry is greater than the median.

In both cases, we begin by allocating a new node and copying data from the end of the original node to the beginning of the new node. Then we insert the new entry, found in upEntry, into either the original node or the new node. Finally, we copy the median entry to upEntry. Note that when we enter Algorithm 10-4, upEntry contains the data being inserted into the overflow node; after the node has been split, upEntry contains the data to be inserted into the parent when we return.

When the new key is less than or equal to the median key, the new data belong in the left or original node. On the other hand, if the new key is greater than the median key, the new data belong in the new node. At Statement 11, therefore, we test the location for the new entry (entryNdx) and call the insert entry algorithm passing it either the original node or the new node.

If you study Figure 10-8 carefully, you will note that regardless of which situation occurred, the median value is always in the same place, identified by the minimum number of entries. Also, the right pointer in the median entry is always the new node's pointer. It is thus easy to build the median entry.

The test cases in Figure 10-8 are found in a larger context in Figure 10-9, on page 453. Figure 10-8(a) is the last insertion in Figure 10-9(c), and Figure 10-8(b) is the same as Figure 10-9(b).

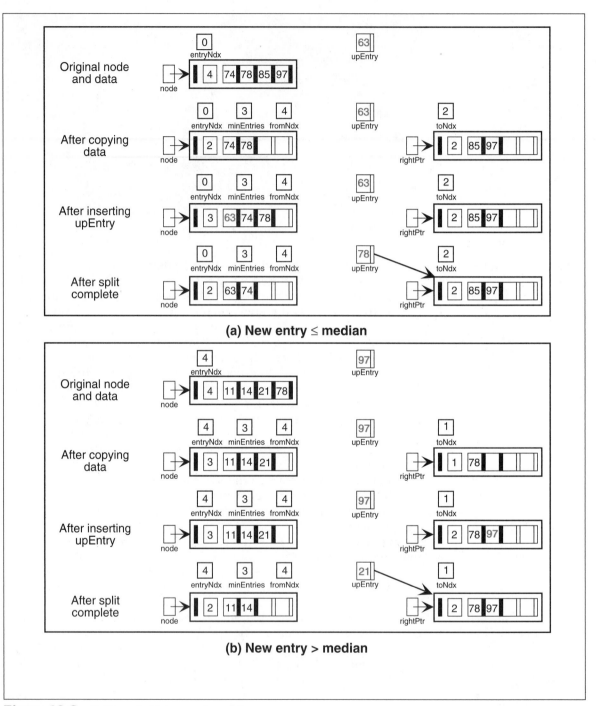

Figure 10-8   Split node B-tree order of 5

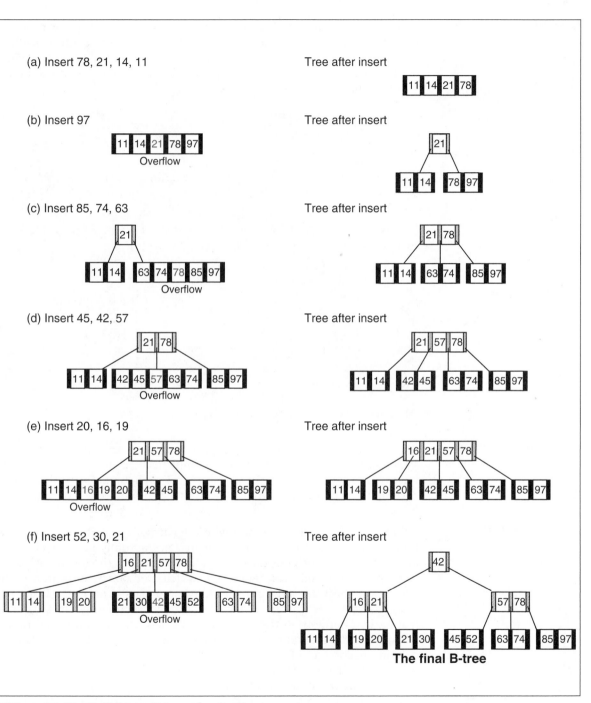

Figure 10-9   Building a B-tree of order 5

Insert Entry

Insert entry receives the node, a new entry, and the new entry's correct location in the node. It then shifts entries to the right until it reaches the correct location, at which point it inserts the new entry. It concludes by increasing the count for the number of entries in the node. The code is shown in Algorithm 10-5.

```
algorithm insertEntry (val node       <pointer>,
                       val entryNdx  <index>,
                       val newEntry  <entry>)
Inserts one entry into a node by shifting nodes to make room.
    Pre     node is pointer to node to contain data
            newEntry contains data to be inserted
            entryNdx is index to location for new data
    Post    data have been inserted in sequence
  1 shifter = node->numEntries
  2 loop (shifter > entryNdx)
    1   node->entries[shifter] = node->entries[shifter - 1]
    2   shifter = shifter - 1
  3 end loop
  4 node->entries[shifter] = newEntry
  5 return
end insertEntry
```

Algorithm 10-5   B-tree insert entry

Insertion Summary

We have now looked at all of the algorithms necessary to insert data into a B-tree. As a summary, we build a complete B-tree in Figure 10-9. You have already seen some of the trees in previous figures. Study this figure carefully to ensure you can build a similar tree with different data.

B-Tree Deletion

There are three considerations when deleting from a B-tree. First, we must ensure that the data to be deleted are actually in the tree. Second, if the node does not have enough entries after the delete, we need to correct the structural deficiency. A deletion that results in a node with fewer than the minimum number of entries is an **underflow.** Finally, as we saw with the binary search tree, we can only delete from a leaf node. Therefore, if the data to be deleted are in an internal node, we must find a data entry to take their place. The design for the B-tree deletion is shown in Figure 10-10. We suggest that you study this design before proceeding with its algorithms.

Note that there are two levels of recursion. The first traverses the tree looking for the node to be deleted and, if it is found at a leaf, simply deletes it. The second recursion is used when the data to be deleted are

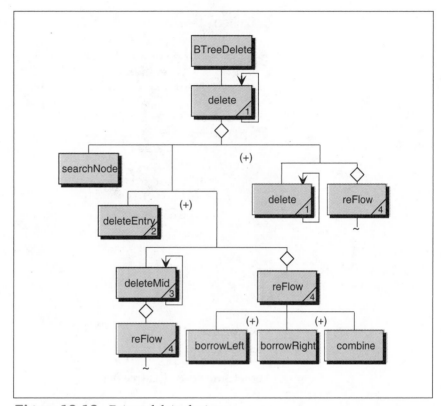

Figure 10-10   B-tree delete design

not at a leaf. The algorithm may be written with only one recursion, but it is more complex to follow.

Now study the node delete logic. It searches for the data to be deleted. If they are not found, then it prints an error message and terminates the recursion. This is the first base case. The second base case is the data have been found and deleted. In either case, the delete must determine whether it has caused an underflow and set a return Boolean—true if underflow occurred or false if the node is okay.

The underflow processing takes place as node delete backs out of the recursion. After each return, it checks the node to make sure it has not underflowed. If an underflow occurred, then it corrects the underflow and continues. With this understanding of the big picture, we are now ready to look at the algorithms.

B-Tree Delete

Like the insert, the B-tree delete requires two algorithms, a user interface and a recursive delete function. The high-level user interface calls the recursive delete and then checks for root underflow. It is shown in Algorithm 10-6.

```
algorithm BTreeDelete (ref tree     <pointer>,
                        val dltKey <key>)
Delete entry with key target from B-tree.
    Pre     tree is a pointer to a B-tree
            dltKey is the key of the entry to be deleted
    Post    data deleted or error message printed
    Return  pointer to B-tree
 1 if (tree empty)
   1   return false
 2 end if
 3 delete (tree, dltKey, success)
 4 if (success)
   1   if (tree->numEntries is zero)
       Tree is shorter--delete root
       1   dltPtr = tree
       2   tree   = tree->firstPtr
       3   recycle (dltPtr)
   2   end if
 5 end if
 6 return success
end BTreeDelete
```

Algorithm 10-6   B-tree delete

Algorithm 10-6 Analysis

B-tree delete has two responsibilities. First, it starts the delete process by calling node delete. Then, when the delete process is complete, it determines whether the root has underflowed. If it has, then the new root is found in the first pointer. After setting the tree to the new root, it recycles the old root node and terminates.

Node Delete

The heart of the delete process is seen in the recursive delete algorithm. If delete reaches a null subtree, it has not found the data to be deleted. It therefore prints an error message and returns underflow false.

If the root is not null, then delete searches the node to see if the data to be deleted are in it. This is the same algorithm we used for the insert search (see Algorithm 10-3, "B-tree search node," on page 449). The search returns either 0 (false), indicating that the delete key is less than the first entry in the node, or an entry index for a node that is less than or equal to the delete key. When the delete key is not in the current node, delete calls itself recursively with a new subtree. If the delete key has been found, it is deleted by calling either deleteEntry or deleteMid. After deleting the node, delete checks for underflow and if necessary repairs the underflow by calling reFlow. The pseudocode is shown in Algorithm 10-7.

```
algorithm delete (ref root        <pointer>,
                  val deleteKey   <key>)
                  ref success     <Boolean>
Recursively locates node containing deleteKey; deletes data.
    Pre    root is a pointer to a non-null B-tree
           deleteKey is key to entry to be deleted
    Post   data deleted--success true; or success false
    Return underflow--true or false
  1 if (root null)
        Leaf node found--deleteKey key does not exist
    1   return false
  2 end if
  3 entryNdx = searchNode (root, deleteKey)
  4 if (deleteKey equal root->entries[entryNdx].data.key)
    Found entry to be deleted
    1   success = true
    2   if (root->entries[entryNdx].rightPtr is null)
        Entry is a leaf node
        1   underflow = deleteEntry (root, entryNdx)
    3   else
        Entry is in internal node
        1   if (entryNdx > 0)
            1   leftPtr = root->entries[entryNdx - 1].rightPtr
        2   else
            1   leftPtr = root->firstPtr
        3   end if
        4   underflow = deleteMid (root, entryNdx, leftPtr)
        5   if (underflow)
            1   underflow = reFlow (root, entryNdx)
        6   end if
    4   end if
  5 else
    1   if (deleteKey < root->entries[0].data.key)
        deleteKey less than first entry
        1   subtree = root->firstPtr
    2   else
        deleteKey is in right subtree
        1   subtree = root->entries[entryNdx].rightPtr
    3   end if
```

Algorithm 10-7   B-tree node delete

```
    4   underflow = delete (subtree, deleteKey, success)
    5   if (underflow)
        1   underflow = reFlow (root, entryNdx)
    6   end if
  6 end if
  7 return underflow
end delete
```

Algorithm 10-7   B-tree node delete *(continued)*

Algorithm 10-7 Analysis

This delete algorithm calls four different algorithms, including itself. The recursive call is found in Statement 5.4. Note that after the recursive calls, we must test for underflow. This logic is important. Although the underflow is detected when a node underflows, it is handled *after the logic flow returns to the parent*. It is handled at this point because to resolve an underflow, we need the parent, the left subtree, and the right subtree.

Delete Entry

Delete entry removes the entry from a node and compresses it; that is, it moves the entries on the right of the deleted entry to the left. After adjusting the number of entries in the node, it tests for underflow and returns a Boolean—true if underflow occurred and false if the node is okay. The code is shown in Algorithm 10-8.

```
algorithm deleteEntry (val node      <pointer>,
                       val entryNdx  <index>)
Deletes entry at entryNdx from leaf node.
    Pre    node is pointer to node containing data to be deleted
           entryNdx is index of entry in node
    Post   entry deleted
    Return underflow <Boolean>
  1 shifter = entryNdx + 1
  2 loop (shifter <= node->numEntries)
    1   node->entries[shifter - 1] = node->entries[shifter]
    2   shifter = shifter + 1
  3 end loop
  4 node->numEntries = node->numEntries - 1
  5 if (node->numEntries < minimum entries)
    1   return true
  6 else
```

Algorithm 10-8   B-tree delete entry

```
    1   return false
    7 end if
end deleteEntry
```

Algorithm 10-8   B-tree delete entry *(continued)*

Delete Mid

As we saw earlier, all deletions must take place at a leaf node. When the data to be deleted are not in a leaf node, then we must find substitute data. There are two choices for substitute data: either the immediate predecessor or the immediate successor. Either would do, but it is more efficient to use the immediate predecessor because it is always the last entry in a node and no shifting is required when it is deleted. We will therefore use the immediate predecessor.

The immediate predecessor is the largest node on the left subtree of the entry to be deleted. The initial calling algorithm, delete, determines the left subtree and passes it as a parameter along with the node containing the data to be deleted and the index to its entry. Delete mid then recursively follows the left subtree's right pointer in the last entry until it comes to a leaf node.

Finding a leaf node is the recursion base case for delete mid. At this point, it replaces the deleted data with the data in the leaf's last entry and uses the delete entry to physically delete the predecessor from the leaf node. The underflow Boolean returned by delete entry is then returned to the calling algorithm. The pseudocode for delete mid is shown in Algorithm 10-9.

```
algorithm deleteMid    (val node     <pointer>,
                        val entryNdx <index>,
                        val subtree  <pointer>)
Deletes entry from internal node in tree.
    Pre   node is pointer to node containing delete entry
          entryNdx is index to entry to be deleted in node
          subtree is pointer to root's subtree
    Post  delete data exchanged with immediate predecessor and
          predecessor deleted from leaf node
    Return underflow <Boolean> (number of entries below minimum)
Find entry to replace node being deleted
  1 if (subtree->firstPtr null)
    Leaf located. Exchange data and delete leaf entry.
    1   deleteNdx = node->numEntries - 1
    2   root->entries[entryNdx].data
            = subtree->entries[deleteNdx].data
```

Algorithm 10-9   B-tree delete mid

```
   3   subtree->numEntries = subtree->numEntries - 1
   4   underflow = subtree->entries < minimum entries
 2 else
   Not located. Traverse right to locate predecessor.
   1   right = subtree->numEntries - 1
   2   underflow = deleteMid
          (node, entryNdx, subtree->entries[right].rightPtr)
   3   if (underflow)
     1   underflow = reFlow (root, entryNdx)
   4   end if
 3 end if
 4 return underflow
end deleteMid
```

Algorithm 10-9   B-tree delete mid *(continued)*

Algorithm 10-9 Analysis

This algorithm is rather simple. As we have seen in other algorithms, the base case is handled first in Statement 1. The recursive search for a leaf node is found in Statement 2. Note that both the base case and the general case determine whether underflow has occurred and pass the underflow status to the return statement at the end of the code.

Figure 10-11 shows the interaction of the B-tree delete, delete, and delete mid algorithms. You may want to study it before going on.

Reflow

When underflow has occurred, we need to bring the underflowed node up to a minimum state by adding at least one entry to it. This is perhaps the most difficult logic in the B-tree delete. To understand it we need to review two concepts, **balance** and **combine.** Balance shifts data among nodes to reestablish the integrity of the tree. Because it does not change the structure of the tree, it is less disruptive and therefore preferred. Combine joins the data from an underflowed entry, a minimal sibling, and a parent in one node. Combine thus results in one node with the maximum number of entries and an empty node that must be recycled.

When we enter reFlow, the root contains the parent to the node that underflowed, identified by the entry index. We begin by examining the left and right subtrees of the root to determine whether one has more than the minimum number of entries. If either one does, we can order the tree by balancing. If neither the left nor the right subtree has more than the minimum entries, we must combine them with the parent. The pseudocode is shown in Algorithm 10-10.

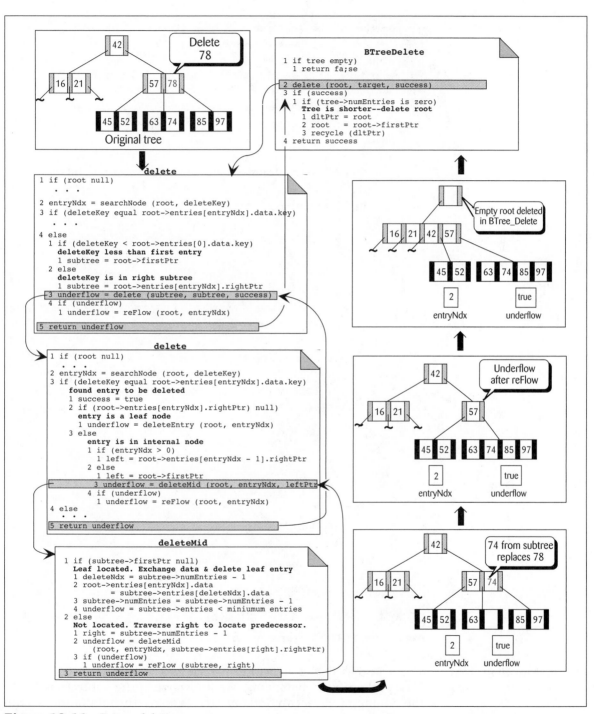

Figure 10-11 B-tree deletions

```
algorithm reflow (val root      <pointer>,
                  val entryNdx  <index>)
```

An underflow has occurred in one of the subtrees to the root
identified by the entry index parameter. Correct underflow by
either balancing or combining subtrees.

   Pre   underflow has occurred in a subtree in root
                entryNdx identifies parent of subtree with underflow

   Post   underflow corrected

   Return underflow <Boolean> root node has underflowed

Try to borrow first. Locate subtree with available entry.

```
1 if (entryNdx equal 0)
   1   leftTree  = root->firstPtr
2 else
   1   leftTree  = root->entries[entryNdx - 1].rightPtr
3 end if
4 rightTree = root->entries[entryNdx].rightPtr
5 if (rightTree->numEntries > minimum entries)
   1   borrowRight (root, entryNdx, leftTree, rightTree)
   2   underflow = false
6 else
```

   Can't balance from right. Try left.

```
   1   if (leftTree->numEntries > minimum entries)
      1   borrowLeft (root, entryNdx, leftTree, rightTree)
      2   underflow = false
   2   else
```

      Can't borrow. Must combine entries.

```
      1   combine (root, entryNdx, leftTree, rightTree)
      2   if (root->numEntries < minimum entries)
         1   underflow = true
      3   else
         1   underflow = false
      4   end if
   3   end if
7 end if
8 return underflow
end reflow
```

Algorithm 10-10   B-tree underflow reflow

Algorithm 10-10 Analysis   The first part of the algorithm determines whether it is possible to correct the tree by balancing. We know one of the subtrees is below the minimum. If we can find one that is above the minimum, we can balance. We first check the right subtree, and if it is above the minimum we call the borrow right algorithm. If it is not, then we check the left subtree. Again, if it is above the minimum, we call the borrow left algorithm to restore order. If neither of the subtrees has an extra entry, then we must combine them by calling a separate combine algorithm.

Underflow can occur only when the nodes are combined. Because borrowing takes place from a node with more than the minimum number of entries, it cannot underflow. Therefore, when we borrow, either from the left or from the right, underflow is set to false. On the other hand, when we combine nodes, we delete the parent entry from the root. We must therefore check to make sure it has not underflowed. If it has, we return underflow true.

Balance

We balance a tree by rotating an entry from one sibling to another through the parent. In reFlow, we determine the direction of the rotation. The simplest implementation, therefore, is to write separate algorithms, one for rotating from the left and one for rotating from the right. The rotations are graphically shown in Figure 10-12.

The code for borrow left is shown in Algorithm 10-11, and the code for borrow right is shown in Algorithm 10-12.

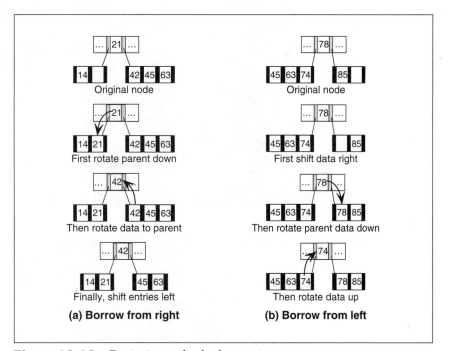

Figure 10-12   Restoring order by borrowing

```
algorithm borrowLeft (val root      <pointer>,
                      val entryNdx  <index>,
                      val left      <pointer>,
                      val right     <pointer>)
```
It has been determined that the right subtree of root has underflowed. Borrow a node from the left subtree and rotate through the parent.

Pre   root is parent of node that underflowed
           entryNdx is parent entry
           left subtree that contains at least one extra node
           right subtree that underflowed

Post   subtrees are balanced

Shift entries right to make room for new data
```
1 shifter = right->numEntries
2 loop (shifter > 0)
  1   right->entries[shifter] = right->entries[shifter - 1]
  2   shifter = shifter - 1
3 end loop
```
Move parent data down and reset right pointer
```
4 right->entries[0].data      = root->entries[entryNdx].data
5 right->entries[0].rightPtr  = right->firstPtr
```
Moved entry's rightPtr becomes right tree first pointer
```
6 fromNdx            = left->numEntries - 1
7 right->firstPtr    = left->entries[fromNdx].rightPtr
8 right->numEntries  = right->numEntries + 1
```
Move data from left to parent
```
 9 root->entries[entryNdx].data = left->entries[fromNdx].data
10 left->numEntries             = left->numEntries - 1
11 return
end borrowLeft
```
Algorithm 10-11   B-tree borrow left

```
algorithm borrowRight (val root      <pointer>,
                       val entryNdx  <index>,
                       val left      <pointer>,
                       val right     <pointer>)
```
It has been determined that the left subtree of root has underflowed. Borrow a node from the right subtree and rotate through the parent.

Algorithm 10-12   B-tree borrow right

```
Pre     root is parent of node that underflowed
        entryNdx is parent entry
        left subtree that underflowed
        right subtree that contains at least one extra node
Post    subtrees are balanced
Move parent and subtree pointer to left tree
 1  toNdx = left->numEntries
 2  left->entries[toNdx].data     = root->entries[entryNdx].data
 3  left->entries[toNdx].rightPtr = right->firstPtr
 4  left->numEntries = left->numEntries + 1
Move right data to parent
 5  root->entries[entryNdx].data = right->entries[0].data
Set right tree first pointer and shift data
 6  right->firstPtr = right->entries[0].rightPtr
 7  shifter = 0
 8  loop (shifter < right->numEntries - 1)
    1    right->entries[shifter] = right->entries[shifter + 1]
    2    shifter = shifter + 1
 9  end loop
10  right->numEntries = right->numEntries - 1
11  return
end borrowRight
```

Algorithm 10-12   B-tree borrow right *(continued)*

Algorithm 10-11 and Algorithm 10-12 Analysis

The code for these two algorithms is rather straightforward, but care must be taken with the pointers. When we balance from the right, the parent node entry's data, but not its pointer, moves down to the left. The right pointer of the new left subtree entry must come from the first pointer in the right subtree. Then, the right subtree's first pointer becomes the right pointer of the first entry, whose data has been copied to the parent. Similarly, when we balance from the left, the data in the last entry of the left subtree is copied to the root entry's data, but its pointer becomes the first pointer of the right subtree. We suggest that you create several balancing situations and follow the algorithms carefully until you are comfortable with the rotation and pointer manipulation.

Combine

When we can't balance, we must combine nodes. Figure 10-13 shows the logic for underflow combine. As you study it, note that the two subtrees and the parent entry are all combined into the left node. Then, the parent entry is deleted from its node, which may result in an underflow. What is not apparent from the figure is that the right subtree node is then recycled. The code for combine is found in Algorithm 10-13.

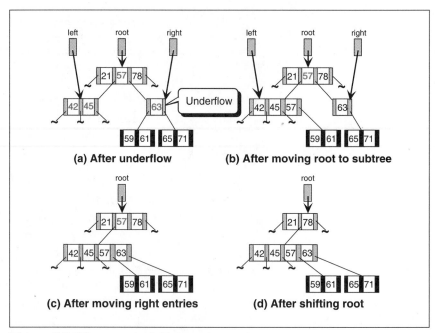

(a) After underflow

(b) After moving root to subtree

(c) After moving right entries

(d) After shifting root

Figure 10-13   B-tree delete combine

```
algorithm combine (val root      <pointer>,
                   val entryNdx  <index>,
                   val left      <pointer>,
                   val right     <pointer>)
Underflow has occurred and we are unable to borrow an entry.
The two subtrees must be combined with the parent.
    Pre    root contains the parent of the underflowed entry
           entryNdx identifies the parent entry
           left and right are pointers to left and right subtrees
    Post   parent and subtrees combined
           right tree node has been recycled
Move parent and set its rightPtr from right tree
  1 toNdx = left->numEntries
  2 left->entries[toNdx].data     = root[entryNdx].data
  3 left->entries[toNdx].rightPtr = right->firstPtr
  4 left->numEntries = left->numEntries + 1
  5 root->numEntries = root->numEntries - 1
Move data from right tree to left tree
  6 frNdx = 0
```

Algorithm 10-13   B-tree combine

```
 7  toNdx = toNdx + 1
 8  loop (frNdx < right->numEntries)
    1   left->entries[toNdx] = right->entries[frNd]
    2   toNdx = toNdx + 1
    3   frNdx = frNdx + 1
 9  end loop
10  left->numEntries = left->numEntries + right->numEntries
11  recycle (right)
Now shift data in root to the left
12  shifter = entryNdx
13  loop (shifter < root->numEntries)
    1   root->entries[shifter] = root->entries[shifter + 1]
    2   shifter = shifter + 1
14  end loop
15  return
end combine
```

Algorithm 10-13   B-tree combine *(continued)*

Algorithm 10-13 Analysis

Once again the most difficult part of this algorithm is the pointer manipulation. Regardless of which subtree has underflowed, we combine all nodes into the left subtree so we can recycle the right subtree.

Study the pointer manipulation in Statement 3. We have just moved the parent data to the first empty entry in the left subtree. Its right pointer then becomes the first pointer of the right subtree. Remember that the first pointer identifies the subtree whose entries are greater than the parent and less than the first entry. This pointer must therefore become the right pointer when the parent is moved to the left subtree. Beyond this one pointer manipulation, the rest of the logic simply copies data from one place to another and adjusts counts.

Figure 10-14 is a summary of the B-tree deletions. It contains an example of each of the major algorithms required to delete data from a B-tree. Study it carefully until you understand the concepts.

Traverse B-Tree

Now that we have a B-tree, let's look at the logic to traverse it. Because the B-tree is built on the same structure as the binary search tree, we can use the same basic traversal design, the inorder traversal. The major difference, however, is that with the exception of leaf nodes, we don't process all of the data in a node at the same time. Therefore, we must remember which entry was processed whenever we return to a node and continue from that point. With recursion, this logic is relatively simple. Figure 10-15 shows the processing order of the entries as we "walk around" the tree. In this figure, each entry is processed as we walk below it. Note that, as expected, the data are processed in sequential order. The traversal logic is shown in Algorithm 10-14.

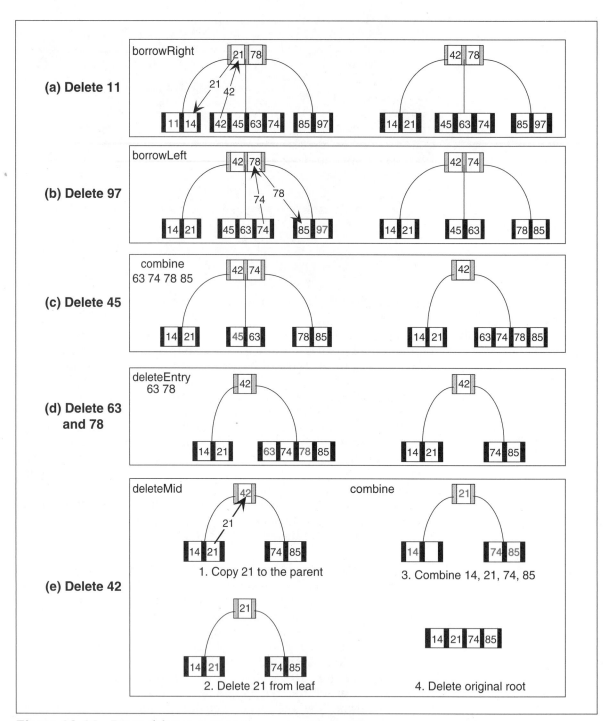

Figure 10-14 B-tree deletion summary

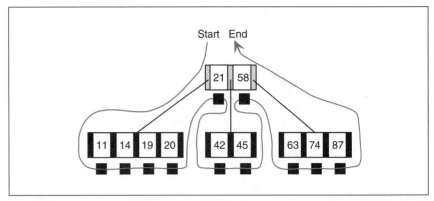

Figure 10-15 Basic B-tree traversal

```
algorithm BTreeTraversal (val root <pointer>)
Process tree using inorder traversal.
    Pre    root is pointer to B-tree; it may not be null
    Post   every entry has been processed in order
  1 scanCount = 0
  2 ptr = root->firstPtr
  3 loop (scanCount <= root->numEntries)
    Test for subtree
    1   if (ptr not null)
        1    BTreeTraversal (ptr)
    2   end if
    Subtree processed--get next entry
    3   if (scanCount < root->numEntries)
        1    process (root->entries[scanCount].data)
        2    ptr = root->entries[scanCount].rightPtr
        3    scanCount = scanCount + 1
    4   end if
  4 end loop
  5 return
end BTreeTraversal
```

Algorithm 10-14   B-tree traversal

Algorithm 10-14 Analysis   In the inorder traversal, data are processed after the left subtree and before the right subtree. The left subtrees are processed in the recursive call found in Statement 3.1.1. When we return from processing a subtree, therefore, we are ready to process the parent entry. We do so by checking the scan count and, if it is less than the number of entries in the node, calling an algorithm to process the data (Statement 3.3.1). We then process the right subtree by setting the traversal pointer (`ptr`) to the right subtree and continuing the loop in Statement 3.

It is tempting to think that the loop can terminate when the scan count becomes equal to the number of entries in the node. Although this is true when we are processing a leaf node, it is not true for internal nodes. The loop cannot terminate because when we have processed the data in the last entry of a node, we still need to process its right subtree.

B-Tree Search

We have seen an algorithm to search a node, but we have not seen one to traverse the entire tree looking for a target key. When we searched a binary search tree, we simply returned the node that contained the target data. Because there are multiple entries in a B-tree node, however, returning the node is not sufficient; we must also return the entry that contains the target. Algorithm 10-15 therefore uses reference parameters for the located node and its entry index.

```
algorithm BTreeSearch (val root      <pointer>,
                       val srchKey    <key>,
                       ref node       <pointer>,
                       ref foundLoc   <index>)
Recursively search a B-tree for the srchKey key.
    Pre      root is a pointer to a tree or subtree
             srchKey is the data to be located
    Post     if found--
                 node is pointer to located node
                 foundLoc is entry within node

             if not found--
                 returns false
    Return   found <Boolean>
  1 if (empty tree)
    1    return false
  2 end if
  3 if (srchKey < first entry)
    1    return BTreeSearch (root->firstPtr,
                             srchKey, node, foundLoc)
  4 end if
  5 foundLoc = root->numEntries - 1
  6 loop (srchKey < root->entries[foundLoc].data.key)
```

Algorithm 10-15   B-tree search

```
   1    foundLoc = foundLoc - 1
 7 end loop
 8 if (srchKey equal root->entries[foundLoc].data.key)
   1    node  = root
   2    return true
 9 end if
10 return BTreeSearch (root->entries[foundLoc].rightPtr,
                             srchKey, node, foundLoc)

end BTreeSearch
```

Algorithm 10-15 B-tree search *(continued)*

Algorithm 10-15 Analysis The logic for Algorithm 10-15 is similar to the design we saw in Algorithm 10-3, "B-Tree Search Node," on page 449. Both algorithms search from the end of the node toward the beginning. The major difference is that we must search the subtrees as well as the current node. Thus we need two different recursive calls in the algorithm, the first when the target is less than the first entry (Statement 3.1) and the second when it is greater than the current entry (Statement 10).

There are two base cases: we reach a null subtree, which indicates that the target doesn't exist, or we find the target entry. The first base case is handled in Statement 1. In this case, we simply return false.

The equal base case is shown in Statement 8. Because we have set the entry number in the loop, we need only set the node address to the current root pointer and return true.

One final point: Study Statement 6 carefully. What prevents the loop from running off the beginning of the array? The answer to this question is found in Statement 3.1. The target's key must be equal to or greater than the first entry's; if it were less, we would have followed the first pointer to the left subtree. Because we know that the target's key is equal to or greater than the first entry's, it becomes a sentinel that will stop the loop. Therefore, we don't need to test for the beginning of the loop, which makes the loop very efficient—it need test only one condition.

10-3   SIMPLIFIED B-TREES

Computer scientists have assigned unique names to two specialized B-trees: 2-3 trees and 2-3-4 trees. We discuss them briefly. Both are well suited to internal search trees.

2-3 Tree The **2-3 tree** is a B-tree of order 3. It gets its name because each nonroot node has either two or three subtrees (the root may have zero, two, or three subtrees). Figure 10-16 contains two 2-3 trees. The first is

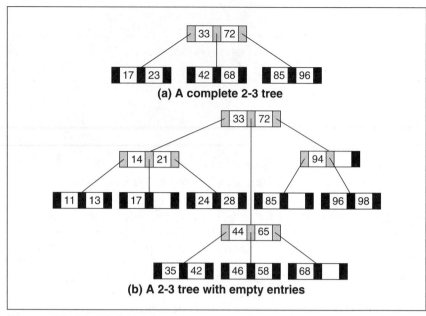

Figure 10-16   2-3 trees

complete; that is, it has the maximum number of entries for its height. The second has more than twice as many entries, but some of the entries are empty. Note also that subtree 94 has only two descendents.

2-3-4 Tree

Figure 10-17 contains a B-tree of order 4. This type of tree is sometimes called a 2-3-4 tree because each node can have two, three, or four children.

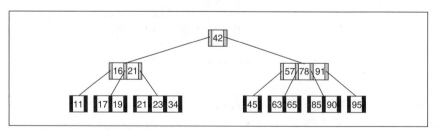

Figure 10-17   2-3-4 tree

10-4   B-TREE VARIATIONS

There are two popular variations on the B-tree. Although their manipulation is beyond the scope of this text, you should be aware of the variations.

B*Tree

When we use a B-tree to store a large number of entries, the space requirements can become excessive because up to 50% of the entries can be empty. The first variation, the **B*tree,** addresses the space usage for large trees. Rather than each node containing a minimum of one-half the maximum entries, the minimum is set at two-thirds.[2]

In a B*tree, when a node overflows, instead of being split immediately, the data are redistributed among the node's siblings, delaying the creation of a new node. Splitting occurs only when all of the siblings are full. Furthermore, when the nodes are split, data from two full siblings are divided among the two full nodes and a new node, with the result that all three nodes are two-thirds full. Figure 10-18 shows how redistribution is handled when a node in a B*tree of order 5 overflows.

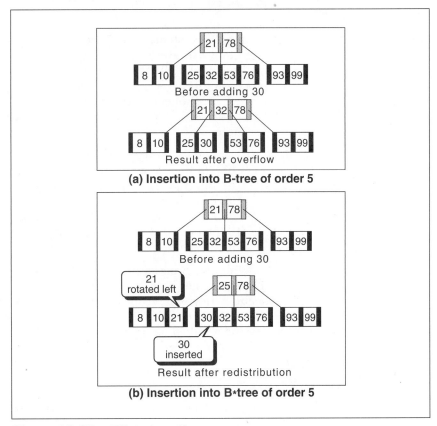

Figure 10-18   B*tree insertion

---

2. Note that when the root in a root-only tree is split, its two subtrees are only half full.

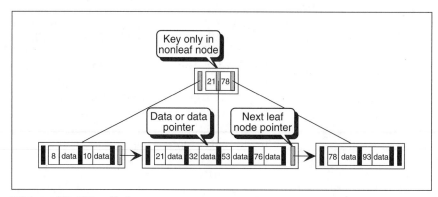

. **Figure 10-19**   B+tree

B+Tree

In large file systems, data need to be processed both randomly and sequentially. In these situations, the most popular file organization methods use the B-tree to process the data randomly. However, much processing time is taken up moving up and down the tree structure when the data need to be processed sequentially. This inefficiency has led to the second B-tree variation, the **B+tree.**

There are two differences between the B-tree and the B+tree:

1. Each data entry must be represented at the leaf level, even though there may be internal nodes with the same keys. Because the internal nodes are used only for searching, they generally do not contain data.
2. Each leaf node has one additional pointer, which is used to move to the next leaf node in sequence. This structure is shown in Figure 10-19.

When we process the data randomly, we modify the tree search to find the target data only at a leaf. The search time is thus increased slightly. However, to process the data sequentially, we simply locate the leftmost entry and then process the data as though we were processing a linked list in which each node is an array.

10-5   LEXICAL SEARCH TREE

Instead of searching a tree using the entire value of a key, we can consider the key to be a sequence of characters, such as a word or a nonnumeric identifier (e.g., a telephone number). When placed in a tree, each node has a place for each of the possible values that the characters in the lexical tree can assume. For example, if a key may contain the complete alphabet, each node has 26 entries, one

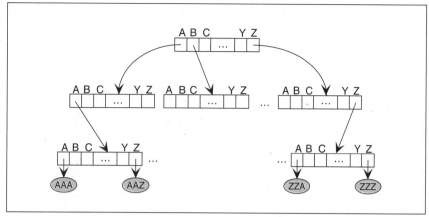

Figure 10-20   The lexical tree structure

for each of the letters of the alphabet. This is known as a **lexical 26-ary tree**.

Each entry in the lexical tree contains a pointer to the next level. In addition, each node of a 26-ary tree contains 26 pointers, the first representing the letter A, the second the letter B, and so forth until the last pointer, which represents Z. Because each letter in the first level must point to a complete set of values, the second level contains 26×26 entries, one node of 26 entries for each of the 26 letters in the first level. Similarly, the third level has $26 \times 26 \times 26$ entries. Finally, we store the actual key at a leaf.

If a key has three letters, there are at least three levels in the tree. If a key has ten letters, then there are ten levels in the tree. Because a lexical tree can contain many different keys, the largest word determines the height of the tree. Figure 10-20 contains a lexical tree.

Tries

The problem with the lexical *m*-ary tree is that after a few levels it becomes very large. To prevent this, we **prune** the tree; that is, we cut all of the branches that are not needed. We identify a pruned branch with a null pointer. For example, if no key starts with the letter X, then at level 0 the X pointer is null, thus eliminating its subtree completely. Similarly, after the letter Q, the only valid letter is U (we will not worry about the very few exceptions). All of the pointers in the Q branch except U are therefore set to null, again eliminating all but the U subtree from level 1 down. The resulting structure is called a **trie** (short for *reTRIEval* and pronounced *try*).

As an example, let's create a spell checker using a trie. A spell checker is not a dictionary; it contains only words and not their definitions. Each word in our spell checker is one entry in the trie, the correct spelling of a word. To demonstrate the idea, let's build a small spell checker trie that checks only the spelling of a few words containing the letters A, B, C, E, and T.

Here we need a 5-ary trie because we have a total of five characters in these words (A, B, C, E, and T). The trie must have four levels because each word has at most three characters. Our trie is shown in Figure 10-21.

Although Figure 10-21 contains the complete spelling for each word, we have eliminated the third and fourth levels of the trie for the letter A because it can be fully identified by the first level under A. This is another form of pruning. Similarly, we have eliminated the third and fourth levels for *EAT* because it's the only word starting with E.

To search our spell checker for the word *CAB*, we check the first level of the trie at the letter C. Because it is not null, we follow the pointer to the second level, this time checking for the letter A. Again, there is a valid pointer at A, so we follow it to the node representing CA and check the B position. At this point, we check the entry pointer and find *CAB*.

Now let's try to find *CTA* in our spell checker. We begin by checking the C position in the first node and find a valid pointer to the C node. However, when we check the T location in the second level, we find that the pointer is null. We then check the entry pointer, which is null, indicating that there is no valid word *CTA* in our spell checker.

Trie Structure

From the above discussion, we derive the structure for a trie. Each node needs two pointer types, one to the subtrees of the trie and one to the data. Each letter in the alphabet for the trie must be represented in each node. This gives us the node structure shown below.

```
trie

    entryPtr        <data pointer>

    ltrPtrs         <array of trie pointers>

end trie
```

Trie Search

Let's write an algorithm to search our trie in Figure 10-21. We need two parameters, one for the dictionary trie and one for the word to be looked up. We use the trie structure shown above for the dictionary and a simple string for the word. The pseudocode is shown in Algorithm 10-16.

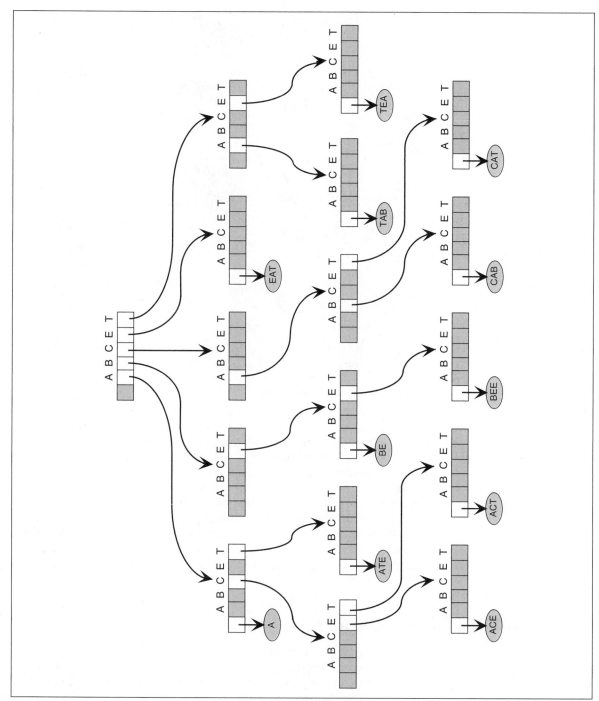

Figure 10-21   A spell checker trie

```
algorithm searchTrie (val dictionary  <trie pointer>,
                      val word         <string>)
Search the dictionary trie for word.
    Pre      dictionary is a valid trie with alphabet ABCET
    Return   true if word in dictionary, false if not
1  root   = dictionary
2  ltrNdx = 0
3  loop (root not null)
    1    if (root->entryPtr->data equal word)
        1    return true
    2    end if
    3    if (ltrNdx > length(word))
        1    return false
    4    end if
    5    chNdx = word[ltrNdx]
    6    root = root->ltrPtrs[chNdx]
    7    ltrNdx = ltrNdx + 1
4  end loop
5  return false
end searchTrie
```

Algorithm 10-16   Trie search

Algorithm 10-16 Analysis   This algorithm's simplicity demonstrates the power of trees. As we search down the tree, we first compare the word associated with the trie node with our target word to see if we have found it. If not, we test to see if the dictionary word length at the current level, represented by the variable index ltrNdx, is greater than the word length. If it is, we know that the word is not in the dictionary.

The implementation of the code in Statements 3.5 and 3.6 varies depending on the language. Most languages have a method of turning a letter into an index. Once the next letter in the word has been converted to an index (chNdx), we can use it to pick up the pointer to the next trie level.

10-6   B-TREE ABSTRACT DATA TYPE

With an understanding of how a B-tree works, it should be no surprise that the B-tree implementation is rather complex. In this section we develop code for the key algorithms. Some are left for you to develop. Figure 10-22 provides the complete list of functions.

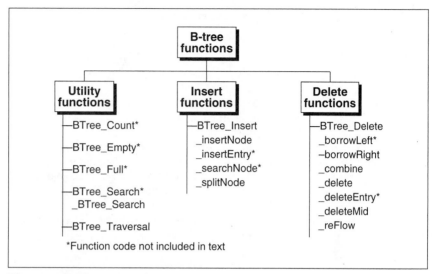

Figure 10-22 B-tree function family

Header File

The header file for the B-tree abstract data type (ADT) class contains the class declaration, along with its data structures, the prototype declarations for its private functions, and the prototype declarations for the user interface functions. It is shown in Program 10-1.

```
1    /* This library contains the code for the B-tree ADT.
2          Written by: G & F
3          Date:       2/98
4    */
5    #include <stdlib.h>
6
7    /* ==================== B-Tree.h ====================
8      This header file contains the functions for the
9      B-tree abstract data type.
10   */
11
12   // ================== CONSTANTS & MACROS ==============
13   const int ORDER       = 3;
14   const int MIN_ENTRIES = (((ORDER + 1) / 2) - 1);
15
16   // ==================== STRUCTURES ==================
17   template<class TYPE>
18   struct NODE;                        // Forward Declaration
19
20   template<class TYPE>
```

Program 10-1 B-tree header file

```
21  struct Entry
22    {
23     TYPE          data;
24     NODE<TYPE>  *rightPtr;
25    }; // Entry
26
27  template<class TYPE>
28  struct NODE
29    {
30     NODE           *firstPtr;
31     int            numEntries;
32     Entry<TYPE>    entries[ORDER - 1];
33    };   // NODE
34
35  template <class TYPE, class KTYPE>
36  class BTree
37    {
38     private:
39         int            count;
40         NODE<TYPE>  *tree;
41
42     bool   _BTree_Search  (NODE<TYPE>   *root,
43                            KTYPE          srchKey,
44                            NODE<TYPE>   **foundNode,
45                            int&           foundLoc);
46
47     void _traversal       (NODE<TYPE>   *root,
48                            void (*process) (TYPE dataProc));
49
50     bool _insertNode      (NODE<TYPE>   *root,
51                            TYPE dataIn, Entry<TYPE>& upEntry);
52
53     int  _searchNode      (NODE<TYPE>   *nodePtr,
54                            KTYPE          srchKey);
55
56     void _splitNode       (NODE<TYPE>   *root,
57                            int            entryNdx,
58                            bool           toRight,
59                            Entry<TYPE>   &upEntry);
60
61     void _insertEntry     (NODE<TYPE>    *root,
62                            int            entryNdx,
63                            Entry<TYPE>&  upEntry);
64
65     bool _delete          (NODE<TYPE> *root,
66                            KTYPE          dltKey,
```

Program 10-1   B-tree header file *(continued)*

```
67                                    bool&         success);
68
69      bool  _deleteMid      (NODE<TYPE>  *root,
70                             int          entryNdx,
71                             NODE<TYPE>  *leftPtr);
72
73      bool  _deleteEntry    (NODE<TYPE> *node, int entryNdx);
74
75      bool  _reFlow         (NODE<TYPE> *root, int entryNdx);
76
77      void  _borrowRight    (NODE<TYPE>  *root,
78                             int          entryNdx,
79                             NODE<TYPE> *leftTreePtr,
80                             NODE<TYPE> *rightTreePtr);
81
82      void  _borrowLeft     (NODE<TYPE>  *root,
83                             int          entryNdx,
84                             NODE<TYPE> *leftTreePtr,
85                             NODE<TYPE> *rightTreePtr);
86
87      void  _combine        (NODE<TYPE>  *root,
88                             int          entryNdx,
89                             NODE<TYPE> *leftTreePtr,
90                             NODE<TYPE> *rightTreePtr);
91
92      void  _destroyBtree (NODE<TYPE> *root);
93
94      public:
95              BTree (void);
96              ~BTree (void);
97
98      bool      BTree_Insert     (TYPE   dataIn);
99      bool      BTree_Delete     (KTYPE  dltKey);
100     void      BTree_Traversal
101                     (void (*process) (TYPE dataProc));
102     bool      BTree_Search     (KTYPE  srchKey,
103                                  TYPE&  dataFound);
104     bool      BTree_Empty     (void);
105     bool      BTree_Full      (void);
106     int       BTree_Count     (void);
107     }; // BTree class
```

Program 10-1   B-tree header file *(continued)*

Utility Functions

There are several B-tree utility functions. We discuss only B-tree search and B-tree traversal and do not develop the code for the constructor, destructor, empty, full, and count. These functions are very similar to those developed in Chapter 8 for the AVL abstract data type class.

Search

The search function is interesting in that it requires an ADT interface function and an internal recursive search function. From the application function's point of view, all search needs to supply is the key to the data to be located. The internal search, however, needs to know which tree node it is processing at any given time in the search. The user interface must therefore receive the request from the application, call the internal search, and then return the results to the application. Its code is shown in Program 10-2.

```
1    /* ================ BTree_Search ====================
2       Search the tree for the node containing the
3       requested key and return matching data.
4          Pre      targetKey is data to be located
5                   dataFound is variable to receive data
6          Post     tree searched and data returned
7          Return   true if found; false if not found
8    */
9
10   template <class TYPE, class KTYPE>
11   bool  BTree<TYPE, KTYPE> :: BTree_Search
12                              (KTYPE   srchKey,
13                               TYPE&   dataFound)
14   {
15   // Local Declarations
16      int           foundLoc;
17      NODE<TYPE> *foundNode;
18
19   // Statements
20
21      if ( _BTree_Search (tree, srchKey, &foundNode, foundLoc))
22          {
23           dataFound = foundNode->entries[foundLoc].data;
24           return true;
25          } // if found
26      else
27          return false;
28
29   } // BTree_Search
```

Program 10-2 B-tree search ADT interface

The internal search function matches the pseudocode in Algorithm 10-15, on page 470. Whereas the internal algorithm returns the key's node address and entry index, in the user interface above we return the data. (Remember that the application does not have access to the node structure.) The internal search implementation is shown in Program 10-3.

```
 1    /* ==================== _BTree_Search ====================
 2       Search tree for node containing requested
 3       key and return its data to the calling function.
 4           Pre     root is pointer to current root node
 5                   srchKey is search argument
 6                   foundNode is pointer to address of node area
 7                   foundLoc is reference to index of key's entry
 8           Post    tree searched and node pointer/index returned
 9           Return  true if found; false if not found
10    */
11
12    template <class TYPE, class KTYPE>
13    bool BTree<TYPE, KTYPE> :: _BTree_Search
14             (NODE<TYPE>    *root,
15              KTYPE          srchKey,
16              NODE<TYPE>   **foundNode,
17              int&           foundLoc)
18    {
19    // Statements
20       if (!root)
21          return false;
22
23       if (srchKey < (root)->entries[0].data.key)
24          return _BTree_Search (root->firstPtr,
25                                srchKey,
26                                foundNode,
27                                foundLoc);
28
29       foundLoc = root->numEntries - 1;
30       while (srchKey < root->entries[foundLoc].data.key)
31          foundLoc--;
32       if (srchKey == root->entries[foundLoc].data.key)
33          {
34             *foundNode = root;
35             return true ;
36          } // if
37
38       return _BTree_Search (root->entries[foundLoc].rightPtr,
39                             srchKey,
40                             foundNode,
41                             foundLoc);
42    } // _search
```

Program 10-3 B-tree search internal function

Program 10-3 Analysis   First, note the name of the function. It begins with an underscore. It is reasonable to assume that a programmer using the ADT may decide to use the same name as one of our ADT functions. Therefore, to prevent duplicates, we prefix all of our internal names with the underscore.

The search begins by testing whether the search argument found in the key pointer is less than the first entry in the node. If it is, we follow the first pointer to the left. If it is not, we must search the entry array for the matching entry or the correct right subtree to continue the search. The entry array search we use is an adaptation of the ordered list search we studied in Chapter 2. The major difference is that it starts from the last entry and works forward.

Traversal   The B-tree traversal is interesting for three reasons. First, once again it requires two functions, one for the ADT interface and one for the internal traversal. Second, we must pass the name of the function that is to be used to process each node. The user interface code, including receiving the process function's address as a parameter, is shown in Program 10-4.

```
 1  /* ============== BTree_Traversal ====================
 2     Process tree using inorder traversal.
 3         Pre    tree has been created (may be null)
 4                process used to "visit" nodes during traversal
 5         Post   entries processed in LNR (inorder) sequence
 6  */
 7
 8  template <class TYPE, class KTYPE>
 9  void    BTree<TYPE, KTYPE>
10     ::  BTree_Traversal (void (*process) (TYPE dataProc))
11  {
12  // Statements
13     if (tree)
14        _traversal (tree, process);
15     return;
16  }  // end BTree_Traverse
```

Program 10-4   B-tree traversal user interface

The third interesting point in the traversal logic is that as we traverse the tree, using a variation of the inorder traversal, we must deblock each entry. We studied the deblocking logic in Algorithm 10-14, "B-Tree Travnsversal," on page 469. The code is shown in Program 10-5.

```
1    /* =================== _traversal  ===================
2       Traverse tree using inorder traversal. To "process"
3       node, the process function is received as a parameter.
4          Pre    tree validated in BTree_Traversal
5                 root is pointer to B-tree node
6                 process is function to process entry
7          Post   all nodes processed
8    */
9
10   template <class TYPE, class KTYPE>
11   void BTree<TYPE, KTYPE> ::  _traversal
12           (NODE<TYPE> *root, void (*process) (TYPE data))
13   {
14   // Local Declarations
15      int          scanCount;
16      NODE<TYPE> *ptr;
17
18   // Statements
19      scanCount = 0;
20      ptr = root->firstPtr;
21
22      while (scanCount <= root->numEntries)
23         {
24         // Test for subtree
25         if (ptr)
26            _traversal  (ptr, process);
27
28         // Subtree processed--get next entry
29         if (scanCount < root->numEntries)
30            {
31             process  (root->entries[scanCount].data);
32             ptr     = root->entries[scanCount].rightPtr;
33            } // if scanCount
34         scanCount++;
35         } // while
36      return;
37   } // _traversal
```

Program 10-5   B-tree traversal internal function

Insert Algorithms

The insertion logic requires several algorithms. We develop all but two of them in this section. Insertion requires a search that returns the index entry of the matching node. Because the logic is the same as we saw for Program 10-3, "B-Tree Search Internal Function," on page 483, we do not develop it here. The other function that we do not develop inserts an entry into the entry array.

ADT Interface Function

Once again, we need an ADT interface function and an internal function. The interface requires only the data to be inserted. The internal function also requires the current node and the entry to be inserted. The ADT interface function is shown in Program 10-6.

```
1   /* ===================== BTree_Insert ======================
2      This function inserts new data into the tree.
3         Pre    dataIn contains data to be inserted
4         Post   data have been inserted or memory overflow
5         Return true if inserted; false if overflow
6   */
7
8   template <class TYPE, class KTYPE>
9   bool  BTree<TYPE, KTYPE> ::  BTree_Insert (TYPE dataIn)
10  {
11  // Local Declarations
12     int    i;
13     bool   taller;
14
15     NODE<TYPE> *newPtr;
16     Entry<TYPE> upEntry;
17
18  // Statements
19     if (tree == NULL)
20         // Empty tree. Insert first node.
21         {
22          newPtr = new NODE<TYPE>;
23          if (newPtr)
24             {
25              newPtr->firstPtr           = NULL;
26              newPtr->numEntries         = 1;
27              newPtr->entries[0].data    = dataIn;
28              newPtr->entries[0].rightPtr = NULL;
29              tree                       = newPtr;
30              count++;
31
32              for (i = 1; i < ORDER - 1; i++)
33                  newPtr->entries[i].rightPtr = NULL;
34              return true;
35             } // if newPtr
36         else
37             // Overflow
38             return false;
39         } // if tree == null
40
41     taller = _insertNode (tree, dataIn, upEntry);
42     if (taller)
```

Program 10-6   B-tree insert ADT interface

```
43          {
44              // Tree has grown. Create new root.
45              newPtr = new NODE<TYPE>;
46              if (newPtr)
47                  {
48                   newPtr->entries[0]   = upEntry;
49                   newPtr->firstPtr     = tree;
50                   newPtr->numEntries   = 1;
51                   tree                 = newPtr;
52                  } // if newPtr
53              else
54                  // Overflow
55                  return false;
56          } // if taller
57
58      count++;
59      return true;
60  }  // BTree_Insert
```

Program 10-6   B-tree insert ADT interface *(continued)*

Program 10-6 Analysis

The insert ADT interface is more complex than those we have seen so far. It performs four different processes compared with only two in the pseudocode design. First, it handles the insert into a null tree. This code is shown in Statements 21 through 39. If you compare the C++ code with the pseudocode found in Algorithm 10-2, on page 446, you will note that the pseudocode handles insert into a null tree as a simple variation on all other inserts. This is one example of how a specific language implementation can be much more complex than the pseudocode.

The second process involves inserting all nodes after the first. It consists of a single call (Statement 41) to the internal insert function. This code is identical in the pseudocode version of the ADT.

Once the new node has been inserted, the insert interface ADT must determine whether a new root needs to be created. The internal insert function returns a Boolean indicating whether the height of the tree has increased. If it has, the new root is built in Statements 43 through 56. Again, the code parallels the pseudocode.

Finally, if the insert was successful, the B-tree count must be updated. If other metadata, such as the maximum number of elements ever held in the B-tree, were necessary, they would also be handled here. This logic is not required in the pseudocode.

Internal Insert Processing

The insert design is shown in Figure 10-6, "B-Tree Insert Design," on page 456. You might want to review it before studying the functions in this section. Although the functions are rather long, they closely follow the algorithm design and should be easy to understand.

Insert Node Function

The code for the internal insert function is shown in Program 10-7.

```
 1    /* ===================== _insertNode =====================
 2       This function uses recursion to insert the new data into
 3       a leaf node in the B-tree.
 4          Pre     application has called BTree_Insert, which
 5                  passes root and data pointers
 6          Post    data have been inserted
 7          Return taller Boolean
 8    */
 9
10    template <class TYPE, class KTYPE>
11    bool BTree<TYPE, KTYPE>
12            :: _insertNode (NODE<TYPE> *root, TYPE dataIn,
13                            Entry<TYPE>& upEntry)
14    {
15    // Local Declarations
16       bool newEntryLow;
17       int  entryNdx;
18       bool taller;
19
20       NODE<TYPE> *subtreePtr;
21
22    // Statements
23       if (!root)
24          {
25           upEntry.data     = dataIn;
26           upEntry.rightPtr = NULL;
27           taller           = true;
28           return  taller;
29          } // if NULL tree
30
31       entryNdx = _searchNODE (root, dataIn.key);
32       newEntryLow =
33          (dataIn.key < root->entries[entryNdx].data.key);
34       if (entryNdx > 0 || (!newEntryLow))
35           subtreePtr = root->entries[entryNdx].rightPtr;
36       else
37           subtreePtr = root->firstPtr;
38       taller = _insertNode (subtreePtr,
39                             dataIn, upEntry);
40
41       if (taller)
42          {
43           if (root->numEntries >= ORDER - 1)
44              {
45               _splitNode (root,          entryNdx,
46                           newEntryLow, upEntry);
```

Program 10-7 B-tree internal insert function

```
47              taller = true;
48            } // node full
49        else
50          {
51            if (newEntryLow)
52                _insertEntry(root, entryNdx, upEntry);
53            else
54                _insertEntry(root, entryNdx + 1, upEntry);
55            (root->numEntries)++;
56            taller = false;
57          } // else
58      } // if taller
59
60    return taller;
61  } // _insertNode
```

Program 10-7   B-tree internal insert function *(continued)*

Program 10-7 Analysis
As we discussed when we studied the pseudocode version (Algorithm 10-2, on page 446), you will need to walk through an example to fully understand this algorithm. We suggest that you use Figure 10-9, on page 453.

Split Node Function

The code for splitting a node is shown in Program 10-8.

```
 1  /* ================== _splitNode ==================
 2     Splits node when node is full.
 3         Pre    node has    overflowed; split node
 4                entryNdx    contains new data index loc
 5                newEntryLow indicates new data is < entry
 6                upEntry     reference to insert data
 7         Post   NODE split and upEntry contains entry to
 8                be inserted into parent
 9             -or- program aborted if memory overflow
10  */
11
12  template <class TYPE, class KTYPE>
13  void BTree<TYPE, KTYPE> ::  _splitNode
14                              (NODE<TYPE>  *node,
15                               int         entryNdx,
16                               bool        newEntryLow,
17                               Entry<TYPE>& upEntry)
18  {
19  // Local Declarations
20    int fromNdx;
21    int toNdx;
```

Program 10-8   B-tree split node function

```
22
23      NODE<TYPE> *rightPtr;
24
25  // Statements
26      rightPtr  = new NODE<TYPE>;
27      if (!rightPtr)
28         cout <<  "Overflow Error 101 in _splitNode\a\n",
29               exit (100);
30
31  // Build right subtree node
32      if (entryNdx < MIN_ENTRIES)
33          fromNdx  = MIN_ENTRIES;
34      else
35          fromNdx  = MIN_ENTRIES + 1;
36      toNdx = 0;
37      rightPtr->numEntries = node->numEntries - fromNdx;
38      while (fromNdx < node->numEntries)
39         rightPtr->entries[toNdx++]
40                     = node->entries[fromNdx++];
41      node->numEntries = node->numEntries
42                        - rightPtr->numEntries;
43
44      if (entryNdx < MIN_ENTRIES)
45         {
46         if (newEntryLow)
47            _insertEntry (node, entryNdx, upEntry);
48         else
49            _insertEntry (node, entryNdx + 1, upEntry);
50         } // if
51      else
52         {
53         _insertEntry (rightPtr,
54                     entryNdx - MIN_ENTRIES,
55                     upEntry);
56         (rightPtr->numEntries)++;
57         (node->numEntries)--;
58         } // else
59
60      upEntry.data      = node->entries[MIN_ENTRIES].data;
61      upEntry.rightPtr  = rightPtr;
62      rightPtr->firstPtr
63                  = node->entries[MIN_ENTRIES].rightPtr;
64
65      return;
66  } // _splitNode
```

Program 10-8 B-tree split node function *(continued)*

Program 10-8 Analysis

Several interesting logical elements in this algorithm require further study. For example, we must add 1 to the node's number of entries when we insert upEntry into the right node (Statements 52 through 58), but not when we insert it into the left node (Statements 45 through 49). The reason is that the left node contains the median entry to be inserted up into the parent and therefore we don't need to add 1. If we did, we would just have to subtract 1 after we deleted the median entry.

In a similar vein, when we insert into the left node, we need to know whether the new data key is less than the entry key. If it is, we pass the entry index to insert entry (Statement 47); if it is not, we pass the entry index plus 1 (Statement 49). To understand the reason for this difference you will need to construct two examples and follow the insertion logic carefully.

Delete Algorithms

Deletion from a B-tree is potentially much more work than insertion. In this section we describe six of the seven functions required to delete.

ADT Delete Interface

As we have seen several times, deletion requires both an ADT interface function and an internal recursive function. The delete interface function, however, is much simpler than the one we saw for the insert. Its code is shown in Program 10-9.

```
 1   /* =================== BTree_Delete ===================
 2      Delete entry with key target from B-tree.
 3          Pre     dltKey contains key to be deleted
 4          Post    data deleted and data space freed
 5                  -or- an error code is returned
 6          Return success (true) or not found (false)
 7   */
 8
 9   template <class TYPE, class KTYPE>
10   bool    BTree<TYPE,   KTYPE>
11      ::  BTree_Delete (KTYPE dltKey)
12   {
13   // Local Declarations
14      bool           success;
15      NODE<TYPE>   *dltPtr;
16
17   // Statements
18      if (!tree)
19          return false;
20
21      _delete (tree, dltKey, success);
22
23      if (success)
```

Program 10-9   B-tree delete ADT interface function

```
24        {
25          count--;
26          if (tree->numEntries == 0)
27             {
28               dltPtr      = tree;
29               tree = tree->firstPtr;
30               delete dltPtr;
31             } // root empty
32          } // success
33       return success;
34    }  // BTree_Delete
```

Program 10-9 B-tree delete ADT interface function *(continued)*

Program 10-9 Analysis

Although the recursive delete function uses an underflow Boolean to determine when a node is below the minimum, the root has no minimum. Therefore, in this function, our only concern is that all entries in the root may have been deleted. We handle this situation in Statements 26 through 31.

Internal Delete Function

The internal delete function searches the B-tree for the entry to be deleted. If it finds the entry in a leaf node, the delete is simple. If it finds the entry in an internal node, however, a substitute in a leaf must be found. As we explained earlier, we search the left subtree for the immediate predecessor of the entry to be deleted. Once the substitution has been made, we can delete the entry we know to be in the leaf. The code is shown in Program 10-10.

```
 1    /* ==================== _delete ====================
 2       Delete entry with key dltKey from B-tree.
 3          Pre    root is pointer to tree or subtree
 4                 dltKey is key of entry to be deleted
 5                 success is Boolean--entry deleted
 6          Post   the node is deleted and space freed
 7                 -or- if not found, tree is unchanged
 8          Return underflow true/false
 9                 success    true/false
10    */
11
12    template <class TYPE, class KTYPE>
13    bool BTree<TYPE, KTYPE> ::  _delete (NODE<TYPE>  *root,
14                                         KTYPE          dltKey,
15                                         bool&          success)
16    {
17    // Local Declarations
18       NODE<TYPE> *leftPtr;
19       NODE<TYPE> *subTreePtr;
```

Program 10-10 B-tree internal delete

```
20
21      int entryNdx;
22      bool  underflow;
23
24  // Statements
25      if (!root)
26          {
27           success = false;
28           return    false;
29          } // null tree
30
31      entryNdx   = _searchNODE (root, dltKey);
32      if (dltKey == root->entries[entryNdx].data.key)
33          {
34            // found entry to be deleted
35            success = true;
36            if (root->entries[entryNdx].rightPtr == NULL)
37                // entry is a leaf node
38                underflow = _deleteEntry (root, entryNdx);
39            else
40                // entry is in an internal node
41                {
42                  if (entryNdx > 0)
43                     leftPtr =
44                         root->entries[entryNdx - 1].rightPtr;
45                  else
46                     leftPtr = root->firstPtr;
47                  underflow =
48                      _deleteMid (root, entryNdx, leftPtr);
49                  if (underflow)
50                     underflow = _reFlow (root, entryNdx);
51                } // else internal node
52          } // else found entry
53      else
54          {
55            if (dltKey < root->entries[0].data.key)
56                // delete key < first entry
57                subTreePtr = root->firstPtr;
58            else
59                // delete key in right subtree
60                subTreePtr = root->entries[entryNdx].rightPtr;
61
62            underflow = _delete (subTreePtr, dltKey, success);
63            if (underflow)
64                underflow = _reFlow (root, entryNdx);
65          } // else not found
66
67      return underflow;
68  } // _delete
```

Program 10-10   B-tree internal delete *(continued)*

Delete Middle

Called by the internal delete function, delete middle locates the predecessor node on the left subtree and substitutes it for the deleted node in the root, as shown in Program 10-11.

```
1   /* ===================== _deleteMid =====================
2      Deletes entry from internal node in B-tree.
3         Pre    root is pointer to node containing delete data
4                subtreePtr is pointer to root's subtree
5                entryNdx is entry to be deleted
6         Post   immediate predecessor data replaces delete data
7                predecessor deleted from tree
8         Return underflow true/false
9   */
10
11  template <class TYPE, class KTYPE>
12  bool  BTree<TYPE, KTYPE> :: _deleteMid (NODE<TYPE>  *root,
13                                     int          entryNdx,
14                                     NODE<TYPE>  *subtreePtr)
15  {
16  // Local Declarations
17     int    dltNdx;
18     int    rightNdx;
19     bool   underflow;
20
21  // Statements
22     if (subtreePtr->firstPtr == NULL)
23         {
24         // Leaf located. Exchange data and delete leaf entry.
25           dltNdx = subtreePtr->numEntries - 1;
26           root->entries[entryNdx].data =
27                 subtreePtr->entries[dltNdx].data;
28           --subtreePtr->numEntries;
29           underflow  = subtreePtr->numEntries < MIN_ENTRIES;
30         } // if leaf
31     else
32         {
33         // Not located. Traverse right for predecessor.
34           rightNdx  = subtreePtr->numEntries - 1;
35           underflow = _deleteMid
36                          (root,
37                           entryNdx,
38                       subtreePtr->entries[rightNdx].rightPtr);
39           if (underflow)
40               underflow = _reFlow (subtreePtr, rightNdx);
41         } // else traverse right
42     return underflow;
43  } // _deleteMid
```

Program 10-11   B-tree delete middle

Program 10-11 Analysis

Delete middle contains one of the most sophisticated pieces of logic in the B-tree ADT class. Study the logic in Statements 35 through 41 carefully. We recursively call delete middle until we find a leaf. When we return, we know that we have deleted the substitute entry. Now we must back out of the tree, testing for underflow at each node. If we detect underflow, we must reflow the nodes and then proceed up the tree until we reach the node that originally contained the data to be deleted. At that point, we return to delete, which will also continue backing out of the tree until it reaches the root.

Reflow Function

When an underflow occurs, we must reflow the nodes to make sure they are valid. Reflow first tries to balance by borrowing from the right, then from the left; if both fail, it combines the siblings. The code is shown in Program 10-12.

```
 1   /* ======================= _reFlow =======================
 2       An underflow has occurred in a subtree to root. Correct
 3       by balancing or concatenating.
 4          Pre    root is pointer to underflowed tree or subtree
 5                 entryNdx is parent of subtree with underflow
 6          Post   underflow corrected
 7          Return underflow true/false
 8                 success    true/false
 9   */
10
11   template <class TYPE, class KTYPE>
12   bool    BTree<TYPE, KTYPE> :: _reFlow  (NODE<TYPE> *root,
13                                           int          entryNdx)
14   {
15   // Local Declarations
16      NODE<TYPE> *leftTreePtr;
17      NODE<TYPE> *rightTreePtr;
18      bool        underflow;
19
20   // Statements
21      if (entryNdx == 0)
22         leftTreePtr = root->firstPtr;
23      else
24         leftTreePtr = root->entries[entryNdx - 1].rightPtr;
25      rightTreePtr   = root->entries[entryNdx].rightPtr;
26
27      // Try to borrow first
28      if (rightTreePtr->numEntries > MIN_ENTRIES)
29         {
```

Program 10-12 B-tree reflow

```
30          _borrowRight (root,            entryNdx,
31                          leftTreePtr, rightTreePtr);
32          underflow = false;
33         } //  if borrow right
34     else
35        {
36         // Can't borrow from right--try left
37         if (leftTreePtr->numEntries > MIN_ENTRIES)
38            {
39             _borrowLeft (root,            entryNdx,
40                           leftTreePtr, rightTreePtr);
41             underflow  = false;
42            } // if borrow left
43         else
44            {
45             // Can't borrow. Must combine nodes.
46             _combine (root,            entryNdx,
47                         leftTreePtr, rightTreePtr);
48             underflow = (root->numEntries < MIN_ENTRIES);
49            } // else combine
50        } // else borrow left
51     return underflow;
52  } // _reFlow
```

Program 10-12   B-tree reflow *(continued)*

Borrow Left or Right

When we underflow, we first try to balance the tree by borrowing a node from the right sibling. If that doesn't work, we try to borrow from the left. These two functions are mirror logic; they are identical except for the direction. The logic for borrow right is shown in Program 10-13.

```
 1  /* ================== _borrowRight ==================
 2     Root left subtree underflow. Borrow from right and rotate.
 3        Pre     root          contains parent to underflow node
 4                entryNdx      is parent entry
 5                leftTreePtr   is subtree that underflowed
 6                rightTreePtr is subtree with extra entry
 7        Post    underflow corrected
 8  */
 9
10  template <class TYPE, class KTYPE>
11  void BTree<TYPE, KTYPE> :: _borrowRight
12                          (NODE<TYPE> *root,
13                           int          entryNdx,
14                           NODE<TYPE> *leftTreePtr,
```

Program 10-13   B-tree borrow right

```
15                              NODE<TYPE> *rightTreePtr)
16   {
17   // Local Declarations
18      int toNdx;
19      int shifter;
20
21   // Statements
22      // Move parent and subtree pointer to left tree
23      toNdx = leftTreePtr->numEntries;
24      leftTreePtr->entries[toNdx].data
25           = root->entries[entryNdx].data;
26      leftTreePtr->entries[toNdx].rightPtr
27           = rightTreePtr->firstPtr;
28      ++leftTreePtr->numEntries;
29
30      // Move right data to parent
31      root->entries[entryNdx].data
32           = rightTreePtr->entries[0].data;
33
34      // Set right tree first pointer. Shift entries left.
35      rightTreePtr->firstPtr
36           = rightTreePtr->entries[0].rightPtr;
37      shifter = 0;
38      while (shifter < rightTreePtr->numEntries - 1)
39         {
40          rightTreePtr->entries[shifter]
41               = rightTreePtr->entries[shifter + 1];
42          ++shifter;
43         } // while
44      --rightTreePtr->numEntries;
45      return;
46   } // _borrowRight
```

Program 10-13   B-tree borrow right *(continued)*

Combine

If we can't borrow a node from a sibling, we must combine two nodes. The logic to combine nodes is shown in Program 10-14.

```
1   /* ==================== _combine ====================
2      Underflow cannot be corrected by borrowing.
3      Combine two subtrees.
4         Pre  root is node of parent to node that underflowed
5              entryNdx is parent entry
6              leftTreePtr and rightTreePtr are subtree pointers
```

Program 10-14   B-tree combine nodes

```
 7            Post   parent and subtrees combined; right node freed
 8     */
 9
10     template <class TYPE, class KTYPE>
11     void BTree<TYPE, KTYPE> :: _combine
12                               (NODE<TYPE> *root,
13                                int          entryNdx,
14                                NODE<TYPE> *leftTreePtr,
15                                NODE<TYPE> *rightTreePtr)
16     {
17     // Local Declarations
18        int toNdx;
19        int fromNdx;
20        int shifter;
21
22     // Statements
23        // Move parent and set its right pointer from right tree
24        toNdx = leftTreePtr->numEntries;
25        leftTreePtr->entries[toNdx].data
26              = root->entries[entryNdx].data;
27        leftTreePtr->entries[toNdx].rightPtr
28              = rightTreePtr->firstPtr;
29        ++leftTreePtr->numEntries;
30        --root->numEntries;
31
32        // Move data from right tree to left tree
33        fromNdx = 0;
34        toNdx++;
35        while (fromNdx < rightTreePtr->numEntries)
36            leftTreePtr->entries[toNdx++]
37               = rightTreePtr->entries[fromNdx++];
38        leftTreePtr->numEntries += rightTreePtr->numEntries;
39        delete rightTreePtr;
40
41        // Now shift data in root to the left
42        shifter = entryNdx;
43        while (shifter < root->numEntries)
44            {
45             root->entries[shifter] = root->entries[shifter + 1];
46             shifter++;
47            } // while
48        return;
49     } // _combine
```

Program 10-14 B-tree combine nodes *(continued)*

10-7   SUMMARY

■   An *m*-way tree is a search tree in which
  a. Each node has 0 to *m* subtrees
  b. Given a node with $k < m$ subtrees, the node contains *k* subtree pointers, some of which may be null, and $k - 1$ data entries
  c. The key values in the first subtree are all less than the key in the first entry; the key values in the other subtrees are all greater than or equal to the key in their parent entry
  d. The keys of the data entries are ordered $key_1 <= key_2 <= \ldots <= key_k$.

■   A B-tree is an *m*-way tree in which
  a. The root is either a leaf or it has 2 . . . *m* subtrees
  b. All internal nodes have at least $\lceil m/2 \rceil$ nonnull subtrees and at most *m* nonnull subtrees
  c. All leaf nodes are at the same level; that is, the tree is perfectly balanced
  d. A leaf node has at least $\lceil m/2 \rceil - 1$ and at most $m - 1$ entries

■   B-tree insertion takes place at a leaf node. An insert to a full node creates a condition known as overflow. Overflow requires that the leaf node be split into two nodes, each containing half of the data.

■   Three points must be considered when we delete an entry from a B-tree. First, we must ensure that the data to be deleted are actually in the tree. Second, if the node does not have enough entries after the delete, we need to correct the structure deficiency (underflow). Third, we can only delete from a leaf node.

■   Because a B-tree is a search tree, we use the inorder traversal to traverse the tree and visit each node in order.

■   There are two special B-trees: 2-3 tree and 2-3-4 tree.

■   The 2-3 tree is a B-tree of order 3. Each node except the root can have two or three subtrees.

■   The 2-3-4 tree is a B-tree of order 4. Each node except the root can have two, three, or four subtrees.

■   There are two popular variations of the B-tree: B*tree and B+tree.

■   In a B*tree, each node contains a minimum of two-thirds of the maximum entries allowed for each node.

■   In a B+tree, data entries are only found at the leaf level and each leaf node has an additional pointer that is used to connect to the next leaf.

■   The lexical *m*-ary tree is a tree in which the key is represented as a sequence of characters. Each entry in the lexical tree contains a pointer to the next level.

■   A trie is a lexical *m*-ary tree in which the pointers pointing to nonexisting characters are replaced by null pointers.

10-8   PRACTICE SETS

Exercises

1. Calculate the maximum number of data entries in a
  a. 3-way tree of height 3
  b. 4-way tree of height 5
  c. *m*-way tree of height *h*

2. Calculate the maximum number of data entries in a
   a. B-tree of order 5 with a height of 3
   b. B-tree of order 5 with a height of 5
   c. B-tree of order 5 with a height of h
3. Draw the B-tree of order 3 created by inserting the following data arriving in sequence:

   92 24 6 7 11 8 22 4 5 16 19 20 78

4. Draw the B-tree of order 4 created by inserting the following data arriving in sequence:

   92 24 6 7 11 8 22 4 5 16 19 20 78

5. Draw two B-trees of order 3 created by inserting data arriving in sequence from the two sets shown below. Compare the two B-trees to determine whether the order of data will create different B-trees.

   89 78 8 19 20 33 56 44
   44 56 33 20 19 8 78 89

6. Draw two different B-trees of order 3 that can store seven entries.
7. Create a B*tree of order 5 for the following data arriving in sequence:

   92 24 6 7 11 8 22 4 5 16 19 20 78

8. Create a B+tree of order 5 for the following data arriving in sequence:

   92 24 6 7 11 8 22 4 5 16 19 20 78

9. Draw a trie made from all 3-bit binary numbers (000 to 111).
10. Using the B-tree of order 3 shown in Figure 10-23, add 50, 78, 101, and 232. In each step show the resulting B-tree.

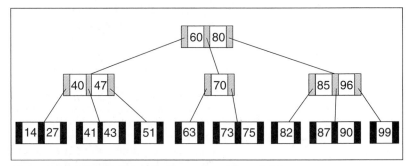

Figure 10-23   B-Tree for Exercises 10 and 11

11. Using the B-tree of order 3 (without the updates in Exercise 10) shown in Figure 10-23, delete 63, 90, 41, and 60. In each step show the resulting B-tree.

Problems

12. Rewrite the B-tree insertion algorithm using a stack instead of recursion.
13. Rewrite the B-tree deletion algorithm using a stack instead of recursion.
14. Write the search algorithm for a B+tree.
15. Write an algorithm that will traverse a trie and print all of its words in lexical order.
16. Write the C++ code for a B-tree count algorithm.

17. Write the C++ code for _insertEntry.
18. Write the C++ code for _searchNode.
19. Write the C++ code for _borrowLeft.
20. Write the C++ code for _deleteEntry.

Projects

21. Using the B-tree ADT, create a B-tree of order 7 that has 100 entries. Use a random number generator to randomly create the keys between 1 and 1000. Then create a menu-driven user interface that allows the user to delete, insert, and retrieve data or print the tree.

22. Create an ADT for a B+tree. In the tree structure, provide an additional metadata variable that identifies the address of the leftmost node in the file. Then modify the traversal function to use the address of the leftmost node and the next node pointers to traverse the tree.

23. The B-tree structure we studied can be used to create an indexed file. An indexed file contains an index structure to search for data in the file. Each entry in the index contains the data key from the file and the address of the data record in the file. The index can be created when the file is opened or it can be stored as a separate file on the disk.

Write a program that uses the B-tree ADT to create a file index in dynamic memory. When the program starts, it reads the file and creates the B-tree index. After the index has been created, provide a menu-driven user interface that allows the user to retrieve a specified record, insert new records, delete records, and traverse the file, printing all of the data. You may use any appropriate application data, such as a collection of CDs or library books, for the file.

24. In Project 23 we created a B-tree index by reading the file. Rather than reading the file each time the program starts, we could store the index as a separate file on the disk. In this case, when the program starts the index is read and inserted into the B-tree. When the program is done, the updated B-tree index is written back to the disk. Modify the program from Project 23 to store the index on the disk.

25. The B-tree index project can be maintained on a disk rather than in dynamic memory. The first record on the index file should contain metadata about the index, including the location of the root entry in the file and the address of the compare function for the data. Modify the B-tree ADT to maintain the B-tree on a disk. In this version of the ADT, the create B-tree function will be replaced by an open file function. The compare function must be defined when the file is opened.

26. As a final variation on the B-tree index project, rework Project 25 as a B+tree.

11 Advanced Sorting Concepts

One of the most common applications in computer science is **sorting,** the process through which data are arranged according to their values. We are surrounded by data. If the data were not ordered, we would spend hours trying to find a single piece of information. Imagine the difficulty of finding someone's telephone number in a telephone book that had no internal order.

The history of sorting dates back to the roots of computing, Herman Hollerith's electric tabulating machine, which was used to tally the 1890 U.S. Census and was one of the first modern sorting machines. Sorting was also on the scene when general-purpose computers first came into use. According to Knuth, "There is evidence that a sorting routine was the first program ever written for a stored program computer."[1] Although computer scientists have not developed a major new algorithm in more than 30 years (the newest algorithm in this book is heap sort, which was developed in 1964), sorting is still one of the most important concepts in computing today.

---

1. Donald E. Knuth, *The Art of Computer Programming,* vol. 3, *Sorting and Searching* (Reading, MA: Addison-Wesley, 1973), 384.

11-1 GENERAL SORT CONCEPTS

We discuss six internal sorts in this chapter: insertion sort, bubble sort, selection sort, shell sort, heap sort, and quick sort. The first three are useful only for sorting very small lists, but they form the basis of the last three, which are all useful general-purpose sorting concepts. After discussing the internal sorts, we will introduce the basic concepts used in external sorts.

Note

> Sorting is one of the most common data-processing applications.

Sorts are generally classified as either internal or external sorts. An **internal sort** is a sort in which all of the data are held in primary memory during the sorting process. An **external sort** uses primary memory for the data currently being sorted and secondary storage for any data that will not fit in primary memory. For example, a file of 20,000 records may be sorted using an array that holds only 1000 records. During the sorting process, only 1000 records are therefore in memory at any one time; the other 19,000 are kept in a file in secondary storage.

Note

> Sorting algorithms are classified as either internal or external.

Internal sorting algorithms have been grouped into several different classifications depending on their general approach to sorting. Knuth identified five different classifications[2]: insertion, selection, exchanging, merging, and distribution sorts. In this text we cover the first three. Distribution sorts, although interesting, have minimal use in computers. The different sorts are shown in Figure 11-1.

Sort Order

Data may be sorted in either ascending sequence or descending sequence. The **sort order** identifies the sequence of the sorted data, ascending or descending. If the order of the sort is not specified, it is assumed to be ascending. Examples of common data sorted in ascending sequence are the dictionary and the telephone book. Examples of descending data are percentages of games won in a sporting event such as baseball or grade point averages for honor students.

---

2. See Donald E. Knuth, *The Art of Computer Programming*, vol. 3, *Sorting and Searching* (Reading, MA: Addison-Wesley, 1973), 73–180.

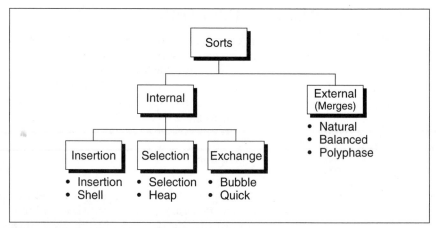

Figure 11-1   Sort classifications

Sort Stability

Sort stability is an attribute of a sort indicating that data with equal keys maintain their relative input order in the output. Stability is best seen in an example. In Figure 11-2(a) the unsorted data contain three entries with identical keys (212). If the data are sorted with a stable sort, the order in Figure 11-2(b) is guaranteed. That is, 212 *green* is guaranteed to be the first of the three in the output, 212 *yellow* is guaranteed to be the second, and 212 *blue* is guaranteed to be the last. If the sort is not stable, records with identical keys may occur in any order, including the stable order shown in Figure 11-2(b). Figure 11-2(c) is one example of the six different sequences that could occur in an unstable sort. Note that in this example, blue comes out first even though it was the last of the equal keys. Of the sort algorithms we will discuss in this text, the `insertionSort` (page 507), `selectionSort` (page 519), and `bubbleSort` (page 528) are stable; the others are unstable.

Sort Efficiency

Sort efficiency is a measure of the relative efficiency of a sort. It is usually an estimate of the number of comparisons and moves required to order an unordered list. We discuss the sort efficiency of each of the internal sorts we cover in this chapter. Generally speaking, however, the best possible sorting algorithms are on the order of $n\log_2 n$; that is, they are $O(n\log_2 n)$ sorts.[3] Three of the sorts we study are $O(n^2)$. The best, quick sort, is $O(n\log_2 n)$.

---

3. As a project, we discuss an interesting sort, radix sort, which is $O(n)$. However, its extensive overhead limits its general use.

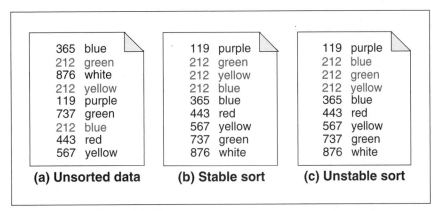

(a) Unsorted data	(b) Stable sort	(c) Unstable sort
365 blue	119 purple	119 purple
212 green	212 green	212 blue
876 white	212 yellow	212 green
212 yellow	212 blue	212 yellow
119 purple	365 blue	365 blue
737 green	443 red	443 red
212 blue	567 yellow	567 yellow
443 red	737 green	737 green
567 yellow	876 white	876 white

Figure 11-2   Sort stability

Passes

During the sorting process, the data are traversed many times. Each traversal of the data is referred to as a **sort pass.** Depending on the algorithm, the sort pass may traverse the whole list or just a section of the list. Also, characteristic of a sort pass is the placement of one or more elements in a sorted list.

11-2   INSERTION SORTS

Insertion sorting is one of the most common sorting techniques used by card players. As they pick up each card, they insert it into the proper sequence in their hand. (As an aside, card sorting is an example of a sort that uses two pieces of data to sort: suit and rank.) The concept extends well into computer sorting. In each pass of an insertion sort, one or more pieces of data are inserted into their correct location in an ordered list. In this section we study two insertion sorts, the straight insertion sort and the shell sort.

Straight Insertion Sort

In the **straight insertion sort,** the list is divided into two parts: sorted and unsorted. In each pass, the first element of the unsorted sublist is transferred to the sorted sublist by inserting it at the appropriate place. If we have a list of n elements, it will take at most $n - 1$ passes to sort the data. This concept is shown in Figure 11-3. In this figure, we have placed a visual wall between the sorted and unsorted portions of the list.

Straight Insertion Sort Example

Figure 11-4 traces the insertion sort through a list of six numbers. Sorting these data requires five sort passes. Each pass moves the wall

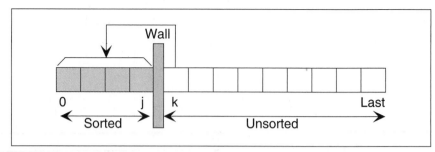

Figure 11-3   Insertion sort concept

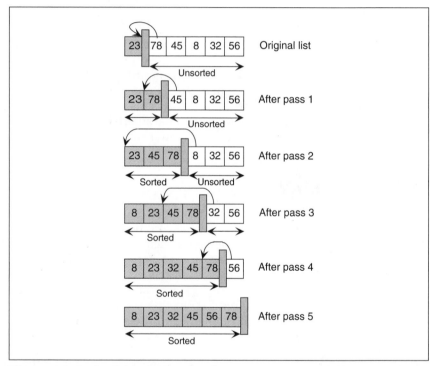

Figure 11-4   Insertion sort example

one element to the right as an element is removed from the unsorted sublist and inserted into the sorted sublist.

Insertion Sort Algorithm

The design of the insertion sort follows the pattern in the example. Each execution of the outer loop inserts the first element from the unsorted list into the sorted list. The inner loop steps through the sorted list, starting at the high end, looking for the correct insertion location. The pseudocode is shown in Algorithm 11-1.

```
algorithm insertionSort (ref list  <array>,
                         val last  <index>)

Sort list[0...last] using insertion sort. The array is divided
into sorted and unsorted lists. With each pass, the first
element in the unsorted list is inserted into the sorted list.

    Pre     list must contain at least one element
            last is an index to last element in the list

    Post    list has been rearranged

 1 current = 1
 2 loop (current <= last)
   1   hold  = list[current]
   2   walker = current - 1
   3   loop (walker >= 0 AND hold.key < list[walker].key)
       1   list[walker + 1] = list[walker]
       2   walker           = walker - 1
   4   end loop
   5   list[walker + 1] = hold
   6   current = current + 1
 3 end loop
 4 return
end insertionSort
```

Algorithm 11-1   Straight insertion sort

Algorithm 11-1 Analysis

Two design concepts need to be explored in this simple algorithm. At some point in their execution, all sort algorithms must exchange two elements. Each exchange takes three statements, which can greatly impact the sort efficiency when many elements need to be exchanged. To improve the efficiency, therefore, we use a hold area. The beginning of the exchange moves the data currently being sorted to the hold area. This typical first move in any exchange is shown in Statement 2.1. The inner loop (Statement 2.3) shifts elements to the right until it finds the correct insertion location. Each of the shifts is one exchange move. Finally, when the correct location is found, the hold area is moved back to the array (Statement 2.5). This is the third statement in the exchange logic and completes the exchange.

Note

> In the straight insertion sort, the list at any moment is divided into sorted and unsorted sublists. In each pass, the first element of the unsorted sublist is inserted into the sorted sublist.

Another point you should study is the workings of the inner loop. To make the sort as efficient as possible, we start with the high end of the sorted list and work toward the beginning of the sorted area. For the first insertion, this approach requires a maximum of one element to be shifted. For the second, it requires a maximum of two elements. The result is that only a portion of the list is examined in each sort phase.

Shell Sort

The **shell sort** algorithm, named after its creator, Donald L. Shell, is an improved version of the straight insertion sort. It was one of the first fast sorting algorithms.[4]

Note

> The shell sort is an improved version of the straight insertion sort in which diminishing partitions are used to sort the data.

In the shell sort, a list of N elements is divided into K **segments,** where K is known as the **increment.** Each segment contains N/K or more elements. Figure 11-5 contains a graphic representation of the segments in a shell sort. Note that the segments are dispersed throughout the list. In Figure 11-5, the increment is 3; the first, fourth, seventh, and tenth elements make up segment 1; the second, fifth, and eighth elements make up segment 2; and the third, sixth, and ninth elements make up segment 3. After each pass through the data, the data in each segment are ordered. Thus, if there are three segments, as we see in Figure 11-5, there are three different ordered lists. If there are two segments, there are two ordered lists; if there is only one segment, then the list is sorted.

Shell Sort Algorithm

Each pass through the data starts with the first element in the array and progresses through the array, comparing adjacent elements in each segment. In Figure 11-5, we begin by comparing elements 1 and 4 from the first segment, then 2 and 5 from the second segment, and then 3 and 6 from the third segment. We then compare 4 and 7 from the first segment, 5 and 8 from the second segment, and so forth until finally we compare elements 7 and 10. If the elements are out of sequence, they are exchanged. Study Figure 11-5 carefully until you see each of these comparisons. Be sure to note also that the first segment has four elements, whereas the other two have only three. The number

---

4. Shell's algorithm was first published in *Communications of the ACM* 2, no. 7 (1959): 30–32.

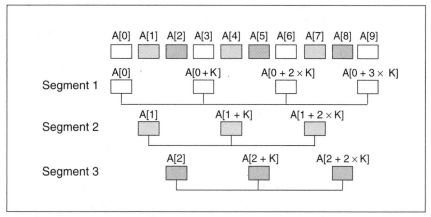

Figure 11-5 A segmented array

of elements in the segments varies because the list size (10) is not evenly divisible by the increment (3).

To compare adjacent keys in a segment, we add the increment to the current index, as shown below.

```
list[cur] : list[cur + incre]
```

After each pass through the data, the increment is reduced until, in the final pass, it is 1. Although the only absolute is that the last increment must be 1, the size of the increments influences the efficiency of the sort. We will discuss this issue separately later. The diminishing increment[5] is shown for an array of ten elements and increments of 5, 2, and 1 in Figure 11-6.

After each pass through the data, the elements in each segment are ordered. To ensure that each segment is ordered at the end of the pass, whenever an exchange is made, we drop back one increment and test the adjacent elements. If they are out of sequence, we exchange them and drop back again. If necessary, we keep exchanging and dropping back until we find two elements are ordered. We now have all of the elements of the shell sort. Its pseudocode is shown in Algorithm 11-2.

---

5. Knuth gave this sort the name "diminishing increment sort," but it is better known simply as the shell sort.

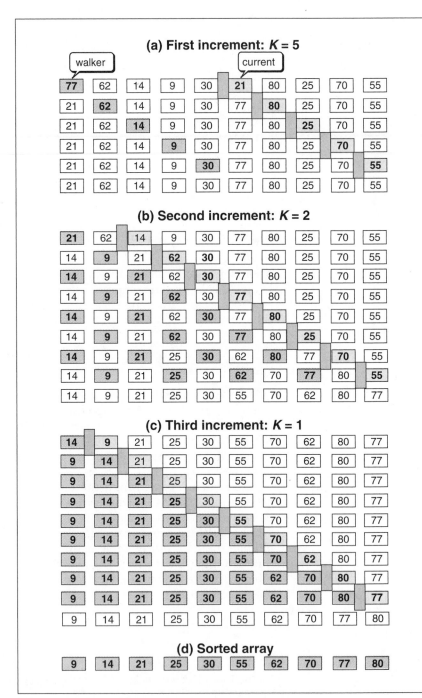

Figure 11-6 Diminishing increments in shell sort

```
algorithm shellSort (ref list  <array>,
                     val last  <integer>)
```
Data in list[0], list[1], ..., list[last] are sorted in place.
After the sort, their keys will be in order, list[0] ≤
list[1] ≤ ... ≤ list[last].

    Pre   list is an unordered array of records
              last is index to last record in array

    Post list is ordered on list[i].key

```
1 incre = last/2
```
Compare keys "increment" elements apart.
```
2 loop (incre not 0)
  1   current = incre
  2   loop (current <= last)
    1   hold   = list[current]
    2   walker = current - incre
    3   loop (walker >= 0 AND hold.key < list[walker].key)
```
            Move larger element up in list.
```
        1   list [walker + incre] = list [walker]
```
            Fall back one partition.
```
        2   walker = walker - incre
    4   end loop
```
        Insert hold record in proper relative location.
```
    5   list [walker + incre] = hold
    6   current = current + 1
  3   end loop
```
      End of pass--calculate next increment.
```
  4   incre = incre/2
3 end loop
4 return
end shellSort
```

Algorithm 11-2   Shell sort

Algorithm 11-2 Analysis

Let's look at the shell sort carefully to see how it qualifies as an insertion sort. Recall that insertion sorts insert the new data into their correct location in the ordered portion of the list. This concept is found in the shell sort: the ordered portion of the list is a segment with its members separated by the increment size. To see this more clearly, look at Figure 11-7. In this figure, the segment is seen as the shaded elements in an array. The new element, $A[0 + 3 * K]$, is being inserted into its correct position in the ordered portion of the segment.

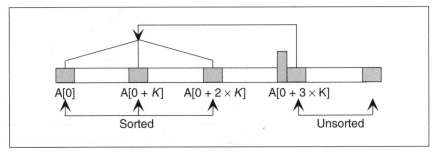

Figure 11-7   Ordered segment in a shell sort

Furthermore, if you compare the code in Algorithm 11-2 with the code in Algorithm 11-1, "Straight insertion sort," on page 507, you will see that, other than the increment, the code is identical.

One of the most important parts of the shell sort is falling back to ensure that the segment is ordered. This logic takes place in Statement 2.2.3.2. If this logic is not included, the resulting list will not be completely sorted.

Selecting the Increment Size

First, recognize that no increment size is best for all situations. The overriding considerations in the sort are to complete the sort with the minimum number of passes (increments) and to minimize the number of elements that appear in more than one segment. One method to eliminate completely an element being in more than one list is to use prime numbers. Unfortunately, the dynamic calculation of prime numbers is a relatively slow process.

Most texts use the simple series we proposed in Algorithm 11-2, setting the increment to half the list size and dividing by 2 each pass. Knuth suggests, however, that you should not start with an increment greater than one-third of the list size.[6] Other computer scientists have suggested that the increments be a power of 2 minus 1 or a Fibonacci series. These variations may result in a slightly more efficient sort, but they are relatively complex. One simple variation of the division-by-2 approach would be to add 1 whenever the increment is even. Doing so would tend to reduce the number of elements that appear in multiple segments.

Although you can use more complex increment-setting algorithms, the efficiency of a shell sort will never approach that of a quick sort. Therefore, if the objective is to obtain the most efficient sort, the solution is to use the quick sort rather than trying to optimize the increment size in the shell sort. On the other hand, the shell sort is a much simpler sort and at the same time is reasonably efficient.

6. Donald E. Knuth, *The Art of Computer Programming*, vol. 3, *Sorting and Searching* (Reading, MA: Addison-Wesley, 1973), 93.

Insertion Sort Algorithms

Sort algorithms determine the **sort effort** for a given sort. **Sort effort** is defined as the relative efficiency of a sort. It can be determined in several ways, but we will use the number of loops in the sort. Another common measure is the number of moves and compares needed to sort the list. Of course, the best measure would be the time it takes to actually run the sort. Time, however, varies by the efficiency of the program implementation and the speed of the computer being used. For analyzing different sorts, therefore, the first two measures are more meaningful. Let's now analyze the straight insertion and shell sort algorithms to determine their relative efficiency.

Straight Insertion Sort

Referring to Algorithm 11-1, "Straight insertion sort," on page 507, we find the following two loops:

```
2 loop (current <= last)
    ...
    3 loop (walker >= 0 AND hold.key < list[walker].key)
```

The outer loop executes $n - 1$ times, from 1 through `last`. For each outer loop, the inner loop executes from 0 to `current` times, depending on the relationship between `hold.key` and `list[walkerl].key`. On the average, we can expect the inner loop to process through the data in half of the sorted list. Because the inner loop depends on the outer loop's setting for `current`, we have a dependent quadratic loop, which is mathematically stated as

$$f(n) = n\left(\frac{n+1}{2}\right)$$

In big-O notation, the dependent quadratic loop is $O(n^2)$.

Note

> The straight insertion sort efficiency is $O(n^2)$.

Shell Sort

Now let's look at Algorithm 11-2, "Shell sort," on page 511. This algorithm contains the nested loops shown below.

```
2 loop (incre not 0)
    ...
    2 loop (current <= last)
        ...
        3 loop (walker >= 0 AND hold.key < list[walker].key)
```

Because we are dividing the increment by 2 in each loop, the outer loop is logarithmic; it is executed $\log_2 n$ times. The first inner loop executes $n - \text{increment}$ times for each of the outer loops; the first time it loops through 50% of the array ($n = (n/2)$), the second time it loops through 75% of the array ($n - (n/4)$), and so forth until it loops through all of the elements. The total number of iterations for the outer loop and the first inner loop is shown below.

$$\log_2 n \times \left[\left(n - \frac{n}{2}\right) + \left(n - \frac{n}{4}\right) + \left(n - \frac{n}{8}\right) + \cdots + 1 \right] = n\log_2 n$$

The innermost loop is the most difficult to analyze. The first limit keeps us from falling off the beginning of the array. The second limit determines whether we have to loop at all: We loop only when the data are out of order. Sometimes the inner loop is executed zero times, sometimes it is executed anywhere from one to `incre` times. If we were able to derive a formula for the third factor, the total sort effort would be the product of the three loops. The first two loops have a combined efficiency of $O(n\log_2 n)$. However, we still need to include the third loop. We can see, therefore, that the result is something greater than $O(n\log_2 n)$.

Knuth[7] tells us that the sort effort for the shell sort cannot be derived mathematically. He estimates from his empirical studies that the average sort effort is $15n^{1.25}$. Reducing Knuth's analysis to a big-O notation, we see that the shell sort is $O(n^{1.25})$.

Note

> The shell sort efficiency is $O(n^{1.25})$.

Summary

Our analysis indicates that the shell sort is more efficient than the straight insertion sort. Table 11-1 shows the number of loops for each sort with different array sizes.

	Number of Loops	
n	Straight Insertion	Shell
25	625	55
100	10,000	316
500	250,000	2364
1000	1,000,000	5623
2000	4,000,000	13,374

Table 11-1 Comparison of straight insertion and shell sorts

7. Donald E. Knuth, *The Art of Computer Programming*, vol. 3, *Sorting and Searching* (Reading, MA: Addison-Wesley, 1973), 381.

One important point to note in analyzing Table 11-1 is that big-O notation is only an approximation. At small array sizes, it may not accurately indicate the relative merit of one sort over another. For example, heuristic studies indicate that the straight insertion sort is more efficient than the shell sort for small lists.

Insertion Sort Implementation

In this section we write C++ implementations of the straight insertion sort and the shell sort.

Straight Insertion Sort

The straight insertion sort's implementation follows the pseudocode very closely. To test the sort, we created an array of random integers. The parameter is therefore changed to integers and the comparisons reference list without a key qualification. The code is shown in Program 11-1.

```
 1    /* ==================== insertionSort ====================
 2       Sort list using insertion sort. The list is divided into
 3       sorted and unsorted lists. With each pass, first element
 4       in unsorted list is inserted into sorted list.
 5          Pre    list must contain at least one element
 6                 last contains index to last element in the list
 7          Post   list has been rearranged
 8    */
 9    void insertionSort (int list[],
10                            int last)
11    {
12    // Local Definitions
13        int current;
14        int hold;
15        int walker;
16
17    // Statements
18        for (current = 1; current <= last; current++)
19           {
20            hold = list[current];
21            for (walker = current - 1;
22                 walker >= 0 && hold < list[walker];
23                 walker--)
24              list[walker + 1] = list[walker];
25            list [walker + 1] = hold;
26           } // for current
27
28        return;
29    } // insertionSort
```

Program 11-1   Insertion sort

Program 11-1 Analysis

We implement both loops using a *for* statement. When we begin the sort, the sorted list contains the first element. Therefore, we set the loop start to position 1 for the unsorted list (Statement 18). In the inner loop, the limiting condition is the beginning of the array, as seen in Statement 22.

Shell Sort

The shell sort implementation, which also uses an array of integers, is shown in Program 11-2.

```
 1   /* ==================== shellSort ====================
 2      List[0], list[1], ..., list[last] are sorted in place.
 3      After the sort, their keys will be in order, list[0].key
 4      <= list[1].key <= ... <= list[last].key.
 5          Pre    list is an unordered array of integers
 6                 last is index to last element in array
 7          Post   list is ordered
 8   */
 9   void shellSort (int list [],
10                       int last)
11   {
12   // Local Definitions
13      int hold;
14      int incre;
15      int curr;
16      int walker;
17
18   // Statements
19      incre = last / 2;
20      while (incre != 0)
21          {
22           for (curr = incre; curr <= last; curr++)
23               {
24                hold = list [curr];
25                walker = curr - incre;
26                while (walker >= 0 && hold < list [walker])
27                    {
28                       // Move larger element up in list
29                       list [walker + incre] = list [walker];
30                       //  Fall back one partition
31                       walker = (walker - incre);
32                    } //  while
33                // Insert hold in proper relative position
34                list [walker + incre] = hold;
35               } // for
36          //  End of pass--calculate next increment.
37          incre = incre / 2;
38          } // while
39      return;
40   } //  shellSort
```

Program 11-2   Shell sort

Program 11-2 Analysis

Although more complex than the straight insertion sort, the shell sort is by no means a difficult algorithm. There are only two additional complexities over the straight insertion sort. First, rather than a single array we have an array of partitions. Second, whenever an exchange is made, we must fall back and verify the order of the partition.

11-3 SELECTION SORTS

Selection sorts are among the most intuitive of all sorts. Given a list of data to be sorted, we simply select the smallest item and place it in a sorted list. These steps are then repeated until we have sorted all of the data. In this section we study two selection sorts, the straight selection sort and the heap sort.

Straight Selection Sort

In the straight selection sort, the list at any moment is divided into two sublists, sorted and unsorted, which are divided by an imaginary wall. We select the smallest element from the unsorted sublist and exchange it with the element at the beginning of the unsorted data. After each selection and exchange, the wall between the two sublists moves one element, increasing the number of sorted elements and decreasing the number of unsorted ones. Each time we move one element from the unsorted sublist to the sorted sublist, we say that we have completed one sort pass. If we have a list of n elements, therefore, we need $n - 1$ passes to completely rearrange the data. The selection sort is graphically presented in Figure 11-8.

Note

> In each pass of the selection sort, the smallest element is selected from the unsorted sublist and exchanged with the element at the beginning of the unsorted list.

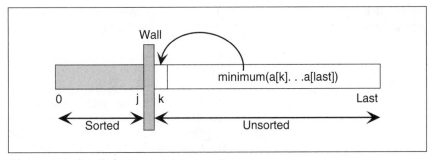

Figure 11-8   Selection sort concept

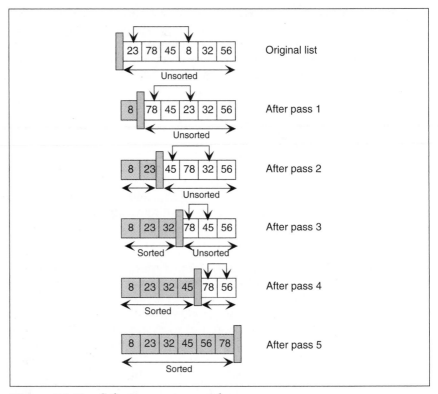

Figure 11-9   Selection sort example

Figure 11-9 traces our set of six integers as we sort them. It shows how the wall between the sorted and unsorted sublists moves in each pass. As you study the figure, you will see that the array is sorted after five passes, one less than the number of elements in the array. Thus, if we use a loop to control the sorting, our loop has one less iteration than the number of elements in the array.

Selection Sort Algorithm

If you knew nothing about sorting and were asked to sort a list on paper, you would undoubtedly scan the list to locate the smallest item and then copy it to a second list. You would then repeat the process of locating the smallest remaining item in the list and copying it to the new list until you had copied all items to the sorted list.

With the exception of using two areas, this is exactly how the selection sort works. Starting with the first item in the list, the algorithm scans the list for the smallest element and exchanges it with the item at the beginning of the list. Each selection and exchange is one sort pass. After advancing the index (wall), the sort continues until the list is completely sorted. The pseudocode is shown in Algorithm 11-3.

```
algorithm selectionSort (ref list  <array>,
                         val last  <index>)
Sorts list[0...last] by selecting smallest element in unsorted
portion of array and exchanging it with element at the
beginning of the unsorted list.
    Pre   list must contain at least one item
          last contains index to last element in the list
    Post  list has been rearranged smallest to largest
1 current = 0
2 loop (current < last)
   1   smallest = current
   2   walker = current + 1
   3   loop (walker <= last)
       1   if (list[walker] < list[smallest])
           1   smallest = walker
       2   walker = walker + 1
   4   end loop
   Smallest selected: exchange with current element.
   5   exchange (list, current, smallest)
   6   current = current + 1
3 end loop
4 return
end selectionSort
```

Algorithm 11-3   Selection sort

Heap Sort

In Chapter 9 we studied heaps. Recall that a heap is a tree structure in which the root contains the largest (or smallest) element in the tree. (You may want to review Chapter 9 before studying heap sort.) As a quick review, Figure 11-10 shows a heap in its tree form and in its array form.

The **heap sort** algorithm is an improved version of straight selection sort. The straight selection sort algorithm scans the unsorted elements and selects the smallest element. Finding the smallest element among the n elements requires $n - 1$ comparisons. This part of the selection sort makes it very slow.

The heap sort also selects an element from the unsorted portion of the list, but it is the largest element. Because the heap is a tree structure, however, we don't need to scan the entire list to locate the largest key. Rather, we reheap, which moves the largest element to the root by following tree branches. This ability to follow branches makes the heap sort much faster than the straight selection sort.

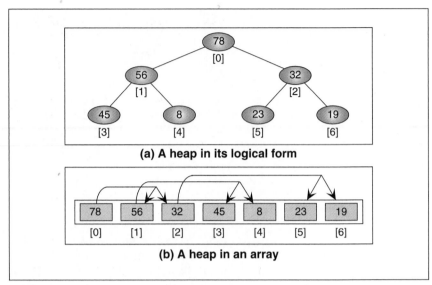

Figure 11-10   Heap representations

Heap sort begins by turning the array to be sorted into a heap. The array is turned into a heap only once for each sort. We then exchange the root, which is the largest element in the heap, with the last element in the unsorted list. This exchange results in the largest element being added to the beginning of the sorted list. We then reheap down to reconstruct the heap and exchange again. The reheap and exchange process continues until the entire list is sorted.

Note

> The heap sort is an improved version of the selection sort in which the largest element (the root) is selected and exchanged with the last element in the unsorted list.

The heap sort process is shown in Figure 11-11. We first turn the unordered list into a heap. You should verify for yourself that the array is actually a heap.

Because the largest element (78) is at the top of the heap, we can exchange it with the last element in the heap and move the heap wall one element to the left. This exchange places the largest element in its correct location at the end of the array, but it destroys the heap. We therefore rebuild the heap. The smaller heap now has its largest element (56) at the top. We exchange 56 with the element at the end of the heap (23), which places 56 in its correct location in the sorted array. The reheap and exchange processing continues until we have sorted the entire array.

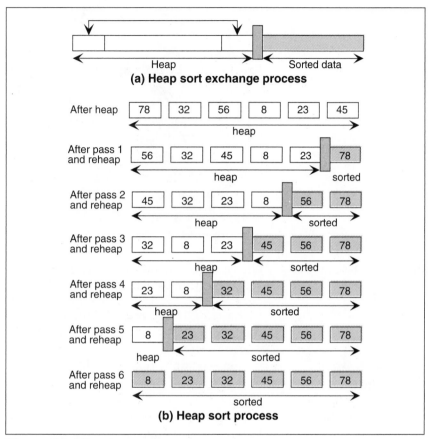

Figure 11-11 Heap sort process

Heap Sort Algorithm

Algorithm 11-4 contains the pseudocode for heap sort. It uses two algorithms defined in Chapter 9, Algorithm 9-1, "reheapUp," on page 414, and Algorithm 9-2, "reheapDown," on page 415.

```
algorithm heapSort (ref heap <array>,
                    val last <index>)
Sort an array, list[0 ... last], using a heap.
    Pre    array is filled
           last is index to last element in array
    Post   array has been sorted
Create heap
 1 walker = 1
 2 loop (walker <= last)
```

Algorithm 11-4 Heap sort

```
    1   reheapUp (heap, walker)
    2   walker = walker + 1
  3 end loop
Heap created. Now sort it.
  4 sorted = last
  5 loop (sorted > 0)
    1   exchange (heap, 0, sorted)
    2   sorted = sorted - 1
    3   reheapDown (heap, 0, sorted)
  6 end loop
  7 return
end heapSort
```

Algorithm 11-4   Heap sort *(continued)*

Algorithm 11-4 Analysis

Whereas the heap-array structure is relatively complex, the heap sort algorithm is deceptively simple. The algorithm begins by using `reheapUp` to turn the array into a heap. It then sorts the array by exchanging the element at the top of the heap with the element at the end of the heap and rebuilding the heap using `reheapDown`.

Selection Sort Algorithms

In this section, we examine the sort efficiency for the selection sorts.

Straight Selection Sort

The code for the straight selection sort is found in Algorithm 11-3, "Selection Sort," on page 519. It contains the two loops shown below.

```
  2   loop (current < last)
      ...
    3   loop (walker <= last)
```

The outer loop executes $n - 1$ times. The inner loop also executes $n - 1$ times. This is a classic example of the quadratic loop. Its search effort, using big-O notation, is $O(n^2)$.

Note

> The straight selection sort efficiency is $O(n^2)$.

Heap Sort

The heap sort code is shown in Algorithm 11-4. Ignoring the effort required to build the heap initially, the sort contains two loops. The first is a simple iterative loop; the second is a recursive loop:

```
5   loop (sorted > 0)
    ...
3     reheapDown (heap, 0, sorted)
```

The outer loop starts at the end of the array and moves through the heap one element at a time until it reaches the first element. It therefore loops n times. The inner loop follows a branch down a binary tree from the root to a leaf or until the parent and child data are in heap order. The probability of the data being in order before we reach the leaf is very small so we will ignore it. The difficult part of this analysis is that for each of the outer loops, the heap becomes smaller, shortening the path from the root to a leaf. Again, except for the largest of heaps, this factor is rather minor and will be eliminated in big-O analysis; therefore, we will ignore it also.

Following the branches of a binary tree from a root to a leaf requires $\log_2 n$ loops. The sort effort, the outer loop times the inner loop, for the heap sort is therefore

$$n(\log_2 n)$$

When we include the processing to create the original heap, the big-O notation is the same. Creating the heap requires $n\log_2 n$ loops through the data. When factored into the sort effort, it becomes a coefficient, which is then dropped to determine the final sort effort.

Note

The heap sort efficiency is $O(n\log_2 n)$.

Summary

Our analysis leads to the conclusion that the heap sort is more efficient than the other sorts we have discussed. The straight insertion and straight selection sorts are both $O(n^2)$ sorts, the shell sort is $O(n^{1.25})$, and the heap sort is $O(n\log_2 n)$. Table 11-2 offers a comparison of the sorts. Note that according to a strict mathematical interpretation of the big-O notation, heap sort surpasses shell sort in efficiency as we approach 2000 elements to be sorted. Remember two points, however: First, big-O is a rounded approximation; all coefficients and many of the factors have been removed. Second, big-O is based on an analytical evaluation of the algorithms, not an evaluation of the code. Depending on the algorithm's implementation, the actual run time can be affected.

	Number of Loops		
n	Straight Insertion Straight Selection	Shell	Heap
25	625	55	116
100	10,000	316	664
500	250,000	2364	4482
1000	1,000,000	5623	9965
2000	4,000,000	13,374	10,965

Table 11-2 Comparison of insertion and selection sorts

Selection Sort Implementation

We now turn our attention to implementing the selection sort algorithms in C++. We first implement the straight selection sort and then the heap sort.

Selection Sort C++ Code

The code for the selection sort is shown in Program 11-3.

```
 1  /* ==================== selectionSort ====================
 2     Sorts list[0...last] by selecting smallest element in
 3     unsorted portion of array and exchanging it with element
 4     at the beginning of the unsorted list.
 5        Pre   list must contain at least one item
 6              last contains index to last element in the list
 7        Post list has been rearranged smallest to largest
 8  */
 9  void selectionSort  (int list[],
10                            int last)
11  {
12  // Local Definitions
13     int current;
14     int smallest;
15     int holdData;
16     int walker;
17
18  // Statements
19     for (current = 0; current < last; current++)
20        {
21         smallest = current;
22         for (walker = current + 1;
23              walker <= last;
24              walker++)
25           if (list[walker] < list[smallest])
26              smallest = walker;
```

Program 11-3   Selection sort

```
27
28              // Smallest selected: exchange with current
29              holdData        = list[current];
30              list[current]   = list[smallest];
31              list[smallest]  = holdData;
32          } //  for current
33      return;
34  } // selectionSort
```

Program 11-3   Selection sort *(continued)*

Heap Sort C++ Code

The heap sort program requires a driver function, which we call heap sort, and two functions we disccused earlier, reheap up and reheap down. We have tailored them here for the sorting process.

Heap Sort Function

The heap sort function accepts an array of unsorted data and an index to the last element in the array. It then creates a heap and sorts it using reheap up and reheap down. The heap sort algorithm is shown in Program 11-4.

```
1   /* ===================== heapSort =====================
2      Sort an array, list[0...last], using a heap.
3          Pre    list must contain at least one item
4                 last contains index to last element in the list
5          Post   list has been rearranged smallest to largest
6   */
7   void heapSort  (int  list[],
8                   int  last)
9   {
10  // Local Definitions
11     int sorted;
12     int holdData;
13     int walker;
14
15  // Statements
16     // Create heap
17     for (walker = 1; walker <= last; walker++)
18         reheapUp (list, walker);
19
20  // Heap created. Now sort it.
21     sorted = last;
22     while (sorted > 0)
23         {
24         holdData    = list[0];
25         list[0]     = list[sorted];
26         list[sorted] = holdData;
```

Program 11-4   Heap sort

```
27          sorted--;
28          reheapDown (list, 0, sorted);
29        } // while
30    return;
31  } // heapSort
```

Program 11-4   Heap sort *(continued)*

Program 11-4 Analysis   The heap sort implementation follows the pseudocode closely. Using an index, we walk through the array, calling reheap up to create the heap. Once the heap has been created, we exchange the element at the top of the heap with the last element in the heap and adjust the heap size down by 1. We then call reheap down to recreate the heap by moving the root element down the tree to its correct location.

11-4   EXCHANGE SORTS

The third category of sorts, exchange sorting, contains the most common sort taught in computer science, the bubble sort, and the most efficient general-purpose sort, quick sort. In exchange sorts, we exchange elements that are out of order until the entire list is sorted. Although virtually every sorting method uses some form of exchange, the sorts in this section use it extensively.

Bubble Sort

In the **bubble sort**, the list at any moment is divided into two sublists: sorted and unsorted. The smallest element is bubbled from the unsorted sublist and moved to the sorted sublist. After moving the smallest to the sorted list, the wall moves one element to the right, increasing the number of sorted elements and decreasing the number of unsorted ones (Figure 11-12). Each time an element moves from the unsorted sublist to the sorted sublist, one sort pass is completed. Given a list of n elements, bubble sort requires up to $n - 1$ passes to sort the data.

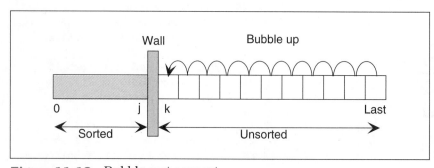

Figure 11-12   Bubble sort concept

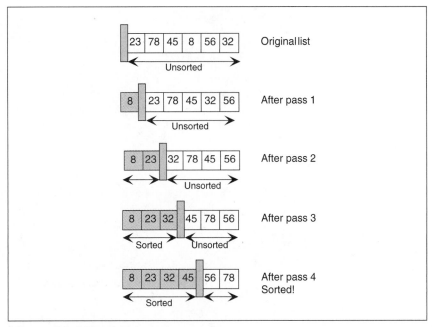

Figure 11-13 Bubble sort example

Figure 11-13 shows how the wall moves one element in each pass. Looking at the first pass, we start with 32 and compare it with 56. Because 32 is less than 56, we exchange the two and step down one element. We then compare 32 and 8. Because 32 is not less than 8, we do not exchange these elements. We step down one element and compare 45 and 8. They are out of sequence, so we exchange them and step down again. Because we moved 8 down, it is now compared with 78 and these two elements are exchanged. Finally, 8 is compared with 23 and exchanged. This series of exchanges places 8 in the first location and the wall is moved up one position.

Note

In each pass of the bubble sort, the smallest element is bubbled from the unsorted sublist and moved to the sorted sublist.

Bubble Sort Algorithm

Like the insertion and selection sorts, the bubble sort is quite simple. In each pass through the data, the smallest element is bubbled to the beginning of the unsorted segment of the array. In the process, adjacent elements that are out of order are exchanged, partially ordering the data. When the smallest element is encountered, it is automatically bubbled to the beginning of the unsorted list. The sort then continues by making another pass through the unsorted list. The code for bubble sort is shown in Algorithm 11-5.

```
algorithm bubbleSort (ref list <array>,
                      val last <index>)
Sort an array, list[0...last], using bubble sort. Adjacent
elements are compared and exchanged until list is
completely ordered.
   Pre    list must contain at least one item
          last contains index to last element in the list
   Post   list has been rearranged in sequence low to high
1 current  = 0
2 sorted   = false
3 loop (current <= last AND sorted false)
  Each iteration is one sort pass.
  1   walker  = last
  2   sorted  = true
  3   loop (walker > current)
      1   if (list[walker] < list[walker - 1])
          Any exchange means list is not sorted.
          1   sorted = false
          2   exchange (list, walker, walker - 1)
      2   end if
      3   walker = walker - 1
  4   end loop
  5   current = current + 1
4 end loop
5 return
end bubbleSort
```

Algorithm 11-5   Bubble sort

Algorithm 11-5 Analysis

If you have studied other bubble sort algorithms, you may have noticed a slight improvement in this version of the sort. If an exchange is not made in a pass (Statement 3), then we know the list is already sorted and the sort can stop. At Statement 3.2, we set a Boolean, `sorted`, to true. If at any time during the pass an exchange is made, `sorted` is changed to false, indicating that the list was not sorted when the pass began.

Another difference you may have noticed is that we started from the high end and bubbled down. As a historical note, the bubble sort was originally written to "bubble up" the highest element in the list. From an efficiency point of view, it makes no difference whether the largest element is bubbled down or the smallest element is bubbled up. From a consistency point of view, however, comparisons between the sorts are easier if all three of our basic sorts (insertion, selection, and exchange) work in the same manner. For that reason, we have chosen to bubble the lowest key in each pass.

Quick Sort

In the bubble sort, consecutive items are compared and possibly exchanged on each pass through the list, which means that many exchanges may be needed to move an element to its correct position. **Quick sort** is an exchange sort developed by C. A. R. Hoare in 1962. It is more efficient than the bubble sort because a typical exchange involves elements that are far apart, so fewer exchanges are required to correctly position an element.

Each iteration of the quick sort selects an element, known as **pivot,** and divides the list into three groups: a partition of elements whose keys are less than the pivot's key, the pivot element that is placed in its ultimately correct location in the list, and a partition of elements greater than or equal to the pivot's key. The sorting then continues by quick sorting the left partition followed by quick sorting the right partition. This partitioning is shown in Figure 11-14.

Hoare's original algorithm selected the pivot key as the first element in the list. In 1969, R. C. Singleton improved the sort by selecting the pivot key as the median value of three elements: left, right, and an element in the middle of the list. Once the median value is determined, it is exchanged with the left element. We implement Singleton's variation of quick sort.

Note

> Quick sort is an exchange sort in which a pivot key is placed in its correct position in the array while rearranging other elements widely dispersed across the list.

Knuth suggests that when the sort partition becomes small, a straight insertion sort be used to complete the sorting of the partition.[8] Although the mathematics to optimally choose the minimum partition size are quite complex, the partition size should be relatively small; we recommend 16.

Quick Sort Algorithm

We are now ready to develop the algorithm. As you may have anticipated from our discussion, we will use a recursive algorithm for quick sort. In addition to the basic algorithm, two supporting algorithms are required, one to determine the pivot element and one for the straight insertion sort. We discuss these two algorithms first.

8. Donald E. Knuth, *The Art of Computer Programming*, vol. 3, *Sorting and Searching* (Reading, MA: Addison-Wesley, 1973), 116.

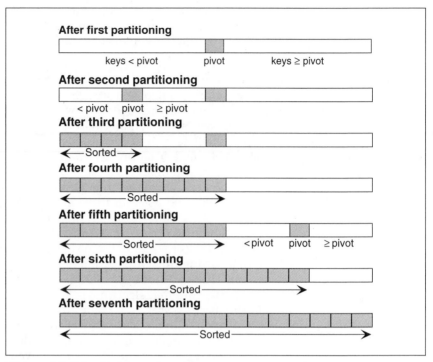

Figure 11-14   Quick sort partitions

Straight Insertion Module   The straight insertion sort is a minor variation on the algorithm developed earlier, which always sorted a list beginning at location 0. Because the partition to be sorted in the quick sort can be found anywhere in the array, we must be able to sort partitions beginning at locations other than 0. We therefore add a parameter that specifies the starting location of the location to be sorted in addition to its ending location. The modified code is shown in Algorithm 11-6.

```
algorithm quickInsertion (ref list   <array>,
                          val first  <index>,
                          val last   <index>)
Sort list[first...last] using insertion sort. The list is divided
into sorted and unsorted lists. With each pass, first element
in unsorted list is inserted into sorted list. This is a special
version of the insertion sort modified for use with quick sort.
    Pre    list must contain at least one element
           first is an index to first element in the list
           last is an index to last element in the list
```

Algorithm 11-6   Quick sort's straight insertion sort module

```
    Post    list has been rearranged
1 current = first + 1
2 loop (current <= last)
    1   hold   = list[current]
    2   walker = current - 1
    3   loop (walker >= first AND hold.key < list[walker].key)
        1   list[walker + 1] = list[walker]
        2   walker           = walker - 1
    4   end loop
    5   list[walker + 1] = hold
    6   current = current + 1
3 end loop
4 return
end quickInsertion
```

Algorithm 11-6   Quick sort's straight insertion sort module *(continued)*

Determine Median of Three

The logic to select the median location requires three tests. First, we test the left and middle elements; if they are out of sequence, we exchange them. Then, we test the left and right elements; if they are out of sequence, we exchange them. Finally, we test the middle and right elements; if they are out of sequence, we exchange them. At this point, the three elements are in order.

$$\text{array[left]} \le \text{array[middle]} \le \text{array[right]}$$

We see, therefore, that this logic is based on the logical proposition that if a is less than b and b is less than c, then a is less than c. Finally, before we leave the algorithm, we exchange the left and middle elements, thus positioning the median valued element at the left of the array. The pseudocode is shown in Algorithm 11-7.

```
algorithm medianLeft (ref sortData  <array>,
                      val left       <index>,
                      val right      <index>)
Find the median value of an array, sortData [left ... right], and
place it in the location sortData[left].
    Pre    sortData is an array of at least three elements
           left and right are the boundaries of the array
    Post   median value located and placed at sortData[left]
Rearrange sortData so median value is in middle location.
```

Algorithm 11-7   Median left

```
1 mid = (left + right)/2
2 if (sortData[left].key > sortData[mid].key)
     1   exchange (sortData, left, mid)
3 end if
4 if (sortData[left].key > sortData[right].key)
     1   exchange (sortData, left, right)
5 end if
6 if (sortData[mid].key > sortData[right].key)
     1   exchange (sortData, mid, right)
7 end if
Median is in middle location. Exchange with left.
8 exchange (sortData, left, mid)
9 return
end medianLeft
```

Algorithm 11-7   Median left *(continued)*

Algorithm 11-7 Analysis

The logic to determine a median value can become unintelligible very quickly. The beauty of this algorithm is its simplicity. It approaches the determination of the median value by performing a very simple sort on the three elements, placing the median in the middle location. It then exchanges the middle element with the left element.

Quick Sort Algorithm

We now turn our attention to the quick sort algorithm itself. It contains an interesting program design that you will find useful in other array applications. To determine the correct position for the pivot element, we work from the two ends of the array toward the middle. Because we have used the median value of three elements to determine the pivot element, the pivot may end up near the middle of the array, although this is not guaranteed. Quick sort is most efficient when the pivot's location is the middle of the array. The technique of working from the ends to the middle is shown in Figure 11-15.

As you study Figure 11-15, note that before the exchanges start, the median element is in the middle position and the smallest of the three elements used to determine the median is in the right location. After calling the median left algorithm, the median is in the left position and the smallest is in the middle location. The pivot key is then moved to a hold area to facilitate the processing. This move is actually the first part of an exchange that will put the pivot key in its correct location.

To help follow the sort, envision two walls, one on the left just after the pivot and one on the right (see Figure 11-15). We start at the left wall and move right while looking for an element that belongs on the right of the pivot. We locate one at element 97. After finding an element on the left that belongs on the right, we start at the right wall and move left while looking for an element that belongs on the left of the pivot.

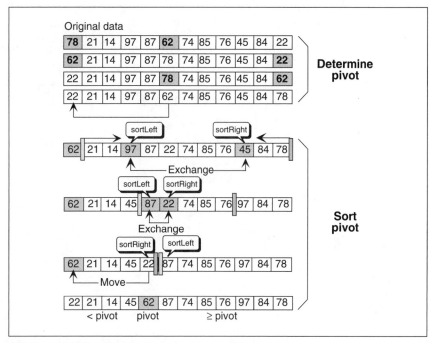

Original data

Figure 11-15 Quick sort pivot

We find one at element 45. At this point we exchange the two elements, move the walls to the left of element 87 and the right of element 76, and repeat the process.

This time, as we move to the right, the first left element, 87, belongs on the right. When we move down from the right, we find that element 22 belongs on the left. Again, we exchange the left and right elements and move the wall. At this point, we note that the walls have crossed. We have thus located the correct position for the pivot element. We move the data in the pivot's location to the first element of the array and then move the pivot back to the array, completing the exchange we started when we moved the pivot key to the hold area. The list has now been rearranged so that the pivot element (62) is in its correct location in the array relative to all of the other elements in the array. The elements on the left of the pivot are all less than the pivot, and the elements on the right of the pivot are all greater than the pivot. Any equal data would be found on the right of the pivot.

After placing the pivot key in its correct location, we recursively call quick sort to sort the left partition. When the left partition is completely sorted, we recursively call quick sort to sort the right partition. When both the left partition and the right partition have been sorted, the list is completely sorted. The data in Figure 11-15 are completely sorted using only quick sort in Figure 11-16. The pseudocode is shown in Algorithm 11-8.

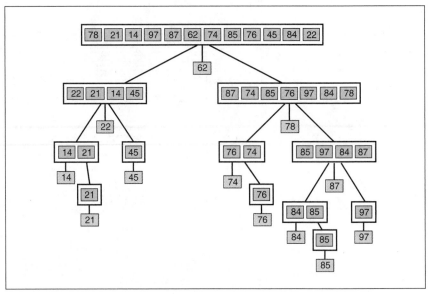

Figure 11-16   Quick sort operation

```
algorithm quickSort (ref list  <array>,
                     val left  <index>,
                     val right <index>)
An array, list [left...right] is sorted using recursion.
    Pre    list is an array of data to be sorted
           left and right identify the first and last elements
           of the list, respectively
    Post   list is sorted
  1 if ((right - left) > minSize)
    quick sort
    1   medianLeft (list, left, right)
    2   pivot           =  list [left]
    3   sortLeft        =  left + 1
    4   sortRight       =  right
    5   loop (sortLeft  <= sortRight)
        Find key on left that belongs on right
        1   loop (list[sortLeft].key < pivot.key)
            1   sortLeft = sortLeft + 1
        2   end loop
        Find key on right that belongs on left
        3   loop (list[sortRight].key >= pivot.key)
```

Algorithm 11-8   Quick sort

```
        1   sortRight = sortRight - 1
    4   end loop
    5   if (sortLeft <= sortRight)
        1   exchange(list, sortLeft, sortRight)
        2   sortLeft   =   sortLeft + 1
        3   sortRight  =   sortRight - 1
    6   end if
6   end loop
Prepare for next phase
7   list [left]            = list [sortLeft - 1]
8   list [sortLeft - 1]  = pivot
9   if  (left < sortRight)
    1   quickSort (list, left, sortRight - 1)
10  end if
11  if (sortLeft < right)
    1   quickSort (list, sortLeft, right)
12  end if
2 else
    1   insertionSort (list, left, right)
3 end if
4 end quickSort
```

Algorithm 11-8   Quick sort *(continued)*

Algorithm 11-8 Analysis   In addition to the design that works from both ends to the middle, two aspects of this algorithm merit further discussion. The loops used to determine the sort left and sort right elements (Statements 1.5.1 and 1.5.3) test only one condition. Most loops that process an array must also test for the end of the array, but we can omit the test in this algorithm based on selection of the pivot key. The pivot key is guaranteed to be the median value of three elements, the first, the last, and the one in the middle. Therefore, the median key cannot be less than the leftmost key nor greater than the rightmost key. At worst, it will be equal to the leftmost or rightmost key.

Assume that we had the worst case: all of the elements in a partition have the same key value. In this case, the pivot key would be equal to the leftmost and the rightmost keys. When we start on the left to move up the list, we stop immediately because the pivot key is equal to the sortLeft key. When we then start on the right and move down, we will move beyond the beginning of the list when all keys are equal. However, because the two elements have crossed, we will not exchange elements. Rather, we will move to Statement 1.7. In this case, we never use the sort right index that has moved off the beginning of the array.

Hoare's original algorithm was not recursive. Because he had to maintain a stack, he incorporated logic to ensure that the stack size was kept to a minimum. Rather than simply sort the left partition, he determined which partition was larger and put it in the stack while he sorted the smaller partition. We are not concerned with minimizing the stack size for two reasons. First, we have chosen the pivot key to be the median value. Therefore, the size of the two partitions should be generally the same, thus minimizing the number of recursive calls. More important, because we are using recursion, we do not need to determine the size of the stack in advance. We simply call on the system to provide stack space.

Exchange Sort Algorithms

In the exchange sorts we find what Knuth called the best general-purpose sort, quick sort. Let's determine their sort efforts to see why.

Bubble Sort

The code for the bubble sort is shown in Algorithm 11-5, "Bubble Sort," on page 528. As we saw with the straight insertion and straight selection sorts, it uses two loops to sort the data. The loops are shown below.

```
3   loop (current <= last AND sorted false)
    ...
3   loop (walker > current)
```

The outer loop tests two conditions, the current index and a sorted flag. Assuming that the list is not sorted until the last pass, we loop through the array n times. The number of loops in the inner loop depends on the current location in the outer loop. It therefore loops through half the list on the average. The total number of loops is the product of both loops, making the bubble sort efficiency

$$n\left(\frac{n+1}{2}\right)$$

In big-O notation, the bubble sort efficiency is $O(n^2)$.

Note

> The bubble sort efficiency is $O(n^2)$.

Quick Sort

The code for the quick sort is shown in Algorithm 11-8, "Quick Sort," on page 534. A quick look at the algorithm reveals that there are five loops (three iterative loops and two recursive loops). The algorithm also contains the straight insertion sort as a subroutine. Because it is possible to use the quick sort to completely sort the data—that is, it is possible to eliminate the insertion sort—we analyze the quick sort portion as though the insertion sort weren't used. The quick sort loops are shown below.

```
5    loop (sortLeft <= sortRight)
     ...
     1   loop (list[sortLeft].key < pivot.key)
         ...
     2   end loop
     3   loop (list[sortRight].key >= pivot.key)
         ...
     4   end loop
     ...
6    end loop
9    if (left < sortRight)
     1   quickSort (list, left, sortRight - 1)
10   end if
11   if (sortLeft < right)
     1    quickSort (list, sortLeft, right)
12   if (sortLeft < right)
```

Recall that each pass in the quick sort divides the list into three parts, a list of elements smaller than the pivot key, the pivot key, and a list of elements greater than the pivot key. The first loop (Statement 5), in conjunction with the two nested loops (Statements 5.1 and 5.3), looks at each element in the portion of the array being sorted. Statement 5.1 loops through the left portion of the list; Statement 5.3 loops through the right portion of the list. Together, therefore, they loop through the list n times.

Similarly, the two recursive loops process one portion of the array each, either on the left or the right of the pivot key. The question is how many times they are called. Recall that we said that quick sort is most efficient when the pivot key is in the middle of the array. That's why we used a median value. Assuming that it is located relatively close to the center, we see that we have divided the list into two sublists of roughly the same size. Because we are dividing by 2, the number of loops is logarithmic. The total sort effort is therefore the product of the first loop times the recursive loops, or $n\log_2 n$.

Note

> The quick sort efficiency is $O(n\log_2 n)$.

Algorithmics does not explain why we use the straight insertion sort when the list is small. The answer lies in the algorithm code and the overhead of recursion. When the list becomes sufficiently small, it is simply more efficient to use a straight insertion sort.

11-5   SUMMARY

Our analysis leads to the conclusion that the quick sort's efficiency is the same as that of the heap sort. This is true because big-O notation is only an approximation of the actual sort efficiency. Although both are on the order of $n\log_2 n$, if we were to develop more accurate formulas to reflect their actual efficiency, we would see that the quick sort is actually more efficient. Table 11-3 summarizes the six sorts we discuss in this chapter.

	Number of Loops		
n	Straight Insertion Straight Selection Bubble Sorts	Shell	Heap and Quick
25	625	55	116
100	10,000	316	664
500	250,000	2364	4482
1000	1,000,000	5623	9965
2000	4,000,000	13,374	10,965

Table 11-3 Sort comparisons

We recommend that you use the straight insertion sort for small lists and the quick sort for large lists. Although the shell sort is an interesting sort that played an important role in the history of sorts, we would not recommend it in most cases. As you will see when we discuss external sorting, algorithms such as the heap sort play an important niche role in special situations and for that reason also belong in your sorting tool kit.

Exchange Sort Implementation

Let's look at the C++ code for the bubble sort and quick sort algorithms.

Bubble Sort Code

The bubble sort code is shown in Program 11-5.

```
1  /* ==================== bubbleSort ====================
2     Sort list using bubble sort. Adjacent elements are
3     compared and exchanged until list completely ordered.
4        Pre    list must contain at least one item
5               last contains index to last element in list
6        Post   list rearranged in sequence low to high
7  */
```

Program 11-5 Bubble sort

```
 8  void bubbleSort  (int list [],
 9                       int last)
10  {
11  // Local Definitions
12     int    current;
13     int    walker;
14     int    temp;
15     bool   sorted;
16
17  // Statements
18     // Each iteration is one sort pass
19     for (current = 0, sorted = false;
20          current <= last && !sorted;
21          current++)
22       for (walker = last, sorted = true;
23            walker > current;
24            walker--)
25         if (list[walker]  < list[walker - 1])
26            // Any exchange means list is not sorted
27            {
28             sorted             = false;
29             temp               = list[walker];
30             list[walker]       = list[walker - 1];
31             list[walker - 1]   = temp;
32            } // if
33     return;
34  } // bubbleSort
```

Program 11-5   Bubble sort *(continued)*

Quick Sort Code

In this section we implement the three quick sort algorithms described earlier. The sort array is once again a simple array of integers.

The first function is quick sort, shown in Program 11-6. The modified version of the straight insertion sort is shown in Program 11-7, and the median function is shown in Program 11-8.

```
 1  /* Array sortData[left..right] is sorted using recursion.
 2       Pre    sortData is an array of data to be sorted
 3              left identifies the first element of sortData
 4              right identifies the last element of sortData
 5       Post   sortData array is sorted
 6  */
 7  void quickSort  (int   sortData[],
 8                    int   left,
 9                    int   right)
10  {
```

Program 11-6   Quick sort

```
11   #define MIN_SIZE 4
12
13   // Local Definitions
14      int sortLeft;
15      int sortRight;
16      int pivot;
17      int hold;
18
19   // Statements
20      if ((right - left) > MIN_SIZE)
21         // quick sort
22         {
23          medianLeft (sortData, left, right);
24          pivot      = sortData [left];
25          sortLeft   = left + 1;
26          sortRight  = right;
27
28          while (sortLeft <= sortRight)
29             {
30              // Find key on left that belongs on right
31              while (sortData [sortLeft] < pivot)
32                 sortLeft++;
33              // Find key on right that belongs on left
34              while (sortData[sortRight] >= pivot)
35                 sortRight--;
36              if (sortLeft <= sortRight)
37                 {
38                  hold = sortData[sortLeft];
39                  sortData[sortLeft]    = sortData[sortRight];
40                  sortData[sortRight]   = hold;
41                  sortLeft++;
42                  sortRight--;
43                 } /* if */
44             } // while
45          // Prepare for next phase
46          sortData [left] = sortData [sortLeft - 1];
47          sortData [sortLeft - 1] = pivot;
48          if  (left     < sortRight)
49              quickSort (sortData, left, sortRight - 1);
50          if (sortLeft < right)
51              quickSort (sortData, sortLeft, right);
52         } // if right > minimum
53      else
54          quickInsertion (sortData, left, right);
55      return;
56   } // end quickSort
```

Program 11-6 Quick sort *(continued)*

```
 1  /* Sort list[0...last] using insertion sort. The list is
 2     divided into sorted and unsorted lists. With each pass,
 3     first element in unsorted list is inserted into sorted
 4     list. This is a special version of the insertion sort
 5     modified for use with quick sort.
 6        Pre    list must contain at least one element
 7               first is an index to first element in the list
 8               last is an index to last element in the list
 9        Post   list has been rearranged
10  */
11  void quickInsertion (int sortData[],
12                       int first,
13                       int last)
14  {
15  // Local Definitions
16     int current;
17     int hold;
18     int walker;
19
20  // Statements
21     for (current = first + 1;
22          current <= last;
23          current++)
24        {
25         hold    = sortData[current];
26         walker  = current - 1;
27         while (walker >= first
28             && hold   <   sortData[walker])
29            {
30             sortData[walker + 1] = sortData[walker];
31             walker--;
32            } // while
33         sortData[walker + 1] = hold;
34        } // for
35     return;
36  } // end quickInsertion
```

Program 11-7   Modified straight insertion sort for quick sort

```
 1  /* Find the median value of an array, sortData[left..right],
 2     and place it in the location sortData[left].
 3        Pre  sortData is an array of at least three elements
 4             left and right are the boundaries of the array
 5        Post median value placed at sortData[left]
 6  */
```

Program 11-8   Median left for quick sort

```
 7   void medianLeft (int sortData[],
 8                    int left,
 9                    int right)
10   {
11   // Local Definitions
12      int mid;
13      int hold;
14
15   // Statements
16      //  Rearrange sortData so median is in middle location
17      mid = (left + right) / 2;
18      if (sortData[left] > sortData[mid])
19         {
20          hold            = sortData[left];
21          sortData[left]  = sortData[mid];
22          sortData[mid]   = hold;
23         } // if
24      if (sortData[left] > sortData[right])
25         {
26          hold            = sortData[left];
27          sortData[left]  = sortData[right];
28          sortData[right] = hold;
29         } // if
30      if (sortData[mid]  > sortData[right])
31         {
32          hold            = sortData[mid];
33          sortData[mid]   = sortData[right];
34          sortData[right] = hold;
35         } // if
36      // Median is in middle. Exchange with left.
37      hold            = sortData[left];
38      sortData[left]  = sortData[mid];
39      sortData[mid]   = hold;
40
41      return;
42   } // medianLeft
```

Program 11-8   Median left for quick sort *(continued)*

11-6   EXTERNAL SORTS

All of the algorithms we have studied so far have been internal sorts—that is, sorts that require the data to be entirely sorted in primary memory during the sorting process. We now turn our attention to external sorting, sorts that allow portions of the data to be stored in secondary memory during the sorting process.

The term *external sorting* is somewhat of a misnomer. Most of the work spent ordering large files is not sorting but actually merging. To understand external sorting, therefore, we must first understand the merge concept.

Merging Ordered Files

A **merge** is the process that combines two files ordered on a given key into one ordered file on the same given key. A simple example is shown in Figure 11-17.

File 1 and file 2 are to be merged into file 3. To merge the files, we compare the first record in file 1 with the first record in file 2 and write the smaller one, 1, to file 3. We then compare the second record in file 1 with the first record in file 2 and write the smaller one, 2, to file 3. The process continues until all data have been merged in order into file 3. The logic to merge these two files, which is relatively simple, is shown in Algorithm 11-9.

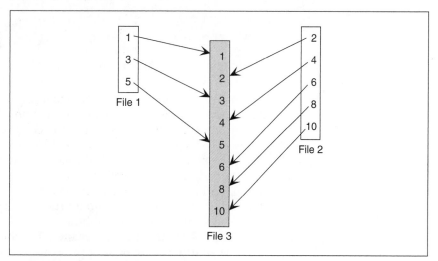

Figure 11-17   A simple merge

```
algorithm mergeFiles
Merge two ordered files into one file.
    Pre     input files are ordered
    Post    input files sequentially combined in output file
 1 open files
 2 read (file1 into record1)
 3 read (file2 into record2)
 4 loop (not end file1 OR not end file2)
```

Algorithm 11-9   Merge files

```
    1   if (record1.key <= record2.key)
        1   write   (file3 from record1)
        2   read    (file1 into record1)
        3   if (end of file1)
            1   record1.key = +∞
        4   end if
    2   else
        1   write   (file3 from record2)
        2   read    (file2 into record2)
        3   if (end of file2)
            1   record2.key = +∞
        4   end if
    3   end if
  5 end loop
  6 close files
end mergeFiles
```

Algorithm 11-9   Merge files *(continued)*

Algorithm 11-9 Analysis

Although merge files is a relatively simple algorithm, one point is worth discussing. When one file reaches the end, there may be more data in the second file. We therefore need to keep processing until both files are at the end. We could write separate blocks of code to handle the end-of-file processing for each file, but there is a simpler method. When one file hits its end, we simply set its key value to an artificially high value. In the algorithm this value is identified as +∞ (see Statements 4.1.3.1 and 4.2.3.1). Then, when we compare the two keys (Statement 4.1), the file at the end will be forced high and the other file will be processed. The high value is often called a **sentinel.** The only limitation to this logic is that the sentinel value cannot be a valid data value.

Merging Unordered Files

In merge sorting, however, we usually have a different situation than that shown above: The input files are not completely sorted. The data will run in sequence, and then there will be a sequence break followed by another series of data in sequence. This situation is demonstrated in Figure 11-18.

The series of consecutively ordered data in a file is known as a **merge run.** In Figure 11-18, all three files have three merge runs. To make them easy to see, we have spaced and colored the merge runs in each file. A **stepdown** occurs when the sequential ordering of the records in a merge file is broken. The end of each merge run is identified by a stepdown. For example, in Figure 11-18, there is a stepdown in file 2 when key 16 in the first merge run is followed by key 9 in the

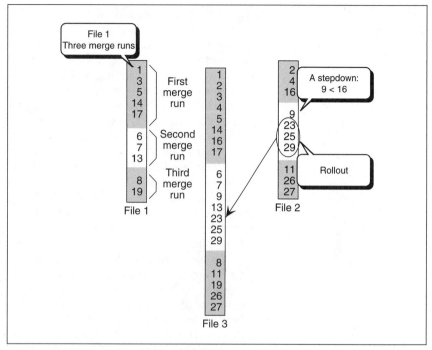

Figure 11-18   Merging files example

second merge run. An end of file is also considered a stepdown. Finally, in the merging of a file, the process of copying a consecutive series of records to the merge output file after a stepdown in the alternate merge input is known as a **rollout**. In Figure 11-18, after record 13 has been copied to the output file and a stepdown occurs, the remaining records (23, 25, and 29) in the second merge run in file 2 are rolled out to the merge output. Now let's look closely at the merge process in Figure 11-18. When merging files that are not completely ordered, we merge the corresponding merge runs from each file into a merge run in the output file. Thus, we see that merge run 1 in file 1 merges with merge run 1 in file 2 to produce merge run 1 in file 3. Similarly, merge runs 2 and 3 in the input files merge to produce merge runs 2 and 3 in the output.

When a stepdown is detected in an input merge file, the merge run in the alternate file must be rolled out to synchronize the two files. Thus, in merge run 2, when the stepdown between record 13 and record 8 is detected, we must roll out the remaining three records in file 2 so that we can begin merging the third merge runs.

Finally, it is important to note that the merge output is not a completely ordered file. In this particular case, two more merge runs are required. To see the complete process, we turn to a higher-level example.

The Sorting Process

Assume that a file of 2300 records needs to be sorted. In an external sort, we begin by sorting as many records as possible and creating two or more merge files. Assuming that the record size and the memory available for our sort program allow a maximum sort array size of 500 records, we begin by reading and sorting the first 500 records and writing them to a merge output file. As we sort the first 500 records, we keep the remaining 1800 records in secondary storage. After writing out the first merge run, we read the second 500 records, sort them, and write them to an alternate merge output file. We continue the sort process, writing 500 sorted records (records 1001 to 1500) to the first merge output file and another 500 sorted records (records 1501 to 2000) to the second merge output file. Finally, we sort the last 300 records and write them to the first output merge file. At this point we have created the situation we see in Figure 11-19. This first processing of the data into merge runs is known as the **sort phase**.

After completing the sort phase of an external sort, we proceed with the merge phase. Each complete reading and merging of the input merge files to one or more output merge files is considered a separate **merge phase.** Depending on how many merge runs are created, there will be zero or more merge phases. If all of the data fit into memory at one time, or if the file was sorted to begin with, then there will be only one merge run and the data on the first merge output file are completely sorted. This situation is the exception, however; several merge phases are generally required.

Computer scientists have developed many different merge concepts over the years. We present three that are representative: natural merge, balanced merge, and polyphase merge.

Natural Merge

A **natural merge** sorts a constant number of input merge files to one merge output file. Between each merge phase, a **distribution phase** is

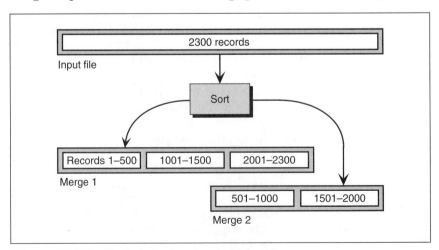

Figure 11-19   Sort phase in an external sort

required to redistribute the merge runs to the input files for remerging. Figure 11-20 is a diagram of our 2300 records as they would be sorted using a natural two-way merge—that is, a natural merge with two input merge files and one output merge file.

Note

> In the natural merge, each phase merges a constant number of input files into one output file.

In the natural merge, all merge runs are written to one file. Therefore, unless the file is completely ordered, the merge runs must be distributed to two merge files between each merge phase. This processing is very inefficient, especially because reading and writing records are among the slowest of all data processing. The question, therefore, is how can we make the merge process more efficient. The answer is found in the balanced merge.

Balanced Merge

A **balanced merge** uses a constant number of input merge files and the same number of output merge files. Any number of merge files can be used, although more than four is uncommon. Because multiple merge files are created in each merge phase, no distribution phase is required. Figure 11-21 sorts our 2300 records using a balanced two-way merge.

Note

> The balanced merge eliminates the distribution phase by using the same number of input and output merge files.

Four merge files are required in the balanced two-way merge. The first merge phase merges the first merge run on file 1 with the first merge run on file 2 and writes it to file 3. It then merges the second merge run on file 1 with the second merge run on file 2 and writes it to file 4. At this point, all of the merge runs on file 2 have been processed, so we roll out the remaining merge run on file 1 to merge file 3. This rollout of 300 records is wasted effort. We would like to be able to eliminate this step to make the merge processing as efficient as possible. We can if we use the polyphase merge.

Polyphase Merge

In the **polyphase merge**, a constant number of input merge files are merged to one output merge file and input merge files are immediately reused when their input has been completely merged. Polyphase merge is the most complex of the merge sorts we have discussed.

Note

> In the polyphase merge, a constant number of input files are merged to one output file. As the data in each input file are completely merged, it immediately becomes the output file and what was the output file becomes an input file.

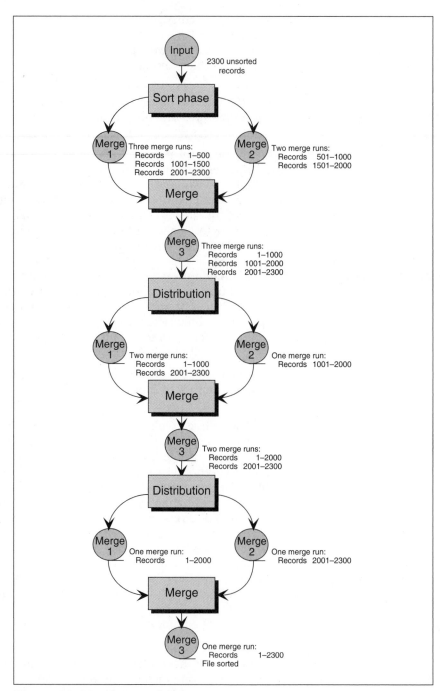

Figure 11-20 A natural two-way merge sort

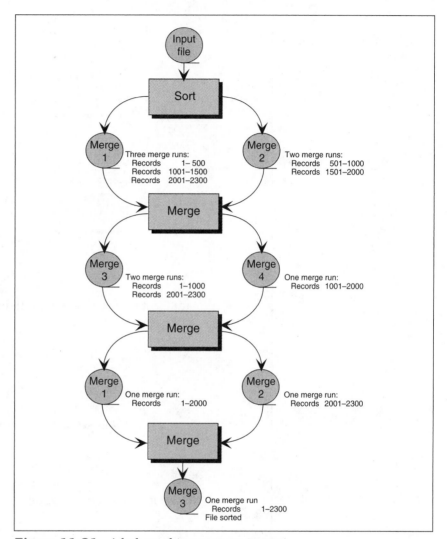

Figure 11-21 A balanced two-way merge sort

To demonstrate the process, let's study Figure 11-22 carefully. The processing begins as it does for the natural two-way merge. The first merge run on file 1 is merged with the first merge run on file 2. Then the second merge run on file 1 is merged with the second merge run on file 2. At this point, merge 2 is empty and the first merge phase is complete. We therefore close merge 2 and open it as output and close merge 3 and open it as input. The third merge run on file 1 is then merged with the first merge run on file 3, with the merged data being written to merge 2. Because merge 1 is empty, merge phase 2 is complete. We therefore close merge 1 and open it as output while closing

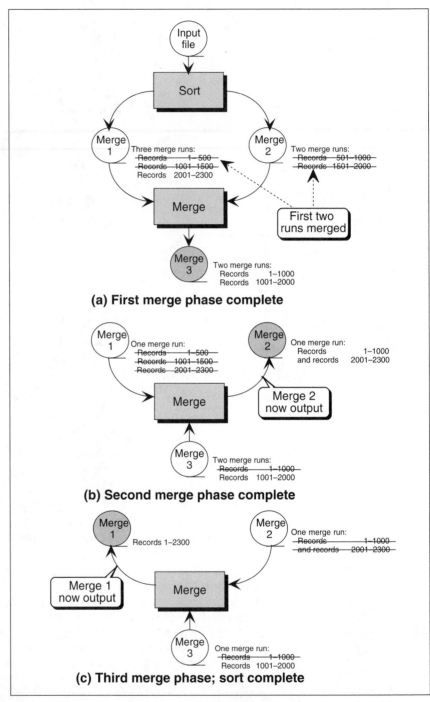

Figure 11-22   The polyphase merge sort

merge 2 and opening it as input. Because there is only one merge run on each of the input files, the sort is complete when these two merge runs have been merged to merge 1.

Sort Phase Revisited

With the polyphase sort, we have improved the merge phases as much as possible. We now return to the sort phase and try to improve it. Let's assume that we used the fastest possible sort in the sort phase. Even if we were able to double its internal sort speed, little would be gained. With today's modern computers operating in picosecond speeds and file processing operating in microsecond speeds, little is gained by improving the sort speed. In fact, the opposite is actually true. If we slow up the sort speed a little using a slower sort, we can actually improve overall speed. Let's see how this is done.

One class of sorts, tree sorts, allows us to start writing data to a merge file before the sort is complete. By using tree sorts, then, we can write longer merge runs, which reduces the number of merge runs and therefore speeds up the sorting process. Because we have studied one tree sort, the heap sort, let's see how it could be used to write longer merge runs.

Figure 11-23 shows how we can use the heap sort to write long merge runs. Given a list of 12 elements to be sorted and using a heap of 3 nodes, we sort the data into 2 merge runs. We begin by filling the sort array and then turning it into a **minimum** heap. After creating the heap, we write the smallest element, located at the root, to the first merge file and read the fourth element (97) into the root node. We again reheap and this time write 21 to the merge file. After reading 87 and rebuilding the heap, we write 78 to the merge file.

After reading 62, we have the heap shown in Figure 11-23(g). At this point, the data we just read (62) is smaller than the last element we wrote to the merge file (78). Thus it cannot be placed in the current merge run in merge 1. By definition, it belongs to the next merge run. Therefore, we exchange it with the last element in the heap (87) and subtract 1 from the heap size, making it two elements. We indicate that the third element, containing 62, is not currently in the heap by shading it. After we reheap, we write 87 to merge 1. We then read 94, reheap, and write it to merge 1. When we read 85, we discover that it is less than the largest key in merge 1 (94) so it must also be eliminated from the heap. After exchanging it with the last element in the heap, we have the situation shown in Figure 11-23(l).

After writing 97 to merge 1, we read 76. Because 76 is less than the last element written to the merge file, it also belongs to the next merge run. At this point, all elements in the array belong to the second merge run. The first merge run is therefore complete, as shown in Figure 11-23(m).

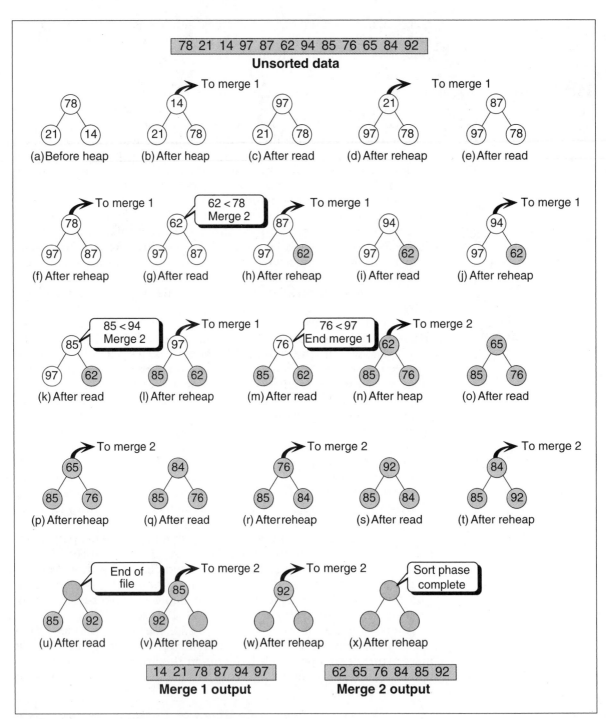

Figure 11-23 External sort phase using heap sort

After rebuilding the heap, we write the first element to merge file 2. We continue reading, reheaping, and writing until we write 84 to the merge file. At this point, we have read all of the data to be sorted and the input file is at the end of the file, as shown in Figure 11-23(u). We therefore move the last element to the heap, subtract 1 from the heap size, and reheap. After writing 85 to the merge run, we move the last element in the heap to the root, reheap, and write it to the merge file. Because the heap is now empty, the sort is complete.

If you examine the merge runs created in this example, you will note that they are both twice as long as the array size. As a rule of thumb, our heuristic studies have indicated that the average merge run size will be twice the size of the array being used for the sort. These longer merge runs will eliminate one merge pass, which is a significant time saver.

11-7   SUMMARY

■   One of the most common applications in computer science is sorting.
■   Sorts are generally classified as either internal or external.
   ■   In an internal sort, all of the data are held in primary storage during the sorting process.
   ■   An external sort uses primary storage for the data currently being sorted and secondary storage for any data that will not fit in primary memory.
■   Data may be sorted in either ascending or descending order.
■   Sort stability is an attribute of a sort indicating that data with equal keys maintain their relative input order in the output.
■   Sort efficiency is a measure of the relative efficiency of a sort.
■   Each traversal of the data during the sorting process is referred to as a pass.
■   Internal sorting can be divided into three broad categories: insertion, selection, and exchange.
■   Two methods of insertion sorting were discussed in this chapter: straight insertion sort and shell sort.
   ■   In the straight insertion sort, the list at any moment is divided into two sublists: sorted and unsorted. In each pass, the first element of the unsorted sublist is transferred to the sorted sublist by inserting it at the appropriate place.
   ■   The shell sort algorithm is an improved version of the straight insertion sort, in which the process uses different increments to sort the list. In each increment, the list is divided into segments, which are sorted independent of each other.
■   Two methods of selection sorting were discussed in this chapter: straight selection sort and heap sort.
   ■   In the straight selection sort, the list at any moment is divided into two sublists: sorted and unsorted. In each pass, the process selects the smallest element from the unsorted sublist and exchanges it with the element at the beginning of the unsorted sublist.
   ■   The heap sort is an improved version of the straight selection sort. In the heap sort, the largest element in the heap is exchanged with the last element in the unsorted sublist. However, selecting the largest

element is much easier in this sort method because the largest element is the root of the heap.

■ Two methods of exchange sorting were discussed in this chapter: bubble sort and quick sort.

  ■ In the bubble sort, the list at any moment is divided into two sublists: sorted and unsorted. In each pass, the smallest element is bubbled up from the unsorted sublist and moved to the sorted sublist.

  ■ The quick sort is the new version of the exchange sort in which the list is continuously divided into smaller sublists and exchanging takes place between elements that are out of order. Each pass of the quick sort selects a pivot and divides the list into three groups: a partition of elements whose key is less than the pivot's key, the pivot element that is placed in its ultimate correct position, and a partition of elements greater than or equal to the pivot's key. The sorting then continues by quick sorting the left partition followed by quick sorting the right partition.

■ The efficiency of straight insertion, straight selection, and bubble sort is $O(n^2)$.

■ The efficiency of shell sort is $O(n^{1.25})$, and the efficiency of heap and quick sorts is $O(n\log_2 n)$.

■ External sorting allows a portion of the data to be stored in secondary storage during the sorting process.

■ External sorting consists of two phases: the sort phase and the merge phase.

■ The merge phase uses one of three methods: natural merge, balanced merge, and polyphase merge.

  ■ In natural merge, each phase merges a constant number of input files into one output file. The natural merge requires a distribution process between each merge phase.

  ■ In the balanced merge, we eliminate the distribute processes by using the same number of input and output files.

  ■ In polyphase merge, a number of input files are merged into one output file. However, the input file, which is exhausted first, is immediately used as an output file. The output file in the previous phase becomes one of the input files in the next phase.

■ To improve the efficiency of sort phase in external sorting, we can use a tree sort, such as the minimum heap sort. This sort allows us to write to a merge file before the sorting process is complete, which results in longer merge runs.

11-8   PRACTICE SETS

Exercises

1. An array contains the elements shown below. The first two elements have been sorted using a straight insertion sort. What would be the value of the elements in the array after three more passes of the straight insertion sort algorithm?

       3 13 7 26 44 23 98 57

2. An array contains the elements shown below. Show the contents of the array after it has gone through a one-increment pass of the shell sort. The increment factor is $k = 3$.

23 3 7 13 89 7 66 2 6 44 18 90 98 57

3. An array contains the elements shown below. The first two elements have been sorted using a straight selection sort. What would be the value of the elements in the array after three more passes of the selection sort algorithm?

7 8 26 44 13 23 98 57

4. An array contains the elements shown below. What would be the value of the elements in the array after three passes of the heap sort algorithm?

44 78 22 7 98 56 34 2 38 35 45

5. An array contains the elements shown below. The first two elements have been sorted using a bubble sort. What would be the value of the elements in the array after three more passes of the bubble sort algorithm? Use the version of bubble sort that starts from the end and bubbles up the smallest element.

7 8 26 44 13 23 57 98

6. An array contains the elements shown below. Using a quick sort show the contents of the array after the first pivot has been placed in its correct location. Identify the three sublists that exist at that point.

44 78 22 7 98 56 34 2 38 35 45

7. After two passes of a sorthing algorithm, the following array:

47 3 21 32 56 92

has been rearranged as shown below.

3 21 47 32 56 92

Which sorting algorithm is being used (straight selection, bubble, straight insertion)? Defend your answer.

8. After two passes of a sorting algorithm, the following array:

80 72 66 44 21 33

has been rearranged as shown below.

21 33 80 72 66 44

Which sorting algorithm is being used (straight selection, bubble, straight insertion)? Defend your answer.

9. After two passes of a sorting algorithm, the following array:

47 3 66 32 56 92

has been rearranged as shown below.

3 47 66 32 56 92

Which sorting algorithm is being used (straight selection, bubble, straight insertion)? Defend your answer.

10. Show the result after each merge phase when merging the following two files:

6 12 19 23 34 · 8 11 17 20 25 · 9 10 15 25 35

13 21 27 28 29 · 7 30 36 37 39

11. Starting with the following file, show the contents of all of the files created using external sorting and the natural merge method:

37 9 23 56 4 5 12 45 78 22 33 44 14 17 57 11 35 46 59

12. Rework Exercise 11 using the balanced merge method.

13. Rework Exercise 11 using the polyphase merge method.

Problems

14. Modify the insertion sort C++ code on page 515 to count the number of data moves needed to order an array of 1000 random numbers. A data move is movement of an element of data from one position in the array to another, to a hold area, or from a hold area back to the array. Display the array before and after the sort. At the end of the program, display the total moves needed to sort the array.

15. Repeat Problem 14 using the shell sort on page 516.

16. Repeat Problem 14 using the selection sort on page 524.

17. Repeat Problem 14 using the heap sort on page 525.

18. Repeat Problem 14 using the bubble sort on page 538.

19. Repeat Problem 14 using the quick sort on page 539.

20. Change the bubble sort algorithm on page 538 as follows: Use two-directional bubbling in each pass. In the first bubbling, the smallest element is bubbled up; in the second bubbling, the largest element is bubbled down. This sort is known as the **shaker sort.**

21. Write an algorithm that applies the incremental idea of the shell sort to selection sort. The algorithm first applies the straight section sort to items $n/2$ elements apart (first, middle, and last). It then applies it to $n/3$ elements apart, then to elements $n/4$ apart, and so on.

22. Write a recursive version of the selection sort algorithm on page 524.

23. Rewrite the insertion sort algorithm on page 515 using a singly linked list instead of an array.

Projects

24. Merge sorting is an example of a divide-and-conquer paradigm. In our discussions, we used merge only as an external sorting method. It can also be used for internal sorting. Let's see how it works. If we have a list of only two elements, we can simply divide it into two halves and then merge them. In other words, the merge sort is totally dependent on two processes, distribution and merge. This elementary process is shown in Figure 11-24.

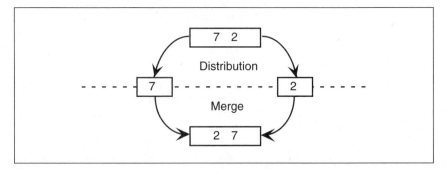

Figure 11-24   Split and merge for Project 24

Given a list longer than two elements, we can sort by repeating the distribution and merge processes. Because we don't know how many elements are in the input list when we begin, we can distribute the list originally by writing the first element to one output list, the second element to a second output list, and then continue writing alternatively to the first list and then the second list until the input list has been divided into two output lists. The output lists can then be sorted using a balanced two-way merge. This process is shown in Figure 11-25. It could be called the *sortless sort* because it sorts without ever using a sort phase.

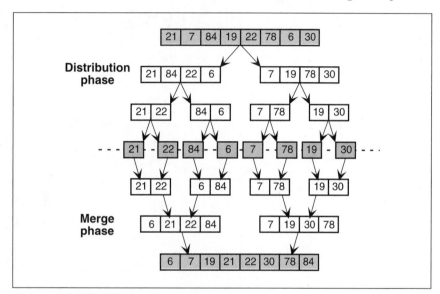

Figure 11-25 The sortless sort

Write a C++ program to sort an array of 500 random numbers using this approach. Print the data before and after the sort.

25. Write a program that sorts an array of random numbers using the shell sort and the quick sort. Both sorts should use the same data. Each sort should be executed twice. For the first sort, fill the array with random numbers between 1 and 999. For the second sort, fill the array with a nearly ordered list. Construct your nearly ordered list by reversing elements 19 and 20 in the sorted random number list. For each sort, count the number of comparisons and moves necessary to order this list.

   Run the program three times, once with an array of 100 items, once with an array of 500 items, and once with an array of 1000 items. For the first execution only (100 elements), print the unsorted data followed by the sort data in 10 × 10 matrixes (10 rows of 10 numbers each). For all runs, print the number of comparisons and the number of moves required to order the data.

To make sure your statistics are as accurate as possible, you must analyze each loop limit condition test and each selection statement in your sort algorithms. The following notes should help with this analysis:

a. All loops require a count increment in their body.

b. Pretest loops (*while* and *for*) also require a count increment either before (recommended) or after the loop to count the last test.

c. Remember that C++ uses the shortcut rule for evaluating Boolean and/ or expressions. The best way to count them is with a comma expression, as shown below. Use similar code for the selection statements.

```
while ((count++, a) && (count++, b))
```

Analyze the heuristics you generated and write a short report (less than one page) concerning what you discovered about these two sorts. Include the data in Table 11-4, one for the random data and one for the nearly ordered data. Calculate the ratio to one decimal place.

	Shell	Quick	Ratio (Shell/Quick)
Compares			
100			
500			
1000			
Moves			
100			
500			
1000			

Table 11-4 Sorting statistics format for Project 25

26. Repeat Project 25 adding heap sort and using your computer's internal clock. For each sort algorithm, start the clock as the last statement before calling the sort and read the clock as the first statement after the sort. Write a short report comparing the run times with the suggested algorithmics in the text. If your results do not agree with the algorithmics, increase the array size in 1000-element increments to get a better picture.

27. Radix sorting—also known as digit, pocket, and bucket sorting—is a very efficient sort for large lists whose keys are relatively short. If fact, if we consider only its big-O notation, which is $O(n)$, it is one of the best. Radix sorts were used extensively in the punched-card era to sort cards on electronic accounting machines (EAMs).

In a radix sort, each pass through the list orders the data one digit at a time. The first pass orders the data on the units (least significant) digit. The second pass orders the data on the tens digit. The third pass orders the data on the hundreds digit, and so forth until the list is completely sorted by sorting the data on the most significant digit.

In EAM sorts, the punched cards were sorted into pockets. In today's systems, we would sort them into a linked list, with a separate linked list for each digit. Using a pocket or bucket approach, we sort eight four-digit numbers in Figure 11-26.[9]

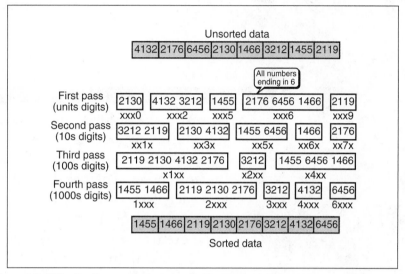

Figure 11-26   Radix sorting example for Project 27

If you analyze this sort, you will see that there are k sort passes, where k is the number of digits in the key. For each sort pass, we have n operations, where n is the number of elements to be sorted. This gives us an efficiency of kn, which in big-O notation is $O(n)$.

Write a program that uses the radix sort to sort 1000 random digits. Print the data before and after the sort. Each sort bucket should be a linked list. At the end of the sort, the data should be in the original array.

28. Modify Project 26 to include the radix sort. Build a table of sort times and write a short paper explaining the different sort timings and their relationship to their sort efficiency.

---

9. Note: For efficiency, radix sorts are not recommended for small lists or for keys containing a large number of digits.

12

Graphs

We have studied many different data structures. We started by looking at several data structures that deal with linear lists, lists in which each node has a single successor. Then we looked at tree structures in which each node could have multiple successors but just one predecessor. In this last chapter, we turn our attention to a data structure, **graphs**, that differs from all of the others in one major concept: Each node may have multiple predecessors as well as multiple successors.

Graphs are very useful structures. They can be used to solve complex routing problems, such as designing and routing airlines among the airports they serve. Similarly, they can be used to route messages over a computer network from one node to another.

12-1   TERMINOLOGY

A **graph** is a collection of nodes, called **vertices,** and a collection of line segments, called **lines**, connecting pairs of vertices. In other words, a graph consists of two sets, a set of vertices and a set of lines. Graphs may be either directed or undirected. A **directed graph,** or **digraph** for short, is a graph in which each line has a direction (arrow head) to its successor. The lines in a directed graph are known as **arcs**. In a directed graph, the flow along the arcs between two vertices can follow only the indicated direction. An **undirected graph** is a graph in which there is no direction (arrow head) on any of the lines, which are known as **edges**. In an undirected graph, the flow between two vertices can go in either direction. Figure 12-1 contains an example of both a directed graph (a) and an undirected graph (b).

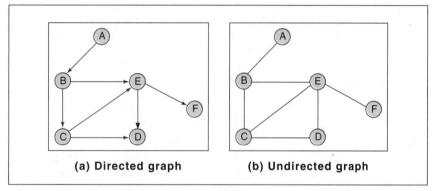

(a) Directed graph   **(b) Undirected graph**

Figure 12-1   Directed and undirected graphs

Two vertices in a graph are said to be **adjacent vertices** (or neighbors) if an edge directly connects them. In Figure 12-1, A and B are adjacent, whereas D and F are not.

> **Note**
>
> A graph is a collection of nodes, called vertices, and line segments, called arcs or edges, that connect pairs of nodes.

A **path** is a sequence of vertices in which each vertex is adjacent to the next one. In Figure 12-1, {A, B, C, E} is one path and {A, B, E, F} is another. Note that both directed and undirected graphs have paths. In an undirected graph, you may travel in either direction.

A **cycle** is a path consisting of at least three vertices that starts and ends with the same vertex. In Figure 12-1(b), B, C, D, E, B is a cycle. Note, however, that the same vertices in Figure 12-1(a) do not constitute a cycle because in a digraph, a path can only follow the direction of the arc, whereas in an undirected graph, a path can move in either direction along the edge. A **loop** is a special case of a cycle in which a single arc begins and ends with the same vertex. In a loop, the end points of the line are the same.

Note

> Graphs may be directed or undirected. In a directed graph, each line, called an arc, has a direction indicating how it may be traversed. In an undirected graph, the line is known as an edge and it may be traversed in either direction.

Two vertices are said to be **connected** if there is a path between them. A graph is said to be connected if, suppressing direction, there is a path from any vertex to any other vertex. Furthermore, a directed graph is **strongly connected** if there is a path from each vertex to every other vertex in the digraph. A directed graph is **weakly connected** if at least two vertices are not connected. (A connected undirected graph would always be strongly connected, so the concept is not normally used with undirected graphs.) A graph is **disjoint** if it is not connected. Figure 12-2 contains a weakly connected graph (a), a strongly connected graph (b), and a disjoint graph (c).

The **degree** of a vertex is the number of lines incident to it. In Figure 12-2(a), the degree of vertex B is 3 and the degree of vertex E is 4. The **outdegree** of a vertex in a digraph is the number of arcs leaving the vertex; the **indegree** is the number of arcs entering the vertex. Again, in Figure 12-2(a) the indegree of vertex B is 1 and its outdegree is 2; in Figure 12-2(b) the indegree of vertex E is 3 and its outdegree is 1.

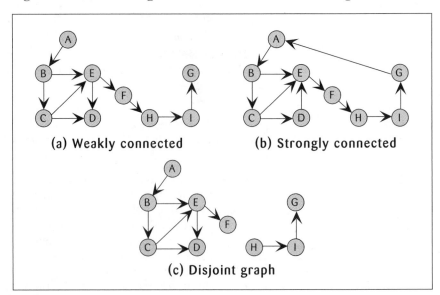

(a) Weakly connected   (b) Strongly connected

(c) Disjoint graph

Figure 12-2   Connected and disjoint graphs

12-2   OPERATIONS

In this section we define six primitive graph operations that provide the basic modules needed to maintain a graph: add a vertex, delete a vertex, add an edge, delete an edge, find a vertex, and traverse a graph. As we will see, the graph traversal involves two different traversal methods.

Add Vertex

Add vertex inserts a new vertex into a graph. When a vertex is added, it is disjoint; that is, it is not connected to any other vertices in the list. Obviously, adding a vertex is just the first step in an insertion process. After a vertex is added, it must be connected. Figure 12-3 shows a graph before and after a new vertex is added.

Delete Vertex

Delete vertex removes a vertex from the graph. When a vertex is deleted, all connecting edges are also removed. Figure 12-4 contains an example of deleting a vertex.

Add Edge

Add edge connects a vertex to a destination vertex. If a vertex requires multiple edges, then add an edge must be called once for each adjacent vertex. To add an edge, two vertices must be specified. If the graph is a digraph, then one of the vertices must be specified as the source and

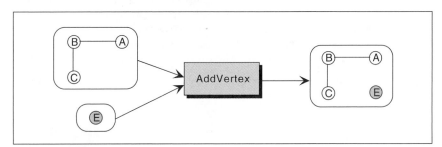

Figure 12-3   Add vertex

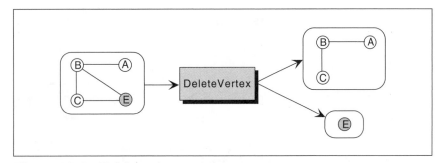

Figure 12-4   Delete vertex

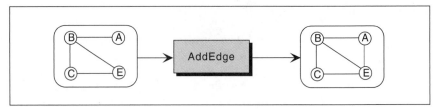

Figure 12-5 Add edge

one as the destination. Figure 12-5 contains an example of adding an edge, {A, E}, to the graph.

Delete Edge

Delete edge removes one edge from a graph. Figure 12-6 contains an example that deletes the edge {A, E} from the graph.

Find Vertex

Find vertex traverses a graph looking for a specified vertex. If the vertex is found, its data are returned. If it is not found, an error is indicated. In Figure 12-7, find vertex traverses the graph looking for the vertex C.

Traverse Graph

There is always at least one application that requires that all vertices in a given graph be visited; that is, there is at least one application that requires that the graph be traversed. Because a vertex in a graph can have multiple parents, the traversal of a graph presents some problems not found in the traversal of linear lists and trees. Specifically, we must somehow ensure that we process the data in each vertex only once.

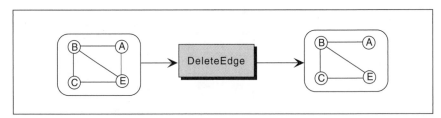

Figure 12-6   Delete edge

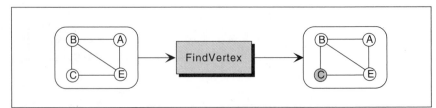

Figure 12-7   Find vertex

However, because there are multiple paths to a vertex, we may arrive at it from more than one direction as we traverse the graph. The traditional solution to this problem is to include a visited flag at each vertex. Before the traversal, we set the visited flag in each vertex off. Then, as we traverse the graph, we set the visited flag on to indicate that the data have been processed.

The two standard graph traversals are depth first and breadth first. Both use the visited flag.

Depth-First Traversal

In the **depth-first traversal,** we process all of a vertex's descendents before we move to an adjacent vertex. This concept is most easily seen when the graph is a tree. In Figure 12-8, we show the preorder traversal, one of the standard depth-first traversals.

In a similar manner, the depth-first traversal of a graph starts by processing the first vertex of the graph. After processing the first vertex, we select any vertex adjacent to the first vertex and process it. As we process each vertex, we select an adjacent vertex until we reach a vertex with no adjacent entries. This is similar to reaching a leaf in a tree. We then back out of the structure, processing adjacent vertices as we go. It should be obvious that this logic requires a stack (or recursion) to complete the traversal.

The order in which the adjacent vertices are processed depends on how the graph is physically stored. When we discuss the insertion logic later in the chapter, you will see that we insert the arcs in ascending key sequence. Because we are using a stack, however, the traversal will process adjacent vertices in descending (last in–first out [LIFO]) order.

Note

> In the depth-first traversal, all of a node's descendents are processed before moving to an adjacent node.

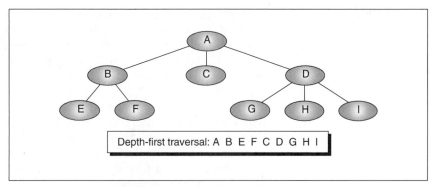

Depth-first traversal: A B E F C D G H I

Figure 12-8 Depth-first traversal of a tree

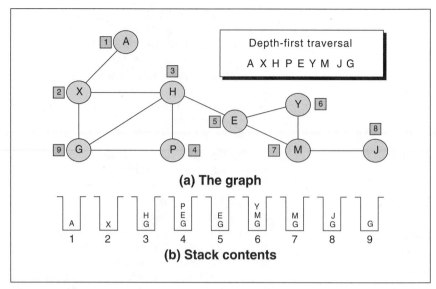

Figure 12-9   Depth-first traversal of a graph

Let's trace a depth-first traversal through the graph in Figure 12-9. The number in the box next to a vertex indicates the processing order. The stacks below the graph show the stack contents as we work our way down the graph and then as we back out.

1. We begin by pushing the first vertex, A, into the stack.
2. We then loop, pop the stack, and, after processing the vertex, push all of the adjacent vertices into the stack. To process X at Step 2, therefore, we pop X from the stack, process it, and then push G and H into the stack, giving the stack contents for Step 3 as shown in Figure 12-9(b)—H G.
3. When the stack is empty, the traversal is complete.

Breadth-First Traversal

In the **breadth-first traversal** of a graph, we process all adjacent vertices of a vertex before going to the next level. We also saw the breadth-first traversal of a tree in Chapter 7. Looking at the tree in Figure 12-10, we see that its breadth-first traversal starts at level 0 and then processes all the vertices in level 1 before going on to process the vertices in level 2.

The breadth-first traversal of a graph follows the same concept. We begin by picking a starting vertex; after processing it, we process all of its adjacent vertices. After we process all of the first vertex's adjacent vertices, we pick the first adjacent vertex and process all of its vertices, then the second adjacent vertex and process all of its vertices, and so forth until we are finished.

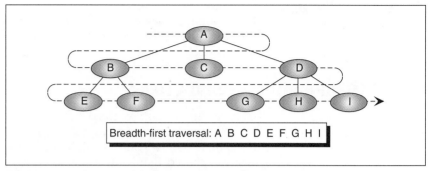

Figure 12-10   Breadth-first traversal of a tree

In Chapter 7 we saw that the breadth-first traversal uses a queue rather than a stack. As we process each vertex, we place all of its adjacent vertices in the queue. Then, to select the next vertex to be processed, we delete a vertex from the queue and process it. Let's trace this logic through the graph in Figure 12-11.

1. We begin by enqueuing vertex A in the queue.
2. We then loop, dequeuing the queue and processing the vertex from the front of the queue. After processing the vertex, we place all of its adjacent vertices into the queue. Thus, at Step 2 in Figure 12-11[b]), we dequeue vertex X, process it, and then place vertices G and H in the queue. We are then ready for Step 3, in which we process vertex G.
3. When the queue is empty, the traversal is complete.

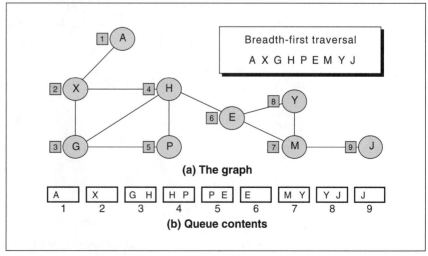

Figure 12-11   Breadth-first traversal of a graph

| Note | In the breadth-first traversal all adjacent vertices are processed be-fore processing the descendents of a vertex. |

12-3   GRAPH STORAGE STRUCTURES

To represent a graph we need to store two sets. The first set represents the vertices of the graph, and the second set represents the edges or arcs. The two most common structures used to store these sets are arrays and linked lists. Although the arrays offer some simplicity and processing efficiencies, the number of vertices must be known in advance. This is a major limitation.

Adjacency Matrix

The **adjacency matrix** uses a vector (one-dimensional array) for the vertices and a matrix (two-dimensional array) to store the edges (see Figure 12-12). If two vertices are adjacent—that is, if there is an edge between them—the matrix intersect has a value of 1; if there is no edge between them, the intersect is set to 0.

If the graph is directed, then the intersection in the adjacency matrix indicates the direction. For example, in Figure 12-12(b), there is an

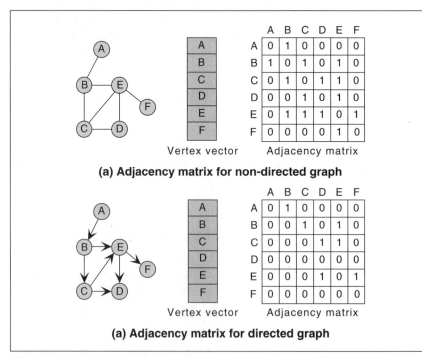

Figure 12-12   Adjacency matrix

arc from source vertex B to destination vertex C. In the adjacency matrix, this arc is seen as a 1 in the intersection from B (on the left) to C (on the top). Because there is no arc from C to B, however, the intersection from C to B is 0. On the other hand, in Figure 12-12(a), the edge from B to C is bidirectional; that is, you can traverse it in either direction because the graph is nondirected. Thus, the nondirected adjacency matrix uses a 1 in the intersection from B to C as well as in the intersection from C to B. In other words, the matrix reflects the fact that you can use the edge to go either way.

Note

> In the adjacency matrix representation, we use a vector to store the vertices and a matrix to store the edges.

In addition to the limitation that the size of the graph must be known before the program starts, there is another serious limitation in the adjacency matrix: Only one edge can be stored between any two vertices. Although this limitation does not prevent many graphs from using the matrix format, some network structures require multiple lines between vertices.

Adjacency List

The **adjacency list** uses a two-dimensional ragged array to store the edges. An adjacency list is shown in Figure 12-13.

The **vertex list** is a singly linked list of the vertices in the list. Depending on the application, it could also be implemented using doubly linked lists or circularly linked lists. The pointer at the left of the list links the vertex entries. The pointer at the right in the vertex is a head pointer to a linked list of edges from the vertex. Thus, in the

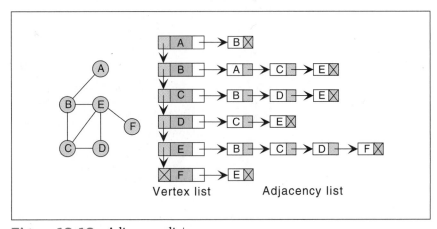

Figure 12-13   Adjacency list

nondirected graph on the left in Figure 12-13, there is a path from vertex B to vertices A, C, and E. To find these edges in the adjacency list, we start at B's vertex list vertex and traverse the linked list to A, then to C, and finally to E.

Note

> In the adjacency list, we use a linked list to store the vertices and a two-dimensional linked list to store the arcs.

12-4   GRAPH ALGORITHMS

In this section we develop a minimum set of algorithms that are needed to create and maintain a directed graph. In addition to the operations described in Section 12-2, "Operations," on page 563, we include several, such as create graph, that are required in programming graph applications. Depending on the requirements for the graph, several other algorithms could be needed. For example, it may be necessary to write algorithms that return the vertex count or a vertex's indegree or outdegree.

Before we discuss the algorithms, we need to design the data structure we use for storing the graph. The most flexible structure is the adjacency list implemented as a singly linked list. In addition to the vertex and adjacency structures shown in Figure 12-13, we also include a head structure. The head structure stores metadata about the list. For our algorithms, we store only a count of the number of vertices in the graph. Examples of other metadata that could be stored include a rear pointer to the end of the vertex list and a count of the total arcs in the graph. The graph data structure is shown in Figure 12-14.

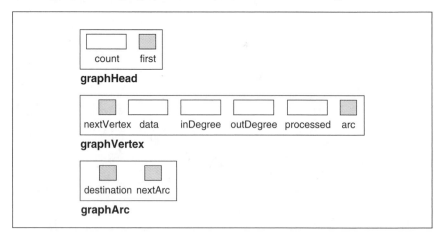

Figure 12-14   Graph data structure

Note that the graph data, if any, are stored in the vertex node. These data pertain only to the vertex. Later we will see a structure that requires that we store data about an arc. In that case, we will store the arc data in the arc vertex. The pseudocode for the graph structure is shown in Algorithm 12-1.

```
graphHead
    count  <integer>
    first  <pointer to graphVertex>
end graphHead


graphVertex
    nextVertex     <pointer to graphVertex>
    data           <dataType>
    inDegree       <integer>
    outDegree      <integer>
    processed      <0, 1, 2>
    arc            <pointer to first graphArc>
end graphVertex


graphArc
    destination    <pointer to graphVertex>
    nextArc        <pointer to graphArc>
end graphArc
```

Algorithm 12-1   Data structure for graph

In addition to the data and pointers, each vertex entry contains a count of the number of arcs pointing to it, the indegree, and the number of arcs leaving it, the outdegree. The indegree count serves a very useful purpose. When we delete a vertex, we must ensure that there are no arcs pointing to it. If there are, any reference to the deleted vertex using the arc pointer would cause the program to fail. Therefore, our delete algorithm will not allow a vertex to be deleted if any arcs are pointing to it.

Finally, we have a field, `processed`, that is used only for traversals. It indicates that the data in a vertex are waiting to be processed or have already been processed during the current traversal.

Create Graph

Create graph initializes the metadata elements for a graph head structure. The code is shown in Algorithm 12-2.

```
algorithm createGraph  (ref graph <metadata>)
   Initializes the metadata elements of a graph structure.
   Pre    graph is a metadata structure
   Post   metadata elements have been initialized
 1 count = 0
 2 first = null
end createGraph
```

Algorithm 12-2   Create graph

Insert Vertex

Insert vertex adds a disjoint—that is, an unconnected—vertex to the graph. The arcs associated with the vertex must be inserted separately. The pseudocode is shown in Algorithm 12-3.

```
algorithm insertVertex (ref graph   <metadata>,
                        val dataIn  <dataType>)
Allocates memory for a new vertex and copies the data to it.
   Pre    graph is a graph head structure
          dataIn contains data to be inserted into vertex
   Post   new vertex allocated and data copied
   Return +1 if successful
          -1 if memory overflow
 1 allocate (newPtr)
 2 if (allocate successful)
   1   newPtr->nextVertex = null
   2   newPtr->data       = dataIn
   3   newPtr->inDegree   = 0
   4   newPtr->outDegree  = 0
   5   newPtr->processed  = 0
   6   newPtr->arc        = null
   7   graph.count        = graph.count + 1
 3 else
   Out of memory
   1   return -1
 4 end if
Now find insertion point
 5 locPtr = graph.first
 6 if (locPtr null)
   Empty graph. Insert at beginning.
```

Algorithm 12-3   Insert vertex

```
       1   graph.first = newPtr
   7 else
       1   predPtr = null
       2   loop (locPtr not null AND dataIn.key > locPtr->data.key)
           1   predPtr  = locPtr
           2   locPtr   = locPtr->nextVertex
       3   end loop
       4   if (predPtr null)
              Insert before first vertex
           1   graph.first = newPtr
       5   else
           1   predPtr->nextVertex = newPtr
       6   end if
       7   newPtr->nextVertex = locPtr
   8 end if
   9 return 1
 end insertVertex
```

Algorithm 12-3   Insert vertex *(continued)*

Algorithm 12-3 Analysis

This is the basic singly linked list insertion algorithm. After allocating memory for the new vertex, we move in the data and set all of its metadata values to null.

Because the graph does not contain an integrated header structure, we must handle insertions into a null graph and insertions before the first vertex as special cases. The insertion into a null list is handled in Statement 6.1. Inserting before the first vertex is handled in Statement 7.4.1.

As a final point, study the returned values. If the insertion is successful, we return 1. We use the same success return value throughout all of the graph algorithms. If memory overflows, then we return a –1. As you study the rest of the algorithms, you will note that all of the error return values are negative. There is a consistency to their values, however. Regardless of which algorithm we are in, we use a consistent return value for a given condition. Thus, you will see that memory overflow is always –1 and that destination key not found is always –2. The reverse is not necessarily true, however. A –1 could have other meanings than overflow.

Delete Vertex

Like any other delete algorithm, the first thing we have to do to delete a vertex is to find it. Once we have found it, however, we also need to make sure that it is disjoint; that is, we need to ensure that there are no arcs leaving or entering the vertex. If there are, we reject the deletion. The pseudocode is shown in Algorithm 12-4.

```
algorithm deleteVertex (ref graph  <metadata>,
                        val key    <keyType>)
Deletes an existing vertex only if its degree is 0.
    Pre      graph is a pointer to a graph head structure
             key is the key of the vertex to be deleted
    Post     vertex deleted (if degree zero)
    Return   +1 if successful
             -1 if degree not zero
             -2 if key not found
 1 if (graph.first null)
   1   return -2
 2 end if
Locate vertex to be deleted
 3 predPtr = null
 4 locnPtr = graph.first
 5 loop (locnPtr not null AND key > locnPtr->data.key)
   1   predPtr  = locnPtr
   2   locnPtr  = locnPtr->nextVertex
 6 end loop
 7 if (locnPtr null OR key not equal locnPtr->data.key)
   1   return -2
 8 end if
Found vertex to be deleted. Test degree.
 9 if (locnPtr->inDegree > 0 OR locnPtr->outDegree > 0)
   1   return -1
10 end if
Okay to delete vertex
11 if (predPtr null)
   1   graph.first = locnPtr->nextVertex
12 else
   1   predPtr->nextVertex = locnPtr->nextVertex
13 end if
14 graph.count = graph.count - 1
15 recycle (locnPtr)
16 return 1
end deleteVertex
```

Algorithm 12-4   Delete vertex

Algorithm 12-4 Analysis   This is a basic singly linked list delete algorithm. The only complexity is that we can't delete a vertex if its degree is greater than 0. This requirement is easily handled by testing the indegree and outdegree in the vertex, as seen in Statement 9.

Insert Arc

Once we have a vertex, we can connect it to other vertices. To insert an arc, we need two points in the graph, the source vertex (`fromPtr`) and the destination vertex (`toPtr`). Each vertex is identified by its key value rather than by its physical address. This system of identification gives us more flexibility in working with the graph and provides a degree of data structure hiding that makes it easier to implement the algorithms. The insertion logic is shown in Algorithm 12-5.

```
algorithm insertArc (ref graph    <metadata>,
                     val fromKey  <keyType>,
                     val toKey    <keyType>)
Adds an arc between two vertices.
    Pre     graph is graph head structure
            fromKey is the key of the originating vertex
            toKey is the key of the destination vertex
    Post    arc added to adjacency list
    Return  +1 if successful
            -1 if memory overflow
            -2 if fromKey not found
            -3 if toKey not found
  1 allocate (newPtr)
  2 if (allocate fails)
    1   return -1
  3 end if
Locate source vertex
  4 fromPtr = graph.first
  5 loop (fromPtr not null AND fromKey > fromPtr->data.key)
    1   fromPtr = fromPtr->nextVertex
  6 end loop
  7 if (fromPtr null OR fromKey not equal fromPtr->data.key)
    1   return -2
  8 end loop
Now locate to vertex
  9 toPtr = graph.first
 10 loop (toPtr not null AND toKey > toPtr->data.key)
    1   toPtr  = toPtr->nextVertex
 11 end loop
 12 if (toPtr null OR toKey not equal toPtr->data.key)
    1   return -3
 13 end if
```

Algorithm 12-5   Insert arc

```
From and to vertices located. Insert new arc.
14 fromPtr->outDegree    = fromPtr->outDegree + 1
15 toPtr->inDegree       = toPtr->inDegree + 1
16 newPtr->destination   = toPtr
17 if (fromPtr->arc null)
   Inserting first arc
   1   fromPtr->arc      = newPtr
   2   newPtr->nextArc   = null
   3   return 1
18 end if
Find insertion point in adjacency (arc) list
19 arcPredPtr = null
20 arcWalkPtr = fromPtr->arc
21 loop (arcWalkPtr not null
          AND toKey >= arcWalkPtr->destination->data.key)
   1   arcPredPtr  = arcWalkPtr
   2   arcWalkPtr  = arcWalkPtr->nextArc
22 end loop
23 if (arcPredPtr null)
   Insertion before first arc
   1   fromPtr->arc = newPtr
24 else
   1   arcPredPtr->nextArc = newPtr
25 end if
26 newPtr->nextArc = arcWalkPtr
27 return 1
end insertArc
```

Algorithm 12-5   Insert arc *(continued)*

Algorithm 12-5 Analysis   We begin this lengthy algorithm by ensuring that there is memory for the new arc. If there isn't, we immediately return –1 indicating memory overflow.

If there is memory, we locate the from vertex and the to vertex. This logic involves simple linked list searches. If either search fails, we return the appropriate value, –2 for from vertex not found and –3 for to vertex not found.

After we locate both vertices, we update their degree counts and set the new arc's destination pointer to the destination vertex. We are then ready to insert the new arc into the adjacency list. Our design for the adjacency list requires that the arc vertices be in sequence by destination key. We therefore search the arc lists, comparing the new destination key with the destinations already in the list. When the new destination becomes less than a destination in the adjacency list, we know we have found the insertion location. Note that this logic places duplicate arcs in the list in first in—first out (FIFO) order. On the other hand, some applications may not allow duplicate arcs. If they are not allowed, the logic would need to be changed and an additional error code created.

Delete Arc

The **delete arc** algorithm removes one arc from the adjacency list. To identify an arc, we need two vertices. The vertices are identified by their key. The algorithm therefore first searches the vertex list for the start vertex and then searches its adjacency list for the destination vertex. After locating and deleting the arc, the degree in the from and to vertices is adjusted and the memory recycled. The pseudocode is shown in Algorithm 12-6.

```
algorithm deleteArc (ref graph    <metadata>,
                     val fromKey  <keyType>,
                     val toKey    <keyType>)
Deletes an arc between two vertices.
    Pre    graph is a pointer to a graph head structure
           fromKey is the key of the originating vertex
           toKey is the key of the destination vertex
    Post   vertex deleted
    Return +1 if successful
           -2 if fromKey not found
           -3 if toKey not found
  1 if (graph.first null)
    1   return -2
  2 end if
Locate source vertex
  3 fromVertex = graph.first
  4 loop (fromVertex not null AND fromKey > fromVertex->data.key)
    1   fromVertex = fromVertex->nextVertex
  5 end loop
  6 if (fromVertex null OR fromKey < fromVertex->data.key)
    1   return -2
  7 end if
Locate destination vertex in adjacency list
  8 if (fromVertex->arc null)
    1   return -3
```

Algorithm 12-6   Delete arc

```
 9  end if
10  prePtr = null
11  arcPtr = fromVertex->arc
12  loop  (arcPtr not null
         AND   toKey > arcPtr->destination->data.key)
    1   prePtr  = arcPtr
    2   arcPtr  = arcPtr->nextArc
13  end loop
14  if (arcPtr null OR toKey < arcPtr->destination->data.key)
        1    return -3
15  end if
16  toVertex = arcPtr->destination
fromVertex, toVertex, and arcPtr all located. Delete arc.
17  fromVertex->outDegree  = fromVertex->outDegree - 1
18  toVertex->inDegree      = toVertex->inDegree - 1
19  if (prePtr null)
    Deleting first arc
    1   fromVertex->arc  = arcPtr->nextArc
20  else
    1   prePtr->nextArc  = arcPtr->nextArc
21  end if
22  recycle (arcPtr)
23  return 1
end deleteArc
```

Algorithm 12-6   Delete arc *(continued)*

Algorithm 12-6 Analysis   There are three processes in this algorithm: (1) locate the source vertex, (2) locate the to vertex, and (3) delete the arc. The source vertex is located by searching the vertex list. Once we have located it, we search the adjacency list for an arc that points to the destination vertex. As we search the adjacency list for an arc that points to the to vertex, we keep a predecessor pointer so that we can delete the arc when we find it. Once we find the correct arc, we adjust the degree fields in the from and to vertex entries and then delete the arc.

Retrieve Vertex

Retrieve vertex returns the data stored in a vertex. Given the key of the vertex, the data are placed in the output area specified in the call. The pseudocode is shown in Algorithm 12-7.

```
algorithm retrieveVertex (ref graph     <metadata>,
                          val key       <keyType>,
                          ref dataOut   <dataType>)
Data contained in vertex identified by key passed to caller.
    Pre        graph is a pointer to a graph head structure
               key is the key of the vertex data
    Post       vertex data copied to dataOut
    Return     +1 if successful
               -2 if key not found
  1 if (graph.first null)
    1   return -2
  2 end if
  3 locnPtr = graph.first
  4 loop (locnPtr not null AND key > locnPtr->data.key)
    1   locnPtr = locnPtr->nextVertex
  5 end loop
  6 if (key equal locnPtr->data.key)
    1   dataOut = locnPtr->data
    2   return 1
  7 else
    1   return -2
  8 end if
end retrieveVertex
```

Algorithm 12-7   Retrieve vertex

Algorithm 12-7 Analysis   Retrieve vertex is a typical linked list search algorithm. If the search is successful, the data in the vertex are placed in the output area specified in the calling sequence and success (+1) is returned. If the list is null or if the data can't be located, key not located (–2) is returned.

First Arc

The arcs associated with a vertex are maintained in the adjacency list in ascending destination key sequence. **First arc** therefore returns the key value of the destination with the lowest destination key. The pseudocode is shown in Algorithm 12-8.

```
algorithm firstArc (ref graph      <metadata>,
                    val key        <keyType>,
                    ref destKey    <keyType>)
Key of first arc source vertex located and passed back to caller.
    Pre       graph is a pointer to a graph head structure
              key is the key of the vertex data
              destKey is the destination key of the first arc
    Post      destKey passed back
    Return    +1 if successful
              -2 if key does not exist
              -3 no destination key (no arcs)
  1 if (graph.first null)
    1    return -2
  2 end if
  3 locnPtr = graph.first
  4 loop (locnPtr not null AND key > locnPtr->data.key)
    1    locnPtr = locnPtr->nextVertex
  5 end loop
  6 if (locnPtr not null AND key equal locnPtr->data.key)
    1    if (locnPtr->arc not null)
      1    toPtr   = locnPtr->arc
      2    destKey = toPtr->destination->data.key
      3    return 1
    2    else
      1    return -3
    3    end if
  7 else
    1    return -2
  8 end if
end firstArc
```

Algorithm 12-8   First arc

Algorithm 12-8 Analysis   The logic in first arc is very similar to the search we saw in retrieve vertex. The only difference is that when we locate the source vertex, we retrieve the key of the arc destination. Because the vertex may be disjoint and not connected to any other vertices in the list, we first verify that there is at least one arc. We then use the vertex arc pointer to retrieve the destination vertex key and place it in the output area. If we locate an arc, we return success (+1). If we are unsuccessful, we return –2 if we could not find the vertex key or –3 if we found the vertex but it did not have any arcs.

Depth-First Traversal

The depth-first traversal was described on page 565. It visits all of the vertices in a graph by processing a vertex and all of its descendents before processing an adjacent vertex.

There are two ways to write the depth-first traversal algorithm: we can write it recursively or we can write it using a stack. We have decided to use the stack in this implementation. When we reach a vertex, we push its address into a stack. Then we pop the stack, process the vertex, and push all of its adjacent vertices into the stack.

The problem is that a vertex may be reached by more than one path through the graph. Consequently, we must ensure that each vertex is processed only once. When we created the structure for the vertex (see page 571), we included a processed flag. When we begin the traversal, we set the processed flag to 0. When we push a vertex into the stack, we set its processed flag to 1, indicating that it is in the stack awaiting its turn. This prevents us from pushing it more than once. Finally, when we process the vertex, we set its flag to 2. Now, if we arrive at a vertex more than once, we will know that we either pushed it or processed it earlier and not push or process it a second time. The traversal logic is shown in Algorithm 12-9.

```
algorithm depthFirst (val graph <metadata>)
Process the keys of the graph in depth-first order.
    Pre     graph is a pointer to a graph head structure
    Post    vertices "processed"
 1  if (empty graph)
    1    return
Set processed flags to not processed
 2  walkPtr = graph.first
 3  loop (walkPtr)
    1    walkPtr->processed = 0
    2    walkPtr            = walkPtr->nextVertex
 4  end loop
Process each vertex in list
 5  createStack (stack)
 6  walkPtr = graph.first
 7  loop (walkPtr not null)
    1    if (walkPtr->processed < 2)
        1    if (walkPtr->processed < 1)
             Push and set flag to stack
             1    pushStack (stack, walkPtr)
```

Algorithm 12-9   Depth-first traversal

```
      2   walkPtr->processed = 1
   2  end if
Process vertex at stack top
   3  loop (not emptyStack(stack))
      1   popStack(stack, vertexPtr)
      2   process (vertexPtr->dataPtr)
      3   vertexPtr->processed = 2
      Push all vertices from adjacency list
      4   arcWalkPtr = vertexPtr->arc
      5   loop (arcWalkPtr not null)
         1   vertToPtr = arcWalkPtr->destination
         2   if (vertToPtr->processed is 0)
            1   pushStack(stack, vertToPtr)
            2   vertToPtr->processed = 1
         3   end if
         4   arcWalkPtr = arcWalkPtr->nextArc
      6   end loop
   4  end loop
   2  end if
   3  walkPtr = walkPtr->nextVertex
 8  end loop
 9  destroyStack(stack)
10  return
end depthFirst
```

Algorithm 12-9   Depth-first traversal *(continued)*

Algorithm 12-9 Analysis

Depth-first traversal begins by setting all vertices to not processed. We then set our walker pointer to the first vertex and begin the traversal in Statement 7. If you are guaranteed that the graph is strongly connected, then this loop is not necessary. However, if there is not a path from the first vertex to all other vertices, or if there are disjoint vertices, then we need to ensure that all vertices have been processed by looping through the vertex list. That is the main purpose of the loop in Statement 7.

As a vertex is selected for processing, we first ensure that it has not been previously pushed or processed as a descendent of an earlier vertex. If not, then we push it into the stack in Statement 7.1.1.1. We then process the vertex at the top of the stack and push all of its adjacent vertices into the stack. Note that because we are using a stack to hold the vertices, we will not only process them in depth-first order but also process the adjacent vertices in descending order. (Remember that we build the adjacency list in ascending key sequence, so adjacent vertices are pushed in ascending sequence and popped in descending sequence.)

When the stack is empty, we advance the vertex walker and return to Statement 7 to ensure that all vertices have been processed.

Breadth-First Traversal

The breadth-first traversal, described on page 566, processes a vertex and then processes all of its adjacent vertices. Whereas we used a stack for the depth-first traversal, we use a queue to traverse a graph breadth first. The pseudocode is shown in Algorithm 12-10.

```
algorithm breadthFirst (val graph <metadata>)
Processes the keys of the graph in breadth-first order.
   Pre    graph is pointer to graph head structure
   Post   vertices processed
 1 if (empty graph)
    1  return
 2 end if
First set all processed flags to not processed
Flag: 0--not processed, 1--enqueued, 2--processed
 3 createQueue (queue)
 4 walkPtr = graph.first
 5 loop (walkPtr not null)
    1  walkPtr->processed  = 0
    2  walkPtr             = walkPtr->nextVertex
 6 end loop
Process each vertex in vertex list
 7 walkPtr = graph.first
 8 loop (walkPtr not null)
    1  if (walkPtr->processed < 2)
       1  if (walkPtr->processed < 1
          Enqueue and set process flag to queued (1)
          1  enqueue (queue, walkPtr)
          2  walkPtr->processed = 1
       2  end if
       Now process descendents of vertex at queue front
       3  loop (not emptyQueue (queue))
          1  dequeue (queue, vertexPtr)
          Process vertex and flag as processed
          2  process (vertexPtr)
          3  vertexPtr->processed = 2
```

Algorithm 12-10   Breadth-first traversal

```
            Enqueue all vertices from adjacency list
      4     arcPtr = vertexPtr->arc
      5     loop (arcPtr not null)
            1   toPtr = arcPtr->destination
            2   if (toPtr->processed zero)
                1   enqueue (queue, toPtr)
                2   toPtr->processed = 1
            3   end if
            4   arcPtr = arcPtr->nextArc
      6     end loop
   4     end loop
 2     end if
 3     walkPtr = walkPtr->nextVertex
 9  end loop
10  destroyQueue (queue)
11  return
end breadthFirst
```

Algorithm 12-10   Breadth-first traversal *(continued)*

Algorithm 12-10 Analysis

The code in a breadth-first traversal begins as the depth-first algorithm does by setting all of the processed flags to 0. Note, however, that three flags are used in this algorithm: If the vertex has not been processed, we set the flag to 0. If it has been placed in the queue but is not yet processed, we set the flag to 1. This prevents a vertex from being placed in the queue more than once. When it is processed, we set the flag to 2. After setting the processed flags to 0, we create a queue using the standard algorithms we developed in Chapter 4.

As we loop through the vertex list (Statement 8), we first check whether the vertex has been processed (Statement 8.1). If it has, then we advance to the next vertex (Statement 8.3) and loop back to check again. As we saw in the depth-first traversal, this loop allows us to pick up disjoint vertices or other vertices in a weakly connected graph.

If the vertex has not been processed, we test to see if it has been placed in the queue already (Statement 8.1.1); if not, we enqueue it. We then process all descendents of the vertex at the front of the queue with a loop (Statement 8.1.3) that dequeues and processes the vertex at the beginning of the queue, places all of its unprocessed adjacent vertices in the queue, and repeats the loop until the queue is empty.

After processing all of the descendents of the vertex at the front of the queue, we advance to the next vertex and loop back to Statement 8 to complete the processing of the vertex list.

12-5   NETWORKS

A **network** is a graph whose lines are weighted. It is also known as a **weighted graph.** The meaning of the weights depends on the application. For example, an airline might use a graph to represent the routes between cities that it serves. In this example, the vertices represent the cities and the edge a route between two cities. The edge's weight could represent the flight miles between the two cities or the price of the flight. A network for a small hypothetical airline is shown in Figure 12-15. In this case, the weights represent the mileage between the cities.

Note

> A network is a graph whose lines are weighted.

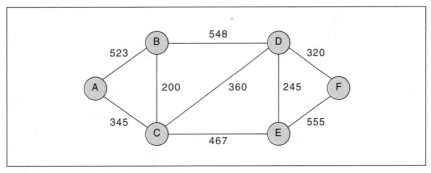

Figure 12-15   City network

Because the weight is an attribute of an edge, it is stored in the structure that contains the edge. In an adjacency matrix, the weight would be stored as the intersection value. In an adjacency list, it would be stored as the value in the adjacency linked list. The representation of the city network in these two formats is shown in Figure 12-16.

We now turn our attention to two applications of networks, the minimum spanning tree and the shortest path through a network.

Minimum Spanning Tree

We can derive one or more spanning trees from a connected network. A **spanning tree** is a tree that contains all of the vertices in the graph.

One interesting algorithm derives the **minimum spanning tree** of a network such that the sum of its weights are guaranteed to be minimal. If the weights in the network are unique, then there will be only one minimum spanning tree. If there are duplicate weights, then there may be one or more minimum spanning trees.

There are many applications for minimum spanning trees, all with the requirement to minimize some aspect of the graph, such as the

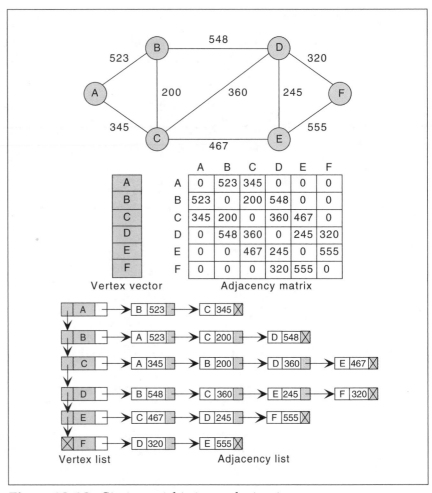

Figure 12-16 Storing weights in graph structures

distance among all of the vertices in the graph. For example, given a network of computers, we could create a tree that connects all of the computers. The minimum spanning tree gives us the shortest length of cable that can be used to connect all of the computers while ensuring that there is a path between any two computers.

Note

A spanning tree is a tree that contains all of the vertices in a graph. A minimum spanning tree is a spanning tree in which the total weight of the lines is guaranteed to be the minimum of all possible trees in the graph.

To create a minimum spanning tree in a strongly connected network—that is, in a network in which there is a path between any two vertices—the edges for the minimum spanning tree are chosen so that the following properties exist:

1. Every vertex is included.
2. The total edge weight of the spanning tree is the minimum possible that includes a path between any two vertices.

Minimum Spanning Tree Example

Before going into the formal algorithm definition, let's manually determine the minimum spanning tree shown in Figure 12-17.

We can start with any vertex. Because the vertex list is usually key sequenced, let's start with A. Then we add the vertex that gives the minimum-weighted edge with A in Figure 12-17, AC. From the two vertices in the tree, A and C, we now locate the edge with the minimum weight. The edge AB has a weight of 6, the edge BC has a weight of 2, the edge CD has a weight of 3, and the edge CE has a weight of 4. The minimum-weighted edge is therefore BC. Note that in this analysis, we do not consider any edge to a vertex that is already in the list. Thus, we did not consider the edge AC.

To generalize the process, we use the following rule: From all of the vertices in the tree, select the edge with the minimal value to a vertex not currently in the tree and insert it into the tree. Using this rule, we add CD (weight 3), DE (weight 2), and DF (weight 3) in turn. The steps are graphically shown in Figure 12-18.

Figure 12-18(g) shows the minimum spanning tree within the original network. If we sum the weights of the edges in the tree, the total is 13. Because there are duplicate weights, a different spanning tree may have the same weight, but none will have a lesser weight.

Minimum Spanning Tree Data Structure

To develop the algorithm for the minimum spanning tree, we need to decide on a storage structure. Because it is the most flexible, we use the adjacency list.

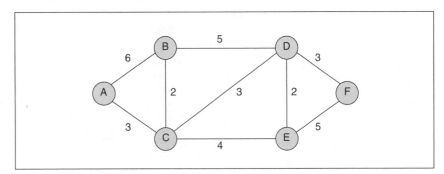

Figure 12-17 Spanning tree

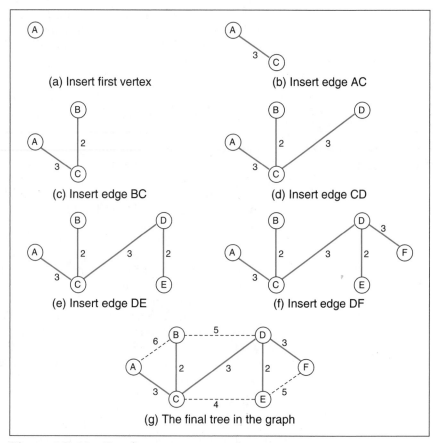

Figure 12-18   Developing a minimum spanning tree

We will need to add some additional elements to determine the minimum spanning tree. Each vertex node will need a Boolean flag indicating that the vertex has been inserted into the spanning tree. In addition, each arc will need an in-tree Boolean. We name both of these fields inTree. Finally, because the structure represents a network, each edge must have a weight. The resulting structure is shown in Algorithm 12-11.

```
graphHead
    count   <integer>
    first   <pointer to graphVertex>
end graphHead
```

Algorithm 12-11   Data structure for spanning tree graph

```
graphVertex
    nextVertex      <pointer to graphVertex>
    data            <dataType>
    inDegree        <integer>
    outDegree       <integer>
    inTree          <Boolean>
    edge            <pointer to first graphEdge>
end graphVertex


graphEdge
    destination     <pointer to graphVertex>
    weight          <integer>
    inTree          <Boolean>
    nextEdge        <pointer to graphEdge>
end graphEdge
```

Algorithm 12-11   Data structure for spanning tree graph *(continued)*

Minimum Spanning Tree Pseudocode

The minimum spanning tree algorithm follows the concept outlined earlier. It begins by inserting the first vertex into the tree. It then loops until all vertices are in the tree, each time inserting the edge with the minimum weight into the tree. When the algorithm concludes, the minimum spanning tree is identified by the in-tree flags in the edges. The pseudocode is shown in Algorithm 12-12.

```
algorithm spanningTree (val graph <metadata>)
Determine the minimum spanning tree of a network.
    Pre     graph contains a network
    Post    spanning tree determined
  1 if (empty graph)
    1   return
  2 end if
  3 vertexPtr = graph.first
  4 loop (vertexPtr not null)
    Set inTree flags false.
    1   vertexPtr->inTree  = false
    2   edgePtr            = vertexPtr->edge
    3   loop (edgePtr not null)
```

Algorithm 12-12   Minimum spanning tree of a graph

```
           1    edgePtr->inTree  = false
           2    edgePtr          = edgePtr->nextEdge
       4   end loop
       5   vertexPtr = vertexPtr->nextVertex
   5 end loop
```
Now derive spanning tree.
```
   6 vertexPtr           = graph.first
   7 vertexPtr->inTree   = true
   8 treeComplete        = false
   9 loop (not treeComplete)
       1   treeComplete  = true
       2   chkVertexPtr  = vertexPtr
       3   minEdge       = +∞
       4   minEdgePtr    = null
       5   loop (chkVertexPtr not null)
```
       Walk through graph checking vertices in tree.
```
           1   if (    chkVertexPtr->inTree    true
                   AND chkVertexPtr->outDegree > 0)
               1   edgePtr = chkVertexPtr->edge
               2   loop (edgePtr not null)
                   1   if (edgePtr->destination->inTree false)
                       1   treeComplete  = false
                       2   if (edgePtr->weight < minEdge)
                           1   minEdge    = edgePtr->weight
                           2   minEdgePtr = edgePtr
                       3   end if
                   2   end if
                   3   edgePtr = edgePtr->nextEdge
               3   end loop
           2   end if
           3   chkVertexPtr = chkVertexPtr->nextVertex
       6   end loop
       7   if (minEdgePtr not null)
```
       Found edge to insert into tree.
```
           1   minEdgePtr->inTree                = true
           2   minEdgePtr->destination->inTree  = true
       8   end if
  10 end loop
  11 return
end spanningTree
```

Algorithm 12-12   Minimum spanning tree of a graph *(continued)*

Algorithm 12-12 Analysis

This rather long algorithm is easily broken into two sections. The first section prepares the graph for processing by setting all of the in-tree flags to false.

The second section loops (see Statement 9) through the vertex graph inserting edges into the spanning tree. As we begin the loop, we set the tree-complete flag to true. If we find a vertex that is not yet in the tree, we set it to false (Statement 9.5.1.2.1.1). On the last pass through the graph, no new edges will be added and the tree-complete flag will remain true, thus terminating the vertex loop. Because we need to remember the edge with the minimum weight, at the beginning of the loop we also set a minimum edge variable to a value larger than any possible weight, plus infinity in the pseudocode. At the same time, we set a pointer to the minimum edge to null.

Within the loop, the edges from each vertex already in the tree are tested with an inner loop that traverses the edges looking for the minimum valued edge. Each edge that is not in the tree is tested to determine whether its weight is less than the current minimum we have located. If it is, we save the weight and the location of the edge. At the end of the loop (Statement 9.7), we set the flags for both the newly inserted vertex and its associated edge.

Shortest Path Algorithm

Another common application used with graphs requires that we find the shortest path between two vertices in a network. For example, if the network represents the routes flown by an airline, when we travel we would like to find the least expensive route between home and our destination. When the weights in the route graph are the flight fare, our minimum cost is the shortest path between our origin and our destination. Edsger Dijkstra developed a classic algorithm for just this problem in 1959.[1] His algorithm is generally known simply as Dijkstra's shortest path algorithm.

Note

> The Dijkstra algorithm is used to find the shortest path between any two nodes in a graph.

Shortest Path Manual Example

Before we develop the formal algorithm, let's walk through an example. We use the same graph we used for the minimum spanning tree. In this example, we want to find the shortest path from vertex A to any other vertex in the graph. The result will be a tree with a root of vertex A. The result of our analysis is shown in Figure 12-19.

---

1. E. W. Dijkstra, "A Note on Two Problems in Connection with Graphs," *Numerische Mathematik* 1 (1959): 269–271.

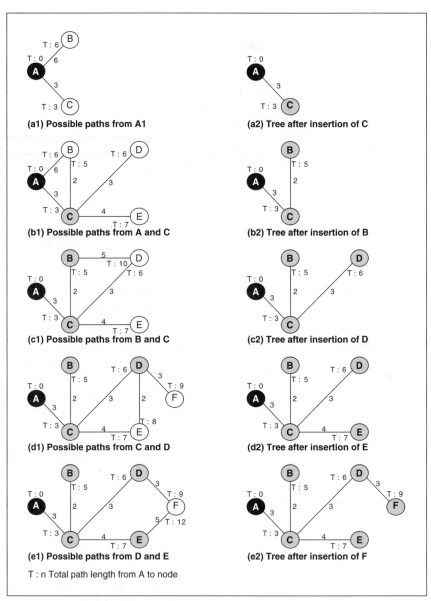

Figure 12-19 Determining shortest path

The algorithm is similar to the minimum spanning tree algorithm. We begin by inserting the starting point into the tree. We then examine the paths to all vertices adjacent to the starting point and insert the path with the minimum weight into the tree. We now have two vertices in the tree, as shown in Figure 12-19(a2).

We then examine all of the paths from the two vertices in the tree, A and C, to all of their adjacent vertices. Rather than determining the shortest path to the next vertex as we did in the spanning tree, however, we determine the total path length to the adjacent vertices. The total path length to each vertex is shown in Figure 12-19 with the notation T : n next to the destination vertex. If you examine Figure 12-19(b1), you will see that there are four paths: AB with a total weight of 6, CB with a total weight of 5, CD with a total weight of 6, and CE with a total weight of 7. We select the minimum path length, CB (T : 5), and place it in the tree. The resulting tree is shown in Figure 12-19(b2).

In the third pass through the graph, we examine the paths from the vertices in the tree (A, C, and B) to vertices not already in the tree (D and E). There are no paths from A. From B we have one path, BD, with a total weight of 10. From C we have two paths, CD with a total weight of 6 and CE with a total weight of 7. We select the minimum path, CD, with a total weight of 6.

Let's try to generalize the steps we have been following.

1. Insert the first vertex into the tree.
2. From every vertex already in the tree, examine the total path length to all adjacent vertices not in the tree. Select the edge with the minimum total path weight and insert it into the tree.
3. Repeat Step 2 until all vertices are in the tree.

Following these steps, we insert edge CE (Figure 12-19[d2]) next and then edge DF (Figure 12-19[e2]) last.

Shortest Path Data Structure

To determine the minimum path, we need to add one more field to the vertex structure, a total path length to the vertex. We call it `pathLength` (see Algorithm 12-13).

```
graphHead
    count   <integer>
    first   <pointer to graphVertex>
end graphHead

graphVertex
    nextVertex    <pointer to graphVertex>
    data          <dataType>
    inDegree      <integer>
    outDegree     <integer>
    inTree        <Boolean>
    pathLength    <integer>
```

Algorithm 12-13   Data structure for shortest path algorithm

```
    edge              <pointer to first graphEdge>
 end graphVertex

 graphEdge
    destination       <pointer to graphVertex>
    weight            <integer>
    inTree            <Boolean>
    nextEdge          <pointer to graphEdge>
 end graphEdge
```

Algorithm 12-13   Data structure for shortest path algorithm *(continued)*

Shortest Path Pseudocode

We are now ready to develop the algorithm. The pseudocode is shown in Algorithm 12-14.

```
algorithm shortestPath (val graph <metadata>)
Determine shortest path from a network vertex to other vertices.
    Pre     graph is pointer to network
    Post    minimum path tree determined
 1 if (empty graph)
    1   return
 2 end if
 3 vertexPtr = graph.first
 4 loop (vertexPtr not null)
    Initialize inTree flags and path length.
    1   vertexPtr->inTree     = false
    2   vertexPtr->pathLength = +∞
    3   edgePtr               = vertexPtr->edge
    4   loop (edgePtr not null)
        1   edgePtr->inTree = false
        2   edgePtr         = edgePtr->nextEdge
    5   end loop
    6   vertexPtr = vertexPtr->nextVertex
 5 end loop
Now derive minimum path tree.
 6 vertexPtr            = graph->first
 7 vertexPtr->inTree    = true
 8 vertexPtr->pathLength = 0
 9 treeComplete         = false
10 loop (not treeComplete)
```

Algorithm 12-14   Shortest path

```
 1   treeComplete  = true
 2   chkVertexPtr  = vertexPtr->edge
 3   minEdgePtr    = null
 4   pathPtr       = null
 5   newPathLen    = +∞
 6   loop (chkVertexPtr not null)
     Walk through graph checking vertices in tree.
     1   if (    chkVertexPtr->inTree true
             AND chkVertexPtr->outDegree > 0)
         1   edgePtr = chkVertexPtr->edge
         2   minPath = chkVertexPtr->pathLength
         3   minEdge = +∞
         4   loop (edgePtr not null)
             Locate smallest path from this vertex.
             1   if (edgePtr->destination->inTree false)
                 1   treeComplete = false
                 2   if (edgePtr->weight < minEdge)
                     1   minEdge    = edgePtr->weight
                     2   minEdgePtr = edgePtr
                 3   end if
             2   end if
             3   edgePtr = edgePtr->nextEdge
         5   end loop
             Test for shortest path.
         6   if (minPath + minEdge < newPathLen)
             1   newPathLen  = minPath + minEdge
             2   pathPtr     = minEdgePtr
         7   end if
     2   end if
     3   chkVertexPtr = chkVertexPtr->nextVertex
 7   end loop
 8   if (pathPtr not null)
     Found edge to insert into tree.
     1   pathPtr->inTree                     = true
     2   pathPtr->destination->inTree        = true
     3   pathPtr->destination->pathLength    = newPathLen
 9   end if
11 end loop
12 return
end shortestPath
```

Algorithm 12-14   Shortest path *(continued)*

Algorithm 12-14 Analysis   As we saw in the minimum spanning tree, the shortest path algorithm begins with an initialization loop that sets the in-tree flags to false and initializes the vertex path length to a number greater than the maximum possible length (+∞).

Once we have initialized the vertices, we are ready to determine the shortest path to all vertices. We start with the first vertex in the graph, as indicated by the graph first pointer. If we needed to determine the shortest path from another vertex, we would have to pass the starting point to the algorithm.

Each loop through the graph (Statement 10) inserts the vertex with the shortest path to any connected vertex, initially only A. For each vertex in the tree (Statement 10.6), we test all of its adjacent vertices and determine the minimum weight to a vertex not already in the tree (Statement 10.6.1.4). As we locate each path edge, we test to see whether it is less than any previous path edge (Statement 10.6.1.6); if it is, we save the new path length and the pointer to the edge.

When we locate the shortest path edge, we insert it (Statement 10.8) and loop back to check the graph again (Statement 10).

12-6   ABSTRACT DATA TYPE

We are now ready to discuss the abstract data type (ADT) class for a graph. You will find this one very simple, especially in comparison with the ADT for B-trees. It uses simple linked list concepts, with the stack and queue ADTs incorporated for the graph traversals.

The graph data structure is an adjacency list, as described on page 568. The data structures and the prototype declarations are declared in a graph header file, which we name `graphs.h`. The header file is shown in Program 12-1.

```
 1 | /* This header file contains the declarations and prototype
 2 |    functions for the graph ADT class.
 3 |       Written by:
 4 |       Date:
 5 | */
 6 | #include "queueADT"
 7 | #include "stackADT"
 8 |
 9 | // ==================== STRUCTURES ====================
10 | template <class TYPE>
11 | struct Vertex;
12 |
13 | template <class TYPE>
```

Program 12-1   Graph header file

```
14   struct Arc;
15
16   template <class TYPE>
17   struct Vertex
18     {
19      Vertex<TYPE>   *pNextVertex;
20      TYPE            data;
21      int             inDegree;
22      int             outDegree;
23      short           processed;
24      Arc<TYPE>      *pArc;
25     }; // Vertex
26
27   template <class TYPE>
28   struct Arc
29     {
30      Vertex<TYPE>        *destination;
31      Arc<TYPE>           *pNextArc;
32     }; // Arc
33
34   template <class TYPE, class KTYPE>
35   class Graph
36     {
37      private:
38        int      count;
39        Vertex<TYPE>   *first;
40
41      public:
42        Graph  (void);
43       ~Graph  (void);
44
45         int  insertVertex    (TYPE dataIn);
46         int  deleteVertex    (KTYPE dltKey);
47         int  insertArc       (KTYPE   fromKey, KTYPE   toKey);
48         int  deleteArc       (KTYPE   fromKey, KTYPE   toKey);
49         int  retrieveVertex  (KTYPE   key,     TYPE& DataOut);
50         int  firstArc        (KTYPE   key,     TYPE& DataOut);
51         bool emptyGraph      (void);
52         bool graphFull       (void);
53         int  graphCount      (void);
54
55         void depthFirst      (void (*process)(TYPE dataProc));
56         void breadthFirst    (void (*process)(TYPE dataProc));
57     }; // Graph
```

Program 12-1   Graph header file *(continued)*

We discuss most of the ADT functions in the following sections. Several of them, however, are very simple and parallel functions developed for other ADTs. They are not developed here.[2]

Insert Vertex

In the building of a graph, the first process is to insert the vertices (see Program 12-2).

```
1   /* ==================== insertVertex ====================
2       This function inserts new data into the graph.
3           Pre     dataIn contains data to be inserted
4           Post    data have been inserted or memory overflow
5           Return +1 if successful; -1 if memory overflow
6   */
7
8   template <class TYPE, class KTYPE>
9   int Graph<TYPE, KTYPE> ::  insertVertex (TYPE dataIn)
10  {
11  // Local Definitions
12     Vertex<TYPE>   *newPtr;
13     Vertex<TYPE>   *locPtr;
14     Vertex<TYPE>   *predPtr;
15
16  // Statements
17     newPtr = new Vertex<TYPE>;
18     if (newPtr)
19         {
20          newPtr->pNextVertex  = NULL;
21          newPtr->data         = dataIn;
22          newPtr->inDegree     = 0;
23          newPtr->outDegree    = 0;
24          newPtr->processed    = 0;
25          newPtr->pArc         = NULL;
26          count ++;
27         } // if new
28     else
29         // Memory overflow
30         return -1;
31     //  Now find insertion point
32     locPtr = first;
33     if (!locPtr)
34     // Empty graph. Insert at beginning.
35         first = newPtr;
```

Program 12-2   Insert vertex

---

2. Specifically, the graph constructor and destructor, `emptyGraph`, `graphFull`, `graphCount`, `retrieveVertex`, and `firstArc` are not included.

```
36      else
37         {
38           predPtr = NULL;
39           while (locPtr && dataIn.key > (locPtr->data).key)
40              {
41                predPtr = locPtr;
42                locPtr  = locPtr->pNextVertex;
43              } // while
44           if (!predPtr)
45              // Insert before first vertex
46              first = newPtr;
47           else
48              predPtr->pNextVertex = newPtr;
49           newPtr->pNextVertex = locPtr;
50         } // else
51      return 1;
52   } // insertVertex
```

Program 12-2   Insert vertex *(continued)*

Program 12-2 Analysis   Insert graph parallels the pseudocode. Although it is not logically necessary to set the processed flag to 0 at this time (see Statement 24), we did so for consistency. The rest of the logic in the function inserts the vertex into a singly linked list.

Delete Vertex

Delete vertex deletes a vertex from a graph, provided that its degree is 0. If another vertex points to it, or if it points to another vertex, then it cannot be deleted. The logic for delete vertex is shown in Program 12-3.

```
1   /* ==================== deleteVertex ====================
2      Deletes an existing vertex only if its degree is 0.
3         Pre     dltKey is the key of the vertex to be deleted
4         Post    vertex deleted if degree 0
5                 -or- an error code is returned
6         Return success +1 if successful
7                        -1 if degree not 0
8                        -2 if dltKey not found
9   */
10
11  template <class TYPE, class KTYPE>
12  int  Graph<TYPE, KTYPE> ::  deleteVertex (KTYPE dltKey)
13  {
14  // Local Definitions
15     Vertex<TYPE>   *predPtr;
16     Vertex<TYPE>   *walkPtr;
```

Program 12-3   Delete vertex

```
17
18    // Statements
19    if (!first)
20        return -2;
21
22    // Locate vertex to be deleted
23    predPtr = NULL;
24    walkPtr = first;
25    while (walkPtr && dltKey > (walkPtr->data).key)
26        {
27          predPtr = walkPtr;
28          walkPtr = walkPtr->pNextVertex;
29        } // walkPtr &&
30    if (!walkPtr || dltKey != (walkPtr->data.key))
31        return -2;
32
33    // Found vertex. Test degree.
34    if ((walkPtr->inDegree > 0) || (walkPtr->outDegree > 0))
35        return -1;
36
37    // Okay to delete
38    if (!predPtr)
39        first = walkPtr->pNextVertex;
40    else
41        predPtr->pNextVertex = walkPtr->pNextVertex;
42    count--;
43    delete walkPtr;
44    return 1;
45 }   // deleteVertex
```

Program 12-3   Delete vertex *(continued)*

Insert Arc

This rather lengthy function is really quite simple. To insert an arc we need to know the source vertex and the destination vertex. Much of the code locates the source and destination vertices. Once we are sure that they both exist, then we simply insert a new arc in the source adjacency list in destination vertex sequence. The code is shown in Program 12-4.

```
1  /* ===================== insertArc =====================
2     Adds an arc vertex between two vertices.
3        Pre    fromKey is key of start vertex
4               toKey is key of destination vertex
5        Post   arc added to adjacency list
6        Return success  +1 if successful
```

Program 12-4   Insert arc

```
 7                              -1 if memory overflow
 8                              -2 if fromKey not found
 9                              -3 if toKey not found
10   */
11
12   template <class TYPE, class KTYPE>
13   int Graph<TYPE, KTYPE> :: insertArc (KTYPE fromKey, KTYPE
     toKey)
14   {
15   // Local Definitions
16      Arc<TYPE>  *newPtr;
17      Arc<TYPE>  *arcPredPtr;
18      Arc<TYPE>  *arcWalkPtr;
19
20      Vertex<TYPE>  *vertFromPtr;
21      Vertex<TYPE>  *vertToPtr;
22
23   // Statements
24      newPtr = new Arc<TYPE>;
25      if (!newPtr)
26         return (-1);
27
28      // Locate source vertex
29      vertFromPtr = first;
30      while (vertFromPtr
31             && fromKey > (vertFromPtr->data).key)
32         vertFromPtr = vertFromPtr->pNextVertex;
33      if (!vertFromPtr || fromKey != (vertFromPtr->data).key)
34         return (-2);
35
36      //  Now locate to vertex
37      vertToPtr   = first;
38      while (vertToPtr
39             && toKey > (vertToPtr->data.key))
40         vertToPtr   = vertToPtr->pNextVertex;
41      if (!vertToPtr
42          || toKey !=  (vertToPtr->data).key)
43         return (-3);
44
45      // From and to vertices located. Insert new arc.
46      ++vertFromPtr->outDegree;
47      ++vertToPtr->inDegree;
48      newPtr->destination = vertToPtr;
49      if (!vertFromPtr->pArc)
50         {
51         // Inserting first arc for this vertex
52         vertFromPtr->pArc = newPtr;
```

Program 12-4 Insert arc *(continued)*

```
53        newPtr-> pNextArc = NULL;
54        return 1;
55       } // if new arc
56
57    // Find insertion point in adjacency (arc) list
58    arcPredPtr = NULL;
59    arcWalkPtr = vertFromPtr->pArc;
60    while (arcWalkPtr
61      && toKey >= (arcWalkPtr->destination->data.key))
62       {
63        arcPredPtr = arcWalkPtr;
64        arcWalkPtr = arcWalkPtr->pNextArc;
65       } // arcWalkPtr &&
66
67    if (!arcPredPtr)
68        // Insertion before first arc
69        vertFromPtr->pArc     = newPtr;
70    else
71        arcPredPtr->pNextArc = newPtr;
72    newPtr->pNextArc = arcWalkPtr;
73    return 1;
74  } // insertArc
```

Program 12-4 Insert arc *(continued)*

Delete Arc

Delete arc is another lengthy function for a relatively simple process. As with the insert arc function, we identify an arc by its source and destination vertices. Once we locate the source vertex and verify that there is an arc to its destination, we use a simple linked list deletion algorithm to delete the arc. The code is shown in Program 12-5.

```
 1  /* ==================== deleteArc ====================
 2     Deletes an existing arc.
 3        Pre     fromKey is key of start vertex and toKey is
 4                key of the destination vertex to be deleted
 5        Post    arc deleted
 6        Return success +1 if successful
 7                        -2 if fromKey not found
 8                        -3 if toKey not found
 9  */
10
11  template <class TYPE, class KTYPE>
12  int Graph<TYPE, KTYPE> :: deleteArc (KTYPE   fromKey,
13                                       KTYPE   toKey)
14  {
15  // Local Definitions
```

Program 12-5 Delete arc

```
16      Vertex<TYPE>    *fromVertexPtr;
17      Vertex<TYPE>    *toVertexPtr;
18      Arc<TYPE>       *preArcPtr;
19      Arc<TYPE>       *arcWalkPtr;
20
21   // Statements
22      if (!first)
23          return -2;
24
25      //Locate source vertex
26      fromVertexPtr = first;
27      while (fromVertexPtr
28             && fromKey > (fromVertexPtr->data).key)
29          fromVertexPtr = fromVertexPtr->pNextVertex;
30
31      if (!fromVertexPtr
32          || fromKey != (fromVertexPtr->data).key)
33          return -2;
34
35      //  Locate destination vertex in adjacency list
36      if (!fromVertexPtr->pArc)
37          return -3;
38
39      preArcPtr  = NULL;
40      arcWalkPtr = fromVertexPtr->pArc;
41      while (arcWalkPtr
42         && toKey > (arcWalkPtr->destination->data).key)
43         {
44          preArcPtr  = arcWalkPtr;
45          arcWalkPtr = arcWalkPtr->pNextArc;
46         } // while arcWalkPtr &&
47      if (!arcWalkPtr
48          || toKey  != (arcWalkPtr->destination->data.key))
49          return -3;
50      toVertexPtr = arcWalkPtr->destination;
51
52      // fromVertex, toVertex, and arcPtr located. Delete arc.
53      --fromVertexPtr->outDegree;
54      --toVertexPtr->inDegree;
55      if (!preArcPtr)
56          // Deleting first arc
57          fromVertexPtr->pArc  = arcWalkPtr->pNextArc;
58      else
59          preArcPtr->pNextArc = arcWalkPtr->pNextArc;
60      delete arcWalkPtr;
61      return 1;
62   }  // deleteArc
```

Program 12-5   Delete arc *(continued)*

Depth-First Traversal

As you study the depth-first traversal, you may want to refer back to Figure 12-9, "Depth-First Traversal of a Graph," on page 566. One of the interesting aspects of this algorithm is its use of the stack ADT class. Recall that we need to completely process a vertex and all of its descendents from start to finish before we process any adjacent vertices. We therefore must place a vertex into a stack and then pop the stack to process it. The logic is shown in Program 12-6.

```
 1    /* ==================== depthFirst ====================
 2       Process the data in the graph in depth-first order.
 3          Pre        nothing
 4          Post       vertices "processed"
 5    */
 6
 7    template <class TYPE, class KTYPE>
 8    void Graph<TYPE, KTYPE> :: depthFirst
 9               (void (*process)(TYPE dataProc))
10    {
11     // Local Definitions
12        bool                    success;
13        Vertex<TYPE>            *walkPtr;
14        Vertex<TYPE>            *vertexPtr;
15        Vertex<TYPE>            *vertToPtr;
16        Stack<Vertex<TYPE>*>    stack;
17        Arc<TYPE>               *arcWalkPtr;
18
19     // Statements
20        if (!first)
21            return;
22
23        //  Set processed flags to not processed
24        walkPtr = first;
25        while (walkPtr)
26           {
27            walkPtr->processed = 0;
28            walkPtr             = walkPtr->pNextVertex;
29           } // while
30
31        // Process each vertex in list
32        walkPtr = first;
33        while (walkPtr)
34           {
35            if (walkPtr->processed < 2)
36               {
```

Program 12-6 Depth-first traversal

```
37          if (walkPtr->processed < 1)
38             {
39             // Push and set flag to pushed
40             success = stack.pushStack (walkPtr);
41             if (!success)
42                cout << "\aStack overflow 100\a\n",
43                   exit (100);
44             walkPtr->processed = 1;
45             } // if processed < 1
46          } // if processed < 2
47       // Process descendents of vertex at stack top
48       while (!stack.emptyStack ())
49          {
50          stack.popStack(vertexPtr);
51          process (vertexPtr->data);
52          vertexPtr->processed = 2;
53
54          // Push all vertices from adjacency list
55          arcWalkPtr = vertexPtr->pArc;
56          while (arcWalkPtr)
57             {
58             vertToPtr = arcWalkPtr->destination;
59             if (vertToPtr->processed == 0)
60                {
61                success = stack.pushStack(vertToPtr);
62                if (!success)
63                  cout << "\aStack overflow 101\a\n",
64                     exit (101);
65                vertToPtr->processed = 1;
66                } // if vertToPtr
67             arcWalkPtr = arcWalkPtr->pNextArc;
68             } // while arcWalkPtr
69          } //  while !emptyStack
70       walkPtr = walkPtr->pNextVertex;
71       } // while walkPtr
72    return;
73 } // depthFirst
```

Program 12-6   Depth-first traversal *(continued)*

Breadth-First Traversal

Again, we suggest that you study Figure 12-11, "Breadth-First Traversal of a Graph," on page 567, as you work with this function. Because we want to process all of the adjacent vertices of a vertex before moving down the structure, we use a queue. The logic is shown in Program 12-7.

```
 1  /* ==================== breadthFirst ====================
 2     Process the data of the graph in breadth-first order.
 3        Pre   graph is a pointer of a graph head structure
 4        Post  graph has been processed
 5  */
 6
 7  template <class TYPE, class KTYPE>
 8  void Graph<TYPE, KTYPE> ::  breadthFirst
 9                  (void(*process) (TYPE dataProc))
10  {
11  // Local Definitions
12     bool             success;
13     Vertex<TYPE>    *walkPtr;
14     Vertex<TYPE>    *vertexPtr;
15     Vertex<TYPE>    *vertToPtr;
16     Arc<TYPE>       *arcWalkPtr;
17
18     Queue<Vertex<TYPE>*> queue;
19
20  // Statements
21     if (!first)
22        return;
23
24     // Set processed flags to not processed
25     walkPtr = first;
26     while (walkPtr)
27        {
28         walkPtr->processed = 0;
29         walkPtr            = walkPtr->pNextVertex;
30        } // while
31
32     // Process each vertex in list
33     walkPtr = first;
34     while (walkPtr)
35        {
36         if (walkPtr->processed < 2)
37            {
38             if (walkPtr->processed < 1)
39                {
40                 // Enqueue and set flag to queue
41                 success = queue.enqueue(walkPtr);
42                 if (!success)
43                    cout << "\aQueue overflow 100\a\n",
44                    exit (100);
45                 walkPtr->processed = 1;
46                } // if processed < 1
```

Program 12-7 Breadth-first traversal

```
47          } // if processed < 2
48
49      // Process descendents of vertex at queue front
50      while (!queue.emptyQueue ())
51          {
52          queue.dequeue(vertexPtr);
53          process (vertexPtr->data);
54          vertexPtr->processed = 2;
55
56          // Enqueue all vertices from adjacency list
57          arcWalkPtr = vertexPtr->pArc;
58          while (arcWalkPtr)
59              {
60              vertToPtr = arcWalkPtr->destination;
61              if (vertToPtr->processed == 0)
62                  {
63                  success = queue.enqueue(vertToPtr);
64                  if (!success)
65                      cout << "\aQueue overflow 101\a\n",
66                      exit (101);
67                  vertToPtr->processed = 1;
68                  } // if vertToPtr
69              arcWalkPtr = arcWalkPtr->pNextArc;
70              } // while arcWalkPtr
71
72          } // while !emptyQueue
73      walkPtr = walkPtr->pNextVertex;
74      } // while walkPtr
75  return;
76 } // breadthFirst
```

Program 12-7   Breadth-first traversal *(continued)*

12-7   SUMMARY

- A graph is a collection of nodes, called vertices, and a collection of line segments connecting pairs of nodes, called edges or arcs.
- Graphs may be directed or undirected. A directed graph, or digraph, is a graph in which each line has a direction. An undirected graph is a graph in which there is no direction on the lines. A line in a directed graph is called an arc.
- In a graph, two vertices are said to be adjacent if an edge directly connects them.
- A path is a sequence of vertices in which each vertex is adjacent to the next one.
- A cycle is a path of at least three vertices that starts and ends with the same vertex.

■ A loop is a special case of a cycle in which a single arc begins and ends with the same node.

■ A graph is said to be connected if, for any two vertices, there is a path from one to the other. A graph is disjointed if it is not connected.

■ The degree of a vertex is the number of vertices adjacent to it. The outdegree of a vertex is the number of arcs leaving the node; the indegree of a vertex is the number of arcs entering the node.

■ Six operations have been defined for a graph: add a vertex, delete a vertex, add an edge, delete an edge, find a node, and traverse the graph.

   ■ Add a vertex operation inserts a new vertex into a graph without connecting it to any other vertex.

   ■ Delete a vertex operation removes a vertex from a graph.

   ■ Add an edge operation inserts an edge between a source vertex and a destination vertex in a graph.

   ■ Delete an edge operation removes an edge connecting the source vertex to the destination vertex in a graph.

   ■ Find vertex operation traverses a graph looking for a specified vertex.

   ■ Traverse graph visits all nodes in the graph and processes them one by one.

■ There are two standard graph traversals: depth first and breadth first.

   ■ In the depth-first traversal, all of a node's descendents are processed before moving to an adjacent node.

   ■ In the breadth-first traversal, all of the adjacent vertices are processed before processing the descendents of a vertex.

■ To represent a graph in a computer, we need to store two sets of information: the first set represents the vertices and the second set represents the edges.

■ The most common methods used to store a graph are the adjacency matrix method and the adjacency list method.

   ■ In the adjacency matrix method, we use a vector to store the vertices and a matrix to store the edges.

   ■ In the adjacency list method, we use a linked list to store the vertices and a two-dimensional linked list to store the edges.

■ A network is a graph whose lines are weighted.

■ A spanning tree is a tree that contains all of the vertices in the graph.

■ A minimum spanning tree is a spanning tree in which the total weight of the edges is the minimum.

■ Another common algorithm in a graph is to find the shortest path between two vertices.

12-8   PRACTICE SETS

Exercises

1. In the graph in Figure 12-20 find
   a. All noncyclic paths from A to H
   b. All noncyclic paths from C to E
   c. All noncyclic paths from B to F

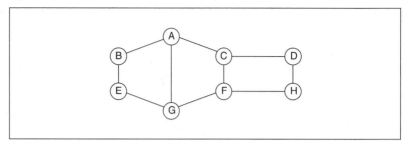

Figure 12-20   Graph for Exercises 1 through 8.

2. In the graph in Figure 12-20, find all nodes adjacent to
   a. Node A
   b. Node F
   c. Node G
3. In the graph in Figure 12-20, find the degree, outdegree, and indegree of
   vertices A, E, F, G, and H.
4. Give the depth-first traversal of the graph in Figure 12-20, starting from
   vertex A.
5. Give the breadth-first traversal of the graph in Figure 12-20, starting
   from vertex A.
6. Draw three spanning trees that can be found in the graph in Figure
   12-20.
7. Give the adjacency matrix representation of the graph in Figure 12-20.
8. Give the adjacency list representation of the graph in Figure 12-20.
9. Find the minimum spanning tree of the graph in Figure 12-21.

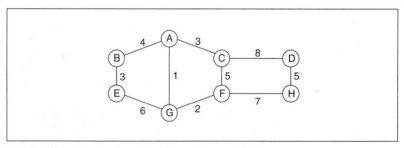

Figure 12-21   Graph for Exercises 9 through 12

10. Find the shortest path between node A and all other nodes in the graph
    in Figure 12-21.
11. Give the adjacency matrix representation of the graph in Figure 12-21.
12. Give the adjacency list representation of the graph in Figure 12-21.
13. Draw the directed graph for the adjacency matrix representation in
    Figure 12-22.

	A	B	C	D	E	F
A	0	3	4	0	2	1
B	0	0	2	0	0	3
C	0	0	0	2	6	1
D	2	6	1	0	1	2
E	0	0	0	0	0	3
F	0	0	0	0	0	0

Figure 12-22   Adjacency matrix for Exercise 13

14. A graph can be used to show relationships. For example, from the following list of people belonging to the same club (vertices) and their friendships (edges), find

```
People = {George, Jim, Jean, Frank, Fred, John, Susan}
Friendship = {(George, Jean), (Frank, Fred),
              (George, John), (Jim, Fred),
              (Jim, Frank),   (Jim, Susan),
              (Susan, Frank)}
```

   a. All friends of John
   b. All friends of Susan
   c. All friends of friends of Jean
   d. All friends of friends of Jim

Problems

15. Write an algorithm that determines whether a node is disjoint.
16. Write an algorithm that disjoints a node.
17. Write an algorithm that finds the sum of the degrees for a node using the adjacency list representation.
18. Both the depth-first and breadth-first traversals process disjoint graphs. Write an algorithm, connected, that traverses a graph and returns true if the graph is connected and false if it is disjoint.
19. Write an algorithm, connected, that determines whether there is at least one arc pointing to a specified vertex. Hint: This is a very simple algorithm.
20. In a weakly connected graph, it may not be possible to start at one vertex and reach another. Write an algorithm that given the graph, a source vertex, and a destination vertex determines whether there is at least one path from the source to the destination.
21. Algorithm 12-9, "Depth-First Traversal," on page 582, uses a stack to traverse the graph. Rewrite the algorithm to use recursion. Hint: You will need two algorithms, one to interface with the using algorithm and one for the recursion.

Projects

22. Write the C++ code for Algorithm 12-12, "Minimum Spanning Tree of a Graph," on page 589, using the ADT given in the text.

23. Write the C++ code for Algorithm 12-14, "Shortest Path," on page 594, using the ADT given in the text.

24. Write an algorithm that prints the minimum spanning tree of a graph. At the end, print the weight of the spanning tree. A suggested report format is shown below.

source vertex	To Vertex	Weight
A	B	2
A	C	4
B	D	3
D	E	1

Total weight of spanning tree: 10

25. Revise the graph ADT using the adjacency matrix as the data structure.

26. One of the tools used to manage large projects is known as the critical path method (CPM). In CPM, the manager builds a network of all phases of a project and then evaluates the network to determine critical aspects of the project.

In a CPM network, each vertex is an event, such as the start or completion of a task. The arcs connecting the vertices represent the duration of the activity. Unlike the examples in the text, they also store the name of the activity. To better understand the concept, let's look at a possible CPM plan to build a house. The network for this project is shown in Figure 12-23.

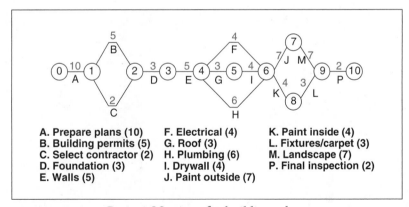

A. Prepare plans (10)   F. Electrical (4)   K. Paint inside (4)
B. Building permits (5)   G. Roof (3)   L. Fixtures/carpet (3)
C. Select contractor (2)   H. Plumbing (6)   M. Landscape (7)
D. Foundation (3)   I. Drywall (4)   P. Final inspection (2)
E. Walls (5)   J. Paint outside (7)

Figure 12-23   Project 26: steps for building a house

In the plan, we see that it will take 10 days to prepare the building plan (A) and 5 days to get it approved (B). Furthermore, we can't start building until we have selected the contractor (C).

We could construct the shortest path from the start to the end for our plan, but it would be of little value. On the other hand, if we determined the maximum path—that is, the path with the greatest sum of the weights—we would know which steps in our plan are critical. If a critical step slips even 1 day, we slip our end date. We can slip noncritical dates, however, without slipping our end date, as long as the slip does not change the critical path for the project.

Modify Algorithm 12-12, "Minimum Spanning Tree of a Graph," on page 589, to determine the maximum path through the graph. Then provide a menu that will allow the project manager to answer the following questions:

a. What is the shortest possible completion time (SPCT)? The SPCT is the longest path through the graph from beginning to end.

b. What is the earliest start time (EST) for each activity? The EST is the sum of the weights in the maximum spanning tree up to the activity.

c. What is the latest start time (LST) for each activity? The LST is the SPCT for the whole project minus the SPCT for the rest of the project (starting from the current activity).

d. What is the slack time for each activity? The slack time is LST – EST.

e. Is an activity a critical path item? Critical path items have a slack time of zero.

f. What is the critical path for the project? The critical path is the subgraph consisting of the maximum spanning tree.

27. The graph is another structure that can be used to solve the maze problem (see Project 23, on page 611). Every start point, dead end, goal, and decision point can be represented by a node. The arcs between the nodes represent one possible path through the maze. A graph maze is shown in Figure 12-24.

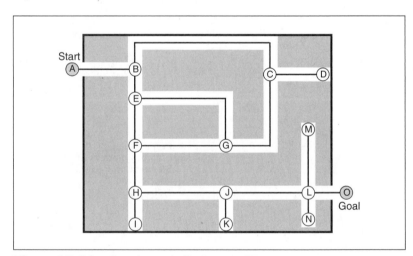

Figure 12-24   Graph maze for Project 27

Write a program that simulates a mouse's movement through the maze using a graph and a depth-first traversal. When the program is complete, print the path through the maze.

28. A computer company in the Silicon Valley area (see Figure 12-25) needs to route delivery vehicles between cities on the shortest route. Having studied data structures, you recognize that this is an application for Dijkstra's shortest path algorithm. To demonstrate your proposal, you decide to implement it on your computer. To do so you must complete the following tasks:

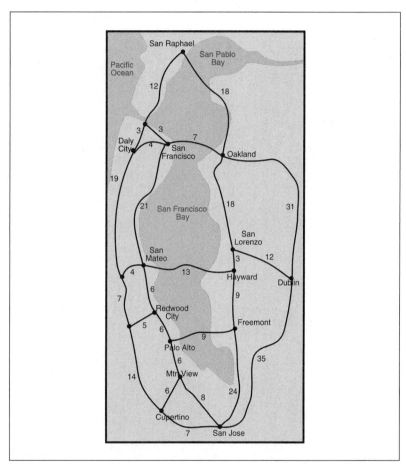

Figure 12-25   Map of Silicon Valley area

   a. Convert the map in Figure 12-25 to a network and present it to management.
   b. Modify the graph ADT to store weights in the arc nodes.
   c. Write an interactive program that given the start and destination will display the shortest route between them.

ASCII Tables

This appendix contains the American Standard Code for Information Interchange (ASCII). Table A-1 indicates the decimal, hexadecimal, octal, and symbolic codes with an English interpretation, if appropriate. Table A-2 gives a hexadecimal matrix of all values.

A-1   ASCII CODES (LONG FORM)

Decimal	Hexadecimal	Octal	Symbol	Interpretation
0	00	00	null	NULL value
1	01	01	SOH	Start of heading
2	02	02	STX	Start of text
3	03	03	ETX	End of text
4	04	04	EOT	End of transmission
5	05	05	ENQ	Enquiry
6	06	06	ACK	Acknowledgment
7	07	07	BEL	Ring bell
8	08	10	BS	Backspace
9	09	11	HT	Horizontal tab
10	0A	12	LF	Line feed
11	0B	13	VT	Vertical tab
12	0C	14	FF	Form feed
13	0D	15	CR	Carriage return
14	0E	16	SO	Shift out
15	0F	17	SI	Shift in
16	10	20	DLE	Data link escape
17	11	21	DC1	Device control 1
18	12	22	DC2	Device control 2
19	13	23	DC3	Device control 3
20	14	24	DC4	Device control 4
21	15	25	NAK	Negative acknowledgment
22	16	26	SYN	Synchronous idle
23	17	27	ETB	End of transmission block
24	18	30	CAN	Cancel
25	19	31	EM	End of medium
26	1A	32	SUB	Substitute
27	1B	33	ESC	Escape
28	1C	34	FS	File separator
29	1D	35	GS	Group separator
30	1E	36	RS	Record separator
31	1F	37	US	Unit separator
32	20	40	SP	Space
33	21	41	!	
34	22	42	"	Double quote

Table A-1   ASCII codes

Decimal	Hexadecimal	Octal	Symbol	Interpretation
35	23	43	#	
36	24	44	$	
37	25	45	%	
38	26	46	&	
39	27	47	'	Apostrophe
40	28	50	(	
41	29	51	)	
42	2A	52	*	
43	2B	53	+	
44	2C	54	,	Comma
45	2D	55	−	Minus
46	2E	56	.	
47	2F	57	/	
48	30	60	0	
49	31	61	1	
50	32	62	2	
51	33	63	3	
52	34	64	4	
53	35	65	5	
54	36	66	6	
55	37	67	7	
56	38	70	8	
57	39	71	9	
58	3A	72	:	Colon
59	3B	73	;	Semicolon
60	3C	74	<	
61	3D	75	=	
62	3E	76	>	
63	3F	77	?	
64	40	100	@	
65	41	101	A	
66	42	102	B	
67	43	103	C	
68	44	104	D	
69	45	105	E	
70	46	106	F	

Table A-1   ASCII codes *(continued)*

Decimal	Hexadecimal	Octal	Symbol	Interpretation
71	47	107	G	
72	48	110	H	
73	49	111	I	
74	4A	112	J	
75	4B	113	K	
76	4C	114	L	
77	4D	115	M	
78	4E	116	N	
79	4F	117	O	
80	50	120	P	
81	51	121	Q	
82	52	122	R	
83	53	123	S	
84	54	124	T	
85	55	125	U	
86	56	126	V	
87	57	127	W	
88	58	130	X	
89	59	131	Y	
90	5A	132	Z	
91	5B	133	[	Open bracket
92	5C	134	\	Backslash
93	5D	135	]	Close bracket
94	5E	136	^	Caret
95	5F	137	_	Underscore
96	60	140	`	Grave accent
97	61	141	a	
98	62	142	b	
99	63	143	c	
100	64	144	d	
101	65	145	e	
102	66	146	f	
103	67	147	g	
104	68	150	h	
105	69	151	i	
106	6A	152	j	

Table A-1   ASCII codes *(continued)*

Decimal	Hexadecimal	Octal	Symbol	Interpretation
107	6B	153	k	
108	6C	154	l	
109	6D	155	m	
110	6E	156	n	
111	6F	157	o	
112	70	160	p	
113	71	161	q	
114	72	162	r	
115	73	163	s	
116	74	164	t	
117	75	165	u	
118	76	166	v	
119	77	167	w	
120	78	170	x	
121	79	171	y	
122	7A	172	z	
123	7B	173	{	Open brace
124	7C	174	|	Bar
125	7D	175	}	Close brace
126	7E	176	~	Tilde
127	7F	177	DEL	Delete

Table A-1   ASCII codes *(continued)*

A-2   ASCII TABLE (SHORT FORM)

	0	1	2	3	4	5	6	7	8	9	A	B	C	D	E	F
0	null	SOH	STX	ETX	EOT	ENQ	ACK	BEL	BS	HT	LF	VT	FF	CR	SO	SI
1	DLE	DC1	DC2	DC3	DC4	NAK	SYN	ETB	CAN	EM	SUB	ESC	FS	GS	RS	US
2	SP	!	"	#	$	%	&	'	(	)	*	+	,	–	.	/
3	0	1	2	3	4	5	6	7	8	9	:	;	<	=	>	?
4	@	A	B	C	D	E	F	G	H	I	J	K	L	M	N	O
5	P	Q	R	S	T	U	V	W	X	Y	Z	[	\	]	^	_
6	`	a	b	c	d	e	f	g	h	i	j	k	l	m	n	o
7	p	q	r	s	t	u	v	w	x	y	z	{	|	}	~	DEL

Table A-2   Short ASCII table (hexadecimal)

B Structure Charts

This appendix documents the structure chart concepts and styles used in this book. It includes the basic symbology for our structure charts and some guidelines on their use. Obviously, it is not a tutorial on the design process.

The structure chart is the primary design tool for a program. As a design tool, it is used before you start writing your program. An analogy will help you understand the importance of designing before you start coding.

Assume that you have decided to build a house. You will spend a lot of time thinking about exactly what you want. How many rooms will it need? Do you want a family room or a great room? Should the laundry be inside the house or in the garage? To make sure everyone understands what you want, you will prepare formal blueprints that describe everything in detail. Even if you are building something small, like a dollhouse for your child or a toolshed for your backyard, you will make some sketches or plans.

Deciding what you want in your house is comparable to determining the requirements for a large system. Drawing up a set of blueprints parallels the structure chart in the design of a program. All require advance planning; only the level of detail changes.

Professionals use the structure chart for another purpose. When you work in a project team environment, you must have your design reviewed before you start writing your program. This review process is called a structured walk-through. The review team consists of the systems analyst responsible for your area of the project, a representative of the user community, a system test engineer, and one or two programmers from the project.

Your design walk-through serves three purposes. First, it ensures that you understand how your program fits into the system by communicating your design to the team. If there are any omissions or communication errors, they should be detected here. If you invite programmers who must interface with your program, the walk-through will also ensure that the interprogram communication linkages are correct.

Second, it validates your design. In creating your design, you will have considered several alternative approaches to writing your program. The review team will expect to see and understand the different designs you considered and hear why you chose the design you are proposing. They will challenge aspects of the design and suggest approaches you may not have considered. The result of the review will be the best possible design.

Third, it gives the test engineer the opportunity to assess the testability of your program. This step in turn ensures that the final program will be robust and as error free as possible.

B-1   STRUCTURE CHART SYMBOLS

Figure B-1 shows the various symbols used to write a structure chart. We describe each of these symbols in this section. In addition to discussing the symbols themselves, we cover how to read a structure chart and several rules to follow in your structure charts.

Modules

Each rectangle in a structure chart (see Figure B-2) represents a module *that you will write*. Modules that are a part of the implementation language, such as read, write, and square root, are not shown in your structure chart. The name in the rectangle is the name you will give to the module. It should be meaningful. The software engineering principle known as *intelligent names* states that the names used in a program should be self-documenting; that is, they should convey their intended usage to the reader. Intelligent names should be used for both modules and data names within your program.

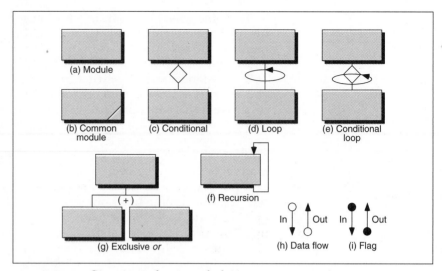

Figure B-1   Structure chart symbols

Although all names should be descriptive, we are going to break our own rule because we want to concentrate on the format of a structure chart rather than a particular program application. The names you see in Figure B-2 identify the various symbols for discussion.

Note

> **Structure charts show only module flow; they contain no code.**

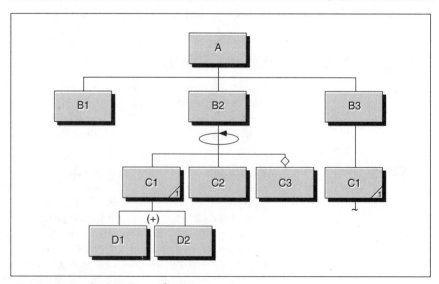

Figure B-2   A structure chart

At this point, it is helpful to discuss an important structure chart rule: No code is contained in a structure chart. A structure chart shows only the module flow through the program. It is not a block diagram or a flowchart. As a map of your program, the structure chart shows only the logical flow of the modules. The algorithm design shows exactly how each module does its job. Another way of looking at it is that a structure chart shows the big picture; the details are left to algorithm design.

Reading Structure Charts

Before discussing the rest of the symbols, let's look at how to read structure charts. Structure charts are read *top-down, left-right.* Thus, referring to Figure B-2, Module A (the first rectangle at the top) consists of three submodules, B1, B2, and B3. According to the left-right rule, the first call in the program is to B1. After B1 is complete, the program calls B2. When B2 is complete, the program calls B3. In other words, the modules on the same level of a structure chart are called in order from the left to the right.

The concept of top-down is demonstrated by B2. When B2 is called, it calls C1, C2, and C3 in turn. Module C2 does not start running, however, until C1 is finished. While C1 is running, it calls D1 or D2. In other words, all modules in a line from C1 to D2 must be called before Module C2 can start.

Common Modules

There are ten modules in Figure B-2. Two of them, however, are the same module (C1). When a module is used in more than one place in your design, it is repeated. In other words, if you need to call a common module from several different places within a program, each call is represented by a rectangle in your structure chart. To identify a common module, draw a line in the lower right corner of the rectangle (see Figure B-1[b]). If multiple modules are used multiple times, it helps to add a unique number for each module. We have numbered C1 in Figure B-2 even though it is not necessary in this example just to illustrate this technique.

One final point about common modules: When common modules call several other modules, their design can become quite large. Rather than redraw all of the submodules each time a common module is called, you can simply indicate that modules are called by including a line below the rectangle and a cut (~) symbol. This concept is also shown in Figure B-2. In this hypothetical design, Module C1 is called by both Module B2 and Module B3. Rather than repeat the design of C1, however, we simply indicate that it calls other modules with a cut symbol when we call it from B3.

Conditional Calls

In Figure B-2, Modules B1, B2, and B3 are always called. Often, however, a module is sometimes called and sometimes passed over. We call this condition a conditional call. It is shown in Figure B-2 when Module B2 calls Module C3. To identify a module as conditional, we use a small diamond, the same symbol used in a flowchart to indicate a selection statement. The code that implements this design is a simple *if* statement, as seen below.

```
1  if (condition)
   1    call C3
2  end if
```

Exclusive Or

Two or more modules are often called exclusively. For example, the design for our program in Figure B-2 requires that we call either D1 or D2 but not both. This design could be implemented with the following statements in Module C1:

```
1  if (condition)
   1    call D1
2  else
   2    call D2
3  end if
```

It is obvious from the code that either D1 or D2 will be called but not both. We need some way to describe this design in the structure chart. The symbol that we use to indicate exclusive calls is (+). Note that if several calls were grouped exclusively, such as in a multiway selection (a *switch* or nested *if* statements in C++), then we would use the same symbol.

Loops

Very often a design requires that a module be called in a loop. For example, assume that in Figure B-2, B2 calls C1, C2, and C3 while processing a file. It must loop, therefore, until all of the data have been read. The loop symbol is an oval. We use an arrow on our oval, but it is not required. The implementation code for our loop would look something like the following piece of code:

```
1  loop (not end of file)
   1    call C1
   2    call C2
   3    if (condition)
      1    call C3
   4    end if
2  end loop
```

Conditional Loops

Sometimes we loop conditionally. For example, consider the following piece of code in which we test for a null linked list before beginning a search. The structure chart symbol for this code combines the conditional diamond with the loop oval, as shown in Figure B-1(e).

```
1 if (list->first not null)
   1    walker = list->first
   2    loop (walker not null)
        1    ...
2 end if
```

Recursion

The last of the module symbols represents a recursive module. It is shown in Figure B-1(f). To see a use of the recursion symbol and as a final example of a structure chart, consider the design of the AVL tree insert as seen in Chapter 8. It is repeated in Figure B-3. This structure chart contains all of the possible structure chart symbols except for a loop. It also presents some interesting design points.

Note that there are two recursive calls in the module, both in the second level. We need two calls because the first one has the left subtree as a parameter and the second one has the right subtree as a parameter. We have used an optional variation of the recursion symbol in this figure, one that doesn't come all the way to the bottom of the rectangle. Also, you should note that the recursion symbol is not generally used on the top rectangle that identifies the name of the module, although it would not be considered wrong to do so.

In this design we are inserting a node on either the left or right branch of the tree. (If you haven't studied trees yet, you may find it a little difficult to understand the following discussion.) Because this is an *exclusive or* design, we place the (+) between the two vertical lines below "AVL Insert."

Looking at the design for inserting on the left, we see that we have a recursive call and then a conditional call to balance the tree. If the tree is still in balance after the insert, we don't need to balance it. To show

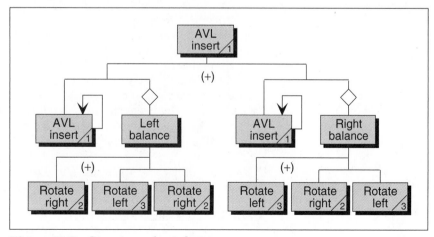

Figure B-3   Structure chart design

that these two calls are grouped together, we connect them with a horizontal line, which also separates the *exclusive or* design.

Now look at the design for "Left Balance." Once again we see an *exclusive or,* this time indicating that we have a single rotation to the right or a double rotation to the left and the right. Again, note the use of the horizontal line to group the design steps and isolate the *exclusive or* logic.

Data Flows and Flags

At this point, we have covered all of the symbols except for data flows and flags. As a general rule, we do not use them because they quickly break down and are often not maintained. We include them here for completeness.

Data flows and flags represent parameters passed to and from the module. Input parameters are shown on the left of the vertical line connecting the modules, and output parameters are shown on the right of the line. The only difference between them symbolically is that the data flows have a hollow circle, whereas the flags have a solid circle. In either case, the names of the data flows and flags should be included on the structure chart.

B-2   STRUCTURE CHART RULES

The rules described in this section are summarized in Table B-1.

1. Each rectangle in a structure chart represents a module written by the programmer. Standard modules provided as a part of the language translator are not included.
2. The name in the rectangle is an intelligent name that communicates the purpose of the module. It is the name that will be used in coding the module.
3. The structure chart contains only module flow. No code is indicated.
4. Common modules are indicated by a crosshatch or shading in the lower right corner of the module's rectangle.
5. Common calls are shown in a structure wherever they will be found in the program. If they contain submodule calls, the complete structure need be shown only once.
6. Data flows and flags are optional. When used, they should be named.
7. Input flows and flags are shown on the left of the vertical line; output flows and flags are shown on the right.

Table B-1   Structure chart rules

Program Standards and Styles

This appendix documents the programming standards and styles used throughout this book. Most companies have their own documented standards and styles. Obviously, when you work for a company, you need to follow its standards.

Our intent with these standards is to suggest some well-proven standards and styles that will enable you to program in a clear and readable form. They form the basis of a discipline that will be needed when you program professionally.

On the other hand, we also encourage you to experiment within the framework of these standards and develop a style that suits you.

For discussion, we have grouped the standard and style comments by program section.

C-1   GLOBAL AREA

Standard

The global area of a program is to be used only for interprogram and interfunction communication (see Program C-1).

1. Place comments at the beginning of the program that document:
   a. The purpose of the program
   b. The author of the program
   c. The date the program was written
   d. The date and a description of all changes

2. Preprocessor commands:
   a. All includes are placed at the beginning of the program
   b. Defined constants are placed at the beginning of the program
   c. Macros are placed here and within functions as required

3. Prototype declarations are placed in the global area at the beginning of the program.
4. All structure definitions are placed either in the global section at the beginning of the program or in a header file.

Standard

Variables are not to be placed in the global section of the program. The only variables allowed in the global section of the program are for external communication. *No internal variables may be placed in this section.*

```
 1   /* This program ...
 2          Written by:
 3          Date:
 4
 5      Change History:
 6         mm/dd/yy: Authority: Change request #nn.
 7                        Program modified to ...
 8   */
 9   #include ...
10
11   // Constants
12
13   // Prototype Declarations
14
15   // Macros
16
17   // Interprogram Communication Variables
```

Program C-1   Contents of global program area

C-2   PROGRAM MAIN LINE

Standard   The only definitions found in `main` are those that need to be passed between functions called by `main` (see Program C-2).

Standard   The only statements found in `main` are

1. A start-of-program message
2. Function calls
3. An end-of-program message

```
1   int main (void)
2   {
3   // Local Definitions
4
5   // Statements
6      cout << "\nBegin program <name of program>\n\n";
7
8      <function calls only>
9
10     cout << "\nEnd of program <name of program>\n\n";
11     return 0;
12  } // main
```

Program C-2   Standards for `main`

C-3   GENERAL CODING STANDARDS

Standard   Do not crowd your code:

1. Provide at least one space before and after every operator.
2. Provide at least one space at the beginning and end of every expression.
3. Align the operator and second operand in a series of assignment statements to make the code more readable.
4. Group related statements by placing blank lines before and after them. (Think of a series of statements as sentences in a paragraph and break them up into small groups that deal with only one process within the function.)

Standard   Only one declaration or definition may be coded on a line.

Standard   With the obvious exception of *for* and the conditional expression, only one statement may be coded on a line.

Style   Group variable declarations by type. Order them alphabetically by type and place a blank line between types.

Style   Adopt a consistent identifier naming style. The preferred style is lower-case, with the first letter of each identifier segment after the first identifier capitalized.

Style   Adopt consistent naming conventions, such as

1. `fpName` for file pointers
2. `pName` for variable pointers

Style   Abbreviate only when identifiers become long. A good abbreviation style is

1. Remove all vowels unless they start a word.
2. Represent double consonants by a single consonant.

Standard   Minimize the number of statements within a function.

Style   The statement portion of a function should fit on one screen.

Standard   Code that depends on a statement is indented at least three spaces. (Exception: Only the first "*else if* . . ." is indented.)

Standard   All blocks are terminated with a comment.

1. End a function block with a comment that contains the name of the function, such as `// main`
2. End *if* statements with `// if` or `// if <condition>`
3. End *else* statements with `// else` or `// else <condition>`
4. End *while* statements with `// while`
5. End *for* statements with `// for`
6. Comment intrafunction blocks at the beginning and at the end.

Standard   Avoid using *continue* and *break* statements within loops.

Standard   Never use *goto*.

C-4   VARIABLES AND STRUCTURES

Standard   Use intelligent identifier names.

1. Avoid single-character identifiers except for loop counters in a *for* statement.
2. Identifiers should clearly convey their contents and use.

     Hint: If you feel that you need to add a comment to explain the name of a variable, the name is inadequate. Change the name.

Style   Indent components within a structure definition to show their relationship in the definition.

C-5   FUNCTION DEFINITION

Standard   Always explicitly code the return type.

Standard   Begin each function, except `main`, with comments that identify its purpose and explain its parameters and return value.

Standard   Within the function definition, place each formal parameter on a different line. Align the parameter types and identifiers.

Style   Place the parameters within a function prototype statement on multiple lines only when there are too many. In that case, place each parameter on a separate line and align the types and identifiers.

Standard   Clearly document the declarative portion of all functions (see Program C-3).

Style   Within a function, use comments only to explain a block of code. Place comments at the beginning of the code that needs explanation. *Do not place comments on lines.*

Standard   Terminate all functions with a *return* statement.

Style   Avoid multiple *return* statements within a function.

Standard   Place a visual identifier at the beginning of each function (see Program C-3).

Standard   Clearly mark the end of the program (see Program C-3).

```
 1   /* ================= <function name> =================
 2      <function purpose>
 3         Pre  <explanation of all parameters>
 4         Post <explanation of all output actions and return value>
 5   */
 6   int doIt (int    p1,
 7             float p2)
 8   {
 9   // Local Definitions
10
11   // Statements
12
13      return 0;
14   } // <function name>
15   // ================= End of Program =================
```

Program C-3   Function format

C-6   CLASS DECLARATIONS

Standard   Data members in classes should be private or protected.

Standard   Overloaded operators should be logical and intuitive.

Standard   Inline functions should be used only when the code is expected to be called from multiple locations.

Style   Develop a clearly identifiable naming convention for class names. We use a style in which the first letter of a class is always uppercase. For example, our fraction class is named `Fraction`.

Random Numbers

Random numbers are found in many data structure applications. For example, hashed lists use random numbers both as a hashing method and for collision resolution. This appendix documents random number generation.

D-1   RANDOM NUMBERS IN C++

C++ provides an excellent facility for generating random numbers. This section documents the standard C++ functions *rand* and *srand*.

srand

The ***srand*** function, seed random, creates the seed for a pseudorandom number series. A pseudorandom series is a repeatable series of numbers with random properties. Each seed will produce a different series when the **random number** generator (*srand*) is called (see below). To generate a truly random number series, therefore, the seed must be a random number. The most common technique for generating a random number is to use a seed that is a function of the current date or time of day.

The seed random prototype is

```
void srand (unsigned int seed);
```

Example: To generate random numbers, use the following call before your first call to *rand*. (The time function requires the *time* header file.)

```
srand(time(NULL));
```

To generate a pseudorandom number series, seed random is called with a constant, preferably a large prime number:

```
srand (997);
```

Regardless of the series you want, *srand* should be *called only once* in for each random number series you generate. Usually, it is called only once in a program.

rand

The ***rand*** function returns a pseudorandom integer between 0 and RAND_MAX, which is defined in the standard library as the largest number that *rand* can generate. The ANSI standard requires that it be at least 32,767. Each call generates the next number in a random number series.

The random number prototype is

```
int rand (void);
```

If *srand* is not called before the first call to *rand*, the series will be based on the seed 1. Thus, you will always generate the same series of numbers.

D-2　CUSTOM RANDOM NUMBER GENERATOR

Sometimes it is necessary to write your own random number generator. For example, if you are using a language that doesn't have a random number generator, you will need to write your own. Even when you are using a language such as C++ that has a random number facility, if you want the random numbers to be standard across hardware platforms, you may need to write your own random number generator. In this section we provide a simple random number generator based on the formula

$$y = ax + c$$

where y is the random number, a and c are prime number constants, and x is the random number seed. The pseudocode for this random number generator is shown in Algorithm D-1.

```
algorithm random (seed <integer>)
Generate the next number in a pseudorandom number series.
   Pre    seed is an integer
   Post   next number in series returned
 1 randomNumber = 7919 × seed + 997
 2 if (randomNumber < 0)
   1    randomNumber = absolute (randomNumber)
 3 end if
 4 return randomNumber
end random
```

Algorithm D-1　　A pseudorandom number generator

Algorithm D-1 Analysis　　As you study the algorithm, you may wonder why we are concerned about negative numbers. Addresses in a list are always positive. We need to ensure that the number developed in Statement 1 did not overflow the numeric field and result in a negative number. If it did, we fix it by taking its absolute value.

D-3　SCALING A RANDOM NUMBER

Often you will need to generate a series of numbers in a narrower range. To create your own range, you must scale and shift, if necessary, what is returned from the random number generator algorithm. The scaling is done by the modulus operator. For example, to produce a random number in the range 0–50, you simply scale the random number as shown below.[1]

```
rand () modulo 51
```

Modulus works well when your range starts at 0. But what if you need a different range? In that case, you must shift the result. For example, suppose you want a random number between 3 and 7 (Figure D-1). If you call *rand* and then use modulus 8, your range will be 0 through 7. To convert to the correct range, you first determine your modulus factor by subtracting the starting point (3) from the modulus divisor (8) and then adding the starting point to the resulting number. Thus, for our example, we subtract 3 from 8, which makes the modulus divisor 5.

Generalizing the algorithm, we get

```
rand() modulo ((max + 1) - min) + min
```

where min is the minimum number and max is the maximum number in the desired range. Of course, if you desire a range starting at 0, the minimum value (min) is 0 and therefore ignored. For example, to create a random number in the range 20 to 30 using C++, we would use the expression shown below.

```
rand() % ((30 + 1) - 20) + 20 ⇨ rand() % 11 + 20
```

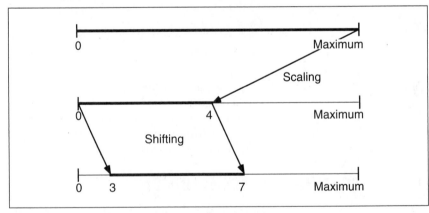

Figure D-1   Random number scaling for 3–7

---

1. The C++ code would be rand () % 51.

Program D-1 demonstrates the generation of random numbers.

```
1   /* Demonstrates the generation of random numbers in
2      three different series:
3          3 and  7
4         20 and 50
5         -6 and 15
6      After generating three numbers, it prints them.
7         Written by:
8         Date:
9   */
10  #include <iostream>
11  #include <stdlib.h>
12
13  int main (void)
14  {
15  // Local Definitions
16      int  a;
17      int  b;
18      int  c;
19
20  // Statements
21      srand (997);
22      // range is 3 through 7
23      a = rand () % 5  +  3 ;                    // 8 - 3 = 5
24
25      // range is 20 through 50
26      b = rand () % 31 + 20;                     // 51 - 20 = 31
27
28      // range is -6 through 15
29      c = rand () % 22  - 6 ;                    // 16 - (-6) = 22
30      cout << "Range 3  to 7:  " << a << endl;
31      cout << "Range 20 to 50: " << b << endl;
32      cout << "Range -6 to 15: " << c << endl;
33      return 0;
34  } // main
```

```
Results:
Range 3  to 7:  3
Range 20 to 50: 34
Range -6 to 15: 2
```

Program D-1   Scaling for random number generation

Program D-1 Analysis   Note that we have used *srand* to generate pseudorandom numbers. The seed we used, 997, is a prime number. Generally speaking, prime numbers generate better random number series than non-prime numbers. However, using a seed does not guarantee that you will get the same results if you run the program on a different computer. It only guarantees that when you run the program repetitively on the same computer, you will always get the same set of random numbers. Given the same seed, different compilers may generate different random series depending on their random number algorithm.

Standard C++ Libraries

This appendix documents two important C++ libraries.

E-1   LIMITS.H

The limits library (Table E-1) documents the minimum and maximum values for C++ integral types.

Meaning	Identifier	16-bit word [a]	32-bit word [a]
Bits in a char	CHAR_BIT	8	8
Short char minimum	SCHAR_MIN	–128	–128
Short char maximum	SCHAR_MAX	127	127
Unsigned char maximum	UCHAR_MAX	255	255
Char minimum	CHAR_MIN	–128	–128
Char maximum	CHAR_MAX	127	127
Short int minimum	SHRT_MIN	–32,768	–32,768
Short int maximum	SHRT_MAX	32,767	32,767
Unsigned short maximum	USHRT_MAX	65,535	65,535
Int minimum	INT_MIN	–32,768	–2,147,483,648
Int maximum	INT_MAX	32,767	2,147,483,647
Unsigned int maximum	UINT_MAX	65,535	4,294,967,295
Long minimum	LONG_MIN	–2,147,483,648	–2,147,483,648
Long maximum	LONG_MAX	2,147,483,647	2,147,483,647
Unsigned long maximum	ULONG_MAX	4,294,967,295	4,294,967,295

[a] Libraries contain unformatted numbers (no commas), often expressed in hexadecimal.

Table E-1   Contents of limits.h

E-2   FLOAT.H

The float library (Table E-2) documents the minimum and maximum values for the C++ floating-point data types.

Meaning	Identifier	Typical value 32-bit word
Digits of precision	FLT_DIG	6
	DBL_DIG	16
	LDBL_DIG	16
Size of mantissa	FLT_MANT_DIG	24
	DBL_MANT_DIG	56
	LDBL_MANT_DIG	56
Largest integer for negative exponent (float radix)	FLT_MIN_EXP	−127
	DBL_MIN_EXP	−127
	LDBL_MIN_EXP	−127
Largest integer for negative exponent (base 10)	FLT_MIN_10_EXP	−38
	DBL_MIN_10_EXP	−38
	LDBL_MIN_10_EXP	−38
Largest integer for positive exponent (float radix)	FLT_MAX_EXP	127
	DBL_MAX_EXP	127
	LDBL_MAX_EXP	127
Largest integer for positive exponent (base 10)	FLT_MAX_10_EXP	38
	DBL_MAX_10_EXP	38
	LDBL_MAX_10_EXP	38
Largest possible real number	FLT_MAX	1.701412e+38
	DBL_MAX	1.701412e+38
	LDBL_MAX	1.701412e+38
Smallest possible real number	FLT_MIN	2.938736e-39
	DBL_MIN	2.938736e-39
	LDBL_MIN	2.938736e-39
Smallest possible fraction	FLT_EPSILON	5.960464e-08
	DBL_EPSILON	1.387779e-17
	LDBL_EPSILON	1.387779e-17

Table E-2   Contents of `float.h`

C++ Function Prototypes

In this appendix we list most of the standard functions found in the C++ language. We have organized them by library so that related functions are grouped together. For your convenience, we have also listed them alphabetically in the function index table shown in Section F-1. Note that not all functions are covered in this appendix.

F-1   FUNCTION INDEX

Function/Page		Library	Function/Page		Library	Function/Page		Library
abort	648	stdlib	fwrite	645	stdio	realloc	648	stdlib
abs	647	stdlib	gcount	647	iostream	remove	645	stdio
acos	644	math	get	646	iostream	rename	645	stdio
asctime	649	time	getc	645	stdio	resetiosflags	647	iomanip
asin	644	math	getchar	645	stdio	rewind	645	stdio
atan	644	math	getline	647	iostream	scanf	644	stdio
atan2	644	math	gets	645	stdio	seekg	646	iostream
atexit	648	stdlib	gmtime	649	time	seekp	646	iostream
atof	648	stdlib	good	646	iostream	setf	646	iostream
atoi	648	stdlib	hex	647	iostream	setfill	647	iomanip
atol	648	stdlib	ignore	647	iostream	setw	647	iomanip
bad	646	iostream	isalnum	643	ctype	setprecision	647	iomanip
calloc	648	stdlib	isalpha	643	ctype	setiosflags	647	iomanip
ceil	644	math	iscntrl	643	ctype	sin	644	math
clear	646	iostream	isdigit	643	ctype	sinh	644	math
clearerr	644	stdio	isgraph	643	ctype	sprintf	644	stdio
clock	649	time	islower	643	ctype	sqrt	644	math
close	645	fstream	isprint	643	ctype	srand	647	stdlib
cos	644	math	ispunct	643	ctype	sscanf	644	stdio
cosh	644	math	isspace	643	ctype	strcat	648	string
ctime	649	time	isupper	643	ctype	strchr	649	string
dec	647	iostream	isxdigit	643	ctype	strcmp	649	string
difftime	649	time	labs	647	stdlib	strcpy	648	string
div	647	stdlib	ldexp	644	math	strcspn	649	string
endl	647	iostream	ldiv	647	stdlib	strlen	649	string
eof	646	iostream	localtime	649	time	strncat	648	string
exit	648	stdlib	log	644	math	strncmp	649	string
exp	644	math	log10	644	math	strncpy	648	string
fabs	644	math	malloc	648	stdlib	strpbrk	649	string
fail	646	iostream	memchr	648	string	strrchr	649	string
fclose	644	stdio	memcmp	648	string	strspn	649	string
feof	644	stdio	memcpy	648	string	strstr	649	string

Function/Page		Library	Function/Page		Library	Function/Page		Library
ferror	644	stdio	memmove	648	string	strtod	648	stdlib
fgetc	645	stdio	mktime	649	time	strtol	648	stdlib
fgets	645	stdio	modf	644	math	strtoul	648	stdlib
flags	646	iostream	oct	647	iostream	system	648	stdlib
floor	644	math	open	645	fstream	tan	644	math
flush	647	iostream	pcount	647	iostream	tanh	644	math
fill	646	iostream	peek	646	iostream	tellg	646	iostream
fmod	644	math	pow	644	math	tellp	646	iostream
fopen	644	stdio	precision	646	iostream	time	649	time
fprintf	644	stdio	printf	644	stdio	tmpfile	645	stdio
fputc	645	stdio	put	646	iostream	tmpnam	645	stdio
fputs	645	stdio	putback	646	iostream	tolower	643	ctype
fread	645	stdio	putc	645	stdio	toupper	643	ctype
free	648	stdlib	putchar	645	stdio	ungetc	645	stdio
frexp	644	math	puts	645	stdio	unsetf	646	iostream
fscanf	644	stdio	rand	647	stdlib	width	646	iostream
fseek	645	stdio	rdstate	646	iostream	write	646	iostream
ftell	645	stdio	read	646	iostream	ws	647	iostream

F-2   CHARACTER LIBRARY

The following functions are found in `ctype`:

isalnum	int	isalnum (int a_char);
isalpha	int	isalpha (int a_char);
iscntrl	int	iscntrl (int a_char);
isdigit	int	isdigit (int a_char);
isgraph	int	isgraph (int a_char);
islower	int	islower (int a_char);
isprint	int	isprint (int a_char);
ispunct	int	ispunct (int a_char);
isspace	int	isspace (int a_char);
isupper	int	isupper (int a_char);
isxdigit	int	isxdigit (int a_char);
tolower	int	tolower (int a_char);
toupper	int	toupper (int a_char);

F-3   MATH LIBRARY

The following functions are found in `math`:

ceil	double	ceil (double number);
exp	double	exp (double number);
fabs	double	fabs (double number);
floor	double	floor (double number);
fmod	double	fmod (double number1, double number2);
frexp	double	frexp (double number, int* exp);
ldexp	double	ldexp (double number, int* exp);
log	double	log (double number);
log10	double	log10 (double number);
modf	double	modf (double number, double* divisor);
pow	double	pow (double number1, double number2);
sqrt	double	sqrt (double number);
sin	double	sin (double number);
sinh	double	sinh (double number);
asin	double	asin (double number);
cos	double	cos (double number);
cosh	double	cosh (double number);
acos	double	acos (double number);
tan	double	tan (double number);
tanh	double	tanh (double number);
atan	double	atan (double number);
atan2	double	atan2 (double number1, double number2);

F-4   TRADITIONAL C INPUT/OUTPUT LIBRARY

We have divided the traditional C input/output (I/O) library `stdio` by the type of data being read.

General I/O

The following are general input/output functions that apply to all files:

clearerr	void	clearerr (FILE *fp);
fclose	int	fclose (FILE *fp);
feof	int	feof (FILE *fp);
ferror	int	ferror (FILE *fp);
fopen	FILE	*fopen (const char *extn_name, const char *file_mode);

Formatted I/O

The following convert text data to/from internal memory formats:

fprintf	int	fprintf (FILE *fileOut, const char *format_string, . . .);
printf	int	printf (const char *format_string, . . .);
sprintf	int	sprintf (char * to_loc, const char *format_string, . . .);
fscanf	int	fscanf (FILE *fileIn, const char *format_string, . . .);
scanf	int	scanf (const char *format_string, . . .);
sscanf	int	sscanf (const char *from_loc, const char *format_string, . . .);

Character I/O

The following read and write one character at a time:

fgetc	int	fgetc (FILE *fp);
fputc	int	fputc (int, FILE *fp);
getc	int	getc (FILE *fp);
getchar	int	getchar (void);
putc	int	putc (int, FILE *fp);
putchar	int	putchar (int char_out);
ungetc	int	ungetc (int char_out, FILE *fp);

File I/O

The following functions work with binary files:

fread	size_t	fread (void *in_area, size_t size, size_t count, FILE *fp);
fwrite	size_t	fwrite (const void *out_data, size_t size, size_t count, FILE *fp);
fseek	int	fseek (FILE *fp, long offset, int from_loc);
ftell	long	ftell (FILE *fp);
rewind	void	rewind (FILE *fp);

String I/O

The following functions read and write strings:

gets	char	*gets (char *string);
puts	int	puts (const char *string);
fgets	char	*fgets (char *string, int size, FILE *fp);
fputs	int	fputs (const char *string, FILE *fp);

System File Control

The following system commands create and delete files on the disk:

tmpnam	char	*tmpnam (char *fp);
tmpfile	FILE	*tmpfile (void);
remove	int	remove (const char *file_name);
rename	int	rename (const char *old_name, const char *new_name);

F-5   C++ I/O LIBRARY

The following functions are found only in C++. For a complete discussion of the C++ class library design, refer to Appendix K, on page 685.

General

close	void	fstream :: close (void);
close	void	ifstream :: close (void);
close	void	ofstream :: close (void);
open	void	fstream :: open (const char* fs_ID, int mode);
open	void	ifstream :: open (const char* fs_ID, int mode);
open	void	ofstream :: open (const char* fs_ID, int mode);

File Status

bad	int	ios :: bad (void);
fail	int	ios :: fail (void);
eof	int	ios :: eof (void);
flags	long	ios :: flags (void);
flags	long	ios :: flags (long new_flag);
good	int	ios :: good (void);
setf	long	ios :: setf (long new_flag);
setf	long	ios :: setf (long new_flag, long mask);
unsetf	long	ios :: unsetf (long flag);
rdstate	int	ios :: rdstate (void);
clear	int	ios :: clear (int = ios :: goodbit);

Output Formatting

fill	int	ios :: fill (char fill_char);
precision	int	ios :: precision (void);
precision	int	ios :: precision (int new_precision);
width	int	ios :: width (void);
width	int	ios :: width (int new_width);

Block I/O

read	istream&	read (char* data);
read	istream&	read (signed char* buffer, int size);
read	istream&	read (unsigned char* buffer, int size);
write	ostream&	write (const char* buffer, int size);
write	ostream&	write (const signed char* buffer, int size);
write	ostream&	write (const unsigned char* buffer, int size);
tellg	streampos	istream :: tellg (void);
tellp	streampos	ostream :: tellp (void);
seekg	istream&	istream :: seekg (streampos position);
seekg	istream&	istream :: seekg (long offset, seek_dir where_from);
seekp	ostream&	ostream :: seekp (streampos position);
seekp	ostream&	ostream :: seekp (long offset, seek_dir where_from);

Character I/O

get	istream&	istream :: get (char& character);
get	istream&	istream :: get (signed char& character);
get	istream&	istream :: get (unsigned char& character);
put	ostream&	ostream :: put (char character);
put	ostream&	ostream :: put (signed char character);
put	ostream&	ostream :: put (unsigned char character);
peek	int	istream :: peek (void);
putback	istream&	istream :: putback (char character);

Line I/O

get	istream&	istream :: get (char* buffer, int n, char stop = '\n');
get	istream&	istream :: get (signed char* buffer, int n, char stop = '\n');

get	istream&	istream :: get (unsigned char* buffer, int n, char stop = '\n');
getline	istream&	istream :: getline (char* buffer, int n, char delimiter = '\n');
getline	istream&	istream :: getline (signed char* buffer, int n, char delimiter = '\n');
getline	istream&	istream :: getline (unsigned char* buffer, int n, char delimiter = '\n');

Miscellaneous I/O

gcount	int	istream :: gcount (void);
pcount	int	ostream :: pcount (void);
ignore	istream&	ignore (int count = 1, int stop = EOF);
flush	ostream&	ostream :: flush (void);

Manipulators

This section lists the manipulators that can be used with the input/output classes. They are not function prototypes—they just show the usage format.

oct	oct
dec	dec
hex	hex
ws	ws
endl	endl
flush	flush
setfill	setfill (fill_char)
setw	setw (width)
setprecision	setprecision (size)
setiosflags	setiosflags (flags)
resetiosflags	resetiosflags (flags)

F-6   STANDARD LIBRARY

The following functions are found in `stdlib`:

Math Functions

The following math functions are found in `stdlib`:

abs	int	abs (int number);
div	div_t	div (int numerator, int divisor);
labs	long	labs (long number);
ldiv	ldiv_t	ldiv (long numerator, long divisor);
rand	int	rand (void);
srand	void	srand (unsigned seed);

Memory Functions

The following are memory allocation functions:

calloc	void	*calloc (size_t num_elements, size_t element_size);
free	void	free (void *);
malloc	void	*malloc (size_t num_bytes);
realloc	void	*realloc (void * stge_ptr, size_t element_size);

Program Control

The following functions control the program flow:

exit	void	exit (int exit_code);
abort	void	abort (void);
atexit	int	atexit (void (* function_name) (void));

System Communication

The following function communicates with the operating system:

| system | int | system (const char * system_command); |

Conversion Functions

The following functions convert data from one type to another:

atof	double	atof (const char * real_num);
atoi	int	atoi (const char * real_num);
atol	long	atol (const char * real_num);
strtod	double	strtod (const char * str, char ** next_str);
strtol	long	strtol (const char * str, char ** next_str, int base);
strtoul	unsigned long	strtoul (const char * str, char ** next_str, int base);

F-7　STRING LIBRARY

The following functions are found in `string`:

Copying Data

The following functions all copy strings or memory:

memcpy	void	*memcpy (void * to_mem, const void * fr_mem, size_t bytes);
memmove	void	*memmove (void * to_mem, const void * fr_mem, size_t bytes);
strcpy	char	*strcpy (char * to_str, const char * fr_str);
strncpy	char	*strncpy (char * to_str, const char * fr_str, size_t bytes);
strcat	char	*strcat (char * to_str, const char * fr_str);
strncat	char	*strncat (char * to_str, const char * fr_str, size_t bytes);

Comparing Data

The following functions all compare strings or memory:

| memchr | void | *memchr (const void * mem, int a_char, size_t bytes); |
| memcmp | int | memcmp (const void * mem1, const void * mem2, size_t bytes); |

strchr	char	*strchr (const char * str, int a_char);
strrchr	char	*strrchr (const char * str, int a_char);
strcmp	int	strcmp (const char * str1, const char * str2);
strncmp	int	strncmp (const char * str1, const char * str2, size_t bytes);
strpbrk	char	*strpbrk (const char * str1, const char * str2);
strstr	char	*strstr (const char * str1, const char * str2);

String Lengths

The following functions return the length of strings or substrings:

strlen	size_t	strlen (const char * str);
strspn	size_t	strspn (const char * str1, const char * str2);
strcspn	size_t	strcspn (const char * str1, const char * str2);

F-8   TIME

The following functions are found in `time`:

clock	clock_t	clock (void);
difftime	double	difftime (time_t time_start, time_t time_end);
mktime	time_t	mktime (struct tm * cal_time);
time	time_t	time (time_t * num_time);
asctime	char	*asctime (const struct tm * cal_time);
ctime	char	*ctime (const time_t * num_time);
gmtime	struct tm	*gmtime (const time_t * num_time);
localtime	struct tm	*localtime (const time_t * num_time);

G

Classes Related to Input and Output

This appendix documents the input/output classes, as shown in Figure G-1. We describe each class and show the prototype declarations for each method used in the text.

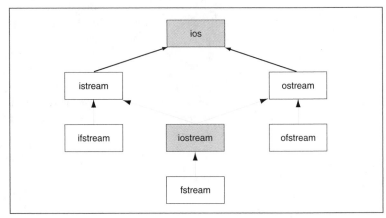

Figure G-1   ios class and derived classes

This discussion is not intended to be comprehensive. There are many more classes than those discussed here.

G-1   ios CLASS

The ios class is the base class for all C++ input and output. It provides the data members and methods to manage stream objects in the classes derived from it:

- Error-state flags
- Mode flags
- Seek flags
- Format flags
- Format parameters

Error-State Flags

Input/output error status is stored in a data member with three flags, as shown in Table G-1.

Flag	Description
bad	I/O: operation invalid
fail	I/O: transmission error
eof	Input: end of file detected

Table G-1   Error-state flags

Given this design, the user can check or clear these flags using the following methods:

```
int ios :: good    (void);
int ios :: eof     (void);
int ios :: fail    (void);
int ios :: bad     (void);
int ios :: rdstate (void);
int ios :: clear   (int = ios :: goodbit);
```

Mode Flags

The ios class also handles the mode of a stream object. The eight ios mode flags are described in Table G-2. These flags can be set only by the open method defined in the inherited classes.

Mode	Description
ios::in	input mode (default for istream)
ios::out	output mode (default for ostream)
ios::ate	file marker positioned at end
ios::app	append mode
ios::trunc	delete data in existing file

Table G-2   Mode flags

Mode	Description
`ios::nocreate`	file must exist: if not, error
`ios::noreplace`	file must not exist: if it does, error
`ios::binary`	binary mode (default is text)

Table G-2   Mode flags *(continued)*

Seek Flags

The ios class contains a set of seek flags (Table G-3) that are used by the inherited classes to determine how the seek operates. The seek flags are stored in eight bits. These flags are used by the *seekg* and *seekp* methods.

Flag	Description
`beg`	I/O: seek from beginning of file
`cur`	I/O: seek from current file position
`end`	I/O: seek from end of file

Table G-3   Seek flags

Format Flags

The 15 flags used to designate the data formats for input (only *skipws*) and output are listed in Table G-4.

Flag	Description
`skipws`	input: skip leading white space characters
`left`	output: left justification
`right`	output: right justification
`internal`	output: fill char fill after sign or base
`dec`	output: display integer value in decimal
`oct`	output: display integer value in octal
`hex`	output: display integer value in hexadecimal
`showbase`	output: display base indicator octal (0) or hex (0X)
`showpoint`	output: display floating-point decimal, even on zero
`uppercase`	output: display hex base indicator/value in uppercase display scientific notation E in uppercase
`showpos`	output: display plus (+) for positive numbers
`scientific`	output: display floating-point values in exponential format
`fixed`	output: display floating-point values in fixed-point format
`unitdef`	output: flush data immediately
`stdio`	output: allows use of C and C++ output in same stream

Table G-4   Format flags

The ios class provides the following five methods that can be used to test or store data in the format flags:

```
long ios :: flags   (void);
long ios :: flags   (long setMask);
long ios :: setf    (long flags);
long ios :: setf    (long flags, long mask);
long ios :: unsetf  (long flags);
```

Format Parameters

The ios base class also contains three variable members that are used to format output: width, fill, and precision. They are shown in Table G-5.

Variable	Description
width	output: length of display area in characters
fill	output: padding character for nondata positions
precision	output: number of digits after decimal point

Table G-5   ios variable members

To store setting in these members, the ios class provides the three methods shown below.

```
int ios::width     (...);
int ios::fill      (...);
int ios::precision (...);
```

G-2   CLASSES DERIVED FROM ios

In this section we describe the two classes directly derived from the ios class: the input stream (*istream*) and the output stream (*ostream*).

Input Stream

The input stream class (*istream*) is derived from the ios class. It contains functions and operators for extracting data from an input stream along with several member data and methods to handle input operations.

```
istream&   istream :: operator>> (...);
int        istream :: gcount (...);
istream&   istream :: get (...);
istream&   istream :: getline (...);
istream&   istream :: ignore (...);
int        istream :: peek (...);
istream&   istream :: putback (...);
istream&   istream :: read (...);
istream&   istream :: seekg (...);
streampos  istream :: tellg (...);
```

Output Stream

The output stream class (*ostream*) is derived from the ios class. It contains functions and operators for inserting data into an output stream along with several member data and methods to handle output operations.

```
ostream&  ostream :: operator<< (...);
int       ostream :: pcoun (...);
ostream&  ostream :: put (...);
ostream&  ostream :: seekp (...);
streampos ostream :: tellp (...);
ostream&  ostream :: write (...);
```

G-3   CLASSES DERIVED FROM istream AND ostream

In this section we describe the input file stream, the input/output file stream, and the output file stream.

Input File Stream

The input file stream (*ifstream*) is designed to process stream objects that are associated in input files. It inherits the properties from both *istream* and *ios*. The primary functions supported by *ifstream* open and close input streams. Their prototype declarations are shown below.

```
void ifstream :: open (...);
void ifstream :: close (...);
```

Input/Output File Stream

The input/output file stream (*iostream*) is derived from both istream and ostream (see Figure G-1, on page 650). It is designed to allow the instantiation of stream objects for both input and output and is the most common stream included in your programs. It contains no data members or methods of its own. It is simply used as a convenience.

Output File Stream

The output file stream (*ofstream*) is designed to process stream objects that are associated with output files. It inherits the properties from both *ostream* and *ios*. The primary functions supported by *ofstream* open and close output streams. Their prototype declarations are shown below.

```
void ofstream :: open (...);
void ofstream :: close (...);
```

G-4   CLASSES DERIVED FROM iostream

The file stream (*fstream*) is derived from the iostream class and through it the *istream*, *ostream*, and *ios* classes. It is used primarily for stream objects that process files opened for both input and output. The prototype declarations for its open and close methods are shown below.

```
void fstream :: open (...);
void fstream :: close (...);
```

The String Class

This appendix creates a string class and overloads the operators so that we can use the assign and compare operators with strings just like we can with other types. We should point out, however, that you don't need to create your own string class. A string class is included in the C++ Standard Template Library; we provide our own string class for completeness.[1]

We could have used array code to manipulate the strings in our class, but we decided to use the standard C++ string functions to do so. Therefore, when we need to assign one string class to another, we use the string copy function. When we need to compare two strings, we use the string compare function.

---

1. This material is extracted from our text *Computer Science: A Structured Programming Approach Using C++* (Pacific Grove: Brooks/Cole, 2000) 631–642.

H-1   THE STRING CLASS

The data for our string class are quite simple: one string pointer and one length field. The string pointer is created when a member of the string class is defined. Although its contents vary depending on the initializers provided in the application code, the memory for the string itself is always allocated out of dynamic memory. If the size of the string is changed in any way, we delete the current string in memory and allocate a new one.

In addition to the two fields, our class needs 14 functions. We discuss the functions in the following sections. The class declaration is shown in Program H-1.

```
 1  #include <string.h>
 2  #include <ctype.h>
 3
 4  class String
 5  {
 6    private:
 7        char *str;
 8        int   len;
 9
10    public:
11          String  (void);
12          String  (const String& strIn);
13          String  (const char *strAry);
14          ~String  (void);
15
16          friend bool operator<  (const String& string1,
17                                   const String& string2);
18          friend bool operator>  (const String& string1,
19                                   const String& string2);
20          friend bool operator== (const String& string1,
21                                   const String& string2);
22
23          String& operator=   (const String& stringIn);
24          void    operator+=  (const String& concatString);
25          char    operator[]  (int pos);
26          String  operator()  (int fromLoc, int toLoc);
27
28          friend String operator+ (const String& s1,
29                                          const String& s2);
30
31          friend ostream& operator<< (ostream& fsOut,
32                                          String&  string);
33          friend istream& operator>> (istream& fsIn,
34                                          String&  string);
35  } ; // class String
```

Program H-1   String class declaration

H-2   STRING CLASS CONSTRUCTORS

There are three string constructors: the default constructor, the copy constructor, and the initialization constructor.

Default Constructor

The default constructor creates a string object with a null string in it. To create a null string object, we allocate a 1-byte string from the heap and set its contents to a null character. We also set the string length variable to 0. The code is shown in Program H-2.

```
1   /* ============= String :: String (void) =============
2      Default string constructor.
3         Pre    nothing
4         Post   null string created
5   */
6   String :: String (void)
7   {
8      str = new char [1];
9      *str = '\0';
10     len  =   0;
11  } // String :: String
```

Program H-2   String default constructor

Copy Constructor

The copy constructor creates a new string object and copies the string from the object passed as a parameter. Note that we use the standard string library to copy the string. The code is shown in Program H-3.

```
1   /* ============= String :: String (String&) =============
2      String copy constructor.
3         Pre    strIn is a string class to be copied
4         Post   string str allocated and strIn copied
5   */
6   String :: String (const String& strIn)
7   {
8      str     = new char [strIn.len + 1];
9      strcpy (str, strIn.str);
10     len     = strIn.len ;
11  } // String copy constructor
```

Program H-3   String copy constructor

Initialization Constructor

The initialization constructor creates a string object and converts a string array by copying it to the string object. Its code is shown in Program H-4.

```
1  /* ============ String :: String (strAry) =============
2       Convert string character array to string class.
3            Pre    strAry is a character string
4            Post   string str allocated and strAry copied
5  */
6  String :: String (const char *strAry)
7  {
8      len = strlen (strAry);
9      str = new char [len + 1];
10     strcpy (str, strAry);
11 } // String copy string array
```

Program H-4   String initialization constructor

String Class Destructor

The string class destructor frees the memory allocated for a string and sets the string pointer in the string object to null. The code is shown in Program H-5.

```
1  /* ================= String destructor =================
2       String destructor.
3            Pre    application has called free (string)
4            Post   string deleted
5  */
6  String :: ~String (void)
7  {
8      delete [] str;
9      str = NULL;
10 } // String destructor
```

Program H-5   String destructor

H-3   STRING OPERATORS

We need ten string operators. They are defined in this section.

String Compare Operators

We overload three basic compare operators in our string class: equal (==), less than (<), and greater than (>). All three use the standard compare function to compare two string objects and return true or false. Their definitions are shown in Programs H-6 through H-8.

```
1  /* =============== String friend operator< ===============
2       Compare class string less than parameter string.
3            Pre    nothing
4            Post   compare result returned
```

Program H-6   String compare less than

```
 5    */
 6    bool  operator< (const String& string1,
 7                         const String& string2)
 8    {
 9       return (strcmp (string1.str, string2.str) < 0);
10    }  // String friend compare <
```

Program H-6   String compare less than (continued)

```
 1    /* =============== String friend operator> ===============
 2       Compare class string greater than parameter string.
 3          Pre    nothing
 4          Post   compare result returned
 5    */
 6    bool operator>  (const String& string1,
 7                         const String& string2)
 8    {
 9       return (strcmp (string1.str, string2.str) > 0);
10    }  // String friend compare >
```

Program H-7   String compare greater than

String Equal

```
 1    /* =============== (String friend operator==) =============
 2       Compare class string equal to parameter string.
 3          Pre    nothing
 4          Post   compare result returned
 5    */
 6    bool operator== (const String& string1,
 7                         const String& string2)
 8    {
 9       return (strcmp (string1.str, string2.str) == 0);
10    }  // String friend string ==
```

Program H-8   String compare equal to

Compare Complements

To determine the complement relations of each of these string operators, you would use the *not* operator. For example, to test for not equal, you would write the following code:

```
if (!(string1 == string2))
```

We do not need to overload the *not* operator because it is already defined for integer values, and the value returned by the equal operator is a Boolean (true or false).

Assignment Operator

The assignment operator (=) assigns the contents of one string object to another. Before we can complete the assignment, however, we must first delete the current string and free its memory. We can then copy the new string into the string object and set its length field. The definition is shown in Program H-9.

```
 1  /* ============== (String :: operator=) ==============
 2     Copy string in parameter to this string.
 3         Pre    nothing
 4         Post   string copied
 5  */
 6    String& String :: operator= (const String& stringIn)
 7  {
 8  // Statements
 9    if (this != &stringIn)        // If !copying to itself
10        {
11         delete [] str;
12         len = stringIn.len;
13         str = new char [len + 1];
14         strcpy (str, stringIn.str);
15        } // if
16
17    return *this;
18  } // String copy (=)
```

Program H-9   String copy function

Program H-9 Analysis

There is a very subtle validation in this function. Note that in Statement 9 we compare the address of the current object, represented by the this variable, with the address of the object that we are copying. If they are the same, then we don't need to copy the object because it is already there. Furthermore, because the first thing we do is delete the string in the current object, it would be a fatal error to try to copy it after we deleted it.

Concatenation Operators

There are two concatenation operators: concatenate to current string and concatenate two strings.

Concatenate to Current String

Concatenate to current string concatenates the string object in the parameter to the end of the string in the current object. It has only one parameter. Because it closely resembles the complex add/assign operator (+=), we use it for this function. Its definition is shown in Program H-10.

```
 1 | /* =============== String :: operator+= ==============
 2 |    Concatenate parameter class to current object.
 3 |       Pre    nothing
 4 |       Post   parameter object concatenated
 5 | */
 6 | void String :: operator+= (const String& concatString)
 7 | {
 8 | // Local Definitions
 9 |    char *temp;
10 |    int   size;
11 |
12 | // Statements
13 |    size   = len + concatString.len + 1;
14 |    temp   = new char [size];
15 |    strcpy (temp, str);
16 |    strcat (temp, concatString.str);
17 |    delete [] str;
18 |    str    = temp;
19 |    len    = size - 1;
20 |    return;
21 | } // String concatenate (+=)
```

Program H-10   Concatenate to current string

Concatenate Two Strings

The second concatenation operator, concatenate two strings, joins two strings passed as parameters and places them in a third string. We use the plus (+) operator for it. Note that this function must be declared as a friend by the string class (see Statement 28 in Program H-1, on page 656). The definition is shown in Program H-11.

```
 1 | /* =============== String friend operator+ ===============
 2 |    Create new string from two strings.
 3 |       Pre    nothing
 4 |       Post   new string contains string1 + string2
 5 |       Return address of new string class
 6 | */
 7 | String  operator+ (const String& s1,
 8 |                         const String& s2)
 9 | {
10 | // Local Definitions
11 |    String newS;
12 |
13 | // Statements
14 |    newS.len = s1.len + s2.len;
```

Program H-11   Concatenate two strings

```
15      newS.str = new char [newS.len + 1];
16      strcpy   (newS.str, s1.str);
17      strcat   (newS.str, s2.str);
18      return newS;
19  } // String friend concatenate two strings (+)
```

Program H-11   Concatenate two strings *(continued)*

Substring Operators

There are two substring operators: extract character and extract substring.

Extract Character

Extract character returns the character found at a specified position in the string. For example, a request to return the fourth character in the string *concatenate* would return the second *c*, which is the character at the index location 3. Because this operation parallels array indexing, we use the index brackets for it. Its definition is shown in Program H-12.

```
 1  /* =============== String :: operator[] ==============
 2     Character operator.
 3        Pre    pos contains string position (relative to 0)
 4        Post   String[pos] returned
 5           -or-  nil character returned (pos < 0 or pos > len)
 6  */
 7  char String :: operator[] (int pos)
 8  {
 9  // Local Definitions
10     char c;
11
12  // Statements
13     if (pos >= 0 && pos <= len)
14        c = *(str + pos);
15     else
16        c = '\0';
17     return c;
18  } // String char extraction ([])
```

Program H-12   Extract character from string

Program H-12 Analysis

Once again we use extensive data validation to ensure that the correct data is extracted. If the position of the character is not in the string, then we return a null character indicating that the character doesn't exist.

Substring Extraction

The second extraction function locates and returns a substring from the string object given its start location and its end location (both relative to 0). The tokens for this operator are the parentheses. It returns a new string object. The code is shown in Program H-13.

```
 1    /* ============== String :: operator() ==============
 2       Extract substring from string.
 3             Pre    fromString/toString contain index locations
 4                    fromString <= toString
 5             Post   returns new string; if successful, new
 6                    object contains copied substring;
 7                    if not, it contains a null string
 8    */
 9    String String :: operator() (int fromLoc,
10                                  int toLoc)
11    {
12    // Local Definitions
13       int     i;
14       int     strLen;
15       String tempString;
16
17    // Statements
18
19       // Validate indexes
20       if (fromLoc < 0 || fromLoc > len)
21           return tempString;
22       else if (toLoc   < 0 || toLoc   > len)
23           return tempString;
24       else if (fromLoc > toLoc)
25           return tempString;
26
27       strLen    = toLoc - fromLoc + 1;
28       tempString = new char [strLen + 1];
29       for (i = 0; i < strLen; i++)
30           tempString.str[i] = str [fromLoc + i];
31       tempString.str[strLen] = '\0';
32       return tempString;
33    } // String substring extraction ()
```

Program H-13   Extract substring from string

Program H-13 Analysis

Once again we must validate the parameters to ensure that the start and end positions are good. If they are not, we return the temporary string we created in Statement 15. This is very subtle logic. Because we create the temporary string with no initial values, the default constructor is executed. This constructor creates a single-character null string. Therefore, when the parameters are invalid, we return a string object that contains a null string. On the other hand, if everything is okay, we use a *for* loop to copy the string in the parameter, character by character, to the temporary string.

H-4   STRING INPUT/OUTPUT OPERATORS

To provide for string input/output we override the extraction (>>) and insertion (<<) operators.

String Extraction Operator

The extraction operator presents some design problems. First, how big do we make the area for the input string? We decided that 256 characters should be sufficient. Remember, the extraction operator skips leading white space and stops at the first white space character. A user is highly unlikely to input more than 256 characters without any white space.

On the other hand, as firm believers in Murphy's Law,[2] we must check to make sure that the user in fact did not exceed our limit. We verify that the length is acceptable with a set width specification. After the read, we check the next character in the input stream to make sure that it is white space. If it isn't, then the user exceeded our string limit and we abort the program. As an aside, how would you check this logic? We simply set the width specification to a low number, such as 5, and then tested by entering more than five characters. After making the test, we restored the limit to 256. The definition of extraction operator is found in Program H-14.

```
 1  /* ============ String friend operator>> ============
 2     Read string into string class.
 3         Pre    fsIn is an open file stream
 4         Post   string read and placed in string class
 5  */
 6  istream& operator>> (istream& fsIn,
 7                            String&  stringCl)
 8  {
 9  // Local Definitions
10     char inArea[256];
11     char whiteSpace;
12
13  // Statements
14     fsIn >> setw(256) >> inArea;
15     whiteSpace = fsIn.peek();
16     if (isspace (whiteSpace))
17        {
18         delete[] stringCl.str;
19         stringCl.len = strlen (inArea);
20         stringCl.str = new char [stringCl.len + 1];
21         strcpy (stringCl.str, inArea);
```

Program H-14   Read string

---

2. Whatever can go wrong will.

```
22         } // if read okay
23      else
24         {
25          cout << "\a\aError Str101. Max Length in Read\n";
26          exit(101);
27         } // else too much data
28      return fsIn;
29  } // String read
```

Program H-14   Read string *(continued)*

String Insertion Operator

Although the string extraction operator is complex, the string insertion operator is simple. Its code is shown in Program H-15.

```
1   /* ============= String friend operator<< ============
2      Write string to a file stream.
3          Pre    fsOut is an open file stream
4          Post   string written to fsOut
5          Return success or failure from <<
6   */
7   ostream& operator<< (ostream& fsOut,
8                           String&  string)
9   {
10     fsOut << string.str;
11     return fsOut;
12  } // write string to file stream
```

Program H-15   Write string

Pointers to Functions

Functions in your program occupy memory. The name of the function is a pointer constant to the first byte of memory. For example, imagine that you have four functions stored in memory: main, fun, pun, and sun. This relationship is seen graphically in Figure I-1. The name of each function is a pointer to its code in memory.

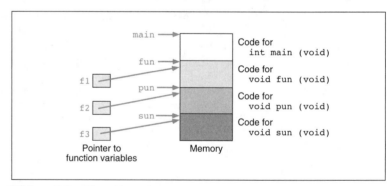

Figure I-1   Functions in memory

As with all other pointer types, we can define pointers to function variables and store the address of fun, pun, and sun in them. The syntax for declaring **pointers to functions** is different. To declare a pointer to a function, you code it as if it were a prototype definition, with the function name and its pointer token in parentheses. This format is shown in Figure I-2. The parentheses around the function name are important: without them, C++ would interpret the function return type as a pointer. Pointers to function variables are also shown in Figure I-1.

f1 is a pointer to a function with no parameters that returns void

```
...
// Local Definitions
void (*f1) (void);
void (*f2) (void);
void (*f3) (void);
...
// Statements
...
f1 = fun;
f2 = pun;
f3 = sun;
...
```

Figure I-2 Pointers to functions

Program I-1 shows how our three functions, fun, pun, and sun, can be executed when they are passed as a parameter. Analyze the prototype declaration for strange carefully. The parameter, ptrToFunction, is a pointer to a function that has no parameters and returns nothing. Consequently, strange expects to receive the address (a pointer) of the function that it is going to execute. To pass the function's address, we simply use its name as the parameter: The function name is a pointer constant.

```
/* Demonstrate use of pointers to functions.
      Written by:
      Date:
*/
#include <iostream.h>

// Prototype Declarations
```

Program I-1 Demonstrate pointers to functions

```
 8  void strange (void(*ptrToFunction)(void));
 9  void fun   (void);
10  void pun   (void);
11  void sun   (void);
12
13  int main (void)
14  {
15  // Statements
16  strange (fun);
17  strange (pun);
18  strange (sun);
19
20  return 0;
21  } // main
22  /* ================= strange =================
23     This function will call whatever function is passed
24     to it by the calling function.
25     Pre    ptrFun is a pointer to the function to be executed
26     Post   requested function has been executed
27  */
28  void strange (void(*ptrToFunction)(void))
29  {
30     (*ptrToFunction)();
31     return;
32  } // strange
33  /* ================= fun =================
34     Prints a simple message about fun.
35     Pre    nothing
36     Post   message has been printed
37  */
38  void fun (void)
39  {
40     cout << "Fun is being with good friends.\n";
41     return;
42  } // fun
43  /* ================= pun =================
44     Prints a simple message about pun.
45     Pre    nothing
46     Post   message has been printed
47  */
48  void pun (void)
49  {
50     cout << "Pun is a play on words.\n";
51     return;
52  } // pun
53
```

Program I-1   Demonstrate pointers to functions *(continued)*

```
54   /* ================= sun =================
55      Prints a simple message about sun.
56      Pre     nothing
57      Post    message has been printed
58   */
59   void sun (void)
60   {
61      cout << "Sun is a bright star.\n";
62      return;
63   } // sun
```

Results:

Fun is being with good friends.
Pun is a play on words.
Sun is a bright star.

Program I-1   Demonstrate pointers to functions *(continued)*

J

Inheritance

What makes classes powerful is the ability to extend one so that it creates a new class while at the same time retaining the basic characteristics of the original. This concept of extending a class is known as **inheritance**. To carry the concept even further, a derived class not only has all of the capabilities of the original class, but it may also take on new attributes and processes of its own. Thus the derived class becomes more powerful than the original.

J-1   BASIC CONCEPTS

To set the stage for the discussions that follow, let's look at a simple example. At the same time, we will use an example to define the terminology commonly used when referring to inherited objects.

We are all familiar with polygons, two-dimensional objects that can have from three to as many sides as needed. Simple examples of polygons are the triangle, square, and rectangle.

Every polygon has two basic attributes, area and perimeter. The area is a measure of the space within the borders of the polygon; its perimeter is the sum of the lengths of all of its sides. Figure J-1 shows three simple polygons.

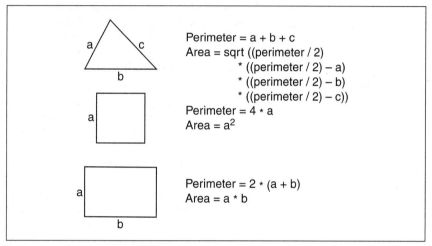

Figure J-1   Simple polygons

With this information, we are ready to create a polygon class. It needs two attributes, area and perimeter. It also needs two application functions. In addition to constructors and destructors, it needs functions to print the area and the perimeter. The polygon class is shown in Program J-1.

```
1   class Polygons
2   {
3      protected:
4          double area;
5          double perimeter;
6      public:
7          void printArea (void);
8          void printPeri (void);
9   }; // Class Polygons
```

Program J-1   Declaration for the polygon class

Program J-1 Analysis

So that `area` and `perimeter` are available when they are inherited, they need to be in an inheritance type known as *protected*.

Base and Derived Classes

Our polygon class is known as a **base class** because it contains all of the common attributes and functions that form the basis for the derivation of other classes. Although polygons all have areas and perimeters, each different type of polygon requires different calculations to determine these values. For example, the calculation for the area of a triangle is different than the calculation for the area of a rectangle. We therefore need to define new objects for the different polygons. Each of these new classes is known as a **derived class** because it has access to the attributes and functions in the base class while having its own attributes and functions to process data.

For example, we declare a derived class, triangle, that needs three sides as attributes and two functions, one to calculate the area and one to calculate the perimeter. The relationship between the base class and its derived classes is shown in Figure J-2.

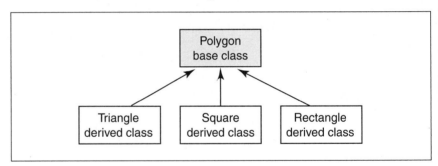

Figure J-2   Base and derived classes

In our polygon example, each derived class has only one base class. When a derived class is created from only one base class, it is known as **simple inheritance**. It is also possible for a derived class to inherit data and functions from multiple classes, in which case it is known as **multiple inheritance**. The code for triangle, square, and rectangle is shown in Program J-2.

```
1   class Triangle : public Polygons
2   {
3     private:
4         double sideA;
5         double sideB;
6         double sideC;
7     public:
8         void calcArea (void);
```

Program J-2   Derived polygon classes

```
 9        void calcPeri (void);
10   }; // Class Triangle
11   class Square : public Polygons
12   {
13      private:
14         double side;
15      public:
16         void calcArea (void);
17         void calcPeri (void);
18   }; // Class Square
19   class Rectangle : public Polygons
20   {
21      private:
22         double sideA;
23         double sideB;
24      public:
25         void calcArea (void);
26         void calcPeri (void);
27   }; // Class Rectangle
```

Program J-2   Derived polygon classes *(continued)*

Inheritance Syntax

Let's look at the inheritance syntax carefully. To declare a derived class, we specify the keyword *class* followed by the class name. This is the standard syntax to create a new class. To relate it to the base class and make it a derived class we use a colon (:), followed by the inheritance type and the name of the base class. The inheritance type may be *public*, *protected*, or *private*. We discuss the meaning of the different inheritance types in "Inheritance Types—Private, Protected, Public" on page 679. The syntactical format for a derived class is shown below. Three examples are provided in Program J-2 (Statements 1, 11, and 19).

```
class derived_class_name : inheritance_type base_class_name
```

Once a derived class has been declared, it is a known type that can be used wherever it is in scope. Thus, to define an instance of our polygon objects, we would use the following code:

```
Triangle    triangle;
Square      square;
Rectangle   rectangle;
```

Inheritance Rules

Because the derived classes can access the attributes and functions in the base class, they are said to have **inherited** them. A copy of the base class object is created (inherited) and then extended with the new object elements required by the derived class. Figure J-3 shows the inheritance for our triangle and rectangle examples.

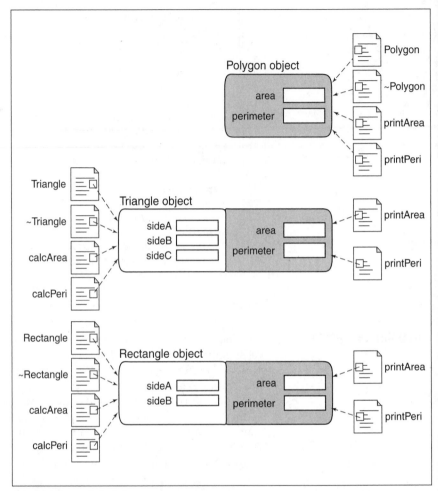

Figure J-3   Inheritance

As you study Figure J-3, look for examples of the following inheritance rules:

1. All data members of the base object are inherited.
2. All function members of the base object are inherited, except
   a. Constructors
   b. Destructors
   c. Friend functions
   d. Assignment operator

In Figure J-3, we see that both `area` and `perimeter` are inherited, which follows Rule 1. When we examine the function prototypes, however, we see that only the two print functions are inherited; the constructor and destructor are not, which follows Rules 2.a. and 2.b.

Because there are no friend functions and the assignment operator was not defined, these examples are not shown.

Polygon-Triangle Implementation

It's now time to write our first inheritance program. To demonstrate the concept, we first develop the polygon class and the triangle class. Then we write a short implementation to demonstrate their operation.

Polygon Base Class

The polygon base class is very simple. It defines the two class variable members and uses no constructors or destructors and only two functions: `printArea` and `printPeri`. It is shown in Program J-3.

```
 1  class Polygons
 2  {
 3     protected:
 4         double area;
 5         double perimeter;
 6
 7     public:
 8         void printArea (void);
 9         void printPeri (void);
10  }; // Class Polygons
11  /* ============== Polygons :: printArea ==============
12     Prints the area of a polygon.
13         Pre    area calculated and stored in area
14         Post   area printed
15  */
16  void Polygons :: printArea (void)
17  {
18  // Statements
19     cout << "The area of your polygon is "
20         << area << endl;
21     return;
22  } // Polygons printArea
23
24  /* ============== Polygons :: printPeri ==============
25     Prints the perimeter of a polygon.
26         Pre    polygon perimeter calculated and stored
27         Post   perimeter printed
28  */
29  void Polygons :: printPeri (void)
30  {
31  // Statements
32     cout << "The perimeter of your polygon is "
33         << perimeter << endl;
34     return;
35  } // Polygons printPeri
```

Program J-3 Polygon base class

Triangle Class

Now that we have built the base class, we are ready to define the triangle derived class. Although both classes would be put into the same header file, we show them separately.

The triangle class inherits the polygon base class's data variables and its two print functions. If we had used any constructors or destructors in the base class, they would not be inherited. We provide an initialization constructor to store the data and calculate the area and perimeter for future use. The triangle class is shown in Program J-4.

```
 1   class Triangle : public Polygons
 2   {
 3      private:
 4          double sideA;
 5          double sideB;
 6          double sideC;
 7
 8          void calcArea (void);
 9          void calcPeri (void);
10
11      public:
12          // initialization constructor
13          Triangle (double sideAIn, double sideBIn,
14                    double sideCIn);
15   };  // Class Triangle
16   /* ============== Triangle :: Triangle ==============
17      Initialization constructor for triangle class
18      Stores sides. Calculates area and perimeter.
19          Pre    Given sideA, sideB, and sideC
20          Post   data stored; area and perimeter calculated
21   */
22   Triangle :: Triangle (double sideAIn,
23                         double sideBIn,
24                         double sideCIn)
25   {
26   // Statements
27      sideA = sideAIn;
28      sideB = sideBIn;
29      sideC = sideCIn;
30
31      calcPeri();
32      calcArea();
33
34      return ;
35   } // Triangle initialization constructor
36
37   /* ================ Triangle :: calcArea ================
```

Program J-4   Triangle class definition

```
38        Calculates triangle area and stores in base class area.
39            Pre   sideA, sideB, sideC, and perimeter available
40            Post  area calculated and stored
41   */
42   void Triangle :: calcArea (void)
43   {
44   // Local Definitions
45      double calcPeri;
46
47   // Statements
48      calcPeri = perimeter / 2;
49      area = (  calcPeri
50               * (calcPeri - sideA)
51               * (calcPeri - sideB)
52               * (calcPeri - sideC) );
53      area = sqrt (area);
54      return;
55   } // Triangle calcArea
56
57   /* =============== Triangle :: calcPeri ===============
58      Calculates perimeter and stores in base class area.
59            Pre   sideA, sideB, and sideC available
60            Post  perimeter calculated and stored
61   */
62   void Triangle :: calcPeri (void)
63   {
64   // Statements
65      perimeter = sideA + sideB + sideC;
66      return;
67   } // Triangle :: calcPeri
```

Program J-4   Triangle class definition *(continued)*

Program J-4 Analysis   It is important to understand what does and does not need to be done in a derived class. We must provide any necessary constructors and destructors because they can't be inherited. For triangle, we need only the initialization constructor.

The functions to calculate the perimeter and area of the polygon are not provided in the base class. Therefore, we must write them for each derived class. Conversely, the base class provides the functions to print the perimeter and area of the polygon so we don't need to write them. They are inherited.

One final note: We must calculate the perimeter before we calculate the area because the calculation of the area requires that we know the perimeter. We could recalculate the perimeter when we calculate the area, but it would not be efficient programming.

Polygon Implementation

Now that we have created a polygon class and a derived triangle class, let's put them in a simple program. In this program, we assume that the polygon class has been defined in a header file that we include. The code is shown in Program J-5.

```
1   /* Demonstrate use of inheritance
2          Written by:
3          Date:
4   */
5   #include <iostream.h>
6   #include <math.h>
7   #include "polygon.h"
8
9   int main (void)
10  {
11  // Local Definitions
12     Triangle tri (3, 4, 5);
13
14  // Statements
15     cout << "Start Polygon Demonstration\n\n";
16
17     tri.printArea();
18     tri.printPeri();
19
20     cout << "\nEnd Polygon Demonstration\n";
21     return 0 ;
22  } // main
23  // ================== End of Program =====================
```

```
Results
   Start Polygon Demonstration

   The area of your polygon is 6
   The perimeter of your polygon is 12

   End Polygon Demonstration
```

Program J-5   A polygon—triangle implementation

Program J-5 Analysis

As is typical with class objects, most of the work is done in the classes themselves. When we define the triangle (Statement 12), we pass it the triangle's side lengths. These data are then stored in the triangle derived class by the constructor. Once the data have been stored, the constructor then calls the functions to calculate and store the perimeter and area of the triangle. All of this work is done in the class itself, however, and all that our program sees is that we define a triangle and then print its area and perimeter.

Inheritance Types—Private, Protected, Public

We commented earlier that it was necessary for the data variables in our polygon class to have protected access. If we had put them in public, they would not have been protected. For example, if the data were public, there would be nothing to stop a program from changing them after we calculated the area of a polygon. On the other hand, if we put the data variables in private, they would not have been accessible to derived classes. (You can prove this to yourself by copying Program J-3 and running it with the variable definitions in the private access section.) Protected is halfway between public and private. In this section, we explain how these three inheritance types work.

The meaning of private and public inheritance with derived types is unchanged. If data or functions in a derived type are private, they can only be used by functions that belong to the class. If data or functions are public, they can be accessed by any function within their scope. The access that needs to be understood is how base class data and functions are treated in the derived class. The inheritance type for the derived class is specified in its class header after the colon and before the base class identifier, as shown below.

```
class derivedClassID : inheritance_type baseClassID
```

To understand how the base class access is combined with the inheritance access types, refer to Table J-1.

Inheritance Type	Base Access Type	Derived Access Type
private	Private	Inaccessible
	Protected	Private
	Public	Private
protected	Private	Inaccessible
	Protected	Protected
	Public	Protected
public	Private	Inaccessible
	Protected	Protected
	Public	Public

Table J-1   Inherited access rules

Inheritance Type Private

When the inheritance type is private, the inherited access for base class data and functions is highly limited. If the base type access is private, neither the data nor the functions can be referenced from the derived class: Private functions are totally inaccessible and the only way to access the data is through the public base class functions.

If the functions and data are protected or public in the base class, they may be accessed by the derived type, but the access is private. The effect of this protection is that the derived class cannot pass on access to any of its derived classes.

Private is the default inheritance type. Therefore, to make the triangle class private, we can either omit the inheritance type or explicitly code it as private. We prefer the latter, as shown below.

```
class Triangle : private Polygons
{
 ...
}; // Triangle
```

Inheritance Type Protected

When the inheritance type is protected and the base class type is private, then the base class functions and data are again inaccessible. For protected and public base types, however, the derived class access type is set at protected. Consequently, types derived from it have access to the base class data and types but cannot pass that access on further.

In our triangle class definition, we specified public inheritance. To make the inheritance protected, we would use the code shown below.

```
class Triangle : protected Polygons
{
 ...
}; // Triangle
```

Inheritance Type Public

This third rule may be a little surprising at first glance. If the inheritance access is public and the base class access is private, then the functions and data are still inaccessible. A little reflection on the rules, however, should bring you to the logical conclusion: If the base type access is private, then nobody can access it under any circumstances.

On the other hand, for a public inheritance type, the base access type is passed on directly to the derived class. If the base type is protected, then the derived type is protected; if the base type is public, then the derived type is public.

Constructors and Destructors

Because constructors and destructors are not inherited, you must write new ones if the class requires special initialization. Furthermore, you need to understand how these functions are called, especially in relation to the base class constructors and destructors.

Constructors

Every class has at least one constructor. If a constructor is not provided, then the compiler generates a default constructor that does nothing. Alternately, we can write one or more of our own constructors. When we write constructors for both the base class and the derived class, we need to fully understand how they are invoked. The basic rule is that the base class constructors are called first, followed by the derived class constructors.

To demonstrate this rule, let's write a very simple program that includes an employee class. We have two types of employees, salaried and hourly. Salaried employees are paid on a monthly basis regardless of how many hours they work. Hourly employees, on the other hand, are paid only for the time that they actually spend on the job.

In this program, we have three classes. The employee base class has all of the data that apply to all employees, in this case only the employee ID. A derived salary class has the data that pertain only to salaried employees, and a derived hourly class contains data that apply only to hourly employees. The design of the classes is shown in Figure J-4.

When a derived class constructor is executed, it must first execute the constructor for the base class. Some of the data established when the derived class is created belong in the base class and some belong in the derived class. Because the derived class may need to use the base class data even in its constructor, these data need to be in place before the derived class is constructed. The question is how to pass the data from the derived class to the base class. A special initialization list known as a **base member initialization list** is used. To pass data from a derived class to the base class, we include the base member initialization list as a part of the header. It is really nothing more than a call to the base class initialization constructor. The format is shown below.

```
derivedClass :: derivedClass (parameter list)
             : baseClass (base parameter list)
```

The base class constructor parameter list does not need to contain all of the parameters in the derived class and in fact seldom will. It needs to contain all of the data required by the base class initiator, however; the parameters must match the parameters in the base class initiator function just like any parameters passed to any function.

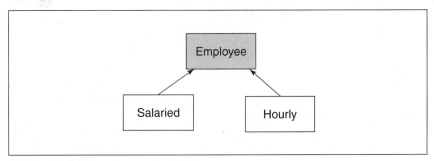

Figure J-4 Employee class design

Now that we understand how to pass data from the derived class to the base class, we are ready to code the class definition. The code is shown in Program J-6.

```
 1   /* Demonstrate use of derived constructors
 2          Written by:
 3          Date:
 4   */
 5
 6   // Class Declarations
 7   class Employee
 8   {
 9      protected:
10         int id;
11
12      public:
13          Employee (int idIn);
14          ~Employee (void);
15   }; // Employee
16
17   // ============= Employee constructor ==============
18      Employee :: Employee (int idIn)
19   {
20      id = idIn;
21      cout << "Base constructor for id    : "
22          << idIn << endl;
23
24   } // Employee constructor
25   // ============= Employee destructor ==============
26   Employee :: ~Employee (void)
27   {
28      cout << "Base destructor for id    : " << id << endl;
29   } // Employee Destructor
30
31   // =============== SalaryEmp Class ================
32   class SalaryEmp : public Employee
33   {
34      protected:
35         int   salary;
36
37      public:
38          SalaryEmp (int idIn, int   salaryIn);
39          ~SalaryEmp (void);
40   };
41   // ============= SalaryEmp constructor ==============
42   SalaryEmp :: SalaryEmp (int idIn,
```

Program J-6 Employee class definitions

```
43                            int    salaryIn)
44              : Employee (idIn)
45  {
46     salary = salaryIn;
47     cout << "Derived constructor for id : "
48         << id << " Salary: " << salary << endl;
49  } // SalaryEmp constructor
50
51  // ============= SalaryEmp destructor =============
52  SalaryEmp :: ~SalaryEmp (void)
53  {
54     cout << "Salary destructor for id   : " << id << endl;
55  } // SalaryEmp destructor
56
57  // ============= HourlyEmp Class ===============
58  class HourlyEmp : public Employee
59  {
60     protected:
61        float   payRate;
62        float   hours;
63
64     public:
65         HourlyEmp (int   idIn,
66                    float payRateIn);
67         ~HourlyEmp (void);
68  }; // HourlyEmp Class
69
70  // ============= HourlyEmp constructor =============
71  HourlyEmp :: HourlyEmp (int    idIn,
72                          float payRateIn)
73              : Employee (idIn)
74  {
75     payRate = payRateIn;                     //Derived data
76     hours   = 0.0;
77     cout << "Derived constructor for id : "
78         << id << " Pay Rate: " << payRate << endl;
79  } // HourlyEmp constructor
80
81  // ============= HourlyEmp destructor =============
82  HourlyEmp :: ~HourlyEmp (void)
83  {
84     cout << "Hourly destructor for id   : " << id << endl;
85  } // HourlyEmp destructor
86  // ============= End Employee classes ============
```

Program J-6 Employee class definitions *(continued)*

Program J-6 Analysis

To demonstrate that the constructors and destructors are working correctly, we have included print statements in their functions. These statements should not be part of the production coding, however.

Destructors

Because destructors do not have any parameters, they are easier to write. When a derived object is destroyed, its destructors are invoked. They in turn invoke the base class destructors. Note that this is the reverse of how the constructors work. Constructors are called starting with the base class and moving toward the derived classes. Destructors are called starting with the derived class and moving toward the base class.

Employee Class Program

To demonstrate how the base and derived class initiators and destructors work, let's write a simple program. This program contains one salaried and one hourly employee definition. As the class objects are created and destroyed, we print out a message (see Program J-6). The output from the program is shown at the end of Program J-7.

```
 1    /* Demonstrate use of inherited constructors with a
 2       base member initialization list.
 3          Written by
 4          Date
 5
 6    */
 7    #include <iostream.h>
 8    #include "P12-09.h"
 9
10    int main (void)
11    {
12    // Local Definitions
13       SalaryEmp  slryEmp (1234, 43000);
14       HourlyEmp  hrlyEmp (5678, 15.76);
15
16    // Statements
17       return 0 ;
18    } // main
```

```
    Results
       Base constructor for id      : 1234
       Derived constructor for id : 1234 Salary: 43000
       Base constructor for id      : 5678
       Derived constructor for id : 5678 Pay Rate: 15.76

       Hourly destructor for id     : 5678
       Base destructor for id       : 5678
       Salary destructor for id     : 1234
       Base destructor for id       : 1234
```

Program J-7   Run employee demonstration

C++ Templates

In C++, templates are a model of a function or an object that can be used to create actual functions or objects. During the compilation, C++ uses the template to create one or more blocks of code. For example, given a function template, one, two, or more actual functions can be created for use in the program. This concept is shown in Figure K-1.

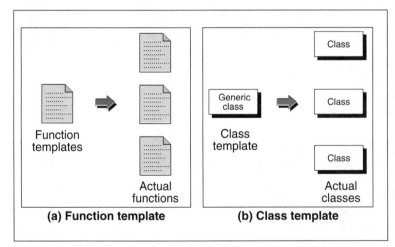

(a) Function template   **(b) Class template**

Figure K-1   Basic template concepts

K-1   FUNCTION TEMPLATE

A basic program concept is that a function applies actions to one or more objects and may create and return one object. In other words, a function can be defined by the

◆ Actions that are applied
◆ Objects that are involved

For example, a function that returns the larger of two integers applies logic to find the larger of two integers passed as arguments. Given such a function, however, if we need to find the larger of two long integers, we need to write a second function. Similarly, if we need to find the larger of two floats, we need to write a third function. Figure K-2 shows this situation.

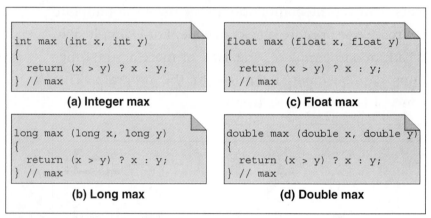

```
int max (int x, int y)
{
   return (x > y) ? x : y;
} // max
```
(a) Integer max

```
float max (float x, float y)
{
   return (x > y) ? x : y;
} // max
```
(c) Float max

```
long max (long x, long y)
{
   return (x > y) ? x : y;
} // max
```
(b) Long max

```
double max (double x, double y)
{
   return (x > y) ? x : y;
} // max
```
(d) Double max

Figure K-2   Multiple max functions

In C++ we can increase productivity by writing one generic function using a template. The compiler can then use the generic function to create different functions based on the need of the application program. Program K-1 shows such a generic function.

```
1   /* Create max function template
2          Written by:
3          Date:
4   */
5   template <class TYPE>
6   TYPE max (TYPE x, TYPE y)
7   {
8      return (x > y) ? x : y;
9   } // max template
```

Program K-1   max template

In this template definition, TYPE is used as a generic type. Based on the need of the application program, the compiler produces the appropriate function code and inserts it into the program. Note that the word class does not mean here the object class but a set of functions.

Let's see how we can use the generic function to create a set of different functions. Program K-2 creates some random integer, long integer, float, and double numbers and then displays the larger of each.

```
 1    /* Demonstrate function templates
 2           Written by:
 3           Date:
 4    */
 5    #include <iostream.h>
 6    #include <iomanip.h>
 7    #include <stdlib.h>
 8
 9    template <class TYPE>
10    TYPE max (TYPE x , TYPE y)
11    {
12        return (x > y ) ? x : y ;
13    } // max template
14
15    int main (void)
16    {
17    // Local Definitions
18        int    i1;
19        int    i2;
20        long   lg1;
21        long   lg2;
22        float  f1;
23        float  f2;
24        double d1;
25        double d2;
26
27    // Statements
28        i1  = rand();
29        i2  = rand();
30        lg1 = rand();
31        lg2 = rand();
32        f1  = rand() / 3.3;
33        f2  = rand() / 3.3;
34        d1  = rand() / 3.3;
35        d2  = rand() / 3.3;
36
37        cout << "Given "      << setw(5) << i1
38             << " and "       << setw(5) << i2   << ": "
39             << max(i1, i2)   << " is larger\n";
```

Program K-2 Demonstrate templates

```
40      cout << "Given "        << setw(5) << lg1
41           << " and "         << setw(5) << lg2  << ": "
42           << max(lg1, lg2) << " is larger\n";
43      cout << "Given "        << setw(5) << f1
44           << " and "         << setw(5) << f2   << ": "
45           << max(f1, f2)   << " is larger\n";
46      cout << "Given "        << setw(5) << d1
47           << " and "         << setw(5) << d2   << ": "
48           << max(d1, d2)   << " is larger\n";
49      return 0;
50  } // main
```

```
Results
Given 16838 and  5758: 16838 is larger
Given 10113 and 17515: 17515 is larger
Given 9409.39 and 1705.15: 9409.39 is larger
Given 6972.73 and 2248.18: 6972.73 is larger
```

Program K-2   Demonstrate templates *(continued)*

Program K-2 Analysis

As you study this simple program, note that there are no functions other than main and the template max. Without the template, we would have had to create four different functions, as shown in Figure K-3. Each of these functions created by the function template is known as an instance of the template.

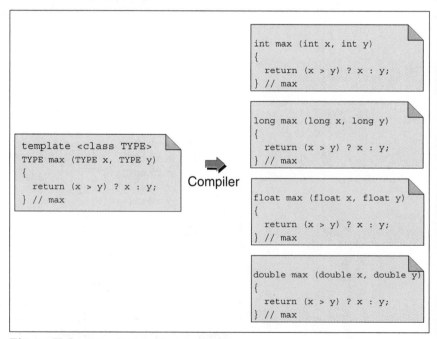

Figure K-3   Function instances

Template Format

Study Figure K-3 carefully. Note that the template parameters are different than normal parameters. Although they can contain standard types, they generally contain one or more generic types as declared in the template class. When they are instantiated, the compiler first replaces the template parameter types with the appropriate types required by a call. This substitution creates a function, with the correct types matching the calling function. When the call is made, the corresponding parameters are replaced by the actual data as in any function call. This function generation and call are shown in Figure K-4.

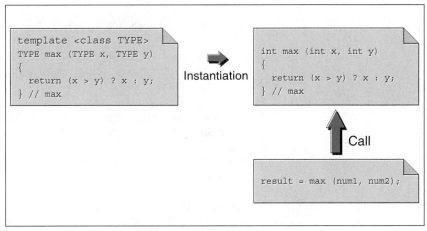

Figure K-4   Function template generation

K-2   CLASS TEMPLATE

We can also have class templates. The general syntax of a class template closely follows the syntax for the function template. The class declaration is immediately preceded by a template that specifies the generic types to be associated with the class. The class then uses these generic types to complete its declaration. Program K-3 contains a simple class template declaration.

```
1   template <class TYPE1, class TYPE2, class TYPE3>
2   class Test
3   {
4      private:
5         TYPE1  x;
6         TYPE2  y;
7         TYPE3  z;
8         int    t;
9
```

Program K-3   Class template declaration and use

```
10       public:
11          Test (void);
12          ~Test (void);
13          TYPE1 doIt (TYPE1 a, TYPE2 b);
14          ...
15          ...
16          ...
17    }; // class Test
```

Program K-3   Class template declaration and use *(continued)*

The template types are a part of the class declaration. To write the functions for the class, we must code the template with the function header and use the template types as part of the definition. This code is shown in Program K-4, which outlines the format for the class constructor for Test.

```
 1    template <class TYPE1, class TYPE2, class TYPE3>
 2    Test <TYPE1, TYPE2, TYPE3> ::  Test (void)
 3    {
 4    // Code for test constructor
 5    } // Test constructor
 6
 7    template <class TYPE1, class TYPE2, class TYPE3>
 8    Test <TYPE1, TYPE2, TYPE3> :: ~Test (void)
 9    {
10    // Code for test destructor
11    } // Test destructor
12
13    template <class TYPE1, class TYPE2, class TYPE3>
14    TYPE1 Test <TYPE1, TYPE2, TYPE3> ::  doIt (TYPE1 a,
15                                              TYPE2 b);
16
17    {
18    // Code for doIt
19    } // doIt
```

Program K-4   Functions for test class

Program K-4 Analysis

As you study the three examples in Program K-4, note that in declaring the scope for Test, all three of the template generic types must be referenced. They must all be referenced, even if the function uses only one or two of them. For example, the definition of doIt in Statement 14 uses only TYPE1 and TYPE2. Nevertheless, the function header's scope specifies all three generic types. Failure to reference all of the generic types associated with the class will result in an unidentified class error during compilation.

Instantiation of Objects

After we have defined the class templates and related function templates, we can create instances of class objects. Once again, when defining the objects, we must provide one standard or derived type for each of the template parameters, three in the case of `Test`. Program K-5 demonstrates how we can create different instances of the `Test` class.

```
 1    int main (void)
 2    {
 3    // Local Definitions
 4       Test <int,    float,  int>     test1;
 5       Test <float,  float,  int>     test2;
 6       Test <double, double, String> test3;
 7       Test <int,    float,  int>     testA;
 8
 9       ...
10       ...
11       ...
12    }  // main
```

Program K-5   Using class templates

Program K-5 Analysis

Note that the template parameters are enclosed in pointed brackets after the class identifier. They match one for one with the generic types specified in the template. In `test3`, we specified the `String` class as the third type. Obviously, this requires that the `String` class be included in the compilation unit.

Not so apparent is that Program K-5 defines three different objects, all derived from the `Test` class template. As with function templates, as long as one of the types being instantiated is different, the classes are different. On the other hand, both `test1` and `testA` are instances of the same type because they have exactly the same types defined in the pointed brackets. A graphical representation of the classes is shown in Figure K-5.

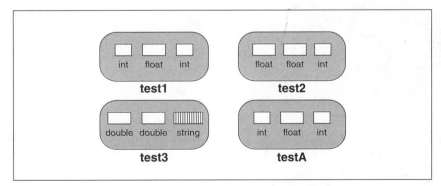

Figure K-5   Classes for Program K-5

L Standard Template Library

The Standard Template Library (STL) is a collection of template classes and template functions that can be used to implement common data structures and their corresponding algorithms. It is included with ANSI/ISO implementations of C++.

STL has five components: containers, container adaptors, iterators, generic algorithms, and function objects.

L-1   CONTAINERS

Containers are objects that store a collection of other objects. There are two broad categories of containers: sequence containers and associative containers.

Sequence Containers

A sequence container is an unsorted, linear collection of objects, all of the same type. The three standard sequence containers are vector, deque, and list.

vector

A vector is a sequence container that supports random access iterators. It is optimized for insertions and deletions at the end of the collection. Insertions and deletions anywhere else in the collection, such as the beginning or middle, take linear time. Storage management is handled automatically.

The vector template class declaration in Template L-1 has been simplified: We have omitted some details and several methods.

```
template <class T >
class vector
{
  public:
// ================= constructor and destructor =================
                    vector  ();                        // default
                    vector  (size_type n, const T& t);
                    vector  (input_iterator first,
                               input_iterator last);
                    vector  (const vector<T>& x);
                    ~vector (void);

// ================= assignment =================
  vector<T>&        operator= (vector<T>&, x);
  void              assign    (input_iterator first,
                                 input_operator last);
  void              assign    (size_type n, const T& t);

// ================= capacity =================
  size_type         size      (void);    // check current size
  size_type         max_size  (void);    // check maximum size
  void              resize    (size_type n);
  bool              empty     (void);
  size_type         capacity  (void);

// ================= create iterators =================
  iterator          begin     (void);              // forward
  iterator          end       (void);              // forward
  reverse_iterator  rbegin    (void);              // reverse
  reverse_iterator  rend      (void);              // reverse
```

Template L-1   vector class

```
// ================= element access ==================
   reference          front       (void);              // first
   reference          back        (void);              // last
   reference          operator[]  (size_type n);       // middle
   reference          at          (size_type n);       // middle

// ================= modifiers ==================
   void               push_back   (const T& t);        // at back
   iterator           insert      (iterator i,         // at middle
                                   const T& x);
   void               insert      (iterator i,         // at middle
                                   size_type n,
                                   constant T& x);
   void               insert      (iterator i,         // at middle
                                   iterator start,
                                   iterator end);
   void               pop_back    (void);              // from back
   iterator           erase       (iterator postion);  // from middle
   iterator           erase       (iterator start,     // range
                                   iterator end);       // start...end
   void               swap        (vector<T>&, x);
   void               clear       (void);              // remove all
} // vector
```

Template L-1   vector class *(continued)*

Template L-2 contains the relational operators associated with the vector class.

```
// ================= relational operators ==================
   bool               operator==  (const vector <T>& x,
                                   const vector <T>& y);
   bool               operator!=  (const vector <T>& x,
                                   const vector <T>& y);
   bool               operator<   (const vector <T>& x,
                                   const vector <T>& y);
   bool               operator>   (const vector <T>& x,
                                   const vector <T>& y);
   bool               operator<=  (const vector <T>& x,
                                   const vector <T>& y);
   bool               operator>=  (const vector <T>& x,
                                   const vector <T>& y);
```

Template L-2   vector class relational operators

deque

A deque is a sequenced container that supports random access iterators. It provides highly efficient insert and delete operations at the beginning or at the end of the data. Insert and delete at the middle require linear time. Thus a deque is optimized for inserting and erasing elements at the beginning or at the end. Storage management is handled automatically.

Template L-3 contains a basic template class declaration for deque. We omit some of the details and methods for simplicity.

```
template <class T>
class deque
{
  public:
// ================= modifiers =================
                  deque ();                              // default
                  deque (size_type n, const T& t);
                  deque (input_iterator first,
                         input_iterator last);
                  deque (const deque<T>& x);             // copy
                  ~deque (void);

// ================= assignment =================
  deque<T>&       operator= (deque<T>&, x);
  void            assign    (input_iterator first,
                             input_operator last);
  void            assign    (size_type n,   const T& t);

// ================= capacity =================
  size_type       size     (void);                      // current size
  size_type       max_size (void);
  void            resize   (size_type n);
  bool            empty    (void);

// ================= iterators =================
  iterator          begin  (void);                      // forward
  iterator          end    (void);                      // forward
  reverse_iterator  rbegin (void);                      // reverse
  reverse_iterator  rend   (void);                      // reverse

// ================= element access =================
  reference       front     (void);          // first element
  reference       back      (void);          // last element
  reference       operator[] (size_type n);  // middle element
  reference       at        (size_type n);   // middle element

// ================= modifiers =================

  void            push_front (const T&    t); // insert front
  void            push_back  (const T&    t); // insert back
  iterator        insert     (iterator    i, // insert middle
                              const T&    x);
  void            insert     (iterator    i,
                              size_type   n,
                              constant T& x);
  void            insert     (iterator    i,
                              iterator    start,
```

Template L-3   deque class

```
                                    iterator      end);

      void              pop_front (void);
      void              pop_back  (void);
      iterator          erase     (iterator postion); // from middle
      iterator          erase     (iterator start,
                                    iterator end);
      void              swap      (deque<T>&, x);
      void              clear();                       // removing all
    }; // deque
```

Template L-3   deque class *(continued)*

The relational operators in Template L-4 are associated with the deque.

```
// ================= relational operators =================
   bool              operator== (const deque <T>& x,
                                  const deque <T>& y);
   bool              operator!= (const deque <T>& x,
                                  const deque <T>& y);
   bool              operator<  (const deque <T>& x,
                                  const deque <T>& y);
   bool              operator>  (const deque <T>& x,
                                  const deque <T>& y);
   bool              operator<= (const deque <T>& x,
                                  const deque <T>& y);
   bool              operator>= (const deque <T>& x,
                                  const deque <T>& y);
```

Template L-4   deque relational operators

list

A list is a sequenced container that supports bidirectional iterators with constant time insert and delete operations anywhere in the list; however, it does not support random access to elements. Thus a list is especially designed for sequential access. Storage management is handled automatically.

Template L-5 contains a simplified template class declaration for list, omitting the allocators for simplicity.

```
template <class T >
class list
{
   public:
// ================= constructor and destructor =================
                    list  ();
                    list  (size_type n,
                           const T& t);
                    list  (input_iterator first,
```

Template L-5   list class

```
                               input_iterator last);
                  list  (const list<T>& x);
                  ~list (void);

// ================= assignment ================
   list <T>&      operator= (list<T>&, x);
   void           assign (input_iterator first,
                          input_operator last);
   void           assign (size_type n, const T& t);

// ================= capacity ================
   size_type      size     (void);         // current size
   size_type      max_size (void);          // maximum size
   void           resize   (size_type n);
   bool           empty    (void);

// ================= iterators ================
   iterator          begin  (void);                   // forward
   iterator          end    (void);                   // forward
   reverse_iterator  rbegin (void);                  // backward
   reverse_iterator  rend   (void);                  // backward

// ================= element access ================
   reference      front  (void);
   reference      back   (void);

// ================= modifiers ================
   void           push_front (const T& t);
   void           push_back  (const T& t);
   iterator       insert     (iterator i,            // middle
                              const T& x);
   void           insert     (iterator i,            // middle
                              size_type n,
                              constant T& x);
   void           insert     (iterator i,            // middle
                              iterator start,
                              iterator end);

   void           pop_front  (void);
   void           pop_back   (void);
   iterator       erase      (iterator postion);     // middle
   iterator       erase      (iterator start,
                               iterator end);
   void           swap       (list<T>& x);
   void           clear      (void);          // delete all

// ================= special list operations ================
   void           splice     (iterator postion,
                              list<T>& x);
   void           splice     (iterator postion,
                              list<T>& x,
```

Template L-5 list class *(continued)*

```
                                          iterator i);
      void              splice     (iterator postion,
                                    list<T>& x,
                                    iterator first,
                                    iterator last);
      void              remove     (const T& value);
      void              remove_if (Predicate pred);
      void              unique     (BinaryPredicate binary_pred);
      void              merge      (list<T>& x);
      void              merge      (list<T>& x, Compare comp);
      void              sort       (Compare comp);
      void              reverse    (void);
}; list
```

Template L-5   list class *(continued)*

The relational operators for the list class are shown in Template L-6.

```
// ================= relational operators =================
   bool              operator== (const list <T>& x, const list<T>& y);
   bool              operator!= (const list <T>& x, const list<T>& y);
   bool              operator<  (const list <T>& x, const list<T>& y);
   bool              operator>  (const list <T>& x, const list<T>& y);
   bool              operator<= (const list <T>& x, const list<T>& y);
   bool              operator>= (const list <T>& x, const list<T>& y);
```

Template L-6   list class relational operators

Associative Containers

An associative container is a collection of sorted objects that allows fast retrieval using a key. In each container, the key must be unique. There are four standard associative containers: *set*, *multiset*, *map*, and *multimap*.

set

A set is an associative container (Template L-7) that supports unique key and bidirectional iterators. It provides fast retrieval on keys. Only the key is stored in the container; there are no other data.

```
template <class Key>
class set
{
public:

// ================= constructor and destructor =================
                set  ();
                set  (input_iterator first,
                         input_iterator last);
                set  (const set<Key>& x);               // copy
                ~set (void);
```

Template L-7   set class

```
// ================= assignment =================
   set<Key>&           operator= (set<Key>&, x);
   void                assign    (input_iterator first,
                                  input_operator last);
   void                assign    (size_type    n,  const Key& t);

// ================= capacity =================
   size_type           size      (void);            // current size
   size_type           max_size  (void);
   bool                empty     (void);

// ================= iterators =================
   iterator            begin (void);                // forward
   iterator            end (void);                  // forward
   reverse_iterator    rbegin (void);               // reverse
   reverse_iterator    rend (void);                 // reverse

// ================= modifiers =================
   pair <iterator, bool> insert (const value_type & x);
   iterator            insert (iterator i, const value_type & x);
   void                insert (InputIterator start,
                               InputIterator end);

   void                erase  (iterator postion);   // middle
   void                erase  (const Key& x);
   void                erase  (iterator start, iterator end);
   void                swap   (set<Key>&, x);
   void                clear  (void);               // remove all

// ================= observers =================
   key_compare         key_comp   (void);
   value_compare       value_comp (void);

// ================= special set operations =================
   iterator            find        (const key_type& x);
   size_type           count       (const key_type& x);
   iterator            lower_bound (const key_type& x);
   iterator            upper_bound (const key_type& x);
   iterator            equal_range (const key_type& x);
}; // set
```

Template L-7   set class *(continued)*

Template L-8 contains the relational operators for the set class.

```
// ================= relational operators =================
   bool                operator== (const set <Key>& x,
                                    const set <Key>& y);
   bool                operator!= (const set <Key>& x,
                                    const set <Key>& y);
```

Template L-8   Relational operators for set class

```
     bool                operator<  (const set <Key>& x,
                                     const set <Key>& y);
     bool                operator>  (const set <Key>& x,
                                     const set <Key>& y);
     bool                operator<= (const set <Key>& x,
                                     const set <Key>& y);
     bool                operator>= (const set <Key>& x,
                                     const set <Key>& y);
```

Template L-8   Relational operators for set class *(continued)*

multiset

A multiset, shown in Template L-9, is an associative container that supports duplicate keys and bidirectional iterators. It provides fast retrieval on key searches. As with the set, only the key is stored.

```
template <class Key>
class multiset
{
  public:
// ================= constructor and destructor =================
                      multiset  ();
                      multiset  (input_iterator first,
                                 input_iterator last);
                      multiset  (const multiset<Key>& x); // copy
                      ~multiset (void);

// ================= assignment =================
   multiset<Key>&     operator= (multiset<Key>&, x);
   void               assign    (input_iterator  first,
                                 input_operator  last);
   void               assign    (size_type       n,
                                 const Key&      t);

// ================= capacity =================
   size_type          size     (void);              // current size
   size_type          max_size (void);
   bool               empty    (void);

// ================= iterators =================
   iterator           begin  (void);                       // forward
   iterator           end    (void);                       // forward
   reverse_iterator   rbegin (void);                       // reverse
   reverse_iterator   rend   (void);                       // reverse

// ================= modifiers =================
   pair <iterator, bool> insert (const Key& x);
   iterator              insert    (iterator i, constant Key& x);
   void                  insert    (InputIterator start,
                                    InputIterator end);
```

Template L-9   multiset class

```
    void            erase      (iterator postion);    // middle
    void            erase      (const Key& x);
    void            erase      (iterator start, iterator end);
    void            swap       (multiset<Key>& x);
    void            clear      ();                     // remove all

    // ================= observers =================
    key_compare     key_comp   (void);
    value_compare   value_comp (void);

    // ================= special operations =================
    iterator        find            (const key_type& x);
    size_type       count           (const key_type& x);
    iterator        lower_bound     (const key_type& x);
    iterator        upper_bound     (const key_type& x);
    pair<iterator, iterator> equal_range (const key_type& x);
}; // multiset
```

Template L-9   multiset class *(continued)*

Template L-10 contains the relational operators for the multiset class.

```
    // ================= relational operators =================
    bool            operator== (const multiset <Key>& x,
                                const multiset<Key>& y);
    bool            operator!= (const multiset <Key>& x,
                                const multiset<Key>& y);
    bool            operator<  (const multiset <Key>& x,
                                const multiset<Key>& y);
    bool            operator>  (const multiset <Key>& x,
                                const multiset<Key>& y);
    bool            operator<= (const multiset <Key>& x,
                                const multiset<Key>& y);
    bool            operator>= (const multiset <Key>& x,
                                const multiset<Key>& y);
```

Template L-10   Relational operators for multiset

map

A map is an associative container (Template L-11) that supports unique key and bidirectional iterators. It provides fast retrieval of values of another type T based on the keys. The key is an index to the data in the container; the key is not stored.

```
template <class Key, class T>
class map
{
  public:
```

Template L-11   map class

```
// ================ constructor and destructor ================
                   map ();
                   map (input_iterator first,
                        input_iterator last);
                   map (const map<Key, T>& x);          // copy
                   ~map (void);

// ================ assignment ================
   map<Key, T>&    operator= (map<Key, T>& x);

// ================ capacity ================
   size_type       size     (void);          // current size
   size_type       max_size (void);
   bool            empty    (void);

// ================ iterators ================
   iterator        begin    (void);           // forward
   iterator        end      (void);           // forward
   reverse_iterator rbegin  (void);           // reverse
   reverse_iterator rend    (void);           // reverse

// ================ element access ================
   T&              operator[](const key_type& k);

// ================ modifiers ================
   pair <iterator, bool> insert (const value_type & x);
   iterator        insert (iterator i, const value_type & x);
   void            insert (InputIterator start,
                           InputIterator end);

   void            erase (iterator postion);   // from middle
   size_type       erase (const key-type& k);
   void            erase (iterator start,
                          iterator end);
   void            swap  (map<Key, T>& x);
   void            clear ();                   // remove all

// ================ observers ================
   key_compare     key_comp   (void);
   value_compare   value_comp (void);

// ================ special map operations ================
   iterator        find (const key_type& x);
   size_type       count (const key_type& x);
   iterator        lower_bound (const key_type& x);
   iterator        upper_bound (const key_type& x);
   pair <iterator, iterator> equal_range (const key_type& x);
}; // map
```

Template L-11   map class *(continued)*

Template L-12 contains the relational operators for the map class.

```
// ================ relational operators ================
   bool                operator== (const map <Key, T>&x,
                                   const map <Key, T>&y);
   bool                operator!= (const map <Key, T>&x,
                                   const map <Key, T>&y);
   bool                operator<  (const map <Key, T>&x,
                                   const map <Key, T>&y);
   bool                operator>  (const map <Key, T>&x,
                                   const map <Key, T>&y);
   bool                operator<= (const map <Key, T>&x,
                                   const map <Key, T>&y);
   bool                operator>= (const map <Key, T>&x,
                                   const map <Key, T>&y);
```

Template L-12   Relational operators for map

multimap

A multimap is an associative container (Template L-13) that supports duplicate keys and bidirectional iterators. It provides for fast retrieval of the values of another type T based on keys. The key is an index.

```
template <class Key, T>
class multimap
{
   public:
// ================ constructor and destructor ================
                       multimap ();
                       multimap (input_iterator first,
                                 input_iterator last);
                       multimap (const multimap<Key, T>& x);// copy
                       ~multimap (void);

// ================ assignment ================
   multimap<Key>&      operator= (multimap<Key, T>&, x);
   void                assign    (input_iterator first,
                                  input_operator last);
   void                assign    (size_type    n, const Key& t);

// ================ capacity ================
   size_type           size     (void);           // current size
   size_type           max_size (void);
bool                   empty    (void);

// ================ iterators ================
   iterator            begin (void);               // forward
   iterator            end (void);                 // forward
```

Template L-13   multimap class

```
    reverse_iterator  rbegin (void);                    // reverse
    reverse_iterator  rend (void);                       // reverse

 // ================= modifiers =================
    pair <iterator, bool> insert (const key_value& x);
    iterator          insert (           iterator   i,
                                 constant key_value& x);
    void              insert (InputIterator start,
                                 InputIterator end);

    void              erase (iterator postion);   // from middle
    void              erase (const key_value& x);
    void              erase (iterator start,
                                 iterator end);
    void              swap  (multimap<Key, T>& x);
    void              clear ();                     // remove all

 // ================= observers =================
    key_compare       key_comp   (void);
    value_compare     value_comp (void);

 // ================= special multimap operations =================
    iterator              find       (const key_type& x);
    size_type             count      (const key_type& x);
    iterator              lower_bound (const key_type& x);
    iterator              upper_bound (const key_type& x);
    pair<iterator, iterator> equal_range (const key_type& x);
}; // multimap
```

Template L-13   multimap class *(continued)*

The relational operators for the multimap class are shown in Template L-14.

```
 // ================= relational operators =================
    bool              operator== (const multimap <Key, T>&x,
                                     const multimap <Key, T>&y;
    bool              operator!= (const multimap <Key, T>&x,
                                     const multimap <Key, T>&y;
    bool              operator<  (const multimap <Key, T>&x,
                                     const multimap <Key, T>&y;
    bool              operator>  (const multimap <Key, T>&x,
                                     const multimap <Key, T>&y;
    bool              operator<= (const multimap <Key, T>&x,
                                     const multimap <Key, T>&y);
    bool              operator>= (const multimap <Key, T>&x,
                                     const multimap <Key, T>&y);
```

Template L-14   Relational operators for multimap

L-2   CONTAINER ADAPTORS

Programmers often need to use other objects, such as a stack, queue, or priority queue, whose interfaces are more limited than those of standard containers. For example, a stack object needs only four types of operations: *push, pop, top*, and *empty.* The STL contains template classes for stack, queue, and priority queue and has made them generic by allowing the programmer to choose the desired sequence container (*vector, deque,* or *list*). These generic classes are called *container adaptors.*

stack

A stack is a sequenced object in which insertions and deletions both take place at one end, known as the top. STL defines a container adaptor that can be adapted to any container that supports *back, push_back*, and *pop_back* operations. Any of the three containers—list, vector, or deque—can be used. The default container is deque. The stack class is shown in Template L-15.

```
template <class T, class Container = deque <T> >
class stack
{
   protected:
   Container c;

   Public:
// ================= constructor =================
                       stack (const Container& = Container ());

// ================= interfaces =================
   size_type          size  (void)
                             {return c.size ();}
   bool               empty (void)
                             {return c.empty ();}
   value_type&        top   (void)
                             {return c.back ();}
   void               push  (const value_type& x)
                             {c.push_back (x);}
   void               pop   (void)
                             {c.pop_back ();}
}; // stack
```

Template L-15   stack class

Relational Operators

The stack uses the same relational operators as those found in the containers—equal (==), not equal (!=), less than (<), less than or equal (<=), greater than (>), and greater than or equal (>=)—to compare two stacks.

queue

A queue is a sequenced container in which insertion takes place at one end (the rear) and deletion takes place at the other end (the front). The STL defines a container adaptor that can be used with any container that supports *front, back, push_back*, and *pop_front.* The best candidates are list and deque; vector is not suitable because *pop_front* is not supported by a vector. The default is deque. The queue class is shown in Template L-16.

```
template <class T, class Container = deque <T>>
class queue
{
   protected:
   Container c;

   Public:
// ================= constructor =================
                     queue (const Container& = Container ());

// ================= interfaces =================
   size_type        size   (void)
                            {return c.size ();}
   bool             empty  (void)
                            {return c.empty ();}
   value_type&      front  (void)
                            {return c.front ();}
   value_type&      back   (void)
                            {return c.back ();}
   void             push   (const value_type& x)
                            {c.push_back (x);}
   void             pop    (void)
                            {c.pop_front ();}
}; // queue
```

Template L-16   queue class

Relational Operators

The queue uses the same relational operators as those found in the containers—equal (==), not equal (!=), less than (<), less than or equal (<=), greater than (>), and greater than or equal (>=)—to compare two queues.

Priority Queue

A priority queue is a queue in which the sequence is created in such a way that the element with the highest (or smallest) priority is at the front, and the rest of the elements are arranged in priority sequence. Entries with equal priorities are processed in FIFO sequence.

The priority queue (Template L-17) can use any container that provides a random access iterator and *front*, *push_back*, and *pop_back* operations. The vector and deque are good candidates. List is not because it does not provide a random access iterator. The default is the vector. No relational operators are provided for priority queue objects.

```
template <class T, class Container = vector<T> >
class priority_queue
{
   protected:
```

Template L-17   priority_queue class

```
    Container c;
    Compare    comp;

    Public:
// ================= constructor =================
                    priority_queue
                            (const Compare& x = Compare(),
                             const Container& = Container ());
                    priority_queue (InputIterator first,
                                    InputIterator last,
                             const Compare& x = Compare(),
                             const Container& = Container ());

//================= interfaces =================
    size_type        size  (void)
                           {return c.size ();}
    bool             empty (void)
                           {return c.empty ();}
    value_type&      top   (void)
                           {return c.front ();}
    void             push  (const value_type& x);
    void             pop   (void);
}; // priority_queue
```

Template L-17   priority_queue class *(continued)*

L-3   ITERATORS

Iterators are objects that provide access to objects stored in a container. They work like regular pointers in C++. They can be used to store and retrieve objects in a container the same way a pointer accesses objects in C++. In this manner, iterators act as the connection between the generic algorithms and the containers. Provided that programmers use the correct iterator, they don't need to know how the objects are stored in the container.

STL defines five different iterators: *input, output, forward, bidirectional,* and *random access,* as shown in Figure L-1.

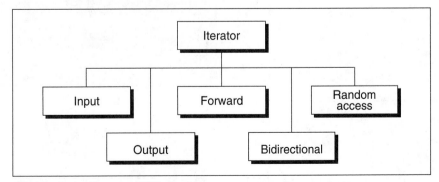

Figure L-1   Types of STL iterators

Input Iterator

An input iterator can be used only to retrieve a value from the input stream; it cannot be used to store a value. It can only move in the forward direction, retrieving the objects one by one. It cannot go backward and it cannot jump. Figure L-2 shows the concept of an input iterator in relation to an input stream.

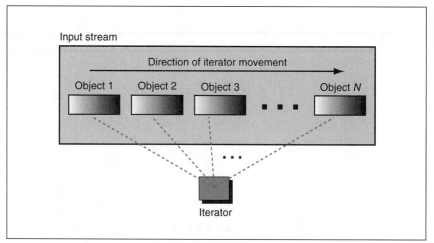

Figure L-2   STL input iterator

Output Iterator

An output iterator can be used only to store a value in an output stream; it cannot be used to retrieve a value. It only moves in the forward direction, storing the objects one by one. It cannot go backward and it cannot jump. Figure L-3 shows the concept of an output iterator in relation to an output stream.

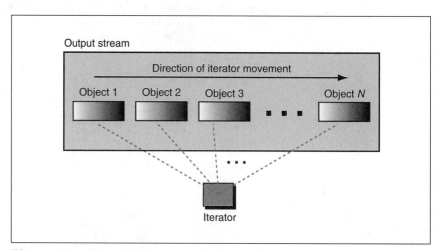

Figure L-3   STL output iterator

Forward Iterator

A forward iterator can be used to both retrieve and store a value. It can only move in the forward direction, visiting the objects one by one. It cannot go backward and it cannot jump. Figure L-4 shows the concept of a forward iterator in relation to a container.

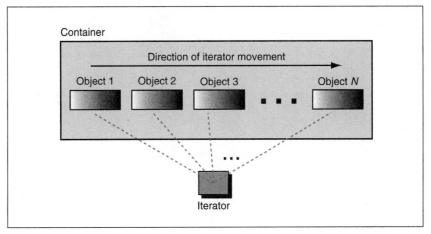

Figure L-4   STL forward iterator

Bidirectional Iterator

A bidirectional iterator can be used to both retrieve and store values. Unlike the forward iterator, it moves backward and forward, one item at a time: It cannot jump. Figure L-5 shows the concept of a bidirectional iterator in relation to a container.

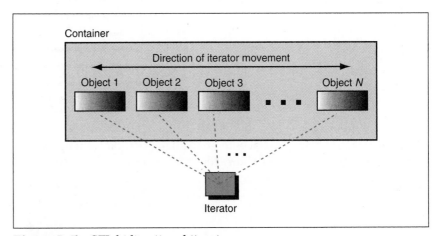

Figure L-5   STL bidirectional iterator

Random Access Iterator

A random access iterator is like a bidirectional operator with one extra capability, it can jump in both direction. Figure L-6 shows the concept of a random access iterator in relation to a container.

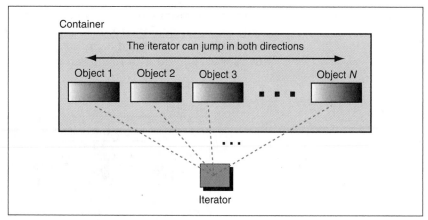

Figure L-6   STL random access iterator

Hierarchical Relation

There is a hierarchical relation between the iterators. Every forward iterator is also an input and an output iterator. Every bidirectional iterator is also a forward iterator. A random access iterator is also a bidirectional iterator. Figure L-7 shows the hierarchical relationship between five different iterators.

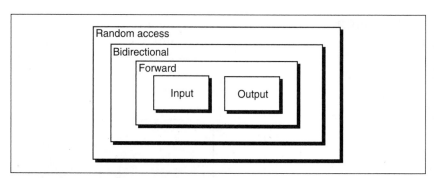

Figure L-7   Iterator hierarchical relationships

Operators Supported by Iterators

Each iterator can support different operators according to its type. Table L-1 shows the types of operators that can be supported by each iterator.

Iterator	Operator
Input	*, =, ++, ==, !=, ->
Output	*, =, ++
Forward	*, =, ++, ==, !=, ->
Bidirectional	*, =, ++, ==, !=, ->, --
Random access	*, =, ++, ==, !=, ->, --, +, -, <, >, <=, >=, []

Table L-1   Iterator operators

L-4   GENERIC ALGORITHMS

STL provides a set of generic algorithms, each of which can operate on a variety of containers. Generic algorithms are normally divided into the groups shown below.

- ♦ Minimum and maximum algorithms
- ♦ Numeric algorithms
- ♦ Nonmutating sequence algorithms
- ♦ Sorting algorithms
- ♦ Set operation on sorted structure
- ♦ Heap operation

L-5   FUNCTION OBJECTS

A function object encapsulates a function. STL uses this strategy to pass a function to a generic algorithm or to a method in a container without using the traditional function pointer. This design is accomplished by overloading the *operator( )* in the corresponding class. A function object can be used in place of a function pointer. Table L-2 shows some of the function objects.

Category	Function	Example
Mathematical	plus<T>	plus <int>
	minus<T>	minus <float>
	multiplies<T>	multiplies <double>
	divides<T>	divides <int>
	modulus<T>	modulus <float>
Relational	equal_to<T>	equal_to <int>
	not_equal_to<T>	not_equal_to <float>
	greater<T>	greater <int>
	greater_equal<T>	greater_equal <string>
	less<T>	less <double>
	less_equal<T>	less_equal <int>
Logical	logical_not<T>	logical_not<bool>
	logical_and<T>	logical_and<bool>
	logical_or<T>	logical_or<bool>

Table L-2   STL encapsulated function objects

Solutions to Selected Exercises

This section contains solutions to selected exercises at the end of each chapter.

Chapter 1 Exercises

1. Both structure charts and pseudocode are tools used in program design. Structure charts give a pictorial representation of the logical flow of an entire program. Pseudocode provides a textual (part English, part structured code) representation of the code.

3. An algorithm in an application program is written specifically for that application and no other. The details of the algorithm are known to the author of the program. The details of an algorithm in an abstract data type are hidden from the programmer who uses that ADT. The only concern is what can be done with the data type and not how it is done.

5. In the C++ language, the composite data types are *pointer*, enumerated type (*enum*), *union*, array, structure (*struct*), and *class*.

7. **a.** 24
   b. $n^{1/2}$
   c. $n\log_2(n)$
   d. $n + n^2 + n^3$

9. $O(n)$

11. $n(5n) = 5n^2 = O(n^2)$

13. $O(n^2\log_2 n)$

15. time $= (1000^3) * 10^{-9}$ seconds $= 1$ second

17. $n_1 = 4096 \qquad n_2 = 16{,}384$
    $f(n_1) = 512 \qquad f(n_2) = 2048$
    $n_2 = 4 * n_1$
    $f(n_2) = 4 * f(n_1)$

    Because $f(n)$ increases proportionally with n, the relationship is linear. The efficiency is also linear, and therefore the big-O notation is $O(n)$.

19. $n_1 = 4096$ $n_2 = 16{,}384$
$f(n_1) = 512$ $f(n_2) = 1024$
$n_2 = 4 * n_1$
$f(n_2) = 2 * f(n_1)$

Because n increases by a factor of 4 while $f(n)$ increases by a factor of only 2, the efficiency is square root(n). The big-O notation is $O(n^{0.5})$.

Chapter 2 Exercises

1. See Table S-1.

Loop Number	First	Mid	Last	Compare
1	0	3 (26)	7	88 > 26
2	4	5 (56)	7	88 > 56
3	6	6 (88)	7	88 = 88
Final	8	6 (88)	7	
locn, 6 (88); found, true.				

Table S-1 Solution to Chapter 2, Exercise 1.

3. Hashing: (List size: 19)
    Modulo Division
    Collision Resolution: Linear Probe
Hashing Calculations
    224562 % 19 = 1
    137456 % 19 = 10
    214562 % 19 = 14
    140145 % 19 = 1 ➮ 2 (1)
    214576 % 19 = 9
    162145 % 19 = 18
    144467 % 19 = 10 ➮ 11 (2)
    199645 % 19 = 12
    234534 % 19 = 17

Hashed List (Collision)
    0 --
    1 -- 224562
    2 -- 140145 (1)
    3 --
    4 --
    5 --
    6 --
    7 --
    8 --

```
 9 -- 214576
10 -- 137456
11 -- 144467  (2)
12 -- 199645
13 --
14 -- 214562
15 --
16 --
17 -- 234534
18 -- 162145
```

Collisions: 2. Density: $9/19 = 47\%$

5. Hashing: (List size: 19)
   Digit Extraction (1, 3, 5) + Modulo Division
   Collision Resolution: Quadratic Probe
   Hashing Calculations

```
224562     ⇌ 246 % 19 = 18
137456     ⇌ 175 % 19 =  4
214562     ⇌ 246 % 19 = 18
 18 + 12   ⇌  30 % 19 = 11  (1)
140145     ⇌ 104 % 19 =  9
214576     ⇌ 247 % 19 =  0
162145     ⇌ 124 % 19 = 10
144467     ⇌ 146 % 19 = 13
199645     ⇌ 194 % 19 =  4
  4 + 12   ⇌  16 % 19 = 16  (2)
234534     ⇌ 243 % 19 = 15
```

Hashed List (Collision)

```
 0 -- 214576
 1 --
 2 --
 3 --
 4 -- 137456
 5 --
 6 --
 7 --
 8 --
 9 -- 140145
10 -- 162145
11 -- 214562  (1)
12 --
```

```
13 -- 144467
14 --
15 -- 234534
16 -- 199645 (2)
17 --
18 -- 224562
```
Collisions: 2. Density: 9/19 = 47%

7. Hashing: (List size: 19)

Mid-Square

Collision Resolution: Random Number (3 * address − 1) % 19

Hashing Calculations

```
224562  ↝  45 = 2025  ↝   2 % 19 =   2
137456  ↝  74 = 5476  ↝  47 % 19 =   9
214562  ↝  45 = 2025  ↝   2 % 19 =   2
  (3 *   2 - 1) % 19  ↝              5 (1)
140145  ↝  01 = 0001  ↝   0 % 19 =   0
214576  ↝  45 = 2025  ↝   2 % 19 =   2
  (3 *   2 - 1) % 19  ↝              5
  (3 *   5 - 1) % 19  ↝             14 (2)
162145  ↝  21 = 0441  ↝  44 % 19 =   6
144467  ↝  44 = 1936  ↝  93 % 19 =  17
199645  ↝  96 = 9216  ↝  21 % 19 =   2
  (3 *   2 - 1) % 19  ↝              5
  (3 *   5 - 1) % 19  ↝             14
  (3 *  14 - 1) % 19  ↝              4 (3)
234534  ↝  45 = 2025  ↝   2 % 19 =   2
  (3 *   2 - 1) % 19  ↝              5
  (3 *   5 - 1) % 19  ↝             14
  (3 *  14 - 1) % 19  ↝              4
  (3 *   4 - 1) % 19  ↝             11 (4)
```

Hashed List (Collision)

```
0 -- 140145
1 --
2 -- 224562
3 --
4 -- 199645 (3)
5 -- 214562 (1)
6 -- 162145
7 --
8 --
```

```
 9 -- 137456
10 --
11 -- 234534 (4)
12 --
13 --
14 -- 214576 (2)
15 --
16 --
17 -- 144467
18 --
```
Collisions: 10. Density: 9/19 = 47%

9. Hashing: (List size: 19)

Fold Shift

Collision Resolution: Linear Probe

Hashing Calculations

```
224562 (22 + 45 + 62) % 19 = 15
137456 (13 + 74 + 56) % 19 = 10
214562 (21 + 45 + 62) % 19 = 14
140145 (14 + 01 + 45) % 19 =  3
214576 (21 + 45 + 76) % 19 =  9
162145 (16 + 21 + 45) % 19 =  6
144467 (14 + 44 + 67) % 19 = 11
199645 (19 + 96 + 45) % 19 =  8
234534 (23 + 45 + 34) % 19 =  7
```

Hashed List (Probe)

```
 0 --
 1 --
 2 --
 3 -- 140145
 4 --
 5 --
 6 -- 162145
 7 -- 234534
 8 -- 199645
 9 -- 214576
10 -- 137456
11 -- 144467
12 --
13 --
14 -- 214562
```

```
15 -- 224562
16 --
17 --
18 --
```
Collisions: 0. Density: 9/19 = 47%

11. Hashing: (List size: 19)
Rotation (right × 2), extract (1, 3, 5), % 19 + 1
Collision Resolution: Linear Probe
Hashing Calculations

```
224562 ⇒ 622245 ⇒ 624 % 19 = 16
137456 ⇒ 561374 ⇒ 517 % 19 =  4
214562 ⇒ 622145 ⇒ 624 % 19 = 16 ⇒ 17 (1)
140145 ⇒ 451401 ⇒ 410 % 19 = 11
214576 ⇒ 762145 ⇒ 724 % 19 =  2
162145 ⇒ 451621 ⇒ 412 % 19 = 13
144467 ⇒ 671444 ⇒ 614 % 19 =  6
199645 ⇒ 451996 ⇒ 419 % 19 =  1
234534 ⇒ 342345 ⇒ 324 % 19 =  1 ⇒ 2 ⇒ 3 (2)
```

Hashed List (Collision)

```
 0 --
 1 -- 199645
 2 -- 214576
 3 -- 234534 (2)
 4 -- 137456
 5 --
 6 -- 144467
 7 --
 8 --
 9 --
10 --
11 -- 140145
12 --
13 -- 162145
14 --
15 --
16 -- 224562
17 -- 214562 (1)
18 --
```
Collisions: 3. Density: 9/19 = 47%

Chapter 3 Exercises

1. `pList` is a unique pointer that is used to keep track of the head (first node) of the list. Executing the statement

   `pList = pList->link`

   modifies `pList` to no longer point to the first node of the list. This may have devastating effects for the entire program. This fact justifies the need for the two walking pointers, `pPre` and `pLoc`, which keep track of the predecessor and the current nodes without altering the head pointer.

3. `pPre->link = pCur->link`
   `recycle (pCur)`

5. 1 `allocate (pNew)`
   2 `...`
   3 `pNew->link  = pPre->link (pPre points to dummy)`
   4 `pPre->link  = pNew`

7. `list1` no longer points to the head of the first list; rather, it points to the head of the second list in the figure. The first list is lost forever.

9. This will create a circularly linked list.

Chapter 4 Exercises

1. See Figure S-1.

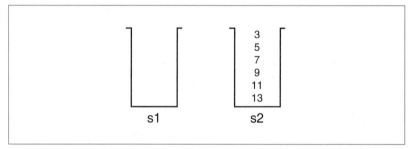

Figure S-1 Solution to Chapter 4, Exercise 1.

3. **a.** Prefix:

   ```
   D - B + C
   ((D - B) + C)
   (+(-D B) C)
   + - D B C
   ```

   Postfix:

   ```
   D - B + C
   ((D - B) + C)
   ((D B -) C +)
   D B - C +
   ```

b. Prefix:

```
A * B + C * D
((A * B) + (C * D))
(+ (*A B) (* C D))
+ * A B * C D
```

Postfix:

```
A * B + C * D
((A * B) + (C * D))
((A B *) (C D *) +)
A B * C D * +
```

c. Prefix:

```
(A + B) * C - D * F + C
((((A + B) * C) - (D * F)) + C)
(+ (- (* (+ A B) C) (* D F)) C)
+ - * + A B C * D F C
```

Postfix:

```
(A + B) * C - D * F + C
((((A + B) * C) - (D * F)) + C)
((((A B +) C *) (D F *) -) C +)
A B + C * D F * - C +
```

d. Prefix:

```
(A - 2 * (B + C) - D * E) * F
(((A - (2 * (B + C))) - (D * E)) * F)
(* (- (- A (* 2 (+ B C))) (* D E)) F)
* - - A * 2 + B C * D E F
```

Postfix:

```
(A - 2 * (B + C) - D * E) * F
(((A - (2 * (B + C))) - (D * E)) * F)
(((A (2 (B C +) *) -) (D E *) -) F *)
A 2 B C + * - D E * - F *
```

5. a.
```
A B * C - D +
2 3 * 4 - 5 +
6 4 - 5 +
2 5 +
7
```

b.
```
A B C + * D -
2 3 4 + * 5 -
2 7 * 5 -
14 5 -
9
```

7. Note: Stacks are shown in top–bottom order.

a.

Original	Stack	Output
D – B + C		
– B + C		D
B + C	–	D
+ C	–	D B
C	+	D B –
	+	D B – C
		D B – C +

b.

Original	Stack	Output
A * B + C * D		
* B + C * D		A
B + C * D	*	A
+ C * D	*	A B
C * D	+	A B *
* D	+	A B * C
D	* +	A B * C
	* +	A B * C D
		A B * C D * +

c.

Original	Stack	Output
(A+B)*C–D*F+C		
A+B)*C–D*F+C	(	
+B)*C–D*F+C	(	A
B)*C–D*F+C	+(	A
)*C–D*F+C	+(	AB
*C–D*F+C		AB+
C–D*F+C	*	AB+
–D*F+C	*	AB+C
D*F+C	–	AB+C*
*F+C	–	AB+C*D
F+C	*–	AB+C*D
+C	*–	AB+C*DF
C	+	AB+C*DF*–
	+	AB+C*DF*–C
		AB+C*DF*–C+

d.

Original	Stack	Output
(A–2*(B+C)–D*E)*F		
A–2*(B+C)–D*E)*F	(	
–2*(B+C)–D*E)*F	(	A
2*(B+C)–D*E)*F	–(	A
*(B+C)–D*E)*F	–(	A2
(B+C)–D*E)*F	*–(	A2
B+C)–D*E)*F	(*–(	A2
+C)–D*E)*F	(*–(	A2B
C)–D*E)*F	+(*–(	A2B
)–D*E)*F	+(*–(	A2BC

```
-D*E)*F          *-(          A2BC+
D*E)*F           -(           A2BC+*-
*E)*F            -(           A2BC+*-D
E)*F             *-(          A2BC+*-D
)*F              *-(          A2BC+*-DE
*F                            A2BC+*-DE*-
F                *            A2BC+*-DE*-
                 *            A2BC+*-DE*-F
                              A2BC+*-DE*-F*
```

Chapter 5 Exercises

1. See Figure S-2.

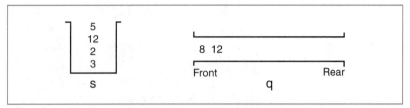

Figure S-2   Solution to Chapter 5, Exercise 1.

3. See Figure S-3.

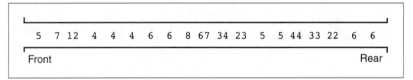

Figure S-3   Solution to Chapter 5, Exercise 3.

5. See Figure S-4.

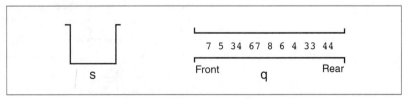

Figure S-4   Solution to Chapter 5, Exercise 5.

Chapter 6 Exercises

1. a. 3 * 4 = 12
   b. (2 * fun1(5) + 7)
   ```
   = (2 * (2 * fun1(0) + 7) + 7)
   = (2 * (2 * (3 * 0) + 7) + 7)
   = 21
   ```

c. (2 * fun1(7) + 7)
        = (2 * (2 * fun1(2) + 7) + 7)
        = (2 * (2 * (3 * 2) + 7) + 7)
        = 45

3. a. -1
  b. -1
  c. (4 * fun3(5, 7))
        = (4 * (5 * fun3(6, 7)))
        = 4 * (5 * (6 * fun (7, 7)))
        = 4 * 5 * 6 * 1 = 120
  d. 1

5. algorithm gcd (val x <integer>,
              val y <integer>)

This algorithm calculates the gcd of two integers.
    Pre   x and y are two integers whose gcd is needed
    Post gcd is calculated
    Return gcd
  1 if (x < y)
    1 return (gcd (y, x))
  2 else if (y = 0)
    1 return (x)
  3 else
    1 return (gcd (y, x mod y))
  4 end if
end gcd

Verification
  a. gcd (4, 28) = gcd (28, 4) = gcd (4, 0) = 4
  b. gcd (22, 4) = gcd (4, 2) = gcd (2, 0) = 2
  c. gcd (22, 5) = gcd (5, 2)
    = gcd (2, 1) = gcd (1, 0) = 1

7. algorithm Ackerman (val M <integer>,
                val N <integer>)

This algorithm calculates the Ackerman number.
    Pre M and N are integers
    Post Ackerman number calculated and returned
  1 if (M equal 0)
    1 return (N + 1)
  2 else if (N equal 0)
    1 return (Ackerman (M - 1, 1))
  3 else
    1 return (Ackerman (M - 1, Ackerman (M, N - 1)))

```
4 end if
end Ackerman
```

Verification

a. `Ackerman (2, 3) = 9`
b. `Ackerman (2, 5) = 13`
c. `Ackerman (0, 3) = 4`
d. `Ackerman (3, 0) = 5`

Chapter 7 Exercises

1. See Figure S-5.

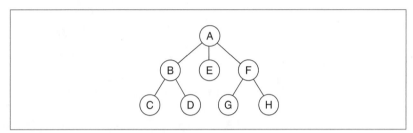

Figure S-5 Solution to Chapter 7, Exercise 1.

3. a. 1
　 b. 1
　 c. I, J
　 d. I
　 e. D, E

5. See Figure S-6.

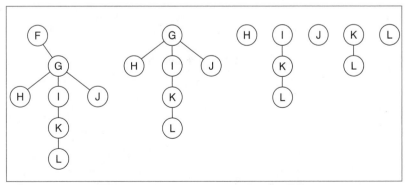

Figure S-6 Solution to Chapter 7, Exercise 5.

7. A (B (C (D E)) F (G (H I (K (L)) J)))

9. $H_{max} = 28$
　 $H_{min} = (\log_2 28) + 1 = 4 + 1 = 5$

11. –2

13. 15

15. A B F C G D E H I J K

17. See Figure S-7. This problem is solved by setting the root of the tree to the first node in the preorder traversal and then, from the inorder traversal, identifying its left subtrees as A B C E D F and the right subtree as G I H. The process is repeated with each subtree until the complete tree is developed.

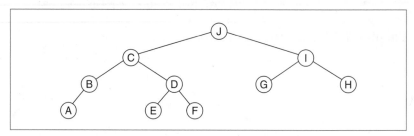

Figure S-7   Solution to Chapter 7, Exercise 17.

19. See Figure S-8. There are several possible solutions to this question. One is shown below. (For a unique solution, you also need to know the inorder traversal.)

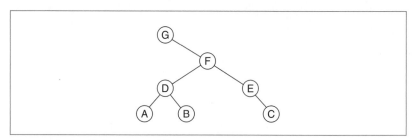

Figure S-8   Solution to Chapter 7, Exercise 19.

21. See Figure S-9.

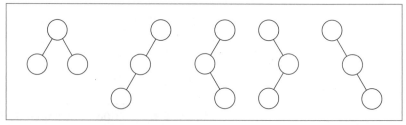

Figure S-9   Solution to Chapter 7, Exercise 21.

23. $H_{min} = (\log_2 42) + 1 = 5 + 1 = 6$

25. Level 5 = $2^5 = 32$

27. See Figure S-10.

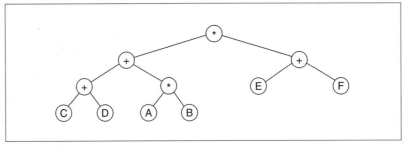

Figure S-10   Solution to Chapter 7, Exercise 27.

Prefix: * + + C D * A B + E F
Postfix: C D + A B * + E F + *

29. See Figure S-11.
Infix: (A * B + C / D) * (E – F)
Prefix: * + * A B / C D – E F

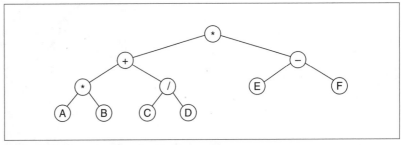

Figure S-11   Solution to Chapter 7, Exercise 29.

31. 2^{H-1}

Chapter 8 Exercises

1. See Figure S-12.

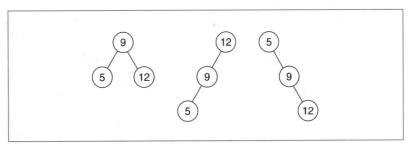

Figure S-12   Solution to Chapter 8, Exercise 1.

3. See Figure S-13.

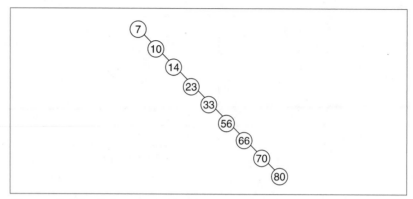

Figure S-13   Solution to Chapter 8, Exercise 3.

5. See Figure S-14.

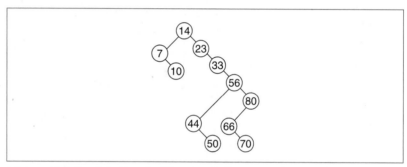

Figure S-14   Solution to Chapter 8, Exercise 5.

7. See Figure S-14.

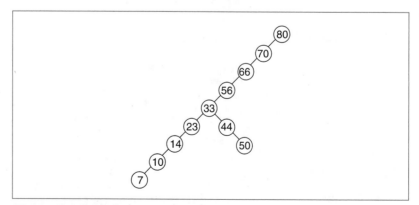

Figure S-15   Solution to Chapter 8, Exercise 7.

9. Left tree invalid (20 < 22).
   Right tree valid.

11. 25, 20, 18, 14, 19
    25, 20, 18, 19, 14

13. See Figure S-16.

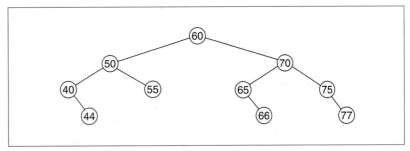

Figure S-16   Solution to Chapter 8, Exercise 13.

15. See Figure S-17.

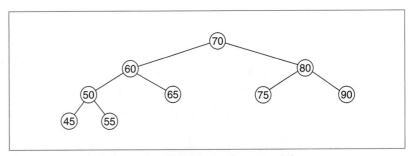

Figure S-17   Solution to Chapter 8, Exercise 15.

17. See Figure S-18.

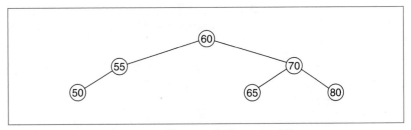

Figure S-18   Solution to Chapter 8, Exercise 17.

19. See Figure S-19.

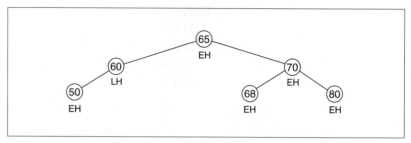

Figure S-19   Solution to Chapter 8, Exercise 19.

Chapter 9 Exercises

1. **a.** Not a heap because it's not nearly complete (empty node on the left)
   b. A heap
   c. Not a heap (13 is greater than its parent 12)
   d. A heap
3. See Figure S-20.

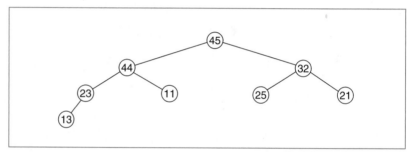

Figure S-20   Solution to Chapter 9, Exercise 3.

5. See Figure S-21.

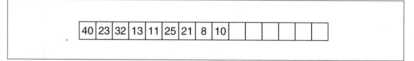

Figure S-21   Solution to Chapter 9, Exercise 5.

7. See Figure S-22.
9. Parent of 11 is 15
   Parent of 20 is 32
   Parent of 25 is 32
11. Index of parent is floor $((37 - 1)/2)$ is 18

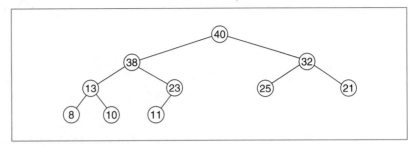

Figure S-22 Solution to Chapter 9, Exercise 7.

13. Item deleted in first delete is 50
     Item deleted in second delete is 40
     Item deleted in third delete is 35

15. See Figure S-23.

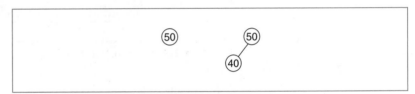

Figure S-23 Solution to Chapter 9, Exercise 15.

17. See Figure S-24.

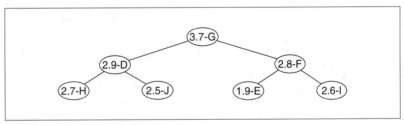

Figure S-24 Solution to Chapter 9, Exercise 17.

Chapter 10 Exercises

1. **a.** $3^3 - 1 = 26$
    b. $4^5 - 1 = 1023$
    c. $m^h - 1$

3. See Figure S-25 on page 730.

5. As shown in Figure S-26 on page 730, the same data entered in different sequences produce different trees.

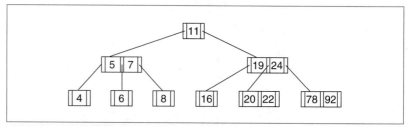

Figure S-25   Solution to Chapter 10, Exercise 3.

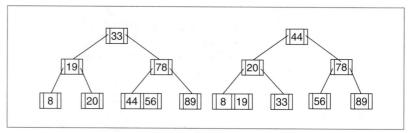

Figure S-26   Solution to Chapter 10, Exercise 5.

7. See Figure S-27.

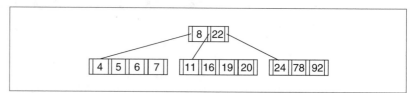

Figure S-27   Solution to Chapter 10, Exercise 7.

9. See Figure S-28.

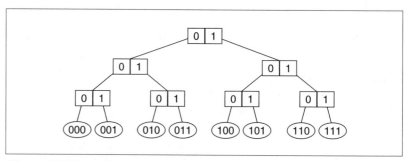

Figure S-28   Solution to Chapter 10, Exercise 9.

11. See Figure S-29.

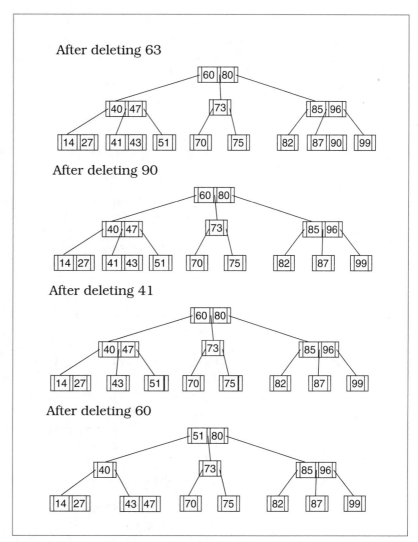

Figure S-29 Solution to Chapter 10, Exercise 11.

Chapter 11 Exercises

1. 3 7 13 26 44 23 98 57

3. 7 8 13 23 26 44 98 57

5. 7 8 13 23 26 44 57 98

7. The sorting algorithm used here could have been straight insertion, selection, or bubble sort because, in this case, these three algorithms give the same result after the first two passes.

9. The algorithm used here is the straight insertion sort because only this sort gives the given sequence after the first two passes.

Selection sort gives

   3   32   66   47   56   92

Bubble sort gives

   3   32   47   56   66   92

11. After sort phase:

File 1: 37 • 4 5 12 45 78 • 14 17 57

File 2: 9 23 56 • 22 33 44 • 11 35 46 59

After merge:

File 3: 9 23 37 56 • 4 5 12 22 33 44 45 78

     - 11 14 17 35 46 57 59

After distribution phase:

File 1: 9 23 37 56 • 11 14 17 35 46 57 59

File 2: 4 5 12 22 33 44 45 78

After merge:

File 3: 4 5 9 12 22 23 33 37 44 45 56 78

     - 11 14 17 35 46 57 59

After distribution:

File 1: 4 5 9 12 22 23 33 37 44 45 56 78

File 2: 11 14 17 35 46 57 59

After merge (sorted)

    4 5 9 11 12 14 17 22 23 33

    35 37 44 45 46 56 57 59 78

13. After sort phase (sort array size of seven):

File 1: 4 5 9 12 23 37 56 • 11 35 46 57 59

File 2: 14 17 22 33 44 45 78

File 3: (empty)

After merge:

File 1: 11 35 46 57 59

File 2: (empty)

File 3: 4 5 9 12 14 17 22 23 33 37 44 45 56 78

After first input file rotation:

File 1: (empty)

File 2: (sorted)

    4 5 9 11 12 14 17 22 23 33

    35 37 44 45 46 56 57 59 78

File 3: (empty)

Chapter 12 Exercises

    1. a. A, B, E, G, F, H
            A, B, E, G, F, C, D, H
            A, C, F, H
            A, C, D, H
            A, G, F, H
            A, G, F, C, D, H
      b. C, A, B, E
            C, A, G, E
            C, F, G, E
            C, F, G, A, B, E
            C, D, H, F, G, A, B, E
            C, D, H, F, G, E
      c. B, A, C, F
            B, A, C, D, H, F
            B, A, G, F
            B, E, G, F
            B, E, G, A, C, F
            B, E, G, A, C, D, H, F

    3. Vertex A: degree = 3, outdegree = 3, indegree = 3
        Vertex E: degree = 2, outdegree = 2, indegree = 2
        Vertex F: degree = 3, outdegree = 3, indegree = 3
        Vertex G: degree = 3, outdegree = 3, indegree = 3
        Vertex H: degree = 2, outdegree = 2, indegree = 2

    5. Assuming that arcs are stored in sequence by their destination, the traversal is
        A, B, C, G, E, D, F, H

    7. See Figure S-30.

	A	B	C	D	E	F	G	H
A	0	1	1	0	0	0	1	0
B	1	0	0	0	1	0	0	0
C	1	0	0	1	0	1	0	0
D	0	0	1	0	0	0	0	1
E	0	1	0	0	0	0	1	0
F	0	0	1	0	0	0	1	1
G	1	0	0	0	1	1	0	0
H	0	0	0	1	0	1	0	0

Figure S-30   Solution to Chapter 12, Exercise 7.

9. See Figure S-31.

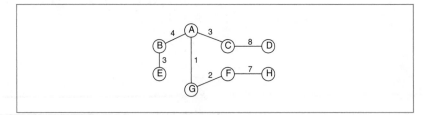

Figure S-31 Solution to Chapter 12, Exercise 9.

11. See Figure S-32.

	A	B	C	D	E	F	G	H
A	0	4	3	0	0	0	1	0
B	4	0	0	0	3	0	0	0
C	3	0	0	8	0	5	0	0
D	0	0	8	0	0	0	0	5
E	0	3	0	0	0	0	6	0
F	0	0	5	0	0	0	2	7
G	1	0	0	0	6	2	0	0
H	0	0	0	5	0	7	0	0

Figure S-32 Solution to Chapter 12, Exercise 11.

13. See Figure S-33.

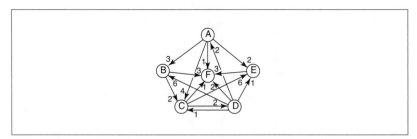

Figure S-33 Solution to Chapter 12, Exercise 13.

Glossary

absolute value: the magnitude of a number, regardless of its sign.

abstract data type: a data declaration packaged together with the operations that are meaningful on the data type.

abstraction: the generalization of an algorithm's operations without a specified implementation.

access specifier: the C++ class specification that designates the class members as private, protected, or public.

accuracy: the quality factor that addresses the correctness of a system.

adjacency list: a method of representing a graph that uses a linked list to store the vertices and a two-dimensional, linked list array to store the lines.

adjacency matrix: a method of representing a graph that uses a vector for the vertices and a matrix (square two-dimensional array) to store the lines.

adjacent vertices: two vertices in a graph that are connected by a line.

ADT: abstract data type.

algorithm: the logical steps necessary to solve a problem in a computer; a module or a part of a module.

algorithmics: the term created by Brassard and Bratley that refers to the study of techniques used to create efficient algorithms.

ancestor: any node in the path from the current node to the root of a tree.

and: a logical operator with the property that the expression is true if and only if the operands are individually true.

ANSI C++: the standard for the C++ language adopted by the American National Standards Institute.

arc: a directed line in a graph. Contrast with *edge*.

array: a fixed-size, sequenced collection of elements of the same data type.

ascending sequence: a list order in which each element in the list has a key greater than or equal to those of its predecessors.

ascending sort: a sort that orders a list in ascending sequence.

ASCII: the American Standard Code for Information Interchange. An encoding scheme that defines control characters and graphic characters for the first 128 values in a byte.

atomic data: data that cannot be meaningfully subdivided.

auxiliary storage: any storage device outside main memory; permanent data storage; external storage.

AVL tree: a height-balanced binary search tree that uses a balance factor to control the balance.

B

backtracking: an algorithmic process, usually implemented with a stack or through recursion, that remembers the path through a data structure and can retrace the path in reverse order.

balance: a tree node attribute representing the difference in height between the node's subtrees.

balance (B-tree): an algorithm that shifts entries among sibling nodes to correct an underflow.

balanced merge: a merge that uses a constant number of input merge files and the same number of output merge files.

base case: in a recursion, any statement that terminates the recursion; the statement that "solves" the problem.

base class: any class from which other classes are derived. Also known as parent class. See also *derived class* and *inheritance.*

batch update: an update process in which transactions are gathered over time for processing as a unit. Contrast with *online update.*

big-O notation: a measure of the efficiency of an algorithm in which only the dominant factor is considered.

bill of materials: a tree representation of a product showing which components are assembled into which parts. A structure chart is an example of a bill of materials.

binary file: a collection of structured data stored in the internal format of the computer. Contrast with *text file.*

binary search: a search algorithm in which the search value is located by repeatedly dividing the list in half.

binary search tree: a binary tree in which (1) the keys of the left subtree are all less than the root key, (2) the keys of the right subtree are greater than or equal to the root key, and (3) the subtrees are binary search trees.

binary tree: a tree in which no node can have more than two children; a tree with a maximum outdegree of 2.

bit: acronym for *Binary digIT.* The basic storage unit in a computer with the capability of storing only the values 0 and 1.

blackbox testing: testing based on the system requirements rather than a knowledge of the workings of a program.

block: in C++, a group of statements enclosed in braces {. . .}.

block comment: a comment beginning with /* and ending with */ that can be used to identify a comment spanning multiple lines. See also *line comment.*

bool: the C++ keyword for the Boolean type.

Boolean: a variable or expression that can assume only the values true and false.

braces: the { and } symbols.

branch: a line in a tree that connects two adjacent nodes.

breadth-first traversal: a graph traversal in which nodes adjacent to the current node are processed before their descendents.

BST: binary search tree.

B-tree: an *m*-way tree in which all nodes except the root have a minimum number of entries and except for leaves each node entry has a nonnull subtree.

B*tree: a B-tree in which each node is at least two-thirds full.

B+tree: a B-tree in which all data are represented at the leaf level and each leaf node has a pointer to the next sequential leaf node in the tree.

bubble sort: a sort algorithm in which each pass through the data moves (bubbles) the lowest element to the beginning of the unsorted portion of the list.

bucket: in a hashing algorithm, a node that can accommodate multiple data occurrences.

buffer: (1) hardware, usually memory, used to synchronize the transfer of data to and from main memory; (2) memory used to hold data that have been read before they are processed or data that are waiting to be written.

bug: a colloquial term used for any error in a piece of software.

byte: a binary character, shorter than a word, usually consisting of 8 bits.

C

call: the process by which one algorithm/function transfers control to another.

call by reference: a parameter passing technique in which an alias, rather than the value, of a variable is passed to a function. See also *call by value.*

call by value: a parameter passing technique in which the value of a variable is passed to a function. See also *call by reference.*

called algorithm/function: in an algorithm/function call, the algorithm/function that is the object of the call.

calling algorithm/function: in a call, the algorithm/function that invokes the call.

cast: a C++ operator that changes the type of an expression.

ceiling: the smallest integral value larger than a floating-point value.

chained list: another term for *linked list.*

character: a member of the set of values that are used to represent data or control operations. See *ASCII.*

child: a node in a tree or graph that has a predecessor.

chronological list: a list that is organized by time—that is, in which the data are stored in the order in which they were received. See also *FIFO* and *LIFO.*

cin: the C++ standard input stream object.

circularly linked list: a linked list in which the last node's link points to the first node in the list.

class: the combination of data and functions joined together to form a type.

class iterator: see *iterator.*

class object: an instantiation of a class with its members.

clustering: the tendency of data to build up unevenly across a hashed list.

collision: an event that occurs when a hashing algorithm produces an address for an insertion and that address is already occupied.

collision resolution: an algorithmic processing that determines an alternative address after a collision.

complete tree: a tree with a restricted outdegree that has the maximum number of nodes for its height.

composite data: data that are built on other data structures; that is, data that can be broken down into discrete atomic elements.

connected graph: a graph is connected if, when direction is suppressed, there is a path from any vertex to any other vertex.

constant: a data value that cannot change during the execution of the program. Contrast with *variable.*

constructor: a class member function that is called when an instance of a class is created or copied.

copy constructor: the constructor that is called whenever class initialization parameters contain an instance of the class object.

counter-controlled loop: a looping technique in which the number of iterations is controlled by a count; in C++, the *for* statement. Contrast with *event-controlled loop.*

cout: the C++ standard output stream object.

CPU: central processing unit.

C++ standard library: any of the libraries that contain predefined algorithms delivered with the system, such as standard library, (stdlib) and standard input and output (iostream).

cycle: a graph path whose length is greater than 1 and that starts and ends at the same vertex.

D

data hiding: the principle of structured programming in which data are available to a function only if it needs them to complete its processing; data not needed are "hidden" from view. See also *encapsulation.*

data name: an identifier given to data in a program.

data structure: an aggregation of atomic and composite data types into a set with defined relationships.

data type: a named set of values and operations defined to manipulate them, such as character and integer.

data validation: the process of verifying and validating data read from an external source.

default argument: a C++ formal parameter that contains an initializer to be used whenever an actual parameter is not supplied in the call.

default constructor: the function called whenever an object is created without explicit initial values.

default value: see *default argument.*

degree: the number of lines incident to a node in a graph.

depth (of tree): see *height.*

depth-first traversal: a traversal in which all of a node's descendents are processed before any adjacent nodes (siblings).

dequeue: delete an element from a queue.

derived class: a class created from a base class through inheritance. The derived class has all of the capabilities of the base class and may also declare and define new data members and functions of its own.

derived type: a composite data type constructed from other types (array, structure, union, pointer, and enumerated type).

descendent: any node in the path from the current node to a leaf.

descending sequence: a list order in which each element in a list has a key less than or equal to that of its predecessor.

descending sort: a sort that orders a list in descending sequence.

destructor: a class member function that is called when an instance of a class is destroyed—that is, when it ceases to exist.

digit extraction: a hashing method in which selected digits are extracted from the key and used as the address.

digraph: a directed graph.

direct hashing: a hashing method in which the key is used without algorithmic modification.

direct graph: a graph in which direction is indicated on the lines (arcs).

disjoint graph: a graph that is not connected.

double hashing: a hashing collision resolution method in which the collision address is hashed to determine the next address.

doubly linked list: a linked list structure in which each node has a pointer to both its successor and its predecessor. Contrast with *singly linked list.*

dynamic allocation: allocation of memory for storing data during the execution of a program. Contrast with *static allocation.*

dynamic memory: memory whose use can change during the execution of the program. (The heap.)

E

EBCDIC: Extended Binary Coded Decimal Interchange Code. The character set designed by IBM for its large computer systems. (Pronounced ebb-see-dic.)

edge: a graph line that has no direction.

empty list: a list that has been allocated but that contains no data. Also known as a null list.

encapsulation: the design concept in which data, functions, and objects, such as text files or linear lists, are maintained separately from the application using them.

end of file: the condition that occurs when a read operation attempts to read after it has processed the last piece of data.

enqueue: insert an element into a queue.

error stream: in C++, the `ostream` instance (cerr) used to display errors; usually assigned to the screen.

event-controlled loop: a loop whose termination is predicated on the occurrence of a specified event. Contrast with *counter-controlled loop*.

exclusive or: a logical operation in which the result is true only when one of the operands is true and the other is false and is false when both are true or both are false.

exponential efficiency: a category of program/module efficiency in which the run time is a function of the power of the number of elements being processed, as in $O(n) = c^n$.

expression: a sequence of operators and operands that reduces to a single value.

external sort: a sort that uses primary memory for the data currently being sorted and secondary storage for any data that will not fit in primary memory.

extraction operator: the C++ operator that reads data from an input stream.

F

factorial: an arithmetic function whose value is the product of the integral values from 1 to the number.

factorial efficiency: a measure of the efficiency of a module in which the run time is proportional to the number of elements factorial, as in $O(n) = n!$.

field: the smallest named unit of data that has meaning in describing information. A field may be either a variable or a constant.

FIFO: first in—first out.

file: a named collection of data stored on an auxiliary storage device. Compare with *list*.

flag: an indicator used in a program to designate the presence or absence of a condition; *switch*.

floating-point number: a number that contains both an integral and a fraction.

floor: the largest integral number smaller than a floating-point value.

flowchart: a program design tool in which standard graphical symbols are used to represent the logical flow of data through a function.

fold boundary: a hashing algorithm in which the left and right folds are reversed before they are added to determine the key.

fold shift: a hashing algorithm in which the key is divided into parts that are added to determine the key.

frequency array: an array that contains the number of occurrences of a value or of a range of values. See also *histogram*.

friend class: a separately declared class that has access to another class, which has granted it friend access.

friend function: a function defined outside a class that is given access to the class's internal data members and functions.

front: when used to refer to a list: a pointer that identifies the first element. In a *queue*, the next element to be removed.

function: a named block of code that performs a process within a program; an executable unit of code.

function member: a function defined in the scope of a class.

G

general case: in recursion, all of the algorithmic logic except the base case.

general list: a list in which data can be inserted and deleted anywhere in the list and for which there are no restrictions on the operations that can be performed.

general tree: a tree with an unlimited outdegree.

goezinta: a colloquial term derived from "goes into" for a bill of material.

graph: a collection of nodes, called vertices, and line segments, called edges or arcs, connecting pairs of nodes.

H

hard copy: any computer output that is written to paper or other readable mediums such as microfiche. Contrast with *soft copy*.

hashed list: a list in which the location of the data is determined by a hashing algorithm.

hashed search: any of the methods used to locate data in a hashed list.

hashing: a key-to-address transformation in which the key, through an algorithmic transformation, directly determines the location of the data.

head pointer: a pointer that identifies the first element of a list.

header node: a node in a list structure, generally located at the beginning of the list, that contains metadata about the list while sharing the pointer structure with the data nodes.

heap: a binary tree in which the root is the largest node in the tree and the subtrees are also heaps. See also *min-heap.*

heap memory: a pool of memory that can be used to dynamically allocate space for data while the program is running. See also *dynamic memory.*

height: a tree attribute indicating the length of the path from the root to the last level; the level of the leaf in the longest path from the root plus 1.

height-balanced tree: a balanced tree in which the balance is controlled through the height of its subtrees. An AVL tree is a height-balanced tree.

hexadecimal: a numbering system with base 16. Its digits are 0 1 2 3 4 5 6 7 8 9 A B C D E F.

high-level language: a (portable) programming language designed to allow the programmer to concentrate on the application rather than the structure of a particular computer or operating system.

histogram: a graphical representation of a frequency distribution. See also *frequency array.*

home address: in a hashed list, the first address produced by the hashing algorithm.

I

identifier: the name of an object. In C++, identifiers can consist only of digits, letters, and the underscore.

include: in C++, a preprocessor command that specifies a library file to be inserted into the program.

inclusive *or*: see *or.*

indegree: the number of lines entering a node.

indentation: a coding style in which statements dependent on a previous statement, such as *if* or *while,* are coded in an indented block to show their relationship to the controlling statement.

index: the address of an element within an array. See also *subscript.*

index range checking: a feature available in some compilers that inserts code to ensure that all index references are within the array.

indirect pointer: a pointer that locates the address of data through one or more other pointers; pointer to pointer.

infinite loop: a loop that does not terminate.

infix: an arithmetic notation in which the operator is placed between two operands.

information hiding: a structured programming concept in which the user does not know the data structure or the implementation of its operations.

inheritance: the ability to extend a class to create a new class while retaining the data objects and methods of the base class and adding new data objects and methods.

inheritance type: the attribute of a derived class (public, protected, or private) that determines the access method of the inherited members.

initialization: the process of assigning values to a variable at the beginning of a program or a function.

initialization constructor: the function invoked when a class is defined with initializers.

inline function: a function whose implementation code is used in place of a call.

inorder: a binary tree traversal in which the root is processed after the left subtree and before the right subtree; an LNR traversal.

input device: a device that provides data to be read by a program.

input stream: the C++ term for any input to a program.

inquiry: a request for information from a program.

insert: the insertion of an element into a data structure or a file.

insertion operator: the C++ operator that receives data from a program and converts it to an external format to be inserted into an output stream.

insertion sort: a sort algorithm in which the first element from the unsorted portion of the list is inserted into its proper position relative to the data in the sorted portion of the list.

instance: the object created when a class is defined. See also *instantiation*.

instantiation: the process of defining an occurrence of a class.

int: the C++ data type for integral numbers.

integer: an integral number; a number without a fractional part.

intelligent name: a data or algorithm name that describes the meaning of the data or the purpose of the algorithm.

internal node: any tree node except the root and the leaves; a node in the middle of a tree.

internal sort: a sort in which all of the data are held in primary storage during the sorting process.

iteration: a single execution of the statements in a loop.

iterator: a C++ object designed to move to the next element in a list with each call.

K

key: one or more fields in a data structure that are used to identify the data or otherwise control its use.

key offset: a hashed list collision resolution method in which the next address is a function of the current address and the key.

L

leaf: a graph or tree node with an outdegree of 0.

level: an attribute of a node indicating its distance from the root.

lexical search tree: a lexicographical search tree in which each node contains only one character rather than an entire key and the complete key is constructed by following a path through the tree.

lexicographical: a data order based on the dictionary. See also *ascending sequence*.

LIFO: Last in—first out.

line: a graph element that connects two vertices in the graph. See also *arc* and *edge*.

line comment: a comment, beginning with //, that must be completed on one line. See also *block comment*.

linear efficiency: a measure of the efficiency of a module in which the run time is proportional to the number of elements being processed, as in $O(n) = n$.

linear list: a list structure in which each element, except the last, has a unique successor.

linear loop: a loop whose execution is a function of the number of elements being processed. See also *linear efficiency*.

linear search: any search algorithm used to locate data in a linear list.

link: in a list structure, the field that identifies the next element in the list.

linked list: a linear list structure in which the ordering of the elements is determined by link fields.

linked list collision resolution: a hashed list collision resolution method that uses a separate area for synonyms, which are maintained in a linked list.

linked list traversal: processing in which every element of a linked list is processed in order.

list: an ordered set of data contained in main memory. Compare with *file*.

LNR: left, node, right. An inorder binary tree traversal.

load factor: in a hashed list, the ratio of the number of data nodes in the list to the number of physical elements in the list, expressed as a percentage.

logarithmic efficiency: a measure of the efficiency of a module in which the run time is proportional to the log of the number of elements being processed, as in $O(n) = \log_2 n$.

logarithmic loop: a loop whose efficiency is a function of the log of the number of elements being processed. See also *logarithmic efficiency*.

logical data: data whose values can be only true or false. See *Boolean*.

loop: in a program, a structured programming construct that causes one or more statements to be repeated; in a graph, a line that starts and ends with the same vertex.

LRN: left, right, node. A postorder tree traversal.

M

m: the order in an *m*-way tree.

m-way tree: a search tree structure with multiple data entries and subtrees per node; the maximum number of subtrees is known as the order of the *m*-way tree.

manipulator: an input/output function that provides functionality to data being read or written.

master file: a permanent file that contains the most current data regarding an application.

max-heap: see *heap*.

member function: a function created within the scope of a class.

merge: to combine two or more sequential files into one sequential file based on a common key and structure format.

merge run: a set of consecutively ordered data in a merge file.

metadata: data about the list or other data structure stored within the data structure itself.

method: a function declared within a class scope.

mid-square hashing: a hashing method in which the key is squared and the address selected from the middle of the squared number.

min-heap: a binary tree in which the root is the smallest node in the tree and the subtrees are also min-heaps. Contrast with *heap* and *max-heap*.

minimum spanning tree: a tree extracted from a connected network such that the sum of the weights is the minimum of all possible trees contained in the graph.

modulo-division hashing: a hashing method in which the key is divided by the list size and the integral remainder is the address.

multidimensional array: an array whose elements consist of one or more arrays.

multilinked list: one physical linked list structure with two or more logical key sequences.

multiway selection: a selection statement that is capable of evaluating more than two alternatives; in C++, the *switch* statement. Contrast with *two-way selection*.

N

natural merge: a merge with a constant number of input merge files and one output merge file.

nearly complete: a tree with a limited outdegree that has the minimum height for its nodes and in which the leaf level is being filled from the left.

nested loop: a loop whose efficiency is a function of the efficiency of a controlling loop.

nested structure: a structure that contains other structures.

network: a graph whose lines are weighted.

NLR: node, left, right. A preorder tree traversal.

node: in a data structure, an element that contains both data and structural elements used to process the list.

O

object: in object-oriented programming, any instantiation of a class, including its members and methods.

octal: a numbering system with a base of 8. The octal digits are 0 1 2 3 4 5 6 7.

one-dimensional array: a simple array in which each element contains only one type value.

online update: an update process in which transactions are processed as they are entered by the user.

open addressing: a collision resolution method in which the new address is in the home area.

operand: an object in a statement on which an operation is performed. Contrast with *operator*.

operator: the action symbol(s) in a statement. Contrast with *operand*.

or: a logical operator with the property that if any of the operands is true, the expression is true.

order: in an *m*-way tree, the maximum number of subtrees allowed for a node.

order (sort): see *sort order*.

ordered list: a list in which the elements are arranged so that the key values are placed in ascending or descending sequence.

outdegree: the number of lines leaving a node in a tree or graph.

output stream: the C++ term for an output from a program.

overflow: the condition that results when an attempt is made to insert data into a full list.

overflow area: in a hashed list, an area separate from the prime area that is used to store synonyms in a linked list.

overloading: the C++ capability that associates multiple function definitions with one function name or one operator.

P

parameter: a value passed to an algorithm/ function.

parent: a tree or graph node with an outdegree greater than 0; that is, with successors.

parse: logic that breaks data into independent pieces for further processing.

pass by reference: a function-coupling technique in which an alias of a field is passed rather than a value.

pass by value: a function-coupling technique in which only a data value is passed to a function.

path: a sequence of nodes in which each vertex is adjacent to the next one.

pointer: a constant or variable that contains an address that can be used to access data.

pointer to function: a pointer that identifies the entry point to a function. It is used to pass a function's address as a parameter.

polynomic efficiency: a measure of the efficiency of a module in which the run time is proportional to the number of elements raised to the highest factor in a polynomial, as in $O(n) = n^k$.

polyphase merge: a merge in which a constant number of input merge files are merged into one output merge file and each input merge file is immediately reused when its input has been completely merged.

pop: the stack delete operation.

postfix: an arithmetic notation in which the operator is placed after its operands.

postorder: a binary tree traversal in which the left subtree is processed before the right subtree and both are processed before the root; an LRN traversal.

posttest loop: a loop in which the terminating condition is tested only after the execution of the loop statements. Contrast with *pretest loop*.

prefix: an arithmetic notation in which the operator is placed before the operands.

preorder: a binary tree traversal in which the root is processed before the left subtree and the left subtree is processed before the right subtree; an NLR traversal.

pretest loop: a loop in which the terminating condition is tested before the execution of the loop statements. Contrast with *posttest loop*.

primary clustering: the buildup of data around the home address in a hashed list. Contrast with *secondary clustering*.

prime area: in a hashed list, the memory that contains the home addresses.

priority queue: a queue in which the elements are organized into groups according to priority numbers and processed such that the highest-priority elements are output first. Within a priority, elements are processed in first in–first out (FIFO) order.

probability search: a search in which the list is ordered according to the probability of the list data being the target of a search, with the most probable targets first.

probe: in a hashing algorithm, the calculation of an address and test for success; in a search algorithm, one iteration of the loop that includes the test for the search argument.

pseudocode: English-like statements that follow a loosely defined syntax and are used to convey the design of an algorithm or function.

pseudorandom collision resolution: a collision resolution method that uses a pseudorandom number generator to determine the next address after a collision.

pseudorandom hashing: a hashing method that uses the key as the variable factor in a pseudorandom number generator to determine the address.

pseudorandom number: one of a repeatable series of numbers with mathematically random properties.

push: the stack insert operation.

Q

quadratic efficiency: a measure of the efficiency of a module in which the run time is proportional to the number of elements squared. Quadratic efficiency is one of the polynomic factors, as in $O(n) = n^2$.

quadratic loop: a loop that consists of two loops, each of which have a linear efficiency, resulting in a loop with quadratic efficiency.

quadratic probe: a collision resolution method in which the increment is the collision probe number squared, giving the series 1^2, 2^2, 3^2, and so forth.

query: inquiry.

queue: a linear list in which data can only be inserted at one end, called the rear, and deleted from the other end, called the front.

queue simulation: a modeling activity used to generate statistics about the performance of a queue.

R

random list: a list with no ordering of the data.

random number: a number selected from a set in which all members have the same probability of being selected.

realtime: processing in which updating takes place at the time the event occurs.

rear: when used to refer to a list, a pointer that identifies the last element; in a queue, the most recent element inserted into the structure.

record: a collection of data treated as a unit.

recursion: a repetitive process in which an algorithm calls itself.

recycle: the pseudocode operation that returns memory dynamically allocated for a structure to the dynamic memory pool. In C++, *delete*.

restricted list: a list in which data can only be added or deleted at the ends of the list and processing is restricted to operations on the data at the ends.

retrieval: the location and return of an element in a list.

return: the statement that causes execution of an algorithm/function to terminate and control to be assumed by the calling algorithm/function.

rollout: merge processing in which a consecutive series of merge input data are copied to the merge output after a stepdown in the alternate merge input.

root: the first node of a tree.

rotation hashing: a hashing method in which the end portion of a key is copied to the front of the key.

S

search: the process that examines a list to locate one or more elements containing a designated value known as a search argument.

search argument: the key value being looked for in a search.

secondary clustering: the buildup of data along a collision path through a hashed list. Contrast with *primary clustering*.

selection sort: the sort algorithm in which the smallest value in the unsorted portion of a list is selected and placed at the end of the sorted portion of the list.

selection statement: a statement that chooses between two or more alternatives, such as an *if . . . else*.

self-referential structure: a structure that contains a pointer to itself.

sentinel: a flag that guards the end of a list or a file. The sentinel is usually the maximum value for a key field and cannot be a valid data value.

sentinel search: a search algorithm in which the search argument is placed in an extra element at the end of the list.

sequential file: a file structure in which data must be processed serially from the first entry in the file.

sequential search: a search technique used with a linear list in which the searching begins at the first element and continues until the value of an element equal to the value being sought is located, or until the end of the list is reached.

siblings: two or more tree nodes with a common parent.

singly linked list: an ordered collection of data in which each element contains only the location of the next element. Contrast with *doubly linked list*.

slack bytes: inaccessible memory locations added between fields in a structure to force a hardware-required boundary alignment.

soft copy: computer output written to a nonpermanent display such as a monitor. Contrast with *hard copy*.

sort: the process that orders a list or file.

sort order: the arrangement of data in a list or file, either ascending or descending.

sort phase: the first pass through the data in an external sort in which a sort algorithm is used to sort data into merge runs for further processing.

sort stability: an attribute of a sort in which input data with equal keys retain their relative order in the sort output.

spanning tree: a tree extracted from a connected graph that contains all of the vertices in the graph.

square brackets: the [and] symbols.

stability: see *sort stability*.

stack: a restricted data structure in which data can only be inserted and deleted at one end, called the top.

stack frame: a logical structure used in a function call that contains the parameters, the local variable values for the calling function, the return statement in the calling function, and the address of the variable to receive any return value.

statement: a syntactical construct that represents one operation in a program.

static allocation: memory whose location is determined by the compiler and therefore preset before run time. Contrast with *dynamic allocation*.

static memory: memory whose use (e.g., for a variable) does not change during the running of a program.

stepdown: an event that occurs when the sequential ordering of the data in a merge file is broken; the end of a merge run. End of file is also considered a stepdown.

stream: the C++ view of a file, consisting of a sequence of characters divided into lines (text stream) or sequences of byte values representing data in their internal memory formats (binary stream).

strongly connected graph: a graph in which there is a path from every node to every other node. Contrast with *weakly connected graph*.

structure: a named collection of fields grouped together for processing; *record*.

structure chart: a design and documentation tool that represents a program as a hierarchical flow of algorithms/functions.

subscript: an ordinal number that indicates the position of an element within an array. See also *index*.

subtraction hashing: a hashing method in which only a constant value is subtracted from the key to determine the address.

subtree: any connected structure below the root of the tree.

switch: see *flag*.

synonym: in a hashed list, two or more keys that hash to the same home address.

T

text file: a file in which all data are stored as characters. Contrast with *binary file*.

this pointer: the specified pointer within a class member function that identifies the invoking instance of the class.

token: any syntactical construct that represents an operation or a flag, such as the plus sign (+).

top: in a stack, the pointer that identifies the newest element in the stack; the pointer that identifies the end of the stack for insertions and deletions.

transaction file: a file containing relatively transient data to be used to change the contents of a master file.

traversal: an algorithmic process in which each element in a structure is processed once and only once.

tree: a set of connected nodes structured so that each node has only one predecessor.

trie: a lexical search tree in which null subtrees are pruned—that is, in which null subtrees are deleted.

two-dimensional array: an array in which each element contains one array. See also *multidimensional array.*

two-way selection: a selection statement that is capable of evaluating only two alternatives, such as the *if . . . else* statement. Contrast with *multiway selection.*

U

underflow: an event that occurs when an attempt is made to delete data from a data structure and it is empty.

undirected graph: a graph consisting only of edges—that is, a graph in which there is no indication of direction on the lines.

update: an action that changes an element in a list.

user-defined function: any function written by the programmer, as opposed to a standard library function.

V

variable: a memory storage object that can be changed during the execution of a program. Contrast with *constant.*

vertex: a node in a graph.

void: the absence of data.

W

weakly connected graph: a graph in which there is at least one node with no path to at least one other node. Contrast with *strongly connected.*

weighted graph: see *network.*

whitebox testing: program testing in which the internal design of the program is considered; *clear box testing.* Contrast with *blackbox testing.*

Index

ABSTRACT DATA TYPES (continued)

B-Tree ADT

Template types are cookie?

Graph ADT